THE WRITING OF ROYALISM,
1628–1660

In *The Writing of Royalism*, Robert Wilcher charts the political and ideological development of 'royalism' between 1628 and 1660. His study of the literature and propaganda produced by those who adhered to the crown during the civil wars and their aftermath takes in many kinds of writing to provide a comprehensive account of the emergence of a partisan literature in support of the English monarchy and church. Wilcher situates a wide range of minor and canonical texts in the tumultuous political contexts of the time, helpfully integrating them into a detailed historical narrative. He illustrates the role of literature in forging a party committed to the military defence of royalist values and determined to sustain them in defeat. *The Writing of Royalism* casts new light on the complex phenomenon of 'royalism' by making available a wealth of material that should be of interest to historians as well as literary scholars.

ROBERT WILCHER is Senior Lecturer in English at the University of Birmingham. He is the author of *Andrew Marvell* (Cambridge University Press, 1985), *Andrew Marvell: Selected Poetry and Prose* (1986) and *Understanding Arnold Wesker* (1991).

THE WRITING OF
ROYALISM
1628–1660

ROBERT WILCHER

CAMBRIDGE
UNIVERSITY PRESS

PUBLISHED BY THE PRESS SYNDICATE OF THE UNIVERSITY OF CAMBRIDGE
The Pitt Building, Trumpington Street, Cambridge, United Kingdom

CAMBRIDGE UNIVERSITY PRESS
The Edinburgh Building, Cambridge CB2 2RU, UK   www.cup.cam.ac.uk
40 West 20th Street, New York, NY 10011–4211, USA   www.cup.org
10 Stamford Road, Oakleigh, Melbourne 3166, Australia
Ruiz de Alarcón 13, 28014 Madrid, Spain

First published 2001

Printed in the United Kingdom at the University Press, Cambridge

Typeset in Baskerville 11/12.5pt [VN]

A catalogue record for this book is available from the British Library

Library of Congress Cataloguing in Publication data
Wilcher, Robert, 1942–
The writing of royalism: 1628–1660 / Robert Wilcher.
p.   cm.
Includes index.
ISBN 0 521 66183 8
1. English literature – Early modern, 1500–1700 – History and criticism.   2. Politics and
literature – Great Britain – History – 17th century.   3. Great Britain – History – Commonwealth
and Protectorate, 1649–1660 – Historiography.   4. Great Britain – History – Charles I,
1625–1649 – Historiography.   5. Propaganda – Great Britain – History – 17th century.   6.
Royalists – Great Britain – History – 17th century.   7. Royalists in literature.   I. Title.
PR438.P65 W55 2001
941.06'2'072–dc21   00-037846

ISBN 0 521 66183 8 hardback

For Miriam, Jessica, Thomasin and Victoria

'Then keep the antient way!'
(Henry Vaughan, 'The Proffer', *Silex Scintillans* 1655)

Contents

Illustrations

Acknowledgements

This book grew out of a general interest in the literature of the seventeenth century that was fostered by the supervisor of my postgraduate work at Birmingham, Elsie Duncan-Jones, and it is to her that I owe my greatest intellectual debt. More particularly, it stems from a fascination with the work of Henry Vaughan, which has been sustained in sporadic pieces of research over the past quarter of a century and greatly encouraged in the past few years by Peter Thomas and Anne Cluysenaar, the moving spirits behind the Usk Valley Vaughan Association, with its annual colloquium and its annual publication, *Scintilla*. During the period in which I have been seriously working on this project, I have profited from conversations with H. Neville Davies and John Roberts, and from the opportunity to discuss parts of it in postgraduate seminars at the universities of Birmingham and Cambridge. I am grateful to my colleagues in the English Department at Birmingham for maintaining the system of Study Leaves, which freed me from teaching responsibilities for two separate terms in the early and later stages of research and writing; and to the staff of the Heslop Room in the University of Birmingham Library for their ready and cheerful assistance. I am also grateful for permission to use material that first appeared in the following publications: 'Daphnis: An Elegiac Eclogue by Henry Vaughan', *Durham University Journal*, new series 36 (1974), 25–40; '"Then keep the ancient way!" A Study of Henry Vaughan's *Silex Scintillans*', *Durham University Journal*, new series 45 (1983), 11–24; 'What was the King's Book for?: The Evolution of *Eikon Basilike*', *The Yearbook of English Studies*, 21 (1991), 218–28; 'Francis Quarles and the Crisis of Royalism', *Critical Survey*, 5 (1993), 252–62; 'Henry Vaughan and the Church', *Scintilla*, 2 (1998), 90–104.

My greatest debt of gratitude, of course, is to my wife and three daughters, who knew when to keep out of the way but were there when I needed them.

Note on the text

Modern scholarly editions or reprints of primary texts are cited when these are available. When seventeenth-century publications are cited, quotations follow the original spelling and punctuation, except for the modernization of consonantal 'i' to 'j', the standardization of 'u'/'v', and the occasional reduction of a capital letter to lower case at the start of an incorporated quotation. To avoid unnecessary proliferation of endnotes, publication details and page references of seventeenth-century works are frequently given in the body of the text and page references for quotations from modern editions of primary texts are given in round brackets in the body of the text once details of publication have been provided in notes to the current chapter.

When a reprint of a scholarly work is cited, the date of original publication will be given in square brackets, thus: Alan Everitt, *The Community of Kent and the Great Rebellion 1640–1660* (Leicester, [1966] 1973). Quotations from Clarendon's *History of the Rebellion and Civil Wars in England* are located by book and paragraph rather than volume and page numbers.

Since the method of this book is to discuss written and printed texts within the historical contexts of their composition and publication, the dates supplied in *A Catalogue of the Pamphlets, Books, Newspapers and Manuscripts Relating to the Civil War, the Commonwealth and Restoration, Collected by George Thomason, 1640–1661* (British Museum Trustees, 1908) are included in square brackets along with details derived from the title-pages of seventeenth-century texts, thus: (London, [16 April] 1646). A Thomason date is that on which a book or pamphlet was received into his collection, usually within a few days of publication. In some cases, when no Thomason date is available, the conjectured date of publication has been taken from Falconer Madan's *Oxford Books: A Bibliography of Printed Works Relating to the University of Oxford or Printed or Published There*, Vol. II (Oxford, 1912), and indicated thus: (Oxford, [Madan 2 October]

1641). For purposes of dating, the year is taken to begin on 1 January, not on March 25 as in the Old Style calendar, and dates for seventeenth-century books published between 1 January and 24 March are emended accordingly.

The following abbreviations have been used for frequently cited editions and secondary texts:

Anselment, *LR*	Raymond A. Anselment, *Loyalist Resolve: Patient Fortitude in the English Civil War* (Newark, 1988)
Ashton, *ECW*	Robert Ashton, *The English Civil War: Conservatism and Revolution 1603–1649* (1978, revised London, 1989)
Bennett, *CW*	Martyn Bennett, *The Civil Wars in Britain and Ireland: 1638–1651* (Oxford, 1997)
BP	*Alexander Brome: Poems*, ed. Roman R. Dubinski, 2 vols. (Toronto, 1982)
Clarendon	*The History of the Rebellion and Civil Wars in England*, ed. W. Macray, 6 vols. (Oxford, 1888)
CP	*The Poems of John Cleveland*, ed. Brian Morris and Eleanor Withington (Oxford, 1967)
CPP	*The Plays and Poems of William Cartwright*, ed. G. Blakemore Evans (Madison, 1951)
CowleyE	*Abraham Cowley: Essays, Plays and Sundry Verses*, ed. A. R. Waller (Cambridge, 1906)
CowleyP	*Abraham Cowley: Poems*, ed. A. R. Waller (Cambridge, 1905)
Fletcher, *Outbreak*	Anthony Fletcher, *The Outbreak of the English Civil War* (London, [1981] 1993)
Gardiner, *History*	Samuel R. Gardiner, *The History of the Great Civil War 1642–1649*, 4 vols. (reprinted London, 1987)
Loxley, *RP*	James Loxley, *Royalism and Poetry in the English Civil Wars: The Drawn Sword* (Basingstoke, 1997)
O Hehir, *EH*	Brendan O Hehir, *Expans'd Hieroglyphicks: A Critical Edition of Sir John Denham's Coopers Hill* (Berkeley and Los Angeles, 1969)

O Hehir, *HD*	Brendan O Hehir, *Harmony from Discords: A Life of Sir John Denham* (Berkeley and Los Angeles, 1968)
QCW	*The Complete Works in Prose and Verse of Francis Quarles*, ed. Revd Alexander B. Grosart, 3 vols. (Edinburgh, 1880–1; reprinted New York, 1967)
Russell, *FBM*	Conrad Russell, *The Fall of the British Monarchies, 1637–1642* (Oxford, 1991)
Smith, *CR*	David L. Smith, *Constitutional Royalism and the Search for Settlement, c. 1640–1649* (Cambridge, 1994)
SNW	*The Works of Sir John Suckling: The Non-dramatic Works*, ed. Thomas Clayton (Oxford, 1971)
Thomas, *JB*	P. W. Thomas, *Sir John Berkenhead 1617–1679: A Royalist Career in Politics and Polemics* (Oxford, 1969)
Wedgwood, *KP*	C. V. Wedgwood, *The King's Peace: 1637–1641* (London, [1955] 1972)
Wedgwood, *KW*	C. V. Wedgwood, *The King's War: 1641–1647* (London, [1958] 1972)
VW	*The Works of Henry Vaughan*, ed. L. C. Martin, 2nd edn. (Oxford, 1957)
Wormald, *Clarendon*	B. H. G. Wormald, *Clarendon: Politics, History and Religion 1640–1660* (Chicago, revised 1964, 1976)

Introduction

Writing in 1981, Ronald Hutton complained that whereas 'the accepted portrait of the parliamentarian party' during the period of the English Civil Wars had 'changed almost beyond recognition' in the previous forty years, 'the accepted view' of the royalist party was 'still that established by Gardiner over a hundred years ago'.[1] In an address to the Royal Historical Society in November 1986, another historian began a 'modest analysis of the Cavalier party in terms of what may be called ideological temperament' with the observation that few 'have paused to consider the kind of people who became Cavaliers and their probable motivation'.[2] A year later, the editors of an interdisciplinary volume of studies noted that in 'their emphasis upon the godly politics of the Puritans, historians have paid too little attention to the Royalists' conviction that they fought God's as well as the king's war'.[3] A similar verdict was reached by Conrad Russell at the end of a study which went some way towards redirecting the emphasis:

In fact, if we look at England in the context of Charles's other kingdoms, the peculiarity which needs explaining is not its revolutionary character: it is the fact that it was the only one of the three kingdoms which created a Royalist party large enough to be an effective fighting force. It is the English Royalists, not the English Parliamentarians, who are the peculiarity we should be attempting to explain.[4]

The informing ideas and principles of royalism were not completely neglected by historians, of course, as the work of Paul Hardacre, James Daly and Joyce Malcolm witnesses.[5] And over the past decade, there have been a number of major advances in our understanding of the origins and nature of the loose coalition of interests that constituted a 'royalist party' in the 1640s.[6]

A parallel development has taken place in the field of literary enquiry since Lois Potter's provocative insight that 'from 1642 to 1660 the source of the most deliberately and consciously subversive publications was the

royalist party' and her comment that 'comparatively little attention has
been paid to the writers of this group'.[7] Important pioneering work had
already been undertaken by Peter Thomas in his analysis of the 'subversive' brilliance of the Oxford propaganda machine organized by
John Berkenhead during the years of Civil War, by Annabel Patterson
in chapters on 'the Royal Romance' and the rise of the familiar letter as
a political genre during the 1640s, by Kevin Sharpe in his investigations
into the literary culture of the Caroline court and by Raymond Anselment in his account of five poets who exemplify a particular aspect of the
royalist temperament and literary endeavour.[8] More recently, the defi-
ciency noted by Potter has been supplied by a number of scholars:
Thomas Corns has given weight to Lovelace, Herrick, Cowley and the
Eikon Basilike alongside Milton, Marvell, and the Levellers; Gerald
MacLean has examined attempts at adapting traditional literary
methods of processing historical events to the new circumstances created by a war between King and Parliament and the judicial execution
of a monarch; Dale Randall and Susan Wiseman have investigated the
continued use of the dramatic medium by royalist authors, whether in
full-length plays or pamphlets in dialogue form, after the closing of the
theatres in 1642; James Loxley has subjected the notion of 'Cavalier
poetry' to historically informed scrutiny; and Steven Zwicker has included the *Eikon Basilike*, the royalist poetics developed by Davenant and
Hobbes, and Walton's *The Compleat Angler* in his study of the way in
which literary texts both reflected and enacted history in the second half
of the seventeenth century.[9]

The purpose of the present study is to offer a more comprehensive
survey than has yet been attempted of the range and diversity of the
partisan writing that was devised to meet challenges to the authority of
Charles I and the institutional integrity of the Church of England, and
later to cope with the social, political, and psychological consequences
of the defeat of the royalist armies, the execution of the King, and the
abolition of the monarchy. A chronological, narrative approach has
been adopted in an effort to locate each text as precisely as possible
within the contexts of its original composition, transmission, and reception – all of which may have a bearing on its interest as a product of or
contribution to the historical phenomenon of 'royalism'. This procedure
follows the advice offered by two influential commentators on Renaissance literature in relation to the politics of its own day: one stresses 'the
importance of an exact chronology in determining what any given text
was likely to mean to its audience at the time of its appearance' and the

other stresses the need to take account of 'authorial intention', insofar as it can be reconstructed, since to ignore its 'substantial and under-acknowledged political element' is 'effectively to depoliticise'.[10] It will be found that, read in relation to other writing generated by the same set of political circumstances, both familiar and neglected works can reveal unexpected insights into the ways in which individuals and groups perceived and tried to influence the course of history during a period of rapid and disorientating change.

Among the new developments that those who enlisted as writers in the service of the royal cause had to confront was the emergence of 'the public sphere', created by rising literacy and the availability of cheap print, as a significant feature of the nation's political and social life.[11] In his study of the dissemination of lyric poetry following the advent of the printing press, Arthur Marotti argues that 'one of the obvious reasons for the persistence of the manuscript system of literary transmission through the seventeenth century was that it stood opposed to the more democratizing force of print culture and allowed those who participated in it to feel that they were part of a social as well as an intellectual elite'.[12] While writers like John Cleveland and Alexander Brome continued to favour manuscript circulation for their satirical and subversive poetry throughout the 1640s and 1650s, Charles I's early commitment to the power of print was an important factor in the proliferation of polemical material in verse and prose that issued from Oxford after it became his headquarters in the autumn of 1642. Although most of this often highly sophisticated propaganda was not aimed at the ill-educated populace, the talents of a genuinely popular writer like John Taylor were also exploited, and the editors of royalist newsbooks and devisers of topical pamphlets were not immune to the effects described by Dagmar Freist: 'In the process of news presentation and the formation of public opinion residues of oral culture and the characteristics of a literate culture began to merge.'[13]

The problem of terminology needs to be addressed at the outset, since the words 'royalist' and 'royalism' are beset with as many difficulties as the words 'puritan' and 'puritanism'. Before the 1640s, there is little evidence of any concerted resistance to the inherited belief in a hier-archical system ordained by God in which, as Thomas Wentworth expressed it in a famous speech to the Council of the North in December 1628, 'the authority of a king is the keystone which closeth up the arch of order and government, which contains each part in due relation to the whole, and which once shaken, infirmed, all the frame falls together into a confused heap of foundation and battlement, of strength and beauty'.[14] Those who were critical of royal policies in the parliaments of the late 1620s would not have contemplated an attack upon the institution of kingship or indeed upon Charles I himself rather than his evil counsellor, the Duke of Buckingham, for fear that any open questioning of the assumptions that sustained the fabric of the state might open the way to 'mutiny and rebellion' by 'the meaner sort' who 'are not easily ruled'.[15] Indeed, John Pym, one of the leading opponents of the government in the House of Commons, had spoken out a few months earlier in defence of the ancient 'form of government' in which 'every part and member' was disposed 'to the common good', giving and receiving 'strength and protection in their several stations and degrees'.[16]

Such a political system was ideologically buttressed by the Protestant emphasis on the decisive role to be played in the defeat of the Roman Antichrist by the Christian Emperor and his Church, which was derived from the millenarian model of history inculcated in John Foxe's highly influential *Book of Martyrs*. In one reading of what happened in 1641, this messianic monarchism, which had been put under increasing strain by the policies of Charles I and his Archbishop of Canterbury, William Laud, was rejected by many puritans in favour of Thomas Brightman's alternative eschatology set forth in *A Revelation of the Revelation* (1615):

> Foxe had created for Puritans an idealised figure of the Godly Prince: the second Emperor Constantine. But Charles I was not Constantine, and Laud was not Cranmer. As faith in Crown and bishop receded, faith in the 'Godly Rule' that both were to create advanced. Puritans turned more and more to Brightman's vision of a reformation that would come, via neither Crown nor Bishop, but via a 'Godly People'.[17]

It is certainly the case, as Conal Condren has demonstrated, that religion was 'the only "colour" under which an army might gather against a lawful magistrate' and that 'Reformation political theology . . . provided a casuistic rhetoric of violence'.[18] One effect of 'the extremities of Civil War' was to upset the 'delicate conceptual balance' of the doctrine of the King's two bodies – the individual ruler and the office of kingship – which was a 'fiction of legal theology . . . designed to explain and legitimise continuity of legally-defined office despite discontinuity of office-holder'. Royalist rhetoric tended to move to one extreme, 'investing Charles with all the sacrosanctity of biblical kingship', while parliamentarians 'for religious reasons, were forced to separate Charles Stuart, that man of blood, from the crown' and to turn 'offices of state' into 'objects of allegiance'.[19] It is not too much to claim that almost everyone was a 'royalist' before events propelled adversaries of Charles I into developing first the case for resistance to a wayward king and then more radical alternatives to the system of monarchy itself. As Sharpe sums up the situation, before 1642 there was no impetus to 'rewrite the *language* of politics', because 'there were no proponents in 1640 of an alternative parliamentary government', and the 'values and discourse' even of those who were 'prepared to try to compel the king to heed good counsel' remained 'traditional'.[20] The term 'royalist', in fact, was not needed until the governing class polarized into parties engaged in an ideological and military contest over the locus of supreme power in the state: on the one side, those who wanted to preserve the ancient prerogatives of the crown; on the other, those who wanted to make the monarch answerable to a parliament which had executive as well as merely legislative authority. The first instance of the word 'royalist' recorded in the Oxford English Dictionary is significantly from William Prynne's *Sovereign Power of Parliaments* in 1643.

Part of the revisionist thrust in re-interpreting the early Stuart period has been the claim that parliamentary history has been 'seriously distorted by hindsight, because historians with their eyes fixed on the Civil War and what followed have been looking for a continuous development of opposition which was not really there'.[21] Focusing on another of the words that have encouraged political and literary commentators to read back the divisions of the 1640s into the preceding decade, Sharpe has insisted that 'there were no cavaliers in the 1630s – if the term is intended to delineate a coherent political group'.[22] He has taken particular issue with the view that there was a deep rift between the culture of the Caroline court, which has been characterized as exclusive, aristocratic and authoritarian, and the culture associated with the 'country' faction in politics, which was heir to the traditions of Elizabethan humanism and puritan in religious orientation. A recent analysis of the cultural significance of chivalric iconography and language at Charles's court tends in the same direction. J. S. A. Adamson points out that the Earl of Newcastle expressed a 'nostalgic "Elizabethanism"' during the 1630s, which he shared with others alienated by court life and which was seriously out of sympathy with the brand of chivalry purveyed in the Caroline masques. This did not prevent him, however, from becoming a leading royalist-in-arms during the 1640s.[23] Further support for this view comes from a study of theatres and plays in the ten years preceding the outbreak of Civil War, in which Martin Butler argues that 'the political possibilities of the period were much more various than the simple Cavalier-puritan polarization allows for' and that 'by trying to distinguish Cavaliers from Roundheads in the 1630s we are applying categories that will not fit, looking for the conflicts of the Civil War in a decade that was not yet fighting them'.[24]

This is another reason for the adoption of a narrative approach in the chapters that follow, since one of the aims of this book is to trace the journeys of individual writers like Davenant, Cowley, Quarles, Taylor, Berkenhead, Denham, Symmons, Cleveland and Vaughan across the decades, as they respond to the unfolding of events which slowly reshape the religious and political landscapes in which they live. Alongside this, there is the related aim of charting the gradual development of different kinds of writing to meet the challenges to the traditional resources of literature posed by a changing political environment. This is why the first two chapters provide a much more selective look at the literary genres that flourished at the Caroline court in the years before 'royalism' began to emerge as a concept, in order to establish the nature of what Malcolm Smuts has called the 'stock of ideas, images, and symbols that lay ready to hand for the publicists of the Civil War period'.[25] It is hoped that by submitting to close scrutiny a substantial body of texts associated with royal occasions, committed to defending or furthering the royalist cause, or merely preoccupied with aspects of royal policy and behaviour, this study will throw some new light on the use of the written, printed, and performed word to influence events or to control the way in which events were interpreted. And behind those public functions of the writing which was designed to support the cause of monarchy in general and of Charles I or Charles II in particular, there will be an occasional glimpse of the more private processes by which individual citizens strove to come to terms with what was happening inside themselves as the familiar world turned upside-down.

CHAPTER I

The halcyon days: 1628–1637

When supporters of the royal cause looked back across the conflicts and defeats of the 1640s, they remembered the years of Charles I's personal rule as a golden age of peace and prosperity. Writing shortly after the death of Oliver Cromwell, Abraham Cowley gave poetic expression to a common nostalgia:

> Ah, happy Isle, how art thou chang'd and curst,
>   Since I was born, and knew thee first! . . .
> When upon Earth no Kingdom could have shown
> A happier Monarch to us than our own.[1]

A similar testimony in prose was given by Sir Philip Warwick, who declared that 'from the year 1628, unto the year 1638, I believe England was never Master of a profounder peace, nor enjoy'd more wealth, or had the power and form of godlines more visibly in it'.[2] Edward Hyde, writing as an exile in the Scillies in 1646, laid particular emphasis on the contrast between continental Europe, ravaged by the Thirty Years War, and the realms of Scotland, Ireland and England over which Charles had reigned in peace:

The happiness of the times . . . was enviously set off by this, that every other kingdom, every other province, were engaged, some entangled, and some almost destroyed, by the rage and fury of arms . . . whilst alone the kingdoms we now lament were looked upon as the garden of the world.[3]

This nostalgia for the decade of rule without Parliament had a cultural as well as a political dimension. As Thomas Corns has pointed out, the posthumously published works of Sir John Suckling and Thomas Carew were presented in 1646 and 1651 as witnesses to a lost world in which the arts had flourished.[4] And when Andrew Marvell cast his mind back from 1648 to the period of his first acquaintance with Richard Lovelace as a young man at Cambridge, he defined the innocence of 'that candid Age' in terms of its literary contrast with a present infested with 'Word-peckers, Paper-rats, Book-scorpions'.[5]

7

From the perspective of a nation embroiled in Civil War or experimenting with new forms of government in the wake of a military coup, such an idealization of the past was natural enough – particularly among the gentry class which, it has been argued, enjoyed a period of 'unparalleled prosperity' during the 1630s.[6] But the myth of a Caroline golden age was not the invention of disconsolate Cavaliers and royalist historians exploiting nostalgia for political purposes.[7] It was created during the period of Charles I's personal rule by writers and painters commissioned by the King or Queen, by poets seeking patronage, and by courtiers simply celebrating their own delight in an environment which favoured the cultivation of the arts.[8] The various components that were to contribute to the making of the myth of the 'halcyon days' were ready to hand when the event which decisively changed the direction of Charles's reign took place.[9]

On 23 August 1628, George Villiers, Duke of Buckingham, was assassinated by a discontented naval officer as he was making preparations for an expedition to relieve the besieged French Protestants at La Rochelle. The strong dependence of Charles upon the friendship and political advice of his father's last favourite had been forged during their abortive escapade to Madrid in 1623 to woo the Spanish Infanta. Buckingham had used his power over both the declining James I and the young prince to secure the subsequent war with Spain and the match with the fifteen-year-old French princess, Henrietta Maria, whom Charles married by proxy on 1 May 1625, a few weeks after succeeding to the throne; and he had continued to be the dominant influence in the new king's political and personal life during the early years of his reign. In the opinion of L. J. Reeve, this relationship was a major factor in undermining the foundations upon which the system of Stuart government had hitherto rested:

> The traditional notion of evil counsel had never been further than the shortest of steps from a reflection upon the monarch. In a situation such as that prevailing in 1628 this distinction could not be sustained. The basis for alarm was that, as events had shown, Charles was *susceptible* to such counsel. ... The removal of Buckingham was to bring those who doubted the king a step closer to recognizing him as the cause of their grievances.[10]

Charles never forgave the House of Commons for impeaching his chief counsellor and closest friend in 1626 and when his own attempt to adjourn his third Parliament on 2 March 1629 was resisted, he retaliated by dissolving it and arresting the leading opponents of his policies. In a series of proclamations, he made it clear that he had no plans to summon another parliament in the immediate future. The death of the major architect of his foreign policy, however, had freed Charles to pursue a different course after the failure of the expedition to La Rochelle and he was ready to face the fact that he simply could not finance any more military adventures abroad. With the support of Richard Weston, who rapidly became the most powerful figure in the government as Lord Treasurer, peace treaties were signed with France in April 1629 and with Spain in November 1630.

The first years of Charles's marriage to Henrietta Maria had not been a success. Mentally and physically immature when she arrived in England in June 1625, the French princess was a Catholic in a Protestant country and initially encountered animosity on all sides. Fearing the loss of his own influence over the King, Buckingham had encouraged distrust of the Queen's French household, and Henrietta Maria herself caused dissension by refusing to attend the Protestant ceremony of her husband's coronation in 1626. By August 1628, however, she was ready to fill the void left in Charles's emotional life by the Duke's death and the royal marriage was soon re-established on a basis of mutual love. Her first pregnancy in January 1629 was said to have made the King 'very forward to have a peace' with France;[11] and the loss of their first-born helped to draw the couple closer together. When the future Charles II was born in 1630, Ben Jonson hailed the young mother as 'Spring / Of so much safety to the realm, and king'.[12] Thereafter there was a minor industry of poems greeting the result of each new confinement.[13] The University of Oxford alone produced no less than five volumes to commemorate royal births between 1630 and 1640 and Henry King struck a representative note when he welcomed Charles back from a visit to Scotland in 1633 with the thought that the offspring of his 'fruitfull Love' for Henrietta Maria were 'Seales of your Joy, and of the Kingdome's Peace'.[14]

The arrival of Peter Paul Rubens in London in 1629 to conduct the peace negotiations on behalf of Spain gave Charles an opportunity to signal the change of foreign policy in cultural terms and to incorporate his improved relationship with his wife into the royal myth that was to be cultivated by court artists and writers throughout the 1630s. His major commission for the painter-diplomat was the decoration of the Banqueting House which Inigo Jones had designed for James I. In addition to the depiction of James as Solomon summoning the allegorical figures of Peace and Plenty, the central oval of the ceiling was to be occupied by the apotheosis of James and the side panels filled with images of the Golden Age. All this was a continuation or revival of the cultural traditions of the previous reign, and it fed into the 'halcyon myth' that came to dominate the imagination of many Caroline courtiers and later royalists.[15] Another of the works started by Rubens during his year in England anticipates a motif that was to run through many of the royal entertainments and much of the panegyric output of academic and court poets in the 1630s. In *A Landscape with Saint George and the Dragon*, Charles is the model for St George and Henrietta Maria is the princess who has inspired his courageous victory over the dragon. Malcolm Smuts decodes the political message embodied in the details of a picture in which 'the landscape represents the kingdom itself', released from the 'devouring monster' of war, and 'the royal couple have already become guardians of peace, in an extended sense which encompasses their personal victories over passion, the defense of the church, and their patronage of the civilizing arts.'[16]

In the field of literature, it is appropriate to find at the threshold of the new age a liminal poem in the form of 'A New-yeares gift. To the King' by the man who has been described as 'the Caroline *arbiter elegantiae*', the number and variety of whose commendatory verses and literary epistles 'testify to the central position he commanded in the artistic life of the court'.[17] Thomas Carew had been personally singled out by Charles for service as a gentleman of the Privy Chamber and evidently enjoyed an intimate relationship with his royal master. The poem he presented to him on 1 January 1631 brings together the themes and motifs of both the commissions that had recently been given to Rubens and sets the cultural agenda for the decade that it ushers in so gracefully. After calling upon the classical god who stands at the gateway between the old year and the new to twine 'auspitious dayes' into a wreath for the monarch, Carew utters a benediction over Charles in his two family roles as husband and father. The joys of the marriage bed and fidelity to his beautiful consort have a direct bearing upon the performance of his kingly duties 'by day', seasoning the 'cares' of public responsibility with private consolation; and the fruits of that happy and stable union will be a blessing to both parents and kingdom, as they grow into the royal inheritance symbolized by their status as 'Suns' in the social and political firmament.[18] Carew then turns to the strategies of international and domestic policy which it will be his task as an artist to endow with cultural values:

Circle with peacefull Olive bowes,
And conquering Bayes, his Regall browes.
Let his strong vertues overcome,
And bring him bloodlesse Trophies home:
Strew all the pavements, where he treads
With loyall hearts, or Rebels heads;
But *Byfront*, open thou no more,
In his blest raigne the Temple dore.

The strength of the self-disciplined monarch will make itself felt on the European stage through the exemplary exercise of virtue rather than military force; and at home these same personal qualities will win the trust of the people, and if necessary put down resistance. The allusion in the final couplet invokes the powerful cultural icon of Augustus Caesar, who ruled over that golden age of Roman civilization during which the arts flourished and the doors of the temple of Janus ('*Byfront*') were closed to signify that there was peace throughout the empire. In this, the poet was very much in tune with the instincts of his royal patron, who placed the impressive portrait of himself in imperial guise by Van Dyck at the end of a gallery lined with Titian's portraits of the Caesars and Guido Romano's smaller series of them on horseback.[19]

But if painting and music were the arts for which Charles I had the deepest regard, the aesthetic medium most characteristic of his court and most instrumental in purveying its ideology of kingly rule was the masque.[20] The two earliest of the Caroline texts to survive are from 1631, the year heralded by Carew as the first in which the reign was blessed by peace. Both were by Ben Jonson and they established a pattern which reflected the other blessing of harmonious love between King and Queen: Charles presented an entertainment to Henrietta Maria at the end of the Christmas celebrations early in January and she reciprocated by presenting one to Charles at Shrovetide. It is made apparent in Jonson's introduction to the printed version of the first of the 1631 masques, *Love's Triumph Through Callipolis*, that the King was quite consciously intent on elevating his new-found feeling towards his wife to mythological status. The poet and his collaborator, Inigo Jones, had been commanded 'to thinke on some thing worthy of his Majesties putting in act, with a selected company of his Lords, and Gentlemen, called to the assistance: For the honor of his Court, and the dignity of that heroique love, and regall respect borne by him to his unmatchable Lady, and Spouse, the Queenes Majestie'.[21] This passage also indicates a major change in the nature of the masque in the Caroline period. The

King had been the chief spectator at the productions of the Jacobean court, but his son would himself be the chief masquer, 'putting in act' the artistic conceptions of his writer and designer, as would the Queen in the works that she commissioned. As the recipient of the masque, Henrietta Maria occupied the central seat on the dais from which she had the most privileged view. In a final piece of stage spectacle, the roses of England and lilies of France united in a *'Crowne imperiall'* at the top of a palm tree; and in a final song, Venus and the Chorus celebrated the propitious effects of mutual love between the principal masquer and the principal spectator. The participation of the monarch himself as a performer meant that he could be fully incorporated into the mythologi-cal fiction as the power which brought about the transformation from disorder to harmony at the climax of the action, when the twelve antimasquers who represented 'deprav'd Lovers' were put to flight by the entry of the fifteen *'perfect* Lovers' led by Charles. And when he and the Queen danced together in the revels, they made manifest in their own ordered movements the effects of a shared and disciplined love and became living symbols of the benefits their marriage bestowed upon the country.

The masques by Jonson and his successors in the early 1630s, per-formed in the majestic setting of the Banqueting House where import-ant ceremonies of state also took place, were thus deliberate attempts to bring the resources of pagan mythology, religious ritual and theatrical art together in a cultural statement about the ideology and the political priorities of the Caroline regime. It has been argued that the Banqueting House itself 'functioned as a temple of royal divinity, expressing the sanctity of the king through an elaborate architectural language'; and that the masques exploited a comparable symbolism, which used the rules of single-point perspective in order to emphasize the central position occupied by the royal spectators in the visual arrangement as well as the dramatic impact of the performance: 'the closer one sat to the monarch, the clearer the masque images became, a way of asserting that the whole masquing world revolves around the king.'[22]

The golden age of peace and love which the new foreign policy and the mutual devotion of King and Queen had supposedly ushered in was also celebrated in poetry of various kinds. Sir Richard Fanshawe's famous ode in response to a royal proclamation requiring gentlemen with no urgent business in London to return to their estates looks forward hopefully to the flowering of literature under the imperial patronage of

Charles, the '*Augustus* of our world', who will be praised by a new Virgil as 'author of peace / And *Halcyon* dayes'.[23] Even a poet like Francis Quarles, who was best known for his biblical paraphrases and moral emblems, celebrated the religious benefits of peace in an eclogue which depicted Charles's kingdom as a haven for the persecuted Huguenots of France: 'How happy! O how more then all the rest, / In the wide world, are *Britaine* Shepheards blest.'[24]

Of all the poetic genres encouraged by the Caroline court, however, the most representative of its ethos was the panegyric. As with the related form of the masque, developments begun during the reign of James I came to full fruition under his son. Not that there had been any shortage of poetic praise for their predecessor, as Ruth Nevo points out, but it had reflected in both form and quality a different kind of relationship between monarch and subject:

> The very tendency of Elizabeth to become Gloriana – that is to say, her significance to her people as a supreme symbol in a total system of values, religious, national, ethical, and sociological – militated against the formal separation of royal panegyric from other kinds of literature. She is pervasively present in prose, verse and drama. And it is not until the break in the dynasty ... that the need is felt for a formal and specific expression of the subject's allegiance and of the values which command it.[25]

This need was created by James's avoidance of any spontaneity in his relationship with his people on public occasions, which was taken further by his son, who introduced into the conduct of the royal household the gravity and ceremonial formality that had appealed to him in the etiquette of the Spanish court.[26]

It is hardly surprising that the Caroline court proved fertile ground for the cultivation of a literary genre which has been described as 'highly conventionalized, embedded in social contexts and hierarchies', and designed to validate power 'by reflecting and disseminating the image power would like to project'.[27] The art of panegyric, as practised by the courtiers and academic poets of the 1630s, was often more than empty flattery by those in search of patronage. The writer who praised a person of influence or celebrated a royal occasion was also affirming his ideological allegiances and laying claim to a place within the privileged circle of the culture that his own talent was helping to create and sustain. In this way, panegyrics served 'a virtually liturgical function, for their authors and the community for which they were written';[28] and like the court masques, they contributed to the separation of that community from the larger society beyond Whitehall and the colleges of Oxford and

Cambridge. The poetry occasioned by Charles's visit to Edinburgh in the summer of 1633 may be taken to typify the methods of the panegyrists who directed encomiums at members of the royal family on almost any pretext – a birth, a miscarriage, an anniversary, the return from a journey or recovery from an illness. The young Cambridge poet, Abraham Cowley, invoked the god-like combination of qualities in England's monarch:

> Yet while our CHARLES with equal Balance reigns
> 'Twixt *Mercy* and *Astraea*; and maintains
> A noble Peace, 'tis he, 'tis only he
> Who is most near, most like the Deity.[29]

For Henry King, the winter created by the King's sojourn in his northern kingdom was ended by his sun-like return; and William Cartwright rejoiced on behalf of his countrymen that 'We are a people now againe, and may / Style our selves Subjects', and went on to imagine how the benighted Scots would boast to their posterity 'that they were seene by Thee'.[30]

Even during these early years of the personal rule, when the death of Buckingham had removed a major grievance and the end of hostilities with France and Spain had eased the pressure on the government to raise money from an unwilling populace, the myth of a harmonious nation ruled by the royal embodiments of virtue, beauty and love was belied by signs of discontent not far beneath the surface. At the very time that negotiations for a peace treaty between England and Spain were nearing completion, renewed impetus was given to the anti-Catholic cause in Europe by the rise of a young military hero, Gustavus Adolphus of Sweden, whose exploits in Germany raised the spirits of Protestants generally and of English supporters of the exiled Elector Palatine in particular. Hopes that the marriage of Charles's sister, Elizabeth, to the Elector Frederick V in 1613 was the signal for England to play a more active role in the Protestant Union had come to nothing, and English public opinion was inflamed when Frederick and Elizabeth, who had been offered the throne of Bohemia, were driven from Prague in 1620 by the forces of the Catholic League. Unable to return to the Palatinate, which had been occupied by the armies of Spain and the League, they became a focus for those in England who distrusted the foreign policy of the Stuart kings. In the context of the recent treaties with the Catholic powers of France and Spain, the victories of Gustavus Adolphus against the forces that had dispossessed James I's daughter were felt as a national reproach by a significant number of Charles's subjects. The shock of the Swedish King's death at the battle of Lutzen on 6 November 1632 resulted in a remarkable outburst of literary activity, some of which speaks with more than formal grief of a loss that seemed to thwart apocalyptic expectations of the final triumph of Protestantism.[31]

In a poem which has been called 'the best known tribute' to the Caroline peace,[32] Carew replies to the suggestion that he should join his fellow poets in honouring 'the dead conquering King'. Aurelian Townshend's 'Elegy on the death of the King of Sweden: sent to Thomas Carew' contains the implication – similar to that in another elegy by Henry King – that the Swedish warrior's achievements have become the measure of true kingship, which is now in short supply.[33] In declining Townshend's challenge, Carew acknowledges Gustavus's great reputation, but rejects the world of victories and defeats as a subject for his own poetry, which, in the reading of Kevin Sharpe, 'has a more sublime purpose and engagement than with the flux of European power politics', being concerned with 'the restoration of a golden age of innocence beside the calm of which the battles of Germany seem but a noise in time'.[34] But the creation of an image of that golden age through art does not preclude an awareness of the facts of the real world. Indeed, it is by confronting those facts with a realism not found in other elegies on Gustavus Adolphus that the value of the poet's task is established.[35] There is the grim fact of a continent laid waste and the certainty that there can be no final victors in a religious war of this kind. Against such a background, the poet's advice to his fellow countrymen has considerable force:

> But let us that in myrtle bowers sit
> Under secure shades, use the benefit
> Of peace and plenty, which the blessed hand
> Of our good King gives this obdurate Land.[36]

Even here, in the juxtaposition of 'good King' and 'obdurate Land', there is a realistic acknowledgement of the difficulties that Charles was experiencing in getting his foreign policy accepted in some quarters. Carew's argument, however, was directed more narrowly at the court poets of England, like Townshend, who had a particular role to play in inculcating the values of a peaceful society in which the civilized arts were encouraged:

> Let us of Revels sing, and let thy breath
> (Which fill'd Fames trumpet with *Gustavus* death,
> Blowing his name to heaven) gently inspire

> Thy past'rall pipe, till all our swaines admire
> Thy song and subject, whilst they both comprise
> The beauties of the *SHEPHERD'S PARADISE.*

In endorsing the genre of pastoral, Carew had in mind the values promoted at court in plays like Walter Montagu's *The Shepheard's Paradise*, which Henrietta Maria acted in during January 1633, and masques like Townshend's own *Tempe Restored*, which had been performed in February 1632; and in reminding his fellow poet that 'Tourneyes, Masques, Theaters, better become / Our *Halcyon* dayes' than 'the German Drum' and 'the thunder of their Carabins', his object was to counter an unthinking enthusiasm for the *idea* of war by writers who owed the very privilege of practising their art in 'calme securitie' to the the foreign policy of 'our good king'.

As the 1630s wore on, voices of criticism began to be raised more insistently against the economic, social, and religious effects of the King's rule without Parliament. Ship Money writs were issued annually from 1634 and for some time proved to be a remarkably successful expedient in the absence of an elected body to vote subsidies.[37] By 1637, however, opposition to what many regarded as an illegal tax was mounting and on 2 February Charles wrote to the judiciary to ask for a ruling on a king's right to compel his subjects to contribute financially to the defence of the realm. All twelve judges confirmed that he had such a right. Armed with this opinion, he allowed a test case to be brought against John Hampden, who had refused to pay his Ship Money assessment. After listening to the arguments from both sides, the judges began to deliver their individual judgements early in 1638, and by June the Attorney-General was able to announce that the legality of the tax had been established by the far from convincing majority of seven to five. Charles had not heard the last of this verdict or of Hampden.

The decision in 1633 to reissue James I's Declaration of Sports, which aimed at promoting the rural festivals and pastimes that were regarded as survivals of paganism and occasions of immorality by the puritan clergy, has been described by a historian of popular culture as part of 'a conservative ideological campaign to repair the vertical ties which bound the social structure together'.[38] David Loewenstein highlights the religious ramifications of this policy, which resulted in 'maypoles themselves' becoming 'symbols of release from godly reformation of the church encouraged by Puritanism'.[39]

A much more audacious puritan assault on the culture of the court itself was launched by William Prynne in *Histriomastix*, which branded women who appeared on the stage as 'notorious whores' and pronounced it 'infamous' for kings 'to act or frequent Playes, or favour Players'. Published in November 1632, only two months before the Queen took part in *The Shepheard's Paradise*, the book was suppressed and its author eventually tried and sentenced to have his ears cropped. Prynne was in trouble again in 1637, when he and two other puritans, John Bastwick and Henry Burton, were brought before Star Chamber for publishing treatises that attacked the ceremonies and government of the national church. Condemned to be whipped, pilloried and mutilated, the three men bore their punishment with such fortitude that they won themselves a reputation as martyrs and fuelled the growing hostility towards the church authorities. There has been a great deal of debate about the extent to which William Laud, the Archbishop of Canterbury since 1633, was to blame for the resentment that boiled over in 1640. Certainly his name was associated with policies that antagonized the puritan element in the Church of England: the placing of the communion table at the east end of the chancel, the railing of altars, the practices of bowing to the altar and kneeling to receive communion. Kevin Sharpe has demonstrated, however, that although Laud was in favour of a renewed stress on the ceremonial aspects of worship, he did not seek to impose his will with such authoritarian strictness as many of his contemporaries believed and later historians have asserted.[40] In some cases, Charles I may have been more insistent on enforcing compliance with controversial measures than Laud himself, but one concern on which they worked closely together was that of the poor condition of many church buildings.[41] In London, the King took the lead in an ambitious project for repairing St Paul's Cathedral and engaged Inigo Jones to design a new west portal.[42] The scheme took on symbolic significance for one poet, who saw in it a summation of Charles I's exemplary conduct as man, king, and churchman.

Edmund Waller's panegyric, 'Upon His Majesty's Repairing of Paul's', recalled that this 'work of cost and piety' had been mooted by James I, but was only now being accomplished 'by his glorious son'.[43] Comparing him with Amphion, whose music raised the walls of Thebes, the poet invoked the image of Charles that had been elaborated in the masques: 'For in his art of regiment is found / A power like that of harmony in sound'. Treated as an emblem of the relationship between the English monarch and the institution that has been entrusted to his care, the act of refurbishment is seen as 'an earnest of his grand design, /

To frame no new church, but the old refine'. And in emphasizing the essentially conservative programme of restoration undertaken by Charles and Laud, Waller sets in stark relief the threat to the ancient fabric of worship by those who were clamouring to frame a 'new church' under the banner of reformation.

The day after the first sentence of mutilation was imposed on Prynne in February 1634, the King had led out the masquers in the performance of a work which has been described as 'the greatest theatrical expression of the Caroline autocracy' and said to mark 'the summer solstice of royal confidence'.[44] It has also been read as 'one of the best examples we have of an ironic and sardonic treatment of the values of the court and of the masques which represented them'.[45] Such contradictory judgements indicate something of the complexity of what is slowly being recognized as a central text for understanding the court culture of the 1630s and the tensions that inhabit the art of its best and most representative poet.[46] Thomas Carew's *Coelum Britannicum* begins with an orthodox presentation of the conceit upon which the masque's action will be constructed. Mercury explains that the 'exemplar life' of Charles and Henrietta Maria has made its influence felt amongst the Olympian gods, who have determined to lay aside their 'wild lusts' and cleanse the firmament, replacing 'infamous lights' with new stars recruited from the present courtiers and past heroes of Britain, who will 'alone dispence / To'th'world a pure refined influence'.[47] Mercury is soon joined by the subversive figure of Momus, however, whose prose has a very different tone from the verse spoken by the messenger of the gods and who scornfully ignores the command to bridle his 'licentious tongue'. Together, from their contrasting perspectives of idealization and satire, Mercury and Momus proceed to purge the heavens and to conduct a series of comic interviews with candidates for the places vacated by the immoral constellations. Eventually, Momus declares that he has grown 'weary of these tedious pleadings' and leaves Mercury to oversee the climactic spectacle in which Charles, his Queen and his courtiers are stellified. A final song celebrates the justice and gentleness with which the 'Royall Turtles' reign over 'their Subjects hearts', and looks to the continuation of the Stuart line far into the future under their heavenly influence: '*Propitious Starres shall crowne each birth, / Whilst you rule them, and they the Earth*'.

There is no doubt that the contending voices and visions of Mercury and Momus reflect the two sides of Carew's own artistic activity as panegyrist and satirist, both promoting and debunking the extreme idealization of female virtue, sexual relations and royal power in the court culture of the 1630s. A question mark remains over the extent to which the sceptical realism of Momus was expected to colour the audience's reception of the undiluted Platonism that takes over once he has withdrawn from the scene. Jennifer Chibnall regards him as a device for exorcising through laughter 'those aspects of social reality which could be brought against the harmonious vision the masque is to present'.[48] Joanne Altieri makes Momus much more central to the experience of the whole masque as Carew's instrument for bringing 'contingent life into contact with the perfected constructions of an idealistically imagined world' and so forcing the audience 'to judge the constructs in terms both of reality and of their self-enclosed consistency'. This is not to say that the voice of Momus is intended to invalidate the voice of Mercury; rather, the realist 'comes on stage to present the realities which both challenge and necessitate idealization'.[49] Whatever judgement is reached about the balance between political scepticism and aesthetic illusion in *Coelum Britannicum*, it no longer seems adequate to dismiss it as a thoughtless reflection of 'the easy Court view' that the King's subjects 'were cheerful, loyal and reverent'.[50] On the contrary, in seriousness of purpose and in the skilful adaptation of an ephemeral form into a vehicle for genuine intellectual debate, it can claim pride of place among the literary artifacts generated from within the culture of the Caroline court.

There had always been antagonism between Henrietta Maria and Richard Weston, now Earl of Portland, who favoured a maritime treaty with Spain, wariness of the French and non-involvement in the European wars. When he fell ill towards the end of 1634, the Queen's court became the focus for increased activity by the anti-Spanish faction led by the earls of Holland and Northumberland.[51] Her closeness to Charles and the lack of any favourite in succession to Buckingham gave her considerable political importance as Portland's deteriorating health made a change of personnel in the higher reaches of the administration imminent. When he died, the two leading contenders for the empty post were Sir Thomas Wentworth, Lord Deputy of Ireland, who was supported by Laud, and Sir Francis Cottington, who was backed by the faction gathered around Henrietta Maria. After a lengthy delay, the Treasurership eventually went to Laud's alternative candidate, William Juxon.

The death of Portland also emboldened those at the English court who had long been advocating more active assistance for the exiled (and now widowed) Elizabeth of Bohemia and her son, Charles Louis, the displaced Elector Palatine, and the outbreak of war between France and Spain in 1635 gave them a new opportunity to press their case. Under mounting pressure from his sister, his wife, and leading courtiers like Hamilton and Holland to make a positive move over the Palatinate, Charles kept diplomatic channels open with both Spain and France. On 21 November 1635, while various negotiations were in progress, Charles Louis arrived in England, only a few weeks short of his majority, and was soon joined by his younger brother, Prince Rupert. The young Elector was widely feted and over the next two years theatrical productions of various kinds played no small part in the demonstrations of political support for his cause.[52] Sharpe considers that this propaganda offensive brought the King closer to 'engaging himself in the spring of 1637 than at any point since the wars of the 1620s'.[53] Events conspired against such an end to the Caroline peace, however, and before the year was over his nephews had been recalled to resume the struggle in Europe without his help and Charles I had become increasingly preoccupied with problems nearer home.

CHAPTER 2

The Bishops' Wars and the Short Parliament: *July 1637 – October 1640*

Edward Hyde's survey of the peace and prosperity enjoyed by Charles I's three kingdoms during the 1630s comes to a dramatic climax with his evocation of the unexpectedness and comprehensiveness of the calamity that brought the period of personal rule to an end:

A small, scarce discernible Cloud arose in the North; which was shortly after attended with such a Storm, that never gave over raging, till it had shaken, and even rooted up the greatest and tallest Cedars of the three Nations; blasted all its Beauty, and Fruitfulness; brought its Strength to Decay, and its Glory to Reproach, and almost to Desolation; by such a Career and Deluge of Wickedness, and Rebellion, as by not being enough foreseen, or, in Truth suspected, could not be prevented.[1]

As we have seen, there were various sources of discontent at court, in the church, and in the country at large which were highlighted by the visit of the Palatine princes and by the cases of John Hampden and the puritans, Burton, Bastwick and Prynne. Whatever the more deep-seated causes of the Civil War may have been, however, the immediate crisis which would eventually result in Parliament's challenge to royal sovereignty was provoked by Charles's mismanagement of affairs in Scotland.

The union of the English and Scottish crowns in 1603 had led to the neglect of the northern kingdom by the Stuart dynasty, so that when Charles I travelled to Edinburgh for his coronation in 1633, it was the first time the inhabitants of Scotland had been favoured with the presence of their King for more than fifteen years.[2] There was already a dangerous gap of knowledge and sympathy separating James's son from the people among whom he had been born, and it was during his brief visit that the seeds of the crisis of 1637 were sown. Charles and his councillors from Whitehall failed to appreciate the dismay caused by the vestments and rites used in the coronation ceremony in Holyrood chapel; they did not understand the extent of the resentment that lay behind petitions about the state of the Kirk; and they ignored the significance of the narrow margins by which the Scottish parliament ratified articles designed to impose conformity on the church in Scotland.

Soon after his return to England, Charles had urged the Scottish bishops to prepare a Book of Common Prayer and canons which would ensure uniformity of discipline in the churches of Scotland. The convocation in Ireland had recently accepted the Elizabethan prayer book and the Articles of 1562, and Charles and his Archbishop of Canterbury, William Laud, now pressed on towards their goal of establishing a common liturgy throughout the three kingdoms. The new book had been completed by the autumn of 1636 and was published in 1637.[3] After the riot that greeted the first attempt to use it in St Giles's Cathedral on 23 July, petitions against the book poured in. Apprized by his Scottish Council of the fierce resistance to what many regarded as popish forms of worship, the King adamantly refused to give way. The situation steadily worsened through the winter months and the National Covenant, a declaration of Scottish commitment to Calvinist doctrines and a Presbyterian system of church government, was signed by lords and gentlemen assembled in Greyfriars Kirk in Edinburgh on 28 February 1638. Within weeks it had been carried all over the southern parts of the country.

As the movement gathered momentum through the spring, Charles realized that he would have to gain time by opening negotiations with the Covenanters, while he made ready to enforce his will by military means. He appointed the Marquis of Hamilton as his Commissioner, with authority to suspend the order for the use of the prayer book and to receive petitions in his name, on condition that the Covenant be repudiated.[4] Early in June, Hamilton reported that far from submitting to the King, the leaders of the rebellion were demanding a parliament and a church assembly. During the summer months, both sides began to raise troops and purchase arms. When the Assembly convened in Glasgow on 21 November, its legality was challenged in a letter from the bishops, who were prevented from taking their seats until a petition indicting them of various crimes had been answered. A week later, Hamilton attempted to dissolve the Assembly and when the Covenanters refused to obey, he withdrew the sanction of royal authority. Over the next three weeks, the Assembly defiantly passed a series of measures which abolished the episcopacy and set up a commission to expel from the church anyone who resisted the Covenant. At the English court, the usual Christmas festivities gave place to preparations for war.

One of the earliest literary responses to the crisis in Scotland came not from a courtier or a professional writer, but from the unknown pen of a scholarly and retiring member of the minor gentry in Yorkshire. The second son of Sir Ingleby Daniel of Beswick, a manor in the East Riding about six miles from Beverley, George Daniel would have been twenty-one years old when he composed his first substantial poem, if the date of 1637 which he claims for it in the manuscript collection of his poetry is to be believed.[5] 'The Genius of this Great and glorious Ile' begins with the description of an earthly paradise in which the poet encounters the beautiful female figure of the title, who relates the history of Great Britain from Roman and Saxon times. It is evident that Daniel is drawing his inspiration from the materials and methods of the court masques that must have been in the library of this obscure but well-read young man.[6] The burden of the story told by 'POORE ALBION' is summed up early in the poem: 'But from the Norman Conquest to these Ages, / How manie wounds! how manie bloodie Stages!' Particular attention is given to the Wars of the Roses and the scars they have left on the armour and the person of 'the Genius'. The emphasis on the iconic aspects of the speaker as a necessary complement to her words looks like a deliberate attempt to imitate the masque as an expressive medium:

> Looke, looke upon this Caske, and see old blowes;
> See the deepe Dints which warre in it hath made;
> Read in my quarter'd face, what speech not showes.

Eventually, the antimasques of war and destruction are superseded by the idyllic vision of a nation at peace under Elizabeth and her successors. Uniting the crowns of England and Scotland after the 'Halcion daies' of the Virgin Queen, the imperial and god-like James I and VI of the masque tradition is celebrated above all as promoter of the arts of writing, both by patronage and by example: 'More then Augustus, Patron to a Muse, / A Muse thy Selfe'. But these great monarchs are only forerunners of the one whose approach dispels the grief caused by the passing of James: 'This, this is Hee / (Sprung from that glorious Stemme) shall bee to mee / Cheife ornament to all Posteritie'. The imagined descent of the current King of England and Scotland, like the entry of the chief dancer in one of Inigo Jones's spectacles, is the climactic event of the pageant of history presented by the Genius of Britain, who exclaims, 'Blest in the Raigne of Charles, I joy and Live'.

The poem does not end like a masque, however, on this note of triumph and harmony. In the final third of the text, the Genius recognizes the tell-tale signs of impending disorder – 'See, how the Malecontents doe Mutinie' – and rebukes as unworthy of their birthright those who 'mutter Treason, and thinke villanie / Against their Prince'. She condemns those whose 'Endeavours' are a threat to the unity of the island, reminding them that 'no Glorie can unto me Accrue / From Seperations'. Whether Daniel has in mind the separatist tendencies of English puritans or the challenge being made to Charles's authority in his northern kingdom, he evidently feels that the principles of monarchical government and divine right need to be asserted:

> Hee is my Guide: Why should I derogate
> From my owne right? 'Tis noe Discoursive thing,
>   High Majestie; but under heaven doth bring
> An awe, and more; a distant Reverence,
> Beyond dispute claiming obedience.

The Genius advises her 'Rebellious Sons' to heed the lessons of their own country's history and to take warning from the present miseries of France and Germany, so that they will 'Bee wise in Time'. Invoking the myth that had been so assiduously created in the literary productions of the Caroline court, the allegorical mouthpiece for Daniel's patriotic fervour declares that there was never yet 'soe blest a government / To silence Envie', even though it suffers detraction by 'the venom\u1d49d tongues / Of Malice'. In imitation of the closing ceremonies of the masque form, the Genius then calls upon the nation's poets to sing the praises of the King from whom 'proceeds, what ever you can boast', greets the 'Royall Mother of the Hopes', and vanishes. The poet concludes with a determination to 'sing / In Louder straine, the Glories of my King'. The final effect of the poem, however, is not to dispel the sense of foreboding but to articulate the fear that the reigns of Elizabeth and James and the early years of Charles may prove to have been no more than a blessed interlude in the 'manie bloody Stages' of British history. The antimasque of Civil War is felt to be waiting in the wings, ready to sweep away the pastoral landscapes and the graces and gods who peopled them in Inigo Jones's illusory evocations of a golden age restored. Daniel's poem stands as one of the first conscious statements of royalism, in the sense of allegiance to the office of the crown and the person of the King at a time when the authority of both was being challenged.

In sharp contrast to the Yorkshire gentleman's troubled mediation between the aesthetic fantasies of Caroline art and the facts of the contingent world, the courtier's welcome tendered by Edmund Waller to Marie de Medici, the Queen Mother, resolutely refuses to acknowledge the embarrassment caused by her arrival in October 1638. The foundering of treaty negotiations with France had led to Henrietta Maria's estrangement from those Puritan politicians who had sought to exploit her influence over the King and a faction of Catholics was now uniting around her at court. At the same time, there were rumours that the King was seeking to enlist the help of Spanish regiments in Flanders and that Sir Thomas Wentworth, Lord Deputy of Ireland, was planning to bring over an army to crush the Covenanters. Several conversions at court in 1638 also contributed to the growing suspicion of a popish conspiracy. It was an inopportune moment for the Queen's mother to settle herself in London and establish another subversive centre of Catholic worship in her chapel. Ignoring the crisis at home which was driving the King towards armed suppression of his Protestant subjects in Scotland, and England's conspicuous failure to give substantial aid to the Protestant cause abroad, Waller welcomes the Catholic mother of Charles's Catholic wife 'to sea-girt Britain's shore'.[7] The poet takes as his central conceit the fact that her offspring wear 'All the chief crowns' of Europe, which means that her 'godlike race must sway the age to come'. This prompts him to imagine a simple resolution of the conflicts that have been devastating the continental mainland for the past twenty years: let Marie's royal progeny 'compose those jars, / And on the growing Turk discharge their wars'. They will soon wrest the 'sacred tomb' in Jerusalem from 'Pagan hands' in a triumphant crusade: 'Our England's Prince, and Gallia's Dauphin, might / Like young Rinaldo and Tancredo fight'. Politics are displaced by aesthetics as Waller transforms contemporary reality into a dream of chivalry, in which 'Christian knights' – untroubled by the distinctions of Protestant or Catholic – slay the dragon of Paganism in the service of Marie de Medici, like heroes from medieval romance. Daniel had invoked the historical past for the bitter lessons it might teach the present; Waller escapes into a past that is already more fantasy than fact in his quest for witty ways of praising a potential patron.

During January, Charles had been appointing his principal officers for a campaign against the Covenanters and on 27 March he set out to join the army that had been raised in Yorkshire. On 3 June, the Earl of

Holland advanced towards Kelso to meet a Scottish force under the command of Alexander Leslie. By the time he got within sight of the enemy with a troop of horse, he had left his infantry far behind. Realizing that he was greatly outnumbered, he had no alternative but to retreat, much to the delight of the jeering Scots. Peace negotiations began a few days later and were concluded with the signing of the Pacification of Berwick on 18 June.[8]

From the early days of the conflict, the leaders of the rebellion had seen the importance of presenting their case to Charles's English subjects as well as winning support for the Covenant in Scotland. Works primarily aimed at a Scottish readership, such as *Reasons for which the Service Book ought to be Refused*, had found their way across the border, but with the publication of *A Short Relation of the State of the Kirk of Scotland . . . to our Brethren in the Kirk of England* later in 1638 a more direct appeal was made to opponents of the King's policy in England. Charles had tried to counter the effect of petitions and seditious sermons with Scottish proclamations in December 1637 and February 1638, and on 27 February 1639 he explained the course of action he was now forced to take against the Covenanters for the benefit of English readers in *A Large Declaration Concerning the Late Tumults in Scotland*. His purpose in leading an expedition against his northern subjects was to tie the two kingdoms united by the Stuart dynasty 'in a stronger bond of love forever together . . . both of them meeting in this point and centre viz. the defence of our person, and of our royal crown and dignity'.[9] These were the traditional terms in which the English monarchy expressed its claims to allegiance, but the propaganda war generated by the Scots' rejection of the prayer book had significant repercussions in England, bringing 'the issues of church government, the nature of authority and obedience, even the right of resistance into the forum of public debate' and eventually transforming 'the perceptions of events and the language and taxonomy of politics'.[10]

One of the earliest attempts to justify the use of force against the Scots was in *God Save the King* (London, 1639), a sermon preached in St Paul's on the day Charles left London. Taking his text from the Old Testament – 'And all the people shouted, and said, God save the King' (1 Samuel 10: 24) – Henry Valentine rehearsed some of the arguments and images that would be endlessly repeated and refuted in the course of the next decade: that the King 'by his *Lawes*, as the *Sun* by his *Beames*, dispels and scatters those deeds of Darknesse which otherwise would cover the face of the Common-wealth'; that the King 'is *Imago Dei*, the bright *Image* of

God, and the most magnificent and conspicuous representation of Divine Majesty'; that a king 'is *Pastor populi*, the *Shepheard* of the *people*' (pp. 5–6). This was the conventional stuff of court panegyric and entertainment. It was now being mobilized not to sustain the idealized self-perception of the royal recipients but to defend the office of the King against men who were challenging the old arguments and over whom such imagery had no persuasive power.

For some of the poets watching and commenting from the sidelines as Charles marched northwards, personalities were of much greater concern than the religious or political issues over which war was about to be waged. Both Waller and Abraham Cowley were apprehensive about the fate of Lucius Cary, Viscount Falkland, who had kept open house at Great Tew and attracted into his circle some of the most learned and talented figures of the age. Edward Hyde was among them and was later to give a glowing account of the man and his cultural significance:

In this time, his house being within ten miles of Oxford, he contracted familiarity and friendship with the most polite and accurate men of that university; who found such an immenseness of wit, and such a solidity of judgment in him, so infinite a fancy bound in by a most logical ratiocination, such a vast knowledge that he was not ignorant in any thing, yet such an excessive humility as if he had known nothing, that they frequently resorted and dwelt with him, as in a college situated in a purer air.[11]

In his panegyrical address 'To My Lord Falkland', Waller sees him as an embodiment of the values that flourished during the 'halcyon days' of peace. His opening gambit is to imagine that Falkland and 'Brave Holland' have been sent on a mission to 'civilize and to instruct the north'.[12] Such a fancy, however, cannot disguise the grim fact that the 'ornaments' which grace a cultivated way of life do not 'make swords less sharp'. Falkland is like Apollo, who not only fosters the arts but also has the courage 'to guard the invaded throne / Of Jove, and cast the ambitious giants down'; but this is little consolation to those who think 'on the blind events of war and thee!' Recoiling from the 'horror' of such a thought, Waller wishes forlornly that the present troubles might be expelled from the stage of history like the wild antics of an antimasque: 'Some happy wind over the ocean blow / This tempest yet, which frights our island so!'

Cowley's 'To the Lord Falkland. For his safe Return from the Northern Expedition against the SCOTS' is spoken by a more distant admirer of 'this great *Prince* of *Knowledge*' than Waller's address to his

'noble friend'. For him, Falkland symbolizes the complete Renaissance
man, whose intellectual achievements are matched by a readiness for
active service; but the exemplary status accorded him in both these
spheres raises unexpected difficulties. The poem begins with a statement
of what is being put at risk by the Scottish campaign: 'Great is thy *Charge*,
O *North*; be wise and just, / *England* commits her *Falkland* to thy trust; /
Return him safe'.[13] After expatiating on the depth and balance of
Falkland's scholarship, the poet turns to his hero's willing commitment
of himself to 'th' noise and business of a State':

> Whilst we who can no action undertake,
> Whom *Idleness* it self might *Learned* make,
> Who hear of nothing, and as yet scarce know,
> Whether the *Scots* in *England* be or no,
> Pace dully on, oft tire, and often stay,
> Yet see his nimble *Pegasus* fly away.

In contrast to Waller's absorption of Falkland into the realms of masque
and myth, Cowley conveys the texture of the existential moment. The
hesitant movement of the verse in the penultimate line betrays the
combination of uncertainty and guilt felt by those left behind, waiting
for news which was slow in filtering south. But the poet does not know
what to make of these unfamiliar feelings, generated by the exposure of
the highly prized man of humane culture to the destructive threat of
war. His only answer to the dilemma posed by Falkland's action is to
demand his safe return from the North and to argue that a sharp
distinction should be maintained between the worlds of cultural and
military service:

> He is too good for *War*, and ought to be
> As far from *Danger*, as from *Fear* he's free.
> Those *Men* alone (and those are useful too)
> Whose *Valour* is the onely *Art* they know,
> Were for sad *War* and bloody *Battels* born;
> Let *Them* the *State Defend*, and *He Adorn*.

As a young man of twenty-one in 1639, who had made a name for
himself with the precocious publication of his first volumes of verse in
1633 and 1636, Cowley was a product of the years of peace. In this
poem, he registers the first tremors of the earthquake that was to wreak
havoc in the lives of many who would have preferred to take no part in
the quarrel between the King and his rebellious subjects. One can feel
the ground of settled assumptions about the centrality of the arts and
scholarship beginning to move under his feet in the impotent assertions
that a man who is 'too good' for war 'ought to be' free to cultivate those

superior talents that make him an adornment to the state. The distaste for the men of valour who are merely born for 'bloody *Battels*' is scarcely concealed by the grudging acknowledgement that they 'are useful too'. Falkland's response to the royal call to arms has provoked the young poet into an uncomfortable scrutiny of the values inculcated by the culture in which he grew to maturity. His attempt to resolve the resulting tensions in the neatly balanced antithesis between those destined to defend and those destined to adorn their country is as fragile as other Caroline efforts to impose aesthetic solutions upon social and political problems. As the expedition against the Scots led on step by step to Civil War in England, the kind of dilemma tentatively explored by Cowley in this troubled poem would become a common experience among those who found that there was no escape from the 'noise and business of a State'.

Among those who responded to Charles's call to arms were three of the courtiers known to later literary history under the collective title of the 'Cavalier Poets': Thomas Carew, Sir John Suckling, and Richard Lovelace. Suckling had already entered the fray as a writer in the autumn of 1638 with two letters, purportedly written by a London Alderman and a Scottish Lord.[14] The first sends 'to enquire how Rebellion prospers', likens Scotland 'to a Hive of swarming Bees, which they say the King watches to reduce them for the better', and records the anxiety bred by rumour and ignorance of what was happening in the North: 'Distance and mens fears have so enlarged the truth, and so disproportioned every thing about the Town, that we have made the little Troop of Discontents a gallant Army, and already measure no *Scotchman* but by his evening shadow'. The Scottish Lord, in his 'letter', sardonically rejects 'the name of Rebels' given to the Covenanters, since they use the conventional formula 'his Majesties most humble Subjects' in the 'Petitions and Messages' which openly challenge royal policies and authority; but, to drive home the satirical point, Suckling makes him add: 'True it is, that in case the King will not do what we would have him, we have provided Arms; and have perswaded those here, and sent to others abroad to assist us'.

When Charles issued his summons at the end of January 1639, Suckling was among the first to volunteer, in the flamboyant manner described by John Aubrey: 'Sir John Suckling, at his owne chardge raysed a Troope of 100 very handsome young proper men, whom he clad in white doubletts and scarlett breeches, and scarlet Coates, hatts,

and feathers, well horsed and armed.'[15] This extension of the masque
world beyond the confines of Whitehall, turning war into spectacle,
provoked a number of lampoons, one of which, in a comic variation on
the serious clash of ideals in Cowley's poem on Falkland, urges the
Cavalier to follow his true vocation as a gambler and lady's man rather
than risk his life as a soldier.[16] While in Yorkshire with the army,
Suckling composed another letter for public consumption entitled 'An
answer to a Gentleman in Norfolk that sent to enquire after the Scotish
business'.[17] Employing the two images most commonly associated with
the activities of the Covenanters, Suckling starts by expressing uncertainty about the true nature of the events in Scotland: 'it is fit you know
that this Northern storm (like a new Disease) hath so far pos'd the
Doctors of State, that as yet they have not given it a name; though
perchance they all firmly believe it to be Rebellion'. His own view,
hinted at in references to pretended religion in the letters of 1638, is that
the question is 'rather *A King or no King*, then *A Bishop or no Bishop*', and
that the King's attempt to impose a new prayer book merely furnished
the conspirators with the excuse they had been looking for. In a private
letter, written between 11 and 17 June, he expresses his dissatisfaction at
the conditions that were being negotiated with the Scots and his scepticism about the desire for peace on either side.[18]

Suckling represents one side of the Cavalier stereotype: the swearing,
gambling, devil-may-care philanderer whose cynicism about love and
politics is strangely at odds with his loyal service to a King whose
shortcomings he had shrewdly weighed up. The poet traditionally
regarded as the embodiment of the other side of the stereotype, epitom-
ized by the last two lines of his best-known poem – 'I could not love thee
(Deare) so much, / Lov'd I not Honour more'[19] – is Richard Lovelace.
He had served in the regiment of George Goring and the song with
which he chose to celebrate the end of hostilities drowns the affront to
his idealism administered by the dubious terms signed at Berwick –
'Now the *Peace* is made at the Foes rate' – in a toast to his superior officer
rather than the King: 'That from all Hearts a health may sound / To
Goring! to *Goring!* see't goe round.'[20] This resort to the fellowship of
hard-drinking comrades-in-arms as an antidote to disappointment and
defeat was to become a common feature of later 'Cavalier' poetry.

The third poet produced not a celebratory paean to his King but 'a
masterpiece of nostalgic control', of which Gerald Hammond writes,
'There are few sadder poems in the century.'[21] Carew's 'To my friend
G. N. from *Wrest*' must have been conceived and completed between

the Pacification of Berwick and 21 November 1639, when Henry de Grey, eighth Earl of Kent, died and his seat at Wrest Park passed into the hands of Anthony de Grey, an octogenarian clergyman of puritan leanings. Henry had inherited the estate in 1623 and had created a flourishing cultural life there not unlike that inspired by Falkland at Great Tew.[22] For the courtier lately returned from the Scottish borders, Wrest Park became a poignant symbol of the social and cultural ideals that were now threatened by the political blunders of the King he had served for so long.

The conventions of masque and country house poem are subtly adapted to express Carew's recognition that the royal myth promulgated by himself and others could not survive recent experiences. The weather and the landscapes he had encountered assume the emblematic status of one of Inigo Jones's stage sets in the opening description of a world distressingly different from his present refuge:

> I Breathe (sweet *Ghib*:) the temperate ayre of *Wrest*
> Where I no more with raging stormes opprest,
> Weare the cold nights out by the bankes of Tweed,
> On the bleake Mountaines, where fierce tempests breed,
> And everlasting Winter dwells.[23]

But instead of a spectacular change of scene, the poet has to make his own retreat into the natural haven of peace and order at Wrest Park, which is not blessed by the magical presence of the King but 'cherisht with the warme Suns quickning heate'. The values of his host and hostess transform the roles played by the King and Queen at Whitehall in Carew's studied denial of the spectacle and illusion that had dangerously obscured the practicalities of political reality in court entertainments: 'The Lord and Lady of this place delight / Rather to be in act, then seeme in sight'. And in another contrast between 'outward gay Embellishment' and 'reall use', Carew seems to be invoking the visual effects of a masque merely to reject them in favour of something more substantial: there is no statue of Ceres 'croun'd with wheaten wreathes' nor figure of Bacchus 'on a Marble Tunne' – in emulation of a sculptured frieze adorning one of Jones's proscenium arches. In place of allegories to be interpreted there are solid pleasures to be enjoyed:

> We offer not in Emblemes to the eyes,
> But to the taste those usefull Deities.
> Wee presse the juycie God, and quaffe his blood,
> And grinde the Yeallow Goddesse into food.

The very language enacts the process of transmuting classical deities back into grape and corn, as if Carew were consciously retrieving the real world from a symbolism that can no longer be sustained.

The closing lines of the poem betray his fear that there are others like his friend G. N. who are not content with the settlement reached at Berwick. Their apparent eagerness to resume the struggle against the Scots will threaten the tranquillity of his country refuge and everything it has come to stand for:

> Thus I enjoy my selfe, and taste the fruit
> Of this blest Peace, whilst toyl'd in the pursuit
> Of Bucks, and Stags, th'embleme of warre, you strive
> To keepe the memory of our Armes alive.

'G. N.' or 'sweet *Ghib*' is a device, like Aurelian Townshend in Carew's poem about Gustavus Adolphus, for defining the stance taken by the poet at a particular historical moment. Joanne Altieri comments perceptively on the contrast between the two literary responses: the poet of 1632 'claims to speak for a cultural group ... to one standing, however momentarily, outside the group's putative values'; the poet of 1639 'is himself the outsider, speaking of a memory of peer efforts now forgone'. Those efforts, she concludes, 'are not repudiated, only their effects are sadly minimized'.[24] Carew was both confirming the system of values he had himself been instrumental in shaping, and dissociating himself from the current policies of the King around whose tastes and personality it had been constructed. In the words of another critic, 'Carew's poem constitutes a farewell, in part disillusioned, in the main elegiac, to a court and culture whose time was past'.[25]

Carew had good reason to be pessimistic about the prospects of a lasting peace. Between the signing of the treaty at Berwick and its proclamation by Hamilton in Edinburgh on 24 June, Charles let it be known that he would not ratify the acts of the 'pretended Assembly' at Glasgow and that he expected them to be annulled by a Scottish parliament and an assembly of the Kirk later in the summer. The Earl of Traquair's official announcement that the bishops would attend the assembly was greeted with riots on 1 July; and when it met in Edinburgh on 12 August, it not only confirmed everything that had been enacted at Glasgow but also asserted that episcopacy was contrary to the law of God. The parliament which Traquair opened in the King's name on 31 August proceeded to give legal sanction to the resolutions of the assembly. With the bishops excluded from holding civil office, the Covenanters were in a position to dominate the small committee known as the Lords of the Articles, which was the real seat of political power in the Scottish system. It was over the King's right to be consulted about appointments to this committee that rivalry first broke out between two of the most prominent figures in the Covenanting movement, the Earls of Montrose and Argyll. In time, Montrose's belief that the authority of the King must be maintained as a check to the ambition of men like Argyll would make him the leader of the royalist cause in Scotland.

Meanwhile, Sir Thomas Wentworth had been recalled from Ireland to become one of Charles's closest advisers and in January 1640 was created Earl of Strafford. Along with Laud and Hamilton, he urged the King to accept that the only practical means of regaining control over his northern kingdom was to call a parliament in England, which could vote the subsidies necessary for a second campaign against the Scots. The decision was taken at a meeting of the Privy Council early in December and writs were issued in February for Parliament to assemble on 13 April 1640. The business of recruiting experienced officers for the army and appointing successors to Lord Coventry, the Lord Keeper, who died on 14 January to be replaced by Sir John Finch, and Sir John Coke, whose position as Secretary of State went to Sir Henry Vane, was not enough to distract Charles and his court from preparations for the last of the Caroline masques. In a letter to the Earl of Leicester dated 9 January, Northumberland complained that the King 'is dayly so im-ployed about the Maske, as till that be over, we shall think of little ellse'.[26]

Devised by William Davenant and Inigo Jones, *Salmacida Spolia* had a topicality which was spelled out in the introduction to the printed version: 'Discord, a malicious Fury, appears in a storm and ... having already put most of the world into disorder, endeavours to disturb these parts, envying the blessings and tranquillity we have long enjoyed.'[27] After an antimasque danced by three 'evil spirits' called up by the Fury, the '*horrid scene*' of uprooted trees and turbulent sea changed to present a pastoral image of the ten years of Caroline harmony now threatened by Discord. Concord and the Good Genius of Great Britain slowly descended, singing of the foolish ingratitude of the people, and of the 'cares of wise Philogenes', whose fate is 'to rule in adverse times, / When wisdom must awhile give place to crimes'.

Another change of scene to a landscape of '*craggy rocks and inaccessible mountains*' heralded the arrival of the Chorus of the Beloved People, who were led by Concord and the Good Genius up to the chair of state and lauded its occupant, Marie de Medici, as the comfort and inspiration of her husband, Henri IV of France: 'Your beauty kept his valour's flame alive; / Your Tuscan wisdom taught it how to thrive.' The top part of the desolate scene then opened to reveal the King and the rest of the masquers on '*the Throne of Honour*'. The third song appears to commend Charles's resolution of the recent crisis in Scotland without shedding the blood of rebellious subjects led astray by the malignant few:

> If it be kingly patience to outlast
> Those storms the people's giddy fury raise
> Till like fantastic winds themselves they waste,
> The wisdom of that patience is thy praise.   (stanza 2)

In the circumstances of the autumn and winter of 1639–1640, with the ignominy of the summer's campaign and the Scottish parliament's challenge to royal authority behind and the uncertainties of an English parliament and a second campaign ahead, it is difficult to know what significance to ascribe to contradictory and ambiguous elements in the words and images of *Salmacida Spolia*.[28] This song, which speaks of patience, mercy and forgiveness, is addressed directly to a king who is seated on a throne of honour adorned with palm trees – symbols of military success – and surrounded by '*captives bound, in several postures, lying on trophies of armours, shields, and antique weapons*'. Since events at Kelso and Berwick hardly constituted a triumph of arms, the visual imagery may represent an inferior course of action that has been rejected or it may be an oblique criticism of the way in which the recent peace was achieved. The reference to Charles's patience with his 'people's giddy fury' is at odds with a context in which he was meeting regularly with a Council of War to plan his next attempt to quell rebellion by force. And how much weight should be given to the introductory 'if' of stanza 2, which casts doubt on the argument that patience is the most 'kingly' policy? The song itself, which praises Charles for exhibiting 'mercy' rather than 'valour' in stanza 5 and for eschewing 'outward force' in stanza 6, is placed between the allusion to Marie de Medici as the inspirer of her victorious husband's valour and the entrance of Henrietta Maria, '*representing the chief heroine, environed with her martial ladies*'. At the close of the fourth song, which greets this group of female masquers '*in Amazonian habits*', the Queen is celebrated like her mother as an inspiration not only to lovers but also to soldiers. The masque ends with a visual prospect of an urban centre of civilization and with a final song paying tribute to the influence of the mutual love between Charles and Henrietta Maria, who have taken their seats next to the Queen Mother:

> All that are harsh, all that are rude,
> Are by your harmony subdued;
> Yet so into obedience wrought,
> As if not forc'd to it, but taught.

The 'if' of the final line, like the 'if' of the third song, permits the thought that force may be needed to teach obedience to those who refuse to learn from the example provided by the King and Queen.

This last royal masque does not abandon the Caroline ideal of a national harmony drawing inspiration from the marital example of the royal pair. Indeed it is the only one in which Charles and his wife both took part as masquers. But it is less blind to the realities of the situation in Scotland and the measures that may have to be taken than the dismissal of its allegory as 'defiantly inept' might suggest.[29]

That having been said, however, there was a widespread feeling of relief and even optimism as the date for the opening of the first parliament for eleven years approached. A popular ballad captured the mood of anticipation in a nation which, in spite of all the resentments that had built up over the past decade, was driven more by an eagerness 'to recapture an idealized vision of an Elizabethan harmony in church, state and the localities'[30] than by a desire for confrontation:

> This happy Aprill will, I trust,
> Give all true subjects reason just
> Of joy to feele a pleasant gust,
> To yeeld them hearts content:
> For we may be assur'd of this,
> If any thing hath beene amisse,
> Our King and State will all redresse
> *In this good Parliament.*[31]

Among the King's advisers, Strafford had had some experience of managing the House of Commons and was confident that a Court party could be organized to secure the subsidies that were the primary objective of royal policy. There were signs, however, that a new awareness of national issues was creating a challenge to the traditional system of clientage that had hitherto dominated the electoral process. In an analysis of the evidence that has survived for 83 of the 233 seats, John Gruenfelder detects 'a diminution of crown influence' in ensuring successful nominations and concludes that the preference for local candidates over court nominees bears witness to a 'developing factionalism' and 'the growth of a more political atmosphere in the England of

1640'.[32] Inevitably, events in Scotland cast their shadow over the English elections and there were many – 'too many', in the view of Bulstrode Whitelocke – who were 'not only favoring but joining with and assisting the proceedings of the Scots Covenanters'.[33] The Scottish demand for the conclusions of the general assembly of the Kirk to be ratified by the Scottish parliament was justified to the English public in a tract entitled *Information from the Estaits of Scotland*, two thousand copies of which were distributed by four commissioners who arrived at court on 12 February to put the Covenanters' case directly to Charles. This propaganda appeal to the people of England was quickly answered by the publication of Bishop Hall's *Episcopacy by Divine Right Asserted*, which had been in preparation for some time on Laud's initiative and which was addressed to readers on both sides of the border.[34]

It is evident from the speech with which the Lord Keeper opened proceedings in the Upper House at Westminster on 13 April that the King and his Council were expecting an immediate grant to meet the threat posed by the Covenanters. Lord Finch decried the 'horrid Treason' of those who had 'taken up Armes against the Lords annoynted their rightfull Prince and undoubted soveraigne'; and he stressed the urgency of voting sufficient funds for 'a powerfull Army to reduce them to the just condicions of obedience and subjeccion' lest 'they gaine more time and advantage to frame their projects with forreine States'.[35] When the Commons assembled on 16 April, Harbottle Grimston, member for Colchester, dismissed the supposed 'defeccion of the Kings naturall subjects' in Scotland as less urgent than 'a case of greater dainger here at home domesticall'. Invoking 'the Charter of our Libertyes called magna charta', he painted a lurid picture of the state of Charles's English kingdom, 'the Gospell and the professors of it persecuted' and the whole nation 'over runne with multitudes and swarmes of projecting cankerwormes and caterpillars, the worst of all the Egyptian plagues'.[36] Sir Benjamin Rudyerd spoke up for those who were hoping to re-establish the balance between 'prerogative and liberty'.[37] But on 17 April, the initiative was firmly seized by those who were determined to assert Parliament's role as guardian of the liberties of the subject against the absolutist tendencies of the Stuart monarchy, when John Pym delivered a devastating indictment of the eleven years of Charles's personal rule, laying out a list of grievances and making it plain that the Commons would not 'Administer any supply untill they bee redressed'.[38] These speeches were followed over the next two days by the presentation of petitions from various counties. On 2 May, an ultimatum was read to the Commons by Sir Henry Vane, in which the King demanded 'a present answere of his Supply', adding that 'a delay was every way as distructive as a deniall'.[39] Further prevarication, together with the rumour that Pym was in close touch with the Scottish commissioners and was on the point of proposing a reconciliation between the King and his northern subjects, persuaded Charles and his Council to bring the Short Parliament to an end on 5 May.[40]

At the end of the month, the Convocation of the clergy, summoned as was customary at the same time as the Parliament and unusually allowed to continue its sitting after the dissolution, finished its work on a new set of canons for the national church.[41] Two of these canons were to ignite further controversy and exacerbate the almost universal hatred of Laud: one spelled out the doctrine of the divine right of kings in a form which set monarchy apart as a system of rule explicitly ordained by God; and the other bound all clergy, schoolmasters and university men by an oath to uphold the doctrine and discipline of the Church of England and never to give their consent 'to alter the government of this Church by archbishops, bishops, deans, and archdeacons, &c., as it stands now established and as by right it ought to stand'. This latter canon in particular antagonized those who wanted further reform of the church, while fear of what might lurk behind the '&c.' fed the general anti-Catholic hysteria that was sweeping through the country.[42]

The outcry against 'the Etcetera Oath' occasioned one of the earliest squibs of a poet whose satirical wit was to make a major contribution to the royalist propaganda campaign in the troubled decade ahead. In 'A Dialogue between two Zealots, upon the &c. in the Oath', John Cleveland mocks the irrational fantasies of two puritan clergymen who fall upon the oath in a frenzy of scriptural excess, identifying the ampersand of the printed text as 'the curled locke of Antichrist' (with a glance at the fashion of ungodly Cavaliers) and discovering in it other apocalyptic implications:

> The Quarrell was a strange mis-shapen Monster,
> &c. (God blesse us) which they conster,
> The Brand upon the buttock of the Beast,
> The Dragons taile ti'd on a knot, a neast
> Of young *Apocryphaes*.[43]

Such satire was a timely reminder of the dangers as well as the absurdities of religious zeal in the months when Charles's counsellors were being threatened by London mobs with placards calling for the abol-

ition of episcopacy, two Catholic officers were murdered by troops
levied in Devon and Dorset, and unruly recruits in the Eastern counties
were breaking church windows, tearing up prayer books and burning
Communion rails.

The decision to press on with a summer campaign against the
rebellious Scots had been taken on 5 May 1640 in what has been
described as 'the most important council meeting of the reign of Charles
I'.[44] Strafford, backed by Laud, argued that a strong offensive action
against the Covenanters was justified to ensure the safety of the realm –
and implied that if need be the King's English subjects must also be
taught obedience to their lawful sovereign. Difficulties in raising money
through June and July, however, caused the muster of troops at York
originally called for 10 May to be twice postponed. Meanwhile, the
Scottish Parliament had reassembled on 2 June without royal authority
and proceeded to pass a series of revolutionary acts which instituted the
meeting of Parliament at least every three years and drew up a new
covenant confirming the legality of the present session. By early August,
members of the Council of War were worried that the Covenanters
might seize the initiative and cross the border before an English invasion
force was ready. On 20 August, the very day that Charles left London, the
Scots crossed the Tweed at Coldstream and by the time he reached York
they had advanced unopposed as far as the Tyne. Determined to take a
lead in the defence of the realm, he marched north toward Newcastle on
27 August, but before he could get there the one decisive engagement of
the Second Bishops' War had taken place at Newburn. On the afternoon
of 28 August, with the help of superior cannon fire, General Leslie routed
a small detachment of English infantry that had hastily dug in on the
south bank of the Tyne and an English cavalry charge could not prevent
the advance of the Scottish army across the river. With his forces in
disarray, Lord Conway decided to abandon Newcastle to the enemy and
withdraw to Durham. Leslie occupied the city on 30 August.

Back again in York, Charles and an ailing Strafford had to face
concerted political opposition as well as military defeat. Already, on 24
August, the Yorkshire gentry had petitioned the King for a new parliament; printed justifications of the military action taken by the Covenanters – *The Intentions of the Army of Scotland* and *The Lawfulness of our Expedition
into England Manifested* – were being widely circulated among English
readers who shared many of their grievances; and a remonstrance,
drafted by Pym and Oliver St John and signed by twelve peers, urged
the King to call a parliament, bring his evil counsellors to account and

make terms with the Scots. Under this mounting pressure, and with Strafford's Irish army stranded in Ulster for lack of shipping, Charles agreed to summon a Great Council of Peers at York. By the time the peers assembled on 24 September, he had accepted the inevitable and the Lord Keeper was ordered to issue writs for a new parliament to meet at Westminster on 3 November.[45]

Sir John Suckling was reported to be among those cavalry officers who made an impetuous attempt to stem the advance of the enemy at Newburn. Some time between the autumn of 1639 and the summer of 1640, he was at work on a play in which the eponymous hero, Brennoralt, was a spokesman for those more headstrong Cavaliers who felt that a firmer line should be taken with the Scots: 'Who puts but on the face of punishing, / And only gently cuts, but prunes rebellion' (I, iii, 73–4).[46] The plot, a romantic farrago of disguise and conflicting loyalites, takes place in the context of a war between Poland and neighbouring Lithuania, which is in rebellion against the Polish crown – a situation that gave Suckling an opportunity to air his disaffected views on the crisis between England and Scotland. But in the central political scene, Brennoralt indignantly resists an attempt to win him over to the rebels' side by playing on his sense of neglect: 'Do'st thinke 'cause I am angry / With the King and State sometimes, / I am fallen out with vertue, and my selfe?' (III, ii, 38–40). And a few lines later, he sets out the programme of hotheads like the poet himself. Scorning the Lithuanians as 'of the wilder sort of creatures', he advocates stern action to curb them: 'What can be used but swords? where men have fal'ne / From not Respecting Royalty, unto / A liberty of offending it?'

Suckling's King of Poland was prepared to listen to this kind of advice, but the King of England found himself committed in the course of October to subsidizing the army of occupation in the northern counties at the rate of £850 per day until terms for their withdrawal could be worked out; and as a final humiliation, the commissioners agreed to transfer their activities from Ripon to London, where the English Parliament could be consulted about the details of a formal peace treaty. When they arrived there, the Scottish representatives were greeted by cheering crowds.[47] This was just one indication of the long-term significance of the storm that broke over Charles I's paradise of peace and plenty at the end of the 1630s. The so-called Bishops' Wars, in the words of their most recent historian, 'demolished the myth of Caroline political consensus and revealed the gulf between King and country'.[48]

CHAPTER 3

The Long Parliament and the trial of Strafford: November 1640 – May 1641

The elections to the new parliament went badly for the King and his ministers, any hope of effective control over the business of the Commons being dashed by the widespread failure to secure the return of candidates sympathetic to the government. According to one count,[1] a mere twenty-seven officials and twenty-two courtiers were elected in the country at large; and in the capital Charles had to stomach not only the success of four members who were violently antagonistic to the Court but also the loss of Sir Thomas Gardiner, the recorder of London, whom he had earmarked as Speaker of the House. Edward Hyde (the future Earl of Clarendon), a young lawyer who had first taken his seat in the abortive assembly of the previous April, was to recall the muted atmosphere that surrounded the opening of what would later be known as the Long Parliament:

It had a sad and melancholic aspect upon the first entrance, which presaged some unusual and unnatural events. The king himself did not ride with his accustomed equipage nor in his usual majesty to Westminster, but went privately in his barge to the Parliament-stairs, and so to the church, as if it had been to a return of a prorogued or adjourned Parliament.[2]

On the afternoon of 3 November 1640, when Charles addressed the assembled lords and representatives of the people, it quickly became evident that the experience of the past six months had taught him nothing. He called upon them to provide financial support to drive the Scottish rebels from the northern counties before he would attend to their grievances. Shocked to find that all did not share his interpretation of the activities of the Scots, he retracted the word 'rebels' and two days later set before the House of Lords a revised proposal to resort to further military action only if the invaders refused to comply with the very terms that they had already rejected. Conrad Russell comments that as 'a political agenda for November 1640' this was simply 'not in the real world', and attributes the King's 'apparent powerlessness' during the first two months of the Long Parliament to his 'entire lack of policy for the situation in which he found himself'.[3] The Earl of Bristol, put in charge of peace negotiations, urged the swift conclusion of a treaty with the Scots, who still posed a serious military threat, and made a case for subsidies to supply both the occupying army and the English troops still quartered in Yorkshire. Charles's attempt to take a personal hand in the talks was blocked and the Lords set up a committee to investigate the background and conduct of the Bishops' Wars.[4]

If many of the peers, headed by the Earls of Bedford, Warwick and Essex and Viscount Saye and Sele, were no longer prepared to tolerate the King's policies or countenance his direction of affairs, the 'irritation and distrust' felt by the gentry 'had only to be voiced by a few in the House of Commons for the overwhelming majority to join in'.[5] And it was not only puritan gentry and opposition lords who were eager to get rid of unpopular ministers and redress the political balance that had swung too far in favour of the royal prerogative: they were joined by 'a body of future royalists', including Hyde, Falkland, Digby and Culpepper, who 'were as deeply opposed to the king in 1640 as his long-standing opponents'.[6]

After the appointment of a reluctant William Lenthall as Speaker of the House of Commons – a man whose 'narrow timorous nature', according to Clarendon, 'contributed as much to the growing mischiefs as the malice of the principal contrivers'[7] – the issues that would dominate the early months of business began to emerge in a series of petitions and debates. In a major speech on 7 November, John Pym reiterated the charges he had made against the King's government in April but with greater emphasis upon a widespread conspiracy 'to alter the kingdom both in religion and government' and to bring about 'a union between us and Rome'. Implicating papists, the 'corrupt part of our clergy', Spanish agents and those who 'are willing to run with Popery' for their own preferment, he denounced the activities of ecclesiastical and secular courts, the breach of ancient parliamentary privileges, the mustering of Roman Catholics and commissioning of papist officers and preparations to use an Irish army 'to bring us to a better order'.[8] On 9 November Sir John Culpepper presented the grievances of Kent, which included the increase in the number of Roman Catholics, new ceremonies introduced into the Laudian church, Ship Money and the canons that had been promulgated by the extended Convocation of the clergy in May. Many of the same complaints were transmitted from Dorset by George Digby. It was this discontented courtier, son of the Earl of Bristol, who mooted the idea of gathering evidence against the ministers responsible for the wayward policies of recent years. A Committee on the State of the Kingdom was set up forthwith and on 11 November the Commons leadership launched its first major offensive against the administration of Charles I by accusing the architect of his war policy, the Earl of Strafford, of high treason.

Strafford had arrived the night before from his base in Yorkshire, and news of the impending impeachment was brought to him while he was at Whitehall in conference with the King. He hurried to Westminster to 'look mine accusers in the face', but as soon as he entered the Lords' chamber the trap closed on him. The charge from the Commons having been read out to him, he was sequestered from the House and placed under restraint. On 20 November the Lords acceded to Pym's demand that the secret proceedings of the King's Privy Council be opened to investigation; on 21 November an emissary from the parliament in Dublin delivered a remonstrance accusing Strafford of oppression and injustice as Lord Lieutenant of Ireland; on 24 November Pym laid the articles of impeachment before the House of Commons; and on 25 November the Lords communicated them to Strafford and consigned him to the Tower of London to await trial.[9] Within a month, Pym and his allies – notable among them John Hampden, Oliver St John, Denzil Holles and the younger Henry Vane – effectively removed most of Charles's other close advisers. Sir Francis Windebank, Secretary of State, was hounded for policies favouring Catholics and fled to France on 10 December; Archbishop Laud was impeached and placed in custody on 18 December; and three days later, Lord Keeper Finch was called before the Commons to answer charges relating to Ship Money, but escaped overnight to The Hague before any move could be made to arrest him.

At some time during these first few weeks, Sir John Suckling wrote an astute assessment of the King's predicament and offered advice on how to deal with it in another of his open letters, 'To Mr Henry German, in the Beginning of Parliament, 1640', addressed on this occasion to a named recipient. Jermyn was one of a group of young courtiers that Henrietta Maria had gathered around herself, and Suckling was perhaps hoping to bring his views to the notice of Charles I through her mediation. Certainly, towards the end, he appeals to those who have influence with the Queen to enlist her support in averting the dangers that ensue when a king is divided from his people: 'For if shee stand aloofe, there will still bee suspitions: it being a receiv'd opinion in the world, that shee hath a great interest in the Kings favour, and power'.[10] Suckling writes as an outsider, like the discontented hero of *Brennoralt*, with undisguised contempt for the closed circle of courtiers who 'give much Counsell, as they beleive the King inclyn'd' and 'determine of his good by his desires'. The main thrust of his own advice is that the King must make some effort to regain the initiative which he has allowed to pass to his adversaries. 'Majestie in an Ecclypse' is under constant observation and Charles's present inertia can only inflict further damage on his political standing in the country: 'To lie still now would att the best shewe but a calmnes of minde, not a magnanimitie'. In an effort to inject some realism into royal strategy by identifying the principal interest of the King as 'a union with his people', he argues that popular demands in two areas of policy must be satisfied – 'Religion and Justice' – and that cannot be done 'by any little Arts, but by reall and Kingly resolutions'. And here Suckling reveals how keenly he has read the current situation. Not only does he know that the nation will not be fobbed off with merely tactical concessions, but he also realises that there are deep-seated grievances across the country which have been tapped by the leadership of the various factions. Convinced that Pym and his colleagues have no personal following beyond Westminster, he argues that the King's best chance of reasserting his own authority over the population at large is to pre-empt the policies of his opponents in London and Edinburgh:

Which done by another hand, (and soe done, that there remaine no jelousie) leaves them where they were, and not much risen in value. And of how great consequence it is for the King to resume this right, and bee the Author himselfe, lett any body Judge: since as *Cumenes* said, those that have the Art to please the people, have comonly the power to raise them.

In response to the realities of late 1640, Suckling has abandoned the bellicose stance that he had taken up during the Scottish campaigns in favour of political concessions that will outflank Covenanters and English parliamentarians alike. He is insistent, however, that the secret of success lies in the King's 'doing something of his owne' – anticipating the desires of the people rather than merely giving way under the pressure of their demands. Once trust has been restored between Charles and his subjects, the power and privilege conceded by the Crown will quickly be restored by a grateful nation. It is like a duel, claims the Cavalier political strategist, 'where the worsted Partie, the other having no ill opinion of him, hath his sword given him again without further hurt, after he is in the others power'. If positive action is not taken now, 'it is not safe to imagine what may followe'. As long as they 'feare, and have the upper hand', the 'timorous' people may be driven into dangerous excesses. Not content 'to fetter onely royaltie', they 'perchance ... will not thinke themselves safe, whiles that [i.e. royalty] is att all'. And this, warns Suckling, 'may bee the present state of things'.

Cautiously broaching a matter 'of soe tender a nature', Suckling identifies one further difficulty that complicates any resolution of the King's present dilemma, 'and that is the preservation of some servants which hee thinkes somewhat hardly torne from him of late'. But political realism – 'as things now stand' – prevails and Suckling advances three arguments for leaving Strafford and his colleagues to their fate: the greater good requires the sacrifice of the lesser; 'whether if hee could preserve these Ministers they can bee of any use to him heereafter'; and, most pertinently, the need to 'bee first right with his people' must take precedence over all other considerations, since 'before the King hath power to preserve, hee must have power'. In a concluding prayer, Suckling reveals a shrewd insight into the personality of the man whose political judgement he had always suspected: 'That the King bee neither too insensible, of what is without him, nor too resolv'd from what is within him'. An inability or refusal to accept political realities and a stubborn conviction that he was in the right were to characterize Charles I's conduct of the first phase of his struggle with Parliament over the crucial twenty months leading up to the declaration of war in August 1642.

A different perspective upon the events of November and December is provided by Dudley North, a member of the House of Lords and one of the group of seventeen peers that had signed a petition calling for new elections after the untimely demise of the Short Parliament. Writing to a friend during 'a little leave of absence from the Parliament',[11] North confesses himself in two minds about some of the issues being raised by the Committee for Religion in the wake of a petition presented to the Commons on 11 December, which put the puritan case against episcopacy 'with all its dependencies, roots and branches'.[12] A third letter, written soon after Christmas, gives an insight into the effects that the first stirrings of political revolution in the capital were having on the day to day lives of the provincial gentry. When Sir Thomas Knyvett wrote from Quidenham in East Anglia to his wife who was nursing her sick mother in London, he was worried by the diligence of the committee set up by the Commons on 5 December to enquire into the rigour with which local officials had undertaken the collection of Ship Money during the previous decade. While out hunting near Larlingford, he had 'compared notes in the open feelde' with John Buxton, who had made many enemies while he was Sheriff of Norfolk in 1638 by his success in gathering arrears of the unpopular tax. Knyvett found him in a dejected frame of mind, 'And, I beleeve, much affray'd his turne of being Question'd for shipp'mony will come'.[13] This encounter prompts some general observations about the 'disturb'd & corrupt consciences' of 'Pollititians' and a sceptical commentary on the political scene in London, in which Knyvett is shrewd enough to see that the current harmony between the Scottish Covenanters and the puritan leadership of the English Commons will not be maintained 'with out loss' to one side or the other when national self-interest is at stake.

During the period when Suckling, North and Knyvett were communicating their various thoughts about the new parliament in the form of letters, a more substantial literary project was being completed by Francis Quarles. Quarles had had connections with the Barringtons of Hatfield Broad Oak in Essex throughout his life, and between December 1639 and the summer of 1640 had received several small sums of money from Lady Barrington.[14] The last of these, recorded in the household account book shortly after 24 August, was given 'to ye Messenger y^t came from Mr Quarles concerneing the Comedy'.[15] This must be a reference to *The Virgin Widow*, the only dramatic work that the poet ever wrote. It was not printed until 1649 and was presumably intended for the private entertainment of the Barrington family. Topical allusions in the text indicate that Quarles was still working on it through the early months of the Long Parliament.[16]

The plot of *The Virgin Widow* is a hotch-potch of theatrical and romantic commonplaces. Kettreena, one of the three daughters of the physician Artesio, is married to an impotent old miser, Pertenax, who is jealous of the attention being paid to her by Evaldus, the King. The King discloses to Kettreena that he is the pilgrim with whom she long ago fell in love, and she reveals that, in spite of her marriage, she has honoured her vow to remain a virgin till he returned. Evaldus's Queen, Augusta, becomes jealous and hires Quack, an apothecary recently dismissed from service by Artesio, to poison Kettreena. Pertenax drinks the poison by mistake and dies. Attempts are made by the plotters to implicate Kettreena in her husband's murder, but the King remains convinced of her innocence. He consults the oracle, and lightning strikes dead both the Queen and her wicked twin sons, Bellarmo and Palladius, who have been fighting over their claims to the throne. In the ensuing confusion, the crown is mysteriously transferred to the head of Kettreena, and Lactusia, one of the plotters, confesses to an earlier crime: '*Kettreena* was the lawfull Queene, whom newly borne, I then her Nurse, exchang'd for *Augusta* your late Wife, who was no other but *Artesio's* daughter' (p. 311). The ambition of Museus, the third of the royal sons who has been scheming to eliminate Bellarmo and Palladius, is thwarted by this discovery; Evaldus resigns his royal authority to Kettreena; and Kettreena herself, taking Evaldus as her consort, assumes her rightful position amid general rejoicing.

Pointing out that the 'Virgin Widow' was a traditional name for the church – the spouse that Christ left behind on earth – Karl Josef Höltgen suggests that Quarles's plot is the vehicle for allegory on two levels: Kettreena is the universal church, left in the power of the lusts of the world (Pertenax) until her eventual reunion with Christ (Evaldus); and, more topically, Kettreena is the English church, temporarily fallen under the control of radical Puritans, but destined to find its way back to its lawful master, the King. He further identifies Artesio as an embodiment of the Arminian party, which has seduced the King into promoting a false view of the church, and Quack as the Roman Catholic interest at court, protected by Queen Henrietta Maria.[17] Gordon Haight had already highlighted the satire on Roman Catholicism in the antics of the fraudulent apothecary and the allusions to the ills afflicting both state and church at the latter end of 1640 in a scene involving Lady Albion and Lady Temple.[18] It should be added that the names of Queen Augusta and Bellarmo, who together grant Quack his licence to practise, were probably chosen to suggest the power of Rome itself (not merely Charles's Catholic wife) and Cardinal Bellarmine, a famous controversialist on behalf of the Roman church during Quarles's youth.

Satire on Catholics, however, is incidental to the main problems that were exercising Quarles in the months immediately before and after the assembling of the Long Parliament. These can be discerned in the underlying structure of the plot: Evaldus, a king misled in matters of religion by his chief counsellor and troubled by the 'factious discords' (p. 294) caused by the rivalry of his three sons (perhaps representing factional interests among courtiers), is rescued from his harmful entanglements with Augusta and Artesio (Catholic and Arminian influences at court and in the church). Kettreena, the 'pure' (i.e. Calvinist)

Church of England from which he has been estranged, spells out the proper relationship between the established church and the monarch who has been appointed its head and defender on earth:

> Being thus ordain'd
> By heavenly Powers to weare
> The sacred Crown of unexpected Care;
> And well-advising, what great dangers waits
> Upon the Scepters of ungovern'd States:
> Conscious of too much weaknesse to command
> So great a Kingdom with a single hand:
> W'are pleas'd to choose a Consort, in whose care
> The Realme hath prosper'd, and to whom we dare
> Commit our self and it. (p. 311)

How far the current head of the family under whose patronage Quarles produced his play would have endorsed Charles I's claim to be a King 'in whose care / The Realme hath prosper'd' is open to debate. Sir Thomas Barrington was to become an active ally of Pym and Oliver St John in the Long Parliament. Perhaps, in the closing months of 1640, he shared Quarles's hope that the removal of Laud's influence and the curbing of the power of the Arminian bishops would bring about the more satisfactory relationship between church and monarch symbolized by comedy's traditional happy ending:

> Mean while, what Art, and Industry can doe
> T' expresse our joyes, and Subjects' full content,
> Let not be wanting: Let us bend our care
> T' advance a publique mirth...
> ... and glorifie the day
> Of Marriage-Royall, solemniz'd between
> New-crown'd *Evaldus*, and his Royall Queen. (p. 312)

It may be significant that the first mention of Quarles's 'Comedy' occurs shortly after another entry in the Barrington household accounts, which reveals a close connection between Sir Thomas and Archbishop Ussher, the poet's former patron, in July 1640.[19] James Ussher, the Primate of Ireland, was to take a lead in promoting a form of 'reduced episcopacy' in an attempt to moderate the more extreme reforms proposed by the 'Root and Branch' petition of 11 December. Certainly the satirical scene at the beginning of Act V, in which Artesio inspects the urine of Lady Albion and Lady Temple, makes it clear that Quarles was no friend to either Separatists or Scottish Presbyterians.

A similar scene occurs in another play which was composed during the same period. *Candia Restaurata* or *Candy Restored* was the second of

seven dramatic entertainments written between 1640 and 1650 by Mildmay Fane, Earl of Westmorland, for performance at his country house
in Northamptonshire. Beneath the Latin title in the manuscript, it is said
to have been 'Presented in a Shewe at Apthorpe the 12th of February
1640 [i.e. 1641] to the Lord and lady of that place by some of their owne
Children and famely'.[20] In Scene ix, Dr Psunodarke (or Synodark),
described in the list of characters as '*A learned Phisitian once banished now
recalld to cure the state*', examines the urine of three sisters, Albinia, Ibernia
and Calidonia, to discover the nature of the disorders that afflict them
and 'suite to each diseas a remedy'. Rhadokein (or Rhodokein) – an
apothecary '*left here dureing his banishment*' – informs him that Albinia
[England] 'hath beene very active / . . . of late to serve and suite her selfe
to the fashion / of other Countries', and in religious practices she has
begun to 'haulfe tune devotion, / to their key' (p. 123). The Doctor
diagnoses an excess of 'opinions', which heat her blood and cause her to
swell with 'empty vayne conceipt'. Rhadokein goes off to organize the
appropriate treatment: 'There is a Surgion skilfull in the trade / of
letting bloode, wher S'ere your worshipp please / although his practis
most be in the neck' (p. 124). While he is away, Psunodarke consults his
'Gloab celestiall' and, in a speech darkened by astrological conceits,
surveys the course of English history from the time of Queen Elizabeth,
under whose influence the country 'was of a healthfull constitution'. The
present diseases of Albinia, 'soe desperate and many', have developed
through a prolonged period of peace; and although the early stages of
her distemper were treated by Psunodarke before his banishment, her
symptoms have since multiplied. References to the measures taken to
raise money by granting monopolies and extending Ship Money to the
inland counties indicate that Fane was far from nostalgic about the
period of Charles I's personal rule in England. Psunodarke obviously
represents the English Parliament, called in 1640 after an interval of
eleven years, and Rhadokein seems to be an embodiment of the constitution or the legal system – left in place by Psunodarke, but unable to act
effectively against 'unlawfull meanes' of imposing taxes without the
safeguard of a parliament to balance the royal prerogative. Restored to
its proper position by the Doctor, the law is ready to hand those guilty of
treason over to the state 'Surgion' for some judicial blood-letting 'in the
neck'.

The play is closer to masque than the romantic tragicomedy of
Quarles. In a prologue, the familiar pastoral imagery of peace and
plenty is pointedly reserved for the reigns of Elizabeth and James, not

Charles I, since old Mother Nip, calculating her age as eighty-three, remembers that when she was forty the isle 'was fram'd of ... reconcilement / In every part' and twenty or even thirty years later there had been 'no great chang'. But the past thirteen years – since the last troubled parliaments in 1628 and 1629 – 'have beene the blasters of our former peace' (p. 109). Then, in a series of pageant-like scenes, the effect of Psunodarke's absence on the lives of ordinary people is enacted: a shepherd complains that 'ther is such pressing upp and downe / for souldiers' and a husbandman declares that he would 'sooner to the gallowes, then / be prest to fight against my owne countrymen'; a captain and a sergeant grumble about the desertion of enlisted recruits and conclude that the world is 'turnd upside downe'; Mother Nip and other cottagers are distressed by the pressing of sons and brothers; and a country squire and his man, Mr Downeright and Tom Telltroth, discuss the 'strange tymes' in which the local economy is undermined by taxes, the church is defiled by 'new worshipp mixt / with hers' and the judges have forfeited their credit 'by broaching their owne fancy lawes and breach / of those the former age established'. Downeright is heartened by the rumour of forthcoming elections – a 'festivall', which 'by unite consent' will secure the 'recall of Psunodark ... to see if he can cure / our malledies' (p. 112) – and a Satyr heralds the arrival of the hero who will reinstate 'auncient lawes' and punish the 'Treachery' that 'hath brought / all this Ile almost to nought' (p. 116). After Rhadokein has taken the measures prescribed by the Doctor, the three sister-kingdoms give thanks to 'the Kinge' for their restoration to health – the freedom to enjoy 'Th'assembly both of people, and of states' and not be troubled by 'monopolye, and project' – and Albinia acknowledges the crucial role played by the Covenanters in ending the period of personal rule:

> I doe confesse the southerne blast
> Had luld me in a Loethargy
> untill the northerne gust wakt me at last
> to seeke a timely remedie. (p. 132)

Calidonia herself pronounces the solution to the ills of Candia, which has been as magically brought about by Charles's summoning of Parliament as the storms of disorder had once been quelled by the entrance of the royal masquer in the Banqueting House at Whitehall:

> Well then I see there is no feare
> But what distempered cloudes did growe
> are vanisht and have left the skye all cleere
> to smile uppon us heere belowe. (p. 132)

In an epilogue, three Sylvans celebrate the return of spring to the 'happie Iland' and bless Cynthia, its tutelary goddess, whose 'handes of Art' have restored 'thes Halcion dayes ... wherein peace shalbe Laureat, jarrs have end' (p. 134).

For Fane's editor, the most remarkable features of the play are the 'glimpses of a restive England in 1641' provided by the early scenes and the genuine optimism of its conclusion; while for Martin Butler the text reveals that Fane was 'a good example of the kind of moderate opinion which Charles and his followers so rashly alienated'.[21] In literary terms, it demonstrates the difficulty of using the masque as a vehicle for understanding the *process* of politics. Just as Charles had expected Parliament and people to support their King without question or delay in a campaign to expel an army of Scottish rebels from English soil, so Fane could only imagine through his idealistic allegory that the election of the Long Parliament signalled the end of an aberrant period of history and a return to the constitutional arrangements that had existed under Elizabeth and James I. As Russell points out, however, Charles's own mistakes precluded any simple restoration of the ancient balance between royal prerogative and elected representatives by altering the perceptions of those engaged in the quest for a settlement:

He had policies only for an imaginary world. When he recovered his touch and began to find policies for the actual situation, he found he had a great deal more power left than was apparent in November and December 1640. In terms of political power, the last two months of 1640 constitute something very like a royal minority, and like other royal minorities, it gave many people a taste of power they were reluctant to abandon when the King was back in action.[22]

From the very different setting of an Oxford college, William Cartwright looked back over the activities of Parliament in those first two months and forward with some apprehension. With a scornful irony beyond the reach of Fane's ponderous muse, he ventured to send 'A New-years-gift to a Noble Lord. 1640',[23] before such 'Presents' were branded as 'Offrings' and howled down as 'Roman Rites' by 'the distemp'red Many', who 'cry they see / The *Missal* in our Liturgie'. In the second stanza, he turns an assault on the investigations being conducted by various committees of the House of Commons into a graceful compliment to the integrity and patriotism of the unnamed recipient of his poem:

> Now an Impartiall Court, deaf to Pretence,
> Sits like the Kingdoms Conscience,
> While Actions now are touch'd, and Men are try'd,

> Whether they can the day abide,
>   Though they should go about
>   To track Offences out,
> In Deeds, in Thoughts, Without, Within,
>   As Casuists, when they search out Sin;
> When Others shake, how safe do you appear,
> And a Just Patriot know no private fear?

From great officers of state like Strafford to local officials like Knyvett's friends in Norfolk, no one could feel safe from a House of Commons that was putting most of its energy into exposing past 'Offences' and regulating what people believed as well as what they did.

A few weeks later, in another letter from Quidenham dated 17 January 1641, Knyvett was despondently confiding to his wife that 'this Parl^mt suerly will settle [i.e. 'knock down dead or stunned', *OED* IV. 5] all Peace & Quiet amongst us'.[24] In the Norfolk churches there is 'like to be such a Purgation of Black-coates' that not enough ministers will be found to fill the empty places; and local JPs are expected to take part in the persecution both of Catholics in general and of individual miscreants. He reports that 'The country is nowe full of warrants for certifycates against B^p Wrenn, sent out by us Justices by command from the Parl^mt' and that he has been summoned to a meeting of 'neighbore Justices' the following Wednesday 'at Larlingford to take in certificates of Recusants'. So few JPs are attending the local courts that 'My Poore Limitt is . . . destitute of Justis' and things are likely to get worse while the present spate of investigations continues: 'These that are left heer I thinke are so afferd of the rodd for what they have done, that some of [them] will nere doe Justis againe.' His distress is evident early in the letter, when he warns his wife that 'if the par^t houlds on' he will retire from public duties: 'I doe fancye a little house by our selves extreamly well, wher we may spend the remainder of our dayes in religiouse Tranquill.'

Within a few days of Knyvett's gloomy account of the provincial consequences of Parliament's unbridled activity, there were signs that Charles I was at last beginning to recognize the need for a new political settlement if he were to reassert some degree of royal authority. On 21 January, rumours that he was about to make ministerial changes at the highest levels of his government were rife in Whitehall. Sir John Temple, an acute observer of the political scene, reported that 'the King is brought into a dislike of those counsels that he hath formerly followed,

and therefore resolves to steer another course'. Confirming the gossip
that the Earl of Bedford would become Lord Treasurer with John Pym
as Chancellor of the Exchequer, and that Lord Saye and Sele would
replace Cottington as Master of the Wards, he commented, 'These
preparatives make us now hope for a happy success of this Parliament,
and I do believe some ways are laid, upon the bringing in of these new
men, to make up an entire union between the King and his people, and
so moderate their demands, as well as the height of that power which
hath been lately used in the government'.[25] In fact, the first foundations
for a scheme to render the King's government more acceptable to the
people by manning it with opposition lords had already been laid in the
early autumn. According to Secretary Windebank's notes, the Privy
Council that met on 1 September 1640 to consider the Petition of the
Twelve Peers had discussed 'whether some of the noblemen not counsellors shall not be called to counsell if it be but to engage them'.[26] On 7
September the Earls of Bedford and Hertford had represented the
signatories of the petition in preliminary talks with the Privy Council.
These moves took place in the absence of the King and were initially
intended to promote a rapprochement between the Court government
and the group of powerful opposition peers. Once the new Parliament
was in session, however, any settlement would have to accommodate
the views of men like Pym and St John, who were long-term associates of
Bedford and had drafted the document to which the peers had set their
names.

There are indications in letters and court gossip during December
that Bedford continued to nurse a scheme that would preserve the
traditional system of government by persuading Charles to appoint a
new team of ministers drawn from leading members of the opposition in
both houses. In Russell's view, it was not until the end of the year that
Charles could bring himself to contemplate such a course and it was
during the first two weeks of January that he 'cleared his own mind
about his negotiating terms', which were 'hammered out in a long series
of Privy Council meetings'.[27] A first indication that the King might be
sympathetic to Bedford's plan came with the appointment of Sir Edward Littleton – a man loyal to the Crown but favourably disposed to a
settlement – to the vacant post of Lord Keeper on 19 January. A few
days later, Charles informed the House of Lords that he was prepared to
'reduce all matters of religion and government to what they were in the
purest times of Queen Elizabeth's days';[28] and on 29 January he made
the conciliatory gesture of choosing Oliver St John as the Solicitor

General. Since the Commons had declared Ship Money illegal on 7 December and threatened to take control of the assignment of customs dues on 29 December, one of the main concessions that he sought from Bedford and his allies was the establishment of a secure basis for the royal finances.

If Bedford, who 'seems to have had friends in all parts of the spectrum',[29] was the leading spirit on the parliamentary side in pressing for a solution to the crisis, on the court side Henry Jermyn and the Marquis of Hamilton were the chief supporters of compromise. Jermyn was one of Henrietta Maria's inner circle and there were reports of his attending secret meetings with the King and Queen and of the Queen's granting private audience to Bedford, Saye and Pym. These clandestine negotiations were at their height during the first two weeks of February and William Davenant's famous poem 'To the Queen'[30] must have been written at about this time. Its message is similar to that contained in Suckling's letter to Jermyn, but with the more persuasive touch of a courtier practised in the art of tempering criticism with flattery. The opening lines are far from uncritical of the King's aloofness, though their edge is slightly blunted by ascribing his stubborn dislike of other people's advice to the isolation inherent in the nature of monarchy, kings being 'so uncompanion'd in a Throne'. Queens were ordained to remedy 'this high obnoxious singleness' by the permanent comfort of their presence, which gives them greater influence than the holder of a political office, whose position is merely temporary. Henrietta Maria therefore performs the role given her 'by Nature' and advances her own 'vertue' when she persuades her husband '(in the Peoples cause) / Not to esteeme his Judges more then Laws'. What amounts to an indictment of Charles's 'extreame obdurateness' is then subtly turned into compliment to both King and Queen by the observation that in 'Jewels' it is 'hardness in excess' that 'makes their price':

> And 'tis perhaps so with obdurate Kings
> As with the best impenitrable things.
> No way to pierce or alter them is found,
> Till we to Di'monds use a Diamond.
> So you to him, who, to new-forme his Crown,
> Would bring no aides less precious then his own.

A note of reservation is sounded in the word 'perhaps', but there can be no doubt about the project which this obdurate King must be persuaded to undertake: to 'new-forme his Crown' in some political accommodation with the opponents of his 'Prerogative' – 'that mystick word'. Only the Queen, 'whose vertues make your Councells thrive', can get Charles to see that the gold coin which bears the ancient stamp of kingship, if it is not to be defaced by those who would test its validity, must be wrought 'to a yieldingness / That shews it fine but makes it not weigh less'.

The passage which brings this 'daring' and 'extraordinarily troubled'[31] poem to a close does not ignore the harsh circumstances in which concessions must be made by the King, the crimes of his ministers must be acknowledged, the judges who have sanctioned illegal measures must be brought to book, the demands of the people must be heeded and scapegoats for unpopular policies must be sacrificed:

> Accurst are those _Court-Sophisters_ who say
> When Princes yield, Subjects no more obey.
> Madam, you that studied Heaven and Times
> Know there is Punishment, and there are Crimes.
> You are become (which doth augment your state)
> The Judges Judge, and Peoples Advocate:
> These are your Triumphs, which (perhaps) may be
> (Yet Triumphs have been tax'd for Cruelty)
> Esteem'd both just and mercifully good:
> Though what you gain with Tears, cost others Blood.

Whether or not Charles and Henrietta Maria ever saw Suckling's letter or Davenant's poem, both were in conciliatory mood. When he spoke to the Lords on 3 February, the King promised to see that the laws against Roman priests and Jesuits were strictly enforced; and on the following day, the Commons received a message from the Queen in which she undertook to work for a reconciliation between her husband and Parliament and to limit the number of English Catholics admitted to her private chapel in Somerset House.[32] Then on 16 February the royal assent was given to the Triennial Act, one of only two bills introduced in the Commons that passed through all their stages during the first three months of the Long Parliament. In providing the mechanisms for calling a Parliament at least every three years, this piece of legislation seriously diminished the sovereignty of the monarch and Charles's acquiescence implies that he had accepted the need for regular consultation with the people's representatives if he were to secure his own authority within a reformed system of government.[33] Three days later, the weeks of bargaining seemed to be nearing a climax when six of the peers who had signed the petition back in August were created members of the Privy Council, including Bedford, Hertford and Saye. A seventh, the Earl of Bristol, was rewarded for his service in the negotiations with the Scots. But Bedford's ultimate aim of filling the major offices of state with royal appointments from the ranks of the opposition was never to be achieved, because on two matters the King had determined not to give in, and they were matters about which Pym was equally adamant: the future of the Church of England and the fate of the Earl of Strafford.

Early in the new year, more root and branch petitions were delivered to the Commons from Kent, Essex and Suffolk and when Charles spoke to members of both Houses on 23 January he made it clear that he would not tolerate any reforms directed either at the right of bishops to vote in the House of Lords or at episcopacy itself. He was prepared to see past misdemeanours punished and even to contemplate some curbing of the bishops' power, 'But this must not be understood, that I shall any way consent that their voices in Parliament should be taken away; for in all the times of my predecessors, since the Conquest and before, they have enjoyed it, and I am bound to maintain them in it, as one of the fundamental constitutions of this kingdom'.[34] Sir Simmonds D'Ewes reflected a common response to this example of the King's tendency to be 'too resolv'd from what is within him' noted by Suckling, which Davenant less delicately termed 'obdurateness': 'This speech filled most of us with sad apprehensions of future evils in case his majesty should be irremovably fixed to uphold the bishops in their wealth, pride and tyranny.'[35]

According to C. V. Wedgwood, the death of Strafford was 'the key to the political strategy of John Pym'.[36] Not only was he held to be the lynch-pin of the Catholic plot, with an Irish army poised to 'reduce this kingdom', but as Anthony Fletcher points out, 'he frightened the leaders of this parliament as no one else did'.[37] More than a month after the impeachment, on 30 January 1641, Strafford was brought from the Tower to hear the details of the case that had been compiled against him. He was granted a fortnight in which to prepare his reply, which was later extended by a further week. On 24 February, with the King in attendance, his answers to each of the charges were read out. A crucial event occurred on that same day, which spelled the end of any serious attempt to arrive at a settlement with Bedford and Pym and was to open a way for the creation of a royalist party in Parliament. In order to bring home to their English friends that a choice must be made between loyalty to the King and support for the religious and political aims of the Covenanters, the Scots published a paper calling for root and branch reform in England and the execution of Strafford. Hyde forced a debate

on this paper in the Commons on 27 February, and it received the active
or tacit support of many of the men with whom Charles had been
hoping to reach an accommodation. The King saw that it would never
be possible for them to agree on the two issues over which he could not
compromise. Although the time was not yet ripe for a formal realign-
ment of interests in the Commons, a turning-point had been reached in
the affairs of the Long Parliament. Russell sums up what had happened:

This debate seems to have brought the settlement scheme to an end.... In
forcing Hampden and the others to make a declaration on the Scots' paper,
Hyde had brought himself a degree nearer the King's favour, and Civil War
several degrees nearer. The King seems to have decided, probably within
hours, on a change of policy. This was not just because his new Councillors had
let him down: it was also because the new wave of anti-Scottish and anti-
Puritan feeling for which Hyde, Culpepper, Strangeways, Hopton and Digby
spoke on 27 February offered him the possibility of raising a party against a
group of people whose outlook had always been profoundly distasteful to him.
It offered him a chance, not to reunite a country much of which he disliked, but
to undertake what he always found the much more congenial task of leading a
party.[38]

Late in February, Pym had brought forward the full articles of
impeachment against Laud and on 1 March the archbishop was trans-
ported by coach through angry crowds to the Tower, where he languished until finally being brought to trial and beheaded in 1645. The
despatch of Strafford was more urgent. On the day that Laud was
lodged in the Tower, the Commons enlisted the power of print to whip
up public opinion against Strafford before he came to trial. They
published the list of charges without Strafford's answers and had them
distributed throughout England, along with copies of the Irish and Scots
remonstrances.[39] The trial eventually began in Westminster Hall on 22
March and for the next seven weeks it absorbed attention countrywide.
In the words of Sir John Temple, writing to the Earl of Leicester on 25
March, 'everyone is engaged, and that passionately, either for my lord
of Strafford's preservation or his ruin'.[40] Among those who had a vested
interest in the latter was Robert Baillie, one of the Scots commissioners,
who was confident that 'when we get his head off all things run
smooth'.[41] Dudley North, writing a 'discourse to the present' on 28
March, took heart from various signs that the nation, 'by God's grace
and the Kings', was now 'upon an indissoluble conjunction of King and
people, *Scotland* and *England*, reconcilement in Religion, and a marriage
with the young Prince of *Orange*, and his Majesties eldest daughter'. But
he was anxious about the 'stain of blood' that would be left by the

execution of Strafford and Laud: 'surely his Majesty is too good and wise ever to readmit (though it were left free unto him) Ministers so hateful, pre-judged and unhappy, as they who now are questioned have been unto him'.[42] North's vision of imminent political and religious harmony seems naively optimistic, but his 'surely' betrays a more shrewd assessment of the King's wisdom, if not his goodness. With less relish than Baillie, he saw how imperative it was to ensure, one way or another, that Strafford would never again be permitted to wield power or influence.

The last of North's signs that things were 'in a happy way' was the result of diplomatic activity that had been going on since the previous December, when Charles had begun to look for alternative methods of financing the army that Parliament was refusing to support. While the Queen was trying to arrange a loan from Rome through her papal envoy, Count Rossetti, Charles was backing the Protestant horse and pursuing a lucrative match for one of his daughters with the heir to the House of Orange. By the middle of January it had become known that Princess Mary was betrothed to the twelve-year-old Prince William. However much the rumoured financial settlement may have strengthened Charles's hand during the abortive talks with opposition leaders during February, the impending marriage was not the harbinger of harmony that North hoped. The King's sister, the exiled Queen of Bohemia, was furious at the snub to her son, who she thought had first claim on the English princess, and matters were made worse when Charles Louis himself arrived at court on 2 March, seeking aid for the Protestant cause in Europe to compensate for his disappointment.

The presence of the Elector Palatine did little to divert public interest from the proceedings in Westminster Hall, which initially went well for Strafford. His courageous conduct of his own defence won the admiration of many and the prosecution case began to crumble. At its centre, enshrined in Article XXIII of the impeachment, was the advice that Strafford was reported to have given Charles on the day he persuaded him to dissolve the Short Parliament:

viz., that having tried the affections of his people, he was loosed and absolved from all rules of government, and that he was to do everything that power would admit, and that his Majesty had tried all ways, and was refused, and should be acquitted towards God and Man, and that he had an army in Ireland ... which he might employ to reduce this kingdom.[43]

This information about what was said behind the closed doors of the Privy Council had been supplied by the younger Vane, who claimed to have found it among his father's notes; but when Secretary Vane himself was called as a witness, his emphasis on the words '*here* to reduce *this* kingdom' was disputed by three other councillors, who categorically denied that there was ever any suggestion of using the Irish army against England rather than Scotland. By the morning of 10 April it had become apparent that without new evidence the charge of treason could not be proved and the court was adjourned. In the afternoon, Sir Arthur Haselrig came before the House of Commons with a Bill of Attainder, which made no new accusations but simply sought to declare by Act of Parliament that the Earl of Strafford was guilty of treasonable behaviour for which the penalty was death. To become effective, the Bill would have to be passed by both Lords and Commons and signed by the King. In the meantime, Strafford had an opportunity to defend himself before his peers on 13 April. With regard to the religious charges against him, he vehemently denied any 'confederacy with the Popish faction' and indeed protested a readiness 'to seal my disaffection to the Church of Rome with my dearest blood'. And as for his 'designs about the State', he eloquently set out his very orthodox views on the constitution:

The prerogative of the Crown and the propriety of the subject have such mutual relations that this took protection from that, that foundation and nourishment from this; and as on the lute, if anything be too high or too low wound up you have lost the harmony, so here the excess of a prerogative is oppression, of a pretended liberty in the subject disorder and anarchy. The prerogative must be used, as God doth his omnipotency, at extraordinary occasions; the laws ... must have place at all other times, and yet there must be a prerogative if there must be extraordinary occasions.[44]

After some hesitation, Pym and Hampden accepted the line of Haselrig and St John in the Commons debates on the Bill of Attainder, and even Culpepper and Falkland spoke in favour of it as a way of ensuring the punishment of treason that was patent if not strictly provable in law. Others who had supported Pym hitherto were uneasy about the tactic and troubled by the prosecution's handling of the evidence relating to Article XXIII, and one them, George Digby, intervened to denounce the leaders of the Commons for 'committing murder with the sword of justice'. When it came to voting on 21 April, he declared 'that my vote goes not to the taking of the Earl of Strafford's life', and so cleared his conscience 'of this man's blood'.[45] Nevertheless, with just over half the members of the Commons taking part, the Attainder was passed by 204 votes to 59. In the Lords, Bedford and Hertford – with other moderate peers like Digby's father, the Earl of Bristol – were again working for a political arrangement by which the

King would appoint their allies to high office in return for sparing Strafford, provided he withdrew from public life. Essex rejected overtures from this group with the notorious remark, 'Stone-dead hath no fellow', and gave his blunt opinion that 'the King was obliged in conscience to conform himself and his own understanding to the advice and conscience of his Parliament'.[46] Meanwhile, Charles had prepared contingency plans for saving Strafford.

During March, two separate groups of conspirators were plotting to use military force if the need arose.[47] Henry Percy and other army officers with seats in the Commons were ready to declare themselves for the King if Parliament continued to withold his revenues and tried to compel him to exclude bishops from the House of Lords or disband the Irish army. The other group, in which Sir John Suckling and Henry Jermyn figured prominently and William Davenant played an obscure role, had a more hot-headed scheme to persuade the Earl of Newcastle, who was governor of the Prince of Wales, to seize command of the army in Yorkshire and march south to occupy London. George Goring, Lovelace's commander in the First Bishops' War and the possible model for Suckling's Brennoralt, was to be Newcastle's Lieutenant-General. Soon after the Strafford trial began, the King seems to have been favourably disposed to the project of presenting an army petition to Parliament and on 29 March an unsuccessful attempt was made in Percy's lodgings in Whitehall to bring the two groups together. At a subsequent meeting with Jermyn and Percy, the King declined to have anything to do with either plan. Goring withdrew, leaked the conspiracy to the parliamentary leadership, and returned to his post as governor of Portsmouth.

The King had by now become convinced that drastic action of some kind would be necessary if he were to honour the promise made to Strafford on the day the Commons passed the Act of Attainder, 'Upon the word of a king you shall not suffer in life, honour and fortune.'[48] On 1 May he made an appeal to the Lords, saying that he could not in his conscience believe that Strafford was guilty of treason and therefore would not be willing to sign a bill that would condemn him to death. Meanwhile, Suckling had been busy raising troops in the capital, ostensibly for service in Portugal.

It was on the tense and troubled Sunday of 2 May, with anti-Catholic mobs of apprentices roaming the streets of London, that nine-year-old Mary was married to Prince William of Orange in a simple ceremony at Whitehall. The couple were brought to bed in the traditional manner, but the young prince was only permitted to kiss his bride, whose nightdress had been sewn up as a precaution.[49] In such circumstances, even the ingenuity of William Cartwright was strained to find an appropriate means of celebrating this particular royal occasion. He makes a forlorn effort to translate it into a symbol of national harmony, but his masque-like dream of 'an Ordred World' struck out of Chaos by the power of love rings less true than his opening evocation of the unfinished drama of Strafford's trial:

> Amids such Heate of Businesse, such State-throng
> Disputing Right and Wrong,
> And the sowre Justle of Unclos'd Affayres;
> What meane those Glorious Payres?
> That Youth? That Virgin? Those All Dresst?
> The Whole, and every Face, a Feast?
> Great Omen! O ye Powr's,
> May this Your Knot be Ours![50]

The joy of this royal occasion, which must have been even more muted by the news that Bedford had been taken seriously ill, was quickly dissipated by the events of the next day. Monday 3 May had been set aside for the Lords to debate the Attainder Bill and Charles decided to make a bid to rescue Strafford. Captain Billingsley, Suckling's confederate and an officer in the Irish army, tried to enter the Tower with a hundred men on the King's authority, but was refused admittance by Sir William Balfour, who was in charge of the garrison. The Lords quickly got wind of this foiled attempt and sent an angry deputation to the King. Meanwhile large crowds were gathering outside both Houses and baying for Strafford's blood. The moment had come for Pym to reveal what he knew. Suckling was hauled before the Commons to explain his recent activities and a committee was set up to enquire into the rumours of a Catholic conspiracy that were sweeping through the city. Fuller details of what quickly became known as the Army Plot were reported on 5 May and a writ for the arrest of the ringleaders was issued on the next day, but by then Suckling and Jermyn were already on their way to France and Percy, too, eventually reached Paris.

The immediate response of the Commons to the panic caused by Pym's revelations was to issue a Protestation, which contained an oath 'to maintain and defend . . . the true reformed religion, expressed in the doctrine of the Church of England, against all Popery and Popish innovation within this realm . . . according to the duty of my allegiance to his Majesty's royal person, honour and estate; as also the power and privilege of Parliament, the lawful rights and liberties of the subjects, and every person that shall make the Protestation in whatsoever he shall do, in the lawful pursuance of the same'.[51] This was to serve a similar function to the Scottish Covenant, in that it bound those who subscribed to it primarily to a cause rather than a person, and it was later interpreted as authorizing them to take arms against the monarch who challenged its principles. To meet the threat that the King might dissolve Parliament if the Attainder Bill was passed by the Lords, the two Houses hurried through another bill vesting the power of dissolution in Parliament itself, and thus removed another vital part of the royal prerogative. This bill passed its final stages in the Upper House on 7 May, the day on which those Lords who had not found excuses to absent themselves voted through the Attainder Bill by a majority of 51 to 9.[52] Strafford's life now depended entirely on the conscience of the King. Aware that more was at stake than his own safety, the statesman had already written to his royal master on 4 May releasing him from his promise:

May it please your Sacred Majesty, I understand the minds of men are more and more incensed against me, notwithstanding your Majesty hath declared that, in your princely opinion, I am not guilty of treason, and that you are not satisfied in your conscience to pass the bill. . . . To set Your Majesty's conscience at liberty, I do most humbly beseech Your Majesty (for preventing of evils which may happen by your refusal) to pass this bill.[53]

During the weekend of 8 and 9 May, while the crowds that had seethed around the Houses of Parliament were clamouring outside Whitehall Palace, Charles consulted the Privy Council and sought spiritual advice from Bishops Ussher, Juxon and Williams. After much inner turmoil, fearful of what might happen to his wife and children, he gave his assent to the Act of Attainder on the morning of 10 May. On the night that Charles was coming to the decision that would haunt him for the rest of his life, the Earl of Bedford succombed to the smallpox that had kept him off the political stage during the momentous events of the previous week. Strafford was beheaded on Tower Hill at noon on 12 May.

The passion and perplexity generated by the career and fall of Strafford resulted in an immediate crop of elegies by some of the leading writers of the age and would continue to reverberate through the literature of the next ten years. The Earl of Bedford, to whom Clarendon was to pay tribute as 'a wise man', who 'would have proposed and advised moderate courses',[54] appears to have been mourned in verse only by Henry

Glapthorne, a minor dramatist and friend of Lovelace. Like Clarendon, Glapthorne celebrated the wisdom of one who, avoiding the hatred let loose 'in this sad distemper of the State', had striven 'with a modest sweetnesse ... to win / All mens affections' and 'Esteemd the truest safety in the meane'. Bedford's political career was driven not by 'pride' but by 'a noble and ambitious zeale, / To encrease the glory of the Common-weale':

> Not like those curious great ones, who create
> Factions and strange distractions in the state,
> Who by malignant Councels strive to bring
> Distempers on the Kingdom and the King:
> Who though their violent Councels overwhelm
> The vessell strive to be advanc'd to th' helme.[55]

Although Glapthorne had once written a dedication to Strafford, it is difficult not to read these lines as an indictment of the recently executed 'evil counsellor', and to find in them yet more evidence of hostility even among future royalists to the path Charles himself had been pursuing under his 'malignant' influence.

   Among those who devoted whole poems to the phenomenon of Strafford, Sir John Denham emphasized the greatness of the fall, the hatred directed against him from all parts of the realm, and the 'feare' of those in 'three kingdomes' who had to resort to a parliamentary device when their attempts to destroy him by due process of law were thwarted. The 'wisdome' and 'eloquence' that he displayed during the trial forced those who were present to listen 'with greater passion then he spoke'; and even those who 'had his death decreed' were affected by his performance: 'So powerfull[y] it wrought, at once they greive / That he should dye, yet feared to let him live.'[56] Having attended the trial, Denham is careful to dissociate himself from Strafford's accusers, sinking his individual identity in the collective responses of those who were dazzled by powers of argument and rhetoric that could 'make / Us heere'.[57] In the last four lines, however, he introduces a more ambivalent note by exploiting the formal qualities of the heroic couplet to create paradoxes and balance one judgement against another:

> Farwell greate soule, the glory of thy fall
> Outeweighes the cause, whom we at once may call
> The enimy and martire of the state,
> Our nations glory and our nations hate.

The greatness of personality exhibited by Strafford in facing both his trial and his execution may be felt to outweigh the case brought against him – but the justice of that case is not necessarily denied; and such doubts are then more sharply focused in the wordplay of the final couplet. Ambiguities multiply within the oxymoron of the penultimate line. Was Strafford actively the enemy of the state because he planned its overthrow or did the state brand him as an enemy in order to get rid of him? Was he martyred *by* or *for* the state – the victim of persecution or a willing sacrifice for the well-being of his country? And how many of his countrymen were bewildered by the mixture of hatred and admiration excited by a career that exposed the inadequacy of simple moral antitheses? When Denham ended his poem with an adaptation of Waller's comment on the disrepair into which St Paul's Cathedral had been allowed to fall – 'Our nation's glory and our nation's crime' – he signalled more than esteem for another's art: he gave notice that his generation of poets was entering uncharted territory in which familiar modes of expression would be put under increasing strain by circumstances that undermined the moral and political assumptions of the past.

Sir Richard Fanshawe was impressed above all by Strafford's decision to make 'a gallant stand' and dispute his enemies' accusations in open court. In the first section of his poem 'On the Earl of *Strafford's* Tryall',[58] he praises Strafford for preferring the '*Touch-stone*' of truth when he might have 'fled at first' or hidden behind the 'skreene' of a 'Royall Master, or a Gracious Queene'. To enlist the 'Powers Divine' of the King and Queen in his rescue would have been to imitate the cheap devices of 'artlesse Poets', who resort to intervention by the gods to resolve their plots and 'play the Mid-wife to their labouring Muse'. Fanshawe conveniently forgets that Charles's actual attempts to save the life of his servant had only proved how limited his power was. In this poetic rendering of events, the protagonist took charge of his own drama and, like a true artist, allowed the plot to unfold to its logical conclusion as he answered each article of the prosecution's case – untying rather than cutting 'the Gordian knot': 'Then if 'twill prove no *Comedy*, at least / To make it of all *Tragedies* the best.' Continuing to refract the political through the aesthetic like so many Caroline poets, Fanshawe turns from the performance in the courtroom to the final performance on the scaffold:

> I know not what past fact
> May speake him lesse, but for his lifes *last act*,
> *Times* shall admiring read it, and *this age*,
> Though now it *hisse*, *claps* when he leaves the Stage;
> So *stand* or *fall*, none *stood* so, or so *fell*;
> This farre-fam'd *Tryall* hath no parallel.

In the pointed rhyming of 'past fact' and '*last act*', Fanshawe comes to the same verdict as Denham, that 'the glory of thy fall / Outweighes the cause': the courage displayed on the platform at Tower Hill cancels any political actions in the past that might 'speake him lesse' and diminish the theatrical impact of Strafford's last moments.

This hint of ambivalence is quickly suppressed, however, as Fanshawe seeks to get the trial into perspective by invoking an historical analogy – but this literary ploy only serves to reinforce his claim that there is 'no parallel'. If Julius Caesar had gone before the Roman Senate and 'been *try'd*, / As he was *stab'd*', then he could have supplied the appropriate comparison. As it is, the scenes in Westminster Hall have turned the usual function of classical allusion upside down, and Strafford becomes the example of what Caesar might have been: 'Thus had great *Julius* spoke, and lookt'. In one respect, however, the reference to Caesar does illuminate the fate of Strafford, since in the end he was virtually assassinated by political opponents who, in Digby's words, committed murder 'with the sword of justice'. But at this juncture, another historical analogue occurs to Fanshawe, which foregrounds the element of self-sacrifice in the death of this patriotic martyr who was greater than the butchered emperor of Rome:

> A *Caesar*? or a *Strafford*? *Hee* resolv'd,
> T' abide no *tryall*: *This*, to be *absolv'd*
> Or *dye*. Herein more like to *Otho* farre,
> Who gave his blood to quench a *Civill Warre*.

Just as he had taken responsibility for his own defence in the trial, so he took responsibility for his own death, as Fanshawe reminds his readers in a marginal gloss: 'The Earles pathetical Letter to the King, which is to be seene in print, wherein hee begges of his Majesty, to passe the Bill for his death, to quiet the Kingdomes.' Using his 'conquering *Eloquence*' against himself, Strafford put to shame all those ranged against him – the '*Three Kingdomes*', 'the *Parliament*' and even the King – when 'to the *Royall*' he chose to 'give his *owne assent*'. While Fanshawe is dimly aware of the unprecedented nature of recent events, he cannot interpret their significance beyond that embodied in the story of Otho: the hero has prevented Civil War at the cost of his own life. But Strafford himself knew that his death would not resolve the power struggle in which he had become merely a pawn. Indeed, as Clarendon reported his speech from the scaffold, he had a dire warning for those who had gathered to see the 'last act' of his tragedy: 'he was come thither to satisfy them with his head; but that he much feared the reformation which was begun in blood would not prove so fortunate to the kingdom as they expected and he wished.'[59]

The finest of all the literary treatments of Strafford's death pursues precisely this insight: that it marked a watershed in a developing historical process rather than the end of a tragic action 'complete in itself'. In order to produce his 'marvelous clarification of what has happened',[60] the author of the famous 'Epitaph on the Earl of Strafford' – probably John Cleveland[61] – weaves the method of paradox and oxymoron into the very texture of his terse couplets:

> Here lies Wise and Valiant Dust,
> Huddled up 'twixt Fit and Just:
> STRAFFORD, who was hurried hence
> 'Twixt Treason and Convenience.
> He spent his Time here in a Mist;
> A *Papist* yet a *Calvinist*.
> His Prince's nearest Joy, and Grief.
> He had, yet wanted all Reliefe.
> The Prop and Ruine of the State;
> The People's violent Love, and Hate:
> One in extreames lov'd and abhor'd.
> Riddles lie here; or in a word,
> Here lies Blood; and let it lie
> Speechlesse still, and never crie.

This Strafford is not an artist orchestrating the effects of a 'labour'd Scene'; he is 'huddled up' and 'hurried hence' by forces beyond his control, and to participants as well as observers it is difficult to draw the moral lines between expediency and justice, treason and convenience. Some of the subsequent paradoxes inhere in the vagaries of popular opinion – 'The People's violent Love, and Hate'; some in the conflicting emotions of a single individual – 'His Prince's nearest Joy, and Grief'; some in divergent interpretations of his political role – 'the Prop and Ruine of the State'. The apparent paradox of the third couplet provides a key to the poem's method: Strafford himself was not uncertain of his religious orientation (he was a Calvinist with little sympathy for Papists);[62] the 'Mist' that shrouds him was deliberately created in the public mind by those who could make political capital out of branding him as the leader of a Catholic conspiracy. This poet finds the significance of Strafford's life and death not in the complexities of his character – as a man he was simply 'Wise and Valiant' – but in the conflicting perceptions of his role and the opacity of the process by which he was removed. The 'Riddles' posed by the trial and execution of Strafford are paradigmatic of the way in which traditional categories of moral and political judgement are being dislocated by revolutionary circumstances.

But if the poet does not pretend to see through the mist and riddles that obscure the events of the recent past, he does hint darkly at their consequences. Behind the appeal of the final couplet to let the blood that has been shed 'lie / Speechlesse still, and never crie' can be heard the Old Testament God of vengeance rebuking Cain for the murder of Abel: 'the voice of thy brother's blood crieth unto me from the ground' (*Genesis*: 4. 10). The 'stain of blood' that North had dreaded and Digby had washed his hands of is an omen of the bloody future that Strafford himself had foreseen.

CHAPTER 4

The beginnings of constitutional royalism:
May – October 1641

For those directly involved in the political crisis that gripped the nation, the period following the execution of Strafford 'was one of deadlock'. The King, having allowed himself on this one issue to be 'pressed beyond his conscience', would be more adamant than ever in his resistance to radical changes in the church; and in the wake of the anti-Catholic hysteria let loose by the revelations of the Army Plot, the safety of his Queen 'took priority over any attempts to restore the political unity of his kingdom'.[1] On the other side, the views of the Lords and Commons on religious reform began to diverge sharply, although they continued to work together to ensure that Charles would never again be able to abuse the royal prerogative or attempt a military coup. For example, an act to abolish the Court of Star Chamber and prevent the Privy Council from interfering in the property rights of individual subjects was passed by both Houses and received the royal assent on 5 July. On 25 May, however, the Lords had voted against a Commons proposal to exclude bishops from the upper house. The Commons retaliated two days later by introducing a Root and Branch Bill to extirpate bishops from the national church, but the impossibility of getting this past the peers, among whom Vicount Saye and Sele was conspicuous in being firmly opposed to episcopacy, meant that it languished in committee all summer. Attempts by the Lords to settle the issue of the King's revenues were blocked by the insistence of the Commons leadership that this must be linked with concessions on the bishops.[2] In the House of Commons itself, future leaders of the King's party like Edward Hyde, who instigated the abolition of the Council of the North, were still prepared to co-operate in dismantling the machinery of political oppression. But on the question of religion a split was beginning to develop. While the younger Vane and Oliver Cromwell were pushing for radical reformation, the case for retaining episcopacy was orchestrated by Hyde's associates, Culpepper, Falkland and Digby.

Sir Edward Dering, who had taken a leading part in the attack on Archbishop Laud and been appointed to the chair of a subcommittee set up to receive complaints from oppressed ministers, had been persuaded by Sir Arthur Haselrig to present the Root and Branch Bill on 27 May.[3] He was later to insist that, in spite of his eagerness to remove bad bishops, he had never advocated the abolition of episcopacy; and by 21 June, he was making a clear distinction between the '*Ruine*' and the '*Reforming*' of 'our present Church-Government' and moving for a rejection of the Bill in its more elaborate form, so that 'we may proceed to reduce again the old original Episcopacy'.[4]

This sense of unease about the direction church reform might take was shared by Francis Quarles, who returned to the form of pastoral debate which he had used extensively during the 1630s for his commentary on ecclesiastical matters. In an eleventh eclogue written in late May or early June, he gives voice to common anxieties in an exchange between Philorthus and Philarchus, shepherds of the Church of England and lovers, as their names proclaim, of orthodoxy and order.[5] Distressed that their calling is 'sleighted' and that their names have become 'the scorn / Of every base Mechanick', Philorthus admits that some of their predecessors among the bishops have brought calamity upon themselves by aiming 'at things / Beyond their pitch' and causing 'combustion in so calme a State', and Philarchus accepts that 'too much wealth' and 'ambitious pride' have 'made the world deride / What late it honour'd' (pp. 233–4). Two couplets express the feeling common among opponents of Laudian innovations that individual bishops should be punished and steps taken to avoid future abuse, but that the institution itself must be left intact:

> Shall some few staines in the full Lampe of night
> Cry downe the Moone, and wooe the Stars for light?
> What if thy too neglected Soile abound
> With noysome Weeds, wilt thou disclaime the ground?   (p. 233)

Quarles clearly prefers the albeit blemished brightness of the full moon of episcopacy to the uncertain favour of a multitude of lesser lights. A bill to do away with Deans and Chapters and dispossess the clergy of their revenues from church property, which was being debated during May, lies behind the fear that their 'fair Livelyhood' is to be 'shortned, if not snatcht away'; and a bitter complaint is exacted by the proposals to implement Root and Branch measures:

> Those Rods of power
> That rul'd our Swains by day, and did secure

Their Folds by night, are threatned from our hands,
And all our Flocks to bow to new Commands. (p. 234)

Philarchus's greatest dread is that the 'settled Government' of the church will give way to 'Confus'd Disorder, – the prodigious Childe / Of factious *Anarchie*' (p. 234).

Philorthus pins his hopes on the collective wisdom of Parliament, which has as its chief priority the 'care of Truth, and zeal of publique Rest' (p. 234). Such confidence is belied, however, by the anxious re-petitiveness with which this chastened pastor, who acknowledges 'the enormous crimes / Of our Profession', clings to the idea that 'the great Assembly's wise'. Surely, because 'they are just and wise', he argues, they will see the practical advantages of a limited reformation: 'far lesse cost and dammage will ensue / To weed old Gardens, then to dig a new'. But his companion cannot forget that the Deans and Chapters Bill is currently being discussed by those who legally hold the nation's land in trust as 'Feoffees of our tottering State':

> True, Shepheard, But they plead for want of dressing
> Our Garden's forfeited, and they are pressing
> Hard for Reentry; They have seal'd a Deed
> Upon the ground, intending to proceed
> Next Tearme t' Ejectment; by which means they'l stand
> Anew possest and re-enjoy the Land. (p. 234)

Philorthus reminds his fellow-bishop that they can turn to the King – '*Pan's Vicegerent*' – if Parliament questions their God-given title, or to 'the high *Chancery*; / That uncorrupted Court' if the common laws are invoked against them. In reply, Philarchus prefers the 'Protection' of God to these human agencies, and glances nervously at the animus against episcopacy displayed both by the populace in numerous Root-and-Branch petitions and by one of the most active radicals in the House of Lords. He prays that Members of Parliament will 'close / Their suits-attending ears' to the clamour of the illiterate mob, whom 'rayling Ignorance, and frantick Zeale / Hath only taught the way to *say*, *and seale*, / And set their marks' [italics added]. Once again Philorthus tries to reassure him that 'our great Assemblie's wise', and only 'com-plies / With the rude Multitude' out of 'policy'; but, true to his name, Philarchus grimly evokes the nightmare that was beginning to haunt the imaginations of moderate reformers:

> I, but *Philorthus*, whilst the State complies
> With the tumultuous Vulgar, tumults rise,
> And rude disorder creeps into our plains;
> Swains will be Shepheards [bishops], Coblers will be Swains [priests];

> Flocks are disturb'd, and pastures are defac'd;
> Swains are despis'd, and Shepheards are disgrac'd,
> *Orders* are laught to scorn; and, in conclusion,
> Our Kingdome's turn'd a *Chaos* of confusion.   (p. 235)

The spokesman for orthodoxy is just launching into another defence
of the policy of the 'wise Assembly' when Philarchus's vision suddenly
materializes in the form of Anarchus, who distils the worst fears of men
like Quarles into the popular rhythms of a revolutionary song, combining religious fanaticism with levelling fervour:

> *Whatere the Popish hands have built*
>   *Our Hammers shall undoe;*
> *Wee'l breake their Pipes & burn their Copes,*
>   *And pull downe Churches too . . .*
> *Wee'l downe with all the 'Varsities,*
>   *Where Learning is profest . . .*
> *Wee'l teach the Nobles how to croutch,*
>   *And keep the Gentry down . . .*
> *The name of Lord shall be abhorr'd,*
>   *For every man's a brother;*
> *No reason why in Church or State,*
>   *One man should rule another.*   (pp. 235–6)

Masoodul Hassan points out that this ballad 'was first published in a
slightly different form in 1642 as "The Round Heads Race" in *The
Distractions of our Times*'.[6] When 'Eclogue XI' was first printed as *The
Shepheards Oracle* in 1644, there was a postscript to the reader in which it
was claimed that the speech of Anarchus had already 'been nois'd by the
Balad-singers, about the streets of London, with some additions of their
owne to make up a full penny-worth'. It is not clear whether Quarles
was adopting an existing revolutionary song into his pastoral, or
whether it was filched from his manuscript and published separately.
Whatever the origin of the song, even the shock of its singer's intrusion
cannot shake Philorthus's faith in Parliament as the best physician for
the nation's ills. The 'great Assemblie's eye' sees the dangers of such
'base Sycophants' as clearly as it sees the threat from Rome; and its
'hand / Feels but, as yet, the *Pulses* of the Land', while it inquires 'where
the peccant humours lye'. Once the Lords and Commons have discovered all the symptoms, 'then, no doubt, / Their active Wisdomes
soon will cast about, / To make a glorious *Cure*'. By a clever exploitation
of his chosen genre of pastoral dialogue, Quarles is able to use two
ideologically similar but temperamentally different speakers to set the
growing fear of extremism against an implicit trust in the wise and

moderating influence of Parliament. The fact that the optimism of Philorthus becomes more and more difficult to sustain, especially after the abstract notion of anarchy has assumed a disturbing dramatic reality in the figure of the Separatist, reveals how Quarles's own views had changed since he composed his play for the Barrington family towards the end of 1640. Then, like many others inside and outside Westminster, he had regarded the new Parliament as an instrument for restoring the church to its pre-Laudian purity. Now, like others who would provide the nucleus for a royalist party in the Commons and in the country, he was alarmed by policies that threatened the foundations not only of the episcopal church but of the traditional order of society.[7]

During the early summer months of 1641, the investigations into the Army Plot continued and further evidence of widespread conspiracy was presented to the Commons in June. Towards the end of July, the committee reported its findings and Suckling, Jermyn and Percy were subsequently voted guilty of high treason on 12 August, by which time Suckling may well have been dead by his own hand.[8] William Davenant, who had been captured at Faversham on his way to the coast, appeared before the Commons on several occasions in May and June. He was named along with the other conspirators in July, but the case against him seems to have been quietly dropped, either because of his slighter involvement or possibly in recognition of the 'Humble Remonstrance', which he addressed 'To the Honorable Knights, Citizens, and Burgesses of the House of Commons, assembled in Parliament'. It may simply have been that by August the Commons had no more time to waste on this least significant of the plotters, who readily confessed that he may have been guilty of 'some mis-becoming words' and 'loose Arguments, disputed at Table perhaps, with too much fancy and heat.' In this remarkable essay in sycophancy and self-justification, the poet even had the audacity to cite in his defence the poem which he had addressed to Henrietta Maria earlier in the year: 'And it is not long since I wrote to the Queenes Majesty in praise of her inclination to become this way the Peoples advocate, the which they presented to her; for the Arguments sake it is extant in good hands, and now mentioned, in hope that it may be accepted as a Record of my integrity to the Commonwealth.'[9]

With the dramatic climax of Strafford's execution behind them, many members were becoming impatient at the unusual length of this parliament and, anxious to return to their families, were pressing for an end to the protracted peace talks with the Scottish commissioners.[10] Charles had been planning for some time to attend the session of the Scottish parliament in July and there was now increased pressure to complete the treaty so that formal ratification could take place during his visit to Edinburgh. Alarmed at the prospect of the King travelling north by way of two discontented armies, Pym devised a scheme for resolving the political crisis in England before his departure, which was originally set for 5 July. His pursuit of the Ten Propositions, which he unveiled on 23 June, became 'the central thread of the summer's politics'.[11] Like the earlier deal promoted by Bedford, the central aims were to settle the royal revenues and to replace evil counsellors with men who had the confidence of Parliament. Distrust of the King's intentions in the wake of the Army Plot led to the postponement of his journey to Scotland until August, by which time it was hoped that terms would be agreed with the Scots and both English and Scottish armies disbanded.

Meanwhile, suspecting that Henrietta Maria might try to raise money for the royal cause abroad, Parliament blocked her plan to accompany Princess Mary when she went to join her husband in Holland. Throughout the summer, rumours of a papist conspiracy in which the Queen herself was implicated continued to circulate and there was a good deal of anti-Catholic activity. Count Rossetti fled to Flanders rather than appear before Parliament in June; and when the Queen's mother, Marie de Medici, left for Cologne in August, a number of English recusants and priests went with her to escape persecution. Pym had made national security a key issue in presenting the Ten Propositions and on 19 July a militia bill was introduced which would remove the King's right to nominate the local commanders of county Trained Bands and vest it instead in the two Houses. Charles resisted attempts to detain him in London for a further two weeks and took his formal leave of the Lords on 7 August. The bill confirming the treaty having been hurried through its final stages on 9 August, he returned to Westminster on the following morning to give it the royal assent and to bid farewell to the Commons before setting out for his northern kingdom. Although some English regiments were dispersed and the Scots had begun to withdraw by the time he left, the last Scottish troops did not cross the border until 25 August and the disbandment of the English army was not completed until 18 September. In the circumstances, it is not surprising that fears of a military coup encouraged Lords and Commons to agree on various measures for the protection of the kingdom against its own King. In spite of differences over church reform, Culpepper and

Falkland joined William Strode, Sir Thomas Barrington and the younger Vane on a committee of defence that was appointed on 14 August. They promptly ordered the Earl of Newport to take up residence in the Tower as Constable, and despatched the Earl of Holland to Hull to assert parliamentary control over the country's largest munitions store. In the event, these fears proved groundless. Charles passed through the northern armies and reached Edinburgh on 14 August. The peace treaty was finally ratified on 7 September.

Before leaving, the King had made further appointments designed to appease the opposition and court moderate opinion. Essex became Lord Chamberlain and was entrusted with military command, and Newcastle, tainted in the eyes of Parliament by possible collusion with the Army plotters, was replaced as Governor of the Prince of Wales by Hertford, who had been elevated to the rank of Marquis. Seymour, Hertford's brother, joined him as a member of the Privy Council on 8 August. Charles had also appealed to popular sentiment by issuing a manifesto on behalf of the Elector Palatine and the Protestant cause in Europe. This received enthusiastic support at a conference of both Houses in July, at which Denzil Holles declared the Commons 'zealous for the Redress of the Prince Elector's Wrongs'.[12] Charles Louis accompanied the King on his visit to Edinburgh, where the manifesto was also endorsed by the Scottish parliament. Some observers wondered whether Charles I was taking precautions against an attempt to depose him in favour of his nephew, but if any such plan was in the wind it came to nothing.[13]

Parliament remained in session throughout August, mainly to oversee the disbanding of the armies, and eventually adjourned on 9 September. Between then and 20 October when it reassembled, the day-to-day business of government was entrusted to a committee which met twice a week under the chairmanship of John Pym. The last act of the lower house before most of its members dispersed to their estates was to issue the text of a Commons' Order on 8 September aimed at undoing many of the religious innovations of the 1630s. Printed for distribution throughout the country, it decreed the removal of altar rails, crucifixes and images of the Virgin Mary from churches, prohibited such Laudian practices as bowing and the placing of communion tables at the east end, and condemned the Book of Sports. Local officials were charged with imposing these policies upon their communities and reporting back to Parliament by the end of October. Conrad Russell sees the attempt to enforce this Order, which had the consent of neither Lords nor King, as an important step in 'making it possible to turn the rule of law into an effective Royalist slogan'.[14]

There is uncertainty among historians about Charles I's own plans as he made his way northwards. Fletcher considers that his public statements during the summer 'hint at an increasingly unyielding stance behind a show of graciousness', but can find 'no good reason' to think that he 'went so far as actively to seek Scottish allies for a coup against the English parliament'.[15] Although in June he had apparently been working to secure Scottish neutrality and engage officers of the northern army in his cause, there seems to be 'no direct evidence to suggest that in August the King had any other plans than disbandment'; and, in Russell's view, he was hoping that the withdrawal of the Scottish army would enable him to 'prorogue, or at least adjourn, the Parliament as soon as he returned from Scotland'.[16] Whether his project in Edinburgh was 'to gain the support of Scotland against the Westminster Parliament' or 'to provoke a challenge to the Covenanter government from within which would result in its overthrow', Bennett argues that the end result would have been the same, 'for surely a Royalist government in Scotland might have begun to dismantle the revolution, and the next logical step would have been to turn the force of this counter-revolution onto the southern kingdom'.[17] Whatever long-term hopes Charles may have been nursing were destroyed by events in his northern and western kingdoms that played into the hands of Pym and the opposition in England: the first was the 'Incident' of 12 October, a foiled plot to seize the earls of Hamilton and Argyle, who headed the alliance against him in Scotland; and the second, far more serious, was the military insurrection in Ireland later in the same month, which triggered a popular rising and widespread violence against Protestant settlers.

Before news of the Incident and the Irish rebellion broke at Westminster, the parliamentary recess from 9 September to 20 October had provided members with 'an opportunity to take stock of the political situation'.[18] Some were already drawing away from Pym over the issue of religion; others were disturbed by the third of his 'propositions', that the power to appoint and dismiss 'officers and counsellors' should be transferred from King to Parliament. David Smith regards the weeks of recess as crucial for the emergence of a group committed to 'constitutional royalism' when the Commons reassembled. Led by Culpepper, Falkland and Hyde, it drew in others who had found themselves asking the question, 'did the Junto now pose a greater threat to the rule of law and to constitutional balance than the King?'[19] Its philosophical basis and political agenda are embodied in a poem which has been called the 'Manifesto of Parliamentary Royalism'.

Sir John Denham's *Cooper's Hill* presents a number of difficulties to interpreters, not the least being that five distinct versions of the text had some kind of public currency during the poet's lifetime. It was first published early in August 1642 and reprinted at Oxford in 1643, but two manuscript versions were in existence prior to that; it was printed in a significantly revised form in 1655; and it appeared again in Denham's collected *Poems and Translations* of 1668 in a text not radically different from that of 1655. Brendan O Hehir, whose comparative edition is the basis of all modern work on the poem, identifies two separate stages of composition and revision which produced what he calls the 'A' Text (Drafts I, II, and III from the early 1640s) and the 'B' Text (printed in 1655 and 1668).[20] Discussion of the 'A' Text in this and subsequent chapters will focus on two related issues: the immediate historical context and the political orientation of each of the three versions. As O Hehir points out, Draft III of *Cooper's Hill* must have been completed by the end of July 1642 at the latest, since it was entered in the Stationers' Register on 6 August 1642 and George Thomason's copy is dated 5 August. It seems logical to infer, as O Hehir does, that the initial composition of the poem must have preceded this publication date 'by a sufficient span of time to allow two distinguishable earlier drafts to have entered separately into manuscript circulation'; and furthermore that the earliest version, of which two copies survive, would not have been released into circulation until Denham 'conceived he had created a finished poem'. Persuaded by internal evidence that the first draft 'was written within the aura of Strafford's trial', O Hehir placed its composition in 'midyear of 1641'.[21]

It has been widely accepted, at least since Earl Wasserman's seminal reading of *Cooper's Hill*, that 'the primary function of its descriptive elements is to create a realizable and meaningful structure for the political concept being poetically formulated'.[22] What has not been so readily agreed is the precise nature of that political concept. Wasserman himself, without the benefit of O Hehir's work on the early drafts, read the first printed text against 'the troubled days of 1642' and concluded that 'Denham's is the basic royalist conception of divine right', although this does not prevent the 'rhetorical function' of the poem being in part 'to caution Charles both against tyranny and against too benevolently yielding up his royal prerogative to the demands of Parliament'.[23]

O Hehir himself considered that it was 'from inception ... a committed Royalist poem' and saw Draft I as 'a poem extremely sympathetic to Charles I'.[24] Insisting that so consciously political a poem 'should reflect the precise circumstances that prompted it', and that the circumstances in 1642 were not the same as those in 1641, John Wallace combed the earliest manuscript version for clues as to its date of origin and was able 'to narrow the period of composition to the three months between the king's departure from London on 10 August 1641 and his return on 25 November, but with a very strong presumption that Denham was writing in September.' He later pinpoints 10 September 1641 as the date by which 'a political climate existed' in which Denham might have undertaken Draft I of his poem.[25] With a timely reminder that 'royalist' is a word which 'begs as many questions as it solves', he argues that Denham 'was no believer in a divine right theory which claimed that kings could do no wrong' and makes a case for his being not 'a "party" poet' but 'a firm believer in the old balanced monarchy which Parliament was fighting for, and which the revolution of 1640–1 had already almost restored'. This means that he belonged ideologically with men like Hyde, Falkland, Culpepper and Sir John Strangeways – the future 'constitutional royalists' – and that during the recess of September–October 1641, 'Denham was voicing the opinions of a growing body of thoughtful men whose principles were equally parliamentarian and royalist'.[26] Ignoring the fact that two distinct manuscript versions were in circulation before the poem was printed in August 1642, James Turner is convinced that it was engendered by events earlier in that year and detects 'stinging satire and sarcasm, directed along party lines', which puts Denham in the same extremist camp as 'the ultra-royalist and provincial George Daniel'.[27]

These diverse readings of Denham's political attitudes have influenced the way in which critics have responded to the literary methods and qualities of the poem. Turner condemns its management of the prospect device as 'dishonest', because 'the eye is obviously led by a political argument and vice versa', and writes dismissively of Denham's provision of an 'aesthetic system' and 'an elaborate display of the art of prospective' for 'those already of his persuasion', rather than a realistic response to the collapse of their political world.[28] O Hehir places the poem in the traditions of the political-didactic georgic, which employed the observed features of 'rural nature as the vehicle for its discourse', and the emblem, which encouraged Denham 'to *read* the landscape "expans'd" before him' and decipher 'the message written in the landscape in God's hieroglyphics'.[29] For Ruth Nevo, the originality of *Cooper's Hill* lay in its adaptation of the idealizing techniques of Caroline court poets like Waller, whose 'eulogistic mythology' obscured rather than illuminated political reality, in an attempt to 'realize the aim of high seriousness through a philosophically rational treatment in an historical context, above the level of hero worship or propaganda or occasional compliment.'[30]

In the opening section of the poem, Denham is at pains to establish the relationship between the poet's vision and the natural scene spread out below him as he stands on Cooper's Hill, overlooking the Thames near his home in the Surrey village of Egham: 'Whose topp when I ascend, I seeme more high / More boundlesse in my Fancy then myne Eye'.[31] The imagination interprets what the eye perceives, so that the poet both sees and *sees into* the landscape; and as his survey of the neighbouring hills and flood-plain proceeds, he will read out of them the political lessons inscribed by the past actions of men upon the natural features created by God. Wallace suggests that the sense of distance implicit in the prospect poem was cleverly deployed by Denham to 'raise his discourse above the fevers of political disputation' and to suggest a stance of impartiality that would reassure the moderate readers he was hoping to attract to his brand of royalism.[32] James Loxley, on the other hand, sees the appeal to the elevated status of the poet as a way of lending 'even greater authority' to the subsequent readings of history.[33] Another recent critic argues that Denham's method was derived from the perspective art of court masques, country house poems and portraits by Van Dyck, in which 'the depiction of landscape' was designed 'to enhance the character of their country subjects':

However, in *Cooper's Hill* the settings are brought into focus by the kings, not the kings by the settings. Kings control the way we look at scenery, not the other way around. The crown is our lens. This is so because its powers shape the course of English history and history, in turn, shapes the prospects which we view along with Denham as he displays the consequences of the acts of kings.[34]

The earliest signal that the tenor of the meanings to be read from the landscape will be political occurs in the fifth line of the poem, which functions rhetorically as a simile amplifying the idea that Parnassus is not a fixed geographical location but comes into existence wherever a poet is inspired to produce poetry: 'And as Courts make not Kings, but Kings the Court, / So where the Muses & their Troopes resorte / Pernassus stands'. In their efforts to place the poem in a specific set of historical circumstances, critics have offered various glosses on line 5. For Wasserman, the context is Charles's efforts in the summer of 1642 to entice members of 'the high *Court* of Parliament' to York after his departure from London; O Hehir more tentatively invokes the dispute during the winter of 1640–1, when Parliament was challenging the 'doctrine of the King as fountainhead of law and justice' and putting Strafford on trial 'as the ultimate High Court of the kingdome'; and Wallace sees an allusion to Charles I's absence in Scotland during the autumn of 1641, which 'had precipitated a fierce debate about the status of the parliament he had left behind'.[35] Perhaps, since the line survives intact in all versions of the text, it is safest not to look for an explanation in any single event, but to recognize with Rockett that it embodies a view of the King's role which became a focus for debate in connection with a variety of specific circumstances during the period leading up to the Civil War:

The constitutional significance of the fifth line of "Cooper's Hill" – "Courts make not Kings, but Kings the Court" – is that the high court of parliament is formed when the king, being present in person, endows the estates assembled in his presence with sovereign authority. However, as Denham and Charles both discovered in the first few weeks of the Long Parliament, this royal power of making courts was an implement with two edges for, once empowered, lords and commons then form a body unified with the sovereignty issuing from the crown. Courts are created by kings, but once they are created sovereignty resides in a complex of shared powers, king and court becoming corporate members of a larger constitutional entity.[36]

After these preliminaries Denham begins his survey with a glance towards London, where the tower of the old St Paul's Cathedral, the tallest building in the city, may have been visible from Cooper's Hill in the seventeenth century:

> So from thy lofty topp my Eye lookes downe
> On Pauls, as men from thence unto the Towne
> My minde uppon the Tumult & the Crowde
> And Sees it wrapt in a more dusky Cloud
> Of busines, then of Smoke, where men like Ants
> Preying on others to supply their wants
> Yet all in vaine, increasing with their Store
> Their vast desires, but make their wants the more.
> Oh happines of Sweete retyr'd content
> To be at once Secure, and Innocent.

The function of this glimpse of London in the earliest draft – whether literally or as a mental picture, since the singular verb 'Sees' fudges the distinction between the perceiving 'Eye' and the conceiving 'minde' – is chiefly, as O Hehir points out, 'to emphasize the happiness of sweet retired contentment'.[37] But already it contains a hint of the political hostility to the city that would be expanded in later drafts: the word 'Tumult' must have recalled the angry mobs that had jostled bishops and peers on their way to the House of Lords and milled around Whitehall during the trial of Strafford; and the fact that '"humble desire" was the invariable expression used by Parliament to petition the king'[38] pushes the distaste for 'vast desires' that increase the more they are satisfied beyond a conventional attack on the acquisitiveness of the business community. In this version of the text, however, the distant view of London is subsidiary to the main structural elements, which are the sight and associations of Windsor Castle to the west and the ruins of Chertsey Abbey to the east, with the River Thames and its adjacent meadows between them.

The first lines about Windsor introduce by way of mythology the fundamental principle that underlies both the aesthetics and the politics of the poem: 'Windsore the next (where Mars with Venus dwells, / Beauty with Strength) above the Valley Swells, / Into myne Eye'. As Wasserman was the first to note in connection with *Cooper's Hill*, the ancient doctrine of *concordia discors* – the cosmic principle of a harmonious balance held between opposite forces – had long been expressed allegorically in the myth of the goddess Harmonia, offspring of the union of Venus and Mars.[39] Since Windsor was a royal castle, Denham must also have had in mind the familiar symbolism of the masques, in which Charles and Henrietta Maria had been identified with the classical deities and their married life celebrated as a source and symbol of national harmony. As the passage develops, however, the more feminine qualities of the hill (with its 'unforct ascent' and 'gentle Bosome'), which 'at once invite / A pleasure & a Reverence from the Sight', are interpreted as aspects of Charles himself, softening the military connotations of the castle that has been erected upon the natural eminence:

> Thy Masters Embleme in whose face I saw
> A frendlike sweetnes & a Kinglike Awe
> Where Majesty & love soe mixt appeare
> Both gently kinde, both Royally Severe.

Denham, in this initial reference to Charles, begins to read him as a living expression of the principle of *concordia discors*, in whom the warmth of friendship and love is balanced by the majesty of kingship, and the necessary severity of office is alleviated by an attractive gentleness of character.

A meditation on the aptness with which Nature provides a succession of heroic occupants for such a perfect combination of site and building

introduces a passage about Edward III, one of the most illustrious
among 'those severall Kings to whome / It gave a Cradle or to whome a
Tombe', who is invoked by Denham to illuminate by parallel and
contrast the nature and achievements of the current owner of Windsor
Castle. He had founded the Order of the Garter and named St George
as its patron. Charles I had always taken a special interest in this order of
chivalry: he had himself been the model for St George in a painting
executed for him by Rubens, and in the frontispiece of Peter Heylyn's
history of the Order of the Garter, published in 1631, there were
matching portraits of Edward III and Charles I together with illustra-
tions of George as soldier and saint.[40] In the emblem devised for the
Order by Edward III, Denham discovers a prophecy of the achievements of the Stuarts. The red cross of St George and England surrounded by a blue garter prefigures the uniting of the island of Great
Britain under one crown, when King James VI of Scotland became
King James I of England in 1603. A marginal note in one of the
manuscripts identifies James as the monarch who bound the two nations
together, but in the lines which follow it is clear that Denham is
extending the prophecy to include Charles I:

> In whose Heroicke face I see the Saint
> Better exprest then in the livelyest paint
> That fortitude which made him famous heere,
> That heavenly Piety which Saints him there:
> Whoe when this Order he forsakes, may hee
> Companion of that Sacred Order bee.

The current King of Scotland and England, who has sealed the work
inaugurated by his father by ratifying the recent treaty between his two
kingdoms, will one day emulate the patron of the earthly Order of the
Garter by joining the ranks of the saints in heaven. At this early date, in
the association of Charles with St George, 'the Martyre & the Souldier',
we may see in embryo the myth of the pious monarch, dying in defence
of the Church of England, that would be exploited to such great effect in
the *Eikon Basilike*.

Edward III also prefigured the present by bringing together in England the royal lineages of Scotland and France in the persons of two
prisoners of war, King David II and King John. Charles and his French
Queen have accomplished a more harmonious version of the same
union in a 'better Fate' that is appropriate to the balance of sweetness
and awe, love and majesty, in their exemplary relationship. It was
clearly destined, proclaims the poet-seer. The peaceful union wrought

by the love of this 'Royall paire', identified in a marginal gloss as the King and Queen 'nowe', is superior to the conquests that Edward achieved by the sword. The disapproval with which Denham writes of victories which involved the bleeding of 'Sister nations' may be intended both to commend the treaty which Charles had just signed with the Scots and to warn against future Civil War; and, in a reference to extending 'the Christian name ... through the Conquered East', Denham may have had in mind the recently revived hope that an end to internal strife might free Charles to support his nephew in the contemporary crusade against the Roman Catholic powers of Europe.

The Windsor section of the poem as a whole, which places Charles in the context of a long line of heroic kings and a glorious national past, makes an appeal, in Wallace's words, 'to feelings that lay much deeper than the animosities that divided the country'.[41] The next section, however, prompted by the ruins on St Anne's Hill, highlights the divisions that *were* becoming more and more apparent with regard to religion. The view across to Chertsey Abbey, a Benedictine foundation which had been destroyed at the dissolution of the monasteries, sets Denham's mind to work comparing the process of reformation in the sixteenth century and the contemporary call for a Root and Branch attack on the established church: 'may no suche storme / Fall on our tymes, where Ruyne must reforme'. The 'storme' which fell upon the church in 'devotions name' is all the more distressing to the poet because it was stirred up by a monarch who had exchanged the 'Learned pen' that had earned him the title 'Defender of the Faith' for the 'much more Learned Sword'.[42] His initial account of Henry VIII's reforming activities creates a deliberate contrast with Charles I's recent dealings with the church. The charges against Henry VIII are essentially moral. Denham does not condemn him for beginning the Protestant reformation of the church in England, but for unworthy motives. Unlike the 'temperate' and 'chast' Charles I, whose personal propriety and devotion to his wife were at the heart of the myth fostered by the court masques, Henry was in no position to be outraged by 'Luxury or Lust' in the church of his day; and although Charles needed money as badly as his Tudor predecessor, and for less self-indulgent purposes, it had been made clear to a meeting of the Privy Council on 24 January that 'ye k. would rather starve than have any of the church lands or livings'.[43]

Turning from the contrasting qualities of kings to the general religious climate, Denham laments the failure to achieve the ideal state of *concordia discors* , either in the time of Henry VIII or in his own day:

> Is there no temperate Region can be knowne,
> Betweene their frigid & our torrid Zone;
> Could wee not wake from that Lethargicke dreame,
> But to be restles in a worse extreame?

Whereas Wallace can find nothing in the first draft of *Cooper's Hill* to
suggest that the poet would have opposed the anti-Laudian stance of
Falkland and Hyde, O Hehir believes that the longed-for 'temperate
Region' was, for Denham, the Laudian church, standing between the
extremes of religious torpor in the late medieval period and the fiery zeal
of contemporary Puritanism.[44] The syntax and punctuation of this
version of the poem often obscure the connections and contrasts that
Denham is intending to make, but the pronoun 'wee' seems to relate to
'*our* torrid Zone' and to refer to the present as distinct from '*their* frigid . . .
Zone' in the early sixteenth century. If this is so, then the poet's
contemporaries have just woken from their own 'Lethargicke dreame',
which parallels the 'Lazie' state that prevailed before the Tudor reformation – and that dream must be the Laudian dispensation of the 1630s.
Denham has no objection to the church waking from this dream, but he
wants a return to Jacobean moderation and not the radical proposals
that Dering had spoken against in June or the fanatical measures that
the Commons had just sought to impose upon local congregations in
their illegal Order of 8 September. Dering had made the same distinction between the '*Ruine*' and the '*reforming*' of the church, and the
metaphor of the 'Lethargicke dreame' for the period of Laud's ascendancy seems to echo similar medical terminology in the work of other
moderate supporters of Parliament's reforms. Fane's Albinia, having
been cured by Dr Psunodarke, had explained how she had been 'in a
Loethargy' until 'the northerne gust wakt me at last'; and a page,
reporting that Quarles's Lady Temple was 'troubled with a *Liturgie*', had
been corrected by Dr Artesio: 'A Lethargie you meane. It is a Chronical
disease, and time must cure it.'[45]

Denham is glad to have his attention diverted from the unedifying
historical spectacle of Henry VIII's greedy despoliation of the church
and the frightening prospect of rampant Puritanism in the future:

> Partinge from thence twixt Anger Shame & fearre
> Those for what's past, & this for what's too neere,
> My Eye descending from the Hill surveyes:
> Where Thames amongst the wanton valleys strayes.

The wonder and delight that result from contemplating the strife between 'huge extreames' in the scene below – 'the steepe and horrid

roughnes of the wood' and 'the gentle Calmenes of the flood' – are an aesthetic response to the principles of *concordia discors* that underlie the art of medicine and the creating activity of Nature herself: 'Wisely shee knew the harmony of things / (Aswell as that of soundes) from discord springs'. Strafford had been relying upon the persuasive power of commonplace when he had invoked the political form of this theory in April: 'and as on the lute, if anything be too high or too low wound up you have lost the harmony, so here the excess of a prerogative is oppression, of a pretended liberty in the subject disorder and anarchy'.[46] And it was by reading the river and the water-meadows in its light that Denham had earlier conjured up an ideal vision of a monarch and his subjects in harmonious relationship – a vision triggered rhetorically by the simile, 'Like Profuse Kings'. The further development of this simile seems to engage more directly with recent events. A concerned husband calming the fears of a weeping Henrietta Maria is the dominant image evoked by the personification of the Thames/King in the following lines:

> And as a parting lover bids farewell
> To his Soules joy, seeing her Eyelidds swell
> He turnes againe to save her falling teares,
> And with a parting kiss secures her feares.

But when the simile of the King is formally applied to the river (the kind of curious inversion of normal rhetorical procedures that is a feature of this poem), the image of the Queen is displaced by (or merges into) an image of the King's metaphorical spouse, the Parliament:

> Soe Thames unwilling yet to be devorc't
> From his lov'd channell, willingly is forc't
> Backward against his proper course to swell,
> To take his second, though not last farewell.

Wallace recognized in these couplets, which do not occur in any of the later versions of *Cooper's Hill*, a highly topical allusion to Charles's two visits to Parliament on 7 and 10 August, at which he took separate leave of the two Houses.[47] Denham purveys the usual royalist claim that Charles was eager to work with his Parliament – to flow in the 'lov'd channell' of the constitution – and, besides implying that he is reluctantly going to Scotland since that is 'his proper course' at this juncture of affairs, also reassures anxious readers that this was not intended to be his 'last farewell' to Parliament.

A political gloss is then put upon two visits associated with the river in another simile which reverses the usual relation of vehicle and tenor, likening 'a wise king' who 'first settles fruitfull peace / In his owne Realmes' and then 'seekes warre abroade' to the Thames, which is a channel for both imports and exports. This simile had obvious topical significance in September 1641 in the wake of the treaty signed in Edinburgh and Charles's declaration of support for the Elector Palatine's cause in Europe. The application of the simile to the Thames is evidently designed to boost commercial confidence in the prospects for trade now that hostilities with Scotland have been formally ended.

The perception of an aesthetic harmony created by Nature from the discordant elements of steeply wooded hillside and calmly flowing river generates yet another simile, which discovers a political parallel in a feature of landscape and leads into the episode that has most exercised interpreters of the poem:

> And as our angry supercilious Lords,
> Big in theire frownes, & haughty in their Words
> Looke downe on those whose humble fruitfull paine
> Their proud & barren greatenes must Sustayne,
> So lookes the hill upon the streame, Betweene
> There lyes a spacious and a firtile greene.

O Hehir was baffled by this reference to 'angry supercilious Lords', and wondered if Denham was looking back to 'the derogatory picture of King Henry VIII' or forwards to 'King John and his tyrannous predecessors'; Wallace is sure that they were 'the lords of the privy council, who had been responsible for many years ... for seeing that the people were properly mulcted of their ship-money'.[48] The word 'our', reinforcing the present tenses, implies a more contemporary significance than the Tudor monarch or the medieval barons, but in the context of September 1641 it is unlikely that Denham was aiming his criticism exclusively or chiefly at the Privy Councillors of the 1630s. Those conspicuous for anger and pride in the more recent past were opposition lords like Saye and Sele, who were seeking to assert their authority over the King – now daring to look down upon the regal stream as well as exploiting the more 'humble' labourers as they had always done.

The sight of Egham Mead, between the river and the hill, reminds Denham of the 'noble heard' of deer (perhaps in contrast to the 'supercilious Lords') that come there to graze; and the thought of the magnificent antlers that adorn their 'sublime & shady fronts' for a brief season prompts him to illustrate from recent history the lesson taught by this natural emblem: 'how soone / Greate things are made, but sooner farre undone.' No reader in 1641 would have missed the aptness of this truism to the rapid rise and fall of Thomas Wentworth, recalled from Ireland to become the King's chief adviser in 1639, elevated to an earldom in 1640 and executed in 1641.

Denham begins, however, by painting what seems to be a familiar scene called into the mind's eye by a particular place: 'Here have I seene our Charles (when great affaires / Give leave to slacken & unbend his Cares) / Chasing the Royall Stagge'. Commentators agree in rejecting any attempt to interpret this episode as a coarse allegory of the trial of Strafford, although O Hehir ventures a 'quasi-allegorical' reading, which admits resemblances or oblique references to details of the impeached earl's fate.[49] In the opening passage of description, the only detail that obviously lends itself to such a reading is the stag's rejection or abandonment by the 'unkindly wise' members of 'the lesser heard', who 'obey'd & fear'd' him when he was at the height of his power. In the next line, however, a formal comparison invites us to remember, as Wasserman puts it, 'that the hunt has a parallel in the world of human affairs':[50]

> (Like a declying [*sic*] Statesman left forlorne
> To his frinds pitty & pursuers scorne)
> Wearied, forsaken & pursu'd, at last
> All Safety in dispaire of safety plact.
> Courrage he then assumes, resolv'd to beare
> All their assaults, when tis in vayne to feare.

This is reminiscent of the Strafford whose fortitude and eloquence had tipped the scales against his possible guilt in Denham's earlier poem on his fall, so that he earned an ambiguous tribute as 'Our nations glory and our nations hate'. In this later poetic evocation of the trial, the poet is more hostile to those who had 'decreed' his death out of fear and to that breed of 'lesser beasts', the 'doggs' who bayed for his blood in the streets of London. He also acknowledges – though without dwelling too long on such troubling aspects of the affair – that when Strafford's rhetoric had failed to secure his release, the promise of friendship made by the King and the plan to use military force had also come to nothing. The simile of a ship sinking in a storm prepares for the conclusion of the narrative, which Nevo sees as carefully designed to convey 'at once apologetic for the King and compassion for the noble quarry, the one as firmly held as the other':[51]

> So stands the stagg among the lesser hounds,
> Repells their force & wounds returnes for wounds,
> Till Charles from his unerring hand letts fly,
> A mortall shaft, then glad & proud to die
> By such a wound, he falls.

As O Hehir points out, this first version of the poem 'emphasizes the fact that Strafford went down fighting'.[52] While noting that the stag is 'glad & proud to die' at the hand of the royal huntsman, Denham here lets slip no hint that Strafford had willingly put his life at the disposal of the King.

The careful wording of the transition to the next section on the signing of Magna Carta by King John confirms for Wallace that the stag stands not for an individual statesman but for a political tendency, which can be seen as exemplified in Charles's fallen minister:

> This a more Innocent & happie chase,
> Then when of ould (but in the selfe same place)
> Faire Liberty pursu'd & meant a prey
> To Tyrany, here turn'd & stood at Bay.

Harking back to the phrase 'Royall Stagge', he argues that the quarry in the 'more Innocent & happie chase' to which Charles, however reluctantly, gave his consent was the panoply of arbitrary power that had been systematically stripped from the monarchy between November 1640 and the summer of 1641.[53] Denham approved of the various parliamentary acts by which the abuse of royal prerogative had been removed, though he could admire the courage shown at the end by the statesman with whom the policy known as 'Thorough' was chiefly identified. It was on this same spot of Runnymede that a stand had been made against tyranny when the barons exacted from King John a guarantee of those rights of subjects that were widely regarded as the cornerstone of English freedom. O Hehir notes that on the very day that Strafford died, 'the Commons authorized, as a deliberate celebration of that death, the publication of the late Sir Edward Coke's *Second Part of the Institutes of the Laws of England*, a work that had been forbidden publication by the King twelve years before'.[54] This book contained Coke's commentary on Magna Carta. But however much Denham may have abhorred the challenge to the laws of the land during the 1630s, he was uneasy about the principle of imposing the people's will upon a monarch by force, even if circumstances might seem to justify it. The example of the barons' resistance to King John was not one that he could comfortably apply to King Charles, especially in the aftermath of military rebellion in Scotland:

> For Armed Subjects can have no pretence,
> Against their Princes, but their just defence:
> And whether then or no I leave to them
> To justifie, who els themselves condemne.

Even if the 'just defence' of the people is the one legally arguable reason for taking up arms against a monarch, Denham still leaves a question mark against the action of the Scots – and by implication against any future action by the English Parliament that had recently made moves towards taking control of the country's militia.

In the distant past, the action of the barons was justified by what was achieved at Runnymede. They succeeded in formulating a constitutional model that reflected the natural principle of *concordia discors*:

> There was that Charter Seal'd, where in the Crowne
> All marks of Arbitrary power layes downe:
> Tyrant, & Slave, those names of hate & feare,
> The happier Stile of King, & Subject beare.

The brutal extremes of tyranny and slavery were exchanged for the civilized balance of royal prerogative and popular allegiance, in which rights and obligations are acknowledged on both sides. But subsequent history was marred by a return to the contest between opposing powers in place of an ideal harmony of complementary interests:

> The Subjects Arm'd, the more theire princes gave,
> But this advantage tooke the more to crave:
> And as by giving the Kings power growes les,
> So by receaving, their demands increase.

If, as royalists of the Suckling stamp believed, Charles I had already given way too readily and too far to the demands of Parliament, then the danger that further demands would drive him towards a military initiative lurks not as a threat but as a warning in a final couplet: 'Till kings (like ould Anteus) by their fall / Reinforc't, their courage from dispaire recall'. The last thing Denham (and men like Hyde and Falkland) wanted was for the fears aroused by Charles's visit to Scotland to be justified. But those fears could be mobilized in the interest of a more moderate and conciliatory policy than that signalled by the militia bill and the Commons' Order of 8 September.

The poem ends with an extended account of a river in flood, which is then applied to the political world of autumn 1641:

> When a Calme River rais'd with suddaine Raines,
> Or Snowes dissolv'd, oreflowes the adjoyninge plaines;
> The husbandmen with high rais'd bankes secure
> Their greedy hopes, & this hee can endure:

> But if with Bays, & Dams they strive to force
> His current to a new or narrow Course,
> No longer then within his banks he dwells,
> First to a torrent then a deluge swells:
> Stronger & fercer by restraint he Roares,
> And knowes no bound, but makes his power his shores.

There was scarcely any need for Denham to apply this description explicitly to the political sphere since inundation as a metaphor for the excessive exercise of royal power was a commonplace, which had figured prominently at the recent show trial in the impeached minister's self-defence. Identifying the 'Prerogatives' of the King and the 'Propriety or Liberty of the Subject' as the forces that must be 'kept in their own wonted Channels' if 'Agreement and Harmony' are to be maintained in the state, Strafford had issued a warning: 'For if they rise above these heights, the one or the other, they tear the Banks, and overflow the fair Meads equally on one side and other.'[55] Denham's stance of objectivity is tilted slightly against the husbandmen by the juxtaposition of their 'greedy hopes' and the tolerance of the king-like river that is prepared to endure much without overflowing banks that have legitimately been raised to restrain its power. It is in the attempt to strike at the very nature of kingship by diverting it into a new course that Denham sees not only the danger of strong retaliatory action by Charles I but the prospect of war between King and Parliament. In a reprise of his earlier account of English history since the signing of Magna Carta, he presses home the lesson that when monarchs impose or subjects demand too much, the balance of the constitution is upset and both are made 'by striving to be greater, lesse'.

The literary achievement of *Cooper's Hill*, as Wasserman almost recognized, was to transcend the outdated masque-like conception of politics that Denham had himself followed in reading Windsor Castle and Chertsey Abbey as static emblems of the ideal king and the tyrant. The stag hunt and the river go beyond this to become 'dynamic symbols', and the latter in particular renders the 'mixed monarchy' as 'a persistent energy' that always tends 'to pull the system into an imbalance'.[56] The power-struggles that constitute history are beginning to be seen as a temporal *process* rather than a series of *pictures*. As an attempt to intervene in that process, the poem is a remarkable document which, as Wallace has convincingly demonstrated, 'is the only statement in this phase of the revolution to give a comprehensive and coherent account of the "new Royalism" at the moment of its inception'.[57] O Hehir sees

Denham's final word as 'an admonition to King Charles's turbulent and provocative subjects';[58] but, in fact, the first version of *Cooper's Hill* closes with an appeal for moderation that is directed with as much urgency at the King and his counsellors as at the people and their representatives in Parliament:

> Therefore their boundles power lett princes draw
> Within the Chanell & the shoares of Lawe:
> And may that Law which teaches Kings to sway
> Their Septers, teach their subjects to obey.

Whatever influence the poem itself may have had in disseminating a particular view of the constitutional crisis that awaited resolution when Charles returned from Scotland, it certainly gave voice to growing fears about the activities of the King's leading opponents and foreshadowed significant political realignments among those who sought to maintain 'a consistent commitment to the rule of law'.[59]

CHAPTER 5

The emergence of the constitutional royalists:
October 1641 – March 1642

Two days before Parliament reassembled, Charles I wrote from Scotland instructing Edward Nicholas, a clerk to the Privy Council who was
under orders to keep him informed of developments in London, to
assure all his servants that he intended to stand firm in defence of the
doctrine and institutions of the Church of England 'as it was established
by Queen Elizabeth and my father'.[1] This is an early indication that
Charles was 'in a mood to assert himself' by the autumn of 1641, and
that the debate about the future of the national church was to be central
to 'the process which brought the emergence of two parties at Westminster and made civil war a possibility'.[2] The contents of the King's letter
were soon available in print under an uncompromising title, *King Charles
his Resolution, Concerning the Government of the Church of England, being contrary
to that of Scotland*, which was designed to calm fears excited by his
endorsement of the Presbyterian system in his northern kingdom, and it
was evident in the first few days of the second session of the Long
Parliament that religious battle lines were being drawn up. On 21
October, Dering launched a general assault on the Order of 8 September.[3] Pym assumed the offensive on the same day with a new bill to
exclude the bishops from the Lords, which was hurried through its
various stages and passed by the Commons on 23 October. His allies
were unable to get it through the upper house, however, and there was a
similar resistance among the peers to a proposal to deprive thirteen
impeached bishops of their vote.[4] On his side, Charles I had shown that
he was determined to back his words with practical action by announcing the appointment of five new bishops, among them Henry King to
Chichester and John Williams, Bishop of Lincoln, to the Archbishopric
of York. This was countered by a Commons motion to prevent their
installation and the debate, which ended in a vote of 71 to 53, was an
early sign that the House was becoming deeply divided over religious
issues.[5]

According to Fletcher, Hyde and Falkland 'were probably in the House more of the time at this period than Pym himself' and they were 'quickly joined, as emerging leaders of a powerful royalist faction, by Sir John Culpepper, Sir John Strangeways and Sir Edward Dering'.[6] David Smith points out that there was no single issue or moment that drew together in opposition to Pym the men who had worked alongside him to dismantle the machinery of arbitrary rule and impeach Strafford and Laud. He identifies two factors above all that drove them towards the King – 'a sense of Charles I as a viable constitutional monarch committed to the Church, and a horror of popular violence against that Church' – and suggests that Culpepper's hatred of Root and Branch 'first translated into a bid to give political assistance to the Crown' as early as July 1641.[7] There has been some disagreement over the timing and the motivation of Hyde's decision to support the King in the House of Commons as a matter of policy. By his own account of his summoning into the royal presence in the summer of 1641, it was his participation in the religious debates of June and July that first brought him to the favourable attention of Charles I.[8] Rejecting the common opinion that Hyde simply changed sides, however, Wormald maintains that he was consistent in his belief that the legislative reforms he had helped to effect in the first session could best be consolidated by pursuing a policy of reconciliation between King and Parliament: 'To suppose that he was any less "parliamentarian" or any more "royalist" is to introduce categories that are both irrelevant and misleading.'[9] The fact that the 'main hindrances' to reconciliation inside the House of Commons 'were the ecclesiastical radicalism and the fear of the King' adequately explains Hyde's open opposition to Pym during late October and November.[10]

Ecclesiastical matters apart, Hyde was concerned to mitigate the effects of the scaremongering that was a standard tactic of the opposition in casting doubt on the integrity of Charles. The Incident in Scotland had given Pym an opportunity to raise the familiar spectre of a widespread Catholic conspiracy as soon as the House of Commons reconvened on 20 October and to heighten the sense of emergency by calling out the Westminster Trained Bands under the Earl of Essex to secure Parliament against a supposed threat from disbanded soldiers.[11] Sir Simmonds D'Ewes was quick to take up the cry that 'darke and evill spirits' were intent on discovering 'the secretts of our State to forraigne parts' and subverting 'the Tru Religion professed amongst us'; and it is from his parliamentary journal that we catch a glimpse of concerted action by Pym's leading opponents to play down an event in which many did not hesitate to implicate the King: 'After I had spoaken the LORD FAULKLAND and Mr. HIDE mooved that wee should leave the busines of Scotland to the Parliament there and not to take upp feares and suspicions without very certaine and undoubted grounds.'[12] Hyde was prominent again in resisting a move to assert parliamentary control over the appointment of the King's councillors, which became 'a central feature of the constitutional struggle' between June 1641 and June 1642.[13] Reporting the debate on 28 October, D'Ewes was obviously shocked by the 'great violence' with which William Strode had seconded this motion: 'it was soe extream a straine as Mr. HIDE did upon the sudden confute most of it: shewing that the choice of the great officers ... [was] ... an hereditarie flowre of the crowne.'[14] On the day after this debate, Nicholas dispatched a letter which made the King aware that there was now the nucleus of a party that could be relied upon to defend the constitutional rights of monarchy as well as the established order of the church: 'I may not forbear to let your Majesty know that the Lo. Falkland, Sir Jo. Strangeways, Mr. Waller, Mr. Ed. Hyde and Mr. Holborne and divers others stood as champions in maintenance of your Prerogative and shewed for it unanswerable reason and undeniable precedents.'[15]

Meanwhile, the fires of fear and suspicion that Hyde was anxious to dampen down were being busily stoked by Pym's revelation on 30 October of another plot involving officers from the northern army, with which Father Philip, the queen's confessor, was said to be associated. Two days later, a shocked Parliament received the first reports of the rebellion that had broken out in Ireland. What had begun on 22 October as a series of concerted military strikes at strategic targets and an attempt to take over the seat of government in Dublin was rapidly developing into a general uprising of the Catholic population. The impact of this turn of events upon the contest between Pym and Charles cannot be underestimated. First of all, it supplied the opposition leader with sensational evidence of a papist conspiracy, which he was quick to exploit in his campaign of suspicion against Henrietta Maria and her entourage. Secondly, and more importantly in the long term, the debate over the right to raise and command an army which it precipitated was 'the context in which two armed forces were created, one under royal and one under parliamentary control'.[16]

Once news of the Irish rebellion had broken, the printing presses of

London played a major part in fanning the flames of rumour and panic. Letters from witnesses in Ireland and 'discoveries' written by dispossessed Protestants who had fled to England made up a large proportion of Thomason's collection of newly published tracts from November 1641 until June 1642, reaching a peak of 37 per cent in April.[17] Stories of massacre and looting were purveyed under such lurid titles as *Bloody Newes from Ireland, Or the barbarous Crueltie By the Papists used in that Kingdome;* and nearer home, the Catholic threat was kept in the forefront of public consciousness by reports of 'a Bloody CONSPIRACY By the Papists in *Cheshire*', a plot 'by the Earle of *Worcester* in *Wales*', and another to rescue Father Philip from the Tower, where he had been lodged after being summoned before the Lords on 2 November. The title of *The Impeachment and Articles of Complaint Against Father Philips The Queenes Confessor* had the effect of implicating Henrietta Maria herself and the publication of an incriminating letter sent from Ireland by the Scottish Earl of Traquair to 'Old Father *Philips,* heere in *England*' seemed to give substance to Pym's conviction that there was a longstanding Catholic design to subvert English Protestantism, which had its roots in the court and its tentacles in all parts of Charles's three kingdoms. On 18 November, the day that Charles set out from Edinburgh on his journey south, the rampant anti-Catholic sentiments in the House of Commons found a political outlet in the measures 'humbly' requested in *A Petition Sent to the Kings Most Excellent Majestie, in Scotland* : 'That all Popish-priests, Jesuits, and other ill affected persons, may instantly be banisht the Kingdome, and not suffered to be in, or neere the Court, at the time of his Majesties Returne into England, so to prevent such dangers as otherwise might ensue throgh [*sic*] their wicked plots and treacherous designes.'[18] The ambiguity about the nature of the dangers that would be prevented by clearing the court of Catholics may well have been deliberate. For many, no doubt, the fear that could not be openly expressed was that those who were 'ill affected' towards the parliamentary reformers would be working *with* rather than *against* the King and his papist Queen.

Distrust of Charles had been increased by the claim of Sir Phelim O'Neill, the leader of the military insurrection in Ulster, that he had a commission from the King himself, bearing the Great Seal and issued in Edinburgh on 1 October. Modern scholars accept that this document, copies of which were widely distributed among O'Neill's followers, was a forgery, but not all are convinced that Charles was ignorant of what was afoot in Ireland. The significant thing for the political situation at

Westminster, however, was that 'the validity of the commission was widely believed at the time'.[19] Charles's supposed complicity in events in Ireland quickly sparked off further clashes between Pym's supporters and the growing faction in the House of Commons that still hoped to avoid an irreconcilable breakdown of relations between Parliament and the monarch. On 5 November, in an item added to five 'instructions' to the Committee of both Houses in Edinburgh, Pym turned the familiar opposition appeal for control over the appointment of government officers into an ultimatum: 'that howsoever wee had ingaged our selves for the assistance of Ireland yet unles the King would remove his evill counsellors and take such councellors as might be approved by Parliament wee should account our selves absolved from this ingagement.'[20] Hyde was immediately on his feet to question this arrogation of parliamentary sovereignty over the King and was backed up by Culpepper and Waller. Pym eventually returned on 8 November with an amended version of this so-called 'Additional Instruction', which removed the threat to abandon the Protestants in Ireland, but registered a deep suspicion of 'such mischievous counsels and designs as have lately been and are still in practice and agitation against us'.[21] The amendment was passed by 151 votes to 110, further evidence that consensus was crumbling under the pressure of controversial assaults on the ancient rights of the crown as well as fundamental features of the established church. That pressure was maintained on the day after Pym's first moving of the Additional Instruction, when Cromwell proposed that Essex's command be extended by direct parliamentary order to all the Trained Bands south of the Trent, a move which signalled the beginning of a protracted contest between Charles and Parliament for power over military as well as governmental appointments.[22]

On the same day that the Commons endorsed the Additional Instruction, the House was presented with what has been described as the 'most illuminating' and the 'most divisive' political document of 1641.[23] The idea of delivering a remonstrance to the King had been mooted by Digby as long ago as November 1640 and preliminary work had been carried out by a parliamentary committee during April and May 1641. A smaller committee of eight had brought it to completion during the autumn and by 8 November Pym was ready to lay before his colleagues this comprehensive account of the misdemeanours of Charles's government since 1625 and the achievements of the current Parliament during its first session.[24] The Grand Remonstrance also contained proposals for reforming the church and the universities and another version of the disputed sixth Instruction. In a preamble, the root of all the 'mischief' of the past sixteen years was traced back to 'a malignant and pernicious design of subverting the fundamental laws and principles of government, upon which the religion and justice of this kingdom are firmly established'.[25]

Fletcher's view is that Pym had hoped 'to bring the House into line behind a document that was designedly conciliatory towards conservative opinion in a number of respects', but that his bid for consensus failed because the royalist faction was alarmed by 'the policies which were believed to lurk beneath the leadership's manifesto'.[26] In his later summary of the contents and effect of the Grand Remonstrance, Hyde certainly remembered it as 'a very bitter representation' of the illegalities of the earlier part of Charles's reign and considered that the publication of 'all the unreasonable jealousies of the present government' was intended to 'disturb the minds of the people'.[27] In the debates that followed over the next fortnight, Hyde played a leading part in the 'trial of strength' between those who sought 'to minimize the sense of danger and distrust' and those who sought 'to maximize it as Pym was doing'.[28] D'Ewes reports more than one occasion on which 'the Episcopall partie were soe strong in the howse' that individual clauses were withdrawn or amended, and when it came to the final vote on the revised draft of the complete document, Hyde – who 'begann and spake very vehemently against it' – was 'seconded by LORD FALKELAND, SIR JOHN CULPEPER and divers others'.[29] Concluding that he must in conscience 'say *NO* to this strange Remonstrance', Dering had given powerful voice to misgivings over the constitutional legality of addressing such a detailed indictment of royal government to the people rather than the King, especially when it had been drawn up by one house alone: 'When I first heard of a Remonstrance, I presently imagined that like faithfull Councellors, we should hold up a glasse unto his Majestie ... I did not dream that we should remonstrate downeward, tell stories to the people, and talke of the King as of a third person.' He concluded on an ominous note: 'The use and *end* of such Remonstrance, I understand not: at least, I hope, I do not.'[30] Culpepper, himself a member of the committee of eight, spoke against its acceptance in terms similar to those of Dering when it had become apparent that Pym was intent on using it as a weapon in a power-struggle with Charles I; and Hyde insisted that 'the end of this Remonstrance is peace'.[31] In the end, those who saw the best hope for the future in a political accommodation between King and Parliament were narrowly defeated by 159 votes to 148, in a division which gave birth to 'the Parliamentarians as a party which fought the Civil War' and marked the demise of Hyde's hopes that 'the body which had taken the initiative in the reform of the State might begin the consolidation of its work by taking the initiative in conciliation'.[32]

The historic vote in the small hours of 23 November did not quite conclude the House's business for the day. One last effort was made to address the Remonstrance to the King, and when this was rejected in favour of a proposal to have it printed for public circulation, Hyde and Culpepper asked for their dissent to be entered in the record of proceedings. Such a step could not be taken without the consent of the House, however, and uproar ensued when Geoffrey Palmer tried to insist on his personal protestation against the majority being recorded. It was agreed to postpone a decision about printing the document, but Palmer was sent to the Tower for inciting a display of partisanship which was still too novel and disturbing a concept for most members of an institution that was accustomed to working by consensus. The 'alternative leadership' offered by Hyde and his faction had initiated a form of adversarial politics that 'men had hardly begun to grasp or accept'. The implications of the parliamentary split that the debate on the Grand Remonstrance had made manifest and the growing 'uncertainty about where power lay' were matters that would only be resolved when the King returned to London.[33]

Over the summer and autumn, disenchantment with the activities of the radical faction in Parliament had spread to the business community and the city officials in London. A visitation of plague and the presence in the capital of unruly soldiers from the disbanded northern army were threatening the stability needed for trade, and the sometimes violent resistance in city parishes to the puritan reforms imposed by the Order of 8 September was breeding discontent with Pym's leadership and a general fear of anarchy. On Nicholas's advice, the King had been lending a friendly ear to the interests of the East India and Levant Companies; and under a newly elected Lord Mayor, a rich silk merchant with pronounced royalist sympathies, the Court of Aldermen and the Common Council decided to mount an elaborate civic welcome for the King when he returned from Scotland. After a reunion with his family at Theobalds, Charles I accordingly set out in state on the last stage of his journey on the morning of 25 November. Having been greeted at Moorgate with expressions of loyalty by Sir Thomas Gardiner, the Recorder of London, the royal party went in procession along

streets lined with liveried members of the City Companies to the
Guildhall, where they were entertained to a sumptuous banquet. In his
speech of thanks, Charles promised to protect the mercantile interests of
the city and repeated his pledge to defend the established church.[34]
These festivities marked 'the climax of the rapprochement between the
crown and the City', but the public display of allegiance was 'official and
organized' rather than spontaneous. A 'strong undercurrent of dissatisfaction' had made itself felt in 'libels against the entertainment' that had
been 'dispersed in the streets', and two companies of the Trained Bands
were on standby to deal with any outbreak of disorder.[35]

Expressions of joy and loyalty poured from the presses, some clearly
designed to make propaganda capital out of the civic reception – like
Ovatio Carolina and *Great Britaines time of Triumph. Or, The Solid Subjects
observation, Shewing in what a magnificent manner, the Citizens of London entertained the Kings most excellent majestie* – and others bearing more personal
witness both to support for Charles and to a widespread anxiety over the
expected political showdown between King and Parliament. John
Taylor, the waterman, had already thrown himself energetically into the
religious struggle on the side of the established church in 'a stream of
witty, scurrilous pamphlets designed to bury the separatists in ridicule
and disgust', and his 'ebullient account of the royal entry' in *England's
Comfort* had inaugurated his 'future career as a popular royalist champion'.[36] Another partisan account had been accompanied by 'a Copie of
Verses congratulating the Kings Return' by one J. H., who combined
panegyric with satire in an attempt to find a viable poetic medium for
the complex political situation of November 1641. Already in the opening ten lines, there is some awkwardness in the management of tropes
and metaphors that had been confidently deployed by Cowley, King
and Cartwright to celebrate Charles's previous return from Scotland
after his coronation in 1633:

> Brave *Charlemains* return'd, me thinks the sound
> Should all our forrain enemies confound;
> And our Domestick foes to friends convert,
> In every breast create a loyall heart.
> These clouds of darknesse, whose resistlesse might,
> In the Suns absence, turn'd the day to night:
> Shall by his presence, vanish, swiftly flie
> Like foggy exhalations of the skie,
> His glorious rayes of Majestie shall shine
> In spight of envy, glorious and divine.[37]

Whereas the youthful Cowley had invoked the names of Caesar and

Alexander to set off the more godlike attributes of Charles, this poet's allusion to Charlemagne prompts an acknowledgement that there are enemies at home as well as abroad, who will not respond as loyal subjects 'should' to the news of the hero's return. For Henry King, the metaphorical winter caused by Charles's absence had been ended by the blessing of his sun-like return; and Cartwright had imagined how the Scots, deprived of the 'Presence' of 'lawfull Majesty' for so long, had eagerly pressed to 'see and know' their monarch. J. H.'s emphasis on the 'resistlesse might' of the 'clouds of darknesse' that have 'turn'd the day to night' during Charles's second visit to Scotland implies that his presence is more a necessity than a blessing in the context of recent political developments. In the expectation that the King's return will stiffen resistance to Pym's faction, the poet abandons 'should' for 'shall' and declares with masque-like confidence that the 'glorious rayes of Majestie' have the power to scatter the 'foggy exhalations' of opposition, although he does not quite lose sight of the 'envy' that will deny both their glory and their divinity.

At this point in the poem, the troubled attempt to sustain the language of panegyric gives way to a more aggressive style in which irony and outright satire are turned against those who have been challenging the King's authority. Seemingly alert to the process of polarization within Parliament that had been taking place during 'our Kings absence', J. H. distinguishes between those who strove 'to expresse their love / And care of us his Subjects' and those who 'were inclin'd / To practise mischief'. Now that Charles has returned, the former will receive a 'Royall guerdon', while the latter can expect a 'Regall judgement' and perhaps even a 'legall grave'. Religion, which was lately tossed 'in blankets', will be rescued from the Church of Rome and from the sectarians, whose spirits are informed by a 'beguiling devill' that makes them withdraw to the refuge of 'a Barn or Stable' in which to hide 'their vile hipocrisie'. As if mindful that he began with the intention of 'congratulating', the poet rather shamefacedly breaks off this twenty-eight-line diatribe against the 'mischief' of the King's opponents – 'But soft I range too farre, the world will frown' – and reverts to the register of panegyric. Even so, he rounds off four lines of prayer for the blessings of a prosperous life and triumphant reign with a challenge to those who do not share his devotion to the crown: 'Long live King CHARLES, true Subjects cry, *Amen.*'

John Bond, identified on the title page as a member of St John's College, Cambridge, begins his poetic welcome[38] with a conventional desire for the skill to 'expresse the joyfull sight / Of your returne' and roots it firmly in the Caroline tradition with apostrophes to Charles as 'Great *Atlas* of Religion' and 'Fountain of peace', descriptions of the rejoicing of 'all the Gods and Goddesses' at his return, and an assertion that as a monarch he is 'nothing earthly, but divine'. But these commonplaces are mingled with fears 'least our Religion should die' and 'least we grow unto some Anarchie'; and the topos of the King as the 'Sun of glory' contains a covert glance at the recent rumours of conspiracy in Scotland: 'those obscure dreames / Of adverse Fortune, unto which we were / Late *incident*'. [italics added] These constitute 'a cloud of feare' only to be dispelled by 'the bright raies of your returne'. References to 'the plots of th' Antichristian Pope' and anxieties about 'Faction' reflect a political perspective in which Charles has a unique role to play as both the bringer of 'concord' and the 'Ark' in which 'sacred truth' will ride out the flood.

In his prose welcome to the King, to which was appended a poem asking for God's mercy on a sinful nation in time of plague,[39] John Cragge's image of Charles is closer to Foxe's Protestant ideal of the Godly Prince. For this pious 'gentleman', the peace 'twixt Scotch and English' has been concluded by 'Our Famous King' only with 'God's assistance'; and Charles is worthy of allegiance because 'He rules in Christ, in Christ he governs well'. Furthermore, Cragge's 'thankes and praise' for the treaty with Scotland and his prayer for an end to 'grudge' and 'repine' in England are both motivated by an apocalyptic vision of a national crusade to restore the Elector Palatine, destroy the power of Rome, and bring in the Kingdom of Christ:

> What better deed by us can now be done,
> Then helpe a Royall Mother, and her Sonne?
> What better fruits may this our peace produce,
> Then Babel punish for her foule abuse?

These three poems alone testify to the various shades of 'royalism' at this time and reveal the strain exerted by a changing world upon traditional modes of poetic discourse. Some of the contributions to the Oxford and Cambridge volumes, *Eucharistica Oxoniensia* (hereafter *EO*) and *Irenodia Cantabrigiensis* (hereafter *IC*) were no doubt written out of a sense of duty to the university as much as to the King, and there is a good deal of recycling of such topoi as the dispersal of mists or night or winter by the arrival of a sun-like king, Charles's personal ability to conquer his foes by wisdom or clemency rather than armed force, the state as a body deprived of its soul at the departure of the King, and the

King himself as a loadstone drawing all hearts after him or a distant star dispensing benign influence. But while many endeavoured, in Loxley's words, 'to reinvigorate the forms of Caroline panegyric', it had also become necessary to reimagine 'the contexts in which the loyal duty of the Christian Royalist takes place'.[40]

In the poem which opened the Oxford volume, Martin Lluellyn sounded a note that was frequently heard in both the university collections: 'Our feares enlarg'd each minute to an age; / And thought your shortest stay a pilgrimage' (*EO*, sig. A1ᵛ). For example, R. Cresswell wrote of a 'Town beset with watches and with fears' (*IC*, sig. L1ʳ); and H. Vaughan (one of three with that surname at Jesus College, Oxford) recalled the 'feares *and* Pantings' with which the '*dire* fame' of 'Irish Tumults, *sword and flame*' (*EO*, sigg. a2ᵛ-a3ʳ) was received.[41] Another Oxford poet, John Dale, adapted the trope of the sun's longed-for return to express the mood of resentment and panic caused by Charles's prolonged sojourn in Edinburgh:

> What crowds of people to each Post did runne
> To know the regresse of their glorious Sunne?
> But when th'unwelcome sound came to their eares
> Of longer stay, all were possess'd with feares.   (*EO*, sig. c1ʳ)

After this striking depiction of a country in the grip of rumour and speculation, the conventional appeal to the image of the Stuart Peacemaker reads like a deliberate evasion of political realities or a dutiful pretence: 'Welcome (*Blest Prince*) whom heav'n sent to compose / All blustring garboyles, making friends of foes' (*EO*, sig. c1ʳ). There is a similarly hollow ring to the assertion by L. T. of Balliol College that the King's entrance upon the scene will resolve the difficulties in Ireland as if they were merely special effects in a court entertainment, put on so that the King can work his magic: 'When your bright rayes breake forth, Those Rebells all / Which like to Meteors rose doe like them fall' (*EO*, sig. a3ᵛ).

More forthright in addressing the fears generated by Charles's return itself was Lluellyn's manipulation of familiar Caroline conceits to counteract Pym's strategy of fomenting distrust:

> Nor doth your bright approach suggest a feare,
> That you who warm'd from Scotland, should scorch here:
> As if the distance lost, your sacred Brow
> Must lay by Temper, and dart lightning now.
> For by a long experience you are knowne,
> To make a Heaven which hath no Torrid zone.   (*EO*, sig. A1ᵛ)

The final phrase echoes line 152 of *Cooper's Hill* – 'Betweene their frigid & our torrid Zone' – and the entire passage looks like an attempt to allay suspicions that Charles might cast aside his carefully nurtured reputation as a man of peace and, in Denham's warning words, grow 'fercer by restraint'. Such an emphasis on the temperate disposition of the King was not mere flattery but a positive move to convey the image of a ruler who could be 'gently kinde' as well as 'Royally severe' and to encourage men like Hyde and Falkland in their policy of keeping open the path to reconciliation. There are hints in several other university poems that Denham's conception of Charles as the ideal embodiment of the principle of *concordia discors* had engaged the imaginations of moderate royalists: Robert Chaundler and Charles Mason attribute the King's success in Scotland respectively to 'his stout meekenesse' (*EO*, sig. A2ᵛ) and to his 'Royall mildnesse' (*IC*, sig. K3ʳ); and I. Goad writes of Charles bringing equilibrium back to the isle of Great Britain (*EO*, sigg. b1ᵛ-b2ʳ). The most striking evidence of the early impact of *Cooper's Hill*, however, is a variation on the controversial fifth line in a pastoral dialogue by F. Palmer: 'for where he resorts, / He creates Kingdomes too, as well as Courts' (*EO*, sig. d1ᵛ).

In his discussion of *Irenodia Cantabrigiensis* and *Eucharistica Oxoniensia*, Loxley points out that the King's return occasioned 'substantial consideration of the nature of his presence in his kingdoms, the ubiquity of his authority and the omnipresence of monarchy' and argues that 'the extensive depiction ... of the royal absence, rather than the royal presence' is even more significant, since it produces 'a King with a spatially specific and therefore limited authority, identified increasingly with the whereabouts of his person'.[42] At Cambridge, T. Yardley affirmed the traditional belief that the King's authority was 'Omnipresent' throughout his realm: 'If not in person to inculcate aw, / Yet by the pow'rfull presence of a law' (*IC*, sig. K4ʳ). While at Oxford, the orthodox view of the monarch's place in a God-given system of correspondences and hierarchies was spelt out by Vaughan in order to provide a natural explanation for the 'fears' alluded to earlier in his poem: 'As *Kings* doe rule like th' *Heavens*, who dispense / To parts *remote* and neare their *influence*, / So doth our CHARLES Move also' (*EO*, sig. a2ᵛ).

Two Cambridge poets responded anxiously to the recent challenges to this conception of kingship. William Fairbrother argued that England was the King's 'proper sphere' and urged that he should 'be by Viceroyes still Ubiquitary', since his absence from the main seat of government had caused such an unfortunate variation in the 'climate' (*IC*, sig. K2ᵛ). Cresswell issued a timely reminder that although the King's 'influence' may be great 'every where', his 'chiefest court' was 'the heart', and his absence in Scotland had demonstrated that not all hearts were responsive to the royal 'life and heat'. His closing advice was that Charles should regard his other kingdoms 'as Innes', but England as his 'home', which he should make his 'constant Presence-chamber' (*IC*, sig. L1ʳ). A number of the Oxford poets were also preoccupied by the political consequences of the King's absence and the disturbing questions about sovereignty that it had raised. In Chaundler's opinion, 'Absence seem'd Oppression' to Charles's neglected northern subjects; and the visit to Scotland could be justified on the grounds that 'none / Can mannage a Kings cause, but he that's One' (*EO.*, sig. A2ʳ). George Barlow was more worried by the effect on the southern kingdom and devoted the bulk of his poem to an energetic satirical diatribe against the various ills that had beset the church while the King was away: 'Tinkers' who have 'Usurp'd the sacred Ephod'; 'woemen' who presume to 'preach, and pray / With th' best who serve at th' altar'; the 'adulterous presse' that pours forth 'bace Pamphlets' containing 'monstrous Calumnies' against the church and the bishops; and the 'furious zeale' of reformers who 'Pull railes, and tables downe'. Having vented his spleen by detailing 'the History / Of those curs'd works of darknesse which were done / Since your departure', Barlow concluded that this 'confusion' had broken out because 'Faith's great defender CHARLES was then away' (*EO*, sigg. A3ʳ⁻ᵛ).

The two most distinguished contributions to *Irenodia Cantabrigiensis*[43] represented two very different literary approaches to the significance of the event that prompted them. Abraham Cowley's relief at the return of those 'Two greatest *Blessings* which this age can know ... *Peace* and *You*' takes up the conventional idiom of Caroline panegyric to transform the awkward substance of political compromise and financial settlement into the consoling fantasies of Stuart myth: 'Others by *War* their *Conquests* gain, / You like a *God* your ends obtain.' Betraying no hint of the insurrection and massacres in Ireland, Cowley concentrates on the treaty between England and Scotland and rejoices particularly that this 'happy *Concord* in no *Blood* is writ'. The miracle has been effected like a spectacular scene-change, restoring the idyllic landscapes where 'the *Northern Hindes*' may once more 'sing and plow' in peace: ''Twas only *Heav'n* could work this wondrous thing, / And onely work't by such a *King*'. The storm of Civil War has at last blown over, as Waller had prayed that it would in his panegyrical address to Lord Falkland when Charles had first taken up arms against the Covenanters in 1639.

In contrast to Cowley's truism that the return of peace and the King are equal blessings, John Cleveland rounded off the volume by challenging the very notion that had supplied the titles and subject matter of many of the poetic tributes elicited by Charles's arrival in London. He adopts a combative stance towards those who regard the time spent by Charles in his northern capital as an absence: '*Return'd?* I'll ne'r believe 't; First prove him *hence*' [italics added]. Cleveland eschews the resources of panegyric, satire, and pastoral in favour of the rhetoric of debate. His versified speech begins by placing the onus of proof on his opponents and then overwhelms their proposition with a plethora of ingenious examples and conceits. The debate centres on the issue that had exercised many of the university poets and Cleveland's opening gambit is to call up some of the commonplaces of Caroline thought (the King as a sun or a star and as the soul of the body politic) in order to confirm that Charles's sovereignty throughout his kingdoms does not depend upon the public display of his person in regal Progress:

> Kings travel by their beams and influence.
> Who says the soul gives out her gests, or goes
> A flitting progresse 'twixt the head and toes?
> She rules by Omnipresence, and shall we
> Denie a Prince the same ubiquitie?

But the nature of this royal 'Omnipresence' is perplexing and the devices of pun and analogy need to be supplemented by paradox as the poem proceeds, in an effort to explain a concept which puts language itself under strain – 'Hither and hence at once'; 'Two realms, like Cacus, so his steps transpose, / His feet still contradict him as he goes'; 'Backward is forward in the Hebrew tongue'. One critic justly observes that the blatant artifice of this stylistic strategy is 'heightened by consciousness that its assertions *are* assailable'; and for another it reveals 'a good deal about Cleveland's own unsettled state of mind'.[44] The literary methods adopted by Cleveland certainly set these verses apart from the others of November 1641. They neither celebrate the King's godlike achievement in conferring peace upon his subjects nor expose the 'mischiefs' that have been rife while he has been away. The poet ends by acquitting him of the charge implied in the first line; he and his English subjects were never truly separated by the journey to Scotland: 'Our souls did guard him northward thus, / Now He the Counterpane [a legal term meaning the counterpart of an indenture] comes South to us'. The dominant impression left by this uncomfortable poem, which effectively conducts a part-legal/part-philosophical enquiry into the nature of a prince's sovereignty, is aptly described as that of a poet 'trying to come to terms with [Charles I] as a phenomenon'.[45]

An anonymous university wit preferred a less academic style, too irreverent perhaps for inclusion in either of the official volumes, which could accommodate classical but not popular models of satire. His poem belongs to a genre that had become firmly identified with the stereotype of the 'Cavalier' by 1656, when it was eventually published in the retrospective miscellany of royalist verse, *Parnassus Biceps*.[46] The second line of the refrain of this drinking catch casts a realistic eye on the King's promise to restore those estates in Londonderry that had been taken from City landowners by the Irish rebels:[47] 'Sing and be merry boyes, sing and be merry, / *London's* a fine Town so is *London-Derry.* ' The anonymous rhymster pours scorn on fanatical reformers like the puritan who looked askance at the sword carried in the manner of a crucifix before the Lord Mayor as the royal party was processing from the banquet to Whitehall, but is also well aware of the element of expediency in Charles's gracious approach to London's commercial magnates. He confirms in his closing comment, however, that he holds Parliament, not the King, to blame for the continuing hostility between them: 'Nothing was wanting if I could but say / The House of Commons had met him half way.'

If the members of the Lower House did not come half-way to meet him – either literally or metaphorically – nor did Charles make any conspicuous effort to conciliate them. He excused himself from an official visit to Parliament on the grounds that he had a sore throat and promptly withdrew with his family and close advisers to Hampton Court. He slighted the Commons further by ignoring the Grand Remonstrance and began to prepare for a trial of strength with Pym by putting the Earl of Dorset in charge of the militia and making a number of changes in his government. Most significantly, Nicholas was knighted and sworn in as Secretary of State to the position left vacant by Windebank's flight and the elder Vane was dismissed from the other Secretaryship. A deputation finally delivered a copy of the Grand Remonstrance to the King at Hampton Court on 1 December, but he pointedly avoided any reference to it during a visit to Westminster on the following day. These ostentatious snubs to Parliament were exacerbated by the measures that Charles was taking to consolidate his new alliance with the City of London. He conferred knighthoods on several aldermen and sheriffs who came in a deputation to Hampton Court on

3 December and acceded to their request to promote confidence and stability in the capital by spending Christmas at Whitehall.[48] This was an urgent priority for both the municipal leadership and the business interests in London, because the ordinary citizens were out again in force demonstrating their agreement with the reformers in Parliament. On 29 November, a large crowd had gathered in the Court of Requests to protest against the bishops and the 'episcopal party', naming Strangeways, Hyde, Falkland and Culpepper as 'persons disaffected to the kingdom'.[49] There was another mass demonstration on 30 November and the tumults continued into the first week of December.

Meanwhile, the contest for influence over men's minds continued with the Commons' decision to print the Grand Remonstrance, which had so far only been circulated in manuscript. It was published on 23 December and on the same day Charles issued his reply. This royal Declaration had been composed by Hyde, according to his own account, 'only to give Vent to his own Indignation, and without the least Purpose of communicating it'. But Lord Digby, who with his father the Earl of Bristol was now part of an inner circle of courtiers, had accidentally had a sight of it and suggested that Hyde allow it to be made public as the King's official answer to the Grand Remonstrance. Hyde claims that he reluctantly agreed, but only on condition that his position in the House of Commons should not be compromised by revealing his authorship. He urged that it should appear with the full authority of the Privy Council in order to disarm those who suspected that the King was still under the spell of evil counsellors.[50] Ashton regards this 'foundation document of constitutional royalism' as a 'masterpiece of conciliation and reasonableness'.[51] For Wormald, it was a 'manifesto of good counsel', which was more concerned with consolidating the recent reforms in church and state than with refuting the indictment of Charles's earlier policies. He argues that its appeals for obedience to the laws and for a united front to deal with the crisis in Ireland were part of Hyde's consistent purpose of encouraging trust between the King and his Parliament as a prerequisite of a political settlement between them.[52]

Unfortunately, this strategy was difficult to pursue in the face of Charles's own behaviour. On the very day that he issued Hyde's conciliatory Declaration in the name of himself and the Privy Council, he antagonized his opponents by removing the pro-parliamentary Constable and Lieutenant of the Tower from their posts and filling the latter position with Colonel Thomas Lunsford, the kind of reckless soldier-courtier that had been involved in the army plots. This brought the apprentices onto the streets on Christmas Day and Charles bowed to the advice of the Lord Mayor that Lunsford be replaced by a less provocative figure. Lunsford remained high in royal favour, however, and during the last days of December was at the centre of several violent skirmishes between the crowds and a group of professional soldiers who had pledged themselves to defend the King. Suspicions about Charles's intentions aroused by the entertainment of these officers at Whitehall were not mitigated by the action of the bishops. Frightened by the tumults, during which Archbishop Williams had been caught up in a scuffle and surrounded by angry citizens, few of the bishops would risk attending the House of Lords and on 30 December Williams led a protest against all the votes taken in their absence. This move, sanctioned by the King, irritated many of the more moderate peers, who joined the minority opposition group in declaring that it constituted a breach of privilege. Twelve bishops were duly impeached for treason by the Lower House and lodged in the Tower, thus permanently damaging Charles's support in the Lords.[53]

The conjunction of the bishops' challenge and the presence of professional army officers at Whitehall created a new sense of emergency, and before the debate on impeachment began, Pym ordered the doors to be shut and 'moved that ... wee might send instantly to the Cittie of London that there was a plott for the destroying of the howse of Commons this day and therfore to desire them to come downe with the Traine Bands for our assistance'.[54] That mutual distrust, which Hyde's document had striven to diminish, had been intensified by Charles's own aggressive stance since its publication. On New Year's Eve, the tension continued to mount: outside the gate of Whitehall a group of 'Cavaliers', a term of abuse first heard on the streets along with the equally pejorative 'Roundheads' during these disturbances,[55] attacked a crowd of citizens armed with swords and staves, and the Commons threatened that if the King would not appoint a guard under the Earl of Essex, they would take whatever measures they deemed necessary for the safety of their House. Russell finds no evidence that either Charles or Pym was planning to make the first move, 'yet both sides, partly because they knew they themselves were willing to fight rather than give in, ended the week believing in the imminence of an armed assault from the other'.[56]

Charles chose this moment to make some significant changes to his government. On 1 January, he made Culpepper Chancellor of the Exchequer and Lord Falkland a Privy Councillor; and the following week Falkland was appointed Secretary of State alongside Nicholas.

Hyde later recalled that through the mediation of Digby, the King and Queen had also tried to recruit him into the government. Adamantly refusing the two posts that were offered to him, he did agree to work behind the scenes with Falkland and Culpepper to co-ordinate the tactics of the anti-Pym faction in the House of Commons.[57] The appointment to senior positions in the Privy Council of two respected parliamentarians, who were both opposed to Pym's policy of confrontation and untainted by connection with the Court, must have encouraged Hyde to hope that the King himself might be persuaded to take a more conciliatory course.[58] Nevertheless, his decision to look after the King's interests in the Commons does not imply that he had become a 'royalist' like Digby, a favoured courtier whose commitment to the royal cause was based on an intimate personal relationship with Charles. The difficulty of finding adequate terminology for Hyde's position at the end of 1641 – and, by implication, the position of other men who were later to join the King's side in the Civil War – is highlighted by Wormald:

There is no call to quarrel with the use of the words 'royalist' and 'parliamentarian' as opposite and mutually exclusive terms. It tallies with events as they shaped themselves in the end. The parliamentarianism of the Parliamentarians known to history, however, was from Hyde's point of view the parliamentarianism of the party of violence, and if we seek a definition of the 'non-violent' attitude, we have but to understand that both in the time of his parliamentary leadership and in the subsequent period of his concern with the membership of the Council, Hyde had worked precisely to prevent the emergence of any such disastrous distinction as came to be established in the end between Parliamentarian and Royalist.[59]

Even if Hyde and his friends were 'deceived', as Wedgwood suggests, into taking at face value 'the King's overtures to them as a welcome sign that he was ready for settlement',[60] they must have been troubled by serious doubts that the crisis could be resolved by a simple return to that political *concordia discors* expressed in Denham's analogy of the river contained in its proper channel. Over the weeks since the first draft of *Cooper's Hill* had been completed, the passing of the Grand Remonstrance by the House of Commons and Charles's more determined attitude towards his enemies had brought the poet's fear of a 'deluge' closer to realization. Parliament's attempts to alter the constitutional landscape – to force the King into a 'course' that increasing numbers of his subjects, inside and outside Westminster, believed to be too 'narrow' or too 'new' – were attended by signs of mobilization for the war of words that would be fought alongside the more bloody encounters on the field of battle.

Since the end of 1640, a revolution had been taking place in the printing trade, which saw a sharp rise in the amount of printed material, much of it in the form of short, inexpensive pamphlets that engaged directly with the current political situation.[61] The Scottish Covenanters had led the way, in a process that Nigel Smith has called 'a "downwards dissemination" of print – a democratizing of its availability',[62] by distributing printed copies of the acts passed by the Glasgow Assembly and launching a 'propaganda offensive' to persuade English readers that the invasion of 1640 was not an act of hostility but a defensive campaign that would help the people of England to resist arbitrary rule.[63] The King's leading opponents in England were not slow to appreciate the power of the printed word and both the speeches in which Pym and St John had set out the case against Strafford and the Protestation of May 1641 had been published by the authority of the House of Commons. An even more important innovation was the publication of parliamentary ordinances, like the notorious Order of 8 September, as Sheila Lambert explains: 'The printing of such ordinances from August 1641 accustomed the reading public to regard these pronouncements as authoritative, particularly since they usually appeared with the King's Printer's imprint, in the familiar style of royal proclamations.'[64] Reports and 'letters' from Ireland continued to pour unchecked from the presses, keeping alive the fear that a Catholic-inspired insurrection would spread to mainland Britain, and the controversy over the Grand Remonstrance shows the growing recognition in both camps that print was a vital weapon in the political arsenal.

Perhaps most significant for the all-out propaganda war that was to be waged over the next few years was the appearance at the end of November of the first of the 'newsbooks'. Foreign news had been published regularly in 'corantos' and 'gazettes' since the 1620s, but the printing of domestic news was forbidden. Although information about events in the capital – including summaries of parliamentary debates – had been communicated to the provinces in the form of manuscript 'newsletters', these were expensive and therefore limited in circulation.[65] The publication of a small pamphlet entitled *The Heads of Severall Proceedings in this Present Parliament* (22–29 November, 1641) was a new phenomenon: a regular survey of events at Westminster produced in larger quantities and more cheaply than the newsletters. This new printing venture quickly spawned imitators – the 'Diurnals', as they came to be called – which began to take on a 'pro-Parliament coloration' early in 1642.[66] Once the Civil War was properly underway, of course, the

London newsbooks and their royalist counterparts produced in Oxford became frankly partisan in their reporting, and sometimes manufacturing, of news.[67]

The situation was somewhat different during the period in which a royalist party was in the process of identifying itself. The literary genres associated with court entertainment and the celebration of the Stuart monarchy had not been designed primarily to influence opinion in the country at large, even if (like masques or verses composed for royal occasions by university poets) they were sometimes committed to print: they had expressed allegiance, sought patronage, confirmed the self-image of the King and his courtiers, discreetly tendered advice or promoted factional policies at court. As we have seen, the Caroline myth that Charles's presence was enough to reconcile differences and quell disorder was difficult to sustain in the verses that greeted his return from Scotland, and the conventions of court panegyric, which rested upon shared assumptions about the role of the monarch in a divinely ordained structure of society, were being rendered obsolete by the emergence of partisan politics and the threat of Civil War. Already, in the verses of J. H. and Barlow, there were indications that more combative methods would be needed for the defence of church and state against anarchy.

It is in the verse satires of John Cleveland that the beginnings of 'a recognisably royalist mode' have been detected.[68] The early stages of this development have been seen in the high-spirited wit with which he ridiculed the Protestation oath of May 1641 in 'A Dialogue between two Zealots' and in the wordplay of his meditation on the 'ubiquitie' of the King. A month or two after the composition of the latter poem, he intervened in the long-running controversy begun by the response of five Presbyterian ministers to Bishop Joseph Hall's justification of the episcopalian system, which he had published in January 1641. Stephen Marshall, Edmund Calamy, Thomas Young, Matthew Newcomen and William Spurstow, whose initials were combined into the pseudonym 'Smectymnuus', had issued *An Answer to an Humble Remonstrance by Joseph Hall* in March, the bishop had replied with *A Defence of the Humble Remonstrance* in April, and during the summer John Milton had weighed in with *Animadversions upon the Remonstrant's Defence Against Smectymnuus*. Cleveland's tactics in 'Smectymnuus, or the Club-Divines'[69] are quite different from those of the prose pamphleteers. He makes no attempt to refute or even engage with the specific arguments of Hall's antagonists, but instead seeks to discredit their entire project as a monstrous aberration that can provoke only astonishment and contempt in rational men. His first shafts of wit are directed at the cover name adopted by the five divines, likening them to 'the Bricklayers that *Babell* built', who were responsible for bringing the curse of linguistic anarchy upon the world: 'SMECTYMNUUS? The Goblin makes me start: / I' th' Name of Rabbi *Abraham*, what art? / *Syriac*? or *Arabick*? or *Welsh*?' As the conceits proliferate, the exuberant mockery of 'a name in Rank and File' – that is, made up of letters arranged in the manner of an acrostic – is infiltrated by puns which hint ominously at the danger of Trained Bands mustering to serve a fanatical cause:

> A Name which if 'twere train'd would spread a mile?
> The Saints Monopolie, the zealous Cluster,
> Which like a Porcupine presents a Muster,
> And shoots his quills at Bishops and their Sees,
> A devout litter of young *Maccabees*.

The allusion to the five sons of the Jewish leader who led the revolt against the tyranny of Syria may be ironic here, as Cleveland's modern editors suppose,[70] but the grotesque simile of the porcupine *shooting* at bishops prompts the more sombre reflection that a 'devout litter' of 'Saints', motivated by self-righteous zeal, may eventually lay aside the 'quills' of pamphlet warfare in favour of guns. Passing from the monstrosity of the name to the monstrous phenomenon it represents, Cleveland goes on to ridicule his multiple opponent as a five-headed freak of nature that might be shown at Stourbridge Fair, as a subject for theological speculation – 'Who must be *Smec* at th' Resurrection' – and as a fitting mate for the '*Et caetera*' oath, upon which he will beget further religious confusion: 'See, what an off-spring every one expects! / What strange Plurality of Men and Sects!' After ninety lines in which he demonstrates 'how variously he can give an aesthetic shape to contempt',[71] he prepares to bring the performance to a close: 'My task is done; all my hee-Goats are milkt.'

The allusion to 'hee-Goats' bears witness to Cleveland's respect for generic decorum, which connected satire by a false etymology with the roughness of the goat-like satyr.[72] His poetic method of accumulating and elaborating witty analogies owes a conscious debt to the 'imperious wit' of Donne, which had been celebrated by Carew and channelled through his poetry into the court culture of the 1620s and 1630s. Margaret Doody has argued that 'the conversion of metaphysical devices and manner to popular and public use' was one of the major literary events of the seventeenth century and has associated Cleveland's religious and political satires with the emergence of such poetry from 'the closet', where it had been 'read with private appreciation by the chosen few'.[73] But Cousins is surely more accurate in claiming that the 'significant originality' of Cleveland lies in the air of intellectual superiority and social exclusiveness with which he 'plays the virtuoso with stylish bitterness' and 'adapts the mannerist aesthetic nurtured by the cavalier world to the defense of that world as it is first threatened then broken'.[74] It is also very much part of the royalist stance of Cleveland's satires that they retain their link with the 1620s and 1630s, when an elitist manuscript culture flourished among the poets associated with the Caroline court.[75] Apart from those written especially for Cambridge volumes, his poems appear to have found their way into print without his supervision or consent, either as anonymous broadsides or in the various collections (often containing spurious items) issued with his name attached from 1647 onwards. Nevertheless, the survival of a large number of contemporary manuscript copies suggests that Cleveland's satires of the 1640s were intended to make an impact on public opinion beyond the court and the academy.[76] The exhibition of erudite wit and linguistic ingenuity in 'Smectymnuus, or the Club-Divines' stands out as an early example of the deliberate flaunting of elitist literary values against the stereotypes of the 'mechanick' preacher and art-hating puritan.

Even as Charles I was appointing leaders of the 'constitutional royalist' faction to the Privy Council at the start of the new year, he was preparing to go onto the offensive against his enemies. Probably at the instigation of Digby and triggered by a flurry of rumours that the Queen was about to be impeached, he determined to strike first and impeach six of his principal opponents on a charge of High Treason. The accusation against Lord Mandeville and five leading members of the Commons (Pym, Hampden, Holles, Strode and Haselrig) was read out in the House of Lords on 3 January and the articles of impeachment, which Wedgwood describes as 'the King's counter-charge to the Grand Remonstrance', were quickly made public.[77] There was a fatal delay in taking the accused men into custody, and by the time Charles and the Elector Palatine entered the Commons' chamber on the afternoon of 4 January, leaving the armed guard that had accompanied them from Whitehall in the lobby, the Five Members had sought sanctuary in the City. On the following day, when the Lord Keeper refused to apply the seal to a royal proclamation demanding the surrender of the fugitives, Charles went himself to the Common Council. Sir Richard Gurney, the royalist Lord Mayor, had effectively lost control of London in the annual Council elections on 21 December and the King was obliged to return empty-handed. The Common Council had already taken the revolutionary step of setting up a Committee of Safety on 4 January and on 6 January the Trained Bands were called out, without Gurney's authority, in response to fears of an imminent Cavalier attack on the City. Charles's attempted coup had brought his capital to the brink of bloody insurrection and, more significantly in the long run, 'the first six days of January were decisive in determining which side the City government would take in the breach between King and Parliament'.[78]

Meanwhile, the Commons had taken refuge in the Guildhall, where, with the cooperation of the new puritan majority on the Common Council, they set about securing control of the armed forces in the City. The effect of all this on Falkland and his colleagues was devastating. Hyde was later to recall their mood in the days that followed: they were caught 'between grief and anger' that 'the violent party' at court had 'gotten great advantage' over them; and they were 'so much displeased and dejected' at the King's failure to consult them that 'they were inclined never more to take upon them the care of any thing to be transacted in the House'. Their strategy of presenting Charles as a monarch dedicated to the rule of law and ready to turn from 'evil counsel' to the advice of moderate parliamentarians was in tatters and their own position was compromised. Their recent elevation to government office meant that 'they could not avoid being looked upon as the authors of those counsels to which they were so absolute strangers, and which they so perfectly detested'. Nevertheless, 'duty and conscience' compelled them to resume the task of trying to calm the 'thousand jealousies and apprehensions' that were rife in the House and the City and to establish trust in the King as the only foundation upon which a peaceful settlement could be built.[79] But there was little they could do in the current mood of crisis, and on 10 January, with the London Trained Bands drilling under the command of Serjeant-Major Skippon and armed watermen thronging the streets in support of Parliament, Charles and Henrietta Maria retreated to Hampton Court with their three eldest children, accompanied only by Secretary Nicholas, the Elector Palatine, a few household servants, and 'thirty or forty of those officers, who had attended at Whitehall for security against the tumults'.[80] On the next day, the Five Members led the House of Commons back to Westminster in triumph to the cheering of crowds, the marching of troops and the beating of drums.[81]

The King's abandonment of his capital is widely regarded as the event which made Civil War inevitable. Russell argues that, given the 'two rival myths' that had taken possession of the main antagonists, compromise was henceforth out of the question: 'Peace could now only come by the surrender of one party, which would only happen if that party was unable to raise a military force to defend itself.'[82] For David Smith, 10 January 'marked a watershed' in the development of a royalist 'party' in the country at large, because 'the physical separation of monarch and Parliament made it far more difficult to reconcile allegiance to both'.[83]

The King himself was still subject to conflicting pressures from factions among his closest supporters. On 12 January, Lord Digby was involved in an abortive attempt to rally Lunsford's cavaliers at Kingston in Surrey, and soon after fled to Holland to avoid impeachment; hopes of securing Portsmouth and the important magazine at Hull were pre-empted by parliamentary instructions despatched to their governors, Colonel Goring and Sir John Hotham; and on 13 January, Charles withdrew to the strategic stronghold of Windsor Castle. The Queen was instrumental in pushing for the military option, and by early February it had been determined that she should go to the Low Countries, where threats against her person could not be used to extort concessions from her husband and where she could purchase arms for the coming struggle.[84] On the other flank, the moderate royalists were still working for an accommodation, and on 20 January the King offered to open negotiations with his enemies in Parliament. This approach was rebuffed, but he made further conciliatory gestures and on 14 February was persuaded by Culpepper to give his assent to bills for the impressment of troops for Ireland and the exclusion of bishops from the House of Lords. By this time, he and the Queen had reached Canterbury on their way to Dover, having set out from Windsor five days before. Henrietta Maria embarked for Holland on 23 February and a few days later Charles was on his way to rally support for his cause in York, taking the Prince of Wales and the Elector Palatine with him.

Like Hyde and others who had been vigorous on behalf of the royal prerogative in the debates of November and December, Sir Edward Dering spoke rarely in a House now dominated by Pym's adherents.[85] But towards the end of January, he caused a stir by publishing a collection of his speeches, including one which he claimed to have prepared but never delivered during the wrangles over church reform the previous summer. His declared purpose was to vindicate his name 'from weake and wilfull calumnie'.[86] This remarkable volume opens with a defiant justification of the shift that had taken place in his attitude to the activities of the reforming Parliament he had once served whole-heartedly: 'I have no end, no ayme to lead me, but faire truth. I have no byas but a conscience warmed with zeale, and therefore when I change, (if I change) it shall be the conquest and victory of truth upon me' (p. 2). He insists that not he but circumstances have altered. In November 1640, the paramount and clear duty of an MP from the county in which Canterbury itself was situated was to bring to justice 'the tallest Cedar on the Churches *Lebanon*', whose crimes 'were many' and manifest (p. 3). And he had not been alone in seeking nothing more than immediate remedies for past wrongs: 'For (the truth is) I did not dreame, at that time of *extirpation* and abolition of any more then his Archiepiscopacy: our professed *rooters* themselves (many of them) at that houre had I persuade my selfe, more moderate hopes then since are entertained' (p. 4). In a postscript, Dering offers himself to the judgement of 'the candid and ingenuous Reader', now that he has made 'a faithfull and clear exposure' of himself 'in matter of Religion' (p. 94). His concluding remarks enunciate the very same fears of the political consequences of radical church reform that were expressed in Quarles's eleventh ec-logue:

These things thus pressed and pursued, I do not see but on that rise of the *Kingship* and *Priestship* of every particular man, the wicked sweetnesse of a popular paritie may hereafter labour to bring the King down to be but as the first among the Lords, and then if (as a Gentleman of the House professed his desire to me) we can but bring the Lords down into our House among us again, *eureka*. All's done. No rather, all's undone, by breaking asunder that well ordered chain of government, which from the chair of *Jupiter* reacheth down by severall golden links, even to the protection of the poorest creature that now lives among us. (p. 96)

As we shall see in the next chapter, Dering was not the only person who would feel impelled – either by 'wilfull calumnie' or by the promptings of his own conscience – into making a 'clear exposure' of himself to 'publike VIEW and CENSURE' (title page) as a result of changed allegiance when the Civil War finally began. Already angered by his 'defection' to the 'party for episcopacy', the Commons condemned Dering's printing of his own annotated speeches as a scandal to the House and hurried him away to the Tower on 2 February.

At about the same time, Sir John Denham must have been revising the text of *Cooper's Hill* to reflect developments in the political situation since September. Brendan O Hehir thinks that Draft II of the poem, which survives in three manuscripts, was 'very likely completed in 1641'.[87] A date in the second half of January or early February 1642, however, is more likely because of a marginal gloss at the start of the passage about Windsor – 'The Kinge and Queene there' – and two substantial additions to the first draft's brief glimpse of London, which change the configuration of the poem by giving the City a structural status and thematic significance equivalent to Windsor and St Anne's Hill.

The first of these additions was inserted after the image of men looking down from the height of St Paul's 'upon the towne':

> Pauls' the late theame of such a Muse whose flight
> Hath bravely reacht & soar'd above thy height,
> Now shalt thou stand, though time or sword or fire
> Or zeale more feirce then they thy fall conspire,
> Secure, while thee the best of Poetts sings
> Preserv'd from ruine by the best of Kings.

Another marginal note – 'Mr Waller's Poem' – makes explicit the allusion to the panegyric in which Waller had interpreted the repairs to the fabric of the cathedral as a symbol of Charles's policy of 'refining' the practices of the English church without altering its fundamental structure. It is the institutional integrity of the church that is now in need of protection by 'the best of Kings' against the conspiracy of zealous reformers.

Line 25 in Draft II (adapted from line 19 of Draft I) names 'London' as the object of the poet's survey; and a subtle change to the original line 22 (now line 28) emphasizes the 'sheer perversity'[88] of the ant-like citizens, who no longer merely prey on others 'to supply their wants' but 'Toyle to prevent imaginary wants'. The claim that their 'vast desires' are never satisfied leads into the next major addition, a rather unwieldy simile which likens London to a diseased body, cramming itself with unhealthy food – a place of confusion, where people frantically pursue malign and self-destructive projects, 'Some to undoe, & some to be undon', and where 'Luxury & wealth' paradoxically breed both 'ruine & increase'. It is because of the power struggle which had delivered the City into the hands of Charles's enemies that London assumes a new prominence in this revision of the text and so creates the tripartite structure perceived by O Hehir, which sets 'the *monarchic* extreme exemplified at St Anne's Hill' and 'the *popular* extreme, equal

and opposite, exemplified in London' against 'the monarchical harmonious balance of Windsor'.[89]

There is one other major change in Draft II, which O Hehir dismisses
without further comment as the replacement of one 'inconsequential'
simile by another.[90] What he does not notice is that these similes, in
which the Thames meeting the sea is likened to a lover parting from his
beloved, refer to two different sets of political circumstances. In Draft I,
as we saw in the previous chapter, lines 179–86 elide the tears of
Henrietta Maria with the separate farewells accorded to the King's
metaphorical spouse, the two Houses of Parliament, when Charles
departed for Scotland in August 1641. The shorter simile in Draft II,
which drops the no longer relevant allusion to 'his second, though not
last farewell', introduces a word that ran like a refrain through exchanges between King and Parliament in the early months of 1642:

> Then like a Lover he forsakes his shores,
> Whose stay with *jealous* eyes his spouse implores,
> Till with a parting kisse he saves hir teares,
> And promising returne secures her *feares*.   [italics added]

Clarendon recalls that 'fears and jealousies' were 'new words' invoked
by Parliament at this time 'to justify all indispositions and to excuse all
disorders'.[91] Since the simile of the 'Lover' describes the activities of the
river (symbol of kingship in the poem), and since it replaces a passage in
which the Thames, unwilling to 'be devorc't' from its 'lov'd channell',
was conceived as the spouse of the monarch, these four lines (with their
allusion to the 'jealous eyes' of the abandoned 'spouse') may be Denham's attempt to adapt his poem to the new situation created by
Charles's withdrawal from Whitehall on 10 January, which severed his
personal contact with Westminster and raised in a more acute form the
question of the continuing legitimacy of parliamentary proceedings,
since 'Courts make not Kings, but Kings the Court'. The reassurance
that the promise of Charles's 'returne' will render 'feares' of a permanent breach groundless may reflect no more than a forlorn hope on
Denham's part that the deluge of Civil War might yet be avoided by a
restoration of the ancient rule of King in Parliament.

After leaving Greenwich, where Hyde had helped him draft a reply to
Parliament's demands in the Militia Bill, Charles spent a few days at
Theobalds before setting out on a leisurely journey northwards. While
there, on 1 March he again refused his consent to a bill that would hand
over control of the country's Trained Bands to his enemies and angrily

threw their reiterated suspicions back in their faces, telling them to consider whether he 'might not likewise be disturbed by fears and jealousies'.[92] The two Houses retaliated by turning the bill into an ordinance, which, as an emergency measure for the defence of the realm, was voted through on 5 March without the need for royal assent. Sixteen members of the House of Lords protested at this violation of the monarch's prerogative to levy troops and the Militia Ordinance has been seen as 'the single most important catalyst' of the eventual decision by leading peers like Hertford and Dorset to join the King.[93] On the other side, the militia itself seems to have had symbolic as well as practical significance for those who were in the process of usurping sovereign authority. The very word, as Bulstrode Whitelocke complained in the Commons on 5 March, was no longer used merely in its traditional sense to denote troops that could be raised in the localities but was coming to mean military power itself, which many now regarded as the key to the current political crisis.[94]

Charles's slow progress towards York, where he finally arrived on 19 March, was punctuated by a series of Declarations, in which each party justified its own position and condemned the other's intransigence. Hyde was responsible for composing many of the royal statements in this war of words and laid great emphasis on the King's affection for the Church of England, determination to abide by the rule of law and readiness to return to London if his own safety could be guaranteed.[95] These Declarations were printed and widely distributed by both sides, but in Russell's opinion they were effective neither as 'a form of public negotiation' nor as appeals for popular support; more concerned with recrimination than persuasion, they expressed 'the continuing amazement of both parties at the absence of any signficiant concession from the other'; and their ultimate effect was to reveal to the disputants 'the depth of their own disagreements' and to raise 'enough sense of their own righteousness to be able to fight'.[96]

Between Newmarket and Huntingdon, the Court had stopped at Cambridge on its way north and on 12 March the Prince of Wales had been treated to a play at Trinity College. Abraham Cowley had been called upon to supply a suitable text at short notice and he had laced his Jonsonian comedy of city life, *The Guardian*, with some timely if rather trite satire on Brownists and Puritans, who 'exclaim upon the sickness of drinking healths, and call the Players rogues, sing psalms, hear lectures', and set up as godly teachers without ever being 'defiled with the Cap and Surplice' of a university degree and priestly ordination.[97] In a

prologue addressed to the young Prince, the poet had mocked the
Roundheads of London for their antipathy to the stage, wondering if a
play, like a sermon, might be acceptable to them if '*made* ex tempore'.[98]

Another play by a writer better known as a poet than a dramatist
seems to be a more considered response to the worsening situation in
early 1642. Denham's *The Sophy*, a tragedy which may have been begun
in 1641, was certainly completed by August 1642 when it was entered in
the Stationers' Register.[99] The plot, derived from an account of intrigue
and murder at the court of the reigning Shah of Persia,[100] revolves
around the schemes of Haly, the King's Favourite, who fosters the
'fears' of the ageing ruler against his popular and virtuous son, Prince
Mirza. Egged on by the cynical politician Mirvan, Haly enlists the aid of
the grand Caliph, who 'will set a grave religious face / Upon the
business' (2. 274–5). Once 'fears' and 'jealousies' have been planted in
the King's mind, he is deaf to the wise voice of caution and takes panic
measures at the rumour that the Prince, who had withdrawn himself
from the 'short and empty pleasures' (2. 38) of the court, is 'posting
hither'. Amid much talk of plots and conspiracies, Prince Mirza is
'imprison'd, and depriv'd of sight' (4. 100) on the orders of his father and
Haly administers poison to him. The repentant King acknowledges his
folly to his dying son – 'he that now / Has poyson'd thee, first poyson'd
me, with jealousie' (5. 328–9) – and when he himself dies of grief, two
good counsellors, who had earlier fallen under suspicion of treason, use
the Prince's loyal army to ensure that the true heir, Mirza's 'most
hopeful Son' (5. 529), is proclaimed King and Haly executed for his
crimes.

O Hehir warns against the quest for any 'direct correspondence' with
the situation in England, but Wallace dates the play's composition to the
first half of 1642 because its plot emphasizes the danger of pursuing
policies based on 'fears and jealousies' and two of the errors openly
regretted by 'friends' of Charles I are reflected in the mistakes made by
Denham's 'arbitrary ruler' and 'good prince' – 'one by letting too much
power fall into the hands of evil counsellors, the other by absenting
himself from the capital at the crucial moment.'[101] Such criticism would
have been endorsed by Hyde and Falkland after the events of 4 and 10
January. There is also considerable urgency in a speech by a 'good
counsellor', which condemns those who conspire with 'popular rage' to
swell 'the torrent' of rebellion and – like the promoters of the Grand
Remonstrance – use the cloak of 'Religion' first to search 'with a saucy
eye' into 'the heart and soul of Majesty' and then to bring the 'actions,

errors, and the end of Kings' to 'a strict account, and censure' (4. 42–50).
Denham follows this with a remarkably perceptive analysis of the spiral
of aggression in which Pym and his allies were now trapped as a
consequence of their own temerity:

> And thus engag'd, nor safely can retire,
> Nor safely stand, but blindly bold aspire,
> Forcing their hopes, even through despair, to climb
> To new attempts; disdain the present time,
> Grow from disdain to threats, from threats to arms;
> While they (though sons of peace) still sound th'alarms.   (4. 55–60)

Elsewhere the text throws into sharp relief other critical moments in
the relentless march of events towards Civil War in England. Haly, for
example, plots to wrest control of the capital from his adversary in words
that must have recalled Lord Mayor Gurney's loss of authority after the
December elections to the Common Council: '*Abdal*, who commands /
The City, is the Prince's friend, and therefore / Must be displac'd' (3.
288–90). Later he uses Pym's tactic of declaring a public emergency in
order to justify a show of military force – 'Go muster all the City-Bands;
pretend it / To prevent sudden tumults' – and Mirvan reminds him that
first the crowds 'must be pray'd and preach'd into a tumult' (5. 441–8).
The King, fearing 'Designs upon my Life and Crown', reacts as Charles
had reacted at the beginning of January to the tumults in London and
the threat to his Queen: 'I must prevent my danger, / And make the first
attempt: there's no such way / To avoid a blow, as to strike first, and
sure' (3. 27–9). The same dislike of extremes – whether sought by 'Kings
or people' (4. 61) – informs both *Cooper's Hill* and *The Sophy*; but whereas
the poem was conceived as a reasoned argument, reading from the
landscapes and history of England salutary lessons about the need for
reconciliation, the tragedy depicts a world that offers a frightening
paradigm of a realm where mutual distrust has become so entrenched
that appeals to reason fall on deaf ears.

Some time during the first half of 1642, Denham put his literary
talents to a rather different use in a set of verses aimed at the leaders of
the parliamentary opposition. Parodying the form that has been described as 'the most potent weapon in the provincial armoury',[102] he
directed a 'humble petition' on behalf of the poets 'To the Five Members of the Honourable House of Commons'. The poem was eventually
printed in a collection entitled *Rump* (1662), but like Cleveland's satires it
enjoyed a considerable circulation in manuscript and marks Denham's
first frankly partisan contribution to the war of words.[103] In an opening

gambit, mockery of puritan resistance to the *Book of Common Prayer* is combined with a hint that the recent campaign of petitioning has been centrally orchestrated: 'Though set form of *Prayer* be an *Abomination*, / Set forms of *Petitions* find great Approbation'. Scorning Parliament's increasingly frequent complaints that its privileges have been violated, by men like Palmer and Dering who had been lodged in the Tower for their inconvenient opinions, Denham raises his voice on behalf of the poets' right to freedom of speech:

> But ours is a *Priviledge* Antient and Native,
> Hangs not on an *Ordinance*, or power *Legislative*.
> And first, 'tis to speak whatever we please
> Without fear of a *Prison*, or *Pursuivants* fees.

With his jaunty rhythms and feminine rhymes, Denham makes more concessions than Cleveland to a popular style and his central conceit is an elaboration of the simple charge that the Five Members have invaded 'our Property' of lying, enshrined in the ancient concept of '*Poetical license*', and made it 'a *Priviledge* of both Houses'. In his critical judgement, Parliament's attempt to usurp literary authority in the recent spate of Declarations – 'those pretty Knacks you compose' – has been a failure. While Pym's propagandists may have learnt to lie 'abundantly', their '*Poems* in prose' lack 'the rhime, the wit and the sense' that distinguish the art of the true poet. In a parting shot, he warns them not to provoke the 'Muse' of King Charles and reminds them that they have come off worse in the verbal contest so far, 'for all the world knows, / Already you have had too much of his *Prose*'.

CHAPTER 6

The beginning of hostilities: March 1642 – April 1643

Things went badly for Charles during his first weeks in York. A mere thirty-nine gentlemen and seventeen guards were in attendance at his court and the local population was lukewarm or hostile to his cause. When he summoned four of his household officers and three other peers to join him in his northern capital, they all refused and, in reprisal, on 23 March Essex and Holland were dismissed from their positions as Lord Chamberlain and Groom of the Stool.[1] The King's attempts to persuade Members of Parliament to adjourn the sitting at Westminster and convene in his presence elsewhere in the kingdom met with a negative response; the suggestion mooted in early April that he might lead the campaign against the Irish rebels in person was strongly resisted on all sides; and by the beginning of June, any hope of winning over the Scottish Council in Edinburgh had evaporated.[2]

Meanwhile, in Kent there were more encouraging signs that his English subjects in localities outside London might rally to his cause. Back in February, Sir Michael Livesey had presented a petition expressing the county's loyalty to Parliament, but this had followed a stereotyped format drawn up in London (the 'set form' denigrated by Denham) and reflected only minority puritan opinion. At the Assizes in Maidstone between 23 and 25 March, a new petition was prepared by a group of local gentry, under the chairmanship of Sir Edward Dering who was back home after his release from the Tower on 11 February. This second Kentish Petition was read out to a crowd of some two thousand which had gathered at the courthouse, and its promoters undertook to print it and collect signatures throughout west Kent before it was delivered to Westminster at the end of April.[3] Although Everitt describes it as 'temperate and conservative' and 'mildly royalist', with its support for 'the solemn Liturgy of the Church of *England*' and 'Episcopal Government' (Clauses 3 and 4) and its requests that 'speedy Consideration' be given to 'His Majesty's Gracious Message of the 20th of *January* last' and that 'a good Understanding' be 'speedily renewed between His Majesty and the Houses of Parliament' (Clauses 13 and 17), it quickly came to be seen as a manifesto of loyalty to the King.[4] Two clauses in particular raised serious constitutional issues and were interpreted at the time as a direct challenge to Parliament. Clause 12 asked that 'the precious Liberties of the Subject' be preserved and 'that no Order, in either or both Houses, not grounded on the Laws of the Land, may be enforced on the Subject, until it be fully enacted by Parliament'. This was clearly an attack on Parliament's assumption of arbitrary power in passing Ordinances that lacked the final sanction of royal assent. Clause 11 was even more provocative in its demand for 'an especial Law' to be framed 'for the regulating the Militia of this Kingdom, so that the Subjects may know how at once to obey both His Majesty and the Houses of Parliament'. In Russell's view, it was in its 'combination of devotion to a "traditional" church and to the rule of law' that the Kentish Petition distilled 'the essence of what was to become the Royalist cause'.[5]

When the proceedings at Maidstone were brought to the attention of Parliament on 28 March, Mr Justice Malet, the Assize Court judge who had presided over the Grand Jury in west Kent, was committed to the Tower, orders were given for the arrest of Dering and three of the other instigators and copies of the petition were burnt by the public hangman.[6] In spite of these measures, the process of subscription continued under the more extreme leadership of a group of younger Cavaliers, and a large crowd assembled at Blackheath on 29 April to choose delegates to carry the demands of the county up to Westminster. On the following day, at the head of 280 Kentish men, Richard Lovelace and William Boteler presented the petition. After being satisfied that this was the same document that had been burnt by order of both Houses, the angry Commons confined Lovelace in the Gatehouse and his companion in the Fleet Prison. The poet was not released on bail until 21 June.[7]

It was during this incarceration that Lovelace composed two of the poems for which he is best known. The contemporary popularity of 'To Althea, From Prison', with its famous fourth stanza – 'Stone Walls doe not a Prison make, / Nor I'ron bars a Cage' – is attested by the existence of twenty seventeenth-century manuscripts, which is unusual for a poet whose work did not circulate widely before it was printed in *Lucasta* in 1649.[8] The first three stanzas express the quintessential values of youthful and idealistic royalism in their celebration of 'the Cavalier trinity of love, wine, and loyalty'.[9] In singing the 'sweetnes, Mercy, Majesty, / And glories of my KING' in stanza 3, however, Lovelace allows ambiguity to complicate praise when he determines 'to voyce aloud, how Good / He is, how Great should be'. The word 'should' may be taken as a loyal lament for the denial of Charles's authority by a rebellious Parliament or as a criticism of Charles for weakly surrendering so many of his prerogatives. The latter reading has some force, since Lovelace's recent activities in Kent, and the drinking song in which he had toasted Goring rather than the King after the debacle of the First Bishops' War, suggest that he had more sympathy with Digby and the dead Suckling than with the moderate faction of Hyde and Falkland.

'To Lucasta. From Prison. An Epode' is also ascribed by modern scholars to the period of Lovelace's imprisonment in 1642.[10] Pursuing the conceit that release from the 'Shackels' of love which bind him to Lucasta will free him to 'fancy all the world beside', he embarks upon a quest for a new object of devotion. The situation beyond the prison walls makes him reject Peace, War and Religion in turn, and Parliament, which he 'would love', has forfeited its claims to his allegiance by its separation from the monarch who gave it constitutional validity: 'Who's he that would be wedded / To th' fairest body that's beheaded?' His Liberty and his 'Birth-right, *Property*' have lost their attractions, since bitter experience has shown that 'There's nothing you can call your owne'; a Reformation of the state machine might have its appeal, provided it were undertaken by the King himself – 'As for our griefes a *Sov'raigne* salve' – rather than an assembly that seems set on a course to 'ore'throw' rather than 'reforme'; and '*Publick Faith*' cannot be trusted because she is 'banke-rupt' and 'couzens all' – an allusion to Parliament's pledge of 'public faith' as security for a loan raised in the City on 10 June. As Margoliouth points out, many of these proposed replacements for Lucasta are dismissed on grounds that reflect clauses in the Kentish Petition.[11] At last, in stanza 11, the poet lights upon a fit object for his love: 'What then remaines, but th' only spring / Of all our loves and joyes? The KING.' The last three stanzas evoke a nation self-blinded by wilfully eclipsing the sun of monarchical 'right' and astray in 'an universall mist / Of Error', which is dangerously edged with 'fury'. Whether or not Hammond is right in detecting the beginnings of a drift towards disillusionment in the last stanza, he is persuasive in his comment that 'Strafford's example must have loomed large for any loyal prisoner':[12]

> Oh from thy glorious Starry Waine
>   Dispense on me one sacred Beame
> To light me where I soone may see
> How to serve you, and you trust me.

This ambivalent apostrophe calls for guidance either to the King by association with the northern constellation known as Charles's Wain or to the mistress addressed in the first stanza, whom he describes in another poem to Lucasta as 'that bright Northerne star'. Any political import in the last line turns on the matter of trust, which runs like a refrain through so many public statements and literary compositions in the first half of 1642, and raises the vexed question of how best to serve the interests of a King whose own trustworthiness was suspect. The root of Lovelace's dilemma, therefore, may not have been simply that he was cut off from active service by imprisonment, but that – in the light of Charles's apparent weakness and in the wake of Parliament's persecution of those involved in the Kentish Petition – he was prey to more fundamental doubts about the viability of the royal cause itself.

In the meantime, heartened, perhaps, by the Marquis of Hertford's decision to bring the little Duke of York to join his father, and alarmed by a parliamentary proposal to transfer the country's major stock of munitions from Hull to the Tower of London, Charles made what one historian regards as his 'first move in the war' and another has described as 'a propaganda exercise'.[13] On 22 April he despatched his second son, with the Elector Palatine and a train of attendants, on a courtesy visit to the governor of Hull. The next morning the King himself arrived outside the walls with a troop of horse, but Hotham closed the gates of the city against him, asserting the authority of Parliament for an act which Charles was quick to condemn as treason. Soon afterwards, the Elector Palatine left York, dissociated himself from the attempt to seize Hull, and made his way to Holland. Another round in the paper war ensued during May, with an exchange of Declarations on the militia and the events at Hull. Both sides were now intent on winning support throughout the country as preparations for armed hostilities began in earnest.[14] The Militia Ordinance was put into effect on 5 May and five days later the City regiments were reviewed by Skippon; on 14 May the King issued a warrant to the gentry of Yorkshire to attend him under arms and soon after created a Lifeguard of Horse to protect his royal person; towards the end of May, he called a halt to any further pretence at working through the two Houses of Parliament by summoning Hyde and loyal peers to York, and over the next few weeks there was a steady exodus of royalist supporters from Westminster, including Falkland, Culpepper, Bristol and even Lord Keeper Littleton, who brought with him the Great Seal with which proclamations were ratified as legal; and in mid-June, Charles countered the Militia Ordinance with the device of Commissions of Array, based on an ancient statute of Henry IV by which local gentry could be charged with the duty of raising troops.[15]

Reactions to the growing signs of mobilization varied, even among those who were already committed to the King. A Kentish call to arms in the aftermath of the famous petition, in which Loxley discerns 'a recuperation of the masculine and chivalric idiom' played down by the court culture of the 1630s, rejoices at the prospect of a military offensive against the King's enemies:[16]

> Give me the man that hangs upon his hilt
> A traitours bloud when his base blood is spilt,
> that dares assist his reason with his sword
> and speake bold Pym to Atomes in a word.

From his lodgings in London, Thomas Knyvett watched the approach of 'this thretning storme' with alarm, while one party grew 'as resolute as the other is obstinate'; and the predicament in which he found himself, communicated by letter to his wife in Norfolk on 18 May,[17] was one shared with 'a great many men of Quality':

Oh' sweete hart, I am nowe in a greate strayght what to doe. Waulk'ing this other mornning at Westminst^r, Sr John Potts, with commissary Muttford, saluted me with a commission from the Lo: of Warwicke, to take upon me (by vertue of an Ordinance of Parlam^t) my companye & command againe. I was surpris'd what to doe, whether to take or refuse. 'Twas no place to dispute, so I tooke it And desierd som'time to Advise upon it. I had not receiv'd this many howers, but I met with a declaration point Blanck' against it by the King.

It was precisely this kind of contradictory claim upon allegiance that Clause 11 of the Kentish Petition wanted a law to resolve, 'so that the Subjects may know how at once to obey both His Majesty and the Houses of Parliament'. For the time being, Knyvett had determined to 'staye out of the way of my newe masters till these first musterings be over'. But when choice became unavoidable, he had no doubts about which way his loyalty would lead him: 'What further commands we shall receive to put this ordinance in execution, if thay runn in a way that trenches upon my obedience against the Kinge, I shall doe According to my conscience, And this is the resolution of All honest men that I can speake with.'

In Cambridge, some time after Hotham's defiance of the King on 23

April, Abraham Cowley was putting the finishing touches to a poem
that may have originated at the time of his entertainment of the Prince
of Wales in March, since it develops in far more vigorous style the
anti-Puritan satire of his play and prologue. Called 'The Puritans
Lecture' in manuscript sources but printed under the title *A Satyre Against
Seperatists* in November 1642, the university panegyrist's first aggressive
expression of his political sympathies found a suitably academic model
in the Horatian epistolary satire as it had been naturalized by Donne in
the 1590s.[18] His target, set up in his opening address, is the institution of
the lectureship, which enabled puritan parishes to hire a preacher if the
orthodox incumbent did not meet their needs. Under Archbishop Laud
many lecturers had been refused licences by diocesan courts, but following the Commons Order of September 1641 they had been flocking to
London to take up preaching appointments:[19]

> I have beene (Sir) where so many *Puritans* dwell,
> That there are only more of them in Hell . . .
> Their blessed liberty they've found at last
> And talk'd for all those yeares of silence past.

The poet's attendance at a lecture provokes him into a comic assault on
the manner, matter and tedious length of a puritan sermon and the
extreme reactions of susceptible auditors: 'They sob aloud, and straite
aloud I snore / Till a kind Psalme telles me the dangers o're'. Escaping
to the hall, where he meets a crowd of 'the brethren', he listens to a
discourse on 'bloudy Popish plots against the State', criticism of the
King or those who lead him astray, tearful memories of 'the losse of the
three worthies Eares' (which he claims was for their own good, in order
to make them 'perfect Round-heads') and the raging of a 'Shee-zealot'
against those 'limbes of Antichrist', the bishops. The arrival of 'the
meate' interrupts this 'hidious storme' and provides the poet with an
opportunity to satirize the length of a puritan grace and the capacity of a
puritan appetite, before a bell rings and they all return to the church for
psalm-singing and an interminable *ex tempore* prayer, in the course of
which the lecturer 'sweats against the state, Church, learning, sence'. In
the sermon that follows, he rails against 'set Prayer', 'Church Government' and the 'malignant party', and finally defies the King. Having
completed his account of a day spent with the Separatists, Cowley
begins to castigate them directly for seeking a reformation 'o'th newest
fashion' from Ipswich or Amsterdam, for condemning 'the humble play
/ Of cat, or footeball on a holyday', for encouraging their women to
petition against 'schollership and learning' and for trying to suppress

burial rites, organs, anthems and the wearing of surplices. He brings his systematic rehearsal of the follies and dangers of rampant Puritanism to a close with an apostrophe to the present times – when the Church is scorned by 'ev'ry *Cade* / And ev'ry *Tyler*', when reason, learning and hospitality are despised and 'the many headed beast *Smectimnius*' is raised against 'learned Fathers', when England's reformed liturgy is 'left for nonsence'. The satire ends with a warning, similar to the one issued by Denham to the Five Members, to beware of the literary fire power that could be mustered by the King's party: cultivated poets like himself would be more than a match for Smectymnuus and the celebrated pamphleteer William Prynne, who had recently published a volume of verse meditations:

> *Oh Times, oh manners! But methinks I stay*
> *Too long with them; and so much for to day:*
> *Hereafter more, for since we now begin,*
> *You'le find wee've Muses too as well as Prinn.*

The exchange of propaganda statements between the two sides came to its climax at the end of May. In Declarations issued on 19 and 26 of that month, the two Houses justified their recent actions as a consequence of the King's refusal to take the advice or attend the meetings of the 'supream court and highest Councell' in the land; and Charles responded (in the last of the documents to be secretly drafted by Hyde, soon after his arrival in York) with 'a brutal exegesis of the parliamentary position', which reduced his opponents' case 'to its absolutist essence' and objected, above all, to the denial of his 'negative voice', so that 'We Our Self must be subject to their Commands'.[20] Parliament's next move was to offer terms to the King for the first time since his departure from London, although Fletcher regards it as 'an ultimatum' rather than 'a serious agenda for negotiation'.[21] The *Nineteen Propositions*, containing some familiar demands that went back to the proposals for settlement formulated by Pym the previous summer, were delivered to Charles on 2 June; and the *Answer to the xix Propositions*, prepared in York by Culpepper and Falkland, was published on 18 June. In what was practically a blueprint for bicameral sovereignty, the King was to be deprived of the rights to choose members of the Privy Council and great officers of state, to levy troops, even to make arrangements for the education and marriage of his children without the consent of Parliament, and was required to acquiesce in any measures the Houses decided upon for the reformation of the church. The result of agreement would have been, in his own words, 'in effect at one to depose both

our self and our posterity'.[22] In their *Answer*, Culpepper and Falkland
caused Hyde some concern by appearing to abandon the ancient estates
theory of the constitution, in which the monarch ruled through a
parliament made up of bishops, nobles and commoners, in favour of a
theory of mixed government by the One (the King), the Few (the Lords)
and the Many (the Commons), which reduced the monarch to being
merely one of three equal estates. In an effort to counter Pym's imposition of a bicameral polity which deprived the King of his veto and other
ancient rights, the two Privy Councillors had, perhaps inadvertently,
substituted a model of government which asserted the need for consent
by all three partners (King, Lords and Commons). They left the door
open, however, to the notion that certain prerogatives belonged uniquely – were 'proper' – to the King, in the reservation that the conveniences
of a mixed government would only obtain 'as long as the balance hangs
even between the three estates, and they run jointly on in their proper
channel'.[23] Whatever Hyde's misgivings, the *Answer* became 'a classic
text in the history of Constitutional Royalism' and stands as 'the official
expression of that commitment to the rule of law' which had motivated
him and his colleagues since November 1640 and which 'now caused
them to rally to the King as a lesser danger to legality than the Junto'.[24]

Other supporters of the royal cause were converging on York during
the summer months: by mid-June thirty-two peers had joined Charles,
including Lord Bristol, whose son had returned to England on a vessel
bringing a cargo of gunpowder purchased by Henrietta Maria in Holland; by the end of June, Lord Digby had been joined by Ashburnham
and Wilmot, fellow conspirators against Parliament who had fled into
exile and become part of the Queen's entourage at The Hague. A 'new
consistency' was now appearing in royal policy, as an alliance between
moderates and extremists was forged in the face of the *Nineteen Propositions* and Parliament's manifest preparations for war.[25] Both sides were
now busy raising troops and appointing officers. On 2 July Charles lost
control of the fleet to the Earl of Warwick; on 4 July a Committee of
Public Safety was set up at Westminster to oversee the defence of the
kingdom; on 9 July Parliament voted to raise a volunteer army; on 11
July Sir Richard Gurney, the Lord Mayor of London, was lodged in the
Tower for daring to proclaim the King's Commission of Array in the
City and a month later was deprived of his office; on 15 July the Earl of
Essex was given overall command of the parliamentary army; and on 26
July 10,000 volunteers paraded in Moorfields. Charles himself was
Captain-General of the Royalist forces; on 3 July he made the Earl of

Lindsey General of the Army, Sir Jacob Astley Major-General of the Foot and Prince Rupert General of the Horse; by August the remaining major posts had been filled by the appointment of the Earl of Newcastle, the Marquis of Hertford and Lord Strange (soon to become Earl of Derby) as commanders in the north-east, west and north-west.[26] Hutton notes that the returned ultra-royalists – Digby, Wilmot, Ashburnham and Percy – received commissions as field officers but were prominent in neither a political nor a military capacity; by choosing 'royalist magnates' with 'national and local prestige' for positions of high command, Charles was banking on them to attract followers through their regional influence.[27]

Hostilities were already breaking out in different parts of the country before war had been openly declared. In pursuit of a plan hatched between Digby and Hotham to surrender Hull to the King, Lindsey made a show of besieging the city, but the governor had second thoughts about betraying his masters at Westminster and on 30 July the royalist soldiers were driven from their positions by Sir John Meldrum, who had brought in reinforcements by sea. While the siege was still in place, the Earl of Holland brought a final request for the King to return to London and resume talks with Parliament, but when the condition that Hull be handed over to him was rejected, Charles declared, 'Let all the world now judge who began this war'. In the north-east, the royalist Earl of Newcastle held the important Tyneside port, while in the south-west, Portsmouth was besieged by a parliamentary force under Sir William Waller after Colonel George Goring had sided with the King in early August.[28] On 8 August, Charles proclaimed the Earl of Essex and all who served under him traitors and rebels and three days later announced the formal raising of the royal standard at Nottingham on 22 August.

Although, as Knyvett had confided to his wife, there were those on both sides who matched resolution with obstinacy in pursuing a course that could only end in open warfare between Charles and Pym's faction, there was a peace party at Westminster. Not only the few moderate royalists who remained in the House, like Edmund Waller, but also longstanding opponents of the King like Harbottle Grimston, Sir Simmonds D'Ewes and Sir Benjamin Rudyerd gave voice to a countrywide 'desire for accommodation', reflected in 'gentry correspondence between March and November 1642', that united 'men and women of widely different political views'.[29] From a position very similar to that of the troubled shepherds in Quarles's 'Eclogue XI', the anonymous

author of *The Round-Head Uncovered* (London, [27 July] 1642) offered on
his title-page a 'moderate triall' of the Roundhead 'spirit' and sought to
distinguish 'betwixt the Round-heads, and such as Papists call Puritans'.
His ideal is 'the reformed Church in generall' and especially the Church
of England, 'which hath so long flourished and shined in the worlds view
in an Orthodox and setled discipline' (p. 4); and he has nothing against
those within the national church who have commonly been 'distinguished from the colder, and more remisse sorte of Protestants, by the
name of Puritans' (p. 5). But he is deeply critical of the 'unconfined
liberty of expounding' the scriptures and 'unseasonable reasoning and
disputing' upon religious matters, from which 'there are now well-nigh
as many Sects and different opinions sprung as there be professors'
(p. 4). This 'crew of Hypocrites' are the true 'Round-heads', who with
their 'lowd whispers', 'libellous Pamphlets', and 'mutinous assemblies'
have 'sent his Highnesse a dangerous voyage into the North' and 'made
a wide overture amongst many of the illiterate People (of *London* especially) to let in Innovations, both of doctrine and discipline into our
Church' (pp. 4–5). Reminding his readers that the word 'roundhead'
had first been heard during the tumults at the end of 1641, he complains
that it has become a term of abuse hurled indiscriminately at 'all
Citizens and many other civill persons that wear no lockes' by the
'Cavaliers and Souldiers of this time' (p. 8). Trying to steer a course
through waters agitated by the language of extremism and confrontation, the author spoke for anti-Laudians who nevertheless accepted 'our
Book of Common Prayer' and prized 'our decent and our orderly
discipline in the House of God' (p. 7). Such men had little sympathy with
either the radical leadership in the Commons or the more flamboyant
supporters of the King, and the pamphlet ends significantly with an
appeal to Englishmen to avoid partisan hatreds.

On the next day, a pamphlet appeared which had a very different
admonishment for undecided readers. Peddling the traditional line that
a king is 'the Father of his Countrey' and 'Gods *Vice-gerent*' (p. 1),
Thomas Jordan[30] quoted the familiar text, 'Touch not mine Anointed'
and showed no respect for a '*John-Indifferent*', who 'dares not hazard his
life & fortunes' (p. 3) when the truth he professes is at stake:

Some still-standing Neuter will answer me very seemingly honest, He will obey
that Text; heaven defend that he should lift and [*sic*] hand against his Soveraigne. But let me justly informe him, He is as guilty in standing stil to see
another doe it. (p. 3)

But even though Jordan is clear about which cause has truth on its side,
he confesses himself 'a Lover of the Commonwealth' as well as 'the

Kings friend' on his title-page, and, in a concluding song, urges his countrymen to unite – presumably against the Irish rebels, whose reported atrocities were a sombre backdrop to the mobilization in England: 'Let's bend our weapons against those / Who are proclaim'd our Countries foes' (p. 6).

During July, Denham must have been making his final revisions to the text of *Cooper's Hill* before its first appearance in print. The bookseller, Thomas Walkeley, entered it in the Stationers' Register along with the same author's play, *The Sophy*, on 6 August; Thomason acquired his copy on the previous day. O Hehir finds no evidence that this third version of *Cooper's Hill* ever circulated in manuscript and concludes that Denham prepared Draft III with publication in mind.[31] Some of the changes to the text of Draft II are in the interests of style, producing a smoother and more elegantly phrased work of literature; but others reveal the poet's concern for the political impact of his poem in the new context of the summer of 1642. For example, the already expanded account of London as a place afflicted with the diseases of extremism, rumour and anarchy gets further elaboration:

> Some study plots, and some those plots t' undoe,
> Others to make 'em, and undoe 'em too,
> False to their hopes, affraid to be secure,
> Those mischiefes onely which they make, endure,
> Blinded with light, and sicke of being well,
> In tumults seeke their peace, their heaven in hell.

O Hehir relates these new lines to the investigations into Suckling's Army Plot in the summer of 1641, but in July 1642 the phrase 'affraid to be secure' would have been construed as an allusion to Pym's strategy of playing upon fears of a widespread Catholic plot in order to maintain a sense of national emergency.

The most significant revision is made to the narrative of the hunt, in which a simile of the cornered stag as a windbound ship sinking at last under a barrage from its pursuers is replaced by a simile which makes the identification of the episode with Strafford's trial more explicit than it was in either of the earlier drafts:

> As some brave *Hero*, whom his baser foes
> In troops surround, now these assaile, now those,
> Though prodigall of life, disdaines to die
> By vulgar hands, but if he can descry
> Some Nobler foe's approach, to him he cals
> And begs his fate, and then contented fals.

This simile not only elevates the status of the quarry from that of 'declining Statesman' (in lines 275–80) to that of 'brave *Hero*', but it also introduces for the first time into *Cooper's Hill* a clear reference to the letter in which Strafford had heroically begged 'his fate' by releasing Charles from his promise of protection. This added detail transforms the implications of the words 'glad and proud to dye / By such a wound', which survive in lines 298–9 from the two earlier drafts: no longer suggestive of 'somewhat hyperbolical pleasure and pride', they recognize the noble self-sacrifice of Charles's minister.[32] As Denham revised his poem for public dissemination, the memory of what could be construed as a damaging betrayal of trust by the monarch would have hampered any effectiveness it might hope to have in rallying support in the imminent war against Parliament. The part played by Charles in signing the fatal Act of Attainder could not be denied, but the moral connotations of the event could be changed by reminding potential readers that Strafford had chosen to die not as a victim at the 'vulgar hands' of the rebellious traitors in the House of Commons but as a dutiful and courageous servant of his King.

The shift in Denham's position, not only since he had written his lines on the trial of Strafford but since he had first conceived *Cooper's Hill* in September 1641, is revealed most clearly in some further additions towards the end of the printed text. A couplet inserted in the section on Magna Carta sums up the constitutional ideal that had informed the poem since its inception: 'Happy when both to the same Center move; / When Kings give liberty, and Subjects love'. But, as Denham goes on to remind his wider readership with a 'therefore' that is new to the text at this point, such a happy state is all too rare in the history of England, which has seen the Charter flouted many times by both kings and subjects. An expanded account of the process by which Charles has been humiliated to the point of armed retaliation prepares for the warning about the danger of flooding when the river of kingship is forced into a new or too narrow channel. In Drafts I and II, Denham had confined himself to a single couplet: 'And as by giving the kings power growes lesse, / Soe by receiving theyr demands increase.' In the six lines which replace this couplet, he spells out for his new readers the parliamentary excesses that have provoked Charles and brought the country to the brink of Civil War:

> Till Kings by giving, give themselves away,
> And even that power, that should deny, betray.
> "Who gives constrain'd, but his owne feare reviles,
> "Not thank't, but scorn'd, nor are they gifts, but spoyles,

And they, whom no denyall can withstand,
Seeme but to aske, while they indeed command.

O Hehir is correct in discerning here the sentiments 'of the Royalist ultras who began to gather around Charles in 1642 as the outbreak of war approached'.[33] They are sentiments with which Digby and Percy – and, indeed, Lovelace – would have agreed; but by August, they were shared by many moderate men whose political principles were embodied in the central philosophy of *Cooper's Hill* and who were now ready to back their King in armed resistance to a Parliament that had become in their eyes an instrument of rebellion against the ancient constitution of church and state.

While Denham was venturing into print on behalf of the royal cause and was about to take a more active role in its service as sheriff of Surrey and governor of Farnham Castle,[34] another royalist poet was more privately assessing the cultural consequences of the impending war and charting the decline into disorder of the pastoral realm that Pan's 'Steward' had 'preserved soe many yeare in Peace'. In the fourth of five eclogues collectively entitled *Polylogia*,[35] George Daniel, the retiring Beswick squire, meditates on the fate of poetry in a world where even 'humble verse / Now carries Danger, to still Jealous Ears'. In the first eclogue, which Daniel dated 1638 in his manuscript, the shepherds Strephon and Amintas had debated the comparative attractions of the country and the city under the guise of two mistresses, named Silvia and Urbana, and Amintas had abandoned Yorkshire for his 'loved London'. Now, denying Damon's request for an example of the art that once 'enricht' their northern air, the returned Amintas explains that his 'Pipe is broke' since Urbana was false to 'her first vowes' and prostituted herself to 'the Grand Paillard'. This allegorical rendering of the City's commitment to a Parliament controlled by Pym is a prologue to the 'Long and Sad' story that Amintas has to tell of the gradual ceding of royal prerogatives by 'our Great Shepherd' to 'Proud Zephirina' who, though 'unfitt / For Soveraigntie', was permitted to 'Sitt / Next to his Throne' and soon turned those 'giddie Heads, who still delight in Change'. While 'Papers' fly from 'everie corner of this Iland', helping to establish the 'yonge Majestie' of Parliament, the rightful sovereign is 'remisse' and hands over the 'Ivorie hooke, / Which even His Father and Himselfe had tooke / Of Pan, with Solemne vow.' On the assumption that 'Power, gives her Right' and emboldened by the defection of 'many Swains' to her party, Zephirina puts the axe 'Unto the Roote', causes the downfall of those who were 'in favour high / To the Great

Shepherd', beheads Philarchus (Strafford, the champion of order) and protects 'Penandro, now her Minion growne' (the Five Members), who must not 'be call'd in Question / For highest Crimes'. The upshot of Zephirina's rise to power is that the King is denounced as the 'worst of Men' and 'forc'd (Soe powerles left) / In this remoter Countrie, thus to shift'. But even here in the north, he is 'thinlie fenced, with Loyall Hearts'; his followers 'want Armes' to defend him against 'the strong Hand / Of Zephirina' and Matho (Hotham) 'stands possest / Of that strong Towne, which by a King once rear'd, / May be anothers Ruine.' Not only in Yorkshire but throughout the country, 'Wee All are Cowed, even Stupifyed with feare', while Zephirina sends 'her late imperious Summons' to 'our Maister' and assembles her 'Voluntarie Troopes' into a 'formidable Armie' to make an attempt on 'His Sacred Person'. Now, 'with the fewe / Willing to serve him', he is marching 'Westward', where he hopes to find 'many a friend'. For all his loyalty to the crown, Daniel cannot disguise the dread that his shepherds are supporting a lost cause, even as Charles bravely 'resolves at once to run / The hazard of his Life'. At the end of his tale, Amintas returns to the treachery of Urbana under Polymorphus (Sir Isaac Pennington, the puritan replacement for the ousted Lord Mayor), who gathers bands of 'Ruffians' from the streets 'to assist / The new-rais'd Tirranie'; and Damon is overcome by 'a darke Extasie'.

In their concluding exchanges, these two survivors from a lost golden age cast a melancholy eye on the options now open to them as poets: they can betray the Muses and 'Celebrate the Glories, of a late / Usurped Power'; or they can fall silent – 'For what is left, to Sing? our Glorie's gon, / Our Loves are Lost, or not worth thinking on'. With a despair deeper than the disillusionment that had begun to afflict the imprisoned Lovelace when he contemplated the condition of Charles and his kingdom, Daniel's shepherds lay aside 'a worne and wearied Quill' and retreat 'homeward'. The 'longer Shadowes' that traditionally brought a pastoral dialogue to a close seem to herald the end of pastoral itself as a viable mode of writing in a dark and dangerous world where kings are 'remisse' and 'Treasons' thrive.

Daniel, a young man in his mid-twenties when the King raised his standard, did not express his family's loyalty actively like his younger brother, Thomas, who became a cornet in the royal army.[36] Nor was the body of narrative and contemplative poetry, which he worked on throughout the 1640s and carefully transcribed into his manuscript book, designed for consumption beyond his family circle. For the rigours of a more active literary service, Charles's supporters among the poets needed the 'sharp lancing quill' that John Taylor boasted could 'make incision, and with art and skill / Search deep for dead flesh and corroded cores'.[37] At about the time that Daniel's shepherds were forsaking their pastoral art in despair, the sixty-four-year-old waterman was holding a mirror up to the topsy-turvy world in which 'Church and State, are by the rabble rout / Abus'd' (p. 4), 'mad Sects' were reviling the 'Protestant Religion' (p. 5) and – as the emblem of Fortune's wheel on his title-page graphically shows – 'Malice, Disloyalty, War and Sects' were in the ascendancy, while 'Religion, Peace, Obedience' were 'ith mire'. Asserting the once commonly acknowledged truths that the King is 'the Lords anointed' and 'God's chiefe vicegerent in his soveraignty', Taylor adjures his rebellious countrymen to 'render *Caesar* what is *Caesars* due' (p. 4) and voices an urgent desire that the proper order of things will soon be restored in London: 'For which I'le hope the Wheele wil turn aboute'.[38]

Thomas Jordan, who had castigated 'neuters' and 'John-indifferents' effectively in prose, also enlisted the muse of satirical verse for one of the mock petitions that were beginning to proliferate.[39] 'The Players Petition to the Long Parliament'[40] scatters its shot widely in the first four lines to strike at the nine or ten 'Heroick Sirs' in the Commons who seek to bend not only the political and cultural life of the country but the language itself to their will by disposing of 'the King or the Kings men' and claiming, with their 'sublimer Rhetorick', that 'Prisons are the Subjects Liberty'. Jordan's actors promise not to jeer at the 'strange Votes' of their antagonists or to 'personate King *Pym*' if the theatres (closed by parliamentary decree in September) are opened again; and they look forward to the stage direction that will terminate the play that is currently absorbing the national audience: '*Enter the King, Exit the Parliament*'. The versatile Jordan could also turn his hand to verse parody. In 'The Resolution', events like Strafford's death and the persecution of the Kentish petitioners are felt not only as political crimes but as a violation of an entire culture when they are recounted in the form of one of Thomas Carew's most popular lyrics:

> Ask me no more, why there appears
> Dayly such troopes of Dragooners? . . .
> Ask me no more (for I grow dull)
> Why *Hotham* keeps the Town of *Hull*,
> I'le answer ye one word for all,
> All things are thus when Kings do fall.[41]

The same stretch of history figures in 'The Humble Petition of the House of Commons', dated 5 October by Thomason but presumably circulated earlier in manuscript like many of these poems.[42] Combining the genre of the mock petition – this one presented to Charles I – with the form of a Cavalier song, it includes ridicule of the 'new new way' of ordering the militia and ends by exposing the sham of the offer of talks brought by the Earl of Holland in August:

> Now, if that you'll make *Hull* your own,
> There's one Thing more we must set down,
>   Forgot before;
> Sir *John* shall then give up the Town,
> If you will but resign your Crown,
>   Wee'll ask no more.

Taylor's vision of a world turned upside down informs the more ballad-like song, 'A Mad World My Masters', which culminates in an aggressive call to arms as the only remedy:

> Arise therefore brave *British* men,
>   Fight for your King and State,
> Against those Trayterous men that strive
>   This realm to Ruinate.[43]

In this literary campaign waged in a variety of genres and with varying degrees of sophistication, specific attacks on Pym, Hotham and others were supplemented by a more general denigration of the enemy as a type, like the prose 'character' of a Puritan which appeared on 12 August, accompanied by 'The Round-Heads Character' and 'The Holy Sisters Character' in satirical couplets.[44] The hacks on the other side counter-attacked with such lurid reports of atrocities as *Nocturnall Occurences Or, Deeds of Darknesse: Committed By the Cavaleers in their Rendezvous* (16 September) and *An exact and true Relation of A most cruell and horrid Murther committed by one of the CAVALIERS on a Woman in Leicester, Billetted in her House* (17 September). In a chapter on the more popular forms of propaganda produced during the first year of fighting, Joyce Malcolm argues that these 'party caricatures', which 'embodied in a stark, emotional manner the goals and fears of party members', worked 'in a self-fulfilling manner driving people to the side to which they seemed to belong' and eventually 'created landmarks of such divergence that two parties speaking the same language came to appear poles apart'.[45]

The two sides, meanwhile, were slowly accumulating enough men under arms for what was expected to be a decisive engagement. After this, either Charles I would re-enter his capital in triumph, punish the rebel faction in the two Houses and re-establish the rule of King in Parliament with a newly elected body of MPs, or a victorious parliamentary army would rescue the King from his evil counsellors and bring him back to Westminster to do the bidding of the present Parliament. For those already committed to the King, the immediate response to the raising of the standard at Nottingham was disappointing, as Clarendon vividly recalled: 'There appeared no conflux of men in obedience to the proclamation; the arms and ammunition were not yet come from York, and a general sadness covered the whole town, and the king himself appeared more melancholic than he used to be.'[46] Nevertheless, while a parliamentary force of 20,000 men was being assembled at Northampton where the Earl of Essex took up his command on 10 September, recruiting to the royal army went forward steadily in Yorkshire, Lincolnshire and the midlands, so that by the time the King left Nottingham for Shrewsbury on 13 September it numbered at least 4,000 men. In an address to his troops at Wellington, which was widely disseminated by royalist clergy and did much to rally further support to his cause, Charles promised 'to maintain the just privileges and freedom of Parliament, and to govern by the known laws of the land, particularly to observe inviolably the laws consented to by me in this Parliament'.[47] During the three weeks that the King had his headquarters in Shrewsbury, regiments raised in North Wales and Cheshire came in and the professional expertise of the army staff was raised by the arrival of Scottish officers, including a respected veteran of the religious wars in Europe, Patrick Ruthven, now the Earl of Forth. When the march towards London began on 12 October, Charles was at the head of thirteen regiments of infantry, ten of horse and three of dragoons, with twenty guns in his Artillery Train.[48]

As the King had drawn towards the Welsh marches to consolidate his strength, Essex had been slowly advancing westward. The first important encounter between the two forces occurred on 23 September, when Prince Rupert, who had sailed from Holland in August and taken command of the cavalry at Nottingham, routed a detachment of parliamentary horse at Powicke Bridge, just south of Worcester. Although this was only a skirmish, and Worcester itself was abandoned to the superior numbers of Essex, it established Rupert's reputation as a vigorous and daring soldier. Both a disciplinarian and an innovative cavalry commander, whose tactics were developed from those of Gustavus

Adolphus, the Prince set about turning the motley collection of cavaliers assembled at Shrewsbury into an efficient fighting force and 'his dynamic activity galvanized the royal cause into new life and raised the morale of the army'.[49]

The cavalry, led by Rupert himself on the right wing and Wilmot on the left, played a conspicuous part in the first major battle of the Civil War at Edgehill on 23 October. Essex had left Worcester on 19 October and caught up with Charles's army half-way between Banbury and Warwick. As night fell, after hours of fierce fighting, it was unclear which side had the advantage. Next morning, however, Essex pulled his forces back towards Warwick, leaving behind some of his artillery. Although, in Peter Young's view, the Earl had thus 'conceded a tactical and moral victory to his enemies', the King's failure to seize 'the best opportunity he was ever to have of retaking his capital' ensured that by mid-November Essex 'had won the campaign'.[50] Instead of heeding the advice of Rupert and Forth and letting the cavalry make a lightning strike on Westminster while the way to London was clear, Charles contented himself with taking the surrender of Banbury, where the Earl of Northampton was installed as governor, and then made his way slowly towards London via Oxford and Reading. This gave Essex time to reach the city before him and on 11 November, reinforced by Philip Skippon's Trained Bands, he moved out to meet the royalist army which was encamped near Brentford. The next day, Rupert stormed the town, allowing his troops to loot and burn, but the King's primary objective was no longer attainable. Faced by vastly superior numbers drawn up on Turnham Green, he withdrew to Reading and, rejecting Parliament's terms for peace, made his way back to Oxford, which was to be his capital for the next four years.

The King now found himself committed to a long war. In addition to the financial burden that this imposed, his strategy would have to take more account of the situation in his other kingdoms. In October 1642, Irish and Old English Roman Catholics had come together in the Confederation of Kilkenny, demanding freedom to practise their religion and claiming that their revolt was against the Parliament in London not against the King. In her letters from Holland, Henrietta Maria urged her husband to accede to their requests in exchange for military assistance against his rebellious subjects in England and Charles made secret approaches to them through the Marquis of Ormond, who commanded the forces of the government in Dublin but maintained a steadfast loyalty to the crown.[51] The Marquis of Argyll, the most powerful member of the Council in Edinburgh, was sympathetic to the English Parliament, but for the time being was in favour of a peaceful settlement of its differences with the King. Charles accepted all too readily the reassurances of Hamilton, his chief adviser on Scottish affairs, that any intervention by the Covenanters could be headed off by taking 'a moderate line with the Scots on domestic policy'.[52]

During December, while the King settled into his new court in Christ Church College, the fighting spread to other parts of England. In Surrey, Denham surrendered Farnham Castle to Sir William Waller, who went on to take Winchester and Chichester. The captured poet was sent to London, but must have been released before April 1643, when he was in Oxford overseeing another edition of *Cooper's Hill*.[53] The royalists fared better in the south-west, where Sir Ralph Hopton, with the help of Sir Bevil Grenville and other influential Cornish gentry, raised a volunteer force that would serve the King's cause beyond the boundaries of Cornwall. In Yorkshire, things were going well for the Earl of Newcastle. Marching south from the Tyne to relieve York, he defeated the younger Hotham on the way and on 6 December drove Sir Thomas Fairfax out of Tadcaster. Towards the end of the month, whilst Charles was keeping Christmas 'with ceremony and splendour',[54] the peace party at Westminster won the approval of the Commons for another attempt to open negotiations. The peace terms finally agreed by both Houses were presented to him at the beginning of February by the Earl of Northumberland. There followed a lengthy period of wrangling over the King's request for a cessation of hostilities rather than disbandment of the armies while talks were in progress, and it was 28 February before new proposals were ready to send to Oxford.[55]

With the peace party in London and the moderates at court engaged in efforts to bring the fighting to an end, the fortunes of war were fluctuating across the country. In the struggle for control of the lucrative wool trade of the West Riding, Bradford, Leeds and Wakefield were taken for Parliament by Lord Fairfax and his son Sir Thomas Fairfax, and the Earl of Newcastle retired to York. On the other side of the Pennines, where Lord Derby's brutality had alienated the local population, Lancaster Castle and Preston fell into the hands of the strong puritan faction in Lancashire; and although Chester was held for the King by Orlando Bridgman, Sir William Brereton dislodged the royalists from Nantwich. Better news was reaching Oxford from the south-west, where Hopton and his 1,500 Cornish volunteers won the first of a series of victories at Braddock Down on 19 January; and on 2 February

Prince Rupert captured Cirencester, a town important for control of the Cotswolds and for communication between Hopton's army and the royalist headquarters. Other gains were made in the midland counties during February, and Parliament received a severe blow on 2 March when one of its more energetic local commanders, Lord Brooke of Warwick Castle, was killed in an assault on Lichfield Cathedral. A similar misfortune was to befall the King's side later in March, when the Earl of Northampton died at the Battle of Hopton Heath in which the Staffordshire royalists repulsed Brereton and captured most of his artillery.[56]

The military contest, which quickly generated the coarse propaganda of the ballad-makers, satirists, and atrocity-mongers, also gave rise to more considered and scholarly attempts to justify the recourse to arms by one side or the other with arguments and precedents derived from human or divine law. Some from the royalist perspective, like *A Vindication of the King* (London, [17 September] 1642), which was advertized on the title-page as being by 'a True Son of the Church of England, and a Lover of his Countries Liberty', continued the line that had been developed by Hyde and his colleagues in the official replies to Parliament's declarations and remonstrances earlier in the year. The writer presents himself as one of those who had looked to 'that Soveraign medicine of a fading State, a Parliament' for a solution to the 'discontents' bred by 'illegal Monopolies' and the ambition of 'ill affected agents' (p. 1). But the King's establishment of 'our Rights and Properties' by the concessions he has already made and his eagerness for 'the setling of Religion in his purity' ought to be 'sufficient ground to desolve our Jealousies if ever we meant to be satisfied' (p. 2). The threat to 'the Rights of Parliament' and 'the fundamentall Lawes of the Kingdom (wherein our Liberty consist)' now comes from those at Westminster who have 'already assumed into their own hands a formall Ordinance countermanding, suspending, nay, creating Acts of Parliament' and in so doing have 'Invested themselves of a power more Arbitrary, then the Monarchicall Government could pretend to' (pp. 3–4). Calling upon the constitutional model promulgated in the *Answer to the xix Propositions*, the anonymous author condemns 'these pretended reformers of the Commonwealth' for undermining 'the health of our State', which 'is admirably ballanced if that have but his due proportion; The Parliament consisting of three bodies, the King, the Lords, and Commons . . . but if either of the two can passe at their pleasure what they will, the third must then of necessitie stand for a Cypher' (pp. 6–7).

Other royalist supporters, like David Owen in *A Persuasion to Loyalty, Or the Subjects Dutie* (London, 1642), merely reiterated the central tenets of their faith – that kings have their authority from God and are not punishable by man – and were content to ground them in proof texts from the Bible, the Fathers and the Protestant reformers rather than develop a theoretical defence of their position. In a preliminary address '*To the dutifull Subject*', Owen offers his systematic marshalling of authorities as an antidote to the wrenching of scripture, which 'the brethren of the enraged opposite faction do indifferently quote, and seditiously apply' (sig. A2ᵛ). In a similar vein, the anonymous author of *The Soveraignty of Kings* (London, [21 November] 1642) brings biblical and classical authorities to bear against the 'ignorant and mechanick Divines', who have stirred up 'faction and dissention in this distracted State' by 'perverting the Scriptures to the confusion of the true Protestant Religion' (sig. A1ᵛ).

It was in response to the challenge thrown down by 'the most notorious pamphlet of the day',[57] however, that a body of theoretical writing in support of constitutional royalism was produced during the first phase of the Civil War. Henry Parker's *Observations upon Some of His Majesties Late Answers and Expresses*, published without his name at the beginning of July 1642, was intended primarily as a reply to both Hyde's analysis of the absolutist tendencies of the parliamentary remonstrance of 26 May and the *Answer to the xix Propositions* by Falkand and Culpepper. But in its 'drift from known law and constitution into equity, popular sovereignty, and the law of nature', it took the debate beyond the statement of entrenched commonplaces, releasing 'what had been the constitutional stream of the official war of words into broader political, religious and (in several senses) moral waters'.[58] A nephew of Viscount Saye and Sele, Parker had emerged as a vigorous opponent of Charles's personal rule and the Laudian clergy in a series of pamphlets printed in the early 1640s.[59] In his famous *Observations*, he begins by locating the origin of power 'in the people' and argues that the authority of an individual ruler does not derive directly from God but from 'a Law of common consent and agreement' (p. 1), by which the limits of his prerogative are determined. Furthermore, the 'Paramount Law' underpinning 'all humane Lawes whatsoever' is '*Salus Populi*' (p. 3); and this 'Charter of nature', which 'intitles all Subjects of all Countries whatsoever to safetie' (p. 4), justifies the resumption of power by a threatened community, for 'if the King will not joyn with the people' in the 'preventing of publike mischiefes', then 'the people may without disloyalty save themselves' (p. 16). Parker proceeds to apply these universal principles to the current crisis in England: 'See if wee are not left as a prey to the same bloudy hands as have done such diabolicall exployts in *Ireland*, or to any others which can perswade the King that the Parliament is not well affected to him, if we may not take up armes for our owne safety, or if it be possible for us to take up armes, without some Votes or ordinances to regulate the *Militia*' (p. 17). This theory of *popular* sovereignty is developed into a theory of *parliamentary* sovereignty in Parker's exposition of the constitutional roles of the three estates identified by Culpepper and Falkland. Arguing that both monarch and aristocracy are subordinate to Parliament (and, more especially, the House of Commons which is the embodiment of the people), Parker asserts the right of this representative body to use its power independently of the other two estates to ensure the security of those it represents.

A debate that extended well into 1643 and continued to reverberate throughout the decade was opened on 9 July by *Animadversions Upon Those Notes Which The Late Observator hath published*. This first assault on Parker's contract theory of monarchy, which had justified resistance to a king who failed in his obligations to the people from whom he derived his authority, scored a direct hit by suggesting that the same principle could be applied to the sovereignty of a representative assembly: 'Well, But good Sir, may not the people withdraw the power of representation, which they granted to the Parliament; was their grant so absolute, and so irrevocable, that they dispossest themselves wholly of taking or exercising that power, their owne proper persons?' (p. 12). Both this argument and the spectre of mob-rule implicit in it provided ammunition for many of Parker's royalist opponents.

One or two other pamphlets took issue with 'the Observator' during August and September, but the first major engagements with the constitutional questions he had raised came towards the end of the year in Henry Ferne's *The Resolving of Conscience* and in *An Answer to a Printed Book*, which has been attributed to Dudley Digges, son of one of the Caroline judges and a member of Falkland's circle at Great Tew in the 1630s. Ferne, a former Fellow of Trinity College, Cambridge, had come to the King's notice when he preached before him at Leicester and had joined the royalist army as a chaplain at Nottingham. As the title of his work indicates, he was chiefly concerned with two aspects of the *moral* dilemma posed by Parliament's challenge to the authority of Charles I, which were set out on his title-page: 'Whether upon such a Supposition or Case, as is now usually made (The King will not discharge his trust but is bent or seduced to subvert Religion, Laws, and Liberties) Subjects may take Arms and resist? and whether that case be now?' Although he rejects Parker's premise that power derives from the people – 'the power it self is of God originally and chiefly, which we prove by Scripture and Reason' (p. 13) – he concedes the subject's right of disobedience in certain circumstances and denies the 'false imputation' that 'all those that appear for the King in this cause' are endeavouring 'to defend an absolute power in him, and to raise him to an Arbitrary way of government; This we are as much against on his part, as against Resistance on the subject's part' (p. 6). Indeed, he is anxious to dissociate himself and likeminded clergy from the further 'imputation' of crying up monarchy as the 'only government to be *jure divino*', although he does find a particular 'excellency' in it as 'the Government God set up over his people in the person of Moses, the Judges and the Kings' (p. 14). The English monarchy, as it has evolved since Saxon and Norman times, has been limited by 'Lawes' and 'Priviledges' granted to the subject people, but this is no basis for arguing, as Parker does, that they have the right to deprive a king of his sovereignty: 'Unto all those [laws] the King is bound. But yet not bound under forfeiture of his power to the people' (p. 15). Under a tyrant who abuses the Ordinance of God from which he derives his power, the Christian conscience might allow a people to protest with 'cryes and prayers to God, petitions to the Prince, denials of obedience to his unjust commands, deniallhs of Subsidies, ayds, and all fair means that are fit for Subjects to use', but in no circumstances should they use 'Arms to resist the Ordinance under pretence of resisting the abuse' (p. 19). Such an extreme situation does not exist in England, however, where King Charles has 'fortified' religion and liberties 'so with many Acts of Grace passed this Parliament, that they cannot be in that danger which is pretended for the raising of this Warre' (p. 22). Therefore, no conscience that listens to the dictates of human or divine law 'can bear a part in this resistance' (p. 26). The threat discerned by the author of *Animadversions* that 'the multitude by this rule and principle now taught them take the Power to themselves' opens up the prospect that a new Cade and Tyler will 'boast themselves Reformers of the Commonwealth, overthrow King and Parliament, fill all with rapine and confusion, draw all to a Folkmoot and make every Shire a severall Government' (p. 18). The best way to prevent the state from falling into such anarchy is to restore 'that excellent temper of the three Estates in Parliament, there being a power of denying in each of them, and no power of enacting in one or two of them without the third' (p. 16).

An Answer to a Printed Book (dated 20 November 1642 by Thomason and ascribed by him to Falkland, Chillingworth, Digges '& ye rest of ye University') shares some ideas with Thomas Hobbes's *De Cive*, which had been published in Paris early in 1642. It accepts Parker's argument that the people were the original source of sovereignty but denies that they might 'upon whatever pretence soever, without manifest breach of divine ordinance, and violation of publique faith, resume that authority, which they have placed in another' (p. 2). Unlike Hobbes, however, Digges and his collaborators defended the mixed constitution, in which the King was bound 'to maintain whatever rights the law doth give us' (p. 12). They also, like Ferne and the anonymous author of *A Vindication of the King*, reassured their readers that whatever 'grievances' they may have 'groaned under' in the past, the 'goodnesse of his Majestie' in accepting reforms meant that there was no 'feare of them for the future' (p. 14).

Many of the same arguments were marshalled, with differing degrees of emphasis, in other royalist contributions to the debate during 1643. Late in January, for example, *A View of a Printed Book Intituled Observations upon His Majesties Late Answers and Expresses* supported the theory of mixed government and warned that Parker's 'doctrine' would 'destroy not only Monarchy, but all Government whatsoever', since the people may 'conclude themselves to be above the Parliament, and at pleasure revoke and controll their power' (p. 14).[60] In February, the anonymous author of *Certain Materiall Considerations* admitted that the two Houses might act alone in an emergency to safeguard the state, but denied that the decision to wrest control of the militia from Charles had been justified by the circumstances prevailing at the time; and in April, Sir John Spelman's *A Review of the Observations* had defended 'our Lawes and auncient setled frame of Government' (p. 8) against Parker's attempt to question the King's constitutional role 'as supream Governour, and first of the three States of Parliament' (p. 24).[61] Ferne had returned to the fray in 1643 with *Conscience Satisfied, that there is no warrant for the armes now taken up by Subjects*, in order to consider the theory that the three estates were 'co-ordinate', which had been promulgated by Charles Herle, a Presbyterian divine, in *A Fuller Answer to a Treatise written by Doctor Ferne* (London, [10 January] 1643). He was prepared to acknowledge an element of co-ordinate power in the mixed constitution, insofar as the consent of King, Lords and Commons was 'necessarily required in the making and declaring Law', but insisted that sovereignty resided in the person and office of the King who, 'notwithstanding such their co-ordination and consent', remained 'the Supreme Head of the Body, Ecclesiastical and Civil, also the only Supreme Governor' (p. 20).

The theory of co-ordinate sovereignty was more energetically refuted by John Bramhall, who has been credited with providing 'a more complete statement of the royalist position than any other man of his day'.[62] A former chaplain to Wentworth in Ireland, he was made Bishop of Derry in 1634, fled to England when the rebellion broke out in 1641, and became a chaplain to Newcastle's northern troops at the start of the Civil War. In *The Serpent-Salve, or, A Remedie for the Biting of an Aspe* (1643), he had mocked the idea of 'two Supreams without subordination one to another' as 'an *Amphisbena*, a Serpent with two heads' (sig. A2^v), and expressed his conception of mixed government in another graphic image: 'The King, like *Solomons* true Mother challengeth the whole Child, not a divisible share, but the very Life of the Legislative Power: The Commons present and pray, The Lords advise and consent, The King enacts' (p. 64). History has taught him that 'to limit a Prince too far is often the cause of much mischief to a State' (p. 148), and that there is danger in upsetting the balance of a constitution which 'is so sweetly tempered and composed of all estates' (p. 136). Reformers should be aware of the consequences of their demands: 'He that shall quite take His Majestyes negative voice away secures us from Tyranny, but leaves us open and starke naked to all those popular evils or Epidemicall diseases which flow from *Ochlocracy*; as Tumults, Seditions, Civill Warres' (p. 136).

In a survey of royalist writing on the nature of the English constitution during the early part of the Civil War, J. W. Allen found few signs – outside the unpublished work of Sir Robert Filmer – that anyone in 1643 'regarded the King as an absolute monarch able to make law as he pleased'; and J. W. Daly goes further, prefacing his study of Bramhall with the remark that 'the most important characteristic of seventeenth-century English royalism was not its defense of the king, but its defense of political moderation and limited government'.[63] In this, the 'talented royalist writers who challenged the Observator'[64] were in a direct line of descent from the poet of *Cooper's Hill* and the moderate parliamentarians who had been drawn into the King's service during the second half of 1641 and drafted his official declarations in the months preceding the Civil War.

While issues of constitutional theory were being debated in terms of scriptural authority, natural law and historical custom, people at all levels of society were faced with the practical problem of choosing sides. On the day after Charles raised his standard at Nottingham, Lord Wharton, who had been levying troops on behalf of Parliament, confessed himself perplexed by the 'riddle' posed when 'those about the king, and those in the Parliament' claimed to be ready to fight for the same things – 'for religion, the king, the law, liberty, and priviledge of Parliament'. He added that 'one of the two must be in the right', and justified his own decision to throw in his lot with the parliamentarians on the grounds that they had 'beene most carefull' of these stated principles 'in theyre constant course of their lives.'[65] The author of a dialogue between 'Cautious a Country-man' and 'Wishwell a Citizen' gave a comic version of the dilemma as it appeared to less exalted members of the commonwealth.[66] In a 'wishing contest', the citizen wishes he were in Turkey, 'Because they say it is a custome there for the people to obey their King' (p. 3) and the countryman admits that he does not want to be a soldier because 'I shall nere be capable to understand what I must fight for' (p. 4). Philip Hunton, a supporter of Parliament who was troubled by the extremist drift of Parker's arguments, could see no constitutional way of resolving the problem of which estate should be deemed sovereign when the system of consensus broke down, since there was 'no legal constituted judge in a mixed government'. Posing the question of 'how this case can be decided', Hunton concludes that if 'non-decision' is intolerable, then 'every person must aid that part which, in his best reason and judgement, stands for public good against the destructive'.[67] Such an appeal to individual choice is implicit in the titles of Ferne's two replies to Parker – *The Resolving of Conscience* and *Conscience Satisfied* – and is made explicitly on the title-page of an anonymous pamphlet which offers to tackle 'some Doubts and Scruples of tender Consciences concerning these times of distraction'.[68]

It was perhaps because the division of allegiances in a Civil War depended for many on individual choice rather than the accident of nationality or class that so much of the polemical material issued during the first year or so of open warfare was presented in the form of a dialogue or a familiar letter. Propagandists in both camps seem to have realized that it might be more effective to enact the process of persuasion in the text than to aim their arguments directly at the reader. In *A Letter sent from a Private Gentleman to a Friend in London* (London, [28 November] 1642), the writer is resentful of the 'chiding invectives' in his correspondent's last letter, and challenges him to take a critical look at his own behaviour: 'I wish you to examine your selfe how farre the profession of so much faith (as those of your opinion are full of) can stand with so little charity, as their censoriousnesse of others expresse' (p. 2). Having established the personal basis of the exchange of letters, the writer rehearses the familiar royalist arguments about the roles of King and Parliament in the constitution and concludes predictably that both law and conscience exempt him from either serving a body that has betrayed the trust of the people or obeying ordinances that lack the assent of the crown. He also makes the standard acknowledgement of 'the past unhappy accidents' of the Caroline regime, for which 'his Majesty hath given abundant satisfaction', and reminds his friend that Charles has 'solemnly protested for the future to be guided by the knowne Lawes of the Land' (p. 7). Signing himself '*Your loving Friend* F', the author prays that they may agree in seeking 'peace' and avoiding the 'obstinacie' and 'sinne' of the parliamentary warmongers (p. 8).

Fiction is a more overt part of the polemical purpose in dialogues like *A New (and too true) Description of England* (London, [15 February] 1643), in which Chrystopher the Cavalier enables Barnaby the Caviller to see through the 'fogg of Ignorance and stupidity' that has blinded him to the truth about 'those mutinous and contumelious outrages, which have driven the King from his Parliament' (n.p.). A more subtle attempt is made to spike the enemy's propaganda guns when a 'Scholler of Oxford' sets out to convince 'a Citizen of London' that it is not the so-called 'malignant party' of 'Cavaliers, and evill Counsellors' but the 'factious meetings and illegall tumults' of 'a rable of Brownists and Anabaptists' that are responsible for the King's withdrawal from 'his great and best Counsell' at Westminster.[69] The two speakers share a desire that the 'throne may be established in righteousnesse' and compare their different political perspectives in a civilized and temperate manner. By the end, neither has abandoned his primary loyalty, but various slanders of the parliamentary press – against Cavaliers and Prince Rupert in particular – have been scotched by the 'Gentleman from Oxford' and the dialogue form itself effectively asserts the need for both sides to be granted full recognition in any peace settlement.

The genre of the familiar letter, like the dialogue, was susceptible to crude or sophisticated use in royalist propaganda. The author of *A Letter written Out of the Country to Mr John Pym Esquire, one of the Worthy Members of the House of Commons, February 1* uses the form to condemn the 'absolute ruine' to which the country has been reduced by those 'who pretended to protect us against all Arbitrary power' (sig. A2^v) and to defend the 'unparallell'd virtues' of a monarch who has 'trebly satisfied' those with genuine grievances (sig. A2ᵛ). A spice of irony is added in the correspondent's initial show of concern that the 'rash Judgments' of Malignants cannot be restrained (sig. A2ʳ) and in the solemn parody of epistolary courtesies at the end:

These things (lest your danger and prevention should have met together) I thought good to acquaint you with, not doubting but your grave wisedome, as it will endeavour the warding of those blowes are aymed at you, so it will take in good part the faithfull advice of *Your most affectonate friend, and humble servant* R. E. (sig. A3ᵛ)

The full weight of academic wit and virtuosity is brought to bear on the task of propaganda when an Oxford scholar writes to his former teacher in the early months of 1643. The language of the schoolroom is gleefully mocked in the opening address to an elderly instructor who must be taught the error of his ways by a former pupil:

Sir, You will esteeme it a *soloecisme* in your *Quondam* schollar, that he should thinke it no false *Syntaxe* to *Catechize* his Master, and may wonder that twenty yeares doe not blush to instruct three-score; but by way of relation to your *many* Lectures, you must pardon my gratitude if I read you *one*; for since the *Act* doth alwayes carry proportion with the *object*, I am sooner to discard my *reverence* to a *Teacher*, then my *Loyalty* to a *Prince*. For whom as I must spend every drop of blood to fight his cause, soe I will shed every drop of inke to assert it.[70]

The 'Scholler' proceeds to flaunt his academic prowess by larding his account of the '*Tragedy*' that has befallen the people of England with classical allusions and quotations and by defending the proposition that 'the King is an absolute Monarch, and by much superiour to both Houses' (p. 7) with a self-conscious display of logical discourse in numbered sequences of 'objections' and 'answers' and 'reasons' and 'corollaries'. Appended to the letter is 'The Schoolemaster's Answer', in which he declares that he is so influenced by 'the *pathos* of your stile ... [and] ... the savage performance of those Rebels ... that I confesse my selfe overcome, and must *Herbam porrigere*' (p. 10). Not content with expressing smug satisfaction that 'I had the *honour* and the *happinesse* to convert you' in a 'Gratulatory Reply to that Answer' (p. 11), the 'Scholler' completes the pamphlet with two more demonstrations of his literary skill and ironic wit in a Latin love elegy from one of the Five Members to his paramour and the lady's repulse of these advances in an English poem which begins, 'What, Latin Sir?' (p. 17).

An example which aims at greater authenticity is *A Coppy of a Letter Writ from Serjeant Major Kirle, to a friend in Windsor* (6 March 1643). Its opening is managed with a fine sense of the dramatic, as the renegade officer sets the scene for his confession to an erstwhile patron in a world where rumours are rife and official information often suspect:

Sir, You were pleased to command a constant account of me, as the onely requitall you would receive for admitting me an Officer in the Parliament Army; and though divers things have come from us, which have been either doubted or contradicted, and seeme to have no other credit then the close Committee; yet what I am now about to tell you, shall run none of those dangers.

He then drops his bombshell and, with a keen sense of the impact it will have, whets his correspondent's appetite for the details of his change of allegiance:

with a great deale of confidence you may report, both in publique to the House, and in private to my friends, that I am now at *Oxford*; nor shall your wonder last long, for by the time I have declared upon what grounds at first I undertooke that service, and upon what reasons I have since deserted it, I shall without doubt (where there is charity or reason) free my selfe from the imputation of dishonour, and undeceive others that are as I was, seduced. (p. 1)

What follows is the story of a young soldier who left his homeland to serve in the Protestant armies in Europe at a time when there were justified 'grievances' against the personal government of Charles I. He had returned during the present 'distempers', ignorant of 'the condition of the Kingdome', to hear the same 'complaints' still being voiced. Not knowing 'that the causes were taken away' by the King's concessions, he had been 'inclinable to receive an imployment from the Parliament' and had risen steadily to the rank of Serjeant Major (p. 1). A strong sense of dramatic control informs the account of his conversion to the royalist cause – or as he puts it, 'a perfect discovery of those false lights, that have hitherto misled me' (p. 2). It was not necessity that drove him into the King's camp, nor ambition, nor malice. It was through the preaching of William Sedgwicke, the radical chaplain of his regiment, that his eyes were opened, 'not by his perswasions or conversion, (for I can assure you, you may still confide in him) but by the spirit (not that pretended to of meeknesse and peace but) of fury and madnesse'. The 'inspired rage' of this fanatical puritan had revealed to him 'the misery of this warre' and 'brake the shell (Religion, safety of the King, Liberty and Propriety) and shewed us the kernell (Atheisme, Anarchy, arbytrary government and confusion)' (p. 2).

After this well-sustained narrative introduction, Kirle goes on to indict the parliamentary side for branding as 'Malignants' anyone who voted against them in the House, for misreporting military defeats as victories, for casting innocent people into prison on the mere word of an informer, and for the transparent deception of 'that strange mistery, that fighting for the safety of the King, was shooting at him, as at *Edgehill* and else where' (pp. 3–4). He has gone into these 'many particulars' of his life, because he wishes to justify himself 'to all the world' (p. 5); and also, as he makes clear in his final paragraph, to convert his correspondent and others by his example:

Sir, I have freely told you my sense, if it have any proportion to yours, and so incline you to that effect it hath wrought in me, I shall take it (next to the condition I am in) as the greatest happinesse, and if I be so fortunate, since in these dangerous times you cannot safely convey it by letters, let me know it by publishing this, whereby also you may happily benefit others; and certainly oblige *Your humble servant*, R. K. (p. 7)

By a witty exploitation of the very nature of the genre – a familiar letter made public in the medium of print – Kirle has the efficacy of this narrative of his own Pauline conversion confirmed. The very fact that it is in print in the hands of the reader is to be interpreted as a profession of royalist commitment by the friend in Windsor.

While the constitutional and moral case against the rebels was being elaborated in prose, the 'muses' mustered under the royal standard were making good Cowley's boast at the end of *A Satyre against Seperatists* in a variety of poetic styles and genres. In October, an anonymous prose satirist had conducted his readers round the empty apartments at Whitehall – 'A Pallace without a Presence!' – and recalled, with mock regret, the days when 'Majesty had wont to sit inthron'd within those glorious Walls, darting their splendour with more awfull brightnesse then the great Luminaries in the Firmament'.[71] This gloating meditation probably provoked the verse lament from the pen of Henry Glapthorne, in which the palace reviews its days of glory as the 'constant Residence o' th' King and Queene' (p. 240).[72] The 'pure Constellations' of success-ive generations of British royalty had made it 'seeme a firmament / Of moving starres' (p. 240), until 'Mischief came thundering from the North' (p. 248) and 'an ere-lasting night' closed in with the departure of the reigning monarch, 'who now in arms, / Exposd is to the dangerous alarms / Of a rude civill-warre.' (p. 249)

Even John Taylor was in a doleful mood in November, when he exhorted King and Parliament in impassioned prose to find some way out of a conflict that was turning the 'fertile fields and pastures' of the 'Paradice of the world' into 'the horrid shapes of so many *Golgotha's*'.[73] His usually resilient muse had been confined to elucidating a woodcut of an amphisboena on the title-page – the same metaphor for these unnatural times that was to serve Bramhall a few months later:

> This double-headed SERPENT is a Wonder,
> It drawes two wayes, and teares the womb in sunder:
> The woful EMBLEM of a troubled STATE,
> Where civill WARRES doe threat to ruinate.

Taylor was not to be kept down, however, and in the new year made his way to Oxford, where he stayed for the rest of the war and 'devoted his energies to the cause of victory, not accommodation'.[74]

Some time over the first winter of the war, a more intellectual muse was deriving creative energy from the problem of writing panegyric in a world which had no use for the traditional values and methods of poetry. In the opening couplets of 'To Prince Rupert' (known in some versions as 'Rupertismus'),[75] Cleveland glances first at a Parliament that has assumed the right to make its own laws – 'O that I could but vote my selfe a Poet! / Or had the Legislative knacke to do it!' – and then at the recruitment of poets from the universities not only as soldiers but also as propagandists, who might be honoured by the King for valiant deeds with the quill as well as the sword. He proceeds to play variations on the conceit that normal meanings and linguistic conventions have been turned upside-down or back-to-front by parliamentary rhetoric: '*Faces about*, saies the *Remonstrant* Spirit; / Allegeance is Malignant, Treason Merit'. His answer to this destabilizing of the medium of communication, in which 'Humble Service' is proffered in public declarations of resistance to sovereign authority, is to 'write a-squint' himself, so he advises Prince Rupert to read him 'but with Hebrew Spectacles': 'Interpret Counter, what is Crosse rehears'd: / Libells are commendations, when revers'd'. Rupert himself, who had remained unscathed in battle, is also proof against 'squibbing Poetrie' and 'th' Artillerie of Verses'; and even his dog, 'that four-legg'd *Cavalier*', is so feared as 'a Devill' – the Prince's familiar spirit – that entire pamphlets have been written against him. In a move typical of this unorthodox panegyric, the remarkable 'Boy' – who 'holds up his Malignant leg at *Pym*' and 'barks against the sense o' the House' – is impeached by the Commons. At the climax of a passage of virtuoso comic fantasy, the delinquent hound is surrounded by his 'Accusers' – 'There *Jowler*, there! ah *Jowler*!' – and the reader is jolted back to the stark realities of power by the memory of another occasion and another poem, 'when the glorious *Strafford* stood at Bay'. Even when Cleveland attempts direct praise of Rupert the warrior in his closing lines, the reductive idiom of satire proves more serviceable than

the outmoded hyperboles of court panegyric: 'Go on brave Prince . . .
Scatter th' accumulative King; untruss / That five-fold fiend, the States
SMECTYMNUUS'. This 'grimly exuberant reconfiguration of royalist
epideictic'[76] cannot sustain the Olympian symbolism of its penultimate
line and permits the poem to fade away to a less exalted sound: 'In fine,
the name of *Rupert* thunders so, / *Kimbolton's* but a rumbling Wheel-
barrow'.

Early in 1643, the less exalted muse of Alexander Brome responded as
cleverly as Cleveland's more academic wit to the topsy-turvy world of
Civil War in making a popular verse form work against its own speaker:

> Fight on, brave soldiers, for the cause,
>   Fear not the cavaliers;
> Their threatnings are as senseless as
>   Our jealousies and fears.
> 'Tis you must perfect this great work,
>   And all malignants slay,
> You must bring back the king again
>   The clean contrary way.[77]

The device of ventriloquism, found in a number of Cavalier poems,[78]
exposes the contradictions and deceptions of parliamentary propaganda
and allows the enemy to damn himself out of his own mouth: ''Tis to
preserve his majesty, / That we against him fight'; 'How often we prince
Robert kill'd, / And bravely won the day'; 'We subjects' liberties
preserve, / By prisonment and plunder'. And at the end of the poem,
the refrain is turned gleefully against those who will receive an appropriate reward for their inverted values:

> But when our faith and works fall down,
>   And all our hopes decay,
> Our acts will bear us up to Heaven,
>   The clean contrary way.

Another popular verse form was adopted by Denham for 'A Speech
Against *Peace* at the Close Committee',[79] in which John Hampden is
made to reveal himself as the instigator, along with Lord Saye and Sele,
of the Scottish invasion of August 1640 and as the chief architect of 'the
whole Design' against the King's authority, with its appeal to 'Necessity', its clever use of petitions and parliamentary committees, and its
orchestration of preaching by 'Zealous Ignorants' to 'stroke the Peoples
ears' and 'raise the price of Fears'. Written in the early months of 1643,[80]
the mock speech identifies Hampden as a leading opponent of peace at
Westminster, where the quest for a settlement threatened 'the main

design' of his faction – 'the ruine of the Church' by the abolition of episcopacy – in pursuit of which he is prepared to destroy the monarchy as well.

Cowley himself participated in this phase of the poets' war with a long formal satire, regarded by his modern editors as 'something of a master-piece' in comparision with the verse squibs of his contemporaries.[81] Completed between 7 December 1642 and 2 March 1643, before Cow-ley left Cambridge, *The Puritan and the Papist* survives in ten seventeenth-century manuscripts and was in print not long after his arrival in Oxford at the end of March.[82] Lacking the narrative dynamic of *A Satyre against Seperatists*, Cowley's second essay in satire devotes two-thirds of its considerable length to the ramifications of the Cleveland-like conceit stated in its opening lines – that the fierce antagonism between the religious extremes of Puritanism and Roman Catholicism conceals an essential kinship, which it will be the task of the poet to uncover:

> So two rude *waves*, by stormes together throwne,
> Roare at each other, fight, and then grow *one*. ...
> Now in a *Circle* who goe contrary,
> Must at the last *meet* of necessity.

Rome permits a '*Pia Fraus*' (a pious lie) if it will 'advance the *Catholicke cause*'; the Puritan 'approves and does the same', but is squeamish about 'the *Latin name*'. This first point of similarity prompts a disquisition on the use of lying to sustain the puritan cause in 'the *Presse*', in 'th' *Pulpit*', and in 'what your small *Poets* have said, or writ'. Whereas the Papist merely claims the 'Power of dispensing *Oaths*', the Puritan's hatred of swearing is such 'that when / You have sworne an *Oath*, ye *breake it* streight agen'. For all his supposed antipathy to the Roman doctrine of justification by good works, the Puritan embraces his own perverted version of it: 'You thinke by *workes* too *justified* to be, / And those *ill workes, Lies, Treason, Perjurie*'; and while the Papist clings to his anti-predestinarian dogma that '*free-will*' is 'the great *Priviledge* of all *mankind*', the Puritan, mindful of his Calvinist inheritance, is 'more *moderate*' in his 'intent, / To make't a *Priv'ledge* but of *Parliament*'. Cowley proceeds in this vein for another 120 lines, revealing the lust for power that binds together the extreme wings of contemporary religious belief and polity in deception and hypocrisy. Subtle links are discovered in their treat-ment of the scriptures and the people ('They *blind obedience* and *blind duty* teach; / You *blind Rebellion* and *blind faction* preach'; in their attitudes towards fasting, holy relics, miracles, transubstantiation, so that it is no contradiction 'if we say, / You goe to *Rome* the *quite Contrary way*'; and above all in their elevation of a single authoritative leader – 'They make the *Pope* their *Head*, you' exalt for him / *Primate* and *Metropolitane*, Master *Pym*'.

Throughout this first phase of the poem, the success of Cowley's satire depends 'largely upon the dexterity with which the couplets turn Puritans into Catholics'.[83] At line 207, this method of using the fear of one religious extreme to expose the extremism of the real enemy is abandoned in favour of a more direct assault on the various kinds of outrage committed by the rebels against the constitution of the English church and state. This shift of gear is, perhaps, an acknowledgement by the humanist poet that the savagery of Civil War demands something more direct and brutal of its men of letters than the careful negotiation of a middle way where wit and irony can flourish. In a final crescendo of partisanship, the subtlety of the learned poet gives way to the sarcasm of the propagandist in a litany of thanks to the puritans for bestowing upon a grateful nation all the evils of Civil War.

The kind of misinformation derided by Cleveland and Brome was disseminated largely by the London newsbooks that had begun to proliferate again during the summer of 1642 after being suppressed by parliamentary order on 28 March. By the end of October, sixteen different diurnals had made an appearance.[84] Charles I was well aware of the power of the printed word and had taken presses with him to York and Shrewsbury.[85] Once he had established a permanent base in Oxford, it was not long before his printer began to issue newsbooks. *The Oxford Diurnal* and *Mercurius Aulicus* were both on sale early in January 1643. The latter, partly financed by the Crown, was not 'a printer's private enterprise' like the London diurnals, and has a significant place in the history of journalism as 'England's first official newsbook'.[86] Peter Heylyn was its original editor, but John Berkenhead, who had worked for Archbishop Laud during the 1630s, was recruited to assist him before the end of January. By September, Berkenhead was in sole charge and quickly acquired a reputation as the 'leading publicist for the Crown', although Heylyn continued to produce odd numbers and Lord Digby also took a hand from time to time.[87] For some months, *Mercurius Aulicus* worked to the agenda set in the first issue: that it would 'proceed with all truth and candor' in the tasks of combating the lies of the 'weekly cheat put out to nourish the abuse amongst the people' and letting the world see 'that the Court is neither so barren of intelligence, as it is conceived; nor the affaires thereof in so unprosperous a condition, as these Pamphlets make them'.[88] Berkenhead's biographer considers that the royalist diurnal was exceptionally 'authoritative and thorough' and that its 'accuracy was at its zenith in 1643, when its punctilious method of citing sources, giving dates and statistics and its full descriptions of important events at once and deservedly established it as England's premier newsbook'.[89]

One of the earliest events to be relayed to the public through the pages of *Mercurius Aulicus* was the safe landing of the King's wife at Bridlington Bay on 22 February (reported under the date on which the news reached Oxford, 27 February). A fuller account was quickly made available by the royal presses at York and Oxford in *A True Relation of the Queen's Majesties Return out of Holland*. Henrietta Maria brought with her the money raised on the crown jewels, several shiploads of arms, and some additions to the company of officers in the northern army, including James King, a veteran of the Swedish armies who quickly became indispensable to Newcastle, and George Goring who had helped with the purchase of munitions and was soon to prove his worth as a soldier by defeating Fairfax at Seacroft Moor. The diurnal made much of the welcome supplies of powder, shot and other kinds of ammunition that the Queen had sent on ahead of her to York. By the time this news reached Oxford on 10 March, she had already settled in the city, where Newcastle maintained an elegant court and she was visited by the Marquis of Montrose and other Scottish royalists eager to enlist her support for a rising against the unpopular regime of Argyll, the King's long-time opponent who was widely suspected of collusion with the English Parliament. In spite of his wife's enthusiasm for such positive action against the rebel government in Scotland, Charles insisted that Montrose be discouraged in the light of assurances from Hamilton, newly arrived in York with a report on the political situation in Edinburgh, that the Covenanters had no plans to intervene in the Civil War in England.[90] Henrietta Maria may have failed to influence the King's policy towards the Scots, but from her base in York she was instrumental in persuading Sir Hugh Cholmley to hand over the castle and port of Scarborough which he had been holding for Parliament. The decision of this country gentleman to change sides has been attributed not only to the Queen's persuasive powers but also to his disappointment at the fading prospects of a 'constitutional compromise' in the long-drawn-out negotiations at Oxford.[91] Henrietta Maria herself, in the very letter which contained the news of Cholmley's defection on 25 March, expressed her determination to return to France if Charles reached any agreement with 'this perpetual Parliament', being unwilling 'to fall again into the hands of those people'.[92] She need not have worried. On 4 April, Secretary Nicholas confided in a letter to Rupert that 'it is most apparent that those at London have no real intentions or inclination to peace . . . their leading (or rather misleading) ministers preaching against it in their pulpits'.[93] The King communicated his final terms to Westminster a week later, and their scornful rejection brought negotiations to an end. The commissioners were recalled from Oxford on 14 April; and on the following day Rupert made an assault on Lichfield, while Essex laid siege to Reading. Soon after the failure of the Treaty of Oxford, Dudley Digges put the finishing touches to his most comprehensive (and most Hobbesian) defence of the King's inviolable sovereignty. Towards the end of *The Unlawfulnesse of a Subjects Taking up Armes*, published posthumously in 1644, he placed the blame for 'our present sufferings and the expectation of growing mischiefs' squarely on the shoulders of those who had embraced Parker's principle of resistance:

Populi salus suprema lex is the engine by which the upper rooms are torn from the foundation and seated upon fancy only, like castles in the air. For the safety of the people is really built upon government; and, this destroyed, the other . . . will soon be swallowed up in the common confusion.[94]

CHAPTER 7

Learning to write the war: April – September 1643

With peace negotiations at an end, the writers of the newsbooks engaged in an ever more vigorous struggle to control public perception of the combatants on both sides and the results of their encounters across the country. In Oxford, the efforts of *Mercurius Aulicus* were reinforced by *Mercurius Rusticus*, launched by Bruno Ryves in May 1643; and among the longer-running titles which first appeared over the next few months in support of the parliamentarian cause were *Mercurius Civicus* (first issued in May), *The Parliament Scout* (26 June), *The Kingdom's Weekly Intelligencer* (3 July), and *Mercurius Britanicus* (5 September). Inevitably, as Joad Raymond points out, all these partisan publications were in the business of 'constructing the world around them, not only by means of polemical invention and political propaganda, but by arranging recent, unrecorded events in a narrative'.[1] At least during their first year in Oxford, those responsible for *Mercurius Aulicus* took pride in giving all the 'particulars' of troop movements and military engagements, including accurate dates and precise casualty figures, 'the better to prevent those mis-reports, which they who use to looke upon the petit losses of His Majestie thorow *Multiplying-glasses*, may chance to make of it' (Week 13, 28 March, p. 158); and Berkenhead in particular 'was trying genuinely to establish a viable technique of war-reporting'.[2] Some entries seem specifically designed to foster a reputation for reliability in the coverage of the war: for example, readers were informed that 'whereas . . . in the last weeke of this *Mercurius* it was related that Sergeant Major Mole with 80 horse was come into *Banbury* (from *Northampton*) to serve his Majesty; on further search into the businesse it proved nothing so' (Week 14, 8 April, p. 180); and news of the loss of Wakefield was held over till 'next weeke' in the interests of accuracy, since there was as yet only 'a rumor' of 'some great blow that had beene given to His Majesty in the Northern parts: but the certainty and particulars not yet fully knowne' (Week 21, 27 May, p. 281). It was duly reported in the next issue as 'the greatest

The Writing of Royalism

losse that hath befallen His Majestie in the *North*, during the course of all this Warre' (Week 22, 28 May, p. 284). This is not to say that *Mercurius Aulicus*, even in 1643, never exaggerated a military success or minimized a reverse. Its writers were quite prepared to increase the propaganda value of Newcastle's victory over the Fairfaxes at Adwalton Moor by adjusting the numbers of those killed and captured, and they paid scant attention to Parliament's achievements in Cheshire and the north midlands during the autumn.[3]

Newsbooks on both sides, of course, accused each other of misreporting and fabrication. In its fourteenth week, *Mercurius Aulicus* could not contain its outrage at the flagrant misinformation emanating from the capital:

In the *London* Diurnall for the last week, ending on Munday *April* 3. it is given out, that in the Earle of *Northampton's* pockets were found three *Crucifixes*, one *Agnus Dei*, and a protection from the *Pope*: a very fine impudent slander, and of no more truth then that Sir *Will. Waller* hath taken *Cyrencester*, which is reported confidently in one of their *Newes-bookes*, and that the Earle of *Essex* came on Sunday seavennight with all his forces unto the very walls of *Oxford*, and stroke up an *Alarme* in our very eares, and that no body durst come out, or shew themselves before his Excellencie: all which are as true as that Prince *Rupert* was buried at *Oxford*: or that Sir *Thomas Lunsford* feedeth upon children. (Week 14, 8 April, p. 180)

Indeed, in the very next issue, the Oxford editors made a point of exposing the 'petit falshoods' that 'most impudently are affirmed for undoubted truths in *London* newes-bookes, which came out this weeke' (Week 15, 15 April, p. 191), and from May onwards this running commentary on the content of rival productions became a regular feature.[4]

Typical of the growing importance of the printing presses in mediating news of the war was the spate of journalistic activity generated by Prince Rupert's storming of Birmingham, which *Mercurius Aulicus* condemned as 'a pestilent and seditious Towne' (Week 14, 5 April, p. 17) because it had made swords and other weapons exclusively for Essex's army. Many of the buildings were set on fire after Rupert's departure – 'contrary to his Pleasure', insisted the royalist newsbook – but the London diurnals seized upon the occasion to lay one more atrocity at his door and the dispute over his personal responsibility was not confined to the weekly publications. Two pamphlets sponsored by Parliament – *A True Relation of Prince Ruperts Barbarous Cruelty against the Towne of Brumingham* and *Prince Ruperts Burning love to England, Discovered in Birminghams Flames* – made political capital out of the event, the latter describing acts of violence committed against civilians and the subsequent night-long revelry of the soldiers, who tyrannized 'over the poore affrighted Women and Prisoners' and 'upon their knees' drank 'Healths to Prince *Ruperts* Dog' (p. 6). A royalist attempt to limit the damage was made in *A Letter Written from Walshall, By a Worthy Gentleman to his Friend in Oxford, concerning BURMINGHAM* ([14 April] 1643), which assured its readers that, before he left, Rupert had given 'expresse Command that no souldier should attempt to fire the Towne' and as soon as he heard what was happening had sent orders for the flames to be quenched (p. 4).

An interesting sidelight on the reporting of the war is provided by the Norfolk JP, Sir Thomas Knyvett, who was among those rounded up at the end of March as part of a conspiracy to seize the port of Lowestoft for the King. He and his fellow-prisoners claimed under questioning that they were merely waiting to take ship to Holland, where other royalist gentry had already sought refuge from persecution.[5] In letters to his wife on 23 and 24 March, sent from the Rose Tavern in Cambridge where the captured 'conspirators' were being held, Knyvett expresses both amusement and anger at the way the 'famous Adventure at Laisstolf' was 'most gloriously set forth in a diurnall':

We are nowe in the midst of the schoole of mars, nothing but drums & Trumpets all the day long. We read our Laistoffe busines in the diurnall with much Joye, because all faulse concerning dangerous plotts for any thing I ever was Acquainted with. God of heaven forgive the devisses of these horrible Lyes to wrong Innocent men.[6]

After taking Lichfield on 21 April, Prince Rupert was diverted from his purpose of clearing a way through the north midlands for Henrietta Maria by the threat to Reading, which commanded the strategically important main road between Oxford and London. By the time the Prince joined his uncle there on 24 April, the town was already on the point of surrendering and when a royalist sally to gain control of Caversham Bridge was repulsed, Charles accepted the terms of capitulation agreed with Essex.

In the latter part of April, the King suffered other setbacks in the south-west, where Sir William Waller marched unopposed into Hereford and Hopton's Cornish army was forced to retire in disorder from an encounter with James Chudleigh on Sourton Down above Okehampton. Parliament was quick to exploit the propaganda value of these events: one London newsbook reported that 'an extraordinary storme of Lightning and Thunder' fell upon Hopton's men, singeing the hair on their heads and firing the powder in their musket pans;[7] and a pamphlet appeared on 29 April with an extravagantly triumphant title,

A Most Miraculous and Happy Victory obtained by James Chudleigh Sergeant Major Generall of the forces under the E. of Stamford, against Sir Ralph Hopton and his Forces. Who with 108 Horse did rout and put to flight 5000 Foot and 500 horse... At the Battle of Stratton on 16 May, however, Hopton won a comprehensive victory over the superior numbers of the Earl of Stamford, Parliament's supreme commander in the west.[8] The literary as well as the military tables were turned and Sir John Denham used his new-found facility with popular verse-forms to mock the terms in which the parliamentary scribblers had rejoiced over Hopton's earlier defeat:

> Do you not know, not a fortnight ago,
>> How they brag'd of a Western wonder?
> When a hundred and ten, slew five thousand men,
>> With the help of Lightning and Thunder....
> There *Hopton* was slain, again and again,
>> Or else my Author did lye...
> But now on which side was this Miracle try'd,
>> I hope we at last are even;
> For Sir *Ralph* and his Knaves, are risen from their Graves,
>> To Cudgel the Clowns of *Devon*.[9]

At about the same time, an anonymous pamphleteer in Oxford was aiming at more than accurate reportage, when he offered the public a 'true and particular Relation of the great defeat given to the Rebels' in *The Roundheads Remembrancer* (Oxford, [June] 1643). His detailed account of the exploits of Hopton and Sir Bevill Grenvile is prefaced by a scornful analysis of the propaganda methods favoured by the puritan rebels, who always contrive to 'fasten their Treasons on *God* and *Religion*': plundered goods are 'the *gifts of God*'; a military defeat is the cue either to '*give thanks for a victory*' or to claim that such small losses are sent by '*speciall Providence to draw the Cavaleirs into further destruction*'; and if they do 'prosper and prevaile over the Kings forces' then 'each thread and particle of their successe is the *Wonderfull worke of God*' (p. 1). It is not, after all, so 'strange' that those who have 'that desperate impudence to shoot at the King, and say it is to save his life' should commit the blasphemy of likening their own puny achievements to the wonders that God wrought for his people in the Old Testament: 'Thus *Wallers* entring *Hereford* is stil'd *as great a Deliverance as the Israelites passage through the Red Sea*; and his *Excellencies* gaining *Reading* they call *no lesse a miracle then the razing downe the walls of Jericho with pitchers and Rams horns*' (p. 1).

Further north, the military picture was less encouraging for the King during May. Cromwell's cavalry had got the better of a superior royalist force under General Charles Cavendish in a skirmish near Grantham, and before the month was out the bad news of Fairfax's surprise attack on Wakefield, in which Goring was taken prisoner, had been compounded by the surrender of Warrington to Sir William Brereton. There were also adverse developments on the political front. During a debate on the contribution of papists to the royal cause on 23 May, the Commons voted to impeach the Queen for High Treason; and a week later, the Committee of Safety uncovered a conspiracy to deliver London to a royalist force. This was said to have been master-minded by Edmund Waller, who was still attending the Commons. Waller and his brother-in-law, Nathaniel Tompkins, were arrested on 31 May, and under interrogation the poet denounced Viscount Conway and the Earl of Portland for their part in a plan to seize Lord Mayor Pennington and the parliamentary leaders and gain control of the capital for the King.[10] Modern historians believe that 'Waller's Plot' was, in fact, 'no plot at all, but the deliberate conflation by Pym of what were almost certainly two entirely separate and disastrously contradictory strands of royal policy'.[11] Waller had been in secret communication with Falkland in an attempt to co-ordinate the efforts of the moderates at Oxford and the peace party at Westminster; but, unknown to his ministers, the King was supporting a plan by Sir Nicholas Crispe 'to execute a royal Commission of Array and provoke an armed rising in London'.[12] Although the Oxford propagandists tried to make light of 'a horrible Treason then discovered against the City and the worthy Members' (*Mercurius Aulicus*, Week 22, 3 June, p. 292), Pym's version of Waller's Plot strengthened the resolve of those in both camps who were determined to continue the war.[13] Waller himself was expelled from the House and kept in custody for many months without trial. He was probably saved from court martial and the fate of Tompkins and another conspirator, who were executed on 5 July, by the speech he delivered at the bar of the House, in which he offered an abject apology and claimed that he had been moved 'to entertaine discourse of this businesse' only by 'impatience of the inconveniences of the present Warre'.[14]

Even more damaging to the King's long-term prospects was the revelation of a wild scheme by the Earl of Antrim, who had been implicated in the rebellion of 1641, to bring together the Irish and Highland branches of the MacDonald clan and the Confederation of Kilkenny in order to defeat the Covenanters in Scotland and the puritans in England. Papers found in his possession when he was captured in County Down in May 1643 connected him with the Scottish royalists who had visited the Queen in York, and the fear of a rising in

Scotland resulted in proposals from the assembly in Edinburgh for a military alliance with the English Parliament.[15] Two immediate consequences of the disclosure of Waller's Plot prepared the way for closer co-operation between Pym and Charles's opponents in his northern kingdom: on 6 June, the Commons formulated a new oath of loyalty to Parliament which was taken by all members of both Houses and forthwith printed for distribution throughout the country; and on 12 June, a parliamentary Ordinance set up an Assembly of Divines to look into ways of reforming the English church along the lines adopted by the Kirk in Scotland.[16]

During this phase of the conflict, the resourcefulness of royalist sympathizers and the professional propagandists at Oxford manifested itself in a number of familiar letters, in which the earlier use of the genre to appeal to the consciences of the undecided gave way to indignant self-justification and denunciation of the moral failings of those who remained at Westminster. A tone of resentment, laced with irony and contempt for the jargon of partisanship that had alienated him from his former colleague, is nicely caught in the opening sentence of *A Letter from a Grave Gentleman once a Member of this House of Commons, to his Friend, remaining a Member of the same House in London* ([4 May] 1643):

Sir, I am extreamly glad that in this time of generall Distraction and Ruine (of which Pragmaticalnesse and want of Charity are both the effect and the cause) there is yet so much Leizure and Kindnesse left, even in the most busy and most ill-natur'd place, to admit a Thought of a Person no more considerable, and to afford a letter to a Malignant and a Cavalier, and that you put me not out either of your Memory or Your Care, when those you live with put me out of the House. (p. 1)

The writer's distress is convincingly communicated as he contemplates what has happened to the man who once had the same values and suffered for the same causes as himself. He reminds him that in the 1620s and 1630s they had both been 'committed about the Loanes' and 'put out of the Commission of the Peace for opposing Shipmony', and 'how sensible We after found the Parliament of all men's sufferings in that kind, and for those causes' (p. 2). But now Parliament itself is penalizing those who resist its own demand for a 'Contribution'; and furthermore, it seems bent on the destruction of 'the whole frame of Monarchy' (p. 3) and 'the totall extirpation of Bishops, Root and Branch' (p. 4). He asks, with poignant repetition, 'did either of us then thinke ... could we ever have thought then' (pp. 2–3) to have seen a Parliament behaving in such a way; and he ends, more in anger than in sorrow, with a vigorous rebuttal of 'that charge of Apostacy (which under other mens names you yourselfe lay upon me)' and an appeal to the judgement of any unbiassed observer, 'whether I left the Houses till they left the Law, and whether to quit the place and retaine the principles, or to quit the principles, and be only constant to the place, be the greater and the truer Apostacy' (pp. 5–6).

Later in the same month, a very different kind of royalist fought back against a hostile world by publishing a defence of his principles in a work which asserted his ideological orientation in its title. It was as *A Loyall Subjects Beliefe* (Oxford, [23 May] 1643), that Edward Symmons, the recently sequestered minister of Little Rayne in Essex, set out his 'Objections for resisting the Kings Personall will by force of Armes' in ninety-four pages of argument. More interesting than this rehearsal of scripture-based commonplaces, however, are the preliminary letter addressed to fellow clergy in the counties of Essex and Hertfordshire and the device of delivering the main body of the text in the form of a personal letter to Stephen Marshall, minister of the neighbouring parish of Finchingfield and a popular preacher before the Commons on its monthly fast days.

Symmons's tone is both hurt and defiant in his complaint that the 'uncharitable times' have caused some of his former associates in the cloth to ostracize him:

'tis counted a prime note of a Malignant to be seene speaking to me, and yet (you know) I have beene some body heretofore, as well as some of you: O but the report goes, I am now growne an Apostate; and why so? because I am (still the same man) obstinate in my way, will not conforme to the example of such and such of my worthy Brethren, preach to promote the warre (as they call it) for the *Parliament*. (sig. 2^r)

He makes no secret of his willingness to endure persecution for his beliefs: 'I may loose my credit, mine outward estate . . . yea and my life too . . . but I am resolved by Gods grace to keep my Conscience; the enemy shall not spoile me of that, let him doe his worst' (sigg. 2^{r-v}). He then relates the humiliations he has been exposed to since he was first called before the Committee for Scandalous Ministers 'upon the bare information of one malicious varlet': he has been 'published in a Diurnall over the Nation', 'voted a Delinquent', and eventually ejected from his living – and all for 'preaching against Lying and Slandering, Pride and Malice' (sigg. 2^v–3^r), which was interpreted as an attack on Parliament. Just as Sir Edward Dering had sought to refute the charge of apostasy by printing his speeches on the issue of church government, so Symmons seeks to make known 'the truth of God which I suffer for' by publishing 'the pith of some 8 Sermons preached in the moneths of June and July last, when my Troubles first begun' (sig. 4^r). One charge against him is that he has reneged on the Protestation of May 1641, which was drawn up at a time when rumours of plots had made many believe that both the Protestant religion and the privileges of Parliament were under serious threat. He had subscribed to this in good faith, but when he later 'saw people inclining to rebellion and strife' and heard 'men unreverently speak of the *Kings Majesties person*', he had raised his voice in defence of the Church of England and the King's honour 'according to my duty and Protestation'. As a result, he was branded with 'the name of a *Malignant*' and 'the title of a *Royalist*, yea of a ranke *Cavaleer*'; and when he inveighed against those who were rending the Prayer Book, he was promptly labelled 'a plaine *Papist*' (sig. 4^v). He dated this epistle 28 March and signed himself, 'Your Brother and Friend in Christ Jesus. E. S.'

In this introductory statement, Symmons makes powerful use of narrative to defend his own conduct before a jury of erstwhile colleagues and to air the injustices to which he and his family have been subjected; the main body of the book is offered specifically to Stephen Marshall (whose initials stood at the head of the pseudonym SMECTYMNUUS) in a spirit of fellowship and humility as a considered intellectual response to 'those things, that were urged at our last meeting, which at that time, I rather heard, then answered' (p. 1); but at the end, the ejected minister expresses a more personal concern for the man who had obtained bail for him when he was first declared a delinquent, exhorting him to abandon the mistaken course he is pursuing: 'And now (deare friend) do not blame me, if I wish your returne unto my selfe into that good old way, wherein we formerly walked together, in which onely you did Christ good service; for by your stepping into this new way, I can assure you that both Christ and you have lost' (p. 90). In a bold appeal to a named correspondent, who was a man of standing and influence both locally and nationally, Symmons moves from self-justification by way of measured argument to a sorrowful indictment (grounded in the specificities of a long-standing relationship) of one who has been instrumental in bringing disaster upon his church and country:

Sir let me beg of you againe (as before by my private letters I have done) and even for Christ his sake, that you would deny your selfe, and speedily put forth your strength to prevent (what in you lies) the ruine of this *Noble Nation*, that bred and fosterd you:... If your *Conscience* tells you, that you have too highly offended your *King*, know that your *Soveraigne* is the Image of your *Saviour* in meeknesse and mercy; O helpe to make up that great breach which you have unadvisedly beene a meanes to widen betweene him and his people. (p. 90)

Symmons was later to develop the idea of his sovereign as the 'Image' of his Saviour at greater length and to become the moving spirit behind the publication of the *Eikon Basilike*.

A Letter from an Officer in His Majesties Army, to a Gentleman in Glocester-shire, which is dated at the end '*from my Quarter this* 10th of April 1643', was also printed in Oxford during May, but unlike Symmons's very personal document, it was a thinly disguised exercise in royalist apologetics by Peter Heylyn, a member of the journalistic team that produced *Mercurius Aulicus*. The 'Officer' is apparently replying to a letter in which a number of questions raised by 'one, who hath a great desire to receive ease and satisfaction', are said to have been causing concern to 'many of whose honesty and publique Affections I have a very good esteem' (p. 1). Although the writer is careful not to alienate readers who may be genuinely exercised by these queries, he quickly exposes the ulterior motives of the 'honest man' who has been using them to undermine the loyalty of potential supporters of the King. The first 'scruple' relates to the Act of 1641 by which Parliament could not be dissolved without its own consent. The loyal 'Officer' denies that by ratifying the Bill passed by the two Houses Charles had obliged himself 'to obey whatever they prescribed' and suggests that they might themselves be held to the principle enunciated by Henry Parker, 'that, the Trust being broken, the power may be reassumed immediately into the hands which reposed the Trust' (p. 2). Was it ever the people's intention that the men elected in November 1640 'should shut the Door, and keep those that sent them for ever from those Counsells?' And did the King, when he summoned a Parliament, 'intend that they should rob, depose & murther him?' (p. 3). Since the present members have manifestly betrayed the trust placed in them by 'the abused King, and injured people', there is a case for declaring 'this Act to be void, and in it selfe against the Fundamentall Lawes of the Kingdom' (p. 3). According to Clarendon, it was only with difficulty that Charles was dissuaded in the spring of 1643 from denying the validity of the Act and ordering the immediate dissolution of Parliament – a course of action which might have put in jeopardy the other reforms that he had conceded since 1640. The advice of the moderates prevailed, however, and the alternative idea of adjourning the Houses 'to some fit and free place' where 'all the members' could meet in safety was outlined in a proclamation of 20 June.[17] Heylyn's letter, which urges 'one of the oldest Parliament men I know' (p. 3) to consider whether those currently sitting at Westminster can any longer be regarded as a legitimate assembly, may be read as preparing the ground for the implementation of one or other of these challenges to Pym's authority. The 'Officer' reminds his correspondent that many of those 'chosen & sent by their Countries' have been turned out of the House 'for not concurring with you in opinion'; and those who remain are mostly 'Persons of such desperate fortunes, and contemptible understandings, as off from those Benches were never thought fit for sober and honest Counsells' (p. 4). Can the people of England be expected to 'look long upon sixscore or sevenscore men (for both Houses doe not containe a greater number) as upon the high Court of *Parliament?*' (p. 4).

The next 'scandall' being noised abroad – that the King is offering protection to 'Delinquents' – provokes another disconcerting question for the man who has been heard to boast of serving in eight Parliaments: 'How many Delinquents have you known sent for in seven of them?' (p. 5). The 'Officer' wonders if this former champion of 'the Lawes of the Kingdome' (p. 3) can admit 'without blushing' that those branded as delinquents by 'this *Parliament*' are 'all such who are not or will not be Traitors to the knowne Lawes' or who 'doe not assist you in your pious worke of murthering the King, and destroying the Common-wealth' (p. 6).

The 'last Scruple' has to be taken more seriously, because it is one which 'startles many well meaning, and well wishing men': it is feared that 'if the King prevailes', the religion of 'the Papists' will have 'too great a countenance and growth, to the scandale of ours' (p. 7). This is a delicate matter, which involves the trustworthiness of Charles and the loyalty of his Queen, and Heylyn treads carefully in assuring anxious readers that the King's 'continued publique Acts of Devotion' and his 'understanding the differences between the Church of *Rome* and us' put him 'above the reach of Envy or Malice, and indeed above your own feares and jealousies' (p. 8). As for Henrietta Maria, she has provided 'soe hopefull and numerous an Issue' and demonstrated her love for her adopted nation so abundantly over fifteen years that she has earned the right to be beyond suspicion (p. 8). Concern about the numbers of Roman Catholics under arms is quickly brushed aside – 'I am confident and I have my Information from no ill hands, that in all His Majesties Armies the Papists cannot make one good Regiment' (p. 10) – and Heylyn ends triumphantly by throwing a familiar shibboleth back in the teeth of the parliamentary preachers and propagandists: if God has endorsed either cause with miraculous 'success', it is that of the King. During the first half of 1642, he had neither arms nor money, whereas the rebels 'had a wanton flourishing Army of 10,000 men within two days March of him'; but 'observe Him in a moment, as if Regiments fell from the Cloudes, hasting his owne March to . . . *Shrewsbury*, view Him at *Edgehill*, with a handfull of men (and if they were more, imagine how he got them) finding out this formidable Army, and dispersing them'; here, indeed, 'is an Argument for a Miracle' (p. 11).

A month after the summoning of Parliament to Oxford had first been mooted in print, the conscience of one of the few peers still attending the Upper House was appealed to in *A Letter to a Noble Lord At London from a Friend at Oxford: Upon occasion of the late Covenant taken by both Houses*, (Oxford, [18 July] 1643). This piece of royalist polemic served the dual purpose of vilifying the new oath of allegiance and undermining the credibility of a constitution in which '*the three vitall parts of the Kingdome*' were no longer 'King, Lords and Commons' but '*The Parliament*, (that is the close Committee) *the City and the Army*' (p. 11). Expressing 'trouble and sadnesse of mind' at receiving a copy of the Covenant 'inclosed in your Letter', the Oxford writer condemns the 'shifts' of those who, like the 'Noble Lord', have forgotten their oaths of allegiance and supremacy to the King and accepted the hypocritical fiction that they have taken up arms against their monarch '*for the defence of the true Protestant Reformed Religion, and Liberty of the Subject*' (pp. 1–2, 5–6). He inquires contemptuously whether this 'defence' began at Edgehill, or earlier, when a 'defensive Army' had been raised by the City to rescue the 'five pretious Members from a legall proceeding' (p. 7). Once the false assumptions behind the wording of the Covenant and the assaults already made by Parliament upon both religion and liberty have been exposed, he hints darkly that those who 'live at a distance have well observed that the principles and foundations for all this mischiefe were laid, long before your Mistresse Necessity was owned by you, long before your Armes were raised', and goads the rebel peer with the question, 'Can you yet look upon that Assembly with reverence?' (pp. 11–12).

The weekly record of the public scene in the diurnals and the need to shape the narrative of recent events to polemical advantage in Oxford and London helped to feed that 'sense of the present as emergent past' which Nigel Smith finds developing by 1644 into 'a historical perspective on the Civil War and its causes'.[18] He cites James Howell's

The Preheminence and Pedigree of Parliament (1644) as an early example of 'the Royalist use of historiography',[19] but Howell himself drew attention to the pioneering nature of a work which he had published in the previous year. In *A Discourse, or Parly, continued betwixt Patricius and Peregrine (upon their landing in France) touching the civill Wars of England and Ireland*, (London, [21 July] 1643), a traveller from Europe had thanked his English companion, Patricius, for giving him a more satisfying account of contemporary Britain than he had been able to glean from 'the most impudent untruths (vouch'd by publike authority)' on one side and the 'many pieces that had good stuffe in them' but 'look'd no further then the beginning of this Parliament, and the particular emergences thereof' on the other:

> But you have, by your methodicall relation, so perfectly instructed and rectified my understanding, by bringing mee to the very source of these distempers, and led me all along the side of the current by so streight a line, that I believe, whosoever will venture upon the most intricate task of penning the story of these *vertiginous* times, will find himselfe not a little beholden to that piece, which, indeed may be term'd a short *Chronicle* rather then a *Relation*. (p. 3)

Peregrine is referring to *The True Informer, Who In the following Discours, or Colloquy, Discovereth unto the World the chiefe Causes of the sad Distempers in Great Brittany, and Ireland* (Oxford, [12 April] 1643), which must have been composed soon after its author was arrested as a Malignant early in the year, since a later reprint claimed that it was '*Written in the Prison of the Fleet, anno 1642*' [i.e. before 25 March 1643].[20] As a man who was widely travelled himself,[21] Howell uses the external viewpoint of Peregrine as a device for spotlighting the folly of a nation that has forfeited the peace and prosperity of the 1630s: 'And was *England* so blind, as not to take warning by so many fearfull combustions abroad?' (p. 5); 'They say abroad that *England* is turned hereby from a *Monarchy* to a *Democracy*, to a perpetuall kinde of *Dictatorship*' (p. 18); 'Nor is it a small disrepute to the *English*, that the word *Cavalier*, which is an attribute that no Prince in Christendome will disdaine, ... is now us'd, not onely in Libels and frivilous Pamphlets, but in publike Parliamentarie Declarations, for a terme of reproach' (pp. 33–4).

For his part, Patricius places the ultimate blame for the present 'unhappy divisions' in England on a conspiracy of 'great *Zelots*' who 'whisper in conventicles' and 'machinators, and engeneers' who will use any means 'for the advancement of their designes, and strengthening their party' (pp. 8–10). A fuller account of 'other externe concurrent causes' (p. 10) leads him into a detailed narrative that begins with the rebellion over the new prayer book in Scotland and ends with the Battle of Edgehill. Peregrine is amazed at 'how his Majestie could beare up all this while, and keep together so many Armies, and still be master of the Field', which gives Patricius the cue for a fulsome tribute to the 'indefatigable' labours of the King in both 'bodie and minde' and the courage of the Queen, whose exploits are 'fitter for a Chronicle, then such a simple *Discourse*' (p. 42). The military success of the King so far must be ascribed 'principally to God Almightie, who is the Protectour of his Anointed' and who 'will doubtlesse continue to steer his course till he waft him to safe harbour againe' (p. 42). In the meantime, however, Patricius decides to accompany Peregrine when he returns to Europe, since 'all things are here growne *Arbitrary*' – as Howell, writing in prison, had good reason to know – and peace 'hath rov'd up and downe this Island, and cannot get a place to lay her head on' (p. 44 [misnumbered 34]).

If Howell, by his own account, was the first to attempt a 'methodicall relation' of the causes and early events of the Civil War, there were other instances in the summer of 1643 of the development of historiography 'under the pressure of controversial needs and inside pamphlet discourse'.[22] William Bridge's *The Truth of the Times Vindicated*, which 'used historical writing to provide considerable evidence of the popular origins of sovereignty',[23] was matched by *A Looking-Glasse for Rebells. Or the true grounds of Soveraignty, Proving The King's Authority to be from GOD only* (Oxford, [18 August] 1643), which derived its argument from the 'Ancient practice of this Kingdom' (sig. A2ʳ) as well as the scriptures.

In *A Plaine Case, Or, Reasons to Convince Any (That would be honest or thrive in the World) which side to take in this present Warre* (Oxford, [1 July] 1643), 'the people of *England*' were invited by an anonymous author to look to the future rather than the past and 'consider what must necessarily follow this warre' (p. 1). A victory for the present Parliament would saddle them with a huge debt incurred 'upon the *publicke faith*' (p. 1) and make them 'perpetually subject to an arbitrary government for the liberty of their persons, and property of their estates' (p. 5); an 'absolute victory' for Charles, on the other hand, would not only entail a much lighter financial burden, but would safeguard the 'ancient Lawes and Religion' of the kingdom, since many supporters of the royal cause 'have beene the most zealous for the liberty of the people and Priviledges of Parliament' (p. 3). The author's buoyant hope that the King will prosper – '(as tis very probable he may) having at this day three armies on foot, any of them able to encounter the Earle of *Essex* in the field' (p. 2) – reflects a growing confidence in royalist quarters as the summer of 1643 wore on.

All three of the royalist armies chalked up notable successes during June and July: on the night of 17–18 June, Rupert raided deep into territory to the east of Oxford and in an engagement on Chalgrove Field the parliamentary statesman and soldier, John Hampden, received a wound from which he died six days later; on 30 June, Newcastle inflicted a crushing defeat on Lord Fairfax and his son at Adwalton Moor, which gave him control of most of Yorkshire, and by 1 August he had advanced into Lincolnshire and taken the surrender of Gainsborough; and in the west, having joined forces with Prince Maurice and the Marquis of Hertford, Hopton's Cornishmen had fought Sir William Waller to a standstill on Lansdown Ridge on 5 July and, with reinforcements from Oxford, virtually destroyed his army at the Battle of Roundway Down on 13 July. Meanwhile, the Queen had at last set out from York early in June with military supplies and a small force of 4,500 men under the command of Henry Jermyn. After breaking her journey at the royalist stronghold of Newark, she was reunited with her husband at Kineton near the battlefield of Edgehill on the same day that Hopton defeated Waller in Wiltshire. Jermyn was granted a peerage, and on 14 July Charles and Henrietta Maria rode into Oxford in triumph.

In the parliamentary capital the mood was very different. Essex's army was ravaged by disease and thinned by desertions, and was continually being harried by the Oxford cavalry. When his own adequacy as Lord General was questioned, Essex offered to resign at the end of June and on 9 July suggested that Charles be approached with the unrealistic alternatives of renewed peace talks on the terms rejected in April or a final resolution of the conflict by a pitched battle between the two main armies.[24] None of these proposals was accepted, and when, at the end of July, Sir William Waller was voted to the command of a new army to be raised by the City, Essex demanded an investigation into the military failure in the west. To make matters worse, Bristol, the second port of England, had surrendered to the royalists after a fierce assault by Prince Rupert and the western army on 26 July. Waller was backed by Henry Marten and the extremists at Westminster and the peace party, reviving under the leadership of the Earl of Holland, sought Essex's support for a deal that would return control of the armed forces to the King.[25]

Optimism that the politicians at Westminster would soon be compelled to accept a settlement favourable to Charles and a corresponding gloom among adherents of Parliament are evident in a variety of private documents during the summer months of 1643. For Lady Sussex, writing to the Verney family on 30 June, 'the death of mr hamden was a most infinet lose beinge so religious and very wise a man', and by 4 August dismay at the reverses suffered by Fairfax and Waller had deepened into foreboding: 'The are very mery att oxfort i hear, and thinke to ovour com all soddonly.' Doll Leeke, by way of contrast, chided Ralph Verney on 10 August for his 'erour' in being 'a violent man against the king' and urged him not to ignore the lessons of recent history: 'Loke upon the king from the begining, and think with your self if god's blising had not gon with him, whether it had bin posible he could have binn in such a condision, as he is now in.'[26] An insight into the effect of Waller's defeat on the morale of Londoners is offered by John Greene, a twenty-seven-year-old lawyer, who studiously avoids revealing his own political sympathies even in the pages of his diary: 'It struck great terror generally, and men were much disheartened with it that were for the Parliament, and the opinion the King would prevaile now stronger than ever, the Citty being much troubled.'[27] As early as 10 June, Secretary Nicholas was informing the Earl of Ormond that the King's forces had 'prospered exceedingly' in the west and predicting that the 'great loss at Wakefield' would be redeemed 'within a short time'; and on 1 August, he reported that 'Yorkshire is all entirely reduced, except only Hull, and a poor town called Beverley' and confided his impression that the tide of public opinion was turning in the King's favour: 'The people have begun to be very sensible and weary of the oppressions of the new projected government, and we doubt not will shortly reject the same, which is now supported but by the Lord Saye, Mr Pym, young Sir H. Vane and a few other factious persons.'[28]

Sir Thomas Knyvett, at liberty once more after the Lowestoft affair, wrote on 20 July to dissuade his wife from attempting to join him in London because 'this place' was 'in greate disturbance by reason of A great rising of people in Kent', which had bred rumours that 'A great part of the Kings horss' was 'Advancing towards this towne'.[29] Although the royalist cavalry did not materialize and the Kentish rebellion against the imposition of the new Covenant had been suppressed by the end of July,[30] Knyvett was in cheerful mood on 3 August, expressing 'rich hopes' that – with the King 'gloriouse in the west', Lincolnshire on the point of being 'secuerd', and Norfolk and Suffolk (his own home territory) about to be 'next askt the Question whether ther be a King or no' – the 'right side' would soon prevail. Like many convinced royalists, his preference was for a political resolution of the conflict and he was hopeful that Charles would embrace any reasonable terms to end the

bloodshed, even though militarily he was 'nowe in so brave A commanding posture'.[31] In the event, Knyvett's 'faier hopes' were dashed
when mobs appeared at Westminster shouting 'No peace!' and the
Commons rejected the Lords' initiative on 7 August.[32] Some of the peers
who had been hanging on at Westminster – either to serve the King's
interests, like Conway and Portland, or in the expectation of a settlement – now began to drift away from London. Of those who had
thrown in their lot with Parliament, Holland and Bedford headed
hopefully for Oxford, where they met with a cold reception from a court
which took its cue from the Queen's open contempt for these refugees
from an assembly of fanatics and traitors.[33]

The moderating influence of Hyde and Falkland, which could still be
exerted on occasion behind the scenes, now made little impact upon the
public voice of royalism as it issued from the Oxford presses. Heylyn and
Berkenhead, under the 'general guidance of Digby and Nicholas', were
'unyieldingly and wittily dismissive' in their treatment of 'political enemies and problems';[34] and even publications that emanated from the
university were not immune to the abrasive spirit of the times. Indeed,
Berkenhead himself contributed a poem to *Musarum Oxoniensium Epiba-
teria*, the volume that celebrated Henrietta Maria's return to England
and arrival in Oxford. Thomason acquired a copy on 31 July, but a
manuscript version may have been presented to her when she was
received into the city on 14 July.[35] In serviceable couplets, the editor of
Mercurius Aulicus had adapted a traditional Caroline motif to the specific
circumstances of summer 1643. The very mention of the word 'Queen'
is enough to shake 'the dark Committee Board', while under her
influence Newcastle had 'purg'd all the North' and Waller 'could but
bleed and fret' (sig. Aa1ʳ). In fact, all the encouraging news items of the
past weeks were attributable to the effects of her approach, from
Hampden's death to the heroic achievements of the Western army:

> When once the *Members* shrunk to *foure*,
> When *Hopton* brought his *Cornish* o're,
> When as Eternall *Grenvill* stood
> And stopt the gap up with his blood,
> When their slye *Conqu'rour* durst not stand,
> We knew the QUEENE was nigh at hand.   (sig. Aa1ᵛ)

Equally alert to the contents of the newsbooks, W. Barker of New
College began his offering with an allusion to the fate of Birmingham,
'Go Burne some Rebell Towne; for such alone / Are Bonfires suiting to

the Joyes we owne'; and in his closing conceit gave a pragmatic gloss to the 'Soveraigne Balme' that Henrietta Maria was said to have brought from 'Forraigne Climates' to heal the nation's wounds: 'And Treason stoop, forc't by commanding Charmes / Either to Kisse your Hands, or Feare your Armes' (sigg. A2^r–A3^r). He was not alone in highlighting her material contribution to the King's cause in sending what one Christ Church poet called 'those Pledges' of her love from overseas – 'the Armes, the Mony, and the Princes [Rupert and Maurice] too' (sig. A3^r). John Dale of Magdalen College was struck by the contrast between the occasions of the present and previous volumes of Oxford poetry:

> The *Muses* heretofore were wont to wait
> Upon you at your Childbed, to relate
> The dangers there o're pass'd, no thought was then
> We should have had such matter for the Penne.   (sig. C3^r)

But for one of the Christ Church wits, she had merely extended her traditional maternal role by nurturing the military capability of the King's party in its infancy:

> Welcome to th' Army you have Nourish'd, when
> CHARLES for his safety but had Naked men:
> The Sinewy strength of Mony You sent o're,
> And cloath'd that strength with Armes, uselesse before.   (sig. C1^v)

By far the most accomplished and dignified of the Oxford responses to Henrietta Maria's return was William Cartwright's tribute to the bravery and resolution with which she had undertaken the task of negotiating with foreign governments and arms dealers and then faced danger in getting her purchases safely through stormy seas and a naval blockade – even coming under fire from parliamentary ships soon after she had disembarked at Bridlington:[36]

> Courage was cast about Her like a Dresse
>   Of solemne Comelinesse;
> A gather'd Mind, and an untroubled Face
>   Did give Her dangers grace.[37]

Such were the times that the most stately panegyric had to accommodate a measure of harsh satirical matter, but Cartwright fashioned even this into a gracefully turned compliment to the qualities of the steadfast Queen:

> Look on Her Enemies, on their Godly Lyes,
>   Their Holy Perjuries,
> Their Curs'd encrease of much ill gotten Wealth,
>   By Rapine or by stealth. . . .
> Look then upon Her selfe; Beauteous in Mind . . .

> Then you'l confesse Shee casts a double Beame,
> Much shining by Her selfe, but more by Them.

While versifiers like Berkenhead wielded the myth of the magical properties of the royal person as a crude journalistic weapon, Cartwright
recognized that the inspiration of Henrietta Maria's personal courage
and commitment could be a genuine asset to the King's cause: 'Her
presence is our Guard, our Strength, our Store; / The cold snatch some
flames thence, the valiant more'.

The fighting in the west country had supplied armed royalism with
another icon in the figure of Sir Bevill Grenvile, a Cornish squire who
had boldly prevented Hopton's cannon falling into enemy hands during
the rout on Sourton Down, led his pikemen in the victorious assault on
Chudleigh's hilltop position at the Battle of Stratton, and been mortally
wounded in another heroic attack on Lansdown Ridge. Grenvile had
once written to his wife, 'I am satisfied I cannot expire in a better cause'
– sentiments which were elaborated after his death in a letter from his
servant and comrade-in-arms, Anthony Payne: 'He fell, as he did often
tell us he wished to die, in the great Stewart cause, for his country and
his King.'[38] Perhaps more than any other individual in the first year of
the war, he came to symbolize those 'concepts of honour and loyalty'
which, in the opinion of G. E. Aylmer, had a greater impact on 'the
strength and fighting spirit' of the King's supporters than the arguments
that were deployed in justification of his cause.[39] For many of the landed
gentry who took up arms in defence of Charles's rights and person, 'the
old service' of the liegeman to his monarch was as compelling a motive
for self-sacrifice as 'that good old way' of Church of England piety and
worship was for Edward Symmons. A recent study of the 'residual,
powerful and sustained sense of loyalty to the Crown' in men like
Grenvile, Sir Edmund Verney (who was killed defending the royal
standard at Edgehill) and Sir Henry Slingsby (who eventually died on
the scaffold) comes to the conclusion that there was no need for the King
to create a royalist party in 1642, 'for it arose itself in opposition to the
spectre of rebellion'.[40] Nevertheless, while it has been demonstrated that
'principle' played a key part in motivating the royalist war effort – just as
'principles' helped to consolidate puritan opposition to Charles in the
early 1640s[41] – the significance of the printed word in disseminating that
principle by giving it 'a local habitation and a name' should not be
underestimated.

The death of 'brave Grenvill' was duly reported in *Mercurius Aulicus*
(Week 27, 8 July, p. 360), but just over a month later the Oxford press

issued a collection of English poems under the title *Verses on the Death of the Right Valiant Sr Bevill Grenvill, Knight. Who was Slaine by the Rebells, on LANSDOWN-hill near Bath. July. 5. 1643.* Grenvile had been a student at Exeter College, but various features of the volume suggest to Loxley that it had 'more than a commemorative role'. The lack of Latin verses, the use of initials rather than names and colleges to identify contributors, and an arrangement of the contents which ignores academic status all indicate that 'it was not constructed primarily as an act of collegiate or university self-representation, but participated instead in the broader polemical strategies of royalism'.[42] A warrior of 'Undaunted Spirit', his face besmeared with 'Dust, Sweat, and Blood', leading his 'stately wood / Of Pikes' up the steep slope 'like a Captaine Oake' until he stood 'like another Hill, or Rock' upon 'the Hill H'had Gain'd'; and an '*Heroick Martyr*', giving his life to convince the half-hearted that, 'when the Right / Of King, and Subject, is suppress'd by Might', the man who 'is not Active, Modestly Rebells' (pp. 18, 1, 2, 18, 20, 8–9) – this composite portrait created by the Oxford poets was certainly 'crafted as a direct riposte, both to the characters of malignant cavaliers written by the London pamphleteers and to the political paralysis of those who re-mained neutral'.[43] One of the minor contributors, however, was uncom-fortably aware of the stylistic challenge of crafting an adequate *poetic* impression of Grenvile's 'famous Actions': 'Could I write as Thou fought'st, the World might see / Perhaps some Picture of thy Deeds, and Thee' (p. 3). The literary model he invokes is that of Homer's treatment of the exploits of Achilles, but his own gestures towards epic style merely transform the brutal carnage of the battlefield into a stage-set, where the heroic actor performs before an admiring audience:

> Methinkes I see Thee shaking thy bold speare
> Against a numerous Host, without their feare
> Who did beset Thee, and the spatious plaine
> Before Thee strow'd with Slaine falne on thy slaine.
> Whil'st all our other Troopes, discharg'd from fight,
> Wonder'd to see the Warre turn'd to a Sight,
> Where one encounter'd many. (p. 5)

In other pieces, the ethos of the newsletter predominated over that of epic. One contributor saw '*Grenvilles* Fall' as a chance for the London hacks to gloat over 'the Greatnesse of Our Blow', making his own efforts redundant: 'What we have Lost in Thee, We need not write, / Thine Enemies will doo't' (p. 12). Dudley Digges used the occasion to deride the social origins of the opposing army, 'the drosse of men' whose deaths bring satisfaction of 'conscience' but no glory to the King's well-born officers: 'for what honour i'st to tell / That here a Sergeant-Major Cobler fell, / There a Mechanick-Colonell dropt downe' (p. 14). And Berkenhead could not let slip the opportunity both to express his distaste for the inferior blood spilled from 'their course Veynes', and also to pepper a variety of familiar targets with verbal grape-shot:

> Let their cheap Legions live (unfit to dye)
> Who like their weapons strike they know not why,
> Give our just Swords more satisfying dust,
> Thread all the bold Committee at one thrust,
> Scatter the Plot, till all the ill-built frame
> Fall downe as tribute to Great BEVILL'S Name,
> That Name (which shames Their malice and our wit)
> Shall last as long as They conspir'd to *sit*.   (p. 17)

Once again, the most substantial and complex poem in the volume came from the pen of William Cartwright, who headed the more literary wing of the propaganda force assembled at Oxford. He begins by celebrating the qualities of the Cornish gentleman as both 'Souldier, and Martyr', drawn into battle not 'in pursuit of Fame' but 'to maintaine Afflicted Right' and driven by 'no Interest but Loyalty'.[44] Even while fashioning his tribute to this ideal champion, however, he feels obliged to include a thrust at wordsmiths in the rival camp who 'blind their Men with specious Lyes, / With Revelations, and with Prophecyes'. Then he casts a 'more intentive Eye' on Grenvile's final heroic deed and deploys a range of rhetorical devices in one of the rare attempts in poetry of the Civil War years to engage imaginatively with the experience of hand-to-hand fighting:[45]

> His Courage work't like Flames, cast heate about,
> Here, there, on this, on that side; None gave out;
> Not any Pike in that Renowned Stand
> But tooke new force from His Inspired Hand;
> Souldier encourag'd Souldier, Man urg'd Man,
> And He urg'd All: so much Example can.
> Hurt upon Hurt, Wound upon Wound did call,
> He was the But, the Mark, the Ayme of All.

But epic yields to polemic once more in the closing section of the poem, when Grenvile's 'Diviner Fury' is contrasted with the empty fanaticism of those who 'boast the Spirit' and yet 'dare not Dye', and the thought of the royalist hero's secure 'Seate' among the 'Valiant' of history prompts a jibe at the fluctuating reputation and authority of Essex, who is either 'a Traitor, or His Excellence' according to the latest 'Reports' in the newsbooks.

At the end of July, some verses said to have been sent from a 'Scholler' in the rival university town to 'his Royall friend at Oxford'[46] reinforced the rather more relaxed image of the 'laughing Cavalier' that was created by *Mercurius Aulicus*, 'a being compounded of heroic loyalty and devil-may-care wit'.[47] This 'Cambridge Royalist' relates how, at a time when fear of Rupert had called the local puritan gentry from 'their rough dunne Wives' to muster in the town, he had been betrayed into 'an act of Vertue' by those notorious Malignants, '*Conscience* and *Reason*' (sig. A1ʳ). Arrested by 'a youth, / With goodly goggle eyes', he was taken to the town hall, where plentiful supplies of beer and sack helped him to keep his fellow-prisoners in good heart: 'How now, who's drooping there? who dares be so / In the Kings Cause?' (sig. A2ᵛ). After leading them in a drinking song, he calls down a curse 'on your Parliament Justice', which refused to release him even though 'the Committee' could bring no plausible case; and he ends with the hope that the 'horrid ills' of 'Sequestration and Proscriptions' will 'sit heavie' on them when they 'meet the King i' th' Field' and that the 'venerable Judge' will be 'drest in most vile Tunes and Rimes' and 'laught at still' by 'Children and Market-maids in after-times' (sig. A4ᵛ).

While the university wits were busy furthering the royal cause in their various ways, the versatile poetic talent of Alexander Brome was casting a critical light on the London scene from the perspective of an insider. Speaking 'in a range of voices from across the social and political spectrum',[48] he managed to combine his subversive literary activities with a successful legal career in the city throughout the 1640s and 1650s. In an early ode, he used an ancient symbol of kingship to taunt those 'blind *Phaetons*', who had dared to drive 'th' foaming Steeds' of 'our Sun' into the 'stables of the North or West', with the prospect of the King's eventual return to his former capital, not to 'light and warme us, with his rayes, but all to burn'.[49] In a satire on Parliament as 'The New Mountebank' ([17 May] 1643), he describes how this 'physician', who 'try'd his skill' first on Strafford, dispenses a drug 'call'd a fundamentall law' which is 'a sovereign antidote' for 'all wounds and all diseases':

> Diurnals are his weekly bills,
> Which speak how many he cures or kills:
> But of the errata he'll advise,
> For cure read kill, for truth read lies.[50]

Mockery of the weekly newsbooks, and in particular of Samuel Pecke's *A Perfect Diurnall* which began publication early in July,[51] was developed into fullblown caricature in 'A New Diurnal', supposedly covering

parliamentary proceedings during the first week of June.[52] Adapting
Denham's claim in his poem on the Five Members that Parliament had
usurped the poet's privilege of invention, Brome explains that he has
decided to put the diurnals into verse in order to 'authorise their lying'.
On Monday, in a debate on 'the raising of money for the state and the
kirk', the Commons had balked at 'the word plunder', but contrived to
'persist in the act, which they blush'd for to name' by calling it 'distrain-
ing'; on Thursday, 'letters were read' which related how 'hundreds were
slain, and hundreds did run' in a victory against Newcastle – information which had been strangely available to Parliament 'ere the battle
begun'; and on Friday, Sir Hugh Cholmley was 'accus'd of treason' for
'being no longer a traitor'. In the postscript, a running gag about the
propensity of the Commons to 'fall' to 'voting' on the slightest pretext
supplies the *coup de grace*, as Brome promises to report their doings
'roundly from Monday to Monday again'. 'And since we have begun,
our Muse doth intend, / To have (like their votes) no beginning nor
end.'

At Oxford, too, the war against the London newsbooks was hotting
up. In a single stanza of his mock-ballad, 'A Second Western Wonder',
Denham killed three birds with one stone – the defeated Sir William
('the Conqueror') Waller, his puritan wife, and *Mercurius Civicus*, which
had recently introduced the practice of enhancing its title-page with
likenesses of military or political leaders:

> When out came the book, which the *News-Monger* took
>   From the *Preaching Ladies* Letter,
> Where in the first place, stood the *Conquerors* face,
>   Which made it shew much the better.[53]

A more sustained comic assault on the parliamentary propagandists
was launched by John Taylor in a prose parody entitled *A Preter-Pluper-
fect, Spick and Span New Nocturnall, or Mercuries Weekly Night-Newes* (Oxford,
[11 August] 1643). Since 'our *London* Diurnals', though written by day-
light, 'often stumble into most grosse errours', he asks the reader to
excuse any 'over-sight' in a 'Night-worke' composed by one who has 'to
grope in the darke, (or at the best in the Moon-shine)' (p. 1). The main
item of Oxford news illuminated by moonshine on Saturday night is the
incursion of 'an Armie of *Mice*' into a stationer's shop near Carfax,
where books and pamphlets printed at York, Oxford and London, all
'stale and past sale', lie in a confused heap, 'friends and foes, Truthes
and Lyes' (p. 2). The discriminating rodents gnaw their way through 'the
Territories of that *Babel*', sparing *Expressions*, *Declarations* and *Exhortations*

by the King and devouring *Remonstrances, Messages* and *Animadverisons* from Westminster, though many were 'almost choak'd with eating of three Words, onely *Cavalier, Malignant,* and *Delinquent*' (pp. 2–3). *Mercurius Civicus* quickly falls victim to their 'sharpe fanges', along with 'the *Observator*' and 'Master *Prin's* 19th and last Volume', but they only nibble at 'Sir *Benjamin Rudiard's* speeches', which are 'luke-warme (too cold for the King, and too hot for the *Parliament*)' (p. 3). Pym's speeches 'were delicious in the palate', but 'wofull experience' soon proved them to be 'more banefull in operation' than 'Rats-bane' or 'venome' (p. 4). At a meeting of 'the Brethren and holy Sisters' on Sunday night, 'one Mistris *Fumpkins* a Porters Wife in Pudding Lane' made 'a short Repetition of almost foure houres' on a lecture given by 'the *New English* Teacher at *Laurence* Church', where 'true Lye, very Lye, She did exceeding Lye, lay open Lye, how zealous Lye, fervent Lye, ardent Lye, and perswasive Lye, he had encouraged his Auditours, vehement Lye, to continue constant Lye, obstinate Lye, rebellious Lye, she said the Gentleman did sweat out most delicate Doctrine' (p. 5). On Tuesday night, 'two old seditious and wicked Ministers' were brought from Gloucestershire by 'three hundred Dragooners' and charged with praying for the King (p. 8); Wednesday night saw the demise of the author of a 'Weake Description of Weekly Newes', whose reputation 'is buried with this Epitaph, *Here Mercurius Civicus lyes in his* throat' (p. 10); and on Friday night, some Cavaliers were accused of plundering water from the proprietress of an alehouse, at which 'some say that *Boy* the Dog of War wagged his taile merrily in a jeering manner at the womans calamitie; and this was the most extraordinary outrage that the Prince or his Armie committed at that or any other time' (p. 17).

The former waterman evidently relished the outlet for his knockabout brand of journalism afforded by the press at Oxford. In another lively pamphlet, he launched a further attack on his London competitors, the factious 'Cavillers', who 'have made bold to make *Mercury* their counterfeit poste, poste-haste and pack-horse' and 'under the names of *Civicus, Britannicus, Scoutes, Scottish Pigeons* [the *Scottish Dove* began publication on 19 October], and other pretty, ill-contrived, sweet, filthy, sophisticated Titles and Epithites, hath beswarmed all the Christian world over with English Lyes'. At the same time, he was eager to play his part in defending the reputation of his new-found comrade, 'the Cavalier', as one who, 'knowing his cause just, applies himselfe onely to Truth, both in fighting and writing'.[54]

John Berkenhead himself may have taken time off from his editorial labours, at the direct behest of the King, in order to back up a Royal Proclamation of 17 July which forbade traffic with London, 'that prodigal and licentious City' as *Mercurius Aulicus* had recently called it (Week 26, 25 June – 1 July, p. 331).[55] In *A Letter from Mercurius Civicus to Mercurius Rusticus: Or, London's Confession but not Repentance* (Oxford, [25 August] 1643), he cleverly exploits the 'collective, social identity' of the Mercury as a 'larger-than-life figure'[56] to expose the moral turpitude of writers who sell their pens in an unworthy cause. Particularly effective is the chastened tone in which Civicus is made to confess his predicament to the country cousin who has chosen to breathe the free air of Oxford:

> *Good Brother* Rusticus, Though there have been some unkinde jars between my brother *Aulicus* and me, yet my earnest desire is to keep a good understanding between your self and me: ... you know how famous we have been here for publishing and printing Lyes, he that will not lye to advantage the great Cause in hand, is not amongst us thought fit to have accesse either to the Pulpit or the Presse. And therefore when I was first set on work to communicate Intelligence to the Kingdom to indear my self to them that imployed me, I played my part reasonable well, I Lyed my share. (p. 1).

After this admission of personal guilt, Civicus enters upon a detailed narrative of the City's involvement in the rebellion from the wresting of power from the Lord Mayor in December 1641 to the recent slighting of the King's terms for peace; and then, in a passionate peroration, he adjures Rusticus to make the truth available to posterity, so that 'if they aske who would have pulled the crown from the *Kings* head, taken the government off the hinges, dissolved Monarchy, inslaved the *Lawes*, and ruined their Countrey; say, "Twas the *proud, unthankefull, Schismaticall, Rebellious, Bloody City of London*"' (p. 32).

The surrender of Bristol by Nathaniel Fiennes, son of Lord Saye and Sele, to the combined forces of Rupert, Maurice and Hopton on 26 July, which was followed by the capitulation of other towns in the region, was the high water mark of royalist success. Instead of advancing directly on London, however, where Essex and Waller were at loggerheads and Pym 'had almost lost control of the situation',[57] the royalist high command decided to consolidate its hold on the west country by investing Gloucester and securing the River Severn for the movement of troops from the recruiting grounds in South Wales. But Charles met unexpected resistance from the young governor, Edward Massey, and the siege which began on 10 August both strengthened the determination of the politicians and military leaders in London and gave them time to augment their dwindling forces. Once the republican Henry Marten, champion of Waller against Essex, had been expelled from the House and briefly lodged in the Tower for speaking too openly against monarchical government, Pym could get on with settling the dispute between the rival generals. This he accomplished with a tactful arrangement whereby Waller received his commission as head of the newly raised army for the defence of London directly from Essex, who was thus confirmed as commander-in-chief and left in control of the main field army.[58] By the end of August Essex was ready to march to the relief of Gloucester with 15,000 men. The cavalry of Wilmot and Rupert failed to halt his progress through the Cotswolds, and he came within sight of the city on 6 September, only to discover that the siege had been hastily abandoned. Charles's priority was now to cut him off before he could get back to his base. Essex eluded his pursuers with a feint towards Worcester and the race for London began. The two armies eventually converged on Newbury, which the King reached first on 19 September. In fierce and confused fighting on the next day, during which Lord Falkland was shot dead by a musket ball, neither side achieved supremacy. At nightfall, dispirited and low on ammunition, Charles withdrew into Newbury, leaving the road clear for his adversary. The parliamentary general was back in London by 25 September, having evacuated the garrison from Reading on the way, while Charles had returned to Oxford. Bulstrode Whitelocke noted that 'most men were of opinion that when the King went to Gloucester, if he had marched up to London, he had done his work'.[59]

The irrepressible John Taylor was in action again during the siege of Gloucester – possibly on 1 September, since he dates his latest pamphlet '*Thursday* the 32th of *August*' on the title-page.[60] In the comic persona of a parliamentary spy – disguised 'in the shape of a Fellow that sels Oranges and Lemmonds' – he passes on to the 'notorious Patriots' in London such 'strange and remarkable Observations' as he has been able to 'sift and picke out of the men' and 'cunningly under-fele and groape out of the women' in Oxford (p. 1). He reports first on the shortage of tobacco pipes and other hardships experienced in the King's capital, where 'they have not one Baker ... that hath the art to bake stale Bread' and 'all manner of Fish (fresh or salt) is at such prices that no man can buy any at all without credit or ready money' (p. 2). Then he points out the mistake of his employers 'in not concealing the losse of *Bristol* from the common People' and advises them not to let this discouraging news 'come to the Eares of Master *Burton*, Master *Pryn*, or Master *Bastwick*' (p. 3). He is also concerned that Henry Marten should not be hanged 'for such small faults as highest Treason', reminding them that 'Master *Martins* Case is many of our Cases, and if we fall to hanging one another, the malignant party will laugh at us' (p. 6). His main anxiety, however, is over the 'world of mischiefe' that has been done to 'our cause' by 'the Printing Presses at *Yorke, Shrewsbury*, and now at *Oxford'*, and more especially by 'those Writers at Oxford' who 'doe out-word us' as successfully as 'their Armies would out-sword us (which they have prettily done of late)' (pp. 6–7). In spite of the sterling service of 'our nimble *Mercurius Civicus'*, who 'hath confest lately that he hath lyed his share for us', the false reports of 'our London Diurnals, and posting *Scout'* are no match for 'their *Mercurius Aulicus, Rusticus* and some other true Relations which are printed every weeke new at *Oxford'* (pp. 6, 7). Parliament's own distortions of the truth in a recent account of the campaign in the west have been exposed to ridicule by opponents who have the temerity to bring 'wit, reason, understanding and scholarship' to bear on the 'triumphant victories' claimed for 'the tenth Worthy (Sir *William Waller*, Sirnamed A Conqueror)' (pp. 11, 7). The practice of holding 'Thanksgivings' for 'invisible Victories', the defection of the Earl of Holland, and the well-reported fact that the 'House doth every where weare thinner and thinner' all lay the spy's 'most deare and laborious Brethren' open to mockery. Their incompetence is capped by their manifest failure to honour his final urgent request 'that you have an especiall care that this Letter be not printed' (pp. 11, 14).

Towards the end of March or soon after, the 'Writers of Oxford', among whom Taylor now proudly numbered himself, had been joined by two notable refugees from Cambridge – Abraham Cowley and John Cleveland.[61] Each played a prominent part in the collective effort to 'out-word' the common enemy during the late summer and autumn. In a 'vicious and uncompromising poem',[62] the latter pits his ingenuity against the monstrous phenomenon of 'The Mixt Assembly' – the 'pye-bald crew' of clergy and laity appointed by Parliament to complete the reformation of the English church – which met for the first time at Westminster on 1 July 1643.[63] 'So mixt they are', scoffs Cleveland, 'one knowes not whether's thicker, / A Layre of Burgesse, or a Layre of Vicar'. '*Black* and *Gray'* like both orders of Friars; half red and half black, like 'parboyl'd Lobsters' or like 'sinners halfe refin'd in Purgatory'; like 'Jewes and Christians in a ship together': even Cleveland's inventive wit is taxed by 'this ridling feature', which can scarcely be represented by 'all th' Adulteries of twisted nature' or called up by any 'Phansie' that is not 'sick'. In the second half of the poem, giving over the attempt to find adequate analogies for this aberrant gathering, he directs his venom at the Earls of Pembroke and Northumberland, two of the peers still attending a House of Lords which 'Looks like the wither'd face of an old hagg, / But with three teeth'; and then, with the cry 'A Jig, a Jig', the poet imagines ill-matched couples – celebrated lay and clerical members – engaging in an 'Antick dance' to 'the Scotch pipes' played by the Prolocutor of the Westminster Assembly, William Twiss. Fielding, a military commander, advances with 'doxy *Marshall*' (Edward Symmons's old neighbour in Essex); Lord Saye and Sele is partnered by 'rumpl'd *Palmer*', a puritan divine with a twisted back; the Earl of Manchester, formerly Lord Kimbolton, 'Must be content to saddle Doctor *Burges*', the vice-president of the Assembly who was notorious as a preacher and adulterer; and Pym leads the other Five Members in an encounter with the five authors who constituted 'Madam *Smec*'. All dancing to the tune of the Scots, the grotesque figures in this antimasque are an obscene travesty of the proper relations of church and state. For A. D. Cousins, Cleveland's descent to the naming of individuals indicates 'a growing bitterness and sense of outrage', in which the 'amused contempt' of his earlier satires has been replaced by 'baffled anger' at an ideology so at odds with his inherited 'Cavalier' view of the world that it is 'finally incomprehensible in its alien motives and forms'.[64]

The precise nature of Cowley's literary activities after his removal to Oxford has only recently come to light. It had been known since 1656, when he published his *Poems* with an apologetic preface, that among the pieces he had written 'during the time of the late troubles' and subsequently 'cast away' there were '*three Books of the Civil War it self*, reaching as far as the first *Battel* of *Newbury*'.[65] An incomplete text of the first book which broke off at line 556 with the note, '*The Author went no further*', was printed under the title 'A Poem on the Late Civil War' in 1679, twelve years after the poet's death.[66] In 1967, Allan Pritchard reported the discovery of all three parts of the lost poem in three manuscript booklets; then another manuscript copy turned up in a seventeenth-century commonplace book; and in 1973 Pritchard's edition of the complete text was published.[67]

Internal evidence indicates that Cowley began work on the text which became Book I during the summer of 1643 and had not yet completed it when Bristol surrendered on 26 July. Pritchard considers that he may have allowed Book 1 to circulate in Oxford while some of the events it dealt with – the death of Hampden, the defeat of Waller at Roundway

Down, the reunion of the King and Queen at Kineton – 'were still relatively fresh'; and that the later books, which take the narrative forward from the storming of Bristol to the Battle of Newbury – were composed soon after the events they describe, since Pym (who died early in December) 'is mentioned as if still alive (2. 545)' and the absence of any reference to Cromwell suggests that the poem had been abandoned before he 'emerged as one of the unmistakably dominant figures in the Parliamentary party and army' during the late autumn.[68]

The earliest critical assessments of *The Civil War* in its entirety pursued the implications of Cowley's statement in the 1656 preface that his planned royalist epic got no further than the third book because 'the succeeding *misfortunes* of the *party*' in the wake of the serious reverse at Newbury 'stopt the *work*; for it is so uncustomary, as to become almost *ridiculous*, to make *Lawrels* for the *Conquered*'.[69] Pritchard himself describes it as a 'unique' attempt 'by a poet of stature to give epic treatment to the great events of the Civil War', which was 'overtaken by history before it was completed'; for Trotter, the enterprise had begun to falter stylistically '*before* history started to provide the wrong plot', since 'the epic frame had been sapped from within by the play of antagonistic rhetorics'; and Anselment, while accepting that 'the heroic and satiric combine' to a degree 'unusual in the traditional epic', sees this mixing of genres as a reflection of 'the complexity of Cowley's commitment'.[70] In taking issue with Trotter's formalist diagnosis of the poem's failure, MacLean argues that the problem facing Cowley 'was not that of an irreconcilable conflict of modes caused by generic variety, but the need to reconcile partisan interest with the formal requirements of an epic design'. His perception that the poet has 'an affective design that generates sympathy for the king's cause' implies that Cowley's text needs to be orientated not only within a literary tradition stretching back to Lucan and Virgil but also within the more immediate context of those popular efforts to supplement 'fighting' with 'writing' that have been explored in this chapter.[71] Norbrook endorses this approach in his observation that, in the process of 'describing a society where ideas are being made widely accessible through the printing press', Cowley conducts 'a fascinating experiment in the possibilities and the limits of representing a modern ideological conflict through the medium of classical epic'.[72]

Pritchard had already identified Cowley's debt to *Mercurius Aulicus* and other Oxford publications (like *The Roundhead's Remembrancer*) for details of particular military actions and to *The True Informer* and *A Letter from Mercurius Civicus to Mercurius Rusticus* for a broader conspectus of recent history. He had also noted that the poem not only adopted 'the emphasis of the Royalist journals and pamphlets' but even exploited the specialized idiom that had been developed 'in the verbal warfare of the period'.[73] Indeed, there is reason to believe that Cowley set out not with a grand design to celebrate the ultimate triumph of royalist arms, but with a more modest and immediately polemical project which only later began to assume the ambitious proportions of an epic. The very fact that 'Book 1' existed as a separate text in at least three manuscripts (two that survive and one that lay behind the 1679 edition) may indicate that Cowley had originally conceived it as a self-contained poem and re-leased it into circulation as soon as it was finished. Although Pritchard established the critical habit of referring to that poem as 'Book 1', he gives the text itself Cowley's heading of 'The Civill Warre' and reserves the label 'Booke' for the two subsequent parts; and he supplies the information that each of the three manuscript 'booklets' has a title inscribed on the verso of the final leaf – 'Civill Warr', '2^d part of the Civil Warr', and 'Civil War 3^d Book', respectively.[74] All this suggests that the continuation of the poem beyond the end of 'Civill Warr' was an afterthought, and that the work's expansion in Cowley's mind into the form and scale of an epic eventually led to the adoption of the term 'book' for its separate sections. In manner and content, 'Book 1' certain-ly has far more in common with other royalist writing of the early 1640s than with Virgil's *Aeneid* or Lucan's *Pharsalia*, the chief classical models for seventeenth-century epic practice. It is significant that almost all of Cowley's specific debts to earlier epics are in Books 2 and 3. Further-more, in one of the manuscripts in which 'Book 1' appears alone under the title 'On the Civill Warr', it is 'preceded by other Royalist verse of the 1640s', including Cowley's own satire, *The Puritan and the Papist*, and poems by Denham and Cleveland.[75]

In its larger structure and in its local detail, 'Book 1' fits comfortably into the context of 'the verbal warfare' of the summer of 1643. It begins with an evocation of the horrors of Civil War (of 'young mens blood' and 'Mothers teares') that appeals to the consciences of true Englishmen on both sides of the conflict; it identifies religious extremism as one of the primary causes of the present troubles; and it glances at the project of uniting the English people behind military support for the Protestants in Europe that Cowley had toyed with in his panegyric of November 1641. Then, following the method pioneered by Howell, Cowley traces the steps by which 'into War we scar'd our selves': the 'darke Quarrell' with the Scots; the Grand Remonstrance, which slandered 'those blest Dayes of *peace*' under Charles's personal rule; the petitions pouring in from 'every *Towne*'; the 'sencelesse Clamours and confused Noyse' that accompanied the trial of Strafford; the 'lowd storme' that 'blew the grave *Miter* downe', made 'great *Mary*' fly across the sea, and 'drove *Charles* into the *North*'. Next, the early stages of the Civil War itself are summarized: the levying of troops; Rupert's skirmish with a parliamentary force near Worcester; Edgehill, which elicits the first set piece of narrative description in the poem; the sacking of Brentford; and Charles's establishment of his headquarters in Oxford.

Up to the Battle of Edgehill, Cowley maintains the relatively objective stance of a moderate and patriotic Engishman, sadly chronicling the progress of the rebellion and infusing a grim note of foreboding into echoes from literature associated with an earlier phase of the conflict – Denham's observation (in his mocking appeal 'To the Five Members') that those who condemn set forms of liturgy have no qualms about encouraging set forms of petition and Cleveland's advice to let the blood of Strafford 'lie / Speechlesse still, and never crie':

> O Happy we! if nether *men* would heare
> Their studied *formes* nor *God* their sudden *Prayer*! . . .
> They call for *blood* which now I feare do's call,
> For *bloud* againe much louder then them all.

But the blood shed at Edgehill – and the failure of that first major clash to bring the war to a swift conclusion – shocks the speaker into the realization that even poets can no longer stand on the sidelines lamenting the 'Sixteene Yeeres' of 'our Happinesse' and deploring the ingratitude and folly of a nation bent on self-destruction: 'This was the day, this the first day that show'd, / How much to *Charles* for our long *peace* we ow'd'. At the centre of a masque-like vision of allegorical figures embodying the values of the armies drawn up against each other at Edgehill – '*Angells*' and '*Fiends*', '*Religion*' and '*Schisme*', '*Loyalty*' and '*Sedition*', '*Learning*' and '*Ignorance*', '*Mercy*' and '*Oppression*', '*Justice*' and '*Rapine* and *Murther*' – is the antagonism, crucial to the humanist man of letters, between 'white *Truth*', clad in the armour of '*Nakednesse*', and '*Lies*' that 'flew thicke like *Cannons* smoaky *Clowd*'. As a refugee from Cambridge – who later entreats Oxford to 'Thinke on thy *Sister*, and shed then a *Teare*' – Cowley accepts the role which history has reserved for men of his kind and vocation:

> Here *Learning* and th'Arts met; as much they fear'd,
> As when the *Huns* of old and *Goths* appear'd.
> What should they doe? unapt themselves to fight,
> They promised noble pens the Acts to write.

A variety of generic weapons will be needed to perform the twofold duty imposed upon those who enlist in this army of scholar-poets: to 'write' the 'Acts' of those engaged in the literal warfare – an essentially com-memorative and celebratory function, calling upon the resources of epic and elegy that had been tried out in the recent volumes dedicated to the Queen and Sir Bevill Grenvile; and the defence of civilization itself against the new barbarians, requiring a direct engagement with those who wield their pens ignobly in the service of anarchy and ignorance. But whether he is describing the heroic exploits of the Cornish army led by 'matchlesse *Hopton*' or mocking the London newsbooks which 'mus-terd up new *Troopes* of fruitlesse *Lies*', Cowley takes up a more aggressive stance after Edgehill. His voice is no longer that of the troubled English-man who – in the early stages of the conflict – could not bear the thought of rejoicing at victory over his fellow countrymen. The plural pronouns assume a new exclusiveness as the poet's language begins to enact and reinforce the divisions within his society: 'If not all this your stubborne hearts can fright, / Thinke on the *West*, thinke on the *Cornish* might'; 'Wee scorn'd their *Thunder*, and the reeking *Blade* / A thicker Smoake then all their *Canon* made'; 'On *Roundway Downe*, our rage for thy great fall, / Whet all our Spirits, and made us *Greenvills* all'. And narrative, even of this partisan kind, gives way to open polemic as the guardian of royalist 'truth' against parliamentary 'propaganda' spurns the writers enlisted on the other side: 'Goe now, your silly Calumnies repeate, / And make all *Papists* whom yee cannot beat.'

In a closing paragraph of direct address, which catches the mood of early August, Cowley challenges the rebels to justify their refusal to consider terms of peace:

> Why will ye die, fond men! why would ye buy
> At this deare Rate your *Countries slavery*?
> Is't *liberty*? what are those threats we heare
> From the base rout? can *liberty* be there? . . .
> Or is't *Religion*? what then meane your *Lies*,
> Your *Sacriledge* and pulpit *Blasphemies*?

Turning to the '*Powers* above', he prays that the three persons of the Trinity will 'allay' the madness that has befallen the nation, 'restore to us our sight' and stay 'the restlesse *Sword*'; but that more conciliatory note is drowned out as the poet joins his voice to the chorus of triumphant royalism that had been issuing from Oxford during the high summer of 1643:

> But if that still their stubborne *Hearts* they fence,
> With new *Earth-workes* and shut thee out from thence,
> Goe on, great *God*, and fight as thou has fought.
> Teach them, or let the *world* by them be taught.[76]

Loxley claims that by setting up 'a mythic framework borrowed from the *Aeneid* and other classical exemplars', Cowley was seeking to establish a distance between the 'form' and the 'subject' of his poem 'which is far removed from the mustered verses of the Oxford polemicists'; and MacLean argues that only after the defeat at Newbury, 'where the royalist party lost control of historical forces', did 'the crown's poet' make a personal appearance in his poem, 'self-consciously confessing that he himself is as much part of the continuing process of history as the events he describes'.[77] But however true this may be of Books 2 and 3, the foregoing analysis has shown that the poem Cowley completed in late July or early August 1643 was consistently focused on the polemical needs of the moment, which it served by revealing how cultured and peace-loving patriots like himself had been drawn by 'the continuing process of history' into active support for armed royalism as their own most cherished values came under increasing threat.

The opening description of Civil War signals the generic change which is effected in Book 2:

> Thus like a *Deluge War* came roaring forth,
> The bending *West* orewhelm'd, and riseing *North*.
> A *Deluge* there; and high red *Tides* the while
> Oreflowd all parts of *Albions* bleeding *Ile*.
> For dire *Alecto*, ris'en from *Stygian* strand,
> Had scatterd *Strife* and *Armes* through all the Land.

At the start of the previous book, it was '*England*' that was torn apart by 'rage', and '*English* Ground' that was soaked by 'young mens blood'. Here, an impersonal narrative voice replaces the urgency of the present tenses and imperatives that frame 'Book 1' and the contemporary is elevated to epic status by the use of extended simile, by transforming England into '*Albions* bleeding *Ile*', and by introducing a classical Fury to preside over the Battle of Hopton Heath and the death of the Earl of Northampton. In the account of the campaigns that followed through the spring and summer, 'Old *Bremigham*' becomes 'black *Vulcans* noysy *Towne*', where 'great *Rupert*' brings about the downfall of 'the barbarous *Cyclops* sooty race'; Charles Cavendish, a young royalist commander who was killed at the siege of Gainsborough, is said to have '*Hector* in his *Hands*, and *Paris* in his *Face*'; 'avenging *Angells*' drive '*Clowds* of pale

Diseases' into the quarters of the '*Essexian Army*' after the loss of Reading; and the capitulation of Exeter to Prince Maurice prompts a long digression on the history of this 'strong, and factious Towne' since its founding by '*Troyes* fatall seed'. This general epic colouring is accompanied by a glorification of the heroic royalist dead, especially the many Cornishmen who lost their lives during the assault on Bristol: 'They joy to *kill* their foes, they joy to *Dy*; / In the deepe *Trenches proud* and *gasping ly*.'

The first half of Book 2, in which Cowley makes his most determined effort at honouring the promise to 'write' the 'Acts' of those who fought for the King, comes to a jubilant climax:

> Th'Imperiall Hoast before proud *Gloc'ester* lay;
> From all parts *Conquest* did her beames display.
> *Feare, Sadnesse, Guilt, Despaire* at *London* meete;
> And in black Smoakes fly thick through ev'ery Street.
> Their best Townes lost, noe Army left to fight!
> *Charles strong* in *Power, invincible* in *Right!*

But even as he records this high noon in the military fortunes of royalism, he knows that events have outstripped the telling; Gloucester has been relieved and the 'sadder *Vict'ry*' of Newbury awaits his pen. The missed opportunity of August 1643, when London lay exposed to victorious armies in the west and north, marks the conscious turning-point of Cowley's projected celebration of the military triumph of Charles I: 'If hee march up, what shall theise wretches doe? / They're trowbled all; and Hell was troubled too'. In the second half of the book, he falls back on the supernatural machinery of epic to explain the recovery of a demoralised foe.

The initial description of an underworld, where 'Lucifer, the mighty Captive reignes', is general enough to be incorporated later into Cowley's biblical epic, *Davideis*. But as he proceeds, the convention is adapted to his current polemical purpose. In this Hell, 'proud Rebellion' is the sin which the fiends 'Love in man, and punish most' and the figure of Rebellion herself – a monster 'with double Face', who 'oft made zealous prayers' with one 'false mouth' and 'curst anoynted Kings' with the other – superintends the endless torments inflicted upon 'an Hoast of plague-strooke Rebells'. These range from Korah, Shimei and Zimri in the Old Testament to the 'thowsand stubborne Barons' who compelled King John to sign Magna Carta and the 'Kets, and Cades, and Tylers' who have led popular insurrections in England. It is at 'a dreadfull Parlament' called by 'the Stygian Tyrant' that the turning of the tide of history is planned. Lucifer chides the assembled devils for 'Suff'ering a Cause soe'unjust to thrive so ill' and despatches them 'to Luds seditious Towne' to put new heart into 'the men who our high bus'ines sway, / Saint-Johns, the Vanes, Kimbolton, Pym, and Say' and rouse 'their Preists' to 'Pray longer, and preach lowder then before'. As Book 2 draws to a close, unwilling or unable to attribute the coming reversal of fortune to mistakes in the King's Council of War, Cowley permits the fiends of epic convention to profit from the caprice of the deity so confidently invoked in expectation of an imminent royalist victory at the end of 'Book 1':

> There's nothing now your great designe to stay,
> God, and his troubl'esome Spir'its are gonne away.
> I heard the voyce, I heard it bid them goe;
> 'Twas a good sound! they left Jerus'alem soe!

The first part of Book 3 describes the effects that 'the Furies' have on the population of London, as they poison the Will, wound the Reason, deface all 'ornaments of Nature, Art, or Grace', and unchain the 'rebell Passions'. With 'Thowsand rich Slanders, thowsand usefull Lies' rising in their brains 'like thick fumes', the leaders of the rebellion hurry to Westminster, and 'fondly there, / Talke, plot, conspire, vote, cov'enant, and declare'. The 'base Mechanicks' take to the streets, crying 'Noe peace', and citizens flock to contribute money or to enlist in the force raised for the relief of Gloucester. In a roll-call of the 'loathsome Haeresies that sent / An Army forth for their deare Parlament' – 'hot-brained Calvinists', Independents, 'Christian Monsters' spawned by the Anabaptists of Munster, Brownists, Adamites, with 'hundred more ill Names of Puritans' – Cowley matches Cleveland's perplexed fury at the unnatural horror of the 'Mixt Assembly' and throws out in passing the ominous comment that 'Who take such helpes might well bring in the Scot'. Glossing over the boldness with which the plan to save Gloucester for Parliament was conceived and executed, the poet has Essex hastening 'homewards' in fear of an encounter with the 'matchlesse King' who abandoned his siege-works 'to meet this wicked rout' in the open field. He makes the most of a skirmish at Aldbourne Chase, where 'valiant Jermin' commanded the Queen's Regiment and, following epic precedent, prefaces the major battle at Newbury with a stirring speech, in which Charles reminds his officers that they 'fight things well establisht to defend' and that their 'births' command them 'to orecome or dy'. The academic poet, who had shown little empathy with those whose *Valour* is the onely *Art* they know' when Lord Falk-

land's participation in the First Bishops' War had first filled him with
unease, bends his own art of words once more to the epic task of
recording the 'dreadfull bus'ines' of warriors in the heat of battle:

> Through dust and Smoake (that Dayes untimely Night)
> The Powders nimble Flames, and restlesse light
> Of glitt'ering Swords, amaze and fright the Eyes;
> Soe through black Stormes the winged Lightning flies.

But when a decisive victory is denied to the King's forces by the
intervention of 'the Furies' – "Twas strange; but yet just Heav'en did soe
dispose' – he descends to mockery of the 'Low, wretched Names, unfit
for noble Verse' of weavers, butchers, dyers, tanners and tailors among
the parliamentary dead.

Elegy succeeds to epic and satire when he comes to the list of
casualties on the royalist side: Colonels Feilding and Morgan, the
twenty-three-year-old Earl of Sunderland, the Earl of Carnarvon, veteran of Edgehill, Lansdown and Roundway Down. The poet's fluent
pen falters, however, when the news of another death reaches him:

> A Muse stood by mee, and just then I writ
> My Kings great acts in Verses not unfit.
> The trowbled Muse fell shapelesse into aire,
> Instead of Inck dropt from my Pen a Teare.
> O 'tis a deadly Truth! Falkland is slaine;
> His noble blood all dyes th'accursed plaine.

The conscientious exercise of public elegy is infused with a more
personal grief at the extinction of the man who had always carried
symbolic significance for Cowley and with whom he had contracted an
'entire friendship . . . by the agreement of their Learning and Manners'
during his months in Oxford.[78] And in the poem's 'most extraordinarily
charged moment', the ambitious and doomed enterprise dissolves into
'an effusive mourning which values the dead man more highly than the
continued pursuit of the King's grand design as that is manifested in the
poem's epic pattern'.[79]

Cowley had always worked against the grain in his dutiful celebration
of the 'Acts' of the sword, being drawn by temperament to the ideals of
civilized learning fostered at Great Tew during the 1630s. The senseless
sacrifice of Falkland, who had been deeply depressed by the failure of all
attempts to negotiate a peace and was said to have deliberately exposed
himself to danger in battle,[80] shocked the Cambridge poet into a revul-
sion against further bloodshed for a cause that God seemed to be
deserting. The closing lines of Book 3, in which the plural pronouns

expand once again to embrace the entire Engish nation, were his last
reflections on the contemporary political scene before going into exile
some time in 1644:[81]

> If this red warre last still, it will not leave,
> Enough behind great Falklands death to grieve;
> Wee have offended much, but there has binne
> Whole Hecatombs oft slaughterd for our Sinne.
> Thinke on our sufferings, and sheath then againe;
> Our Sinnes are great, but Falkland too is slaine.

CHAPTER 8

Declining fortunes: from Newbury to Marston Moor
September 1643 – June 1644

The long and bloody Battle of Newbury, which began soon after dawn and came to a desultory close when darkness fell, was technically a defeat for the King, since his withdrawal from the field left the road clear for Essex to continue his march to London on the following day. As one would expect, however, the presses on either side offered contradictory interpretations to the public. *A True Relation of the Late Battell neare Newbery* (London, [27 September] 1643) advertized on its title-page 'the happy successe of his Excellencies Forces against the Cavaliers' and *A True and Impartiall Relation of the Battaile betwixt, His Maiesties Army, and that of the Rebells neare Newbery in Berkshire* (Oxford, 29 September 1643) argued that while the battle proper was evidence of 'God's blessing upon the justice of His Majesties Armies' and 'may well be counted in it selfe a happy successe', the subsequent skirmishes which sent 'the Rebells back with so much terror, to their nest (*London*) may well bee reputed a great victory' (sig. A4ᵛ). *Mercurius Aulicus* claimed that the King had early on beaten the enemy from an advantageous position on high ground 'in despight of all the Rebels planted Cannons, Foot and Horse' (Week 38, 20 September, p. 527), but in view of the eventual stalemate could only cite the abandonment of 'many barrels of Musket and Pistoll Bullets, and very many Chirurgions Chests full of Medicaments' as 'a further evident Argument of the victory His Majesties Army obtained over the Rebels' (p. 530) and make the most of Rupert's harrying of the rearguard of Essex's army as it pushed on towards Reading. *Mercurius Britanicus* was quick to capitalize on the discomfiture of 'Master *Aulicus*', remarking shrewdly that 'he hath lost his wit, or our last victory hath frighted him out of it, for never came newes so simply into the world from *Oxford* as this weeke, not so much as a *sparkle* of wit' (No. 6, 26 September – 3 October, p. 41).

The individual loss which was of such overwhelming significance to Cowley made less impact upon the writers of the Oxford newsbook, who had little sympathy with Falkland's conciliatory temper and religious tolerance. It was merely reported from Newbury that the 'noble and learned Lord, the L. Viscount *Falkland*' had been 'most unfortunately slaine there, with some other worthy Gentlemen who were also hurt' (Week 38, 20 September, p. 529). Politically, his death and replacement as Secretary of State by Lord Digby strengthened the war party in Oxford, which had been growing in influence since Henrietta Maria's return to court in July so that 'the only civilians admitted to royal councils of war seem to have been Digby and Culpepper, both of whom lined up alongside the military commanders favouring hardline policies'.[1]

If the decision to invest Gloucester before marching on London proved to be the most fatal error in royalist strategy during the autumn of 1643, another important opportunity was lost in Lincolnshire when Newcastle failed to support a rising against Parliament in King's Lynn because his troops were tied up in a fruitless attempt to reduce Hull. This gave the Earl of Manchester time to organize the defence of the counties in the Eastern Association and on 11 October he and Oliver Cromwell got the better of a royalist force from Newark at the Battle of Winceby. On the following day, Newcastle was compelled to raise the siege of Hull after Sir John Meldrum had driven his men from some of their trenches, which were then flooded by a high tide. Parliament's resurgence in the East Midlands and East Anglia continued steadily through October.

The general mood of despondency in Oxford was not lifted by the onset of the 'camp disease' that had afflicted Essex's troops during the summer. Between October and early December, it claimed the lives of, among others, Dudley Digges, and – probably on 29 November – the city's most celebrated poet, William Cartwright. Charles I himself wore black on the day that the Christ Church poet died and was said to have 'dropt a teare at the newes of his death'.[2] In what was presumably his last poem, 'November or, Signal Dayes Observ'd in that Month in relation to the Crown and Royal Family',[3] Cartwright had compiled a Stuart calendar of festival days to light up the month which begins with the liturgical feasts of All Saints and All Souls. The first to be revealed, as in a masque or pageant, is the ill-starred 3 November, anniversary of the assembling of the Long Parliament, which must be anathematized before the celebration of the true Signal Days can proceed: ''Tis the *Third* Day; throw in the Blackest Stone, / Mark it for Curs'd, and let it stand Alone'. 4 November marks the birth in 1632 of Princess Mary, whose alliance as an 'Early Bride' with the House of Orange 'spreads our Glories to another State'; the delivery of James I and his Parliament from the Gunpowder Plot on 5 November prompts a comparison of the destructive 'Zeale' of the Catholic conspirators 'in the Vault' with the ambitious 'Zeale' of the traitors now 'in the chayre' at Westminster, all of whom deserve to have their severed heads on public display; 12 November calls up images of Rupert's sacking of Brentford in the first autumn of the war, falsely branded royal 'Treachery' by the 'Traytor' foe; Henrietta Maria's birthday on 16 November is cause for rejoicing that this 'Most Fruitful Queene' has crossed the seas three times, 'to raise a strength of Princes first, and then / To raise Another strength of Men'; the Accession Day of Elizabeth I on 17 November elicits nostalgia for the 'Comely Order' in the fabric of Church and State, which 'now by Facion [']s torn'; and finally, on 19 November, a prayer is offered on behalf of the subjects of the 'Sonne of the Peaceful *James*' that his own birthday may 'flow to Him as void of Care, / As Feasts to Gods, and Poets are'. Cartwright ends this last of his many poetic tributes to the Stuart family with the typically witty and partisan reflection that the first of the signal days in this month of anniversaries is best remembered by 'Loyall Hearts' in conjunction with the last: 'That gave us *Many Tyrants*, This a KING'.

The focus of military activity during Cartwright's month of red-letter days had switched to the south-west, where the besieged parliamentary outpost of Plymouth repulsed an assault by Prince Maurice on 16 November, and the south-east, where Sir William Waller twice failed to take Basing House, the fortified seat of the Marquis of Winchester which commanded the road between London and Salisbury. As the head of a newly created South-Eastern Association, Waller's chief preoccupation was with the manoeuvres of Hopton's army, which had now reached Hampshire in its slow advance eastwards. By 9 December, Hopton had got as far as Arundel, but his capture of the castle there was to mark the limit of his progress. His campaign to secure the southern approaches to London received a serious setback when Waller took the garrison at Alton by surprise on 13 December and by early January both Chichester and Arundel itself had fallen to the parliamentary general. Meanwhile, having made another vain attempt to break the resistance of Plymouth, Maurice had raised the siege on 22 December.

More significant in the long run, however, were developments in Charles's other kingdoms. On 15 September, the negotiations which the Marquis of Ormond had been secretly conducting with the Confeder-

ation of Kilkenny culminated in a one-year truce between the King and
the Catholic rebels, designed primarily on the part of Charles to release
troops for service in England. Ten days later, members of the House of
Commons and the Assembly of Divines signed a Solemn League and
Covenant with commissioners from Scotland by which the two nations
undertook to preserve the Scottish Church, purify the religion of England and Ireland 'according to the Word of God and the example of the
best reformed Churches', and protect 'the rights and liberties of parliaments'.[4] With the benefit of hindsight, it can be seen that 'only the
failure of the Royalists to exploit their success in the summer had saved
Parliament from defeat', and that the signing of the Solemn League and
Covenant was a decisive moment, which constituted the 'crowning
achievement' of John Pym's career.[5] When Pym succumbed to cancer of
the bowel on 8 December, he 'had taken the measures, financial,
military and parliamentary, which made victory possible'; it was left to
his successors in the leadership of the Commons – Oliver St John, the
younger Henry Vane, who had taken a prominent part in drafting the
Covenant with the Scots and Oliver Cromwell – to ensure that victory
would become a reality.[6]

    In one of the more distasteful episodes of the war of words, the nature
of Pym's disease and the state of his corpse became a matter of conten-
tion between the rival capitals. With an air of mock gravity, *Mercurius
Aulicus* gave notice of the statesman's failing health:

This morning heavy tydings came to Court ... of the lamentable estate of *John
Pym* the sonne of *Agnes*, principall *Member* of the *Foure*, who hath spent him selfe
so much to prevent *Obstructions* in the body Politick, that he hath altogether
neglected his owne health: For by his exceeding temperance and strict diet
(which made him languish and still looke thin) he hath contracted the *Dropsie*,
the *Jaundyes*, and *Pthyriasis*. (Week 46, 17 November, p. 661)

Communicating 'the remarkable newes of *John Pym's* death' three weeks
later, the Oxford writer could not conceal his glee that 'this, I cannot say
famous, but notorious man' had 'died this very day, chiefly of the
Herodian visitation [a morbid condition in which the body is infested
with lice], so as he was certainly a most loathsome and foule carkasse'
(Week 49, 9 December, p. 703). As a parting shot, Aulicus concluded his
customary listing of the lies purveyed by the London newsbooks over the
past seven days with the observation that 'All these are as true, as that
John Pym died an honest man' (p. 705). *Mercurius Britanicus* was filled with
contempt for 'the *lies*, and follies, and Calumnies' of '*Berkenhead* the
Scribe, Secretary *Nicholas* the Informer, *George Digby* the contriver (No.

16, 7–14 December, p. 121). And even the more sober author of what appears to be an official obituary was at pains to scotch the slanders of the Oxford press, insisting that when this 'godly' and 'holy' man went to his eternal reward 'in heaven', he 'left us a clear and faire corps (though malignants would have raised a rumour to the contrary)'.[7] At the end of the month, after a solemn funeral in Westminster Abbey at which Stephen Marshall preached, it was deemed necessary to publish the details of an autopsy in order to lay to rest 'divers uncertaine reports and false suggestions spread abroad, touching the disease and death' of the parliamentary leader.[8] John Taylor could not resist giving a more literary turn to the denigration of Pym's memory by concluding his annotations of the sixteenth number of *Mercurius Britanicus* with a wry glance at the adulatory funeral sermon given by a leading member of the Wesminster Assembly and a sneer at an instance of defective metre in the elegy printed at the end of the London newsbook:

and so I leave my pretty *Wit-Harmaphrodite* made up of Orator and Poet, *to Sacrifice his Elegy at the Hearse of John Pym*. But Sir before you goe to your devotions, you must tell me whether he was Canonized by the *New Assembly* ... or Pope *Marshall*. ... And so having cost my Reader halfe an hower, and my selfe an afternoone (my little City Poet) I leave you as I found you, fit only to write Verses on the Death of M[r] PYM.[9]

While St John did his best to continue the policies of Pym and Hampden, Pym's death 'marked the end of effective moderate leadership' at Westminster; and Pym's final achievement, the terms of the military alliance with the Scots that had been sealed in Edinburgh on 23 November, ensured 'that the war would enter a new phase in the coming months'.[10] Indeed, as Wedgwood points out, the character of what had hitherto been an exclusively English contest was changed by the intrusion of 'the politics of Ireland and of Scotland', which would 'divert the course, alter the objectives, and prolong the duration of the war'.[11] Detachments of seasoned government troops from Ireland, at first mostly Protestants of English descent, had begun to arrive during the autumn through Chester and ports on the Bristol Channel, and by March 1644 more than 17,000 of these auxiliaries had been deployed in various theatres of war. Some went to strengthen Hopton's army in Hampshire; some garrisoned towns in the midlands and Dorset; but the largest numbers came initially under the command of Lord Byron in Cheshire and North Wales and eventually provided the nucleus of an army raised by Rupert for a campaign in Lancashire and Yorkshire. Byron had been despatched to North Wales to counter the threat of Sir

William Brereton, who had seized Wrexham in November as a base for harrassing newly arrived troops from Ireland. After a skirmish near Middlewich on Boxing Day, Brereton retreated into Nantwich where he came under siege early in the new year.

Apprehensiveness about the imminent intervention of the Scots was mounting in many quarters. Nicholas wrote from court on 6 November to inform Prince Rupert of the King's concern over the defensive arrangements in the north, where 'my Lord of Newcastle's army' would be 'put in very great straits' if the Scots were to 'come in' before the royalist hold on Lancashire had been strengthened.[12] At about the same time, the poet and dramatist James Shirley, who was serving with the northern army, gave voice to a common perception of the crucial role allotted to his commander in hailing him as 'great Preserver of the King'.[13] From the different viewpoint of an undeclared royalist sympathiser living in London, John Greene confided his secret hopes and fears to his diary in December:

About the beginning of this month the King grow strong about Sussex and Hampshire. Wee conceive his designe is for Kent, and 'tis feared suddenly for London before the Scots come in, especially if he can prevayle to goe into Kent.[14]

As well as preparing to meet the challenge of a Scottish army under the Earl of Leven, which finally crossed the Tweed on 19 January 1644, Charles and Digby were actively encouraging the revival of a scheme by the Earls of Montrose and Antrim to rally the Macdonalds of Ireland and Scotland in support of a royalist rising against Argyll and the Covenant. Montrose had displaced Hamilton as the King's trusted adviser on affairs north of the border and on 1 February was commissioned as lieutenant general of the royal forces in Scotland.

The most famous literary response to the incursion of a Scottish army upon English soil for the second time in recent years was 'The Rebell Scot', the poem which has been singled out as the poet's 'major statement in defense of the cavalier world'.[15] Announcing that 'A Poet should be fear'd / When angry' and reaching after an image powerful enough to quench his 'rage' and do justice to his loathing of the Scots, Cleveland likens the body of England to the infested corpse of the man who was responsible for this new 'bondage' to 'a Land that truckles under us' [i.e. is subordinate by nature]:

> And where's the Stoick can his wrath appease
> To see his Countrey sicke of *Pym's* disease;
> By Scotch Invasion to be made a prey
> To such Pig-wiggin *Myrmidons* [hired ruffians] as they?

Unable to summon up 'mouth-Granadoes' that are explosive enough to 'expresse a *Scot*', he invokes the 'keen *Iambicks*' of satire as the only artistic medium adequate to the task he has set himself. But no sooner has he whet his pen to 'scratch til the blood come' than he has to remind himself that the 'wildernesse' beyond the Tweed is not completely forsaken by God: 'A Land that brings in question and suspense / Gods omnipresence, but that CHARLES came thence.' Nevertheless, Scotland is a place fit only for exile – 'Had *Cain* been *Scot*, God would have chang'd his doome, / Not forc'd him wander, but confin'd him home'. Having pointedly reminded the King that 'tis steel must tame / The stubborn *Scot*', the poet expends his final shafts of wit and indignation on the religious hypocrisy of 'the Brethren', with their rallying cries of 'the Cause! the Cause!' and 'the Fundamentall Lawes!'

Whereas the Cambridge intellectual had deliberately tuned his satiric instrument to a pitch of 'almost total rage'[16] for his denunciation of the barbarous mercenaries from the north, James Howell adopted a much more sober tone in his defence of the King's readiness to employ reinforcements from across the Irish Sea. He assures 'the wel-temperd READER' that his title – *Mercurius Hibernicus* (printed in Bristol in 1644) – implies no acquaintance, '*much lesse any* Kinred', with the '*mongrell race of* Mercuries *lately sprung up*'. Confident that he will '*be longer liv'd*' than '*those* Ephemeron *creatures*' that '*have commonly but one weeke time for their conception and birth*', he brags that '*there was more time and matter went to my Generation*' (sig. A2ʳ). His stated purpose is to justify the 'late suspension of Arms' in Ireland and 'to make it appeare to any rationall ingenious capacity, (not pre-occupied or purblinded with passion) that there was more of honour and necessity, more of prudence and piety in the said Cessation, than there was either in the *Pacification* or *Peace* that was made with the Scot' (p. 3). But although he carefully traces the origins of the Irish insurrection to the protest against the new Prayer Book in Scotland and the ill-treatment of Catholics in England, the immediate political agenda of his scholarly 'discourse' becomes clear when he not only asserts that most of the troops sent over by Ormond are 'perfect and rigid Protestants' but also defends the enlistment of Papists in the King's 'just cause' (p. 23). And the air of historical objectivity which he strives to establish in his quest for the 'true causes' of the rebellion deserts him when he contemplates recent challenges to his traditional sense of propriety: 'For the World is come now to that passe, that the Foot must judge the Head, the very *Cobler* must pry into the Cabinet Counsels of his *King*; nay, the *Distaffe* is ready ever and anon to arraigne the *Scepter*' (pp. 2–3). So topsy-turvy is the state of affairs in England that any

proposal bearing 'the stamp of royall Authority' will be either 'counter-
manded, cryed down, and stifled' or 'calumniated and aspersed with
obloquies, false glosses and misprisions' (p. 27).

On the political front, important manoeuvres by each side were reported in the Oxford newsbook just before Christmas. Some months
earlier, Parliament had ordered the design of a new Great Seal, the
highest symbol of legislative power in the land, since the original had
been lost to Westminster when Lord Keeper Littleton took it with him to
York. During November, the Houses had determined to assert their
complete independence of the crown's authority by entrusting it to six
commissioners. Now, in the words of the indignant writer of *Mercurius
Aulicus*, they had committed 'thir last act of insolency against His Sacred
Majestie, by putting in execution their forged *Great Seale*' (Week 51, 22
December 1643, p. 728). On the very same page, there was another
piece of 'Newes' which required the 'best notice' of the loyal reader and
brought to fruition the scheme adumbrated by the King on 20 June:
'and it is of His Majesties most gracious *Proclamation for the Assembling the
Members of both Houses at* Oxford.'

   The gathering of 44 Lords and 118 members of the Commons in
Christ Church Hall on 22 January 1644 has been seen as 'a considerable
achievement on Hyde's part', but although the Oxford Parliament
reflected moderate opinion by voting that the Scots had violated the Act
of Pacification and by appealing to the Earl of Essex in an open letter
dated 27 January, it failed to entice members of the peace party away
from Westminster.[17] And even while Hyde was nursing a hope that the
meeting of a parliament in Oxford might strengthen his hand against
the war party there, his sovereign was once more engaged in plots to
provoke a rising in the City, this time by exploiting disaffection among
the Trained Bands and disagreements between Independents and Presbyterians in the Assembly of Divines. Like earlier royalist conspiracies in
the capital, this was betrayed from within and St John's revelation of the
plotters' activities on 6 and 26 January helped to stiffen the resolve of
members in London against both the efforts of their Oxford rivals to
engage Essex as an intermediary and a later approach by the King
himself on 3 March, which proposed that the 'Lords and Commons of
Parliament assembled at Westminster' and the 'Lords and Commons of
Parliament assembled at Oxford' should each appoint commissioners to
devise a way for 'all the members of both Houses' to 'securely meet in a
full and free convention'.[18] Enclosing a printed copy of the King's letter

on 13 March, Sir Thomas Knyvett reported from London to his wife in Norfolk that the 'wisdome of the Parlam^t heer have taken much exceptions against it, to the great greefe of those that wish & pray for Peace' and commented wryly that the main objection was thought to be 'the putting of the members of both housses of Parlam^t assembled at Oxford in equall ballance of title & dignity with the unquestionable parlam^t heer'.[19] On 2 March, Secretary Nicholas informed an unnamed correspondent that the Oxford members 'have sent several messages to London for a Treaty for an accommodation, but have been still refused, whereupon the Londoners say that at Oxford sit the Parliament for Peace and at Westminster the Parliament for War'.[20] The formal rejection of a 'full and free convention of Parliament' on 9 March resulted in a vote three days later by the Oxford members that those who continued to sit at Westminster were guilty of high treason for raising an army under the Earl of Essex, counterfeiting the Great Seal and bringing in the Scots 'in a warlike manner'.[21] The royalist press was quick to capitalize on the manifest reluctance of the London politicians to respond to overtures from Oxford. In spite of its antipathy to the policies of Hyde and its generally 'sparse coverage of the Oxford Parliament',[22] *Mercurius Aulicus* played upon popular dismay that 'the remnant at *Westminster* should delight to sit voting, when all the Kingdome is involved in bloud, and should like it so well, that they'll hang up any that but thinkes of *Peace*' (Week 7, 11 February 1644, p. 827); and the Oxford members themselves exploited the propaganda value of their stance as 'the Parliament for Peace' in a pamphlet issued on 19 March, which began with the declaration that 'We hold our Selves bound to let Our Countries know, what in discharge of Our duty to God and to them, We on Our Parts have done since our comming to *Oxford*, to prevent the further effusion of Christian blood and the desolation of this Kingdome'.[23] In the long run, however, an assembly which was 'essentially the creation of royalist moderates' had little realistic hope of controlling the King or curbing the power of the war faction at court, and by the time it was prorogued for the summer on 16 April it had already 'outlived its usefulness in the eyes of many royalists'.[24]

In the days before the Oxford Parliament assembled, two posthumous contributions to the constitutional debate sparked by Parker's *Observations* found their way belatedly into print. *The Unlawfulnesse of Subjects taking up Armes against their Soveraigne* (Oxford, [15 January] 1644) was the most substantial of Dudley Digges's treatises, written in the aftermath of

the abortive peace negotiations in the first half of 1643. Digges, a victim
of the 'camp disease' on 1 October, was dismissed as 'essentially a
partisan journalist' by Allen, who regarded his last work as 'a sort of
compendium of Royalist argumentation'.[25] A recent historian, however,
takes it more seriously as an attempt to harness political theory to the
needs of practical politics by offering 'an ideological framework which
justified the responses of the Royalist commissioners during the Treaty
of Oxford'.[26] The author had been associated with the moderate group
at court in the composition of *An Answer to a Printed Book* (November
1642), and it may well have been under their auspices that his final work
was printed as part of a campaign to put pressure on those members of
both Houses still meeting at Westminster.

   Digges seeks to invalidate the 'two maine principles, by which the
seduced multitude hath beene tempted to catch at an empty happinesse,
and thereby have pulled upon themselves misery and destruction' (p. 2).
The first, which appeals to 'the law of Nature' to justify the casting off of
any authority which is felt to be 'inconvenient and destructive of native
freedome' (p. 2), is countered with a Hobbesian version of the origins of
'civil unitie' under 'one head' and of the duty this imposes upon a
subject people 'of not using their naturall power but onely as Law shall
require, that is, of not resisting that body in which the supreame power
is placed' (p. 4). The second principle, that killing in self-defence – even
the killing of a king – is permitted by natural law, is refuted on the
grounds that 'this native right' is forfeited once individual human beings
have 'voluntarily' made themselves 'sociable parts in one body' (p. 5)
and so obliged themselves 'not to resist publique authority' (p. 6). Digges
invokes recent experience, which is 'powerfull beyond rhetorick', to
demonstrate the evils which 'flow from this licence to resume our power
against contract' and adds that as 'reason induced men to enter into
such a Covenant... So honesty and religion strictly bind them to
preserve their faith intire, and this contract inviolable' (p. 6). In another
move reminiscent of Hobbes, he points out that the use of the term
'supreame power' in talking about government imposes 'an improper
name' and gives 'occasion for mistakes', because 'there cannot be two
powers and yet the Kingdome remaine one' (pp. 7–8). In a polemical
conclusion, Digges warns those who are currently in arms against the
constitutional and divinely sanctioned authority of Charles I, 'not for
certaine and knowne Lawes, not for a certaine and knowne Religion',
that their resistance 'is most offensive of the Subjects part, and doth
unavoidabl[y] incurre the Apostles sentence, *damnation*' (p. 170).

The second tract published posthumously at this time was *The Case of Our Affaires in Law, Religion, And Other Circumstances Briefly Examined, and Presented to the Conscience* by Sir John Spelman. A London reprint reached Thomason on 29 January but it was probably first issued in Oxford a day or two before the Parliament met. Spelman, who had been an early casualty of the 'camp disease' in July 1643, takes Prynne as his chief antagonist, and this pamphlet is placed, along with Digges's last work, in 'the post-*Observations* phase of royalist polemic' by Mendle.[27] It is evident from the opening gambit why it might have recommended itself to the King's publicists in the month between the summoning and the first sitting of the Oxford assembly:

Our State of *England* (even by the declaration of our Lawes) is a Kingdom, an Empire, a well-regulated Monarchie; the Head thereof a Supreme Head, a Soveraigne, a King whose Crown is an Imperiall Crown, the Kingdom *His* Kingdom, *His* Realm, *His* Dominion, the People *His* People, the Subject *His* Subject, not onely as they are single men, but even when being in Parliament assembled, they make the Body Representative of the whole Kingdom considered apart without the King, so that the very Parliament it self is also by our Lawes called *His* Parliament: the King alone by Law hath power to call together in Parliament that Representative Body, and at his pleasure to dissolve it. (p. 1)

Like Digges, Spelman argues that there can be no 'co-ordination nor co-equality of any Estate, Order or Degree, of the Subject with the Soveraigne' (p. 2), but although he also shares the other constitutional royalists' view that the King's power 'is not absolute' but 'regulated' by the law, he sees this restraint upon the power of English monarchs as the result not of a contract but of 'their voluntary and pious submission of their wills, till constant custome becomming a Law made that which was at first at their will, become an absolute and inevitable limitation of their power, so as that at this day no positive Law can now be made by the King, without the consent of the Peeres and of the Commons' (p. 5). Like Digges, again, he argues that once 'the frame of the State' had been fixed 'in the person of the King' by rational processes, 'then comes in Religion, and fortifies, and enforces all those bonds of duty and obedience, and that under severe menace of damnation ... abundantly set forth in the Scriptures' (p. 17). In his peroration, Spelman urges 'our great *Metropolis* of *London*' to 'deale so effectually with those that there reside in shew of Parliament, as that they bring them to yeeld to the equality of a free and legall Parliament, and so provide against future grievances, without any violation of the Rights of the Crown'; and goes on to advise 'the Citie' that, if the rebels at Westminster refuse, it should 'deliver unto the King the Heads of those opposites that rise up against Him', lest it bring upon itself the 'deplorable destruction' that God has in store (pp. 25–6). The fact that the Oxford edition of this pamphlet has appended to it *A Discoverie of London's Obstinacies and Miseries*, which has been identified as an extract from *A Letter from Mercurius Civicus to Mercurius Rusticus*,[28] strengthens the likelihood that it owes its publication at this juncture of affairs to royalist propaganda needs in the run-up to the Oxford Parliament.

A few months earlier, Henry Ferne – dubbed 'this most effective of Civil War royalist authors' by one commentator[29] – had published a lengthy and considered response to three of his opponents in the controversy over the nature of sovereignty. In *A Reply unto Several Treatises Pleading for the Armes now Taken up by Subjects in the Pretended Defence of Religion and Liberty* (Oxford, [1 November] 1643), Ferne, now a royal chaplain, produced his 'fullest examination of the issue of mixed government' by bringing the constitutional royalists' favourite weapons of reason, history and scripture to bear on *A Treatise of Monarchy* by Philip Hunton, *Scripture and Reason Pleaded for Defensive Armes* by a group of puritan ministers, and the anonymous *Fuller Answer*.[30] As conscious as Digges of the ambivalences and misprisions that abound in the theoretical discourse of the day, he insists that it 'was never my intent ... to plead for absolutenesse of Power in the King, if by absolutenesse of power be meant (as it should be) a power of Arbitrary command, but if by Absolutenesse of Power this Author means (as he doth sometimes) a Power not to be resisted or constrained by force of Armes raised by Subjects, such a power we plead for' (p. 12). He is prepared to follow Hunton in allowing 'a distinction of Monarchies', various kinds of legal government other than monarchical, and the existence of 'a Legall restraint upon the Power of the Monarch in this Kingdome', but he challenges him on the fundamental question of the source of sovereign authority, affirming by reason and scripture that 'Government is not the invention of man, but the institution of God, whereby he rules men by men, set over them in his stead' and that his 'Vicegerents' therefore derive 'their power not from the People ... but from God' (pp. 12–13). He is also anxious to close the door opened by Falkland and Culpepper in the *Answer to the xix Propositions* by carefully glossing the words that had been put forth in the King's name:

Lastly when his Majesty hath spoken of himselfe, as of one of the three Estates, he has but spoken to them in their owne phrase (for they first stiled him so) and that usually in the point of his Negative Voyce; for every Bill comes to him in the third or last place, the Lords spirituall and Temporall, who indeed are two of the three Estates, making a Concurrence in one Vote or Voice. But His Majesty did never use that phrase with any intent of diminution to his Supremacy or Headship; for properly the Prelates, Lords, and Commons, are the three Estates of this Kingdome, under his Majesty as their head. (p. 32)

He ends on a conciliatory note, with a reminder that Charles has 'offered, promised, protested' his determination to ensure 'a just Reformation of all abuses' and with a prayer that God will 'cast out all Councels, and defeat all designes, that are against the restoring of our peace, and the continuance of the true Reformed Religion' (p. 97).

These three voices from 1643 belonged to a phase of the constitutional debate that was already passing into history when they were published. Another defence of royalism appeared in print at the end of January, which had its roots in an older theory of divine right kingship and signalled the ascendancy of apologists for absolute monarchy as the military fortunes of the King began to wane. John Maxwell, formerly a Laudian bishop in Scotland and Ireland, had left Ulster in the early days of the insurrection and found a position as chaplain to the royal court in Oxford. *Sacro-Sancta Regum Majestas: Or, The Sacred and Royall Prerogative of Christian Kings* (Oxford, [30 January] 1644) was the product of his 'formidable theological erudition' and advanced a 'view of the nature of royal authority and the constraints upon it' that was 'significantly different' from that expounded by the 'constitutional royalists' who had hitherto dominated the dispute with Parker.[31] Maxwell lays out five questions at the start of his treatise, which raise the familiar issues of the origin of political power, the nature and limits of sovereignty and the lawfulness of armed resistance by a subject people, but in considering 'the maine grounds, by which the Jesuite and Puritane endeavour by no lesse spurious then specious pretexts ... to robbe Kings of their Sacred and divine Right and Prerogative' (p. 3), he has recourse to scholastic arguments drawn from Aristotle, proof texts from the Old and New Testaments, and a patriarchal theory of the derivation of royal authority from Adam, in whose 'person' the 'power of government' had been 'fixed' by the Creator 'before he had any child or subject to governe' (p. 84). As J. P. Sommerville has shown, the 'crucial equation between civil and patriarchal power was made by James I in a speech of 1610' and the argument that kings derived their right to rule from the right of fathers was developed largely in response to the Catholic theory of civil society promulgated by such writers as Bellarmine and Suarez, which placed the origin of kingly authority in the consent of the people and allowed for deposition if a king failed to abide by the legal conditions laid upon his power.[32] Maxwell's debt to this Jacobean body of theory is

evident in his identification of a twofold enemy – 'the Jesuite and the
Puritane' – and in his insistence that kings are exempt 'from *Coercion
humane*', because God alone has invested them 'with entire Soveraignty'
and God alone has 'set the bounds of it' (pp. 140, 125). The most novel
aspect of his denial that sovereignty is conveyed to the King 'by trust
immediately from the people, and mediately onely from God' is an
elaborate proof, based on the principles of Aristotelian philosophy, that
the only power inherent in the '*Community*' is '*potestas passiva regiminis*, a
capacity or susceptibility to be governed by one or by moe', and that this
capacity 'is attended with an *appetitus naturalis*, and *necessarius ad regimen*, a
naturall necessary and vehement inclination and desire to submit to
Government' (p. 91).

At about the same time that Maxwell was assembling his defence of
the divine right of kings, an even more radical version of patriarchal
kingship was being composed by a landowner in Kent who, 'virtually
alone in his party', not only 'equated absolute with arbitrary monarchy'
but also 'heartily approved of the result'.[33] Sir Robert Filmer was born in
1588 and after inheriting the family estate at East Sutton in 1629 had
become prominent in a circle that included Spelman, Sir Roger Twys-
den and Sir Edward Dering. He seems to have taken no part in the
Kentish Petition of 1642, but since the early 1630s had been privately
compiling the material that was eventually published in 1680 under the
title *Patriarcha*.[34] In the winter of 1643, he was imprisoned in Leeds Castle
on the orders of the local parliamentary Committee and over the
following months prepared a reply to Hunton's *Treatise*, which he kept
by him until 1648, when it was printed as *The Anarchy of a Limited or Mixed
Monarchy*.[35]

Maxwell and Filmer were the most scholarly and systematic but by no
means the only defenders of Charles I who ignored or played down the
legal restraints upon his power and emphasized his God-given rights.
Back in 1643, Thomas Morton had made the scriptural case for non-
resistance in *The Necessity of Christian Subjection*, in which he asserted that
monarchy, derived from Adam, was the only form of government
sanctioned by both nature and God. Gryffith Williams, Bishop of
Ossory, had also argued that absolute monarchy was grounded in the
paternal authority of Adam in *Vindiciae Regum* and *The Discovery of
Mysteries*, published in February and July respectively; and soon after the
Battle of Newbury, an anonymous author had laid out thirty-two
quotations from the Old and New Testaments to convince those with 'a
well rectifyed conscience' that it was 'godly wisdome to refrain from

taking up armes against the King'.[36] In a sermon delivered at Christ
Church on 3 March 1644 and printed a few days later, James Ussher,
Archbishop of Armagh, expounded a familiar verse – 'Let every soule
bee subject to the higher powers: for there is no power but of God'
(*Romans* 13: 1) – to demonstrate that Christian princes 'beare the Sword'
in vain 'if their subjects conscience may question their power' and to
recall any man who had taken up arms against Charles I to his divinely
ordained duty: 'Remember that he is still thy Prince, and since thy
conscience may not yeeld to his command, shew thy selfe his subject in
yeelding to his punishment.'[37]

   A much more ingenious piece of propaganda, which adapted the
simple format of an educational primer to serve the same ends as
Ussher's admonitory sermon, was *The Rebells Catechisme* (Oxford, [6
March] 1644). Peter Heylyn, its unacknowledged author, reassures 'the
Christian Subject' that he has '*contracted into a narrow compass*' the various
arguments that he has '*found scattered and diffused in many and those larger
Tractates*' (p. 1), and proceeds to uncover the origins and nature of
rebellion in a series of questions and answers: Satan was its 'first
Author' (p. 2); it comes in three kinds – 'the *Rebellion* of the *Heart*, the
Rebellion of the *Tongue*, and the *Rebellion* of the *Hand*' (p. 2); the third kind
is manifested in two ways, in 'the composing and dispersing of false and
scandalous *Books* and *Pamphlets*' (p. 5) and in '*a levying of Warre against our
Soveraigne Lord the King*' (p. 6). After these preliminary definitions, the
impersonal mode of catechism gives way to a more dramatic confrontation between the poser of the questions and the supplier of the
answers. The partisan attitude of the questioner begins to make itself
felt in stray phrases – 'as your party calls them', 'we deny not' (p. 8) –
and his questions take on a more urgent tone: 'But tell me seriously,
doe you conceive that all *resistance* of this kind made by *force of Armes*,
may be called *Rebellion*' (p. 9). On his side, the answerer dismisses the
distinction between the 'Kings *Person* and his *Power*' as mere 'folly'
(p. 20) and scornfully rejects the idea that the two Houses of Parliament
are '*co-ordinate* with him' (p. 21). Before long, the adherent to the rebel
cause is ready to be won over if the catechist can provide clear proof
'that the *Parliament* did begin the war, that on their part it was *offensive*,
not *defensive* only or that they had a purpose to destroy the King' (p. 23).
In his response, Heylyn wearily rehearses all the well-worn arguments,
breaking off with the remark that 'it were but labour lost to speake
further in it' (p. 24). More relevant to current political realities is his
answer to the question whether 'the party which remaines at *Westmin-*

ster have not the full authority of the two *houses* of *Parliament*' (p. 26).
This elicits from the wavering rebel a supplementary question in which
the royalist reply is implicit: 'then the remaining party now at *Westminster* consisting seldome of above an hundred *Commons*, and sometimes
not above *three Lords* have challenged and usurped the name of the *two
Houses*?' (p. 27). Predictably, the questioner ends up convinced 'of the
unlawfulnesse of this *warre* against his Majestie' and of the guilt of those
'who either laid the plot thereof, or have since pursued it' (p. 28). One
final question – 'what punishment the *Lawes* do inflict on those who are
convicted of so capitall and abhorred a crime?' – gives the Oxford
propagandist an opportunity to expatiate with graphic detail on the
earthly fate that awaits those whom Digges and Spelman had consigned to damnation: 'his belly to be ripped up, & his bowels to be
taken out, whilest he is yet living, his head and limbes to be advanced
on some eminent places, for a terrible example unto others' (p. 28).
Another anonymous Oxford tract, the work of John Doughty, fellow of
Merton College, warned the rebels of the 'certaine destruction' they
were drawing upon themselves by their double disobedience to God
and Charles I, 'because as by the former we offend God in his owne
person, so by the latter we injure him in the *Person* of his *Substitute* or
immediate Vicegerent here appointed over us'.[38]

While the views of 'an ultra-hard *jure divino* apologist'[39] like Doughty
were a sign of the more uncompromising royalism that was beginning to
make itself heard, two publications at the beginning of April bear
witness to the pressure of events upon the consciences of men with
moderate reformist principles, who had gone along with the early
measures of the Long Parliament but been alienated by the Root and
Branch attack upon the established church. Sir Edward Dering's resignation of his royalist commission had been reported in *The True Informer*
(No. 20, 27 January to 3 February 1644, p. 151) and another diurnal had
revelled in the news of his defection from the court at Oxford: 'Sir
Edward Deering, and Mr *Murry* of the Bedchamber, are come for London
ayre, which is (no doubt) precious to many there who intend to follow;
who know now, that their condition will be exposed to more misery in
the Papists mercy then in the justice of the true old Protestant Parliament.'[40] Dering and Murry were by no means alone in their abandonment of the royal cause during the first half of 1644. In February,
Mildmay Fane, Earl of Westmorland, compounded with Parliament
and the Earl of Holland made his way back to London; others, including

Lord Conway, were soon to follow. Like Fane, Dering was particularly troubled by the truce in Ireland and by the influence of Catholics in the King's counsels at Oxford. In an attempt to justify changing sides for the second time, he explained in print that he had felt it was his 'lawfull Duty' to answer the summons to York in 1642, but that in Oxford he had found the church overrun by 'Romish back-sliders', who were 'yet in love with those specious, pompous, loud, exteriour complements'. Although he would never give up his devotion to the person of Charles I, he now felt compelled to 'onely serve the Parliament in the new great Controversie between them'.[41] Dering was a dying man in February 1644 and may have been partly motivated by a desire to secure his sequestered estate for his widow and children, but he must also have been influenced, like other defectors, by 'a fear that the voice of reason and moderation – never very powerful at Oxford – was now in danger of being completely hushed'.[42]

Perplexity and vacillation are the keynotes of the other confessional text that appeared early in April. In *The Loyall Convert* (Oxford, [Madan 1 April] 1644), Francis Quarles describes how he stood 'amazed' at the '*Riddle*' of two opposed parties, each claiming to preserve 'the true *Protestant Religion*', '*the Liberty of the Subject*' and 'the *priviledges of Parliament*':

I turned mine eyes upon his *Majesty*; and there I viewed the *Lord's Annointed*, sworne to maintaine the established *Lawes* of this *Kingdome*: I turned mine eyes upon the two *Houses*; and in them, I beheld the *Interest* of my Countrey sworne to obey his *Majesty* as their supreme *Governour*.

I heard a *Remonstrance* cryed from the two *Houses*: I read it; I approved it; I inclined unto it; a *Declaration* from his *Majesty*; I read it; I applauded it; I adhered to the justnesse of it: The Parliament's *Answer*; I turned to the *Parliament*: His Majestie's *Reply*; I returned to his *Majesty*.

Thus tost and turned as a *Weathercock* to my own weaknesse, I resolved it impossible to serve two *Masters*.[43]

Eventually, after both reason and policy had failed to supply him with a satisfactory answer, his eye lit upon a verse in the Book of Proverbs which confirmed him in obedience to the King; and further search in the Scriptures soon furnished him 'with such strict *Precepts*, backt with such strong *Examples*', that his 'wavering *Conscience*' was 'throughly convinced'.[44] In a series of observations on the arguments that were being invoked to justify armed opposition to the Crown, Quarles reveals that his views were now close to the brand of royalism expressed by Ferne and Spelman. Towards the end of *The Loyall Convert*, theoretical discussion gives way to a defence of King Charles himself, 'a *Prince*, whom God hath crowned with graces *above his fellowes*; A *Prince*, whom,

for his Piety, few *Ages* could parallel'; and the aging poet finally rests the
case for his conversion on the 'eminent *Graces* and illustrious *Virtues*' that
heaven has bestowed on the person of England's reigning monarch and
the certainty that 'Almighty *God* . . . will not leave a work so forward, so
imperfect; but, will, from day to day, still adde and adde to his transcen-
dent *virtues*, till he appeare the Glory of the *World*; and, after many
yeares, be crowned in the World of *Glorie*.'[45] The perfecting of the
aesthetic and religious *image* that the King would leave behind when he
was finally rewarded with his crown 'in the World of *Glorie*' was to be the
work of men rather than God, however, and in the meantime his
fortunes in this world were in marked decline from the zenith of royalist
success in the summer of 1643.

During the weeks following its arrival in the north of England, the
Scottish army had made little direct impact on the progress of the war,
although its presence was always a threat. Impeded by a heavy snowfall
and flooding, Leven and Argyll found that Newcastle had been well
prepared to withstand a siege when they eventually reached it early in
February; and it was not until the weather improved towards the end of
March that they began to push southwards again. The Marquis of
Newcastle had determined to hold the line of the Tees, but a series of
parliamentary successes in his rear, including the rout of the Yorkshire
royalists at Selby on 11 April, compelled him to withdraw from Durham
into York. Before the month was out, he found himself penned in by the
combined forces of the Scots and the Fairfaxes. In spite of Rupert's
spectacular dash from Chester to Newark, where he inflicted a crushing
defeat on Sir John Meldrum on 21 March, the balance of military
domination was tipping in favour of the rebels. Sir Thomas Fairfax had
helped Brereton to raise the siege of Nantwich on 24 January, capturing
the bulk of Lord Byron's infantry from Ireland and despatching one of
their number – Colonel George Monck – as a prisoner to London; Sir
William Waller had achieved the first major parliamentary victory of
the war when he overwhelmed the army of Forth and Hopton at
Cheriton Wood near Alresford on 29 March and put an end to the
long-standing royalist strategy of advancing on London from the south;
Winchester had capitulated to Waller on the next day; and much of
South Wales had been secured for Parliament by Rowland Laugharne
in the course of March. Oxford was now vulnerable to attack and so it
was decided that the Queen should make her way to Exeter for her
approaching confinement. She and Charles parted for the last time at
Abingdon on 17 April.

Prince Maurice, given the task of reducing the last parliamentary outposts in the south-west, made several unsuccessful attempts to storm Lyme Regis, but naval support enabled the small garrison commanded by Colonel Robert Blake to hold out. With the Queen safe in Exeter and the Earl of Manchester on his way to join the two armies besieging York, it was time for Rupert to put into effect the plan of campaign agreed at a Council of War early in May. Leaving Charles to sit tight in Oxford behind its string of outlying fortresses, he headed northwards from his base at Shrewsbury on 16 May. He picked up men from Lord Byron at Chester and before the end of the month had taken Stockport and Bolton. Once he had been further reinforced by the bulk of the northern horse under Sir Charles Lucas and by Lord Goring, who had been skirmishing in Lancashire since his recent release from captivity, the Prince pressed on to achieve his first two objectives by the second week in June – the relief of the besieged stronghold of Lathom House and the seizure of Liverpool, a port through which Irish troops could be brought in. But now that his forceful nephew was at a distance, Charles listened to the advice of his other officers and withdrew the garrisons from Reading and Abingdon in order to create a more mobile force capable of taking the war to the enemy. Both towns were quickly occupied by Essex and Waller, whose armies began to encircle Oxford itself. Charles narrowly avoided falling into enemy hands whilst hunting at Woodstock and on 3 June he left the city secretly by night and set up a temporary headquarters in Worcester. Shaken by the predicament they had got themselves into, Digby and Wilmot, commander of the cavalry that had accompanied the King in his flight from Oxford, sat down with their royal master on 14 June to draft a letter in which 'the true state' of his affairs was laid before Rupert, along with some rather muddled orders about military priorities:

If York be lost I shall esteem *my crown little less*; unless supported by your sudden march to me; and a miraculous conquest in the South, before the effects of their Northern power can be found here. *But if* York be relieved, and *you beat the rebels' army* of both kingdoms, which are before it; then (but otherwise not) I may possibly make a shift (upon the defensive) to spin out time until you come to assist me. Wherefore I *command and conjure you* ... you immediately march, according to your first intention, with all your force to the relief of York.[46]

In Gardiner's view, it was only the inability of Essex and Waller to work together that saved the King from immediate disaster.[47] Instead of combining their armies to bring him to a decisive battle while Rupert was engaged elsewhere, Essex headed towards Lyme Regis and Waller remained in the midlands to follow the movements of Charles and the

Oxford cavalry. Ignoring orders from London, Essex forced Maurice to raise the siege of Lyme, occupied Weymouth, and advanced upon Exeter, where Henrietta Maria had given birth to a daughter on 16 June.

It appeared to Sir Thomas Knyvett, writing from London on 20 June, that the King of England was being 'hunted indeed like a partridg in the mountaines',[48] but in fact Charles had by now realised that he was in a position to take the initiative. Strengthened by infantry from the Oxford garrison, he played a cat-and-mouse game with Waller until 29 June, when the two forces met in a confused and inconclusive series of actions centred on the bridge over the Cherwell at Copredy. Although the battle itself was hardly a royalist victory, it demoralized Waller's army, which began to disintegrate. Moreover, its propaganda value was seized upon by the Oxford journalists as incontrovertible evidence that Parliament's repeated disclaimer about the true nature of their war aims was a sham. Since Charles had left his courtiers and political advisers behind him in Oxford, 'Sir *William* still being commanded to fight, manifests to the World that it was not the *Evill Counsellours* but the *good King* they fought against; not to rescue him from them, but to remove him from this present world'.[49]

In Yorkshire, however, Culpepper's gloomy comment on the ill-advised letter that the King had sent to Rupert without his approval – 'Why, then, before God you are undone, for upon this peremptory order he will fight whatever comes on't' – was proving to be prophetic.[50] By the end of June, the Prince had crossed the Pennines and reached Knaresborough, a mere twelve miles from York. In a vain effort to prevent him linking up with the Marquis of Newcastle, the allied generals abandoned their siege-works and drew up their armies to bar his path across Marston Moor. Rupert outwitted them by sweeping round to approach the city from the north-west and at nightfall on 1 July made camp beneath its walls. Both Newcastle and Lord Eythin, the former James King, were reluctant to commit their siege-weary soldiers to a pitched battle, but Rupert, mindful of his uncle's letter, was determined to resolve the military situation in the north as quickly as possible. The result was the Battle of Marston Moor, fought through the evening of 2 July 1644 and ending in an overwhelming victory for Parliament and its Scottish allies. The Marquis of Newcastle, who had fought bravely in the battle itself, could not face the ignominy of such a devastating defeat and took ship at Scarborough for a prolonged life of exile. Rupert, with the help of Sir Marmaduke Langdale and Lord Goring, resolutely reassembled the scattered cavalry at York, but on 15

July, soon after their departure for Lancashire, the city surrendered. Apart from a few isolated strongholds, the north was lost to the King.

Writing before the series of disasters that began at Alresford and culminated at Marston Moor, Quarles had reflected a common royalist view in his survey of the war's progress in *The Loyall Convert* – that 'the providentiall hand of God' had been 'visible' both in '*prospering*' the cause of the King and in '*punishing* his Enemies'. He cited the various fates of Hotham, Hampden, Hamilton, Holland and '*Bristoll Fines*' as evidence of judgement on the wicked, and looked for divine wrath to be visited upon Cromwell, 'that profest defacer of Churches ... whose prophane Troopers ... watered their Horses at the *Font*'. But Quarles was uncomfortably aware that charges of 'impious *barbarismes*' could be levelled at some of the King's own followers, 'whereof, no question, too great a number are as equally prophane; whilst all together make up one *body* of wickednesse, to bring a ruine on this miserable Kingdome; for whose impieties His Majestie hath so often *suffered*'.[51]

William Chillingworth, who 'did more to form Falkland's mind and to direct his reading' than any other member of the Great Tew circle,[52] had sounded the same cautionary note in a famous sermon that was printed twice in June 1644 (in Oxford, claiming that it was preached before the King at Reading, and in London, claiming that it was preached 'at a publike fast' in Christ Church College).[53] After a diatribe against the ungodliness of the age in general, he approaches 'a little nearer to the businesse of our times' in an attack on 'the cheife Actours in this bloudy Tragedy, which is now upon the Stage', and then turns his criticism upon those 'that maintain the Kings righteous cause with the hazard of their lives and fortunes, but by their oathes and curses, by their drunkennesse, and debauchery, by their irreligion and prophan-nesse, fight more powerfully against their party, then by all other meanes they do or can fight for it'. His fear is that 'the goodnesse of our cause may sinke under the burthen of our sins' and that God may 'deliver us up to the blind zeale and fury of our Enemies, or else, which I rather feare, make us instruments of his justice each against other, and of our owne just and deserved confusion'.[54] Chillingworth had been taken ill during the siege of Arundel and died in January 1644.[55] By the time his sermon was published, his warning voice had become part of a chorus of royalist preachers, including Henry Leslie, Bishop of Downe, who decried before the Oxford House of Commons 'the carriage of our Soludiers (*sic*)', whose 'godlesse behaviour' discredited 'the good cause' for which they fought; and Henry Ferne, who preached on the '*Divisions* among us' and the 'Wrath provoked by our sin', which cannot all be laid at the door of those who were guilty of 'raising or continuing' the war.[56]

The main drift of Ferne's sermon is to commend the members of the Oxford Parliament, a few days before the summer recess, for their gestures of peace 'towards those from whom wee are *divided*'; but he also feels it his duty to urge their support for further military efforts if peace cannot 'be had with the Refusers of Peace but upon unjust tearmes', in which case they must take '*Resolutions* for a necessarie Warre', since 'the Sword must sometimes make the way for Peace, and the readiest meanes to stay blood, is to strike a veine for the letting of it out' (pp. 24–5). In a sermon before the Prince of Wales, Edward Symmons took an even more aggressive stance against '*The men of Westminster*', who are not to be regarded as the 'Parliament of *England* (as some are pleased to call them;) but only that powerfull faction there abiding'.[57] His first aim, like Heylyn's in the *Catechisme*, is 'to discover out of Gods Booke the nature of Rebellion'; his second is 'to encourage from the Lord the Kings Loyall Subjects, and true hearted Souldiers in their opposing such' (p. 1). He scours the Old Testament to trace the ancestry of 'the men of Westminster' back to 'the first rebell that ever was' (p. 6) – 'Yea so diligent and industrious have they beene that they have acted Satans part, in rebelling themselves and seducing others: *Cains* part in slaying and murdering their brethren; *Cham's* part in mocking their Father, their common Father: they have acted *Achitophell's* part . . . *Absolom* and *Sheba's* part . . . *Doeg's* part . . . *Jeroboam's* part . . . *Rabsakeh's* part in railing against the Lord's Anointed, in the hearing of his Subjects, even on purpose to stirre them up to rebell against him'; and he caps his indictment with a reference to the New Testament which casts Charles I prophetically in the role that he would later come to play in royalist iconography – 'and *Judas* his part in betraying their Master' (pp. 13–14). In pursuit of his second aim, Symmons takes up the baton from Chillingworth and, in the words of Professor Aylmer, comes 'as near to what we might call grass-roots Anglican-Cavalierism as anything we can find'.[58] Declaring that the regiments assembled at Shrewsbury are as much 'Messengers to execute his will' as 'we Ministers, who are God's Messengers in another kinde', he reminds them of their reputation in the London press as 'wicked swearers' and 'vicious livers' (pp. 19–20), and puts before them the 'character' they should strive to emulate:

A Compleat Cavalier is a Child of Honour, a Gentleman well borne and bred; that loves his King for conscience sake, of a clearer countenance, and bolder looke then other men, because of a more Loyall Heart: He dares neither oppose his Princes will, nor yet disgrace his righteous cause, by his carriage or expressions: He is furnished with the qualities, of Piety, Prudence, Justice, Liberality, goodnesse, Honesty . . . in a word, He is the onely Reserve of English Gentility and ancient valour . . . This is a compleat Cavalier and if any of you be not according to this Character, believe mee you be not right, nor the men you ought to be. (pp. 22–3)

Military failures under other royalist commanders are attributed to 'neglect of praier' by their soldiers, and Symmons ends with a rousing appeal to Prince Rupert's troops not to imperil the continued success of 'this Man of men . . . this mirrour of *Europe*' (pp. 42–3). It was, perhaps, because of the notorious 'godliness' of Cromwell's troopers, who were heard singing psalms while the armies were drawn up opposite each other at Marston Moor,[59] that measures were taken to supply the King's followers with suitable printed aids to devotion in the field[60] and to inflict exemplary punishments for misdemeanours, like the hanging of 'two foot-soldiers . . . on the trees in the hedge-row, for pillaging of the country villages', recorded in mid-July by a trooper in the mounted Lifeguards, who accompanied the King when he left Oxford at the beginning of June.[61]

Alongside the spate of proofs from constitutional and divine right monarchists that it was unlawful and damnable to bear arms against the King and the urgent warnings that the rebels might be an instrument of God's wrath against the sins of the entire nation, there ran another stream of pamphlets designed to highlight the dangerous illegality of the attempt to forge a military alliance between the people of England and their northern neighbours. A royal proclamation forbade the tendering or taking of the oath late in October and *A Briefe Discourse Declaring the Impiety and Unlawfulnesse of the New Covenant with the Scots* (Oxford, [26 October] 1643) branded Parliament's new allies as foreign invaders. Further protests appeared after an ordinance was passed on 5 February requiring all Englishmen over the age of eighteen to subscribe to the terms of the document: *The Iniquity of the Late Solemne League, or Covenant Discovered* (Oxford, [Madan 8 March] 1644) interpreted it as a direct threat against the person of the King; *The Anti-Confederacie* (Oxford, [6 April] 1644) provided the public with selections from a longer work which had not yet been printed because 'our Presses here at Oxford' were 'overburdened beforehand, with some incomparable pieces, necessary for the times' (p. 24); and the author of *A Letter from a Member of the House of Commons, To a Gentleman now at London, Touching the New Solemne League and Covenant* (Oxford, [6 May] 1644) adopted a well-tried royalist genre as a vehicle for deriding any misplaced 'confidence' in 'the pretended Houses', whose members no longer behaved like 'Subjects', and consequently were 'not their King's Parliament, which they must be, or none at all' (p. 13). The oppressive tendencies of the illegal regime at Westminster were cleverly exposed by the learned response of a group of Cambridge academics to the vigorous prosecution of the Covenant throughout the university. Under a suitably dispassionate title – *Certaine Disquisitions and Considerations Representing to the Conscience the Unlawfulnesse of the Oath* (Oxford, [Thomason 17 April] 1644)[62] – John Barwick and his colleagues bound themselves in the very words employed in the administration of the Covenant to examine the document and assess whether 'all things therein be true, and withall sufficient to that end for which they were premised' (p. 2). Their scrupulous clause by clause analysis led them to conclude that, as 'Subjects of the Church of *England*', it was not lawful for them 'to assist the Scots, or consent to them in this warre, which assistance is the generall end of this Covenant' (p. 7). The Cambridge scholars who met in Barwick's rooms to conduct their subversive 'disquisitions' went their several ways before the pamphlet was published, and indeed the wholesale removal of fellows and heads of colleges who demonstrated their malignancy by refusing the Covenant was the climax of a systematic cleansing of the university by the Earl of Manchester.

In addition to the royal proclamations, the sermons by royal chaplains, the orders issued by the Oxford Parliament and the Privy Council and the various propaganda items noticed so far in this chapter, a number of other 'pieces, necessary for the times' kept the 'overburdened' presses of Leonard Lichfield and Henry Hall busy during the critical months between the battles at Cheriton and Marston Moor. *An Orderly and Plaine Narration of the Beginnings and Causes of the Warre* (Oxford, [Madan April/ May] 1644) draws upon *A Letter from Mercurius Civicus to Mercurius Rusticus* for its survey of events leading up to the outbreak of hostilities and displays all the signs of authorship by the group that produced the Oxford newsbook, especially in singling out London as 'the Nest and Seminary of the seditious faction' and in the witty sting at the end of its final sentence: 'Now whosoever go about to overthrow Policies long since established, are enemies to mankinde, and fight against God's expressed will, saith the Confession of the Church of *Scotland*.'[63]

Peter Hausted, a Cambridge scholar who had migrated to Oxford in the autumn of 1642, seems to have been the author of the lively couplets

of *Ad Populum: Or, A Lecture to the People* (Oxford, [20 May] 1644), which
are ostensibly aimed at a more popular readership than the usual run of
Oxford publications. The initial apostrophe, however, is openly contemptuous – 'Ye dull Idolators, have ye yet bent / Your Knees enough
to your Dagon Parliament?' (p. 1); and the 'patronizing tone' in which
simple countryfolk are reminded of the 'Golden dayes' before the war
convinces Lois Potter that the writer's real purpose was 'to reinforce the
views of readers considerably more sophisticated and affluent than the
ones the poem purports to be addressing'.[64] The poet shakes his head
sadly over the foolish longing 'to try which were the better Thing, / Five
hundred Tyrants, or one gentle King' (p. 2) and the lost innocence of
those whose hard-bought experience is expressed in a new postlapsarian
language:

> How much the better are ye now, I pray,
> That yee with much expence have learn'd to say
> *Quarter* for *lodging*, and can wisely well
> What *Carbine* signifies, and *Granado*, tell? ...
> Was not your Ale as browne, as fat your Beefe,
> E're Plunderer was English for a Theife? (pp. 3–4)

The freedom of the good old days, when farm labourers could go to
'the Shire Towne' twice a year to 'O'rethrow a Parson, Drink drunke,
and forsweare' themselves (p. 6) is contrasted with the sombre effects of
'Deacon *Cromwells* visitation' (p. 7), and then Hausted challenges his
rustics to 'be ingenious' in weighing their gains and losses: 'Would yee
not give the best horse in your Teame / The three yeares past were
but a fearefull Dreame?' (p. 9). He assures them that their lot can only
get worse, unless they turn back to 'God and King', exchange 'that
painted whore / Who sits at *Westminster*' for the true Parliament that
serves their interests at Oxford, and 'learn to understand' that in the
natural order of things, 'The Plow and Scepter are not for one Hand'
(pp. 15–16).

In what appears to be a more realistic attempt to influence the lower
reaches of society, an anonymous royalist compiled twenty-four pages of
extracts from works by three of the 'first Reformers of the true Protestant Religion', in the hope that 'seduced wretches' might 'see the error
of their new wayes, and returne to their old paths of duty and loyalty to
God'.[65] Underlining the economic and political practicalities of his
project, which was published in London with a counterfeit Oxford
imprint, he explains that he has confined his choice to three authorities
because 'the common sort of people' cannot afford a larger book and

because 'the poore Printers are a little to be considered in these prest oppressing times; for those few of them that are so honest and valiant, as to dare to print ought that savours of loyalty and duty to their Sovereigne are so hunted and persecuted . . . that to imploy them in ought that would long detaine them, were to betray them, and perhaps those that set them on worke'.[66]

Among the genuinely popular writers working in the two capitals, Alexander Brome echoed the bewilderment of Quarles at the 'Strange riddle' of an age in which 'both sides say they love the King' and 'Both say they wish and fight for peace; / Yet wars increase';[67] and John Taylor, although he wept when he sang 'the maddest mad Rebellion, / That ever Story told', related in jaunty verses his own eventful flight from persecution by the 'Nose-wise Scripture Picklers' in London by way of Henley and Abingdon to Oxford, where he was amply rewarded for the perils and hardships of his journey by an encounter with the King himself in Christ Church garden and the privilege of kissing 'his Royall hand'.[68] Another London writer adapted the much more literary form of the complaint by a betrayed woman – 'Oh that my Head did flow with Waters! . . . Oh that I could melt away, and dissolve into Tears, more brackish than those Seas that surround me!' – to express through the mouth of England herself the grief felt by many royalists at the prolongation of 'this unnatural self-destroying War'.[69] As in his previous pamphlets, James Howell offers his readers a European perspective on the folly of the nation that has thrown away the envied peace of the 1630s for all the horrors of a civil and religious war, a historical investigation into the origins of the conflict ('wherein some say, the Crosier, some say the Distaff was too busy'), and a socially bigoted commentary on the lamentable state of Religion in his native land – 'The Vintner and Tapster may broach what Religion they please . . . the Weaver may cast her upon what Loom he pleases . . . the Blacksmith may forge what Religion he pleases'.[70]

A few days before the climactic engagement at Marston Moor, poetic tears were being shed by Edward Walsingham over the loss at Alresford of Sir John Smith, Major General of Hopton's Western Army, who had rescued the royal standard at Edgehill and been an exemplary soldier ever since in the mould of Symmons's 'compleat Cavalier'.[71] Elegies for such men were destined to become an increasingly poignant and prominent feature of the literary output of royalists in the years that followed the disastrous spring and summer of 1644.

Throughout this phase of the war, from the first Battle of Newbury to the surrender of York, the royalist literary machine kept up a constant and varied barrage of printed words against the regime at Westminster and its Scottish allies. But its foremost vehicle, *Mercurius Aulicus*, lost some of its earlier momentum in the wake of serious military reverses and consequent problems in gathering intelligence. Thomas records that it 'began to lag behind events very early in 1644, and from then on appeared anything from a week to a month later than the dates on the title-pages suggest'.[72] Its rivals took notice of this decline and during May and June launched a concerted campaign of mockery against its dwindling size, its failure to appear on time, and its grasping at straws of encouraging news to compensate for major setbacks. *The Spie* was first with a rumour that either '*George Aulicus*, or *Berkenhead Aulicus*' was 'upon his sick Bed' (No. 17, 15–22 May, p. 129) and in its next issue went onto the offensive with all guns blazing, as Essex's army closed in on Oxford:

Every weeke *Aulicus* produces a successful sally made by the Countesse of *Derby*; which indeed is forged at *Oxford* in that fruitfull shop of falshoods, and then the starveling story is fathered upon that starveling Garrison. . . . Their ill successe of late hath made him and the whole *Cavalrie* heart-sicke of Malignancy, and now since my Lord Generalls advance, the Pulse of *Aulicus* his braines beates very faintly and slowly; being hardly able to hold up his reputation with a single sheete. (No. 18, 22–30 May, p. 137)

Mercurius Britanicus weighed in with ridicule of both the Oxford journalists and the unpopular Lord Derby, husband of the redoubtable mistress of Lathom House: 'you will not let the *Countesse* be quiet in her Castle, but father such *prodigious* and masculine *Sallies* upon the *Countesse*, (that the Earle vowes) if all be true I hear, never to appear for them again, for he sayes they give the Lady all the *reputation*, and he was never so much as named' (No. 38, 27 May–3 June, p. 295). A few days later, *The Spie* announced that 'both the Authour and the Pamphlet' were dead (Number 19, 30 May–6 June, p. 145) and *Mercurius Britanicus* trumpeted London's victory in the war of the newsbooks:

The advancement of his *Excellency*, and Sir *William Waller* towards *Oxford* have broken the *braines* and the *heart* of their Intelligencer *Aulicus* . . . his pen dropt out of his hand, and himselfe dropt after it into his *Grave*; . . . thus *Britanicus* hath lived to see *Aulicus* die before him, and hath utterly routed their *Oxford Mercury*, pursued him out of his *two sheets* into his very *winding sheet*. (No. 39, 10–17 June, p. 303)

Even the news from Oxford that '*Aulicus* is risen again' was turned to advantage in the judgement that 'this new upstart Scribe is unworthy the name of his Ghost' and the prediction that 'if ever *George Digby* and *Harry Jermyn* return again to *Oxford* (as tis very unlikely) they will never be perswaded to own him for a competitor' (*The Spie*, No. 21, 13–20 June, p. 161).

One striking indication that things were becoming difficult for those who remained at their journalistic posts in Oxford was the reporting of events in Yorkshire. It was Saturday before the editors received tidings of 'what's done at *Yorke*', and then they allowed themselves to be misled by the tales of fugitives from the parliamentary side who had not stayed to see the early success of Goring's cavalry squandered. Too ready to accept 'the great newes', which was said to be 'certified . . . by Expresse messenger' and 'seconded by many others', *Mercurius Aulicus* announced 'That the great medley body of *Scots* and *English* Rebels, was totally routed upon Tuesday last, by Gods blessing on His Majesties Forces led by His Highnesse Prince RUPERT', at a place neare *Yorke* called *Hesly moore*' (Week 27, 6 July, p. 1072). It was not until the last day of the next issue that the delayed truth was reluctantly imparted, with an attempt to explain away the previous week's blunder as an instance of the untrust-worthiness and cowardice of the foe:

And now we judge it time, we give you an account of what was done last weeke in *Yorkshire*; the particulars whereof you had had last weeke, if the Rebels on the way would have suffered any Messenger to bring us a true Relation. What we then told you was chiefly grounded on the Rebels owne Assertions. . . . All which by vowes and very deepe oaths (for the Rebels can sweare as well as Lye) they laboured to attest. But they who dare not stay to fight, dare not speake Truth. (Week 28, 13 July, p. 1082).

In a muted account of the battle itself, an attempt is made to deflect attention from the true scale of the disaster by questioning the estimates of royalist dead, criticizing the partisan narratives printed in London, and assuring readers that Prince Rupert had united his scattered troops with a fresh force from Cumberland and Westmorland for 'another reckoning with the Remnant of these Brethren, who of all sorts of Rebels are the most perfidious' (pp. 1084–6). No mention is made of the flight of the Marquis of Newcastle or the surrender of York in subsequent issues, and two weeks after the battle the Oxford editors were still trying to defend themselves against the ridicule of their London rivals and lay the blame for their overhasty triumph on 'the divers scores of Rebels' who had fled from the battlefield: 'Tis the first time we gave credit to Rebels, and since their friends are scandall'd at it, we'll never trust them more' (Week 29, 16 July 1644, p. 1090).

CHAPTER 9

Defeat, captivity and exile: July 1644 – September 1647

By the time reliable reports of the disaster in Yorkshire reached Charles I, he was heading for Devon, where the Earl of Essex's army was closing in on Exeter. The Queen, seriously ill after the birth of Princess Henrietta and denied safe-conduct to Bath, made her way in disguise to Falmouth and took ship for France on 14 July.[1] Balked of his immediate objective, Essex pressed on into Cornwall to relieve Plymouth and conquer the peninsula for Parliament. But having got as far as Bodmin, he found himself trapped between the army of Sir Richard Grenvile and the combined forces of the King, Prince Maurice and Lord Hopton. On 3 August, he took up a defensive stance at Lostwithiel on the Fowey estuary and waited for help from the Committee of Both Kingdoms. Charles took advantage of his military predicament to renew the approaches made through the Oxford Parliament in January, this time proposing an alliance to rid England of the Scots and impose a settlement that Westminster would be in no position to refuse.[2] The Lord General replied that he had 'no authority to treat' without instructions from Parliament and could not do so 'without breach of trust'.[3] These moves caused the discontent and rivalry that had been simmering in the royalist high command all summer to boil over. Prince Rupert had for some time suspected the loyalty of Lord Wilmot, Lieutenant General of the horse, and his close associate Lord Percy, Master of the Ordnance, who were no longer whole-hearted supporters of Digby's war policy. There were rumours that Wilmot favoured transferring the crown to the Prince of Wales in order to facilitate a peace agreement, and when it became known that he had been in secret correspondence with Essex, Charles arrested him on 8 August and gave command of the cavalry to Lord Goring. Percy resigned and was replaced by Hopton, and Wilmot was permitted to go into exile.[4]

As the weeks passed, Essex was hemmed in more and more, so that ammunition and reinforcements were unable to reach him by land or sea. At last, after foolishly letting the parliamentary cavalry slip through their lines to the safety of Plymouth in the early hours of 31 August, the royalists drove the infantry back into the Iron Age earthworks of Castle Dore. Essex realized that further resistance was futile and got away by boat, leaving Philip Skippon to negotiate the surrender of his de-moralized troops on 2 September.

Things were going better for the royal cause than could have been hoped even by the ever-sanguine Digby six weeks earlier. Sir Charles Gerrard had strengthened his hold on South Wales against the deprada-tions of Rowland Laugharne, Rupert had been recruiting from Lord Byron's base in Chester, and on the very day of Essex's humiliation at Lostwithiel, Montrose had scored the first success of his remarkable campaign against the Covenanters in Scotland. At the beginning of July, the Earl of Antrim had finally honoured his promise and despatched 1,600 Macdonald clansmen under Alasdair MacColla to the Western Highlands, where they wrought havoc among their bitter enemies, the Campbells. Montrose hurried north from Carlisle and by early August had begun to forge an effective guerrilla army out of MacColla's Irishmen and local highlanders. On 1 September, he routed a much larger force under Lord Elcho at Tippermuir and entered Perth in triumph. A fortnight later, he had taken Aberdeen amid scenes of appalling carnage. The Marquis of Argyll, chief of the Campbell clan as well as the dominant political figure in Scotland, led an army out against him, but Montrose's lightly equipped troops disappeared into the mountains. Once, in late October at Fyvie Castle, he caught up with them, but was driven back and returned to Edinburgh to report his failure. He was not even safe in his own castle at Inverary, and had to escape across Loch Awe when Montrose launched a surprise attack in mid-December and plundered the surrounding villages and farms.[5] This was heartening news for the King, but as Bennett points out, whatever long-term dream Montrose had of riding into England at the head of a royalist Scots army to 'restore Charles to power', in reality he was engaged in 'a Highland civil war' being fought by men who had little reason to be loyal to the Stuart monarchy.[6]

The political and military disarray amongst their opponents gave Charles and Rupert a breathing space to begin the process of rebuilding their position after Marston Moor, although dissension in their own ranks would eventually undo them. The combination of armies that had been victorious in Yorkshire went their separate ways – the Scots to invest Newcastle, Fairfax to mop up in his own county, and Manchester back across the Humber. The Scottish Commissioners in London were antagonistic towards Cromwell, who was becoming identified as the champion of the Independents at Westminster and whose 'Ironsides' had so distinguished themselves in the recent battle that their own troops under Lord Leven were deprived of the prestige needed to strengthen their hand in negotiating the reform of the English church along Presbyterian lines. And the Eastern Association itself, Parliament's most successful military organization, 'was reduced to paralysis in August and September' by Manchester's 'swing to the peace party', when it dawned on him that an outright victory against Charles 'might be followed by something even worse than the tyranny of king and bishops'.[7] The joint forces of Waller, Manchester and Cromwell were unable to prevent the advance of the King and Prince Maurice from the west or to inflict a decisive defeat upon them at the second Battle of Newbury on 27 October; and when Charles returned on 9 November with Rupert, newly appointed Lieutenant General of all the royalist armies in place of the ageing Earl of Forth, the parliamentary commanders held back from a further engagement and allowed them to supply the garrison at Donnington Castle and retrieve the artillery left behind there after the battle. Although Newcastle capitulated to the Scots on 20 October and Liverpool to Sir John Meldrum on 1 November, the King had some reason for satisfaction when the main royalist army took up its winter quarters around Oxford on 23 November.

After Marston Moor and the loss of York, however, there was a marked decline in the volume and quality of Oxford's literary contribution to the war effort, which can only be partly accounted for by the fire which broke out in the city on 6 October and destroyed Leonard Lichfield's printing house. The production of *Mercurius Aulicus* was not affected, since it was printed by Henry Hall, and Berkenhead was quick to turn any propaganda advantage back upon his rivals: 'As for them in print who talke of 300 Oxford *houses burnt to the ground*, others *of* 290, others *of* 400, telling us *all is fired from Saint Gyles, his Church, to Friar Bacon's Study*, we shall onely say, that lately at *Leycester* severall bundles of *London* Pamphlets were throwne into the fire for continuing such open Lyes that the Brethren there were ashamed to have them seene' (Week 41, 6 October 1644, p. 1192). Nevertheless, as Allen long ago noted, the centre of significant debate shifted after the summer of 1644:

From most Parliamentarian points of view the contentions of the Royalists were no longer worth answering.... Already in 1644 the Parliamentarian party showed signs of splitting up; and henceforward, for many years, controversy was to be mainly between its various sections. The dismal prognostications of Royalist writers were already in a way to be fulfilled.[8]

During the second half of the year, there were the usual petitions and official announcements, a few sermons printed by order, and the texts of the letters in which Charles had offered terms for peace to Essex in August and to the Lords and Commons in July and September – the latter reprinted in *Mercurius Aulicus* with the comment, 'What welcome this Gracious message found with them at Westminster is horrible to imagine, for no sooner had they received it, but instantly there followed a fast at Saint *Laurence* his Church, for the *happy proceedings of the Councell of Warre*, that is, for shedding innocent bloud enough' (Week 38, 18 September 1644, p. 1171). Apart from these, very few significant expressions of royalism were issued from Oxford in the months following Marston Moor.

One short pamphlet was little more than a string of quotations from the Book of Homilies and the Confessions of the Reformed Churches, justifying its author against a charge of malignancy.[9] Daniel Featley's much weightier tome is of greater interest. He was a royal chaplain who ignored the King's instruction not to accept a place in the Assembly of Divines, only to be subsequently deprived of his membership for refusing to take the Covenant and for critical remarks in a letter intercepted on its way to Archbishop Ussher at Oxford. In *Sacra Nemesis, the Levites Scourge* (Oxford, [Madan 20 July] 1644), he defends episcopacy, gives his reasons for rejecting the Covenant, and inveighs against the prophanities of sectarians. But, as the titles of this and his earlier work of self-vindication, *The Gentle Lash* (January 1644), indicate, a great deal of his rhetorical energy goes into administering 'discipline' to the 'agents' of the 'close Committee' who have 'a Patent to Lye' in their 'weekly *Curranto's*' (p. 8). At a time when ministers of religion are undergoing the worst persecution since 'a bloody cloud' hung over the church during the reign of Queen Mary, they have to bear the jibes of 'every *hackney* pamphleteer, every mercenary scribler' that sees a profit in casting 'blots on their faces' and adding 'affliction to the afflicted' (sig. A1ʳ). Of these, the 'busiest' is *Britanicus*, who gets a section to himself before Featley turns to the wider censure '*of all the Diurnals and Scouts*' that 'have fastened their *venemous teeth* upon the true Servants of God' (p. 2). No one is spared by such 'snarling Curs' – 'thou *spittest venome* at Majestie it selfe' (p. 2) – but 'at this present', he will confine himself to answering the cowardly slanders against 'a late Member of the Assembly, whose hands thou knowest are so tyed, that he cannot wipe away the *froth* of thy impure discourse, which thus *driveleth* from thee' (p. 3). His almost hysterical contempt for London journalists breaks out again over the letter that had been first stolen and then wilfully misinterpreted:

Lastly, to return to thee, Sir *Britanicus, Civicus,* or *Scoticus,* for thou art a man *omnium nominum & horarum*; tell me in good earnest, what is the Trade, or Profession, or Mysterie, whereby thou livest? Is it not to be Citie-*Spie*, and Intelligencer? And why may it not be as lawfull for the Doctor to send *Theologicall Truths* to *Oxford*, as for thee every week *Civill Lyes* to all parts of the Kingdom? (p. 10)

Rather more restrained is John Maxwell's reply to the request of a 'Worthy Gentleman' for information about the kind of church government being devised by the Westminster Assembly.[10] Most of his lengthy 'letter' is devoted to describing the organization of a presbyterial system, demonstrating that the articles of dogmatic faith associated with it are incompatible with the ancient rights of kings, and arguing that 'this treacherous and damnable Covenant' is a way of inciting 'poore People to act Treason and Rebellion' (p. 78). He does sound one novel note, however, which would be heard again when the Assembly's deliberations produced tangible results in the new year, in his adjuration to well-meaning readers not to 'be so disposed and fixed upon a resolution' that they will 'shake off the true and necessary government instituted by our Lord' merely in order to 'redeem externall Peace' (pp. 1–2). Like Maxwell, Gryffith Williams had already traced the rights of patriarchal kingship back to Adam, and in *Jura Majestatis* (Oxford, [30 October] 1644), he presented it, with the full panoply of citations from the bible and from patristic and classical writings, as the form of government most agreeable to the laws of nature and the will of God.

The New Distemper (Oxford, [Madan 13 November] 1644), among the first items published by Lichfield after the fire, was one of two late polemical works by Francis Quarles to be printed in the weeks following his death in September 1644. In it, he developed the metaphor he had used in *The Virgin Widow* to diagnose the '*disease* of our distempered Church', concluding that the patient was still 'sound' in her 'doctrine of Faith' and that the King, who was performing the role of her 'pious and religious *Nursing Father*', could be trusted to maintain 'the honour of the true Protestant Religion' and preserve the moderate reforms already instituted since 1641 (pp. 148, 156).[11] The other pamphlet by Quarles, entitled *The Whipper Whipt* and published in London, was dedicated to King Charles and conducted a point-by-point defence of a religious

tract dating from 1625 by Cornelius Burges against charges recently
brought by an 'unworthy *Pamphleter*' who 'like a *Fly*, buzzes through his
whole *Larder*, blowing here and there' (p. 161).[12] Gordon Haight thought
that this must have caused offence to 'ardent Royalists' because it lent
support to the ideas of the man who was Vice-president of the Westminster Assembly.[13] But Quarles's systematic method was a clever device for
bringing down two birds with one shot by quoting both the comments of
the pamphleteer and opinions held by Burges nearly twenty years before
– that the path 'to the best Reformation is by prayers and teares' (p. 167);
that those who 'accuse, arraigne and condemne the sacred and dreadfull
person of the Lords Annoynted' are on 'the high way to all Treasons and
Rebellions' (p. 171); that the man who rails unrepentantly 'at Ceremonies, Bishops, and Common-Prayer' will 'never have any true Religion
in him' (p. 177). In his own replies to the 'Calumniator' of these unexcep-
tionable views – views which must have caused some embarrassment to
the reforming divine of 1644 – Quarles pours scorn on a false cause that
is 'stronglyer defended by the *Sword*, then by the *Pen*'. Weighing the
'world of *Pamphlets*, of both sides published', he puts the sound biblical
and secular scholarship of one party in the balance against the '*Wresting*
of Scriptures', the '*obscurity* of stile', and the 'raylings' of the other
(pp. 167–8); and he asks whether the God of Peace, Truth and Order
can possibly be pleased by 'this rabble of rebellious and seditious
Rakeshames, that style themselves by the name of *Mercuries, Scouts, Weekly
Intelligencers, &c.*' and are nothing but 'a pack of *Alebench* Whistlers,
decay'd Captaines, and *masterlesse* Journymen', ready 'for halfe a Crown a
week' to 'fly in the face of God's *Vicegerent*' (pp. 171–2).

As part of his portrait of Charles as a man of 'wisdom, moderation,
and tender piety' in *The New Distemper*, Quarles had argued that the
temperate King not only held his own 'provoked passion' in check, but
that he must have laid a '*restraining* power' upon his supporters, since
'Oxford had and yet hath Pens, sharp enough, and Ink that wanted no
Gall' (p. 156). But it is more likely that the propaganda engine was
beginning to run out of steam. Quite apart from the dispiriting effect of
the serious setbacks at Cheriton and Marston Moor and the loss of York
and Newcastle, Spelman, Falkland, Digges and Cartwright were dead,
Cowley had abandoned his epic and gone abroad, and Digby was in the
field with the King through most of the summer and autumn. The
predicament of those left behind to co-ordinate the literary campaign in
the royalist capital is, perhaps, indicated by the measures taken to
supplement the rather meagre crop of new work in the second half of

1644: the belated publication of a complete text of *The Anti-Confederacy*;
the printing of Falkland's contribution to the Root and Branch debates
of 1641–2; a second edition of *Dodona's Grove*, the prose allegory about
English and European affairs from 1603 up to the spring of 1640, which
had got James Howell arrested in London and branded as 'no friend to
Parliaments'; and the reprinting of Thomas Morton's *The Necessity of
Christian Subjection* as a new sermon by John Berkenhead, fraudulently
claimed to have been preached before the King at Christ Church on 3
November and commanded 'to the Presse' by the Prince of Wales.[14]

Apart from Berkenhead himself, the wielder of the sharpest pen still
active in Oxford in the autumn was John Cleveland, who responded to
the fall of Newcastle with some doggerel verses – 'News news News is
come from the North; / Tis chopping News & new come' – which
suggest to his modern editors that he was parodying a northern news-
sheet.[15] Not long afterwards , in 'The Scots Curanto', the London poet,
Alexander Brome, used a similar device to expose the self-interest of
Parliament's allies and the cracks that were appearing in the alliance:

> Come, come away to the *English* wars,
>   A fig for our Hills and Valleys,
> 'Twas we did begin, and will lengthen their jarrs,
>   We'l gain by their loss and folleys; . . .
> And when at the last we have conquer'd the King,
>   And beaten away the Cavaleers,
> The Parliament next must the same ditty sing,
>   And thus we will set the Realm by the ears.[16]

Cleveland moved into prose for a much more stinging and sustained
attack on the abuse of rational discourse by the hacks on the other side
in the work which first brought him to the notice of a wider public when
it was printed twice in London in 1644 and again in Oxford towards the
end of January 1645.[17] *The Character of a London-Diurnall* begins with an
attempt to define its subject, a tactic frequently employed in Cleveland's
verse satires:

A *Diurnall* is a punie *Chronicle*, scarce pin-feathered with the wings of *time*: It is an
History in *sippets*, the English *Iliads* in a nut-shell; the *Apocriphall Parliaments* book
of *Maccabees* in single sheets; It would tire a *Welch Pedigree*, to reckon up how
many *aps* 'tis removed from an *Annall*: For it is of that *Extract*; onely of the
younger *house*, like a *Shrimp* to a *Lobster*.[18]

Cleveland's point is partly linguistic, partly literary, and, as Sharon
Achinstein argues, wholly political, because the act of naming 'is an
issue of power' and 'whoever controls the language can order the world
as he wants it to be ordered'.[19] None of the generic labels or titles of

specific works traditionally associated with the practice of recording
events for posterity (chronicle, history, *Iliad, Book of Maccabees*, annal) is
appropriate for the brief, ephemeral and fatherless spawn of the printing
houses that are taken in like bastards at Westminster 'by the names of
Scoticus, Civicus, Britannicus' (p. 88). It is no wonder that the '*Country
Carrier*', unfamiliar with this new phenomenon and the word coined to
describe it, 'miscals it the *Urinall*' when he 'buyes it for the *Vicar*'; and yet,
he gets closer than he knows to its true nature as a waste product
symptomatic of the current political sickness, 'for it casts the water of the
State, ever since it staled bloud' (p. 89).

Conscious that his shafts of wit might provide ammunition for his
opponents, Cleveland is careful to distinguish the character of a London
newsbook from its counterpart in Oxford: 'It differs from an *Aulicus*, as
the *Devill* and his *Exorcist*; or as a *black Witch* doth from a *white* one, whose
office is to unravel her *inchantments*' (p. 89). When he turns from the title
to the contents of the 'London-Diurnall', his first ploy is to deconstruct
the specialised idiom of rebellion in order to expose the illegitimacy of its
patron's proceedings: 'It begins usually with an *Ordinance*, which is a *Law
still born*, dropt before quickened by the *Royall assent*: 'Tis one of the
Parliaments by-blows (*Acts* being legitimate) and hath no more *Syre* than a
Spanish Gennet, that's begotten by the wind' (p. 89). After printing the
latest illegitimate decrees, the Diurnal regales its readers with the latest
'plots' – a word which aptly describes the fanciful revelations made by
the leading actors in the Commons, for 'since the *Stages* were *voted* down,
the onely *play-house* is at *Westminster*' (p. 89). Next, through the pages of
the Diurnals 'march their *Adventurers*', the heroes whose incredible
exploits furnish narrative material for 'the *Round-heads Legend*' and 'the
Rebels Romance' (p. 90). The rest of Cleveland's own pamphlet is devoted
to demolishing the reputations of Parliament's military leaders and the
lying propaganda that created them: Stamford, who danced 'a *Morrice*
through the *West* of *England*' early in the war and 'by the help of a
Diurnall, routed his enemies fifty miles off', and Waller that knight errant
and '*Prodigy of Vallour*', who killed Hopton many times over (pp. 90–1);
'his Oxellency', the Earl of Essex (p. 91); Cromwell, who 'is never so
valourous, as when he is making speeches for the Association' (pp. 91–2);
Manchester, commander of sectaries and Independents, 'so every one of
his *souldiers* is a destinct *Church*' (p. 92); Brereton and Gell, 'two of *Mars*
his petty-toes' (p. 93); and Fairfax, along with other lesser 'Puppets that
move by the wyre of a *Diurnall*' (p. 93). At length, he breaks off this
rewriting of 'enemy figures so they appear not in the enemy's language

but in [his] own',[20] and dismisses 'the triumphs of a *Diurnall*' as 'so many imposthumated Fancies, so many Bladders of their own blowing' (p. 94).

However brilliant his counter-measures against the London diurnal-makers – to whom he denies the title of 'authors' in another prose character written around this time[21] – there is something unmistakably defensive in the methods he adopted, which betrays 'a deep anxiety' about 'the waywardness of language'.[22] Since the war of words began in earnest, there had been vigorous and inventive mockery of the enemy newsbooks by *Mercurius Aulicus* and popular writers like Taylor and Brome, who enjoyed the rough-and-tumble of street controversy, but when self-protective abuse creeps into the work of men like Quarles, Featley and Cleveland, the jibe of *Mercurius Britanicus* earlier in the summer that he had 'utterly routed their *Oxford Mercury*', though not literally true at the time, begins to look prophetic of the ebbing of royalist confidence in the literary as well as the military sphere of the conflict.

Essex's humiliation in Cornwall and the ineffectiveness of the other parliamentary generals in following up their success in Yorkshire may have left the Court in a 'generally cheerful' mood as Christmas was celebrated in Oxford.[23] But it was at Lostwithiel that the seeds were sown of the 'palace coup' that would displace Essex and bring about a major change in military organization.[24] According to Viscount Saye and Sele, suspicions planted by the King's approach to Essex in August helped to trigger these developments: 'This with other things then laid the foundation in men's hearts of that resolution, which soon after was put in execution, to new Model the Army, and put the Command into other hands.'[25] The immediate context was the exchange of recriminations on 25 and 28 November between Cromwell and Manchester and a joint move by the Scots and the peace party, now led by Essex and Denzil Holles and identified with the Presbyterians, to impeach Cromwell as an incendiary who sought to divide the alliance; and the first step was taken on 9 December, when Zouch Tate proposed in the Commons that political and religious faction should be removed from the practical business of soldiering by forbidding any member of either House to hold a military command for the duration of the present war. The effect of what became known as the Self-Denying Ordinance would be to deprive Essex, Waller, Manchester and Cromwell of their commissions. A draft Ordinance was passed by the Commons on 19 December, and although there was resistance by the Lords, who did not accept it until 3

April in a revised form, preparations went ahead to reorganize the militia on a national basis. On 21 January, Sir Thomas Fairfax was named as prospective commander-in-chief of the New Model Army, with Philip Skippon as his Major General; his list of officers was accepted on 18 March; Essex, Manchester and Denbigh resigned their commands on 2 April, followed by Waller on 17 April; and on 4 April Fairfax and Skippon took up their commissions.[26]

While these crucial arrangements for the future of the parliamentary war machine were being put in place, yet another attempt to reach a negotiated settlement was in progress. There had been 'a wave of protests, and demands for peace talks' when the Oxford Parliament reassembled in October 1644;[27] and although a delegation from Westminster had received a cool reception in Oxford, the King chose Commissioners in November and talks eventually began at the end of January 1645. The Scottish Covenanters took a leading role in the proceedings, but their policy was governed by two misconceptions, highlighted in a study of the so-called Uxbridge Treaty: 'that they could pressure the English into establishing a church similar in form and spirit to their own' and 'that, given the chance, Charles might be convinced to renounce episcopacy and accept Presbyterianism in its stead.'[28] But since the King was adamantly determined not to abandon episcopal church government and not to yield control of the armed forces to Parliament – two of the conditions set out in the proposals from Westminster – the prospect of a settlement was 'wonderfull improbable, and scarce hoped for by any men of understanding'.[29] The talks accordingly ended in deadlock on 22 February. Even while preparations were in train for the conference at Uxbridge, Parliament was pressing forward with the long-awaited reform of the English church: on 4 January, the Elizabethan Prayer Book was replaced by a new Directory of Worship and on 13 January the Commons adopted a system of parochial Presbyterianism which failed to satisfy the Scots and, in most English counties, 'never really got off the ground'.[30]

This was evidently an anxious time for Laudians and even for more moderate supporters of the established church and in the month before the two sides met, Maxwell's admonition against agreement at the cost of principle was reiterated in print. Afraid that change in church government might be embraced 'as the readiest way to Peace' by some who would enter into the bargain 'blindfold', Henry Ferne spelled out the nature of a presbyterial system and the dangers it entailed for the religious and civil well-being of the kingdom.[31] Henry Hammond made a more emotional appeal, 'in the bowells of compassion to my bleeding Country', to anyone who, though satisfied of the lawfulness of episcopal government, 'doth yet conceive that the parting with it is no *change of Religion*, and consequently, that the standing for it at this time, when it is oppos'd, is but the preferring the interests of some inconsiderable men before the conveniences and common wishes of all'.[32] John Gauden could not agree that the Scottish model of Presbyterianism was 'above all others according to the word of God' and his inquiry into the logical consistency and scriptural legitimacy of the Covenant left him unable 'to subscribe at present with judgement or knowledge of what I vow'.[33] Another examination of the Covenant, undertaken in order 'to rescue . . . the many seduced Souls out of that pit of Destruction into which they are already plunged', was reprinted at Oxford in January as part of an orchestrated campaign to prepare public opinion for the rejection of a settlement on terms dictated by the Scots.[34]

A more individualistic attempt to rescue 'seduced Souls' from error was made by Edward Symmons in a book occasioned by his duties as an army chaplain.[35] In 'The Preface to the Readers', he relates how the previous Easter during a visit to the prison in Shrewsbury, he had been troubled by the misguided zeal of some enemy soldiers, who told him 'that they took up Armes against *Anti-Christ*, and *Popery*; for (said they) *'tis prophesied in Revelation, that the Whore of Babylon shall be destroyed with fire and sword*' (sig. A3^r). They had gone on to justify the armed struggle against the King with other biblical texts, which they said they had learned to apply in this way from a printed sermon by Stephen Marshall. Symmons could not believe their story, 'for though some Weavers and Taylers, and Tinkers and Pedlers, and such like, who were suffered to preach, did abuse and pervert Gods word to their own purposes, yet M. *Marshall* (who was one whom my selfe knew better then they did) I was persuaded had more wisedome, learning, and honesty then so to doe' (sig. A4^r). Several months later, he 'fortuned to be in a Booksellers shop in *Ludlow*', where he 'chanced to see a Sermon of M. *Marshalls*' upon one of the very texts that his 'simple' prisoners had cited. He came to believe that he had been 'called by a speciall Providence to set pen to paper, to vindicate the *Scriptures* of God' for the benefit of 'others of the like ranke and quality, in other places', who might be 'by the same as much misled' (sig. A4^r). His hope is that the ensuing treatise may also bring his once 'deare friend', Stephen Marshall, to 'see more of his errour' (sig. A4^v).

In the body of his vindication, Symmons demonstrates how Marshall has systematically 'misconstrued' his text from the Book of Judges 5: 23 –

'Curse ye Meroz . . .' – a verse that has been 'of great use and estimation' among 'the Ministers of his party' (p. 1) and that, to his 'griefe and sorrow', has been followed in the spirit of Marshall's preaching by too many of the Cavaliers, who 'are most extreamly given over to that hellish sinne' (p. 10). By ingenious turns of argument, he holds this sermon and others like it responsible for the conditions that provoked the insurrection in Ireland and for the lamentable acts of cruelty perpetrated by some of the soldiers in the royalist armies (pp. 13, 56). Recalling the blameless life and worthy ministry of Marshall 'before his ingagement in this rebellious and bloudy businesse' led him to betray 'his *oath of obedience*', he muses on the possibility 'that as these men have beene the Cheife exciters *unto*, and promoters *of* this unnaturall Rebellion, so perhaps the Providence of God hath ordered, that the discovery of them, must be the meanes to appease the storme; we see fighting doth but increase the fire, happily 'tis writing which may quench the flame' (pp. 85–7). He ends with a thought which was to root itself deeply in the royalist imagination over the next few years: that those who serve Christ and the King 'in detecting [the] wickednesse and Hypocrisy' of the 'Pharisees and Saduces' of the present age must expect 'to be *murdered* and *martyred* by these sanguinarious and *bloudy men*' (p. 89).

A compelling instance of just such a fate was reported by *Mercurius Aulicus* on 11 January:

And now we must tell the World, that on *Friday* last (*Jan.* 10) the Rebells murthered the *most Reverend Father in God* William *Lord Arch-Bishop of Canterbury*, on a Scaffold upon *Tower hill*, after they had kept him Prisoner above foure years. . . . At last the Brethren passe over *Tweed*, and then that malitious Scot (*Alexander Henderson*) demands the Arch-Bishops life, as an impediment to their Reformation. (January 5–12, 1645, p. 1332)

Berkenhead, whose own career had been fostered by Laud in the 1630s, drives home the charges of political expediency and illegality against those who made him 'the *King's* and the *Church's Martyr*' (p. 1340) by noting the sinister coincidence of the Ordinance of Attainder – the same device used to declare Strafford a traitor in 1641 – and the Ordinance which removed the cornerstone of worship in the Laudian Church of England. Two things were 'ordained' on 4 January: 'First that the Arch-Bishop of *Canterbury* should suffer death, Secondly, that their *Directory* should be established instead of the Book of *Common-Prayer*, (see how fitly they couple their Votes together)' (p. 1333). After printing the text of Laud's speech from the scaffold, the newsbook pays tribute to his 'Integrity, Learning, Devotion, and Courage' and cannot resist a final thrust at the perpetrators of 'the most groundlesse, malicious, solemne, studied Murther, that ever was committed in this wretched Island' (p. 1340). Passages from the speech were quickly printed as a separate pamphlet by Leonard Lichfield and, restyled as *His Funerall Sermon, Preacht by himself on the Scaffold on Tower-Hill*, by a London publisher. Laud's opponents answered his 'Suttle and Jesuiticall falacies', and gave an account of his execution which assured the righteous that 'as they have seen, so it shall be to all their Adversaries, Archbishops, and Lord Bishops, and to all the enemies of God'.[36] Peter Heylyn, another of Laud's protégés, was stung by such attempts to 'render him more odious to the common people' into compiling a more accurate version 'of his *death* and *sufferings*' and exposing to public view 'those *plots* and *practises* which were set on foote, to plucke a few yeares from a weake old man, and bring him to an unnaturall calamitous end' (p. 2).[37] The narrative of Laud's final years, from the tumults that surrounded his arrest in 1640 to his martyr's death, provided a model for the royalist management of the more spectacular martyrdom of Charles Stuart in 1649, not least in Heylyn's self-conscious transformation of the ephemeral material of the newsbooks into a work of art:

It is a preposterous kind of writing to begin the story of a great mans life, at the houre of his death; a most strange way of setting forth a solemne *Tragedie*, to keepe the *principall Actor* in the *tyring-house*, till the *play* be done, and then to bring him on the *stage* onely to speake the *Epilogue*, and receive the Plaudites. Yet this must be the scope and method of these following papers. (p. 1)[38]

Cleveland's verses 'On the Archbishop of Canterbury' are also characterized by self-conscious rhetoric – about the falsity of sobbing 'in numbers'.[39] He picks up the newsbook's emphasis on the conjunction of the two Ordinances and sees this second judicial murder by Parliament as completing the country's ruin: 'The state in *Strafford* fell, the Church in *Laud*'. His polemical treatment of the archbishop's death, rather wearily marshalling its ingenious metaphors and hyperboles into verse, lacks the personal touch of a comment in the prose defence – '"tis the last Office I shall doe him' – and the notes of genuine loss and admiration that are heard in the couplets that round off Heylyn's act of homage:

> And yet not leave thee thus, I faine would try
> A line or two in way of *Elegie*; . . .
> Nor be thou greiv'd, bless't Soule, that men doe stil
> Pursue thee with black slaunders. . . .
> Or that thou want'st *inscriptions*, and a stone
> T' ingrave thy name, and write thy Titles on.
> Thou art above those trifles . . .   (pp. 28–9)

Heylyn had taken particular exception to the defamation of his old patron by William Prynne. At about the same time that Henry Hall was preparing his *Briefe Relation* for the press, the other Oxford printer was publishing a reply to two more of the Puritan lawyer's 'pestiferous Pamphlets' by John Taylor, who explains in a postscript that his text was ready before John Pym died, but *'the Presse and the Printers'* were *'full of worke of greater Consequence than to curry* Crop-ear'd *Jades'* (p. 40).[40] Taylor offers himself now as the heir to the mantle of Thomas Nashe, the Elizabethan satirist who was employed by the authorities to combat 'a Crew of Rascalls called *Martinists*; whose Laxative Purity did most shamefully in printed toyes, Pamphlets, and Lying Libells, besquitter all *England* over' (p. 2). Because this 'Nest of Mischievous, Malevolent, Malignant *Martins*' has broken loose again and almost overthrown both religion and law, the ghost of Nashe has appeared to him and stirred him up to 'Nip, and Whip, strip and Snip' these 'Matchlesse, Headlesse, Heedless Rebells' (p. 3). Prynne is to be his prime target, and he is charged with the task of distilling the essence of the 'eighty and odde sheets of printed Confusion' which sell at 'ten or twelve shillings' into '12 Leaves in Quarto' which can be acquired at 'sixpence a peece' (p. 3). There follow forty pages of close commentary on the offending volumes. In the light of the postscript and a curious prefatory note – 'There are divers Latine words thrust into this mine Answer ... which words I neither understand, know the Authours, or thanke them for it' (sig. A1ᵛ) – it may be inferred that the propaganda team at Oxford doctored an existing work by Taylor and perhaps encouraged him to increase its appeal by adding a comic prologue, in which a link was forged between the Marprelate conspirators and the contemporary subverters of church and state.

Auguries were not good for the King's cause as the new campaigning season approached. During the winter, the resentment of local communities against war levies and marauding soldiers quartered in their midst had begun to manifest itself in associations of yeomen farmers, who declared themselves ready to fight for their property against both King and Parliament. Although most of these Clubmen were not specifically anti-royalist, their troublesome activities were commonest in the southwest and along the Welsh borders, where the King's armies were concentrated. Goring, for example, met fierce opposition when Dorset was affected by what has been called 'the most massive popular movement of the entire civil war period'.[41] Also bad for morale was the death in January of Sir Henry Gage, the popular deputy governor of Oxford, whose daring raid into Hampshire to supply the beleaguered Basing House was one of the more colourful exploits of the previous autumn; and on 22 February, the day on which the Uxbridge talks were abandoned, Shrewsbury was lost in a surprise attack. Uxbridge, as Rupert was among the first to realize, would prove to be the King's 'last chance of making a treaty that was not a surrender'.[42] The Prince's relations with Digby were rapidly deteriorating, and the personal rivalry between them has been seen as a determining factor in the military disaster of 1645.[43] Charles himself, under the influence of his closest counsellor, remained blindly optimistic. Having sent Hyde off with Culpepper on 4 March to set up a separate Council for the Prince of Wales at Bristol and rid himself of 'our mongrel Parliament here' by an adjournment, he wrote to the Queen on 27 March that 'the general face' of his affairs was improving and that he was in a 'better condition' than at any time 'since this rebellion began'.[44] At a Council of War early in April, however, Rupert added his voice to those calling for a resumption of talks while there was still something to bargain with, but the King and Digby lived in expectations of aid from Ireland or from Henrietta Maria's efforts on the Continent. In the meantime, Montrose was carrying all before him[45] and on 7 May Charles rode out of Oxford with the ultimate objective of a rendez-vous in the north with his Scottish champion.

In the course of May, three different literary strategies were tried to harness the growing anti-war mood by assigning responsibility for the start of the conflict and the failure of the recent treaty to the politicians and preachers in London. One writer posed as a willing supporter of the early reforms, who had taken the Protestation to 'live and dye with the Earle of *Essex*' in a cause that seemed to be 'piously mannaged' by 'religious Patriots' (p. 2).[46] A careful assessment of the progress of the war, in which 'the Battailes we most bragg of' were inconclusive and the King's victories 'were beyond the expectation of reason', has convinced him that he was led astray by 'both Pulpit and Parliament' (p. 3). And when he looks 'backe upon our State Actors, that sit at the helme and direct all things' – Hampden, struck down on Chalgrove Field; 'Patriot Pym, whom the people for his Speech applaud like *Herod*, like *Herod* eaten up of Lice'; Essex himself now scorned and neglected by his own side – and considers the illegality of parliamentary Ordinances and the ignominy of permitting the Scots to 'prescribe us a Church government' (p. 14), he can only resolve 'to leave their party that have misse-led me and my poore Countrymen to our ruine' (p. 16). In another pamphlet, it is a voice from the pre-war world of order and tradition that catches the reader's attention with 'an old Story of the *Horse* & the *Hind*, which I have heard my Grandfather tell many a Winter night, when I was a boy' (p. 1).[47] This tale is applied to the fate of the laity of England, seduced by the 'nimble' arguments of the clergy into setting up the Golden Calf of innovation in church and state but now 'faine [to] returne to their old wonted Lawes and Liberties, if they could tell which way' (p. 5). This writer's main purpose is to deflect blame for the failure at Uxbridge away from the royalist side. Since even 'such a simple man' as himself can see that Parliament's demands were unreasonable, the King's Commissioners had obviously discerned 'that the concession and granting of them must needs inferre, a totall *Alteration and Change*, both in our *Spirituall*, and in our *Civill* Government ... and God deliver me, and every honest man, from living to behold that day' (p. 13).

John Taylor adopts a mock-epic stance when he resumes his vendetta against the disciples of Lucifer and Beelzebub, who have 'disjointed' both church and state by committing the 'foule murther' of first Strafford and now Laud:

> Lo, I the Man, whose stout impartiall quill
> Dares venture to confront the damned Crew,
> Knaves who make will their law, and law their will,
> And from the Presse and Pulpit slanders spew.[48]

The Waterpoet was evidently already conversant with the analogy that would become an ever more prominent feature in royalist propaganda, as its emphasis shifted from the justification of kingship (whether constitutional or divine) to the defence of Charles himself:

> Since God's eternall Son was crucifide,
> No Gracious Prince was ever more abus'd,
> Than good King *Charles*, oppos'd, and vilifide,
> Robb'd, ransack'd, and still wickedly traduc'd.   (p. 6)

Taylor was soon in print again, in the guise of 'a Trusty Wellwisher' of the regime in London, describing how Oxford had been taken 'by lesse then 150 Parliament Souldiers' (p. 6) under the command of Fairfax, 'the admired *Agamemnon* of our Host', and urging *Mercurius Britanicus* to 'Jeere and flourish' (pp. 6–7).[49] In reality, Oxford had not fallen, but it had been surrounded by the forces of Fairfax, Browne, Cromwell and Skippon on 22 May and the situation had been serious enough for Secretary Nicholas to write 'att Midnight' to the King, informing him that the city would soon be in 'very great distress' for lack of 'victuals'.[50] The storming and plundering of Leicester on 31 May had drawn the besieging forces away from Oxford, but the King delayed his northward march, against the advice of Rupert, in order to supply the royalist capital. This gave Fairfax time to secure the appointment of Cromwell as his Lieutenant General, in spite of the Self-Denying Ordinance, and to prepare for the decisive encounter that must soon come. As the New Model Army approached, Rupert argued against giving battle until Goring and Gerrard arrived with reinforcements, but once again Digby's counsels prevailed.[51] On 14 June, near the east midland village of Naseby, the greatly outnumbered royalist force not only suffered a crushing defeat but also lost all its artillery and a great deal of ammunition. The King's main field army was destroyed, leaving three smaller armies under Byron at Chester, Gerrard in South Wales, and Goring in the south-west to continue the struggle. Charles retreated with what was left of the cavalry to Hereford, where the disagreements between his commander-in-chief and his favourite counsellor developed into an open feud. Rupert departed in anger to consult with the Prince of Wales about the defence of the west country, while Digby accompanied the King to Raglan Castle in the hope of recruiting fresh regiments of Welsh infantry to replace those killed and captured at Naseby. Reports came in of Montrose's victory at Alford on 2 July and his welcome into Glasgow on 18 August after destroying the Covenanter army at Kilsyth, but from elsewhere the news was uniformly bad. As Rupert had predicted, Fairfax and Cromwell set out to reduce the south-west: they eliminated Goring's army as an effective fighting force at Langport on 10 July and by the middle of August had taken Bridgewater, Bath and Sherborne. Carlisle fell to the Scots on 25 June and within a month Pontefract and Scarborough Castle had also surrendered. In Pembrokeshire, Laugharne had beaten a royalist force at Colby Moor on 1 August and stormed the castle at Haverfordwest four days later. But the heaviest blow was Rupert's surrender of Bristol. He had been hindered by local Clubmen in stocking the city against the inevitable siege, which began on 21 August, and when the final assault was launched on 10 September, he made terms with Fairfax rather than sacrifice more men in a hopeless defence. With the fall of Bristol, Charles I not only lost his 'last claim to credibility in Europe',[52] where Henrietta Maria was trying to organize assistance, but also his last shreds of confidence in Rupert. Persuaded by Digby that the Prince was conspiring to secure the Crown for his brother, the Elector Palatine, who had been in London since August 1644 and had recently been granted a pension by Parliament, he stripped Rupert of his command and had both him and his close ally,

Colonel William Legge, placed under arrest in Oxford. Having wit-
nessed another defeat at Rowton Heath from the walls of Chester on 24
September, the King made his way to the strongly garrisoned town of
Newark. Digby, newly appointed Lieutenant General of the north, set
out with Langdale and what was left of the northern horse in search of
Montrose, who had once more taken to the mountains after the decimation of his Irish troops at Philiphaugh, where they had been surprised on
13 September by General Leslie and a contingent of cavalry from the
Scots army quartered in the North of England. Digby's own force was
routed at Sherburn in Yorkshire on 15 October, but he pursued his
fruitless quest as far as Dumfries before the hostility of the Scottish
peasantry and the desertion of his own troops forced him to take refuge
on the Isle of Man. From there, he made his way to Ireland and
eventually to France.[53]

Meanwhile, Rupert had been exonerated by a Council of War at
Newark, but a protest by his supporters – among them Prince Maurice
and Sir Charles Gerrard, who had earlier been relieved of his command
in South Wales – over the replacement of the garrison's governor,
another of the Prince's adherents, led to their wholesale dismissal from
the King's service. Rupert and his followers withdrew to Belvoir Castle
and sought permission from Parliament to leave the country. By his
intransigence, 'the King had lost his best cavalry officers and his army
was broken beyond all hope of recovery'.[54] When Newark came under
threat, Charles and his Lifeguard escaped to Oxford on 5 November;
and in the west, the Prince of Wales retreated with his Council into
Cornwall. One by one, the remaining royalist strongholds capitulated:
Basing House in October; Beeston Castle in November; Hereford and
Lathom House in December; Dartmouth in January; Chester and
Torrington in February; Exeter on 9 April. The future Charles II, with
Hyde and his other councillors, sailed for the Scillies on 2 March and
thence to Jersey; and the last royalist armies were surrendered by
Hopton on 13 March and Astley on 21 March. During April, the King
made approaches to both the Independents and the Scots, and even
proposed going to Westminster in person to discuss terms. And then, in
the early hours of 27 April, he slipped out of Oxford dressed as a
serving-man, accompanied only by Michael Hudson and John
Ashburnham, a chaplain and a groom of the bedchamber. On 5 May,
he gave himself up to the Earl of Lothian, who was with the Scots forces
besieging Newark. The garrison surrendered on his orders and within
three days he was heading for Newcastle under the protection of the

Scots army. Oxford had been under siege since early May, and on 20 June, Sir Thomas Glenham signed the Articles for its surrender; on 22 June the Princes Rupert and Maurice, who had not availed themselves of the earlier passes, were permitted to make their way to the coast and take ship for Europe; and on 27 June, Fairfax formally took possession of the keys of the city. Worcester, the last major royalist garrison in England, capitulated on 23 July. The Civil War was over, although Pendennis Castle and Raglan Castle held out until August and it was 13 March 1647 before Harlech, the last of the castles in North Wales, submitted to Parliament.

There had been occasional gaps in the sequence of *Mercurius Aulicus* from late in 1644, but the five weeks following the defeat at Naseby (8 June – 12 July 1645) are a complete blank; and No. 116, covering news for the week 13–20 July, did not appear until 12 August. Thereafter only two more issues were published, nominally dated 10–17 August and 31 August – 7 September. A month after the battle, preaching in St Mary's, Richard Harwood reflected the stunned reaction at Oxford in his meditation on the song with which the Israelites had greeted the Babylonian captivity:

God help us, we are all prisoners in our native country (for what difference is it to be captive in a strange land, and to be used like strangers in our own?) *England* it self, the Paradise of the world, is now become our *Babylon*: And by these waters of *Marah* do we sit down, and weep to remember thee, our *Brittish Sion*.[55]

He counselled a patient retirement into '*the chamber of devotion*' to await 'the salvation of the Lord' (p. 4). But although he was confident that '*God's Anoynted*' would be restored 'to his Crowne and Dignity', he warned that many loyal subjects might have to drink the 'bitter cup' of martyrdom (pp. 11, 17). Published a few days later than this sermon in mid-July, George Wharton's survey of the course of the war up to the commissioning of the New Model Army aimed to fasten guilt for 'the destruction of Houses and Families, the desolation of Cities and Townes, the increase of Widdowes and Orphanes' upon 'this pretended Parliament' and to encourage 'His Majesties loyall Subjects' in their continued defence of 'a good cause'.[56] Drawing heavily upon the Oxford newsbook for facts and perspective, he condemned 'the perfidious *Scots*', blamed 'those of Westminster' for the breakdown of the Uxbridge Treaty, and included a verse elegy on Sir Henry Gage, whose brave exploits at Basing House and Abingdon had distinguished him from 'the wary *Skippon*'. Gage's status as a Cavalier hero, dying for his King, was confirmed by the publication of an extended account of his military career, supplemented with another elegy and a prose 'character' by Edward Walsingham.[57]

The logistical difficulties experienced by Berkenhead and his colleagues after Naseby and the general collapse of morale evident in Harwood's sermon were compounded by the capture of the King's private papers, among them his politically compromising correspondence with Ormond and Henrietta Maria. The printing of these letters, with annotations by Henry Parker, Thomas May and John Sadler,[58] was a major event in the propaganda war. *The King's Cabinet opened: Or, Certain Packets of Secret Letters & Papers, Written with the Kings own Hand, and taken in his Cabinet at Naseby-Field* (London, [10 July] 1645), as its title indicates, exposed the King's private thoughts to public scrutiny and accelerated the shift of emphasis already discernible in some royalist writing from the justification of monarchy to a defence of the King.[59] It was gleefully pointed out in a preface that even 'the most vulgar capacities' would be able to grasp the damning import of 'what the printed papers will themselves utter in their own language' (sig. A4^r); and the annotators revelled in the confirmation that 'the King's Counsels are wholly managed by the Queen' (p. 43). *Mercurius Britanicus* very quickly got in on the act with its own more aggressive brand of commentary, announcing an intention 'to *anatomize* every *Paper*, week after week' and ridiculing the uxoriousness of a monarch who had resigned himself, '*Breeches* and all', into the hands of his wife 'for all eternity' (No. 90, 14–21 July, 1645).[60] In the long term, the most damaging result of these glimpses into Charles's personal opinions and secret projects was to put an end to the 'evasion of blaming evil counsel'; as Joad Raymond goes on to observe, the King himself had been revealed as 'a malignant'.[61]

This public relations emergency stirred the Oxford writers into a flurry of activity. Among the first into print at the beginning of August was the poet, Martin Lluellyn, who poured scorn upon the '*Poor cheap Design*' of Parliament's '*Closet-spies*' and 'bold *Intruders*', and mounted a spirited defence of the Queen's courage, intellectual capacity and religious constancy.[62] Another writer took issue with the 'inferences' of the annotators, arguing that the letters did indeed provide a true 'Mirour of the King's mind', but that only an 'ill humour' could see anything 'unworthy of Him in all that hath passed from Him'.[63] A more imaginative but no less specious ploy to regain the initiative was tried in yet another letter to a friend, in which a long-standing supporter of Parliament confides his anxiety that the publication of Laud's diary and the contents of the King's cabinet 'hath done much mischiefe to our cause', because such writings 'deepely worke into all wise men an exceeding strong beleife of those things which were let fall in so great secrecy' (p. 1).[64] The problem from the supposed author's point of view is that the two books in question, 'though they containe some truths that make for our turne', also demonstrate that the archbishop was 'a man very much a Christian, exemplary in his devotions to God, in his loyalty to his Prince', and that the King is 'sharpe and rationall' in his counsels and 'full of judicious fancy' in his expressions. He is particularly impressed by Charles's 'abilities' with the pen, finding 'his stile' both 'elegant' and 'masculine' – perhaps to counteract the charge of weak dependency on his wife (pp. 2–3). The perusal of the letters and a conversation with another friend – 'A Malignant I confesse' – have left him 'in a great perplexity', not quite 'converted' by the royal case, but uncertain how long his conscience 'will hold out' (p. 22). Dr Thomas Browne took up the cudgels against three members of Parliament for their 'Blasphemous Observations' at a public reading from the stolen correspondence in the Guildhall.[65] He gave a positive welcome to the '*Image* of the Kings very *Thoughts*' that had provided his subjects with a new insight into his fine qualities as 'a *Man*', 'a *Husband*', 'a *Christian*' and 'a *King*' (pp. 51–2). As a parting blow, he predicted that an impartial posterity would find in these letters evidence not only of Charles's true nature but also of the malice and stupidity of his opponents: 'They will never gaine this *Power* over their *beliefe*, or so farre *subdue* their *understanding*, as to think, either that so decryed a King, as He hath been, could *Penne* such Papers, or, that such *wise* Rebells, as they would faine be thought, could *Print* them' (p. 53).

Early in August, Marchamont Nedham stepped beyond the bounds tolerated even by Parliament when he treated the King as a common criminal: 'Where is *King Charles*? What's become of him? . . . it were best to send *Hue and Cry* after him' (*Mercurius Britanicus*, No. 92, 28 July – 4 August 1645).[66] He was reprimanded by the authorities in London and his collaborator, Thomas Audley, the founder of the newsbook, landed in prison. The Oxford team seized the chance to turn the tables on their rival and to keep the name of their own faltering weekly in the public eye with *Aulicus His Hue and Cry Sent forth after Britanicus, Who is generally reported to be a lost Man* (London, [13 August] 1645):

Oyez, Oyez, Oyez, If there be any person or persons that can tell any tidings of a petty penny Clerke, sometime a writer of Writs for a penny a dozen, who hath forgot his owne name, and hath a long time answered to the name of *Britanicus*; hee is a man of low stature, full set, blacke haire, hollow-hearted, empty scull'd, barren of invention, a lover of basenesse, void of grace, and lastly, a Traytor to his King: bring newes to *Aulicus* and expect a reward. (p. 1)

At the same time, they were producing a sustained counterblast to Nedham's scurrilous 'anatomy' of the royal correspondence in the three parts of *Mercurius Anti-Britanicus*, published on 4, 11 and 18 August and largely the work of John Berkenhead.[67] Part I expends its vitriolic wit upon the 'bold, shamelesse, licentious *Scumme* and *Rout*' of writers and preachers who have been the '*Engines*' on which the '*Machine*' of rebellion 'hath all this while turn'd' and singles out the 'unwasht, unhallowed *Pen*' of Britanicus for particular abuse (pp. 3–4); Part II begins the vindication of the King's cabinet against the 'aspersions' of Britanicus; and Part III gloats over his committal to the Gate-house for 'a *Hue and Crye* sent after the King' (p. 31), naming 'Captaine *Audley*' (a cowardly soldier who prefers 'to Storme Townes in a thin *Quarto*') and Nedham ('heretofore an under clerke' at Gray's Inn) as the '*Herm-Aphrodite* Rebell' responsible for 'a strange double-sex'd kind of writing . . . which runnes halfe Military froth, halfe Ale' (p. 26). This composite 'farthing *Historian*' (p. 24) is despised most of all for lacking the manners of a gentleman and divulging 'what the Queene said to her Husband in his Armes' (p. 30). Berkenhead's biographer considers that the 'remarkable volubility of the ridicule betrays the desperation with which Oxford tried to make the best of a bad case'.[68]

A similar desperation is manifest in what was probably Berkenhead's last Oxford publication, in which a Protestant convinces a Puritan and a Papist that the rebellion – 'Conceived in *England*, Borne in *Scotland*, sent back to Nurse in *London*' – will ultimately be cursed by God, even though he has permitted it some temporary success, and that parliamentary glosses on the King's letters have been 'full of Nonsense, Malice and Detraction'.[69] His final contribution to the royalist war-effort before his propaganda team disbanded was to add some notes to one of John Taylor's last Oxford pamphlets, *The Causes of the Diseases and Distempers of This Kingdome* (Oxford, [22 October] 1645).[70] His principal colleague, Peter Heylyn, had recently produced another of his scholarly attempts to 'satisfy' the qualms of an acquaintance who feared that parliamentary meddling may have vitiated the process of reformation in sixteenth-century England.[71] Going back over its history to the time of Henry VIII, he proves that the English church was free from political interference until 'these later times', when members of both Houses have been all too eager to draw 'the managery of all Affairs as well *Ecclesiasticall* as

Civill into their own hands' (p. 33). Before the disastrous summer was over, John Arnway tried to rally a population that was 'weary of Warre and greedy of Peace' (p. 2) with the argument that only a military victory for the King would bring an end to violence and oppression.[72] And in the weeks preceding Charles's flight to the Scots at Newark, one more forlorn effort was made to motivate a stand against the victorious enemy in a 'letter' which quickly degenerated into a diatribe against the misdemeanours of those who had wrested power from the King and 'laid more Taxes on the people' in five years 'then he had done in 17'.[73]

Far from the rival capitals, the nerve centres from which the battle for hearts and minds was being waged, a young poet, who would later assume a prominent role in the literary resistance to the new Commonwealth of the 1650s, temporarily laid aside his pen and took up the sword in defence of the King's failing cause. Breconshire had so far remained unscathed by the Civil War, and after his father had recalled him to South Wales in 1642 from four years of study in Oxford and London, Henry Vaughan had lived quietly in the Usk valley, working as secretary to Sir Marmaduke Lloyd, Chief Justice of the Brecon circuit.[74] Some of his early poems indicate that his two years at the Inns of Court had introduced him to literary circles in which the names of Ben Jonson and Thomas Randolph were revered and wine was celebrated as the 'Spirit of wit'.[75] A verse translation of 'Juvenal's Tenth Satire', probably composed soon after his return to the family home, reflects his first-hand experience of the tumults that surrounded the trial and execution of Strafford, and significant deviations from his source suggest a literary context which includes Cleveland's famous 'Epitaph' and the stag episode in *Cooper's Hill*.[76] At first resentful at being cut off from a fellowship in which his poetic talent was beginning to flourish and then angry and distressed at neglect by his former boon companions, his changing state of mind is vividly charted in an ordered sequence of verses derived from the *Tristia* and *Ex Ponto* epistles of Ovid. The process of translation helped him to articulate his sense of exile ('friendless' in 'a strange Land') and thwarted ambition ('now I must forget / Those pleased *Idoea's* I did frame and set / Unto my selfe').[77] In a second group of poems translated from Boethius and following on seamlessly from the Ovidian set, he took solace and encouragement from another poetic voice that claimed to find in the continued practice of poetry itself an alternative to the fickleness of fair-weather friends. A passage from 'Metrum 4' seems to have a direct bearing on Vaughan's political situation in the summer of 1645, although one of his modern editors sees only a moral significance in the sixth line, which he reads as an attempt to render the idea in the Latin original 'that a man who cannot govern his own passions is a slave to them':[78]

> Dull Cowards then! why should we start
> To see these tyrants act their part?
> Nor hope, nor fear what may befall
> And you disarm their malice all.
> But who doth faintly fear, or wish
> And sets no law to what is his,
> Hath lost the buckler, and (poor Elfe!)
> Makes up a Chain to bind himselfe.

The opening apostrophe is not in Boethius, nor is the adverb 'faintly'. In a verbal context which highlights the need for courage and includes the words 'tyrants' and 'buckler', the expression 'setting a law to what is his' could well mean being ready to fight to preserve rights or beliefs or possessions rather than merely exercising self-control. This reads, indeed, like a poem in which Vaughan was preparing himself psychologically to bear arms against the 'tyrants' who were now dangerously close to taking over the country.

Charles I was in Usk on 25 July and stayed overnight on 5 August at Brecon Priory as the guest of Sir Herbert Price, one of the county's MPs and a colonel in the local royalist army.[79] It was presumably at this time, when the King was on a recruiting drive from Raglan Castle, that Henry Vaughan enlisted, since he is known to have fought in Price's regiment at Rowton Heath near Chester on 24 September and was among the survivors of that disastrous battle who were permitted to march out of Beeston Castle when it surrendered on 16 November.[80] Among those who did not survive was a young friend of Vaughan's, whose 'years … could not be summ'd (alas!) / To a full *score*'.[81] In a remarkable elegy, the poet gave vent to 'a full years griefe', during which he had 'stood / Still on … sandy hopes' that the youthful soldier had escaped with his life, and described his last sight of him in a uniquely personal attempt to record the experience of a Civil War battle in verse:

> O that day
> When like the *Fathers* in the *Fire* and *Cloud*
> I mist thy face! I might in ev'ry *Crowd*
> See Armes like thine, and men advance, but none
> So neer to lightning mov'd, nor so fell on. . . .
> . . . like *shott* his active hand
> Drew bloud, e'r well the foe could understand.
> But here I lost him.

Another poem about Vaughan's brief military career adopts a more
Clevelandesque style to banter with a comrade-in-arms whose gro-
tesquely stiff and voluminous cloak had stood the poet in good stead
during the rigours of the autumn campaign in North Wales:

> Hadst thou been with me on that day, when wee
> Left craggie *Biston*, and the fatall *Dee*,
> When beaten with fresh storms, and late mishap
> It shar'd the office of a *Cloke*, and *Cap*, ...
> I know thou wouldst in spite of that day's fate
> Let loose thy mirth at my new shape and state.[82]

A 'Peaceable Army' of Clubmen had been active in Glamorgan
earlier in the summer and Astley, the royalist commander who replaced
Gerrard in South Wales, reported on 15 August that most of the
Breconshire gentry 'inclined to be neutrall and to join with the strongest
party'.[83] Richard Symonds, still in attendance on the King as a trooper
in the Lifeguards, noted in his diary on 12 November that 'the inhabitants of Brecknockshire had pulld downe the castle of Brecknock, and the
walls of the towne';[84] and when Major General Laugharne reached
Brecon soon after the fall of Beeston Castle, he was given a warm
welcome. On 23 November, the townspeople and local gentry declared
their loyalty to Parliament, but at the end of January, Laugharne
informed Speaker Lenthall that he had left a garrison there to deter any
resurgence of support for the King.[85] This seems to be the situation
reflected in Vaughan's verse epistle, inviting a friend to meet him in
Brecon, where the 'foule, polluted walls' look as if they had been 'sackt
by *Brennus*, and the salvage *Gaules*'.[86] Complaining that the streets ring to
the noise of 'Pigs, Dogs, and Drums', he adds that a time-serving
collection of 'new fine *Worships*' have been appointed to the local bench
in place of the 'old cast *teame* / Of Justices'. He chides his friend for a
long absence, and the rather shrill bravado of his reversion to the old
Cavalier stance of his London days is representative of one kind of
response to the military collapse of royalism:

> Come then! and ... blith (as of old) let us
> 'Midst noise and War, of Peace, and mirth discusse.
> This portion thou wert born for: why should wee
> Vex at the times ridiculous miserie?
> An age that thus hath fool'd it selfe, and will
> (Spite of thy teeth and mine) persist so still.
> Let's sit then at this *fire*, and ... steal
> A Revell in the Town.

The cults of friendship and retirement which became central features of the Cavalier strategy for coping with life under the new dispensation combine with particular poignancy in another of Vaughan's poems that may belong to this period.[87] Addressed to Thomas Powell, rector of the nearby parish of Cantref and the poet's closest friend, it pursues an extended analogy between magnetic attraction and the '*Sympathy*' which draws 'sever'd Friends' towards each other; and it summons Powell from his quiet retreat to share the pleasures of like-minded company in rather more sober terms than the previous invitation to Brecon:

> So from thy quiet *Cell*, the retir'd Throne
> Of thy fair thoughts, which silently bemoan
> Our sad distractions, come: and richly drest
> With reverend mirth and manners, check the rest
> Of loose, loath'd men!

There has been some discussion about the significance of the phrase 'Loyall Fellow-Prisoner' in the poem's title, which is now generally thought to be figurative.[88] As Harwood had lamented in his Oxford sermon, 'we are all prisoners in our native country'.

Charles I was himself literally a prisoner from the time he gave himself up to the Scots in May 1646, and Vaughan was one of three poets who wrote on the subject of his flight from Oxford to Newark. He and George Daniel both seem to have written in the knowledge of 'The Kings Disguise',[89] in which John Cleveland struggled to come to terms with the King's apparent betrayal of both his royal identity, by concealing the majesty that set him apart from ordinary human beings – 'why so coffin'd in this vile disguise? ... / Is't not enough thy Dignity's in thrall, / But thou'lt transcribe it in thy shape and all?' – and his political integrity, by surrendering his person into the hands of his rebellious countrymen – 'May thy strange journey contradictions twist, / And force faire weather from a Scottish mist'. As Judge Advocate to the garrison at Newark since May 1645, the poet was on the spot when Charles turned up there, already 'halfe depos'd' in shabby 'Attire', and the image of 'the Princely Eagle shrunke into a Bat' must have shocked him deeply. Unable to comprehend the propriety or the wisdom of his sovereign's action, he clings to a blind faith that the 'Text Royall' has deliberately obscured itself in 'a darke mysterious dresse' in order to render his secret counsels undecipherable by 'Cabinet-Intruders' and 'Pick-locks'. In the view of Jacobus, this was Cleveland's 'only way to avoid despair', the only alternative 'to renouncing a king who has seemed to renounce himself'.[90]

When 'The King disguis'd' was eventually published in Vaughan's late volume, *Thalia Rediviva,* a headnote claimed that it had been written *'about the same time that Mr* John Cleveland *wrote his'.*[91] The opening couplet employs the same conceit and catches the same tone of bewilderment: 'A King and no King! Is he gone from us, / And stoln alive into his Coffin thus?' The Welsh poet goes further than his original in hinting at a parallel between the 'Royal Saint' in servant's garb and the mystery of the godhead humbled at the Incarnation: 'Poor, obscure shelter! if that shelter be / Obscure, which harbours so much Majesty'. But he shares Cleveland's unease at the image of 'great *Charles'* in 'such a dress' – 'When he was first obscur'd with this coarse thing, / He grac'd *Plebeians,* but prophan'd the King' – and puts his faith in the ultimate wisdom of royal policy: 'Secrets of State are points we must not know'. Like Cleveland, however, his misgivings about Charles's choice of protector are not completely allayed: 'O strengthen not / With too much trust the Treason of a Scot!'

George Daniel's response to the plight of the King was couched in the more expansive form of a pastoral dialogue, in which two northern shepherds combine lamentation with a narrative of the 'Great Battles' and 'strange growth / Of Treasons' since Edgehill:

> Then, in this Night of Sorrow, let us bring
> Our Grones to the Disasters of the King;
> Sigh out a Storie to yᵉ pious Ears
> Of Men, who when wee're dead, may read this verse.[92]

Strephon's grief at the 'Royall Distresses' mingles with despair at the victory of 'Rebell Powers' and horror at the thought that the 'sacred Person' of the King 'must, / Inevitably fall, to their unjust / Tirrannous wills'; and Hilas is sceptical about Charles's hope 'to be Secure; / And to engage that Nation, who has bene / The Greatest Cloud his Glories yet has seene'. After all, 'A Scott's a Scott,' exclaims Hilas, astonished that 'a man / Of his high Reason, (once deceiv'd) ere can / Againe be brought to trust 'em'. Strephon, shocked at this criticism, voices Cleveland's only alternative to despair and renunciation of the royal cause and appeals to the image of the saintly Charles that was beginning to take hold of the royalist imagination: 'This Great King! this Good Man! . . . This Good King Saw a Sphere beyond our Sence . . . Why he thus proceeds / Let not us question.' The anxiety underlying all three of these poems stems from the perception that 'Charles has participated in his own occlusion', which has been related to an important shift in public attitude during the later 1640s: 'If trimming his own beard and hair is to be described as sacrilege or treason, then the King's image must be taken to be as crucial to his royal identity as any inner reality.'[93]

With the surrender of Oxford, Charles and his propagandists lost control of their presses. Among their last appeals to the country were two volumes which together consitituted a comprehensive indictment of the depradations of Parliament and its agents over the past four years. *Querela Cantabrigiensis: Or, A Remonstrance By way of Apologie, For the banished Members of the late flourishing University of Cambridge* (Oxford, [April] 1646), probably by John Barwick, printed documentary evidence of the 'barbarous courses' taken against the academic community, and described the impact on 'the said sufferers' of losing their livelihoods and witnessing the spoliation of their institution: 'this sad prospect did so farre surcharge us with griefe, that it cast us for a long time into a fit of Musing' (sig. A2r). The volume was promptly incorporated into a collected edition of all twenty-one issues of Bruno Ryves's weekly, *Mercurius Rusticus* (May 1643 – March 1644), which contained a separate section on the fate of the cathedrals and a list of persecuted clergy.[94]

The end of the Civil War saw the dispersal and regrouping of the royalist writers who had been actively engaged in the military or literary contest with Parliament. Berkenhead left Oxford before the final siege began in May and was with the garrison at Wallingford when it surrendered on 27 July. By October, after being permitted to visit Charles in Newcastle, he had found a niche for himself in London, helping to foster support for the King among the moderate Presbyterian readership of *The Kingdome's Weekly Intelligencer*, a newsbook edited by Richard Collings, and provoking division between the moderate and extreme parties at Westminster in two pamphlets, *An Answer to A Speech Without Doores* (November 1646) and *The Speech Without Doores Defended Without Reason* (December 1646).[95] John Taylor sought refuge for some time with relatives in East Anglia, before taking over an alehouse near Covent Garden.[96] He supplemented his income and kept the popular royalist flag flying with such occasional publications as *Peace, Peace, and we shall be quiet. Or, Monarchie asserted* (London, [21 May] 1647) and *The Whirligigge Turning To his Points, and Numbers* (London, [August] 1647). John Cleveland drops out of sight after the fall of Newark, although he may have been the author of 'The Scots Apostasie', a verse satire printed as a broadside (London, [10 March] 1647), which called down 'an Epidemick curse' upon all Scotsmen when the Scottish army realized the fears of Cleveland, Vaughan and Daniel by handing Charles over to Parliament on 30 January for a payment of £400,000.

After six months of delay and intrigue on the part of the King, the Scots had finally despaired of persuading him to sign the Covenant and accept a Presbyterian system for the English church, which had been their price for supporting a settlement between Charles and the Presbyterian faction at Westminster against the more radical Independents who dominated the Commons. Even Henrietta Maria was urging her husband to compromise on the question of episcopacy, and in October 1646 a poet was her chosen emissary from the court that had assembled around her in Paris. Since the autumn of 1644, Sir William Davenant had been acting as a royalist agent, carrying letters between Jermyn in France and Digby in England, organizing Goring's passage across the Channel in November 1645, joining Jermyn, Digby and Culpepper on the mission that brought Prince Charles on the last leg of his journey into exile from Jersey to France in June 1646, and despatched to Newcastle by the Queen on a fruitless mission to overcome the King's obdurate conscience.[97]

Once a deal had been struck with Westminster, the Scottish garrison withdrew from Newcastle and within two weeks the entire army was back on its native soil. On 3 February, escorted by Commissioners of the English Parliament, Charles I began his journey to Holdenby House in Northamptonshire, the place appointed for his captivity. All along the route there were cheering crowds and bells were rung in Nottingham and Northampton. Ordinary people everywhere had had enough of bloodshed, high war taxes, and the control over their daily lives exercised by the County Committees. They saw the reconciliation of King and Parliament as the necessary precondition for a return to stable government. Even among those engaged in the political management of the peace, few could imagine any permanent settlement that did not place the King 'at the head of the new order of things'.[98] Over the months that followed, the Presbyterians at Westminster, led by Denzil Holles and Sir Philip Stapleton, tried to negotiate an agreement with Charles based on some variation of the proposals made to him at Newcastle. But the victorious New Model Army was also beginning to act 'as a directly political force, with a sweeping programme of constitutional reform'.[99] There was widespread resistance among troops and officers to a Commons move to disband regiments not needed for service in Ireland; Agitators – some of them with Leveller affiliations –

were appointed to speak for the rank and file at the end of April; and in early June a Council composed of senior officers and elected representatives from each regiment was set up. Since an agreement with the King was the political goal of Army grandees like Cromwell and his son-in-law, Commissary General Henry Ireton, and of the Presbyterians, there was growing concern on both sides about the control of his person. To prevent him being used as a pawn to secure a new military alliance between the Scots and the Presbyterian faction at Westminster, he was abducted from Holdenby on 4 June by Cornet Joyce and a body of 500 horse and taken into the custody of the Army at Newmarket. Cromwell may have been implicated in this action, although Underdown thinks it more likely that 'Joyce was acting on behalf of the radical junior officers and Agitators'. Cromwell and Ireton, however, were more than ready to exploit the opportunity of binding the King 'to an advantageous settlement on their own terms' and avoiding 'the danger of a Presbyterian-Scottish betrayal'.[100] Charles was moved to Caversham early in July, where he had a long private meeting with Cromwell; and a constitutional package, devised by Ireton and approved by the Army Council, was formally presented to him on 28 July, before being published on 1 August under the title *The Heads of the Proposals*. Soon afterwards, he was taken to Oatlands and on 24 August he was moved again to Hampton Court. Towards the end of the month, Parliament made another attempt to interest him in its earlier terms. He had also opened clandestine discussions with the Scots. Ashton sums up the devious game that Charles was playing as summer turned into autumn, 'juggling rather maladroitly with three balls in the air: the parliamentary and Scottish Newcastle (Hampton Court) Propositions; the army's Heads of the Proposals; and ... the possibility of a Scottish military intervention on his behalf'.[101]

Not long after Charles had been surrendered by the Scots into the keeping of the English Commissioners, another of Parliament's prisoners spoke out against violations of Magna Carta by those who were 'elated' by 'the successe of their armes'. Judge David Jenkins was unequivocal in the legal 'positions' that he presented to the Lords and Commons from Newgate, where he had been incarcerated for 'seditious' writings: that it is '*High Treason*' to imprison the King, remove his counsellors by force and alter established laws and religion. Two months later, now lodged in the Tower, he put the weight of 'forty five yeares in the Study of the Lawes of this Land' behind an appeal to the Inns of Court to defend the 'Regality of the Crown of England' against the traitors who were depriving the King of his liberty 'untill he hath yeelded to certain demands'.[102] Another defender of the ancient constitution rehearsed the well-worn argument that the promoters of the war had, from the beginning, 'had a designe against his Majesty and against Monarchy', and showed that the 'Propositions' put to the King at Uxbridge and Newcastle had the consistent aim of settling 'the chiefe Power and Government in the two Houses of Parliament'.[103]

The removal of Charles from Holdenby to Newmarket produced a flurry of pamphlets from across the spectrum of what might be covered by the term 'royalist' in the circumstances of mid-1647. The Welsh judge, still in the Tower, was among the first in the field, pitting the Common Law against parliamentary legislation that was invalidated by its internal contradictions and making the constitutional case against a perpetual Parliament.[104] Robert Grosse mustered the usual array of biblical and classical 'sentences' in favour of obedience to ordained authority and urged a return to the mixed government achieved by the reforms of 1641, in which 'the King may stil enjoy his *Regalities* and *Prerogatives* without farther alteration, and the *Parliament* may still retain their ancient priviledges and immunities without any more interruption'.[105] In the first of a three-part exposure of the 'deep Hypocrisie and hatefull treachery' of the Presbyterians at Westminster, Amon Wilbee spoke for the moderate group of 'Royal Independents' in Parliament, 'whose ends and endeavours, are wholly to set up the *Gospel* in the power of it, to doe *right* to their *King*, and to discharge their trust to the *Kingdome*'.[106] And Michael Hudson, who had accompanied Charles in his clandestine departure from Oxford, devoted nearly two hundred pages to demonstrating that the Holy Scriptures 'afford a more exact and compleat model of *Monarchie*, and more perfect Rules of Government and obedience' than secular philosophers and lawyers; but he betrayed an unease, like that expressed in the verses of Cleveland and Vaughan, about 'the prodigious preposture and confusion' that his own exploit of the previous spring had contributed to, in a topsy-turvy kingdom 'where servants ride on horse-back, and Princes walk on foot; where subjects are clavered up into the Kings Throne, and the King debased below the condition of a free-born subject'.[107]

The pamphlet which points most clearly to the next phase of royalist writing, however, was the work of Jasper Mayne, who followed up the insights that others had begun to formulate in the controversy over the King's cabinet:

I have in my time seen certain *Pictures* with two *faces*. Beheld one way, they have presented the *shape* and *figure* of a *Man*. Beheld another, they have presented the *shape* and *figure* of a *Serpent*. Me thinks, Sir, for some years, whatever *Letters* the King wrote either to the *Queene*, or his *friends*, or what ever *Declarations* he publisht in the defence of his *Rights* and *Cause*, had the ill fortune to undergoe the fate of such a *Picture*. To us who read them impartially, by their own true, genuine *light*, they appeared so many cleare, transparent *Copies* of a sincere and Gallant *Mind*. Look't upon by the People . . . through the *Answers* and *Observations*, and venemous *Comments*, which some men made upon them, a *fallacy* in *judgement* followed very like the *fallacy* of the *sight*, where an *Object* beheld through a false deceitfull *medium*, partakes of the *cosenage* of the *conveyance*, and *way*, and puts on a false *Resemblance*.[108]

As the period of the King's captivity lengthened and the unthinkable possibility that he would be brought to trial by his own subjects edged into the public consciousness, the new goal for polemical writers on either side would be the creation of an image of the 'man of blood' or the 'royal martyr' out of the complex contradictions that made up the character of Charles I.

Lois Potter notes the 'centrality of prison in the lives of the reading public' during this period, when there was a 'stream of pamphlets from the imprisoned levellers', and points out the difference between the prison literature of the Elizabethans and that produced by the mid-century prisoner, who 'could present himself as a guiltless sufferer for reasons of conscience'.[109] Judge Jenkins, signing himself 'Now Prisoner in the Tower', declared his resolution 'to tender' himself a 'Sacrifice' for the Laws of England; while Michael Hudson's prefatory letter to Charles I was dated '*From my Close Prison in the Tower, 9. Sept. 1647*'.[110] James Howell gives a graphic account of his arrest in Number LV of the first edition of his *Familiar Letters* in 1645:

One morning betimes there rush'd into my chamber five armed Men with Swords, Pistols, and Bills, and told me they had a Warrant from the Parliament for me: I desir'd to see their Warrant, they deny'd it: . . . So they rush'd presently into my Closet, and seiz'd on all my Papers and Letters, and anything that was Manuscript; and many printed Books they took also, and hurl'd all into a great hair Trunk, which they carry'd away with them.[111]

He was brought before 'the Committee of *Examination*', but an inquiry 'could find nothing that might give offence'. Nevertheless, 'such was my hard hap, that I was committed to the *Fleet*, where I am now under close restraint' (p. 356). In the next letter, he commiserates with Sir Eubale Thelwall at the Peter-House in London: 'Sir, Tho' we are not in the same *Prison*, yet we are in the same *predicament* of sufferance; therefore I presume you subject to the like fits of melancholy as I' (p. 356). Sad thoughts became the badge of the defeated royalist, and when journalistic activity started up again in the autumn of 1647, the first title to be launched was *Mercurius Melancholicus*, the author of which was said to have recently emerged 'forth from my sad and Loathsome Cell' (No. 7, 9–16 October 1647). Writing to Philip Warwick in November 1645, Howell comments on those who share his fate: 'Moreover, there are here some choice Gentlemen who are my *Co-Martyrs*; for a *Prisoner* and a *Martyr* are the same thing, save, *that the one is buried before his death, the other after*' (Number LVII, p. 369).

From the middle of 1646, those who willingly suffered for the cause could look to Charles himself as a model of patient endurance, an image that was exploited in a variation on Christ's address from the Cross in George Herbert's 'Sacrifice':

> I have been truckt for, bought and sold, yet I
> Am King (though prisoner) pray tell me why
> I am removed now from Holdenby?
>   Never was griefe like mine. . . .
> Causelesse they like a bird have chased me,
> Behold, O Lord, looke downe from heaven and see,
> Thou that hearest prisoners prayers, heare me.
>   Never was griefe like mine.

Sidney Gottlieb describes the entire work, which ranges over various complaints about Charles's treatment by his subjects since 1640 and ends with 'Lamentations of the Church', as 'a kind of miniature *Eikon Basilike*, helping pave the way for the enormously popular later work'.[112]

Howell's letters, although many of them date from the reign of James I, were presented from the start 'as topical, royalist statement'.[113] The related form of the prison poem became a recognizable royalist genre with evident popular appeal. Lovelace's 'To Althea. From Prison' was widely circulated, as was Sir Roger L'Estrange's 'The Liberty and Requiem of an imprisoned Royalist', which reiterates the Stoicism of the earlier lyric but adds the post-1646 motif of sufferings shared with the King himself:

> Locks, bars, walls, lonenesse, tho together met,
> Make me no prisoner, but an Anchoret. . . .
>   When once my Prince affliction hath,
>   Prosperity doth treason seem,
>   And then to smooth so rough a path
>   I can learn patience too from him.

> Now not to suffer shews no loyall heart,
> When Kings want ease subjects must love to smart.[114]

In an address 'To the Lovers of Honour & Poesie', Francis Wortley
excuses the prose 'characters' and translated verses in his *Characters and
Elegies* ([15 July] 1646) as 'fruits of Phansie' rather than 'serious studies',
which served to distract 'the melancholy thoughts of my imprisonment'
(sigg. A3ᵛ–A4ʳ). His collection of original poetry is rounded off with some
lines 'Upon a true and contended Prisoner', which spice their Christian
Stoicism with thoughts of ultimate revenge:

> Art thou imprison'd? looke up thou shalt find,
> Thou hast a strange enlargement in thy mind.
> Th' are more ingaged far, Imprisoned thee;
> And shall come to accompt, when thou art free.   (p. 58)

Wortley was also the author of a drinking-song, printed as a broadside,
in which the 'well try'd loyall blades' in the Tower flouted the lies and
primness of the puritans and celebrated their allegiance to the King:

> Gallant Sir *Thomas* bold and stout,
> (Brave *Lunsford*) children eateth,
> But he takes care, where he eats one,
> There he a hundred getteth. . . .
> Wee'l drink them o're and o're again
> Else we're unthankfull creatures
> Since CHARLES the Wise, the valiant King
> Takes us for loyall traytors.[115]

The names of Wortley and Lunsford are prominent among the
'Prisoners of Warre' who gave vent to their grievances and printed their
petitions in a pamphlet published some time in 1647 under the self-
explanatory title, *A True Relation of the Cruell and unparallel'd Oppression
which hath been illegally imposed upon the Gentlemen, Prisoners in the Tower of
LONDON.*

Verse had been used as a medium for the expression of royalist ideology
throughout the Caroline period and as a weapon in the war between
King and Parliament since the early 1640s. Apart from the university
collections, major set pieces like *Cooper's Hill* and Cowley's *A Satyre
Against Seperatists*, and the broadside doggerel of writers like John Taylor,
however, most of the poetic manifestations of royalism had circulated in
manuscript. Some, like the satires of Cleveland and Denham and the
wittily subversive inventions of Alexander Brome, which addressed
topical issues directly, reached an extensive public; others, like the
Jonsonian epistles and translations of Henry Vaughan and the odes and

eclogues of George Daniel, remained within the orbit of a very private readership. This preference for more or less limited manuscript circulation was the result of the survival into the Stuart period of the 'stigma of print' among Tudor Court poets and socially ambitious 'wits', who did not want to be associated with the new breed of professional writer who 'went to market with his wares'.[116] As a Milton scholar has pointed out, and as Peter Beal's *Index of English Literary Manuscripts* amply illustrates, 'the 1620s and 1630s were the peak decades of a widely and tightly interconnected manuscript culture reflecting the aristocratic and *arriviste* distaste for the print medium'.[117] This situation changed as royalist military resistance petered out in the course of 1646. In his investigation into the effect of print on the transmission of lyric poetry, Arthur Marotti identifies the posthumous appearance of John Donne's *Poems* and George Herbert's *The Temple* in 1633 as 'a watershed event that changed the relationship of lyric poetry to the print medium, helping to normalize within print culture the publication of poetry collections by individual authors'. He argues that the successive editions of the work of these two influential poets over the next twenty-five years 'became part of a process by which courtly and Royalist poets were installed in the literary institution taking shape within print culture' and that instead of being 'a potential embarrassment to Royalist writers', the printed book 'became a safe haven for their work and a sign of political resistance to the authority of those who had defeated the king's forces'.[118]

Marotti goes on to highlight the role of Humphrey Moseley, who published collections of poetry by Waller, Suckling, Crashaw, Shirley, Cowley, Carew, Cartwright, Stanley and Vaughan between 1645 and 1651 and 'portrayed himself as the preserver of an endangered Royalist or loyalist body of texts'.[119] Other critics have commented on Moseley's 'self-advertizing' prefaces, in which 'the royalist sympathies of the author are made explicit', and drawn out the implications of the Latin title given to Suckling's *Fragmenta Aurea* (1646) – 'that is, *Golden Pieces*, the broken remains of a writer and a culture both now perceived to have been destroyed by the political turmoil' – and of the extended title of Moseley's 1651 edition of Carew, which 'reads like the obituary for a way of life': *Poems. With a Maske, by Thomas Carew Esq; One of the Gent. of the privie-Chamber, and Sewer in Ordinary to His Late Majesty. The Songs were set in Musick by Mr Henry Lawes Gent: of the Kings Chappell, and one of his late Majesties Private Musick.*[120] Loxley has recently added the important observation that the political attitudes expressed in individual poems are less important than the propaganda value of an entire volume, like

Mildmay Fane's *Otia Sacra* (1648) or Robert Herrick's *Hesperides* (1648), 'as a single signifying unit which presents the opportunity for the exploration and maintenance of a poetics of activism'.[121] What needs to be further examined is the variety of motivations for going into print in the second half of the 1640s – and this involves distinguishing among the different kinds of volumes of collected poetry that appeared after 1645.

Moseley set up one model in his edition of Waller, taken over from the bookseller Thomas Walkley, who had printed a manuscript that came into his hands in 1644, probably without the author's permission.[122] Waller had been imprisoned for his part in the plot of May 1643 and had gone abroad upon his release in the autumn of 1644. Moseley signalled the royalist connections of the poet on the title-page of his reissue of Walkley's volume in 1645 – 'All the Lyrick Poems in this Booke were set by Mr HENRY LAWES Gent. of the Kings Chappell, and one of his Majesties Private Musick' – and in 'An advertisement to the Reader' reinforced the propaganda over the merely commercial aspects of publishing these poems in his appeal to an appropriate readership, which would share the elite cultural tastes of himself and the exiled poet:

Thus they go abroad unsophisticated, and like the present condition of the Author himselfe, they are expos'd to the wide world, to travell, and try their fortunes: And I beleeve there is no gentle soule that pretends any thing to knowledge and the choycest sort of invention but will give them entertainment and wellcome.[123]

Similarly, he assumes that the readers of his collection of Suckling's 'Incomparable Peeces' will be 'only knowing Gentlemen', who by rejecting the 'Paper prostitutions' of 'this Age' will have become 'qualified' as competent judges of a writer whose name 'is sacred to Art and Honour'[124]; and the title-page of *Steps to the Temple* (1646) presents the poet to the world as a victim of the purge carried out by Manchester in 1644: '*By* Richard Crashaw, *sometimes of* Pembroke *Hall, and late Fellow of* S *Peters Coll. in* Cambridge.'

Following Moseley's lead, John and Richard Marriot published the full set of eleven eclogues by Francis Quarles under the title *The Shepheards Oracles* with the date 1646 on the title-page, although Thomason purchased his copy on 2 December 1645. The first ten of these pastoral dialogues had been written during the 1630s on a variety of ecclesiastical topics and were rather anti-Laudian in tone. But the eleventh, which had already been printed separately in 1644, dramatized the dangers of Separatist anarchy and looked to the King to defend the episcopal system against Root-and-Branch reformers. One passage in particular was exploited in an emblematic frontispiece by William Marshall [see Figure 1] that was designed to secure a sympathetic readership among moderate Protestants like Quarles himself, who had become 'loyal converts' to the King's cause and perhaps even 'professed royalists':

> But think'st thou, Swain, the great Assemblie's eye
> Beholds not these base Sycophants, that lye
> Close gnawing at the root, as well as those,
> That with the *Romish* Axe, strike downright blows
> On the main *body* of Religion's tree?[125]

Although he was neither dead nor, as far as is known, in exile, Cleveland suffered the same fate as Quarles and Waller in having his work launched into the market place without his permission (and, indeed, without his name) in what must have been the major commercial and propaganda success of the period, since there were no less than five reprintings in 1647 alone of *The Character of a London-Diurnall, with several Select Poems by the same Author.* In the same year, the London publisher, Philemon Stephens, issued a second edition of Christopher Harvey's 1640 volume, *The Synagogue,* which was later often sold with the seventh edition of George Herbert's *The Temple,* published under Stephens's imprint in 1656. Herbert's modern editor suggests that Stephens may have already produced an unauthorized version of *The Temple* in 1647, calculating that 'the new edition of *The Synagogue* would go off better if it were bound up with *The Temple*'.[126] Since Harvey's religious poems, written in avowed imitation of Herbert, took a decidedly ideological stance in celebrating church festivals and defending the Book of Common Prayer, the publisher may have seen more than merely financial advantage in forging a link between the work of Harvey and one of the poetic monuments of the 'ancient' Church of England.

In addition to those produced by the enterprise of Moseley and others in the book trade, there are also collections of verse that were apparently undertaken on the initiative of the poets themselves. James Shirley explained in a postscript that he had only let his poems '*proceed to the Publik view*' because corrupt copies of some of them had been '*mingled with other mens ... conceptions in Print*'.[127] Martyn Lluellyn, Francis Wortley and Henry Vaughan, however, all sent to the press volumes which had political designs upon their readers. Lluellyn's *Men-Miracles. With Other Poems* (London [29 June] 1646) was dedicated to the Duke of York, and in several of the commendatory verses, the poet was heralded as the

Figure 1. Frontispiece to Francis Quarles, *The Shepherds Oracles* (1646)

successor to his Christ Church colleague, William Cartwright. A series
of topical satires – on the Oxford fire, the parliamentary newsbooks
('The Spy of the Buttery, Or the Welsh Dove'), and the printing of the
King's letters – were followed by elegies on eminent casualties of the
war, like Sir John Smith and Sir Bevill Grenvile, and on Oxford
scholars, like 'Master R. B. Student of Christ Church' and 'C. W. H.
Slaine at Newark', in whom 'The *Sword* & *Booke*, the *Campe* & *Colledge*
met' (p. 90). The verse elegies in Wortley's *Characters and Elegies*, with
their repetitive praise of courage, duty and 'noble blood' manifested in
'loyal death', make their real impact not as individual tributes but as a
collective honouring of the royalist dead – from popular heroes like the
Earl of Northampton and General Charles Cavendish to 'my dear
Godson and Nephew *Henry Morton*' (p. 50).

Vaughan's gathering of poems from his student days in Oxford and
London, and from his 'retirement' in Breconshire in the early years of
the war, is not so overtly partisan in its contents, but the mode of his
introductory address to 'To all Ingenious Lovers of Poesie' – the *'more
refined* Spirits' that can *'out-wing these dull Times'* and, like the poet, *'revell
... in the* Dregs *of an Age'* – lays claim to a readership among those
connoisseurs of wit and learning who were drawn towards the royal
cause. And his ironic apology for the major piece in the volume, the
translation of a Latin satire, is meant to be understood by those inside
the court culture that Vaughan had once aspired to join:

It is one of his, whose Roman *Pen had as much true* Passion, *for the infirmities of that State,
as we should have* Pitty, *to the distractions of our owne: Honest (I am sure) it is, and offensive
cannot be, except it meet with such* Spirits *that will quarell with* Antiquitie, *or purposely*
Arraigne *themselves: These indeed may thinke, that they have slept out so many* Centuries
in this Satyre, *and are now awaked; which, had it been still* Latine, *perhaps their Nap had
been Everlasting.*[128]

Simmonds has noted the topical significance of the poet's contempt for
those unlearned 'Spirits' – the 'mechanick preachers' of royalist propaganda – who *'quarrel with* Antiquity' in their assaults on the ancient
traditions of church and monarchy and who have up to now been
protected from the force of Juvenal's satire by their ignorance of
Latin.[129] The poem itself is full of topical allusions to the evils of Civil
War and to the 'wrong zeale' of those who commit themselves to
violence by 'idle and superfluous vowes' and stir it up with 'Vaine
dreames, and jealousies'.[130]

Another group of poets were content for the fruits of their lyric
meditations during the years of warfare and defeat to remain in

manuscript. Some wrote for the consolation or entertainment of their immediate circle of family and friends. Ralph Knevet's imitation of 'the best of all Poets', George Herbert, in *A Gallery to the Temple*, marks him as an adherent to the outlawed church which the saintly poet-priest had come to symbolize.[131] Redolent of a more political royalism is a manuscript compiled by Lady Elizabeth Brackley and Lady Jane Cavendish, daughters of the exiled Marquis of Newcastle, and containing not only poems and songs (many of them addressed to their absent father), but also a play entitled *The Concealed Fansyes*, which reflects their experiences when Welbeck Abbey was surrendered to parliamentary forces in August 1644 and retaken for the King in July 1645.[132] After being ejected from his fellowship at Peterhouse in 1644, Joseph Beaumont occupied his enforced retirement with the composition of a long verse narrative, *Psyche or Loves Mysterie*, and a body of lyric poetry which has the air of a private diary, recording his lucubrations on church feastdays, like Whitsunday, and on more personal occasions, like the anniversary of his baptism.[133] George Daniel's *Scattered Fancies* were intended, he tells future readers in a postscript, 'not to the publike Eye, but his owne retired Fancies, to make light that burthen which some grone under'.[134] In the dark years following the execution of Charles I, Henry Vaughan would fashion the collection of lyric poetry into one of the major achievements of royalist art, which creatively blurred the distinctions between private and public, and between religious devotion and political subversion.

CHAPTER 10

Trial and martyrdom: September 1647 – January 1649

During the turbulent summer of 1647, the Army had marched into London to quell a counter-revolutionary move by the City Council to coerce Parliament into restoring Charles I to power. Through the autumn, however, Cromwell and the generals were themselves working with the moderate leaders at Westminster to reach an agreement with the King on the basis of Ireton's *Heads of the Proposals*. The Army grandees were still intent on using constitutional means to achieve a settlement, but much more radical reforms were proposed in the Leveller-inspired *Agreement of the People*, which was drawn up by the Agitators and debated with the Army commanders at the end of October in Putney church. Fearing that his life was in danger, Charles escaped from Hampton Court on 11 November and sought refuge on the Isle of Wight, where he soon found himself once more in captivity, this time in Carisbrooke Castle under the care of the governor, Robert Hammond, who was a cousin of Cromwell. No more able than most of his contemporaries 'to imagine that a settlement could be made without him', he was still manoeuvring 'to sell his support to, and then exploit, the highest bidder'.[1] But he had miscalculated in his flight from Hampton Court, which 'led on all sides to a hardening of positions'.[2] As a result of his contemptuous refusal of Parliament's pre-conditions for further talks in December, there was a vote by 'a revealingly broad coalition in the Commons' on 3 January 1648 that no further 'addresses' should be made to him; by then, however, he had embarked upon 'his ultimate folly', an 'Engagement' with the Scots which he had concluded on 26 December by conceding Presbyterianism in England for three years, during which a final religious solution would be worked out to the satisfaction of himself and the English Parliament.[3]

In the meantime, an outbreak of violence in Canterbury over the Ordinance of 1644 forbidding the celebration of Christmas heralded a spate of petitions and riots against rule of the localities by a centralized system of Committees and in favour of the disbandment of the Army and a treaty with the King. But the Second Civil War of 1648 was 'a series of isolated and unco-ordinated risings', which lacked a 'unified strategic plan', and any hope of returning Charles to power was vitiated by 'the tardiness of the Scottish invasion'.[4] By the time the Duke of Hamilton's Engager army had linked up with Marmaduke Langdale at Carlisle in July, a rising against Parliament in South Wales had been crushed, Fairfax had dispersed the Kentish insurgents at Maidstone, a force raised by the Earl of Holland had been defeated at St Neots, and another group of royalists was besieged in Colchester. With Cromwell's victory over the Scots at Preston on 17–19 August and the surrender of Colchester on 28 August, the fighting was virtually over, although Pontefract Castle held out until 22 March 1649.

While Charles was being held under easier conditions at Hampton Court, where he was attended by his chaplains and allowed to receive visitors,[5] John Taylor directed another of his topical verse pamphlets to his 'Most Gracious (suffering) Sovereign Lord the King', praising his 'patient constancy' and 'Christian Mind Majestical', and hoping that before long 'we may have our Queen and Prince once more / And use them Kinder than we did of yore'.[6] Taylor may also have been involved in *Mercurius Melancholicus*, one of several underground royalist news-books that were launched during the autumn. Among the others were *Mercurius Pragmaticus*, the longest-running successor to *Aulicus* which was produced by Marchamont Nedham (supposed to have been enlisted in the royal cause by Charles himself in an interview at Hampton Court),[7] and *Mercurius Bellicus*, which provided a regular outlet for the talents of John Berkenhead when he took it over in February 1648 to rally military support for the King and brand the Independents as potential regi-cides.[8] The pen of Berkenhead has also been detected in *Melancholicus*, *Pragmaticus* and George Wharton's *Mercurius Elencticus*,[9] and towards the end of 1647 he kept up the Laudian attack on the church-reformers in a satirical portrait of a typical member of the Assembly of Divines – 'nor *Priest*, nor *Burgess*, but a *Participle* that shark's upon both', who 'has sate four years *towards* a new Religion, but in the interim left none at all'.[10]

The composers of popular ballads were also active in the wake of the Army's assertion of its new political role. In 'Lex Talionis: Or, London Revived' (dated 3 September 1647 by Thomason) it was pointed out that just as the King gave 'power to a Parliament' which has now 'Depriv'd him of his government', so Parliament gave power to Fairfax, 'Still presuming he would be / Their servant', only to discover that 'he requites them in each thing, / As they before have serv'd the King'.[11] Alexander Brome chipped in with a mock panegyric on Cromwell (dated 22 September by Thomason), in which a celebration of the Army's entrance into London during August provides a platform for personal attacks on Prynne ('Whose circumcised ears are hardly grown / Ripe for another Persecution') and Cromwell himself with his 'Nose ... dominical [red]', and for general assaults on 'Sequestrating Knaves' that have 'made whole Counties beggarly' and the members of the 'Synod' at Westminster that have 'torn the Church' and 'set up that Calf, your Directory'.[12]

Not long before *Mercurius Pragmaticus* and *Mercurius Bellicus* began stirring up armed rebellion against Parliament and the Army, a loyal clergyman was shaming those who 'served the King ... so long as the sun shined' but have now 'run away to compound & save something', and paving the way for renewed action with an appeal to 'our Gentlemen of the Sword, if ever the King hath occasion to use them againe'.[13] And the author of a 'little Pamphlet' was eager to 'comfort and strengthen' those who were 'apt to misconstrue all things, and to imagine the worst' with 'two considerations' – 'the goodnesse and mercy of our God' and 'the wisedome and pollicy of our King', whose 'sincerity ... to his friends' is the 'maine Axeltree whereon our Kingdome turnes'.[14]

Once the first Civil War was over and the King a prisoner, printed reports of isolated battles and sieges gave way to more considered (if still partisan) appraisals of the entire conflict. Already, before the trial and execution of Charles I, a number of substantial histories appeared in print: *Magnalia Dei Anglicana* (London, 1646) by John Vicars, *A Survey of England's Champions* (London, 1647) by Josiah Ricraft, *Anglia Rediviva* by Joshua Sprigge, and, the most 'comprehensive and ambitious' of these early civil war histories, Thomas May's *History of the Parliament of England: Which began November the third, M.DC.XL* (London, 1647). Most of these celebrated the achievements of the victorious Parliament.[15] Their only strictly royalist competitor was George Wharton's primitive chronicle, *England's Iliads in a Nut-Shell* (Oxford, 1645), but in 1648 Clement Walker, a man of conservative constitutional views who was driven by the extremes of post-war politics into support for the King, published an account of the past few years, divided into two sections on 'The Mystery of the two Junto's, Presbyterean and Independent' and 'The History of Independency'.[16] The uneasiness of this late convert to royalism is apparent in the three separate epistles prefixed to his history. In the first, 'To my dread Soveraigne', he praises a 'mixed' government and condemns kings who enlarge 'their Prerogatives beyond their limits' (sig. A2ᵛ); in the second, '*To His Excellency Sir* THOMAS FAIRFAX, *and the* ARMY *under his Command*', he urges the soldiers to cure 'those *ulcers*', the '2 *factions in Parliament*', that have divided the two Houses and 'the whole Kingdom' (sig. A4ʳ); and in the third, 'To the un-byassed Reader', he invokes the principles that have been betrayed by '*a* prevaricating number of Grandees' (sig. B1ʳ) – order and decency in religion, the rule of law, the liberties of the people.

The major royalist history of these years was not published until the eighteenth century and its author seems to have intended it for a very select readership during his own time. Edward Hyde began work on what became *The History of the Rebellion* in the Scilly Isles during the early weeks of his exile, dating the first page 'March 16, 164[6]'. On 8 March 1648, he completed the seventh book with an account of Prince Rupert's relief of Newark in March 1644, at which point he interrupted his narrative, only to resume it many years later.[17] He was to claim in 1671 that he first undertook this laborious task with the approbation of Charles I, 'by his encouragement, and for his vindication'.[18] But in a letter to Secretary Nicholas on 15 November 1646, making provision for the fate of the manuscript in the event of his death, he implies that his purpose was as much to instruct as to vindicate his royal master: 'that in due time somewhat by your care may be published, and the original be delivered to the King, who will not find himself flattered in it, nor irreverently handled, though the truth will better become a dead than a living man.'[19] A few months before, the aim of privately confirming the faith of fellow 'constitutional royalists' and securing their good name in the future seems to have been uppermost in his mind, when he confided to Sir John Berkeley that his outspokenness would 'make the work unfit in this age for communication, yet it may be fit for the perusal and comfort of some men; and being transmitted through good hands, may tell posterity that the whole nation was not so bad as it will be then thought to have been'.[20] In his preamble to the text itself, these multiple motives jostle for attention in his hopes that 'posterity may not be deceived' and that his work may both contribute to the process of binding up 'the wounds' of the present and also 'serve to inform myself, and some others, what we are to do, as well as to comfort us in what we have done'.[21] George Watson regards Hyde's masterpiece as essentially 'a study in statecraft, in how power is lost and won; in how motive, decision, and outcome are causally linked'; and Nigel Smith argues that, for all their differences in other respects, both Hyde and May, by 'their incorporation of the printed materials which played such a crucial role in the conflict', significantly expanded 'the dimensions of historical writing by acknowledging the communications revolution which had taken place during the course of the 1640s'.[22]

A very different kind of book, published in 1648, distils the experience not only of the preceding decade but of the whole of Charles I's reign into a collection of short songs, epigrams, verse epistles and pastoral dialogues. Dedicated to 'the Most Illustrious and Most Hopefull Prince, CHARLES, Prince of *Wales*', whose birth in 1630 coincided with the appearance of Hesperus in the midday sky, *Hesperides* 'announces Herrick's royalism' in its very title and the contents of the volume 'testify to his political engagement'.[23] Herrick had been ejected from his living in Devonshire during 1647 and Thomas Corns concludes that he must have put the finishing touches to his collection of poetry soon after the end of August, the last datable poem having been occasioned by the King's arrival at Hampton Court, and that it was published 'fairly early in 1648'.[24] Scattered through the volume, which consists largely of *carpe diem* and amatory lyrics, flower poems and epigrams on all manner of topics, are a small number of pieces marking events of historical significance from the perspective of a long-standing royalist: 'To the King: Upon his comming with his Army into the West', 'A Pastorall upon the birth of Prince Charles', 'To Prince Charles upon his coming to Exeter', 'To the King, Upon his taking of Leicester', 'To the King, Upon his welcome to Hampton-Court'. Other poems, addressed to members of the royal family and the aristocracy or to gentlemen like Endymion Porter ('Patron of Poets') and John Crofts ('Cup-bearer to the King'), evoke the court culture of the 1630s; others again call up the lost world of country festivals and pastimes – may-poles, wassails, harvest homes, ceremonies for Candlemass Eve – encouraged by the Book of Sports and frowned upon by the Puritanism that had banned the celebration of Christmas and the worship of the old Church of England.[25] As Corns emphasizes, however, *Hesperides* is 'not simply a great retrospective', nor is it a 'mere repository for the uncritically assembled totality of his output': though many of the poems date back to the 1620s and 1630s, the volume is 'a product of the late 1640s' and 'takes its political significance from the peculiar circumstances of that period'.[26] Both Corns and Summers discover the tensions of these circumstances in individual

poems, like Herrick's poetic effusion on Charles's return to Hampton
Court, which 'manages to be simultaneously a hopeful celebration of
the King as "a still protecting Deitie" and also a sober warning'.[27] Ann
Baynes Coiro goes further and discovers 'a high degree of contemporary
relevance and structural complexity' in the collection as a whole. For
her, the title with its many allusive dimensions – 'the classical image of
the earthly paradise', 'a place where dead heroes are rewarded', the
British Isles – 'creates the overarching structure that the 1,130 poems
inhabit and remains a hermeneutical device against which each individual poem can be read'; and she discerns a gradual shift from lyrics to
'sententious epigrams' as the dominant form, so that the isolated poems
of 'royal praise' become 'more and more hedged in' by criticisms of
Stuart policy, while the *carpe diem* poems 'become more deeply poignant
next to the late poems on the civil war'.[28]

    Herrick's smaller body of religious verse which is appended to *Hesper-
ides* under the separate title, *His Noble Numbers: Or, His Pious Pieces*, has
also been read as an assertion of Laudian Anglicanism against the
joyless zeal of the puritan reformers.[29] Summers sees in one particular
poem, '*Good Friday: Rex Tragicus, or Christ going to His Crosse*', a 'contra-
puntal counterplot' of topical relevance which 'depicts King Charles as
Christomimetes, poignantly anticipating the regicide'.[30] In the months
following Charles's flight from the dangerous proximity of the Army
headquarters at Putney, where the radicals had recently been airing
egalitarian views and murmuring against his life, Herrick's lines must
have voiced the darkest apprehensions of many, like John Taylor, who
saw the image of Christ in their 'Gracious (suffering) Sovereign Lord':

> Go Thy way,
> Thy way, Thou guiltlesse man, and satisfie
> By Thine approach, each their beholding eye. . . .
> Why then begin, great King! ascend Thy Throne,
> And thence proceed, to act Thy Passion.[31]

The emphasis on the *spectacle* of the King's suffering – exposed to each
'beholding eye' – is one frequently encountered at this stage of his 'way'
towards martyrdom. Even Cromwell was reported to have wept at the
'tenderest sight that ever his eyes beheld', when he was present at an
interview between Charles and three of his children that were under the
care of Parliament.[32] Mildmay Fane's poem, 'Upon King Charles's
meeting with the Dukes of York and Gloucester, and the Lady Elizabeth, his three children at Maidenhead, the 15 of July, 1647', describes
'Affection all dissolv'd to Tears';[33] and Richard Lovelace contemplates

not Charles himself, but an artist's rendering of the care-worn but dignified monarch, painted while he was in captivity:

> See! what a *clouded Majesty*! and eyes
> Whose glory through their mist doth brighter rise!
> See! what an humble bravery doth shine,
> And griefe triumphant breaking through each line;
> How it commands the face![34]

Anselment regards Lely's picture as anticipating 'Charles's most famous portrait, *Eikon Basilike*' and argues that both works drew upon the same resources that had been developing through the 1640s; and Corns sees it as 'an enhancement and deepening of the panegyric tradition, such as we find in *Eikon Basilike*'.[35]

Prompted, perhaps, by the royalist parody of Herbert's 'The Sacrifice', Alexander Brome boldly put words into the mouth of the monarch in a poem which found its way into print as *A Copie of Verses, said to be Composed by his* MAJESTIE, *upon his first Imprisonment in the Isle of Wight* (London, [29 September] 1648):

> Imprison me, you traitors! . . .
> Mistaken fools! to think my soul can be
> Grasp'd or infring'd by such low things as ye!
> Alas! though I'm immur'd, my mind is free . . .
>   tho' all your plagues you bring,
> I'll die a martyr, or I'll live a king.[36]

In the course of a lengthy response to the execution of two royalist defenders of Colchester, which soon abandons 'trayling Elegy and mournfull Verse' for satirical outrage at the 'unmanly hate' of those who could murder 'in cold blood', Henry King's thoughts are drawn to the plight of his captive sovereign: 'Fore-telling in These Two some greater ill / From Those who now a Pattent have to Kill'.[37]

Charles himself, who was so adept at promoting his own image through the arts of dancing and painting, had first hinted at the role which had already, by 1648, become far more potent than the memory of the royal masquer. On 2 December 1642, he had written to his cousin, the Marquis of Hamilton, about the uncertain future in which he would 'be either *a Glorious King or a Patient Martyr*' – adding that he did not 'at this present' apprehend the latter potentiality.[38] A significant contribution to the development of this image was made by Edward Symmons who, during 1645 and 1646, had been working on the manuscript of a defence of his royal master against 'those Aspersions cast upon Him by certaine persons, in a scandalous Libel, Entituled, *The Kings Cabinet*

Opened (title-page). Circumstances had more than once prevented him from publishing his work as a direct answer to the offending pamphlet, but in 1647 (as he informs his readers in a prefatory epistle dated 25 October), 'some friends' persuaded him to 'put it to the Presse', and he speculates that 'perhaps God had a speciall Providence in this also, peoples hearts were not then so capable to receive a *Vindication* of their Soveraigne from a fellow-Subject, as now they are even forced to be, by that illustrious eminency of his *graces* which hath beamed forth in his dark condition'.[39] Having argued the case for Charles at painstaking length in twenty-five sections, Symmons abandons ratiocination for a daring experiment in iconography. Up to now, he has been engaged in the task of dismantling a version of the King's character and conduct deliberately created by his enemies, who 'hoped to portray him forth, according to the *Image* of him in their own minds by wresting his expressions to the highest pitch of misconstruction, and charging upon him their own conditions; but (through Gods help) those *filthy Garments* they arrayed him with, are taken off, and sent home to their proper owners' (p. 241). Symmons will, in fact, contest the false image of the King *mis*-constructed in their own image by his denigrators with a *re*-constructed image more in harmony with recent history as perceived by a 'loyal subject':

Wherefore I will present him once againe, as habited in another *mantle*, more truly his, then that other was, though put upon him (for the most part) by the same men; in opposition to that *Act* of theirs, which I have undone, I will set him forth in Christ *Robes*, as cloathed with *sorrows*, and shew what a perfect similitude there hath been and is, between our *Saviour* and our *Soveraign* in the foure last yeares of both their sufferings. (p. 241)

There follows a series of parallels between the period of Christ's public ministry and the experiences of Charles I between 1642 and 1646. And, warns Symmons, the series may not yet be complete:

In a word, as Christ was belyed, slandered, betrayed, bought and sold for money, reviled, mocked, scorned at, spit on, *numbred among transgressors*, and judged to be such a one from his great misery, and from the successe his enemies had against him, and at last put to death; even so hath the King been used in all respects, by his Rebellious people, who have already acted all the parts which the Jewes acted upon the *Son of God*, the last of all only excepted which may also be expected in the end from them, when opportunity is afforded. (p. 246)

Acting on earlier hints, Symmons was here erecting a model for much of the most effective royalist propaganda that was to appear in the wake of the regicide; and by assigning the roles of the Pharisees who persecuted

Christ and the Jews who clamoured for his crucifixion to the members of the Long Parliament and Charles's rebellious subjects, he was (as his earlier metaphors indicated) deliberately stealing the rhetorical clothes of his antagonists, whose preachers had made such capital out of the analogies between their own struggle against episcopacy and tyranny and the Old Testament captivities of the tribes of Israel. The English nation were the new Israelites, indeed, as Protestant typology never tired of proclaiming, but the evidence of four years of Civil War suggested to Symmons that the Chosen People would pursue the biblical parallel to its bitter end in the New Testament and hound the King they had spurned to an ignominious death:

Well, when he is dead, as I think no wise man expects otherwise, but that they will murder him, openly or secretly shorten his dayes, if they can get him, and God doe not in a miraculous manner againe deliver him; (for as nothing but Christ's Crucifixion would please the Jewes of *old* so nothing but the Kings extinction will satisfie the malice of some in this Age,) but I say, when he is dead, we shall in this one thing imitate *Pilate*, and publish to all the world his accusation and cause of his death; This shall be his Title: *Carolus Gratiosus, Rex Anglia:* CHARLES *the Gracious, King of England, was put to death by the Pharisaicall Puritans of his Kingdome, only because he was their King, and in many respects so like unto Jesus Christ the Worlds Saviour.* (p. 250)

The figure of Charles the Martyr, the King of Peace whose patient sufferings and sacrificial death at the hands of his own people could be read as an imitation of Christ, would prove a more potent weapon in the armoury of royalist propaganda than the earlier image of the 'glorious King' created by Inigo Jones and Van Dyck had ever been. Richard Ollard sums up the iconographical division of Charles I's reign:

Both these projections of the King's role have succeeded in acquiring historical substance in their own right, irrespective of truth or falsehood to the figure who conceived and perfected them. In the closing scenes of his life, at his trial and on the scaffold, he rose to the part.[40]

In the course of 1648, 'three distinct but inseparable lines of action converged inexorably'.[41] At Westminster, the political factions continued to manoeuvre; at Newport, the King entered into yet another round of negotiations with parliamentary commissioners on 18 September; and at Windsor, the Army gathered for a prayer meeting in the spring, before going out to meet the renewed royalist challenge of the Second Civil War, and came to the 'very clear and joint resolution' that it was their duty 'to call Charles Stuart, that man of blood, to an account for that blood he had shed, and mischief he had done to his utmost, against the Lord's cause and people in these poor nations'.[42] By the autumn, the victorious Army had become exasperated with both King and Parliament, and on 20 November a Remonstrance drafted by Henry Ireton was delivered to Westminster. As well as condemning the King's policy and rejecting any further attempt to negotiate with him, the Army demanded 'that the capital and grand author of our troubles, the person of the King, by whose commissions, commands or procurement ... and for whose interest only, all our wars and troubles have been ... may be speedily brought to justice, for the treason, blood and mischief he's therein guilty of'.[43] The Presbyterian group, which had a majority in the Commons, delayed discussing the Remonstrance for a week and continued to treat with Charles through their Commissioners on the Isle of Wight. 'Mercurius Pragmaticus' (Marchamont Nedham) articulated the opinions of many who feared the intentions of the Army, when he urged Parliament to assert its authority in his answer to the Remonstrance, *A Plea for the King, and the Kingdome* (London, [20 November] 1648): 'What remaines then, but that the *Lords* and *Commons* in *Parliament*, doe stand up now for their *Priviledges*, the *Laws*, and the maintenance of *Monarchy*, and yet (if it be possible) revive the dying hopes of the *Nation* with an *Argument* by this *Treaty*; for as much as his *Majesty* is (and of necessity must be) the *Basis* of a *settlement*' (pp. 27–8).

The patience of the soldiers was exhausted, however, and on 1 December they removed the King to Hurst Castle on the Solent, and subsequently to Windsor; and once again the capital was occupied. On 5 December, the House of Commons defiantly voted to pursue a treaty with the King, and the next day more than a hundred members were prevented from taking their seats by Colonel Pride and a body of armed troops. Many were allowed to return home; some remained in military custody. There were further exclusions when the House reassembled on 12 and 13 December.[44]

Slowly, in the following weeks, the Army and the 'Rump' of radical Independents put into place the machinery necessary to bring Charles Stuart 'to an account for that blood he had shed': on 15 December, the General Council of the Army agreed that he should be brought to justice; on 23 December, the House of Commons appointed a committee to recommend a way of proceeding; on 28 December, an Ordinance for the trial of the King was passed; on 4 January, the Commons swept aside the Lords' refusal to endorse an Ordinance setting up a High Court of Justice to try the King. What ensued was a public ritual which put the seal on the vesting of supreme power in the single estate of 'the commons of England, in parliament assembled'.[45] The High Court began its sessions on 8 January; the King appeared before it on 20, 22 and 23 January; on 27 January he was sentenced to death; and the sentence was carried out on 30 January. It was forbidden to proclaim his successor, but this did not prevent the governor of Pontefract, still under siege by parliamentary troops, from striking a gold coin for *Carolus Secundus* and the excluded members of the Commons from declaring their allegiance to the new King.[46]

In 'A Postscript to the Reader', presumably added when he was finally preparing *A Vindication of King Charles* for the press, Edward Symmons had chided his fellow-countrymen for their dilatoriness in countering attacks on the reputation of their sovereign: 'it must be acknowledged in very deed, that this way the enemies have been more diligent in defaming, then we have been in defending the King' (p. 306). As earlier chapters have shown, there was no shortage of reasoned support for monarchy and for the role of the king in the English constitution, but little more than the platitudes of the panegyrical tradition had been expended on Charles Stuart as the current embodiment of kingship. The printing of his private correspondence had focused attention on his personal qualities, and during the period of his captivity, as Raymond has illustrated, there was a 'representational shift' which transformed the lineaments of Charles's image 'from a brow-beaten husband into a family man, from a ruler deprived of his rights into a human deprived of affection and compassion, with whom the common reader could ident-ify'.[47] Even during the dark months of December 1648 and January 1649, however, there were few voices raised in positive vindication of the man, as distinct from the constitutional figure-head who must be 'the *Basis* of a *settlement*', if the emergence of either a popular or a military dictatorship were to be avoided. The main protests against the actions being taken by the Army and the Rump came from Presbyterians, who were at best half-hearted royalists, intent on preserving their own influence against the now dominant coalition of generals, Independents and Levellers. William Prynne, of all people, published *A Brief Memento to the Present Unparliamentary Junto* on 1 January; forty-seven Presbyterians issued *A serious and faithful representation of the Judgment of the Ministers of the Gospel within the province of London* on 18 January; nineteen Presbyterians and Independents signed *The humble and earnest desires of certain well-affected Ministers &c of Oxon and Northampton*, which came out on 25 January; and on the eve of the execution, *A Vindication of the Ministers of the Gospel in and about London, from the unjust aspersions cast upon their former actings for the*

Parliament, as if they had promoted the bringing of the King to capital punishment bore the names of fifty-eight men.[48] Underdown cites William Sedgwick and Joshua Sprigge as the best-known among a number of Independent clerics who 'joined in the chorus of opposition'.[49] Excluded bishops and adherents to the former Church of England were strangely silent during these weeks, though Dr Juxon, former Bishop of London, was in faithful attendance on the King throughout the trial and on the scaffold. From his own party, the solitary champions of Charles I to go into print in the weeks leading up to the execution were John Gauden and Henry Hammond.

The Religious & Loyal Protestation, of John Gauden D[r] in Divinity; Against the present Declared Purposes and Proceedings of the Army and others; About the trying and destroying our Soveraign Lord the King (London [5 January] 1649) was sent to a colonel to be presented to Lord Fairfax and his General Council of Officers. In an epistle 'To the Reader', Gauden explains that he is responding to a divine compulsion to speak out, both for himself and for the religion he professes, '*against the crooked and perverse motions of others, in this untoward Generation, which is ready to father upon God and the Christian Reformed Religion, one of the most adulterous, deformed, and prodigious issues, that ever the corrupt hearts of the men of this world conceived, their unbridled power brought forth, or the Sun beheld*' (sig. A1[r]). He is anxious not to be thought to '*have any hand in the midwifery of so monstrous productions*' either by his assent or by his silence. Following the example of Edward Symmons, with whom he was working closely on the most celebrated and significant of all royalist propaganda texts, he offers a New Testament analogy for the present situation: '*Next, to the betraying and killing of Christ, was their sin, who either denied, or deserted Him*' (sig. A1[v]). Then, in an imaginative move that parallels the methods of the *Eikon Basilike*, Gauden puts an emotional plea into the mouth of Charles himself:

Me thinks I heare His Majesty in His Agony, solitude, and expectation of an enforced death, calling to me, and all other His Subjects, You that never believed My Life was sought after in the bottome of this Warre but My safety and Honour, you that never fought for Me, yet professed to abhorre the fighting destinately against Me, or destroying of Me; Cannot you, dare not you now speak one word to save My Life, and your own Soules? shall your silence seem to encourage and make up their suffrages, who therefore pretend they may, and will destroy Me, because it pleaseth you, and the generality of My people? (sig. A2[r]).

In the body of the text, Gauden warns the Army Council against the misplaced confidence of those who take success as justification for their cause 'and interpret Gods permission of what may bee very wicked and un-just, as his approbation and witnessing to their Justice' (p. 2), and goes on to question the legality of the process by which the King is being brought to trial. Then, putting this more reasoned approach aside, he appeals to the feelings and consciences of the officers, and invokes the personal qualities shown by the King in the face of betrayal and confinement:

O let not the World find in the event, that your pretended mercies were intended cruelties. . . . After so long and so hard a restraint which the King hath suffered with so much patience, after so many Concessions to his own dimin-utions, in order to the satisfaction of the *Parliament*, the *Kingdomes*, and the *Armies* Interest, both joynt and severall: how can you in cool bloud, without any colour of due Authority from God or Man, destroy your and our King; who cast himself into His Subjects Armes, and was received with all assurances of safety and Honour? (pp. 6–7)

Once again, the methods are closer to those of Symmons's *Vindication* and the more famous book which the two clerics were even then seeing through the press than to the defences of monarchy as an institution that had occupied apologists for the royal cause during the years of Civil War.

To the Right Honourable, The Lord Fairfax, and His Councell of Warre: The Humble Addresse of Henry Hammond (London, [15 January] 1649) appeared when the sessions of the High Court had already begun, and consists mainly of an examination of the false principles upon which the trial was being conducted. Hammond questions the validity of any claim to divine inspiration by the Army of the Saints and, like Gauden, advises them to beware of misreading their victory, since 'most commonly the prosperity of Armes hath not been *the lot of the* most *righteous*' (p. 5). He uses scripture, reason and precedent to undermine the principle that 'the *community of the People is the Supreme power*' in the state, pointing out that 'all those that have adhered to the KING all this time ... are as much to be considered to the making up the *community* of the *People*, as any others' (pp. 5, 15). It is in dealing with the final principle – that blood must answer for all the blood spilt 'in the late Warres' – that Hammond adopts the new approach to vindicating the King developed by Symmons and exploited by Gauden:

But if *God* should permit you to go on undisturb'd to the *shedding* of *more bloud*, as the *Jewes* did from other lower acts to the *crucifying their King*: How possible were it, not onely that this should prove the provoking of God to *deliver you up for ever to your owne hearts* lusts, but be to the whole *Nation* a *filling up the measure of our iniquities*, and the forerunner of all the *calamities*, that can befall a People. (p. 19)

In January 1649, Gauden and Hammond were lone voices. The situation was to alter dramatically as soon as the King's head was off and the idea of the Royal Martyr had taken hold of the popular imagination.

Information about the events taking place at Westminster and Whitehall was disseminated by the weekly newsbooks, of which there were six licensed by the government censors at the end of 1648. Gilbert Mabbott's *The Moderate*, which promoted the programme of the Levellers, had campaigned for Charles to be brought to trial (14–21 November 1648) and openly called for the death of 'the person called the King' (12–19 December 1648, p. 203). The three numbers from 9 to 30 January carried a full account of the proceedings in the court-room, and the next described Charles's dignified behaviour on the scaffold, but reminded its readers that it is the cause, not the death that makes a martyr. In his *Perfect Occurrences*, Henry Walker provided extensive coverage of the trial, but avoided partisan commentary. During the closing months of 1648, John Dillingham had been cautious in his treatment of the political situation in the pages of *The Moderate Intelligencer*, but his reports on the trial and beheading were, according to Joseph Frank, 'fair and full'; and his narration of 'the famous tragedy ... drawing to a period' (18–25 January 1649, p. 1850) revealed genuine 'sympathy for the chief character'.[50] Richard Collings had indicated support for a treaty between Parliament and the King in *The Kingdomes Weekly Intelligencer* during August and September 1648, and though he later became more circumspect, his relation of the events of January betrayed his political allegiance: 'The King carryeth himself very resolutely and looketh well, although he hath no great reason for it, for he hath not bin in bed these two nights' (6–13 January 1649, p. 1232); 'This Day it did not rain at all, yet it was a very wet day in and about the City of London by reason of the abundance of affliction that fell from many eyes' (30 January – 6 February 1649, p. 1241). No such touches softened Daniel Border's report of the trial in *The Perfect Weekly Account*; but Samuel Pecke's *A Perfect Diurnall*, together with such supplements as *A Perfect Narrative of the whole Proceedings of the High Court of Justice* (23 January) and *A Continuation of the Narrative* (25 January), furnished the basis for accounts that later came out under government sponsorship.

In addition to these six licensed weeklies, there were the unlicensed *Mercuries* written by journalists committed to the royalist cause. These came out at irregular intervals and were printed on small presses that could be moved from place to place to escape the authorities. *Mercurius*

Melancholicus, which had drawn upon the analogy of Christ's betrayal by Judas in the issue of 14–21 August 1648, did not survive to comment on the 'Passion' of Charles I. Wharton's *Mercurius Elencticus* was so hard-pressed by government agents that only two numbers appeared in the early part of January to express horror at the imminence of the trial; after a gap of four weeks, however, it did provide a detailed narrative of the trial and execution, in which the saintliness of the King's end and the righteousness of his cause were given full measure.[51] Nedham had relinquished the editorship of *Mercurius Pragmaticus* at the end of December, and although his former collaborators made some attempt to report the events of January, it suffered from the strong measures taken by the Army to control printing and preaching on the subject of the trial and its outcome.[52]

In spite of royalist charges that the shorthand record of the King's speech from the scaffold had been tampered with, Wedgwood considers that 'so much was printed that reflected credit on the King and discredit on his enemies that it is hard to believe that anything vital had been concealed'.[53] Certainly, the story of Charles's 'deportment' during his last days and minutes, as it was told in the licensed weeklies and eventually made available in pamphlet form under official imprimatur, must have done much to erase less favourable memories from the public consciousness and to prepare the soil in which the myth of the royal martyr would take root.

There was little the authorities could do to lessen the emotional impact of the eloquent and dignified words from the scaffold, in which Charles at last felt free to reply to the charges brought against him in the great hall at Westminster – something he had steadfastly refused to do throughout the trial on the grounds that the court presided over by John Bradshaw had no 'legal Authority warranted by the Word of God the Scriptures, or warranted by the Constitutions of the Kingdom' (p. 7).[54] When the 'Charge of the Commons of England against Charles Stuart, King of England, Of High Treason, and other High Crimes' had first been read out by the Clerk of the Court on 20 January, he had adopted the position that he was to maintain until sentence had been passed on him:

Remember I am your King, your lawful King ... therefore let me know by what Authority I am seated here, and I shall not be unwilling to answer; in the mean time I shall not betray my Trust; I have a Trust committed to me by God, by old and lawful descent, I will not betray it to answer to a new unlawful Authority, therefore resolve me that, and you shall hear more of me. (p. 6)

On 22 January, he reiterated his claim to be honouring his divinely appointed obligations as the guardian of 'the Liberties of the people of England' under the law (p. 12); and on his third appearance, on 23 January, he had entered fully into his role as the champion of the ancient rights of his subjects, destined by his birth to carry a unique burden of responsibility:

For the Charge, I value it not a rush, it is the Liberty of the People of England that I stand for; for me to acknowledge a new Court that I never heard of before, I that am your King, that should be an example to all the people of England for to uphold Justice, to maintain the old Lawes; indeed I do not know how to do it. (p. 19)

Before judgement was passed on 27 January, Charles contrived to dramatize still more poignantly the cost to him as a human being of what he had hitherto borne, and was yet prepared to suffer, as a king loyal to his trust:

This many aday all things have been taken away from me but that that I call more dearer to me then my life, which is my Conscience and my Honor; and if I had respect to my Life more then the Peace of the Kingdom, the Liberty of the Subject, certainly I should have made a particular defence of my self, for by that at leastwise I might have delayed an ugly Sentence, which I beleeve will pass upon me. (p. 25)

His attempts to make a statement after the sentence had been read out were stifled by the Lord President, and his last recorded words before he was led from Westminster Hall reinforced the part he had been playing with increasing conviction throughout the proceedings: 'I am not suffered for to speak, expect what Justice other people will have' (p. 47).

When he was eventually granted the opportunity to speak on the scaffold, he at last undertook to clear himself of guilt, 'both as an honest man, and a good King, and a good Christian' (p. 4).[55] Having answered the political accusations made against him, he embraced his religious role by publicly forgiving those who had brought him to the point of death and invoked the name of the first Christian martyr to underline his selfless concern, even at this extremity, for the well-being of his people: 'I pray God with St *Stephen*, That this be not laid to their charge, nay, not only so, but that they may take the right way to the Peace of the Kingdom, for my charity commands me not onely to forgive particular men, but my Charity commands me to indeavor to the last gasp the Peace of the kingdom' (p. 5). To the end – and most powerfully as the end approached – he maintained his stance as the defender of the people's liberties before the law: 'Sirs, It was for this that now I am come here: If I would have given way to an Arbitrary way, for to have all Laws changed according to the power of the Sword, I needed not to have come here, and therefore I tell you (and I pray God it be not laid to your charge) That I am the Martyr of the People' (p. 6). The immediate popular appeal of the image that had been so skilfully perfected towards this moment is evident in the echoes of Charles's final speech in a stanza from one of the many ballads that circulated in the months following the execution:

> His Foes he did forgive,
>   Graciously, graciously,
> And wisht we all might live
>   in quiet peace.
> He wisht what ere was past,
> That he might be the last,
> No sorrow we might taste,
>   but wars might cease.[56]

On the very day on which Charles I went to the block, copies of a book that was to promote the image of 'the Martyr of the People' throughout Europe were in existence. That book, *Eikon Basilike: The Pourtraicture of His Sacred Majestie in His Solitudes and Sufferings,* has been called 'the most widely read, widely discussed work of royalist propaganda to issue from the English Civil War'.[57] Much of the discussion, however, has concentrated on the question of its authorship and more recently on its effectiveness as a performance which deliberately conceals its status as a printed text and serves to complement both the famous frontispiece by William Marshall [Figure 2] and the theatrical triumph on the scaffold.[58] Steven Zwicker has used a comparison with Milton's *Eikonoklastes* to situate it within various 'streams of contestative rhetoric' and to show how the 'verbal art of the *Eikon Basilike* allows prose to make the man: the rhetoric of moderation and the balance of carefully weighted periods argue refinement of manner, and more purposefully, they express the king's deliberative intelligence'.[59] It is the purpose of the rest of this chapter to interpret some of the stylistic features of the text in the context of what is known about its composition and printing in order to construct an hypothesis about the evolving nature and function of 'the King's book'.

It was at Theobald's, not long after his final departure from London in January 1642, that Charles had first mooted the idea of defending himself with his pen against the libels of his enemies. Some of his most intimate companions questioned the advisability of opening the old

Figure 2. Frontispiece to *Eikon Basilike* (1649).

wound of Strafford's death, but Charles went ahead with his project
and 'the continuation of His Divine Meditations, which He had gone
along with to the Successe of that day', was among the royal papers
which were captured at the Battle of Naseby. This manuscript was
eventually 'recovered above all expectance, and return'd to His Majesties Hand'.[60] There is evidence that the King used the time passed in
close confinement at Holdenby, between 16 February and 4 June 1647,
to resume work on a justification of his actions since the calling of the
Long Parliament, and it is assumed that it was during his subsequent
sojourn at Hampton Court, between 24 August and 11 November 1647,
that he recovered the lost papers.[61] The compiler of the authoritative
modern bibliography of the *Eikon Basilike* is confident that the accumulated evidence 'leaves no further room for doubt as to the existence by
that time of substantial writings of the King, composed at different

times, and comparable in subject-matter, though not identical in form, with the published *Eikon*'.[62] Of particular importance is the testimony of Sir John Brattle, which was first published by Richard Hollingworth in 1692:

In the year 47 King Charles, having drawn up the most considerable part of this book, and having writ it in some loose papers, at different times, desired Bishop Juxon to get some friend of his (whom he could commend to him as a trusty person) to look it over, and to put it into an exact method; the Bishop pitch'd upon Sir John's Father, whom he had been acquainted withal for many years, who undertaking the task, was assisted by this his son, who declares, he sate up with his Father some nights, to assist him methodizing these papers, all writ with the King's own hand: thanks be to God, Sir John is yet alive, and is ready to give the same account to any man that asks him.[63]

There is no way of knowing how far Charles had himself begun to develop the analogy between his own situation and that of Christ in the 'loose papers' that were put 'into an exact method' while he was at Hampton Court, but the later chapters of the *Eikon Basilike* exploit it quite extensively, and it looks as if the printed version of 'the King's book' owed a considerable debt to Symmons's *Vindication*.[64]

It was, in fact, through his association with Symmons, who had been his contemporary at Cambridge in the 1620s and the incumbent of a neighbouring living in Essex at the outbreak of the Civil War, that John Gauden, who later claimed that the 'book and figure was wholy and only my invention, making and designe', first came into contact with the King's writings.[65] A servant later testified that Gauden had made a copy of a manuscript lent to him by Symmons, which must have been the 'methodized' version of the royal papers produced by the Brattles in the autumn of 1647. It is conceivable that Symmons, who had recently prepared his own defence of the King for the press, saw the potential for a more spectacular propaganda coup in a vindication under Charles's own name and recruited his former acquaintance to carry the project through. However he came to be involved, Gauden had completed his redaction of the work by the beginning of June 1648. His plan was to publish it under the title 'Suspiria Regalia', but he was advised by Lord Capel to seek the King's approval before proceeding. The start of the negotiations between Charles and Parliament at Newport provided the necessary opportunity and the manuscript was entrusted to the Marquis of Hertford. The King evidently gave his blessing to the enterprise, since he is said to have 'sometimes corrected and heightened' Gauden's 'sheets', although he apparently urged that it should 'be put out in another name'; and in October, he was making arrangements for the work to be published by Richard Royston, who later affirmed 'that his late Ma^ty of blessed memory King Charles the First did sent to him about Mich[ael]mas before his Martirdome to provide a Presse for hee had a Booke of his owne for him to Print'. The King having been removed from Newport by the Army on 1 December, and the process of bringing him to trial having been set in motion, Gauden, according to his wife's testimony, 'did Resolve to print it with all the sped that might be ... only hee then added the Esay upon denying his Ma: the attendance of his Chaplins, and the Meditation upon Death'. She adds that 'the instrument wch my Hus: imployed to git it printed was one Mr Simons a Devine' – a fact corroborated by Royston himself, who also records that it was on Christmas Eve that the manuscript was delivered into his hands. Printing went ahead forthwith and the proof sheets were with Symmons by 14 January. It was while the book was actually in the printing-shop that Gauden's title of *Suspiria Regalia, or, The Royal Plea* was changed to *Eikon Basilike*, on the advice of Jeremy Taylor.

Charles's hesitation about having his name attached to the fruits of Gauden's labours – even though they were largely derived from his own papers – may well have stemmed from the same considerations that motivated Taylor. As Helgerson has pointed out, King James had broken with tradition in exploiting the new authority of the printed word to disseminate his views in his own person. In *Basilikon Doron* and the other publications that were collected in *The Workes of the Most High and Mightie Prince, James* (London, 1616), Charles's father had deliberately flouted 'the class-coding of print, the association of print with trade and the resultant stigma that marked any gentleman, including a king, who wrote for it'.[66] If Charles were to own his authorship, it was politic to remind his readers of the royal precedent – and also to include within the body of the text occasional indications that he was not writing with publication directly in view. Chapter 17 merely glances at the possibility 'that posterity may see (if ever these papers be public) that I had fair grounds, both from Scripture canons and ecclesiastical examples, whereon my judgement was stated for Episcopal government' (p. 125); Chapter 21, after impugning the civility and humanity of those who had exposed the King's private correspondence 'to public view', hints at the greater benefits that might be derived from his present meditations: 'I wish my subjects had yet a clearer sight into my most retired thoughts, where they might discover how they are divided between the love and care I have, not more to preserve my own rights, than to procure their peace and happiness, and that extreme grief to see them both deceived and destroyed' (pp. 156–7); and Chapter 27 adopts the fiction familiar among aristocratic authors, that the composition is directed not at the undiscriminating world but at an exclusive and personally identified readership – in this instance, indeed, a specific individual, the Prince of Wales:

Son, if these papers, with some others wherein I have set down the private reflections of my conscience and my most impartial thoughts touching the chief passages which have been most remarkable or disputed in my late troubles, come to your hands, to whom they are chiefly designed, they may also be so far useful to you as to state your judgment aright in what hath passed; whereof a pious is the best use can be made; and they may also give you some directions how to remedy the present distempers, and prevent, if God will, the like for the time to come. (p. 191)

In this, the last chapter to be based on the King's own writings[67] – how far 'methodized' by Brattles, revised by Gauden, or finally 'corrected and heightened' by Charles himself we do not know – the work appears before the public as the 'private reflections' of a king preparing to meet death and seeking to ensure that the 'judgment' of his successor will be formed 'aright' by an 'impartial' account of recent history. The taint of writing for the press and the indignity of appealing directly to the judgement of the common reader are thus eschewed as the royal author bequeathes his personal 'papers' to the future monarch for whose edification 'they are chiefly designed'.

As one might expect, the complexity of the process by which 'the King's book' achieved a final form left its mark on the text itself. Although no reference is made to an editor, the intervention of some third party between the 'private reflections' of 'His Sacred Majestie' and their appearance in the public medium of print is implied in the third-person titles at the head of each chapter. There is also a curious inconsistency in the use of tenses, which may betray the variety of hands and the lack of temporal continuity in its composition. The title-page proclaimed the work to be a portrait of the late King 'in His Solitudes and Sufferings'. Such a formula might be taken to suggest that its contents were intended to be read as the fruits of his long captivity. In conformity with this, most of the chapters that dwell upon specific events adopt a retrospective stance and supply a commentary which draws upon the wisdom of hindsight. In Chapter 3, for example, a past tense narration of how he went 'to the House of Commons to demand justice upon the five members' in January 1642 prompts a sad reverie by the later Charles on the subsequent disasters that he had done his best to check with this timely intrusion upon the proceedings of the rebellious Parliament: 'I endeavoured to have prevented, if God had seen fit, those future commotions which I foresaw would in all likelihood follow some men's activity, if not restrained, and so now hath done, to the undoing of many thousands; the more is the pity' (p. 13).

Other chapters, however, are couched in a present tense which creates the impression of an immediate and unresolved situation. For example, the account in Chapter 22 of the King's flight from Oxford to join the Scottish army in the spring of 1646 presents him as ignorant of the sequel: 'I must now resolve the riddle of their loyalty and give them opportunity to let the world see they mean not what they do but what they say' (pp. 134–5). The drama continues to unfold in the present tense in the next chapter, which takes place some eight months later, after he has been handed over to the English and incarcerated at Holdenby:

Yet may I justify those Scots to all the world in this, that they have not deceived me, for I never trusted them further than to men. If I am sold by them, I am only sorry they should do it and that my price should be so much above my Saviour's. . . . The solitude and captivity to which I am now reduced gives me leisure enough to study the world's vanity and inconstancy. (p. 137)

As one would expect, if the bulk of the papers 'methodized' by the Brattles and used by Gauden as material for the text of *Suspiria Regalia* were penned by Charles during 1647 while he was being held at Holdenby, most of the chapters dealing with earlier events consist of past tense narrative and present tense commentary. When the period of 'Solitudes and Sufferings' is approached, it is natural for the present tense to take over, as it does consistently in Chapters 22–8 – a sequence which begins with the King seeking refuge with the Scots and ends with Gauden's fabrication of 'Meditations upon Death, After the Votes of Non-Addresses, and His Majesty's Closer Imprisonment in Carisbrook Castle'. The title of this late addition serves primarily to assign Charles's spiritual preparation for martyrdom to the year 1648, since the move to the Isle of Wight in November 1647 and the circumstances of the vote in the following January make no substantial contribution to the content of the chapter. Other chapters – such as 16, 'Upon the Ordinance against the Common Prayer Book' (mainly a reasoned Anglican defence of set forms of worship), and 20, 'Upon the Reformation of the Times' – are more in the nature of general essays on topics that were of concern throughout the decade.

This leaves a handful of sections that stylistically disrupt the steady development from the philosophically distanced past to the more poignant immediacy of the writer's imprisonment and isolation. Chapters 7, 10 and 11 are concerned with a number of things which happened in the months preceding the outbreak of Civil War in 1642: Henrietta Maria's departure for the Low Countries in February; the seizure of the armed forces by the Militia Ordinance in March; the *Nineteen Propositions* of June. In each of these meditations, retrospective narrative gives way to the more dramatic impact of the present tense. In the first, political circumstances have compelled the Queen to seek refuge overseas. Charles's gloss on the 'scandal of that necessity which drives her away' reads like the work of a man engaged in the process of coming to terms with the shock of what is happening to him, rather than the contemplation of an old sorrow by one looking back over five years of disappointment and defeat:

that she should be compelled by my own subjects and those pretending to be Protestants to withdraw for her safety, this being the first example of any Protestant subjects that have taken up arms against their king, a Protestant. For I look upon this now done in England as another act of the same tragedy which was lately begun in Scotland; the brands of that fire, being ill-quenched, have kindled the like flames here. (p. 30)

The writer of Chapter 10 takes the stance of a beleaguered monarch anxious to prove himself innocent of hostile intent towards his people. Opening with the assertion, 'How untruly I am charged with the first raising of an army and beginning this Civil War', he goes on to protest that his very 'unpreparedness' for any kind of military action 'testifies for me that I am set on the defensive part, having so little hopes or power to offend others that I have none to defend myself' (p. 46). In Chapter 11, the man who meditates on the *Nineteen Propositions* seems to forgo or not have access to the historical perspective provided by his later 'solitudes':

Although there be many things they demand, yet if these be all, I am glad to see at what price they set my own safety and my people's peace, which I cannot think I buy at too dear a rate, save only the parting with my conscience and honour. If nothing else will satisfy, I must choose rather to be as miserable and inglorious as my enemies can make me or wish me.... Here are many things required of me, but I see nothing offered to me by way of grateful exchange of honour or any requital for those favours I have or can yet grant them. (pp. 52–3)

Sandwiched between the retrospective treatment of the King's repulse from Hull in Chapter 8 and the dramatic present of the protestations of Chapter 10 is an account of the outbreak of hostilities, which

mobilizes the resources of both these temporal perspectives. It opens
with the King struggling in the toils of historical circumstance:

I find that I am at the same point and posture I was when they forced me to
leave Whitehall. What tumults could not do, an army must, which is but
tumults lifted and enrolled to a better order but as bad an end. My recess hath
given them confidence that I may be conquered. (p. 38)

Out of the midst of the confusion of 1642 – and the date of the utterance
is pointedly inscribed in the text – he speaks in tones of hurt and baffled
innocence: 'Are the hazards and miseries of civil war in the bowels of my
most flourishing kingdom the fruits I must now reap after seventeen
years living and reigning among them with such a measure of justice,
peace, plenty, and religion as all nations about either admired or
envied?' (p. 39). For several more pages, an analysis of the immediate
past – the activities of the London mobs, the Root and Branch Bill, the
controversy over the right of bishops to sit in the House of Lords – is
presented from the perspective of the summer of 1642. Then there is a
marked transition to the historical vantage-point of the captive king of a
later period, who writes from the bitter experience of more than three
years of fighting and seeks to absolve himself from all responsibility for
starting it: 'This is the true state of those constructions pretended to be in
point of justice and authority of Parliament, when, I call God to witness,
I knew none of such consequence as was worth speaking of a war, being
only such as justice, reason, and religion had made in my own and other
men's consciences' (p. 42). Looking back now, from 1647, he has a
clearer view of the consistent policy of those who were determined to
find a pretext for taking up arms against him: 'That this is the true state
and first drift and design in raising an army against me is by the sequel so
evident that all other pretences vanish' (p. 43). He concludes with an
expression of gratitude that, 'in the midst of all the unfortunate successes
of this war on my side', he has been able to take comfort from the
certainty of his own innocence, which was never 'any whit prejudiced or
darkened' (p. 44).

Two explanations suggest themselves for these shifting time perspectives, one emphasizing the rhetorical strategy, the other the historical
origins of *Eikon Basilike*. The first would argue that Gauden cleverly used
the medium of the present tense to heighten the dramatic appeal of his
subject at crucial moments in the story; the other would ponder how far
Gauden was reflecting the variation of tenses in his source manuscript –
that collection of 'loose papers', composed 'at different times', which
had been organized 'into an exact method' while the King was at

Hampton Court. The Brattles may have done little more than arrange the documents into roughly chronological order. Gauden's contribution may have consisted of devising the format of a series of meditations, which would have entailed a certain amount of rewriting, adding some of the more general essays (such as that on the Book of Common Prayer), and completing the 'Pourtraicture' with Chapters 24 and 28, which highlighted the pathos of the 'solitude they have confined me unto' (p. 141) and brought the narrative more or less up to date.

It may well be that Charles, who was seen working on a manuscript at Holdenby, had there composed the majority of the 'loose papers' dealing with the period 1640 to 1645 – the material written largely from the perspective of 1647 which became Chapters 1–21. The immediacy of the account of the decision to leave Oxford for the safety of the North in Chapter 22 suggests that Charles's resumption of sustained work on the project dated from his sojourn in Newcastle, before he was transferred to Holdenby. The present-tense reflections on his betrayal by the Scots in Chapter 23 locate themselves clearly during the Holdenby period itself. Chapter 26, 'Upon the Army's Surprisal of the King at Holmby', and the letter to the Prince of Wales, which ends 'Farewell till we meet, if not on earth, yet in heaven' (p. 171), are presumably the latest additions not certainly attributable to Gauden's own intervention.

Such a reconstruction of the work's composition leaves open the possibility that drafts of the anomolous present-tense meditations (Chapters 7, 10 and 11, and the first part of 9) antedated by some years the period of confinement at Newcastle and Holdenby which gave Charles the leisure to undertake a retrospective assessment of his career since 1640. Perhaps, if they were among the captured writings that were returned to him at Hampton Court, they were not available when the Brattles 'methodized' the King's 'loose papers', and were only later incorporated into the text by Gauden, who for some reason omitted to harmonize their temporal stance with that of the surrounding material.

There remains the question of the book's purpose. When he first discussed the idea of drawing up a vindication of his actions in 1642, and even when he set about putting his papers in order in 1647, Charles himself can hardly have anticipated that publication would coincide with the final bloody act in his long-drawn-out contest with Parliament. Similarly, Gauden's redaction in the early months of 1648 must have been intended as a contribution to a battle for political power that had not yet been irrevocably lost. Even as late as October, when Charles had approved and corrected Gauden's manuscript and alerted his publisher, the work must have been regarded as a means of strengthening his hand in the negotiations at Newport by exciting popular sympathy for a captive and persecuted monarch. His unexpected removal to Hurst Castle on 1 December and the subsequent acceleration of events confirmed the resolve of Gauden (or should it be Symmons, if he was the moving spirit in the whole enterprise?) 'to print it with all the sped that might be'; and Symmons deposited the augmented manuscript with Royston on the same day that the House of Commons appointed a committee to make arrangements for the trial. Was this a last ditch attempt to rally public opinion to the King's defence, or does the addition of the 'Meditations upon Death' earlier in December indicate that those closest to the King had bowed to the inevitable and were already planning a propaganda coup that would transform the execution into a martyrdom? References to the danger of violent death in earlier chapters had been in the context of military action, as in the comment that 'the hazards of war are equal, nor doth the cannon know any respect of persons' (p. 39). Death on the scaffold seems to have replaced death on the battlefield in the scenario imagined by Gauden in Chapter 28 with its spectators and triumphing adversaries, and the imminent end is now presented as more or less unavoidable:

That I must die as a man is certain. That I may die a king by the hands of my own subjects, a violent, sudden, and barbarous death, in the strength of my years, in the midst of my kingdoms, my friends and loving subjects being helpless spectators, my enemies insolent revilers and triumphers over me, living, dying, and dead, is so probable in human reason that God hath taught me not to hope otherwise as to man's cruelty. However, I despair not of God's infinite mercy. (pp. 173–4)

It may be that the last-minute change of title from *Suspiria Regalia, or, The Royal Plea* to *Eikon Basilike* marks the final acknowledgement by those responsible for producing 'the King's book' that it was too late for any 'plea' to influence the result of the trial. In those last weeks of January, it must have become clear that 'the Pourtraicture of His Sacred Majestie' would enter the public consciousness as a martyred monarch's bequest to a grieving nation rather than the political vindication of a king who would have been prepared to lay down his life for his country's peace.

CHAPTER II

Lamenting the King: 1649

He nothing common did or mean
Upon that memorable Scene:...
This was that memorable Hour
Which first assur'd the forced Pow'r.[1]

Looked at from whatever perspective – and Marvell adopted two in this famous passage – the execution of Charles I on 30 January 1649 was certainly 'memorable'. On 20 November 1648, when there still seemed a chance of outmanoeuvring the radicals in the Army leadership, Marchamont Nedham presented a petition to the House of Commons, reminding the members that although in the past there were examples of 'sovereign Princes' being deposed and assassinated, 'yet in no History can we find a parallel for this, that ever the rage of Rebels extended so far as to bring their Sovereign lord to public trial and execution'.[2] Just a week before the King was summoned to the bar of the High Court of Justice, Captain Joyce was urging the General Council of Officers assembled in Whitehall to trust in God's promises and go forward confidently to accomplish 'such things as were never yet done by men on earth'.[3] A more detached observer, the Venetian Ambassador at Munster, echoed the belief shared by these ideologically opposed Englishmen that something momentous was taking place: 'History affords no example of the like.' But if he was well aware of the temporal significance of that 'memorable *hour*' for the future power relations within the state, the more immediate impact of 'that memorable *scene*' as political theatre – 'so imposing a spectacle' – was not lost on him.[4]

Although the act performed on a platform outside Inigo Jones's Banqueting House may have achieved its political purpose in establishing beyond argument the position of Cromwell and the Army of Saints as the effective authority in the state, such a *spectacle* played into the hands of the supporters of monarchy, who were not slow to exploit the opportunity created by their King's last and most dramatic appearance.

When Clarendon looked back to 'that lamentable tragedy' and Sir Philip Warwick recalled how the 'bloody Independents draw the curtain, and shew, how tragicall their design had bin from the beginning',[5] they were taking up one of the metaphors that had quickly become current as a means of rendering the traumatic episode palatable to the royalist imagination.[6] The dignity with which Charles played his essentially passive role at the centre of a drama controlled by the 'industrious Valour' of one of the 'greater Spirits' of history is given its due in Marvell's 'Ode':

> Nor call'd the *Gods* with vulgar spight
> To vindicate his helpless Right,
>   But bow'd his comely Head,
>   Down as upon a Bed.

Similar associations, apparently undisturbed by the kind of reservations implicit in Marvell's tribute to the '*Royal Actor*', were stirred in the mind of another witness:

The King's deportment was very majestick and steddy; and tho' his tongue usually hesitated, yet it was very free at this time, for he was never discomposed in mind . . . and a Gentleman of my acquaintance . . . protested to me, he saw him come out of the Banquetting-house on the scaffold with the same unconcernedness and motion, that he usually had, when he entered into it on a Masque-night.[7]

Both Marvell and Warwick were attracted more by Charles's manner than his words: the calm suppression of his habitual stammer and the self-control and grace with which he accomplished his final gesture made the most lasting impression on them, just as his elegant movements as the chief masquer had always carried a deeper symbolic meaning than the verse of a Townshend or a Davenant could convey in the entertainments at Whitehall.

Once Charles Stuart was dead, the regicides had to make arrangements for the future government of the country. The Army was now 'the ultimate arbiter of the nation's destinies',[8] but the Generals did not take political power directly into their own hands. The Rump, led by Vane and Haselrig, re-admitted some of the members purged in December and on 6 and 7 February the House of Commons voted to abolish the House of Lords and the monarchy. On 14 February, a forty-one strong Council of State was nominated, on which seven Army Officers were to serve, including Fairfax and Cromwell, but excluding Ireton. It had executive powers to implement domestic and foreign policy, but its membership remained under the control of Parliament.[9] The most pressing task for the new republic, which was formally instituted on 17 March and 19 May by Acts abolishing kingship and declaring England a free Commonwealth, was to secure itself against internal and external threats to its authority. Fairfax had already ordered the summary execution of Sir George Lisle and Sir Charles Lucas for their prolonged resistance at Colchester; five more royalist leaders of the insurrections in 1648 were tried and three of them – Hamilton, Holland and Capel – were executed on 9 March. The challenge from Lilburne and the Levellers was effectively broken when Fairfax and Cromwell stamped out a mutiny in the Army by shooting three of the ring-leaders at Burford on 15 May.[10] In Ireland, the strength of Ormond's Royalist-Confederation alliance was dealt a severe blow at Rathmines on 2 August, and Cromwell began the reconquest of the island by storming Drogheda in September and Wexford in October.[11]

The Officers and the Rump politicians also took measures to control the spread of news and ideas that might harm the regime. On 9 January, Richard Lawrence, Marshall General of the Army, was issued with a warrant to seize all unlicensed presses and on 3 February a Commons committee was appointed to suppress printing and preaching on the King's trial; Treason Acts were passed on 14 May and 17 July, which specified as treasonable any written or printed materials that questioned the legitimacy of the new government; and on 20 September another Act confined legal printing to the city of London and the two universities, and forbade the production and hawking of 'seditious' and 'scandalous' texts.[12] This did not stop the secret royalist presses, however, and the weeklies soon resumed their subversive activities in support of Charles II. Titles from the previous autumn reappeared, to be joined by *Mercurius Militaris*, a resurrected *Mercurius Aulicus*, and John Crouch's *The Man in the Moon*, described as 'the most violent of the royalist Mercuries'.[13]

But the royalist response to the revolution that was taking place was not confined to underground journalists. The trial and execution of Charles I and the illegality of the Commonwealth were denounced with a greater display of rational argument and learning in three defences of monarchy during 1649. Judge David Jenkins appealed to the twin authorities of Scripture and Law to sustain his charge that the 'seeming Legall Proceedings, and executions of Justice' of the 'popular Pre-tenders' who had usurped power were 'indeed, nothing else but Reall, and Revengefull Murders'.[14] Fabian Philipps rehearsed the familiar interpretation of events since 1640 to prove that the 'end hath now verified the beginning', rising to a colourful peroration:

Seaven yeares hypocriticall Promises and Practices, *seaven* yeares Pretences, and *seaven* yeares preaching and *pratling* have now brought us all to this conclusion as well as *Confusion*. The blood of old *England* is let out ... the Trees have made the *Bramble* King and ... have not only slaine the King who was their *Father*, but like *Nero* rip't up the belly of the Common-Wealth which was their *Mother*.[15]

The most interesting and substantial of these publications was the reissue of Clement Walker's *Relations and Observations* with a continuation introduced by a separate title-page as *Anarchia Anglicana: Or, The History of Independency. The Second Part* (1649). Over 256 pages, he narrates the events leading up to and including the execution of Charles I, reprinting the speech from the scaffold and other documents, and listing in red ink the names of those who sat as judges, 'with the Councell and Attendants of the Court' (p. 103). Between pages 112 and 113, he reproduces an engraving in which 'the downfall of King *CHARLES* the 1. ... and in Him of the Royall Government, Religion, Lawes, and Liberties of this auntient Kingdome is Emblematically presented to the Readers view' (p. 113) [Figure 3]. The name of Oliver Cromwell heads the blood-coloured list of regicides in the text, and it is Cromwell who presides over the desecration of the English oak tree by representatives of the soldiery and the common people.

Cromwell was also the primary villain in *The Famous Tragedie of King Charles I* (1649), which advertized its polemical rather than aesthetic approach to the King's fate in some dedicatory verses to his eldest son: 'That by Thy heavy, and Victorious hand / Those Monsters who doom'd Thy great Syre to die / May receive treble vengeance'. A 'Prologue to the Gentry' raised the spectre of social anarchy as well as military oppression:

> For having kill'd their KING, where will they stay
> That thorow GOD, and MAJESTIE, make way,
> Throwing the Nobles, and the Gentry downe
> Levelling, all distinctions, to the Crowne.

The play itself is little more than a series of scurrilous attacks on the ambitious machinations and sexual depravity of Cromwell, aided by his 'fine *facetious Devill*', the Army chaplain Hugh Peters. The cold-blooded murder of Lucas and Lisle by Fairfax (dismissed as a 'silly Foole' by Cromwell) supplies a subplot, the corruption of General Lambert's wife by Peters (acting as Cromwell's pandar) a comic interlude and a tableau of the dead bodies of Charles I, Lord Capel, the Duke of Hamilton and the Earl of Holland, a spectacular finale.[16]

Figure 3. Engraving between pages 112 and 113 in Clement Walker, *Anarchia Anglicana: Or, The History of Independency. The Second Part* (1649).

In Walker's emblem, the cutting down of the oak tree entails the loss of texts crucial to the well-being of the English state – the Bible, Magna Carta, the ancient Laws and Statutes – and hanging alongside them in its branches is the literary embodiment of the King himself, his very own self-portrait in the *Eikon Basilike*. Doubts about the authenticity of 'the King's book' began to circulate, however, from the moment of its appearance on the day of the execution. In June, an anonymous apologist (possibly John Ashburnham) defended it as 'a *Living Memoriall* of Princely piety and devotion', in which Charles had undertaken 'to vindicate His traduced Honour by His Pen'.[17] This was followed in August by the first printed accusation that the work was a forgery in *Eikon Alethine*, which was answered by *Eikon E Piste* in September. By October, John Milton, in his official capacity as Secretary for Foreign Tongues to the Council of State, was ready with *Eikonoklastes*. In a chapter-by-chapter onslaught on the *Eikon Basilike*, he sought to render harmless by ridicule the 'conceited portraiture' of the frontispiece and to demolish by argument the fraudulent attempt 'to make a Saint or Martyr' by publishing 'these overlate Apologies and Meditations of the dead King'.[18]

But as was noted at the tercentenary of the King's death, 'conquered and frustrated people hunger for a myth, and provided they have a symbolical figure and a dramatic immolation they are seldom fastidious about the literal truth or authenticity of the gospel'.[19] The myth so brilliantly fashioned by Symmons, Charles I and Gauden was not only disseminated by the book itself, which went through thirty-five English editions in 1649 alone, but also through sermons and elegies that were preached and printed in spite of the best efforts of Lawrence's pursuivants and the new Treason Acts. Helen Randall suggests that the earliest sermons were designed to fill the 'omission' and repair the 'indignity' of Parliament's refusal to allow an elaborate ceremony or sermon when the King's body was laid to rest in a vault in St George's Chapel at Windsor on 9 February. She discusses four which 'employ an artful obscurantism' for fear of reprisals, two of which drew upon an analogy with the death of King Josiah in the Old Testament and two of which imply without quite stating a parallel with the Passion of Christ.[20] Two that were delivered and printed overseas needed to take no such precautions: Henry Leslie, Bishop of Down, preached before Charles II and his sister, the Princess of Orange, at Breda in June and his sermon was published in The Hague under the title, *The Martyrdome of King Charles, Or, His Conformity with Christ in his Sufferings*; and Richard Watson, chaplain to Lord Hopton, also preached before the dead King's son and daughter in Holland, where his text was later printed as *Regicidium Judaicum Or A Discourse, about the Jewes Crucifying Christ, their King. With An Appendix, or Supplement, upon the late murder of Our Blessed Soveraigne Charles the First* (The Hague, 1649). As well as finding an extraordinary number of similarities between the events of Holy Week and the persecution of Charles as 'a second Christ, an anoynted of God' (p. 23), Watson expatiates on 'the everlasting stupendious monument of a booke, rais'd higher then the Pyramids of Aegypt in the strength of language, and well proportion'd spiring expression' (p. 26). After rather hastily expounding his text (I Corinthians 2: 8), Leslie turns to 'another sad tragedy', which is his real topic for the day, 'a parricide so heinous, so horrible that it cannot be *paralelld* by all the *murthers* that ever were committed since the world began, but onely in the murther of Christ' (pp. 11–12). He, too, invokes the dead monarch's *Divine Meditations*, 'of which Book I dare bold say, that since the spirit of Prophesie ceased, never yet was there any book written; with so great strength of Reason, depth of Judgment, heigth of Devotion, and elegancy of Stile; as that Golden Manual' (p. 14).

For the common reader, consolation was provided in the guise of a 'Letter to a Friend' – unusually specified as a woman, whose 'worthy Husband' and 'Family' are included in the wishes of the clerical writer, perhaps to heighten the pathos of his desire to preserve her 'from fainting under the burthen of those tender thoughts that are in you towards his sacred Majesty' (p. 3).[21] After thanking his correspondent for the 'refuge and comfort' afforded 'in the time of my persecution', he makes the customary gestures of piety: every rose has a thorn; the fact that Charles 'died so good a KING' offers 'some recompense of comfort and solace'; and grief that he 'should suffer by his own *Judas's*' is alleviated by the reflection that he 'suffered so like his own *Jesus*' (p. 5). Having worked through the now familiar list of 'parallels', he pauses to note the 'differences': 'Christ he suffered for the whole World, he but for his three Kingdomes'; Christ died to free mankind from sin and Satan, whereas Charles died 'to free his Kingdomes from a temporal Captivity, and the Tyranny of wicked men' (p. 6).

Alongside the sermons and controversial or consolatory pamphlets generated by the execution, a veritable flood of verse elegies poured from the presses through the spring and summer. Loxley argues that the proper context in which to read these often awkward attempts to raise a monument to the dead monarch is 'the polemical deployment of elegy within royalist poetics in preceding years', in which the genre 'is envisaged as a means of effecting a fundamental military aim'.[22] And Lois Potter points out that the nature of the King's death presented potential elegists with a unique set of difficulties 'in attempting an adequate literary response to the occasion'; the task of instilling an air of sincerity into a public and formal mode – of controlling 'the expression of supposedly uncontrollable grief' and steering a course 'between cliché and hysteria' – became acute when the subject was 'the embodiment of all traditional values on the one hand, and an unprecedented and shocking event on the other'.[23] The note of incredulity is frequently sounded. The full title of one lament, which appeared along with other elegies in *Vaticinium Votivum* (London, [11 March] 1649), spells out not only the year, month, and day of the execution, but also the precise hour at which Charles I was beheaded, as if to imprint this unthinkable occurrence upon the map of history: '*Chronosticon*: Decollationis CAROLI Regis, tricesimo die Ianuarii, secunda hora Pomeridiana, *Anno Dom.* MDCXLVIII'. The text itself emphasizes the unique horror of what has happened – 'Such a Fall / Great Christendome ne're Pattern'd' – and shies away from formulating it in words, taking four stanzas to drag the awful truth into consciousness:

> CHARLES – ah forbear, forbear! lest Mortals prize
> His Name too dearly; and Idolatrize.
> His Name! Our Losse!...
> CHARLES our Dread Sovereign! – hold! lest Out-Law'd Sense
> Bribe and seduce tame Reason to dispense
> With those Celestial Powers...
> CHARLES our Dread Soveraign's murther'd! – Tremble! and
> View what Convulsions Shoulder-shake this Land...
> CHARLES our Dread Soveraign's murther'd at His Gate!
> Fell Feinds! dire Hydra's of a stiff-neck't-State![24]

Henry King went into print soon after the burial at Windsor with 'A Deepe Groane, fetch'd at the Funerall of that incomparable and Glorious Monarch, Charles the First' (London, [16 May] 1649). Apostrophizing the 'Accursed Day' of the murder, he can find no precedent in the annals of secular history for the 'prodigious Villanie' and resorts to the Scriptures: 'Now comes the miscreant Doomes-day of the Land. / Good-Friday wretchedly transcrib'd'. In the more polished 'Elegy upon the most Incomparable King Charles the First', which was begun in 1649 but not published until the Restoration was in sight, the same poet introduces his survey of the King's reign since 1640 with a similar assertion that this is a story 'which through time's vast Kalendar / Must stand without Example or Repair', and scours 'Holy Writ' in vain, discounting David, Solomon, Hezekiah and Joash as fit examples to set beside a king who 'exceeds Judea's Parallels'. Only when he comes to Charles's betrayal by the Scots and the events of the trial does he find appropriate biblical analogues in 'Iscariot' and 'Pilate Bradshaw with his pack of Jews'.[25]

A sense of personal disorientation is rendered in a barrage of questions in the opening lines of the elegy which John Quarles appended to a long narrative poem in which the dreaming poet tries to kiss the King's hand:

> What? do I dream? or does the *fancy* scatter
> Into my various *mind* a reall matter?
> What ails my *thoughts*? what uncorrected *passion*
> Is this that puts my *Senses* out of fashion?
> Where am I hurri'd? what sanguinious *place*
> Is this I breathe in, garnish'd with *disgrace*?
> Why? what's the reason that my *eys* behold
> These waves of *blood*?[26]

Awoken from his dream of Charles into the blood-drenched nightmare of contemporary England, he feels that he is 'in a *desert*' with no guide, and language itself leads him only into a contemplation of the catastrophe that throws his mind into further tumult:

> Great *Charls*, oh happy word, but what's the next
> (Bad's th' application of so good a *Text*)
> Is dead; most killing word, what is he dead?
> Nay more (a more may be) hee's murthered:
> Ah then my thoughts are murther'd ... (p. 40)

Another elegist, thought by Thomason to be Walter Montagu, also asserts that his reason is 'cast away in this *Red floud*, / Which ne'r o'erflowes us all'. He goes on to elaborate both the geographical and the biblical aspects of the allusion – 'This stroke hath cut the only neck of land, / Which between us, and this *Red Sea* did stand, / That covers now our world' – and likens the darkness and blood that have descended upon Britain to two of the plagues of Egypt.[27] A similar image occurs to the author of 'An Elegie On the best of Men, and meekest of Martyrs, CHARLES the I'. Questioning the motives of those who were 'Fed by some Plague, which in blind Mists was hurld / To strew infection on the tainted World', he ends with a vision of Charles invested 'with the Crown of Martyrdome' and enthroned above the darkness that covers this nether world, in what might be a reminiscence of the myth of stellification in Carew's great masque of 1634:

> And death the shade of nature did not shroud
> His Soul in Mists, but its clear Beams uncloud,
> That who a Star in our Meridian shone
> In Heaven might shine a Constellation.[28]

For Henry King, the 'cursed Authors' of the 'Brave Reformation' of recent years are not stars but 'unwholesome Exhalations', which 'onely Plagues beget'.[29]

The image of the saintly monarch, who died to defend the Church of England, was derived in a number of elegies explicitly from Charles's own book. After his narrative of the 1640s, King works a variation on the image of the star directing its light upon the monarch, who is about to pass from his 'Sufferings' to his 'Eternal Crown' in the famous frontispiece:

> Thou from th' enthroned Martyrs Bloud-stain'd Line
> Dost in thy Virtue's bright Example shine.
> And when Thy Darted Beam from the moist Sky
> Nightly salutes Thy grieving People's Eye,
> Thou, like some Warning Light rais'd by our fears,
> Shalt both provoke and still supply our Tears.[30]

And a few lines later, he alludes to the subtitle of the *Eikon Basilike*, 'The Pourtraicture of His Sacred Majestie in His Solitudes and Sufferings': 'Thy better Part / Lives in despight of Death, and will endure / Kept safe in Thy Unpattern'd Portraicture'. Francis Gregory turns a trite disclaimer about the inability of rhetoric to meet the occasion into a compliment to the expressive skill displayed by the royal author:

> Thy Book is our best Language; what to this
> Shall e're be added, is Thy Meiosis [figure of understatement]:
> Thy Name's a Text too hard for us; no men
> Can write of it, without Thy Parts and Pen.[31]

Alexander Brome, in one of his three poems on the death of Charles I, goes even further and finds in 'the King's book' a biblical power:

> Whose leafs shall like the Cybels' be ador'd,
> When time shall open each prophetic word:
> And shall like scripture be the rule of good
> To those that shall survive the flaming flood.[32]

Several of the foregoing motifs occur together in the first of the elegies in *Monumentum Regale* (London, [14 June] 1649). 'Our Sovereign's' is said to be 'like our *Saviour's Passion*'; he shines 'a *Star* more *fixt* & bright / Then where the *year* makes but *one day & night*'; plagues have befallen England as well as Egypt – '*Frogs* and *Lice*, and *Independents* too'; and both his martyrdom and the legacy of his pen will vindicate himself and the religion he lived by and died for: 'His *Book*, his *Life*, his *Death* will henceforth be / The *Church* of *England*'s best *Apology*' (pp. 104–15).

A recent study of the English funeral elegy concludes that 'no matter how many practices and conventions and clichés accumulated', it was 'essentially a form without a form ... a genre defined by its occasion'.[33] There were two major traditions of vernacular elegy in seventeenth-century England flowing from Sidney and Spenser, who 'rediscovered, reinvented, and transformed' the ancient pastoral model, and from Donne, who devised 'a non-pastoral (essentially latinate) funeral elegy'. The former, dwelling on 'continuity, change, loss, and memory', adopted a 'posture of exile, self-questioning, opposition, and obliquity'; and the latter, focusing on 'the particularities of the speaker, the occasion, and the subject', was set 'in an argumentative register appropriate to conversation, satire, and the dramatic expression of inner turmoil'. Followers of both Spenser and Donne had to engage consciously with 'the problem of fitting words to the special requirements of an occasion' – a politically sensitive process when the occasion was a royal death.[34]

Almost all the elegies on Charles I printed in 1649 adopted the 'argumentative register' favoured by Donne, in which 'the *witty* figure' was 'the form prescribed by decorum'.[35] They gave dramatic voice to the 'inner turmoil' of the speaker – so much so that Henry King's modern biographer dismisses his two poems as 'incoherent with rage' and offers them as prime examples 'of the destruction of the form of expression by underlying emotional sincerity'.[36] The Donne tradition certainly encouraged King and others to escape from their intolerable sense of loss by leaning towards satire. The anonymous author of *A Flattering Elegie*, for example, weaves scatological fantasies, in which the devil, treated by an infernal 'Doctor and Apothecary' with a 'Vomit, Clister, and Suppository', very soon 'turn'd our happy Kingdome to his Jakes':

> Here (from his Hellish throat) he spawl'd and spew'd
> Of Sectaries a cursed Multitude...
> And from his gut beneath he vented out
> An ill look't vermine with a fiery snowt...
> A mighty blackfac'd worme he eke did void,
> And those two have our happinesse destroy'd.
> And thus the Divels excrements did vent
> A cursed Army, and a Parliament.[37]

Later, presenting the historical 'particularities' of the situation with the directness that was a feature of the Donne line of elegies, the satirist relates how one of these monsters rounded on the other and brought Fairfax and Cromwell to power: 'So Parliament and City dare not act, / Except great TOM and NOL approve the fact' (p. 6). Henry King names names in his second poem, from 'Hazlerig', 'Cromwel' and 'Hammond' to 'th' unkennell'd crew of Lawless men / Led down by Watkins, Pennington, and Ven'; and by switching his emphasis from praise to blame turns the protean 'form without a form' into a vehicle for indictment and denunciation rather than praise, lament and consolation. Like other elegists of Charles I, King is not content with the traditional image of the earthly monarch lifted 'up to His Eternal Crown' and brings his poem to a close with a call for vengeance:

> But He whose Trump proclaims, Revenge is Mine,
> Bids us our Sorrow by our Hope confine . . .
> It dares Conclude, God does not keep His Word
> If Zimri dye in Peace that slew his Lord.[38]

Alexander Brome also waits upon the justice of the God who has permitted 'those traytors impious hands / To murther his anoynted', and looks forward to the day when 'their headlong and unpitied fall' will make 'the Realms Nuptial of their funerall'.[39] An extreme version of this stance is adopted in one of the most widely disseminated poetic responses to the death of Charles I, in which the Marquis of Montrose deliberately rejects the mode of elegy as inadequate to the present situation:

> Great! Good! and Just! could I but rate
> My griefs, and thy too rigid fate,
> I'de weep the world to such a strain,
> As it should Deluge once again.
> But since thy loud-tongu'd bloud demands supplies,
> More from *Briareus* hands, than *Argus* eyes,
> I'le sing thy Obsequies, with Trumpet sounds,
> And write thy *Epitaph* with *Bloud* and *Wounds*.[40]

The claim that this was written 'with the point of his Sword' reinforces the sentiment that 'the special requirements' of this 'occasion' cannot be met by the pen. As MacLean puts it, 'The poet himself demands an active participation in history, preferring the role of avenging agent rather than that of grief-stricken maker of memorials.'[41]

The last two works to be discussed in this chapter belong to a different order of imaginative power from those poems in which the methods

bequeathed by Donne and the 'polemical' elegists of the Civil War failed
to cope satisfactorily with the unprecedented circumstances of January
1649. Henry Vaughan's choice of the alternative model of Spenserian
pastoral in 'Daphnis: An Elegiac Eclogue', exemplified for his generation by Milton's 'Lycidas', opened up a rich store of poetic resources
which enabled him to avoid the stridency that resulted from the practice
of foregrounding the 'inner turmoil' of an individual speaker and baldly
addressing the 'particularities of . . . the occasion'. Already distanced
from the immediate horror of the event by his retirement to Breconshire,
the pastoral 'posture of exile' came naturally to him; and the virulence of
the persecution in his own locality, where thirteen Malignant ministers,
including his own brother and close friends, were ejected from churches
within six miles of his home, must have recommended to this staunch
supporter of the Church of England both the 'opposition and obliquity'
of the Spenserian mode and its thematic stress on 'continuity, change,
loss, and memory'. Of all the previous examples of pastoral elegy, the
one which has the most direct bearing on Vaughan's elegy is Virgil's
Fifth Eclogue, in which two interlocutors, one of whom is called Menalcas, lament the passing of a shepherd named Daphnis. Although other
candidates have been proposed, the most widely held interpretation of
Virgil's poem (certainly in the seventeenth century) identifies Daphnis as
Julius Caesar, whose 'cruel death' at the hands of his political enemies
and subsequent deification affords an obvious parallel to the martyrdom
of the English King.[42]

The fiction of two shepherds in dialogue creates that sense of grief
shared and alleviated by the communal performance of appropriate
rituals which has been described as 'a healthy work of mourning' – work
which is inscribed in the conventions of a poetic tradition that has its
roots in 'the death and return of the vegetation god' and follows 'the
ancient rites' that took initiates 'through grief or darkness to consolation
and renewal'.[43] The fact of loss is confronted in Menalcas's account of
'the green wood', which 'glitter'd with the golden Sun', being overtaken
by the 'fierce dark showrs' of war, and the consequent silencing of the
nightingale: 'I saw her next day on her last cold bed; / And *Daphnis* so,
just so is *Daphnis* dead!'[44] Damon's reply, adapted from a passage in
Virgil's Fifth eclogue, is a moving lament for all those who have fallen in
the wars of the past decade, especially the young, like Vaughan's friend,
Mr R. W., who had vanished in the smoke at Rowton Heath, and his
own younger brother, William, who probably died of wounds received
in the fighting of 1648:[45]

> So Violets, so doth the Primrose fall,
> At once the Springs pride and its funeral.
> Such easy sweets get off still in their prime,
> And stay not here, to wear the soil of Time.

The linking through this simile of Daphnis/Charles and those who have
given their lives in his cause helps to elucidate the complex imagery of
Menalcas's next speech:

> Souls need not time, the early forward things
> Are always fledg'd, and gladly use their Wings,
> Or else great parts, when injur'd quit the Crowd,
> To shine above still, not behind the Cloud.

The phrase 'or else' implies a distinction between the 'early forward
things' – the young men who 'gladly' accept death – and 'great parts'
who, king-like and sun-like, still shine in glory above the clouds which
seek to obscure them. This second image seems to have haunted
Vaughan's imagination. He had already used it in 'The King Disguis'd',
and in 'An Elegie on the death of Mr *R. Hall*, slain at *Pontefract*, 1648', he
applied it to another young friend:

> But I past such dimme Mourners can descrie
> Thy fame above all Clouds of obloquie,
> And like the Sun with his victorious rayes
> Charge through that darkness to the last of dayes.[46]

But there is something far more significant behind these lines in 'Daphnis' than merely Vaughan's predilection for certain kinds of imagery. In
the engraved frontispiece of the *Eikon Basilike* [Figure 2], there is an
allegorical landscape behind the kneeling figure of Charles I. From a sky
overcast with swirling clouds, a single ray of light – inscribed with the
words '*Clarior e tenebris*' [More brightly out of darkness] – descends upon
the King's head. Above him, on the right, there is a view through a
window: a second ray, labelled '*Coeli specto*' [I look at the heavens],
ascends from the King's eye to a radiant crown of glory, beneath which
the clouds are rolling away. If Vaughan had seen this emblem, and there
is other evidence to suggest that he had, then the couplet from 'Daphnis'
quoted above could well be a direct reference to the saintly Charles's
translation from the troubles of this world into the light that always
shines beyond the clouds.

The next few lines contain a reference to Vaughan's twin brother,
Thomas, and present a number of intriguing possibilities:

> *Men.* And is't not just to leave those to the night,
>   That madly hate, and persecute the light?

Who doubly dark, all *Negroes* do exceed,
And inwardly are true black Moores indeed.
   Da. The punishment still manifests the Sin,
As outward signs shew the disease within.
While worth opprest mounts to a nobler height,
And Palm-like bravely overtops the weight.

The first couplet reads like an attack on the fanatical puritans who were so active in South Wales during the first years of the Commonwealth.[47] The next puns on the name of Henry More, who was involved in a bitter controversy with Thomas Vaughan in 1650.[48] Damon's reply is more puzzling. What is the punishment that 'still manifests the Sin, / As outward signs shew the disease within'? There are hints elsewhere in Vaughan's work that he admired the early poetry of John Milton ('Lycidas' in particular)[49] but later developed a hostility towards him. This exchange between the two shepherds may contain, in addition to the attack on More, a sneer at the 'doubly dark' apologist for regicide, whose spiritual blindess in composing such works as *Eikonoklastes* was known to be costing him his eye-sight – a fitting 'punishment'.

While men like More and Milton were, in their different ways, persecuting the light and reviling the dead King and his devoted followers, 'worth opprest mounts to a nobler height, / And Palm-like bravely overtops the weight'. This is a version of a proverb: 'The straighter grows the Palm the heavier the weight it bears.'[50] But there was one particular application of this image which would have been familiar to faithful royalists like Vaughan. In the lower part of the emblematic landscape in William Marshall's frontispiece to the *Eikon Basilike*, there is a palm-tree with heavy weights suspended from its branches. A scroll bears the elucidating text, *'Crescit sub Pondere Virtus'* [Virtue grows when weighed down]. Beneath the plate, in later editions of the book, there is an 'Explanation of the Embleme' in both Latin and English verses. The English version begins:

Though clogg'd with *weights* of miseries
Palm-like *Depress'd*, I higher rise.
And as th' *unmoved Rock* out-brave's
The boist'rous *Windes* and rageing *waves*:
So *triumph I*. And *shine more bright*
In sad Affliction's Darksom night.

The verbal similarities between the Latin scroll, these lines, and Vaughan's couplet about the palm-tree, and also the closeness to the earlier image of the sun shining 'above still, not behind the Cloud', suggest that Vaughan was deliberately alluding to the *Eikon Basilike* and proclaiming his poem an allegorical elegy on the dead King.

The rest of Damon's speech is an evocation of the poet's boyhood in Breconshire. At the centre of it is 'the great oak' which may, as Hutchinson suggests, be the one which Thomas Vaughan records as growing 'before the courtyard of my father's house', but it does not seem adequate to dismiss this long and eloquent passage as merely 'a description of the pastoral scene'.[51] The oak, like the sun, is a common symbol of kingship, and the way the shepherd talks about this particular tree calls up a vision of the golden age before the fall of Charles I. Those artists who were now bereft of his patronage had indeed found 'a goodly shelter' beneath the monarch's 'stately height and shade'. In 'those happy days', before the outbreak of the Civil Wars, the shepherds – poets like Cartwright and Carew – had practised their art unmolested by the puritans. Old Amphion – Matthew Herbert, rector of Llangattock, who had been schoolmaster to Henry and Thomas Vaughan – along with Thomas himself and Thomas Powell, had been deprived of their livings by 1650. It is to such persecution, through the familiar equation of minders of sheep and pastors of the church, that Vaughan points in a line which echoes the biblical image invoked in many of the printed elegies: 'With all those *plagues* poor shepherds since have known' [italics added].

There are good reasons for reading the last lines of Damon's speech as an allegory of the beheading of Charles and the slaughter of his followers – perhaps the recent executions of Lucas, Lisle and Lord Capel were uppermost in the poet's mind. All the branches of the oak-tree, 'from the trembling top / To the firm brink', were lopped off, and 'the pride and beauty of the plain lay dead'. (There is a parallel tree image, applied explicitly to the death of the King, in 'An Epitaph upon King Charles' by J. H., printed at the end of the *Eikon Basilike*: 'So falls the stately cedar, while it stood / That was the only glory of the wood.')[52] Vaughan may also have been drawing upon the royalist iconography found in the frontispiece to Quarles's collection of eclogues [Figure 1] and the engraving in Clement Walker's *Anarchia Anglicana* [Figure 3] and also widely disseminated in the picture of the British Oak at the front of James Howell's popular political allegory, *Dodona's Grove*, which went into a third edition in 1649 and sported as its motto, 'Let the tree be honoured whose shade protects us'. It is certainly tempting to see references to Cromwell, who directs the pruning and felling of Walker's 'Royall Oake of Brittayne', in the 'curs'd owner' and 'the hated Hewer' of lines 67 and 77. Although the King's supporters – the 'undone Swains' – mourn their loss, however, the royalist cause has not been totally defeated and 'new recruits and succours' are brought into the field. This may be an allusion to the fact that Charles II was proclaimed king in Scotland and in Ireland, where a combined force of Catholics and English and Scottish colonists under Ormond held most of the country and threatened England with invasion during the spring and early summer. At a slightly later date, it could refer to the royalist force led by Charles II that got as far as Worcester in 1651. Read as a pastoral account of the 'halcyon days' and the fall of Charles I, the passage can be seen as a powerful and consistent piece of allegory, standing at the artistic centre of an elegy that mourns not only for the death of a monarch but for the passing of an entire culture and way of life.

Menalcas's reply brings the first half of the poem, which has been concerned with the personal rule, sufferings and death of Charles I, to a strong climax with imagery that once more invokes the *Eikon Basilike*:

> So thrives afflicted Truth! and so the light,
> When put out, gains a value from the Night.
> How glad are we, when but one twinkling Star
> Peeps betwixt clouds, more black than is our Tar?
> And Providence was kind, that order'd this
> To the brave Suff'rer should be solid bliss;
> Nor is it so till this short life be done,
> But goes hence with him, and is still his Sun.

The phrase 'brave Suff'rer' glances at the book's subtitle and the image of the 'one twinkling Star' is derived from the frontispiece, in which the single ray of light is not only a comfort in 'this short life' but also a symbol of the divine light that will irradiate him when he 'goes hence'. Vaughan may also be offering consolation to faithful royalists left behind in the black night of Cromwell's England. The one star in their political firmament was Charles II, the new King, who had gone 'hence' into exile as his father had gone 'hence' into heaven, but was 'still his *Son*'.

Damon's next speech is the structural pivot of the elegy, as the poet moves from his meditation on the past to his resolution for the future and a survey of the grim realities of life under the new regime. A conventional appeal to the shepherds to deck the grave with garlands becomes a defiant call to sing 'pious *Anthems*' and 'be never dumb' in honouring the name of Daphnis in 'the years to come'. The lines which introduce an epitaph on Daphnis direct another shaft at government propagandists like Milton, whose *Eikonoklastes* had slandered the moral character of the dead monarch: 'Write o're his Hearse / For false, foul Prose-men this fair Truth in Verse'. After Damon has spoken the epitaph, Menalcas takes up the theme of the honours due to Daphnis in another passage modelled on Virgil's Fifth Eclogue:

> Let this days Rites as stedfast as the Sun
> Keep pace with Time, and through all Ages run . . .
> And when we make procession on the plains,
> Or yearly keep the Holyday of Swains,
> Let *Daphnis* still be the recorded name
> And solemn honour of our feasts and fame.

But there is more to these lines than literary allusion. The 'procession on the plains' and the 'Holyday of Swains' represent those country festivals and church ceremonies that the puritans were trying to stamp out; and more pointedly, the injunction to celebrate 'this days Rites' on a steadfast yearly basis looks like evidence for the early practice of keeping 30 January as a virtual saint's day, long before it was instituted as a day of annual fasting and humiliation in the Restoration Prayer Book.[53] As the passage develops, however, it becomes a powerful statement of local resistance, rather than merely a promise that Daphnis will not be forgotten:

> Nor will these vocal Woods and Valleys fail,
> Nor *Isca's* lowder Streams this to bewail,
> But while Swains hope and Seasons change, will glide
> With moving murmurs, because *Daphnis* di'd.

In such a context, the phrase 'while Swains hope' implies precise political hopes – the return of Charles II – rather than a generalized religious hope of salvation.

One couplet in Damon's lament over the sad condition of the land stands out as a regret for the drabness of the Christian calendar, deprived of the ancient cycle of church festivals and the colourful vestments of Christmas and Easter: 'Not one short parcel of the tedious year / In its old dress and beauty doth appear'. Menalcas utters an even more bitter cry of despair in lines 143–54. Now that the 'dregs and puddle of all ages' flow over the country, his only solace is the thought that Daphnis at least 'Got through' to eternal life while the streams were still clear and the light not quite gone. Damon continues this gloomy line of thought: with Daphnis, 'the last looks of day / Went hence, and setting (Sun-like) past away', and now only 'feral fires' break the darkness in place of stars. What follows is an angry warning to those in power: in the shadows, men wait and watch for the 'future storms' that will be hatched by 'present sins' – 'Fury that's long fermenting, is most wild'. And the concluding movement of this speech adds a political bite to the motif of gathering dusk traditionally used to close a pastoral poem: 'The shades prevail, each Bush seems bigger grown: / Darkness (like State,) makes small things swell and frown'. Cromwell and his ilk have assumed an unnatural and deceptive eminence in a state where the light of monarchy has been put out.

As the shepherds part, Menalcas looks forward to some future date when joy will return to the saddened earth:

> *Men.* Farewel kind *Damon*! now the Shepheards Star
> With beauteous looks smiles on us, though from far.
> All creatures that were favourites of day
> Are with the Sun retir'd and gone away.
> While feral Birds send forth unpleasant notes,
> And night (the nurse of thoughts) sad thoughts promotes.
> But Joy will yet come with the morning-light,
> Though sadly now we bid good night! *Da.* good night!

Since Vaughan made use of Virgil elsewhere in the poem, it seems appropriate to gloss the first couplet with a reference to the Ninth Eclogue, in which Lycidas mentions the name of Daphnis and alludes to 'the star of Caesar' – a comet that appeared just after the assassination of Julius Caesar and was commonly held to be the dictator's deified soul.[54] If the parallel between Charles and Caesar is accepted, then 'the Shepheards Star' represents the martyred monarch still keeping watch over his faithful followers. Meanwhile, those who were favoured by the dead King – 'favourites of day' – have gone into exile 'with the Sun/ Son'. The country is left, for the time being, to the occupation of the 'feral Birds' and the darkness of the new Commonwealth; but every night is followed by a dawn, and the sun will return bringing the 'morning-light' of a restored monarchy. Once again, the similarity between Vaughan's choice of words and images and a passage in the *Eikon Basilike* seems too remarkable to be a coincidence:

For mine honour, I am well assured that, as mine innocency is clear before God in point of any calumnies they object, so my reputation shall, like the sun (after owls and bats have had their freedom in the night and darker times), rise and recover itself to such a degree of splendour as those feral birds shall be grieved to behold and unable to bear.[55]

The 'feral Birds' of Vaughan's elegy, sending forth 'unpleasant notes', are the 'feral birds' which cast 'calumnies' upon the King, and whose reign of darkness will one day end and permit the reputation of Charles I to shine forth again 'like the sun'.

The other poem on the death of Charles I which stands apart from the ruck of elegies, both in its form and in its poetic quality, has only recently been identified. Pursuing a connection between the title of 'The Unfortunate Lover' and the role of Philogenes (Lover of the People), danced by the King in the last of the Caroline masques in January 1640, Margarita Stocker argues that Andrew Marvell effects 'an ironic inversion of the normal masque movement'.[56] The calm antimasque of 'pleasant . . . dayes' spent 'By Fountains cool, and Shadows green' presented in Stanza 1 is dispelled by the 'masque of quarrelling Elements', which symbolizes the more recent history of a monarch 'by the Malignant Starrs, / Forced to live in Storms and Warrs'.[57] Stocker's reading contains a wealth of valuable insights – relating Stanza 3, for example, both to 'These storms the people's giddy fury raise' in *Salmacida Spolia* and to the frontispiece of the *Eikon Basilike*, which depicts 'the martyrdom of Charles I against a background of stormclouds and a turbulent sea'.[58] In a few particulars, however, it needs an adjustment of historical focus. Certain that 'the "Rock" upon which the state foundered' in Stanza 2 was the illusion of absolutism, she interprets the Lover's victimization by 'Corm'rants black' as a figure for 'Charles' ruin at the hands of the clergy', and insists that he is an 'unfortunate and abject Heir' because he submits 'to episcopal domination'.[59] While it may be consistent with the views Marvell expressed elsewhere that 'Charles' ruin was provoked by Laud and his Arminian colleagues',[60] the words of Stanza 4 surely describe a later phase of his experience, when the Laudian hierarchy was no longer in a position to exert any serious influence over royal policy:

> A num'rous fleet of Corm'rants black,
> That sail'd insulting o're the Wrack,
> Receiv'd into their cruel Care,
> Th' unfortunate and abject Heir:
> Guardians most fit to entertain
> The Orphan of the *Hurricane*.

These lines must refer not to the King's soul 'in the keeping of the "Guardian" bishops',[61] but to the years of captivity when he was literally an 'Orphan of the *Hurricane*' of Civil War. While he was in the 'cruel Care' of the Scots at Newcastle and Parliament at Holdenby, he was denied the service of his own chaplains and subjected to continual efforts to persuade him to sign the Covenant and accept a Presbyterian settlement. It was during the extended period of negotiations, broken off and resumed, with both Presbyterians and Independents, that he was fed 'with Hopes and Air', until 'angry Heaven' made him the central figure in 'a spectacle of Blood' – which, again *pace* Stocker, seems a more apt description of the 'memorable Scene' on the scaffold outside White-hall than of the prolonged conflict of the Civil War. Stocker helpfully relates the imagery of the final stanza to the biblical story of 'Josiah the righteous King' and to some lines from the early masque, *Loves Triumph through Callipolis*, in which it was prophesied that Charles would 'flow forth like a rich perfume / Into your nostrils, or some sweeter sound / Of melting music'.[62] But closer to the time of the poem's composition was the King's own book, which had been lauded in elegies and sermons for both its 'Musick' – the elegance of its style – and its 'Story' of the events that led through 'Love' and 'Warrs' to martyrdom:

> Yet dying leaves a Perfume here,
> And Musick within every Ear:
> And he in Story only rules,
> In a Field *Sable* a Lover *Gules*.

Whatever reservations there might be about occasional details in her analysis, Stocker is convincing in her conclusion that the 'peculiar tone' of this poem, 'with its mixtures of the extravagant and pathetic', is the product of a troubled and honest imagination which was struggling to do justice to both the 'folly' and the 'qualities' of the '*Royal Actor*'.[63]

In the last stanza of 'The Unfortunate Lover', there is an allusion to one of the lyrics published in Lovelace's collection of poetry, *Lucasta* (London, [21 June] 1649), to which Marvell contributed a dedicatory poem. Thomas Corns's perceptive study of the volume as a 'resourceful, resilient, and internally coherent' response to 'the crisis in royalist ideology' leaves no doubt about the poet's commitment to the royal cause, but points out that its strategy for 'ideological survival', in which 'courtly love at once validates militarism and is validated by it', is challenged at the end by the alternative course explored in 'Aramantha. A Pastorall', which 'offers an image of retreat and an escapist fantasy of a lifelong and erotic seclusion'.[64] The final chapter of this survey of royalist writing will be concerned with some of the strategies for 'ideo-logical survival' developed in the 1650s, when the initial shock of the King's execution had passed and writers had to face the day-to-day realities of life in the new republic.

CHAPTER 12

Coping with defeat and waiting for the King: 1649–1660

The history and contents of *Lucasta* are paradigmatic of the situation of
the committed royalist poet as the decade of the Civil Wars approached
its revolutionary climax. The book was licensed on 4 February 1648, but
the title was not entered in the Stationers' Register until 14 May 1649;
and Thomason acquired his copy on 21 June. The delay of more than a
year before publication was due to the insurrection in Lovelace's home
county of Kent during May and June 1648.[1] He was himself committed
to the Peterhouse prison on 9 June – perhaps merely as a precautionary
measure because of his role in the Kentish Petition of 1642 – and was not
released until 10 April 1649.[2] The volume he had prepared for the press
in February 1648 seems to have been designed as an encouragement to
military action. Although the poet had taken no part in the Civil Wars in
England since serving under Goring against the Scots in 1639 and 1640,
he had fought on the continent and been wounded at the siege of
Dunkirk in 1646.[3] A number of commendatory poems were contributed
to *Lucasta* by soldiers and several address him as Colonel Richard
Lovelace.

The collection opens with two songs that mark the beginning of a
soldier's career – 'To Lucasta, Going beyond the Seas' and 'To Lucasta,
Going to the Warres'. In the second of these, the Cavalier leaves 'the
Nunnerie' of his beloved's 'chaste breast' to embrace 'A Sword, a Horse,
a Shield'. Twice, in the body of the volume, he embraces instead a
common strategy of defeated Cavalierism in celebrating a life of hedon-
istic ease at the country house of Endymion Porter (where the sensual
pleasures of tobacco and wine are added to the aesthetic delights of the
courtier's gallery of paintings)[4] and in extending to Charles Cotton the
consolations of a warm hearth and literary conversation (as well as a
revival of forbidden festivities in the depths of winter):

Thou best of *Men* and *Friends*! we will create
  A Genuine Summer in each others breast;
And spite of this cold Time and frosen Fate
  Thaw us a warme seate to our rest. . . .
Dropping *December* shall come weeping in,
  Bewayle th' usurping of his Raigne;
But when in show'rs of old Greeke we beginne,
  Shall crie, he hath his Crowne againe![5]

But while these expedients may have been attractive to royalists in the immediate aftermath of military defeat in 1646, the context in which *Lucasta* was planned in the winter of 1647–8 required a different emphasis. The riots in Canterbury over the Christmas period were the prelude to a renewed effort to re-establish the 'Raigne' of both the king of the midwinter revels and the King of England, and Lovelace closed his collection of poetry with a summons to Lucasta, who is interpreted by one critic as 'an embodiment of the royalist ideals once celebrated in the Caroline masques'.[6] She is adjured to emerge from 'the dire Monument' where her 'vestal flame' is entombed and to display 'all the Standards' of her 'beames'.[7] Metaphors of trumpets, artillery and drums make this a call to arms, and it is also a call to dispel the Cavalier gloom for which wine and song were the usual remedies: 'Awake from the dead Vault in which you dwell, / All's Loyall here, except your thoughts rebell'.[8] *Lucasta* was not published in the spring of 1648, however, perhaps (as Marvell's commendatory verses assert) because of interference by the '*barbed Censurers*' who looked upon it like '*the grim consistory*' and '*on each line cast a reforming eye*'.[9]

When Lovelace was eventually free to see his book through the press in the summer of 1649, not only had the rebellion been crushed and its leaders executed, but the King himself was dead and the monarchy abolished. The altered circumstances in which it appeared are reflected in the poem printed at the end of the volume, which was presumably written in prison and added, as the title-page indicates, to the manuscript licensed in February 1648.[10] The first half of the text describes the rural round of Aramantha as she passes by way of the garden and the dairy to the shade of 'the neighbring Wood' and the seclusion of 'a well orderd stately grove', which is the 'Court oth' Royall Oake'. Here, 'ev'n tyerd with delight', she 'softly layes her weary limbs'; but this idyll is broken by the sound of a 'bitter groan' and 'a trembling Voyce', which complains that the 'gay Livery' of the natural world is at odds with the grief that should be expressed 'at this Funerall'. The speaker is Alexis,

Lovelace's pastoral persona, and he is mourning the loss of Lucasta, but it is hard not to read these lines, written early in 1649, as the Cavalier's lament for his dead King.

In the second half of the poem, Alexis is roused to fury when Aramantha chides him for overvaluing the beauty of Lucasta, only to discover his beloved in this rustic disguise. She tells him that she took refuge in 'this yet living Wood' from the 'sad storm of fire and blood' that blew up when 'HYDRAPHIL' (lover of the multitude) and 'PHIL-ANACT' (lover of the prince) fought 'for the same things' and in the process destroyed the 'glory of this Sicilie'. The soldier-poet determines to give up the futile struggle in the public domain and withdraw with Lucasta into the 'peacefull Cave' that will be 'their Bridall-bed and grave':

> His armes hung up and his Sword broke,
> His Ensignes folded, he betook
> Himself unto the humble Crook:
> And for a full reward of all,
> She now doth him her shepheard call,
> And in a SEE of flow'rs install.

If Lucasta was, indeed, Lovelace's symbol for the values of the court world of the 1630s – that *'candid Age'* regretted by Marvell, in which *'speaking well'* was the goal of literary art – then the poem added to his collection of royalist verse when it was belatedly published in 1649 prescribes the cultivation of retired pleasures as the best strategy for keeping that cultural ideal alive in the new Commonwealth.

This course was widely adopted by former supporters of the King during the 1650s. Many delinquents whose property had been sequestered under an ordinance of 1643 had already compounded for their estates by paying part of the value in order to retain possession of the rest. Under new regulations brought in after Charles's execution, 'composition cases initiated in 1649 and 1650 exceeded those in any other year with the exception of 1646'.[11] Among the first to compound back in 1644 had been Mildmay Fane and he was also among the first to give poetic expression to the positive aspects of such an enforced retirement. In the verse he assembled for his 1648 volume, *Otia Sacra*, he recommended his 'happy Life' to a friend: 'I settle to a Countrey life; / And in a sweet retirement there, / Cherish all Hopes, but banish fear'. In an apostrophe 'To Retiredness' he summed up its advantages:

Thus out of fears, or noise of Warr,
Crowds, and the clamouring at Barr;
The Merchant's dread, th' unconstant tides,
With all Vexation besides;
I hugg my Quiet, and alone
Take thee for my Companion.[12]

In another poem, he had calculated the spiritual profit to be derived from a 'Happy Retreat', in which he could 'cast up' his 'Reck'nings' and assess 'how Arrears increase / In Nature's book, towards the God of Peace'.[13]

In his study of Cavalier poetry, Earl Miner had seen Henry Vaughan as an extreme instance of the tendency exemplified by Fane and enacted in the encounter between Alexis and Aramantha/Lucasta: 'Few supporters of the King can have retreated so far inward as Henry Vaughan … certainly he has moved farther away than Herrick or Lovelace from the times, and in *Silex Scintillans* "The Retreate" into the soul is very nearly complete.'[14] Since these words were written, however, the political dimension of Vaughan's two volumes of devotional lyrics has been gradually opened up. James Simmonds, for example, devotes a chapter to Vaughan's anti-Puritan satire across the entire range of his secular and religious verse; Eluned Brown points out that his adoption of the title 'Silurist' for the first time in the 1650 *Silex Scintillans* may have been an appeal not simply to 'local "pietas"', but also to 'the heroic past of the Silures which he felt to be particularly pertinent at the time of his own defeat and mental and spiritual resistance'; and Jonathan Post sees the poet developing his inheritance from George Herbert along a 'subtly militant line of succession', which incorporated the 'sense of an impending apocalypse' derived from 'The Church Militant' and was 'shaped by an acute recognition of political oppression'.[15]

It is important to remember that there are two parts of *Silex Scintillans*, which are the products of different sets of historical circumstances. The original collection was registered on 28 March 1650 and Simmonds has made a good case for March 1648 as 'the most likely date' for Vaughan's beginning to compose religious lyrics.[16] The poems in the first part of *Silex Scintillans* therefore not only belong to 'a time which was the nadir of Royalist hopes';[17] they also belong to a time when political and personal catastrophes were inextricably combined in the poet's experience. His friend, Mr R. Hall, was killed at the siege of Pontefract; his younger brother died of his wounds; the Second Civil War ended in

disaster; and the King was executed. It is hardly surprising that the bulk
of the poems in the first two-thirds of the 1650 volume turn away from
the contemporary scene to explore the world of inner, spiritual life, in
such poems as 'Regeneration', 'The Search', 'The Retreate' and 'The
Storm'. The poet is preoccupied with his own sinfulness, his need for
justification and illumination, his longing for the peace and innocence of
childhood or the ultimate peace of death. When he does look outwards
to the process of history, his emphasis is on the hopelessness of the
situation, and the one bright spot in the future is to be found in the
universal equivalent of personal death – the Second Coming of Christ
which signals the end of the historical continuum. The mood is established in the group of poems which follow the opening allegory of the
soul's pilgrimage, 'Regeneration'. 'Death. *A Dialogue*', 'Resurrection and
Immortality' and 'Day of Judgement', with their epigraphs from the
Book of Job, the Book of Daniel and the First Epistle of St Peter, direct
attention to '*the land of darknesse*', '*the end of the dayes*' and '*the end of all things*'.

The next group of poems, 'Religion', 'The Search' and '*Isaacs* Marriage', which look back longingly to the 'calme, golden Evenings' and
the 'white dayes' of the Biblical era and contrast the pure spring of the
early Church with the 'tainted sink' of contemporary religion, lead into
a complaint by the personified British Church about the ecclesiastical
consequences of the puritan victory:

> Ah! he is fled!
> And while these here their *mists*, and *shadows* hatch,
>   My glorious head
> Doth on those hills of Mirrhe, and Incense watch.
>   Haste, haste my dear,
>   The Souldiers here
> Cast in their lots again,
>   That seamlesse coat
>   The Jews touch'd not,
> These dare divide, and stain.[18]

The contempt for the puritans, hatching 'their *mists*, and *shadows*', is
obvious enough; and a typological reading of lines 5–10 evinces the
familiar royalist parallel between the crucifixion of Christ and the
martyrdom of Charles I. Less clear-cut is the identity of the 'glorious
head' of the first four lines. One editor provides the succinct gloss,
'Christ', who is, of course, the Head of the universal church; but the
verb 'fled' has connotations which scarcely seem appropriate to the
risen and ascended Son of God. Perhaps Vaughan expected his readers

to pick up more political meanings from the ambivalent phrase and see, behind the figure of the risen Christ, the head of the Anglican Church on earth, who, in the person of Charles II had literally fled to the Continent, and in the person of Charles I had departed this life for heaven. The change from the third person to the personal address of the imperative at line 5, which is maintained throughout the rest of the poem in the urgent appeals 'O get thee wings!' and 'haste thee' in the simile of the 'young Roe' from the Song of Solomon, implies an eschatological solution to the problems of the British Church: its earthly head being dead or in exile, only its spiritual head can set things right at his Second Coming.

As the volume proceeds, this note is frequently sounded: meditations on the poet's own grief and sinfulness or on the corruption and troubles of mankind in this dark and storm-tossed world are punctuated by yearnings for a release from time through death or through apocalyptic intervention. 'The Lampe' looks forward to 'That houre, which must thy life, and mine dispatch' (p. 411); 'Thou that know'st for whom I mourne', the first of a number of elegies on William Vaughan, ends with the poet longing to join his brother in a better world; and the second elegy, 'Come, come, what doe I here?' yearns for death and an end to the miseries of time. Other poems, though not specifically death-directed or eschatological, are heavy with an awareness of time's oppression. 'Joy of my life!' complains that 'the night / Is dark, and long' (p. 423); the Body in 'The Evening-watch' asks of the Soul, 'How many hours do'st think 'till day?' (p. 425); 'Silence, and stealth of dayes!' computes wearily ''tis now / Since thou art gone, / Twelve hundred houres' (p. 425). 'Buriall' looks for time's slow-moving dominion to be cut short by the return of the Saviour: 'Lord haste, Lord come, / O come Lord *Jesus* quickly!' (p. 428); and this tone of urgency in anticipation of the final day runs right through 'The Dawning' from the opening questions: 'Ah! what time wilt thou come? when shall that crie / The *Bridegroome's Comming*! fill the sky?' (p. 451).

A. J. Smith has traced a development in the series of elegies on William Vaughan from a 'strong sense of a general cataclysm' to a renewed faith in life.[19] A similar movement from utter despair to a state of mind in which continuance of life in time can be borne is evident in Vaughan's treatment of the political realities of the day in poems towards the end of the 1650 volume. 'Easter-day' embodies a decisive change of attitude and merits quoting in full:

> Thou, whose sad heart, and weeping head lyes low,
>   Whose Cloudy brest cold damps invade,
> Who never feel'st the Sun, nor smooth'st thy brow,
>   But sitt'st oppressed in the shade,
>   Awake, awake,
> And in his Resurrection partake,
>   Who on this day (that thou might'st rise as he,)
>   Rose up, and cancell'd two deaths due to thee.
>
> Awake, awake; and, like the Sun, disperse
>   All mists that would usurp this day;
> Where are thy Palmes, thy branches, and thy verse?
>   *Hosanna!* heark; why doest thou stay?
>   Arise, arise,
> And with his healing bloud anoint thine Eys,
>   Thy inward Eys; his bloud will cure thy mind,
>   Whose spittle only could restore the blind.   (p. 456)

This is a call to throw off despair – a despair that is associated with political distress through the words 'invade', 'oppressed' and 'usurp'. It is also an act of defiance, in its call for the celebration of one of the traditional Church festivals in a way that was outlawed by the reformers. Vaughan is not looking to an end of political oppression, but to a revival of spirits among the oppressed – the 'Thou' he addresses is not only or chiefly himself. He is not, in the last lines, even stressing the redeeming aspects of Easter Day, but rather the power of Christ's resurrection to open 'inward Eys' and 'cure thy mind': that is, to overcome the deadly despair in which defeated royalists like himself have been imprisoned.

The next two poems, 'Easter Hymn' and 'The Holy Communion', celebrate this revival, the first beginning 'Death, and darkness get you packing', and the second, 'Welcome sweet, and sacred feast; welcome life!' (p. 457). There follow a group of poems which begin to recognize that the current situation has its positive side. In the translation of Psalm 121, the poet realizes that God's blessings can be manifested in defeat as well as victory. 'Affliction', 'The Tempest' and 'Love, and Discipline' are all variations on the theme that 'Sickness is wholsome', 'Kingdomes too have their Physick'; and 'Retirement' contains a reminder from God that all hope need not depend on the cessation of this time-bound existence:

> Now here below where yet untam'd
>   Thou doest thus rove
> I have a house as well
>   As there above,

> In it my *Name*, and *honour* both do dwell
> And shall untill
> I make all new. (p. 463)

Rather than lamenting helplessly that religion is a 'tainted sink' and that the 'glorious head' of the British Church 'is fled', the poet is directed to maintain the continuity of Anglican worship 'here below': 'Up then, and keep / Within those doors, (my doors) dost hear? *I will*' (p. 463). A complex network of intertextual allusions to the poetry of George Herbert turns this poem into a ceremony in which Vaughan accepts a God-given commission as the successor to the great poet-pastor of the Church of England with the words used to affirm personal commitment in the services of Confirmation, Matrimony and Ordination in the Book of Common Prayer: '*I will*.'[20]

The same theme of resolute faith and endurance is taken up in 'The Pilgrimage' which, unlike the opening allegory 'Regeneration', is concerned not with the inward journey in search of personal redemption, but with man's outward journey through life. The poet still longs for God's final appearance, so that 'I may get me up, and go'; but he is now ready to pursue his pilgrimage rather than pinning all his hope on a divine intervention: 'and since I may / Have yet more days, more nights to Count, / So strengthen me, Lord, all the way' (p. 465). Three poems further on, in 'The Mutinie', Vaughan encounters a new problem: how to live on faithfully but with patience in a state of political oppression, when his instinct, now that he has been roused from apathy, is to resist openly and actively. The analogy of the Israelites in Egypt, making bricks for the construction of the pyramids, focuses his own struggle to accept the wellnigh intolerable burden of Christian meekness. Seeing a future of bondage stretching before him, he rebels in a magnificently articulated sentence:

> Weary of this same Clay, and straw, I laid
> Me down to breath, and casting in my heart
> The after-burthens, and griefs yet to come,
>   The heavy sum
> So shook my brest, that (sick and sore dismai'd)
> My thoughts, like water which some stone doth start
> Did quit their troubled Channel, and retire
> Unto the banks, where, storming at those bounds,
> They murmur'd sore. (p. 468)

He grudgingly admits that he must carry on, but not without words of protest, which break angrily across the boundary between stanzas:

> If yet these barren grounds
> And thirstie brick must be (said I)
> My taske, and Destinie,
>
> Let me so strive and struggle with thy foes
> (Not thine alone, but mine too,) that when all
> Their Arts and force are built unto the height
> That Babel-weight
> May prove thy glory, and their shame.   (p. 468)

He does not discount God's power to provide the solution he clung to in his despair – 'Not but I know thou hast a shorter Cut / To bring me home, than through a wildernes' – but the likelihood is now faced that it is the alternative pilgrimage into the desert that awaits him. The Christian answer to his dilemma is obedience to the divine will, which may require him to be 'soft and mild' rather than actively engaging with his and God's foes. In 'The Constellation', which immediately follows 'The Mutinie', the same lesson is set forth in less personal terms, with a concluding prayer that the British who have been 'Commission'd by a black self-wil' and 'disorder'd into wars' by their own 'lusts' may become 'an humble, holy nation' (p. 470). These poems look to a historical future, in which the individual and the people each have a part to play. The eschatological solution has dropped out of sight.

'Misery', almost at the end of the volume, reveals that the commitment to a life of pious retirement is under severe pressure from the new impulse towards action:

> At length I feel my head to ake,
> My fingers Itch, and burn to take
> Some new Imployment, I begin
> To swel and fome and fret within.
> *"The Age, the present times are not*
> *"To snudge in, and embrace a Cot,*
> *"Action and bloud now get the game,*
> *"Disdein treads on the peaceful name,*
> *"Who sits at home too bears a loade*
> *"Greater than those that gad abroad.*
> Thus do I make thy gifts giv'n me
> The only quarrellers with thee,
> I'd loose those knots thy hands did tie,
> And would go travel, fight or die.   (pp. 473–4)

This seems to indicate that the former royalist soldier – the pious recluse and mystic of critical tradition – was, at some time before his collection of poems was registered in March 1650, beginning to itch for a more active role in the struggle against the enemies of God and the church and not a little contemptuous of those royalists who had taken the easy option and gone into exile, leaving the greater burden to be carried by those who stayed '*at home*'. For a man who, in spite of his dedication to the quest for illumination of the spirit, could also feel that '*the present times are not / To snudge in*', some attitude towards the times would have to be found which could give a satisfactory direction to his political commitment. It would not be enough for this 'fierce soul' merely to cultivate the landscape of the mind.

Meanwhile, the poets among those who had gone abroad were not without literary projects and ambitions. There were two main groups of royalist exiles: the so-called 'Louvre' faction, identified with Henrietta Maria and politically controlled by Henry Jermyn, which favoured an alliance with the Scots and a deal with the Presbyterians at Westminster; and the 'Old Royalists' under the leadership of Hyde, Nicholas and Hopton, whose policy was to wait until the tide of national opinion turned against the new regime in London.[21] William Davenant, a long-standing adherent of the Queen, had been occupying himself with the composition of an 'Heroick Poem' and avidly canvassing the views of other exiled writers in Paris – in particular Abraham Cowley, Edmund Waller and the philosopher Thomas Hobbes. By the end of 1649, he had completed two of the projected five books of *Gondibert*, but other enterprizes intervened and early in May 1650 he set sail for the New World to take up an official post in one of the colonies loyal to the Crown.[22] Before he left Paris, unwilling to offer the world an unfinished work, he published a lengthy *Preface to Gondibert*, dated 2 January 1650, in which he laid before Hobbes the literary principles that the conversations of the past year had helped him to formulate. Printed with it was an *Answer* by Hobbes, dated 10 January, praising the poem and endorsing the theory behind it.[23]

Davenant's careful placing of his 'Heroick Poem' in relation to the epic poetry of the past, his rejection of supernatural machinery and the traditional appeal to the Muse and his reasoned justification of a five-part structure derived from tragedy have encouraged commentators to read the Preface as 'the manifesto of neo-classicism', which 'breathes the seventeenth-century spirit of enquiry' and is pervaded by the rationalism of Bacon and Hobbes.[24] This may well be its primary interest in the longer perspective of intellectual history, but some aspects of its literary programme are, as Steven Zwicker has noticed, 'exactly responsive to the circumstances of royalist exiles in 1650' and certain passages are charged with an urgency that goes beyond the desire for 'aesthetic regulation'. Several of the issues taken up in Davenant's exposition of a rational poetics turn out to be 'pretexts for a politicized discussion of literary culture' and 'the force of his arguments and the edge of his language are very political indeed'.[25] In explaining why he 'chose a Story of such Persons as profess'd Christian Religion', for example, he describes the contrasting religion of the Jews in terms which a contemporary reader would have recognized as applicable to the new 'chosen people', the self-proclaimed 'Saints' of the English republic: '[it] doth still consist in a sullen separation of them selves from the rest of humane flesh, which is a fantasticall pride of their owne cleanesse, and an uncivill disdaine of the imagin'd contagiousnes of others' (lines 262–5). The need on occasion to use force against the common people, 'since they are never willing either to buy their peace or to pay for Warre' (lines 366–7), comes up in the course of justifying 'Courts and Camps' as the fittest settings for heroic action; and a disquisition on the moral significance of ambition as a motivating passion in the fable provides the occasion for a criticism of royalists who have opted for quietism: 'for the world is only ill govern'd because the wicked take more paines to get authority, then the vertuous; for the vertuous are often preach'd into retirement; which is to the publique as unprofitable as their sleep' (lines 448–51). But most expressive of 'the courtly position at a moment of crisis and change' is 'the attack on inspiration and the concomitant celebration of wit', which Zwicker highlights in both the Preface and the Answer.[26] For Davenant, 'inspiration' has become 'a dangerous word' over the past ten years for political rather than literary reasons. Originally 'a spirituall Fitt, deriv'd from the ancient Ethnick Poets', it has been hijacked by those 'who now professe the same fury' and 'may perhaps by such authentick example pretend authority over the people' (lines 732–8). '*Witte*', being the product of both 'labour' and 'dexterity of thought' (lines 597–8), does not 'assume such saucy familiarity with a true God' (line 746). Because 'like that of the *Spider*' its thread 'is considerately woven out of our selves' (lines 590–1), it makes no claims that transcend its own rational consistency. Taking his cue from Davenant, Hobbes makes the same connection between the 'foolish custome' of the poets, who desire 'to be thought to speake by inspiration, like a Bagpipe' (lines 147–50), and the less venial deception of puritan divines: 'For when they call unseasonably for *Zeale* there appears a spirit of *Cruelty*; and by the like error instead of *Truth* they rayse *Discord*; instead of *Wisdome, Fraud*; instead of *Reformation, Tumult*; and *Controversie* instead of *Religion*' (lines 137–41). Consequently, his mechanistic model of the creative process, elaborated from Davenant's account of Wit, has good political reasons for eradicating all trace of the mysterious or supernatural: 'Time and education begets experience; Experience begets memory; Memory begets Judgement, and Fancy; Judgement begets the strength and structure; and Fancy begets the ornaments of a Poeme' (lines 151–4). With poetry coming into its own as the main literary support system for royalism in eclipse, the need to enunciate a distinctive poetics was to bear other important fruit in the course of the new decade.

Davenant had ended the Preface with a promise that he would only 'delay the publication of any part of the Poem' until he could send it to Hobbes 'from *America*; whither I now speedily prepare' (lines 1583–5). These hopes were dashed when his ship was intercepted by the Commonwealth's navy and he was imprisoned in Cowes Castle to await trial as a notorious Malignant. Through the summer, he worked on the third book of *Gondibert*, but he broke off at the end of Canto VI with a postscript dated 22 October 1650, at which point he was transferred to the Tower to be tried for capital crimes against the state. Knowing that he was 'threatned with Death', he asked the 'civill' reader 'not to take it ill, that I run not on till my last gasp'.[27] But he also defended the composition of poetry 'in an unseasonable time' with the realistic argument that 'Conquest is the Wheels of the World, on which it has ever run' and that the poet's task is to serve the cause he embraces at different phases of the inevitable 'revolution of Empire'. He reminds the potential reader that '*Poesie* was that Harp of *David*, which remov'd from *Saul*, the Melancholy Spirit' and that 'with *Poesie*, in *Heroick Songs*, the Wiser Ancients prepar'd their Batails'. As a poet living in a time of war, he could not 'sit idle, and sigh with such as mourn to hear the Drum; for if this Age be not quiet enough to be taught Vertue a pleasant way, the next may be at leisure'. Like the other royalist prisoners charged with him, Davenant was not in the end executed, but he was kept in the Tower until October 1652. By then, the completed half of *Gondibert* had been published in London, where it was acquired by Thomason in January 1651. Cowley and Waller loyally supplied poems of commendation, the former obediently making a contrast between the 'Poets Fury' and the 'Zelots Spirit' and the latter censuring the poet's countrymen who 'have impov'rished themselves' by obliging him to sing in 'forraign

Groves';[28] and Henry Vaughan, hailing Davenant as the 'Prince of *Poets*', marvelled at the resilience of a talent that could flourish when 'mur'd in solitarie stones'.[29]

Unfortunately, Davenant's ambition to join the ranks of Homer, Virgil and Tasso with his 'Gift to Posterity' of 'an *Heroick POEM*' was not to be realized. In his own day, it was mocked for its pretensions in a volume mischievously entitled *Certain Verses written by severall of the Authors Friends, to be Re-printed with the second Edition of Gondibert*, published in London in 1653 and largely the work of Sir John Denham, who had held aloof from the literary coterie that surrounded the Queen in Paris.[30] Later critics have found in Davenant's tale of love and honour in eighth-century Lombardy 'the solemn gallantry of the *salon*', derived from the French romances of the time, and have judged it to be written 'much more in the style of the Restoration "heroic play" than in that of the classical epic'.[31] Attempts to read it as a *roman à clef* have been unconvincing, although its modern editor detects a reference to the fate of Charles I in the description of a stag hunt in the second canto, which seems to echo the famous passage in *Cooper's Hill* and at one point certainly hints at a political subtext:

> The Heard deny him shelter, as if taught
> To know their safety is to yield him lost; . . .
> We blush to see our politicks in Beasts,
> Who Many sav'd by this one Sacrifice.[32]

While Davenant and Hobbes were developing a new royalist poetics, the practical business of disseminating the work of royalist poets was being carried on by Humphrey Moseley. In 1650, he reprinted *Cooper's Hill* and published *Clarastella*, the poems of Robert Heath, which he recommended as 'worthy of the publick view' because of 'the gallantness and Ingenuity of the Gentleman' who had written them – qualities which left little doubt as to the poet's cultural and political affiliations;[33] in 1651, he issued a third edition of Carew's *Poems* and published the collected plays and poetry of William Cartwright, the *Poems* of Thomas Stanley and *Olor Iscanus* by Henry Vaughan; and in 1652, he reissued the Stanley volume and published *Theophila*, a long meditative poem by Edward Benlowes which, in its last two cantos, celebrates the quiet and innocence of the countryside, where 'fields of corn' are exchanged for 'fields of combat', and the psychological damage inflicted by Civil War can be repaired: 'Retreating to sweet shades, our shatter'd thoughts we piece'.[34]

Stanley had taken a lead in sustaining the cultural life of defeated royalism after his return from a youthful tour of France in 1646. Although only twenty-one, he became a generous patron of James Shirley and other hard-up writers at that difficult time and gathered about him in London a literary circle that may have included Herrick and Lovelace.[35] He seems to have founded a secret society in which members indicated their sympathy for the plight of the King by wearing a black ribband round their arm. There are allusions to this emblem of loyalty in poems by Herrick, Shirley and John Hall.[36] Stanley himself wrote verses for Shirley's *Poems* and Suckling's *Fragmenta Aurea*, and soon after the death of Charles I he began to versify the prose meditations at the end of each chapter of the *Eikon Basilike*, which he published in 1657 as *Psalterium Carolinum*.

The practice of contributing verses to each other's volumes of poetry as a means of maintaining a sense of cultural identity reached its peak in the fifty-six poems of commendation prefixed to the posthumous works of Cartwright. The massed tributes of John Berkenhead, Henry Vaughan, Alexander Brome, Izaak Walton and many of the writers and scholars who had been part of the war-time community in Oxford was a powerful statement of royalist solidarity. *Olor Iscanus*, which had been prepared for the press as early as December 1647 but for some reason held back from publication,[37] boasted three commendations by alumni of Vaughan's university: his Breconshire neighbour, Thomas Powell, an unidentified I. Rowlandson and his twin brother. Thomas Vaughan apologizes for this rather thin 'guard of *Poets*', assuring Henry that there are many more 'learned *friends*' who would gladly come forward 'were they told of this' and making explicit the political significance that poetry had assumed as a distinguishing activity of royalism during the Interregnum:

> And though this *sullen age* possessed be
> With some strange *Desamour* to Poetrie,
> Yet I suspect (thy fancy so delights)
> The *Puritans* will turn thy *Proselytes*.[38]

The system of government put in place during the spring of 1649 lasted until April 1653. The fatal tension between the radicalized Army with its 'vision of the New Jerusalem' and the social conservatism of the majority of members at Westminster was embodied in the figure of Oliver Cromwell, himself both Rumper and General, who 'was probably never unconscious of the gap between the legitimate aspirations of the saints, which he shared, and the common desires and prejudices of the Country gentry'.[39] At first, the military leadership was preoccupied with

military matters. Leaving Ireton as Lord Deputy in Ireland, Cromwell
returned to England in May 1650 to meet the challenge from Scotland,
where Charles Stuart had abandoned Montrose (soon to be defeated,
captured and executed) in favour of Argyll and the Covenanters, and an
army had been raised under David Leslie. Fairfax resigned rather than
lead a pre-emptive strike against the Scots and Cromwell headed an
expeditionary force across the border at the end of July. He defeated
Leslie at Dunbar on 3 September and soon had control of Edinburgh.
Delayed by illness, he resumed his campaign in June 1651. Charles
slipped past him into England, where the hoped-for royalist rising did
not materialize. Cromwell and Lambert caught up with him at Worcester on 3 September and the young King of the Scots had to flee in
disguise.[40]

In its domestic policies towards the defeated supporters of Charles I,
the Rump had to make a 'choice between the elementary alternatives of
conciliation and repression'.[41] A hardline approach was justified by
Marchamont Nedham, now employed as editor of *Mercurius Politicus*, the
major official newsbook. In one of a series of editorials, eventually
published together in 1656 as *The Excellencie of a Free State*,[42] he summed
up the case for repression:

When a commonwealth is founding, or newly founded, in the close of a civil
war, upon the ruins of a former government; in this case (I say), to make no
distinction between men but to allow the conquered part of the people an equal
right to choose and to be chosen, &c., were not only to take away all proportion
in policy, but the ready way to destroy the commonwealth, and by a promiscuous mixture of opposite interests, to turn all into confusion.[43]

Various measures were put in place to ensure that such a distinction was
made: on 2 January 1650, the Engagement Oath barred from public
office any adult male who refused to bind himself to 'be true and faithful
to the Commonwealth of England, as it is now established, without a
king or House of Lords';[44] on 26 February 1650, all papists and delinquents were banished from the capital and forbidden to travel more
than five miles from their places of residence; on 16 July 1651, the estates
of seventy leading royalists were confiscated; and during 1651 orders
were issued outlawing such country pastimes as horse-racing, cock-
fighting and hunting, for fear that they might become occasions for
plotting against the government.[45] Hobbes, who returned to England
when the military supremacy of the new regime had been confirmed at
Worcester, provided philosophical support for the case made in the
course of the Engagement controversy for submission to the

Commonwealth.[46] Although he did not disown his preference for monarchy, there was no avoiding the implications of the blunt conclusion he enunciated in the English version of his own *De Cive*: 'All judgement, therefore, in a city belongs to him who has the swords; i.e. to him who has the supreme authority.'[47] And political ideas developed in the full exposition of his system in *Leviathan*, published later in 1651, left him with few friends among the ranks of the defeated: 'The Obligation of Subjects to the Soveraign, is understood to last as long, and no longer, than the power lasteth, by which he is able to protect them.'[48]

With Cromwell back at Westminster, Parliament moved 'haltingly toward a general policy of reconciliation with those who would renounce their malignant pasts' by voting through an Act of Oblivion on 24 February 1652.[49] But it also led the Commonwealth into a successful commercial war against the Dutch and with growing confidence in its own legitimacy began to assert itself against the religious radicals in the Army. By 1653, the conservative majority was 'set on a collision course with the soldiers'.[50] The point of impact came at the end of a series of weekly debates on a bill for the dissolution of the Rump and the election of a new parliament. What exactly happened to prompt Cromwell's action is not clear, but on 20 April he hurried to the House of Commons with a file of soldiers, seized the bill, and angrily dismissed the assembled members.[51] This *coup* was not 'the overture to military rule', however, since the Army under Cromwell 'continued to seek some form of civilian government that would heal the nation's political wounds and provide the solid legal and constitutional foundation on which to build lasting reform'.[52] A new Council of State was appointed to carry on the business of government while an assembly of godly men was nominated to prepare the way for the eventual election of a parliament. This assembly, nicknamed 'Barebone's Parliament' after one of its number, was opened by Cromwell on 4 July, but alarmed by the activities of its more radical members, the moderates voted to dissolve it on 12 December. A draft constitution that Lambert had been preparing promptly became the basis for the Instrument of Government by which Cromwell was installed as Lord Protector on 16 December 1653, with a Council of State and provision for a triennial parliament.[53]

The arrangements in Wales during the 1650s were different from those in Ireland, which was 'absorbed *de facto* into the Commonwealth', and Scotland, which was annexed by an Act of Union.[54] Regarded as one of the 'dark corners of the land', it was put into the care of seventy-one commissioners by the Act for the Better Propagation and Preaching of the Gospel in Wales passed on 22 February 1650. John Morrill has pointed out that 'the distribution of ejections' in English parishes during the 1640s 'was determined less by the malignancy of the clergy than by the persecuting temper of local commissioners', and that 'the presence of an individual hardliner could lead to differential levels of sequestration within counties'.[55] In the wake of the new legislation, this was also true of Wales during the 1650s, where the zeal of the propagators was such 'that a high proportion of the ejections which took place . . . during the three years of the Act's life had been effected before the end of 1650', and in total 278 ministers were ejected, 196 of them in South Wales and Monmouthshire, mostly on the grounds of 'moral lapses and political disaffection rather than religious unsuitability'.[56] Since enough educated Welsh-speaking replacements could not be found by the twenty-five 'Approvers', many parishes were left vacant and their needs catered for by a system of itinerant preachers. Breconshire was served by Vavasor Powell, but in Henry Vaughan's home parish of Llansantffraed, from which his brother Thomas had been ejected, the church stood unused.[57] Those loyal to the traditional forms of worship in the county also suffered at the hands of a particularly active Approver in the person of Jenkin Jones of Llandetty.[58]

A study of three generations of 'Church of England' poets concludes that Henry Vaughan, brought up in the 1630s to participate 'in the tradition of liturgical enactment enabled by the Book of Common Prayer', found himself cut off from communal worship and forced by political circumstances to transform himself into 'the chronicler of the experience of that community when its source of Christian identity was no longer available'.[59] Leah Marcus attributes the 'force and poignancy of Vaughan's vision of childhood' to his 'adult conviction that the very years when he had been a child were the years when his religious ideals had been best embodied on British soil', and imagined how, after the Civil Wars, he had 'watched with horror the gradual extinction of the earthly manifestations of Laudian Anglicanism'.[60] But Vaughan did much more than chronicle and watch. He had responded to the invitation to some future poet in George Herbert's 'Obedience' to 'set his hand / And heart unto this deed' – in a poem entitled 'The Match', which Jonathan Post locates at the exact centre of the 1650 *Silex Scintillans*[61] – and, as we have seen, in 'Retirement' he had ritually ordained himself as what Simmonds calls a 'lay preacher of the "underground" church'.[62] This resolution to follow Herbert's example and serve God's 'house' was to bear practical fruit over the next four years in a series of prose works and in the augmented edition of *Silex Scintillans*, at a time when Breconshire was being subjected to the full severity of puritan rule.

It must have been near the beginning of this wave of persecution that Vaughan wrote his most graphic evocation of the Church in all its manifestations as place of worship, human institution and community of worshippers, as it was preserved in the memories of his own childhood and in the writings of George Herbert. It occurs in *The Praise and Happinesse of the Countrie-Life*, one of several prose translations that were added to *Olor Iscanus* when it was belatedly published in 1651:

O what a pious and beautifull work it is, when *holy* and *solemne days* are observ'd in the Country, according to the *sacred rules* and *Ordinances* of *Religion*! The *doore-keepers* of the *house* of *God* set wide open their *beautifull gates*, The *Church-bels* ring, and every pious Soule is ravish'd with the *Musick*, and is sick of *love* untill he come into the *Courts* of the *Lord*. The *Temples* and *Communion tables* are drest, and the *beauty of holinesse* shines every where. The poorest *Country-labourer* honours that day with his best *habit* ... and every one in a decent and Christian *dresse* walks Religiously towards his *Parish Church*, where they heare Divine *Service*. (p. 131)

In this idyllic vision derived from a Spanish original, Vaughan was covertly reminding his readers of what had been lost in the rural parishes of England and Wales since 1640. It had the same function as the message spelt out in the final stanza of 'The Proffer', the fifth of the poems added to the 1655 *Silex Scintillans* and one of his most passionate statements of resistance to the 'black Parasites' who were promoting the 'Commonwealth':

> Then keep the antient way!
> Spit out their phlegm
> And fill thy brest with home; think on thy dream:
> A calm, bright day!
> A Land of flowers and spices! (p. 488)

While the new poems were accumulating, Vaughan entered the public arena with a more direct challenge to the opponents of 'the antient way' of Cranmer and Herbert in a volume of prose meditations and prayers entitled *The Mount of Olives*, which was printed in 1652. Honouring his commitment to affirm the sanctity of '*the House of my God*' (p. 148), he deplored the effects of current church policy in Wales: 'These reverend and sacred buildings (however now vilified and shut up) have ever been, and amongst true Christians still are the solemne and publike places of meeting for Divine Worship' (p. 147). A section on the proper way to prepare for the Eucharist condemns the sacrilegious practices that were being imposed upon the faithful people: 'Such was in our Church, that more strict and holy season, called *Lent,* and such still are the preparation-dayes before this glorious Sabbath in all true Churches' (p. 156). A prayer to be used in time of persecution and heresy spells out the double calamity of closed and defiled church buildings:

The wayes of *Zion* do mourne, our beautiful gates are shut up, and the Comforter that should relieve our souls is gone far from us. Thy Service and thy Sabbaths, thy own sacred Institutions and the pledges of thy love are denied unto us; Thy ministers are trodden down, and the basest of the people are set up in thy holy place. (p. 166)

The subtitle of this work, 'Solitary Devotions', acknowledges that communal worship can no longer take place in the 'sacred buildings' and that 'the Church' must now subsist in the hearts of those who remain faithful to the tradition embodied in the Book of Common Prayer. In a dedication to Sir Charles Egerton, Vaughan reminds those who still dare to '*look* upon, and *commiserate* distressed Religion' that there is good precedent for their exile from the comforts of a 'house' of their own, 'seeing their *Master* himself took up his *nights-lodging* in the cold *Mount* of *Olives*' (p. 138). And he adds a '*short Exhortation*' in an epistle 'To the Peaceful, humble, and pious Reader', which offers the encouragement of shared experience to those who are under pressure to abandon 'the antient way':

That thou wouldest not be discouraged in this way, because very many are gone out of it. Think not that thou art alone upon this Hill, there is an innumerable company both before and behind thee. Those with their Palms in their hands, and these expecting them. If therefore the dust of this world chance to prick thine eyes, suffer it not to blinde them; but running thy race with patience, look to JESUS the Authour and finisher of thy faith, who when he was reviled, reviled not againe. Presse thou towards the mark, and let the people and their Seducers rage; be faithful unto the death, and he will give thee a Crowne of life. (p. 141)

As if to assert the continuing validity of the liturgical calendar that had governed the worshipping life of Anglicanism, he opened his new collection of poems in the second half of the 1655 *Silex Scintillans* with 'Ascension-day' and 'Ascension Hymn', and followed these at intervals with 'White Sunday', 'Trinity Sunday', and 'Palm Sunday'. In a poem on the descent of the Holy Spirit at Pentecost, which immediately precedes the attack on the 'flyes of hell / That buz in every ear' in 'The Proffer', Vaughan reiterates a determination to defend the clarity of his vision of the true church against puritan claims to the authority of inspiration:

Though then some boast that fire each day,
And on Christ's coat pin all their shreds;
Not sparing openly to say,
His candle shines upon their heads:

Yet while some rays of that great light
Shine here below within thy Book,
They never shall so blinde my sight
But I will know which way to look. (p. 485)

Although different in so many ways from Hobbes and Davenant in his spiritual orientation and poetic affiliations, Vaughan was as anxious in 1655 as they were in 1651 to dissociate both his religion and his poetry from those who justified their right to preach and govern by an appeal to divine illumination.

The Breconshire poet was not alone in grieving over the state of the church and using the press to subvert the government's attempt to eradicate its traditions. Thomas Washbourne published his *Divine Poems* in June 1654, with an epigraph from George Herbert on the title-page and an assurance 'To the Reader' that he was 'no pretender to extra-ordinary Gifts of the Spirit, as too many are, who have very little or no evidence to commend or approve them to others: whatsoever high conceits they may have of themselves' (sigg. A3^v–A4^r). Like Vaughan in 'White Sunday', who saw by the light of 'thy Book', he derived his poetic inspiration from the 'the Fountain of the Sacred Scriptures' (sig. A4^r). In a poem about the contemporary church based on Psalm 180, he complains that the 'poor Vine lies wast':

Her Sprigs are dry, the holy Sacraments
Are stopt, or run not free to all ...
Under her shade we did securely rest
And comfort we did take in it.
But now we pine away with grief opprest
To see her in the dust to sit;
Come Lord thine aid we crave,
Come quickly her to save. (p. 17)

'A Dialogue Between the Church and Her Daughters', in which the daughters lament that 'of late / Most men have cast you out of door', concludes with words of faith and hope from the 'widow desolate':

When he shall find it fit to wash off all
My black, and outward grace restore,
Like the Sun after an Eclipse, I shall
Shine brighter then I did before. (p. 30)

Jeremy Taylor, adopting a stance not unlike that assumed by Vaughan, saw himself as one of 'the *Seers* who are appointed to be the Watchmen of the Church' (sig. A2ʳ), and took measures to ensure that when the 'Eclipse' was over there would be a new generation of the faithful to enjoy the sunshine of restored Anglicanism. *The Golden Grove, Or, A Manuall of Daily Prayers and Letanies, fitted to the dayes of the Week... Also Festival Hymns, According to the manner of the Ancient Church* was published in 1655 with a purpose similar to that of Vaughan's *Mount of Olives*, but with a particular emphasis on education: 'we must now take care that the young men who were born in the Captivity, may be taught how to worship the God of *Israel* after the manner of their fore-fathers, till it shall please God that Religion shall return into the Land, and dwell safely and grow prosperously' (sig. A3ʳ).

The Printing Act of September 1649 did not stamp out the royalist newsbooks overnight. John Crouch's *Man in the Moon*, which suspended publication for a few weeks from November, reappeared in January 1650 and it was joined for a while first by *The Royall Diurnall* and then by *Mercurius Elenticus* in rallying support for the expected arrival of Charles II in Scotland. But the arrest of Crouch in June saw its demise as the last of the royalist weeklies.[63] Occasional items of patent propaganda still got onto the streets, like the mock publisher's catalogues compiled by John Berkenhead, *Two Centuries of Paul's Church-Yard* and *Bibliotheca Parliamenti* (1653), which advertized such titles as *Whether Cromwell be not an absolute hater of images, since he hath defaced God's in his own countenance.*[64] In general, however, royalist writers preferred less aggressive ways of maintaining their cause in the medium of print during the 1650s. Vaughan's doctored prose translations and solitary devotions, Taylor's manual of daily prayers and volumes of posthumous or religious poetry were obvious expedients. But, as Zwicker points out, the 'powerful currents released by the wars polemicized a broad range of texts and subjects' and it is no surprise to find that one of the most popular works of the period 'gave classic expression to the culture of sequestered royalism' in the guise of a manual on the art of fishing.[65]

Izaak Walton's *The Compleat Angler* was first published in 1653 and reissued in 1655 in an augmented edition. The new material, expanding the volume by about a half, consisted mostly of practical information for the prospective fisherman, which led one critic to conclude that the book 'was always primarily a handbook on angling'.[66] Recent studies, giving more weight to the subtitle – *The Contemplative Mans Recreation* –

have reached a different conclusion. An enquiry into the generic complexity of the work argues that it 'began as a discourse on retirement and contemplation written in response to the political and religious controversy surrounding the Puritan revolution' and that its 'values of toleration and inclusiveness' are deliberately anti-controversial.[67] In an introductory epistle, Walton stresses that for him the very process of writing the book was 'a recreation of a recreation', but he then assumes a mildly combative stance towards the kind of reader who might take exception to certain passages of 'innocent Mirth' – 'of which, if thou be a severe, sowr complexioned man, then I here disallow thee to be a competent Judg'.[68] Indeed, Zwicker finds 'commemorative and contentious designs' embedded in the hearty conversations about the art of angling and the recitations of favourite verses on the pleasures of the countryside, that take place while Piscator and his companion Viator are sheltering from a shower under a 'high hedg' (p. 88) or enjoying the hospitality of a local inn, where they look forward to a good night's sleep between 'fresh sheets that smel of Lavender' (p. 98). Walton creates 'an image of a community of anglers and a community of texts', which has an unmistakably polemical purpose in the context of 'the triumphant puritanism of the 1650s'.[69]

The poetry of George Herbert is quoted twice, and when Walton's spokesman introduces into the 1655 text a poem about 'our *Book* of *Common Prayer*' by Harvey with the comment that 'he is a friend of mine, and I am sure no enemy to Angling' (p. 260), it becomes apparent that those who belong to 'the brotherhood of the angle' are closely related to the followers of Vaughan's 'antient way'. Earlier, in the 1653 edition, Piscator invokes the example of an Elizabethan dean of St Paul's – 'his Monument stands yet undefaced' – who had spent 'a tenth part of his time in Angling' and had 'made that good, plain, unperplext Catechism, that is printed with the old Service Book' (pp. 75–6). Vaughan's nostalgic vision of Sunday in a rural parish before the war has its secular equivalent in Walton's idyll of life in the English countryside, where a milkmaid and her mother sing to the gentlemen anglers, the lambs frisk in the sunshine, and the merry company of sportsmen call for 'some good Ale' with their supper and sing each other songs in praise of country life (pp. 92–8). The rhythm of the fisherman's sport is governed by the cycles of the day and the seasons which, as Zwicker notes, 'are sharply at odds with the millenarian time of puritan eschatology', so that *The Compleat Angler* 'is an affirmation of recurrence and antiquity'.[70] Like other royalist writers during the Interregnum, Henry Vaughan was to be drawn more and more back into this rhythm of 'seasonal certainty' in the second half of *Silex Scintillans*.

Walton was a man of the older generation, like Francis Quarles, with whom he shared both a dislike of the Laudian innovations of the 1630s and a horror at the Root-and-Branch reforms of the 1640s. Born in 1593, his political sympathies were firmly royalist, but an instinct 'to shun public protest and set an example of dutiful and quiet obedience' held him back from active involvement in the Civil War.[71] For him, true Anglers/Anglicans[72] were 'men of mild, and sweet, and peaceable spirits' (p. 74) and his mildly subversive book of 1653 ended with a blessing 'upon all that hate contentions, and love *quietnesse*, and *vertue*, and *Angling*' (p. 163). The same instinct is expressed by Walton's young friend and proselyte in the art of fishing, the poet Charles Cotton, whose father had been addressed in Lovelace's 'The Grass-hopper' and who would eventually add a Second Part to the final revision of *The Compleat Angler* in 1676.

Born in 1630 at Beresford Hall in Derbyshire, Cotton composed his drinking-songs and celebrations of a retired country life for his own recreation and that of like-minded friends, while they waited for what Earl Miner dubbed 'the Cavalier winter' to pass.[73] His 'Winter Quatrains' sum up the consolations of the royalist gentry, restricted to their estates but keeping up their spirits with conversation and poetry and defiantly preserving their sense of community:

> Whilst we together jovial sit
> Careless, and Crown'd with Mirth and Wit;
> Where though bleak Winds confine us home,
> Our Fancy round the World shall roam.
>
> We'll think of all the Friends we know,
> And Drink to all worth Drinking to:
> When having Drunk all thine and mine,
> We rather shall want Healths than Wine.   (p. 21)

An 'Ode' deliberately flouts the republic's intelligence service that tried to enforce the prohibition on toasting Charles II and the royal family:[74]

> Then lett us drinke, Time to improve,
>   Secure of Cromwell and his Spies,
> Night will conceale our healths, and Love
>   For all her thousand thousand eyes.   (p. 223)

And 'The Litany' petitions for deliverance 'From a Kingdom, that from health / Sickens to a Commonwealth', 'From a Church without Divines, / And a Presbiter that whines', and 'Lastly, from the Poet's Evill, / From his highnesse, and the Devill' (pp. 224–7). The usurpation of a kingly role by 'his highnesse', the Lord Protector, is charted in a sequence of verses that follow the natural cycle in a pastoral countryside from morning to night. In the 'Noon Quatrains', the traditional sun/king symbolism is invoked to condemn rulers in general who, when they have got to the '*Zenith*' of power, 'devour' those 'whom they should protect', and is then applied to the current situation in England:

> Has not another *Phaeton*
> Mounted the Chariot of the Sun,
> And, wanting Art to guide his Horse,
> Is hurri'd from the Sun's due course? (p. 5)

The sequence closes in darkness, when 'all's with Fun'rall Black o'respread' and sound sleep is the reward of the innocent, but the last line – 'For every Day must have its Night' (p. 13) – implies its corollary, that this 'Cavalier night' will also come to an end. In a poem addressed to his '*dear and most worthy Friend*', Cotton pronounces the devotees of Walton's gentle art far 'happier' than those who 'like Leviathans devour / Of meaner men the smaller Fry' (p. 29), and endorses the political philosophy with which it had been imbued in the pages of *The Compleat Angler*:

> If the all-ruling Power please
> We live to see another *May*,
> We'll recompense an Age of these
> Foul days in one fine fishing day. (p. 28)

Another royalist poet of a rather different stamp was an occasional visitor to Beresford Hall and on friendly terms with both Cotton and Walton. When Alexander Brome's collection, *Songs and other Poems*, was published in 1661, it included some pastoral verses by Walton, 'written the 29 of May 1660' to celebrate Charles II's return to London.[75] Brome had contributed a poem to the 1655 edition of Walton's book, in which he gently teased his friends for the '*undisturb'd*' and '*dangerlesse* delight' they enjoyed 'by some gliding *River*', while he, 'not supply'd / With those three grand essentials of your *Art*, / *Luck, Skill* and *Patience*', practised his own art of 'scribling' in a world of power relations where all men 'or *Fish* or *Fishers* be; / And all *neutralitie* herin's deny'd'. It was not in his poetic nature to let slip any opportunity to engage with the enemy:

> Yet I shall hardly *praise*, or *like* thy skill;
> For w'are all prone enough to *catch* and *kill*;

> Thou need'st not make an *Art* on't: they that are
> Once *listed* in the new Saints *Calender*,
> Do't as they *pray* and *preach* by *inspiration*.[76]

Throughout the Interregnum, Brome kept up his subtle mockery of successive constitutional experiments and their social consequences, often by impersonating the targets of his satire. In 'The Safe Estate', for example, a parody of the 'retirement poem' – 'How happy a man is he, / Whose soul is quiet and free, / And liveth content with his own!' – launches a combined attack on the five-mile travel restrictions imposed upon delinquents and on those royalists who obediently compounded and made the best of it:

> The desires of his mind,
> To's estate are confin'd . . .
> And if sad thoughts arise,
> He does only devise
>   With sack to repel 'um.
> Though the times do turn round,
> He doth still keep his ground,
>   Both in a Republique and Realme.[77]

'The New Gentry' exposes 'the upstart Mushromes of our Nation' who profited from the sale of royalist property and those of the traditional landed class who 'tamely will submit' to the new order of things and

> pay and pray
> Great men in power, that they
> Will take our Liberty and trample on her.   (pp. 156–7)

And the cynical counsel offered in 'The Advice' for securing 'a happy life' in 'these dayes of distraction' is to avoid 'Wealth' and 'Wit' – the latter, because a dullard's 'words are ne're taken for treason' and the former, because there is no financial gain in opening legal proceedings against a man 'Whose estate is but small':

> He may do, he may say,
> Having nothing to pay,
> It will not quit costs to arraign him.   (p. 176)

'The Polititian' and 'The Antipolititian' are spoken by representatives of two responses to the new Commonwealth that Brome despised equally. The first makes a Hobbesian submission of principle to force:

> What is't to us who's in the ruling power?
> While they protect, we're bound t'obey,
> But longer not an hower.   (p. 148)

The second is content with 'Good Company and good wine' and a life of political quietism in which he 'can safely think and live, / And freely laugh or sing' (pp. 155–6). Unlike the run-of-the-mill drinking-songs of

such rhymsters as Robert Heath – 'Fill, fill the goblet full with sack! . . .
Let's drink then as we us'd to fight, / As long as we can stand' (*Clarastella*,
London, 1650) – Brome's use of the genre is always ambivalent. The
primary objects of his satire are obvious enough in 'The Prisoners:
Written when O. C. attempted to be King':

> Come a brimmer (my bullies) drink whole ones or nothing,
>   Now healths have been voted down. . . .
> We'l drink their destruction that would destroy drinking,
>   Let 'um Vote that a health if they will.   (p. 150)

But there is clearly no hope of effective action to overturn the Protectorate from the rollicking Cavalier who authors these lines: 'We only
converse with pots and with glasses, / Let the Rulers alone with their
trade' (p. 151).

The work of another of the younger poets of the 1650s has until
recently been regarded as 'apolitical' in its recommendation of a 'chosen
privacy, a cheap content' and a 'retir'd integritie',[78] in spite of her being
'an unswervable friend to Royalists' and 'fervently' devoted to Cavalier
drama and Caroline poetry.[79] The first collected edition of the work of
Katherine Philips, however, has enabled Carol Barash to uncover the
'royalist ideals of monarchy' that are 'symbolically protected by the
"Society of Friendship" created between "Orinda" and her female
friends'.[80] Born Katherine Fowler in London in 1632 and educated at
Mrs Salmon's school for young women in Hackney, she was married at
sixteen to a fifty-four-year-old relative of her mother's third husband,
Colonel James Philips, and transplanted in 1649 to his house in Cardiganshire, where he served in local government under the
Commonwealth and Protectorate regimes.[81] During spells in the capital
when her husband was there on political business, she became acquainted with a circle of writers and musicians surrounding Henry
Lawes, who 'were concerned to preserve the cultural ideals of the
Caroline court';[82] and the fact that her contribution headed the array of
fifty-four commendatory items in Moseley's 1651 edition of Cartwright's
works 'suggests her importance to the royalists who shaped the volume'.[83] This was the first of her poems to be printed and her verses
mostly circulated in manuscript until a pirated collection came out in
1664. By 1653, however, she was already becoming known as 'Orinda',
the name she adopted among the coterie of friends which included John
Berkenhead. Her closest female friend, Anne Owen, was given the
sobriquet 'Lucasia', which Barash derives from Lovelace's 'Lucasta' and
interprets as a complex cover for expressing, along with other things, a
yearning for the return of the absent King.[84]

Among Katherine Philips's earliest surviving poems is 'Upon the double murther of K. Charles, in answer to a libellous rime made by V. P.', in which she presents herself as unconcerned 'which way soever' the 'Helme' of State 'is turn'd', but unable to remain silent when the 'dying Lion' is 'kick'd by every asse' (p. 69). In spite of this opening disclaimer, her political orientation is made manifest in her resentment at the propaganda of the new regime:

> He broke God's lawes, and therefore he must dye,
> And what shall then become of thee and I?
> Slander must follow treason; but yet stay,
> Take not our reason with our king away.
> Though you have seiz'd upon all our defence,
> Yet do not sequester our common sense.   (pp. 69–70)

In an unusual feminization of monarchy, which Barash sees as typical of the way her writing about power serves to destabilize 'both gender and political authority',[85] she describes the last serious effort to restore a Stuart to the throne until 1660 in a poem on the Battle of Worcester entitled 'On the 3d of September 1651':

> So when our Gasping English Royalty
> Perceiv'd her period now was drawing nigh,
> She summons her whole strength to give one blow,
> To raise herself, or pull down others too.   (p. 82)

Some of the poems addressed to members of the coterie 'make women's friendship a very complicated royalist trope'.[86] For example, there is a strong undercurrent of political implication in these lines from 'Lucasia':

> Nor doth discretion put religion down,
> Nor hasty Zeale usurp the Judgment's Crowne:
> Wisedome and friendship have one single throne,
> And make another friendship of their own.   (p. 105)

And the strategy advocated in 'A retir'd friendship, to Ardelia. 23d Augo 1651', which the modern editor relates to a minor rebellion of royalist gentry in Cardiganshire in June, figures friendship in the way that Walton figures angling:

> Here let us sit, and blesse our Starres
>   Who did such happy quiet give,
> As that remov'd from noise of warres
>   In one another's hearts we live....
> In such a scorching Age as this,
>   Whoever would not seek a shade
> Deserve their happiness to misse,
>   As having their own peace betray'd.   (p. 98)

The political realities of Interregnum Wales are an important part of the context of Philips's work. The 'V. P.' whose slander against the dead king provoked her to respond was Vavasor Powell, and she was later perturbed at a threat by the radical Approver, Jenkin Jones of Llandetty, to use her poem to discredit her husband, who was himself one of the more conciliatory members of the commission set up under the Act for the Propagation of the Gospel. She regrets that her 'crimes' should become his 'scandall too', in 'To Antenor, on a paper of mine wch J. Jones threatens to publish to his prejudice', but her penitence for her 'errours' and 'faults' soon gives way to a confident writer's contempt for an inferior talent that is 'below a poet's curse' (p. 117).

Henry Vaughan had probably met Katherine Philips when she was a child, already showing precocious poetic gifts, at her father's house in London, where literary gatherings were held in the years before the outbreak of the Civil War.[87] He published a verse tribute to her in *Olor Iscanus* and she praised both *Poems* (1646) and *Silex Scintillans* (1650) in 'To Mr Henry Vaughan, Silurist, on his Poems'. In the preface designed to introduce the augmented *Silex Scintillans*, dated from Newton by Usk on 30 September 1654, Vaughan condemned the '*idle words*', '*scurrilous conceits*' and '*lascivious fictions*' that too often passed for wit in what he insisted on calling 'this Kingdom', and apologized for his own past '*follies*' in that kind (pp. 388–90). But while emulating 'persons of eminent piety and learning' who had 'long before' his time 'taken notice of this *malady*', he was careful to distinguish between 'the seditious and *Schismaticall*' – men like Prynne and Milton with whom he refused to 'meddle' – and the 'peaceful and obedient *spirits*' with whom he sought to align himself (p. 389). Most eminent among these was 'the blessed man, Mr *George Herbert*, whose holy *life* and *verse* gained many pious *Converts*, (of whom I am the least)' (p. 391). Herbert played a vital part not only in deepening Vaughan's spirituality but also in refashioning his self-image as a writer during the 1650s. Aspiring 'to write (with *Hierotheus* and holy *Herbert*) A *true Hymn*', the Silurist communicated his 'poor *Talent* to the *Church*' and, in words that vibrate with double meanings and political nuances in the context of 1654, put his volume 'under the *protection* and *conduct* of her *glorious Head*: who (if he will vouchsafe to *own* it, and *go along* with it) can make it as useful now in the *publick*, as it hath been to me in *private*' (p. 392). And then, in a ploy typical of a period in which royalist writers needed to shield themselves against charges of sedition, he obliquely urged upon his readers an alertness to the public agenda of this collection of 'private Ejaculations':

> In the *perusal* of it, you will (peradventure) observe some *passages*, whose *history* or *reason* may seem something *remote*; but were they brought *nearer*, and plainly exposed to your view, (though that (perhaps) might quiet your *curiosity*) yet would it not conduce much to your greater *advantage*. (p. 392)

The personal grief and political despair that dominated the earlier part of the 1650 volume have largely been dispelled from the poems added in 1655 and the future is now contemplated with a renewed sense of historical purpose. In 'White Sunday', he calls down the Pentecostal flames that descended upon the Apostles:

> O come! refine us with thy fire!
> Refine us! we are at a loss.
> Let not thy stars for *Balaams* hire
> Dissolve into the common dross!   (p. 486)

This reference to the regime's efforts to absorb the defeated party into the new order is sharpened by the poem's position immediately before 'The Proffer', in which the defiant royalist refuses to cast his 'Crown away' for the 'smooth inducements' of Commonwealth agents and holds out the prospect of recompense and revenge for the man who stands firm: 'But when thy Master comes, they'l finde and see / There's a reward for them and thee' (p. 487). The broadening of the appeal from the sinful 'I' which dominates Part I to a communal 'we' in 'White Sunday' and other poems in Part II is indicative of the change of perspective already foreshadowed in 'The Constellation'. Vaughan is now writing specifically for and on behalf of a body of steadfast royalists who are to be distinguished from 'the common dross' of collaborators.

In 'The Jews', he offers a vision of historical restoration based on the rhythms of nature and the Jewish expectation that a Messiah will come to set them free:

> When the fair year
> Of your deliverer comes,
> And that long frost which now benums
> Your hearts shall thaw...
> O then that I
> Might live, and see the Olive bear
> Her proper branches!...
> And sure it is not far!   (p. 499)

The firm declarative verbs and the note of eager anticipation are in striking contrast to the helpless yearnings for lost 'white days' and an escape from time in the 1650 volume. The 'fair year' that Vaughan looks forward to is no longer apocalyptic, nor is it primarily of significance to the Jews. The British, too, are expecting the arrival of a 'deliverer', in the person of Charles II – the 'Master' of 'The Proffer' – who will thaw the 'long frost' of the Cavalier winter. 'And sure it is not far!'

The dilemma that faced Vaughan at the end of the 1650 *Silex Scintillans* is resolved in this and other new poems by a strategy of patient expectation. Both the natural world and the Bible give assurance that an end to present troubles can be looked for within the continuum of history. A retired life, keeping a belief in the episcopal church and the political system of monarchy alive in the hearts of the faithful, need not be the 'Lethargy, and meer disease' that it seemed to be in 'Misery'. Waiting in quiet confidence can be a positive act of political defiance, particularly when it involves resisting temptations to collaborate and 'Dissolve into the common dross'. This programme is most powerfully expressed in 'The Seed growing secretly' through Vaughan's favourite image of plants weathering hard conditions and putting forth shoots when the season is propitious: 'Dear, secret *Greenness*! nurst below / Tempests and windes, and winter-nights' (p. 511). As the poem approaches its conclusion, the political dimension becomes more overt:

> Glory, the Crouds cheap tinsel still
> To what most takes them, is a drudge;
> And they too oft take good for ill,
> And thriving vice for vertue judge....
> Then bless thy secret growth, nor catch
> At noise, but thrive unseen and dumb;
> Keep clean, bear fruit, earn life and watch
> Till the white winged Reapers come!   (p. 511)

The 'white winged Reapers' are certainly on one (politically safe) level the angels of the Apocalypse, but a typological interpretation can discover in them the agents of a historical rather than an eschatological process, which will relieve those who have been thriving 'unseen and dumb' and holding aloof from 'the Crouds cheap tinsel'. The whole poem, read in the context of a countryside peopled by royalists biding their time until the great day comes when their loyalty will be vindicated, can be seen as wise counsel to other men of Vaughan's persuasion as well as a solution to his own private problem.

Towards the end of the volume, there is a second poem on the Day of Judgement, which no longer sees it in the exclusively personal terms that dominated Vaughan's approach in the companion piece in Part I:

> O day of life, of light, of love!
> The onely day dealt from above!
> A day so fresh, so bright, so brave
> Twill shew us each forgotten grave,
> And make the dead, like flowers, arise
> Youthful and fair to see new skies.   (p. 530)

The ultimate context for this exhilarating vision is the rising of the dead on the Last Day; but within British history, a day of judgement, brought about by the return of 'thy Master' (Charles II rather than Christ), will also 'shew us each forgotten grave', when the royalist dead, like young William Vaughan and Mr R. W., will be properly honoured. In 'L'Envoy', Vaughan prays for a time when 'like true sheep, all in one fold / We may be fed, and one minde hold'. He also prays that the new guides who take over the government may profit from the lessons of this dark period of British history:

> Therefore write in their hearts thy law,
> And let these long, sharp judgements aw
> Their very thoughts, that by their clear
> And holy lives, mercy may here
> Sit regent yet, and blessings flow
> As fast, as persecutions now.
> So shall we know in war and peace
> Thy service to be our sole ease,
> With prostrate souls adoring thee,
> Who turn'd our sad captivity!   (p. 543)

These are the closing lines of *Silex Scintillans*. They look to a historical future in which the termination of 'these long, sharp judgements' will be an example to set beside the deliverance of the Israelites from bondage. The assurance with which Vaughan takes leave of his readers is summed up in the tense of the final verb, which presents the 'sad captivity' of the Interregnum as already a thing of the past, 'turned' decisively by a beneficent and just God.

While Vaughan, as far as is known, took no part in political activity beyond the use of his pen to put heart into those who '*might be discouraged in this way*', a variety of courses were open to those who were determined to participate more actively on behalf of the Stuart cause. There were a number of 'half-baked royalist and Leveller assassination plots'[88] against Cromwell, like those of John Gerard in May 1654 and Miles Sindercombe in January 1657, which were routinely uncovered by Secretary Thurloe's network of spies and informers; and there were several (mostly abortive) plans for armed rebellion, from the rising in Dorset and Wiltshire led by Colonel John Penruddock in March 1655 which was quickly snuffed out, to the more serious attempt by Sir George Booth, who raised a sizeable army in Lancashire and Cheshire in August 1659, but failed to get the support he expected from other parts of the country or from abroad and was defeated by Lambert.[89] Some of the underground activities during the Protectorate were orchestrated by the Sealed Knot, a secret society of six members (mainly younger sons of noble families) that was formed in the winter of 1653–4 and corresponded through undercover agents with Hyde and Nicholas at the court-in-exile. They followed Hyde's strategy of waiting for political occasion to ripen and relying on old royalists rather than seeking an expedient alliance with the presbyterians or backing wild schemes by hotheaded 'blades'. Their caution rendered them ineffective and they disbanded in 1659.[90]

Among those who became involved in clandestine operations, though not necessarily through the Sealed Knot, were the poets, Sir John Denham and Abraham Cowley. Denham returned to England in 1653 and stayed for some time at Wilton, the country seat of the Earl of Pembroke. He attracted the notice of Thurloe and was among those arrested on suspicion of being royalist agents in the aftermath of the Penruddock rebellion, but rather than being confined to the Tower like some of the others, he was merely prohibited from coming within twenty miles of London and seems to have made his way back to France.[91] It was probably at Wilton that he worked on the text of *Cooper's Hill* that was published by Moseley late in 1655. A note 'To the Reader', signed 'J. B.' (possibly John Berkenhead),[92] claims that this *'perfect Edition'* was *'obtained from the* Author's *owne papers'* and makes particular mention of *'that excellent Allegory of the* Royall Stag'.[93] A glance at some of the changes effected in what O Hehir calls a 'radical and massive' revision of the 1642 text will serve to indicate how Denham adapted his poem to the specific circumstances of 1655.

The hill at Windsor no longer reminds him of the 'friend-like sweetnesse' and 'King-like aw' of an accessible but dignified reigning monarch but of the 'meekness, heightned with Majestick Grace' of the royal martyr. The account of Henry VIII's contradictory use of the 'learned Pen' and the 'more learned Sword' in his dealings with the English church is given a topical slant in a rewording which, as O Hehir notes, alludes to a phrase in the Instrument of Government whereby 'the *style* of which person shall be the Lord *Protector* of the Commonwealth', and hints at a parallel between the 'gross religious hypocrisy' of the Tudor despot and the republic's godly ruler:[94] 'Thus he the Church at once protects & spoils: /But Princes swords are sharper than their stiles'. A new passage about the 'desolation' brought upon the church in 'the Name of Zeal' records Denham's horror at the perpetration of the 'Sacriledge' that was only a fearsome prospect in 1642. The expansion of the hunt episode from thirty-eight to eighty-two lines is the most striking of all the revisions and the consistent crediting of the stag 'with human motives, emotions and reactions', along with 'allegorizing detail of precisely the nature dear to the heart of Charles himself', transforms it from an oblique commentary on the fate of Strafford into J. B.'s 'excellent Allegory' of the later years and death of the King.[95] Denham had not contributed to the spate of elegies after the regicide and it may be that his purpose in 1654 was not merely to refashion his most famous text for a new market but to clarify his personal perspective upon the events that had changed the world since he had first committed it to print in August 1642. The poet whose aesthetic and political ideal was summed up in the concept of *concordia discors* and distilled in the emblem of the River Thames – 'Strong without rage, without ore-flowing full' – now abandons his closing exhortation that kings and subjects should work together under the mutual constraints of Law. The time for such advice is long past, and a radical rearrangement of the ending leaves the reader with a grim evocation of the very thing that Denham's poem had originally been written to prevent:

> No longer then within his banks he dwells,
> First to a Torrent, then a Deluge swells:
> Stronger, and fiercer by restraint he roars,
> And knows no bounds, but makes his power his shores.

Cowley fared less happily than Denham and Hobbes. He returned to England in the summer of 1654 on a secret mission for the 'Louvre' faction and managed to arouse the distrust of both sides. When he was arrested in April 1655 in the general round-up of royalist suspects, Jermyn denied all knowledge of his activities. He was taken before Thurloe and Cromwell and then committed to the Tower, where he underwent further interrogation before being released on bail towards the end of the year.[96] During his incarceration, he completed work on a collected edition of his poetry, which was registered on 11 September 1655 and published early in the new year by Humphrey Moseley. *Poems* (1656) consists of four distinct parts and was furnished with a preface which laid the poet open to the charge of political apostasy at the time and has continued to exercise his critics.[97] As early as 10 May 1656, Hyde was commenting on the adverse light it cast on Cowley's loyalty and when Thomas Sprat came to edit his literary remains, he took care to explain away the passage which had permanently damaged Cowley's reputation among fellow royalists and kept him out of favour in 1660.[98] Whatever the implications of *Poems* as a whole for an understanding of the poet's political allegiance, the preface provides evidence of 'how sensitive and contested was the publication of verse in the late 1640s and 1650s'.[99]

In the offending passage, Cowley extends into the period of defeat the concern about the proper role of the poet in time of war that had first been aired in his abortive epic of 1643, when those with literary talent who were 'unapt themselves to fight' were assigned the honourable task of celebrating military exploits with 'noble pens'. Now, in the context of the Engagement controversy and the Act of Oblivion – and perhaps influenced by the 'many examinations "before the usurpers"' which Sprat alludes to'[100] – Cowley argues that it is time to accept what has been determined by 'the event of battel and the unaccountable *Will* of *God*':

> We must lay down our *Pens* as well as *Arms*, we must *march* out of our *Cause* it self, and *dismantle* that, as well as our *Towns* and *Castles*, of all the *Works* and *Fortifications* of *Wit* and *Reason* by which we defended it. *We* ought not, sure, to begin our selves to revive the remembrance of those times and actions for which we have received a *General Amnestie* as a *favor* from the *Victor*. . . . The Names of *Party* and *Titles* of *Division*, which are sometimes in effect the whole quarrel, should be extinguished and forbidden in peace under the notion of *Acts* of *Hostility*. (p. 84)

These words certainly amount to an earnest of good behaviour, if not quite the 'recantation' some claimed, and the question for the biographer or apologist is whether they represent, as Nethercot considered, a genuine move towards embracing the new political order by a man who had absorbed the philosophy of Hobbes and was 'easily swayed by his environment, even weak-willed';[101] or whether, as Sprat insisted in 1668, they were camouflage for a spy who had not abandoned his mission, but who realized that 'inevitable ruine' would befall any premature action against the 'united' enemy of 1656: 'He therefore believed that it would be a meritorious service to the King, if any man who was known to have followed his interest, could insinuate into the Usurpers minds, that men of his Principles were now willing to be quiet, and could perswade the poor oppressed Royalists to conceal their affections for better occasions.'[102] As a document written in 1655 by a poet with a strong sense of his calling, the preface reveals how a certain kind of royalist temperament responded to one of the darkest periods of the Interregnum. The hopes raised by the Penruddock conspiracy had come to nothing and Cromwell had angrily scrapped his policy of reconciliation, divided the country into ten military districts under the control of Major Generals, and imposed a decimation tax on unyielding supporters of the Stuart cause because they were 'implacable in their malice and revenge, and never to be drawn from their adhering to that cursed interest'.[103] Unlike Davenant, who did not 'mourn to hear a drum', Cowley looked back with nostalgia to his tranquil apprenticeship as a poet at Cambridge in the 1630s. He affirmed that the spirit of poetry 'must, like the *Halcyon*, have *fair weather* to breed in' and complained that 'a warlike, various, and a tragical age is best to *write of*, but worst to *write in*'; and he claimed to have been nursing a desire 'to retire ... to some of our *American Plantations*', where he might 'forsake this world for ever' and bury himself 'in some obscure retreat' (pp. 80–2).

In a perceptive account of the entire 'complex and enigmatic' volume, however, Corns points out that Cowley makes no effort to 'disguise, mitigate, or apologize for his loyalty to Charles I or his son' and that the first group of poems, entitled 'Miscellanies' and including pre-war tributes to Falkland, the King and the Prince of Wales, constitutes 'an abiding record of cultural royalism'.[104] And Zwicker contends that the volume as a whole not only 'acknowledges the power of politics in the ordering of the literary and reinforces the royalist poetics of wit', but also takes the further step of assimilating 'some of the poetics of inspiration and the authority of Scripture to its own literary and cultural cause'.[105] Cowley's *Poems* can therefore be seen as a significant attempt to face the predicament of 1655 by combining the new rationalist poetics of Hobbes and Davenant with the Christian poetics expressed in the preface to the 1655 *Silex Scintillans* and embodied in Vaughan's devotional but politically engaged lyrics. *The Mistress* (1647), which is reprinted as the second part of the collection, is absolved in the Preface of 'the two unpardonable vices' that Vaughan had condemned, the '*Obscenity* and *Prophaneness*' that are too common in love poetry; and the next section, containing hitherto unprinted material written in the 1650s, is carefully mediated to the public of 1656: 'For as for the *Pindarick Odes* (which is the third part) I am in great doubt whether they will be understood by most *Readers*; nay, even by very many who are well enough acquainted with the common Roads and ordinary Tracks of *Poesie*' (p. 85–6). The translations and imitations of Pindar are provided with a separate preface which introduces 'the Musick of his *Numbers*' and his flights of fancy, but the poet's anxiety about generic unfamiliarity, like Vaughan's warning that some passages in *Silex Scintillans* 'may seem something *remote*', sounds like a prompt to the 'competent' reader to look beyond the obvious meaning of the text.[106]

Two of the imitations have proved especially problematic for later interpreters, some of whom have found in them further evidence of an ideological shift if not downright apostasy. Nethercot was convinced that in 'Destinie' and 'Brutus', 'under the veil of different allegories', the royalist poet 'continued the recantation he had begun' in the Preface.[107] He read into the chess imagery of the first strophe of 'Destinie' unmistakable allusions to Cromwell (the 'proud *Pawn*' who is admired for 'advancing higher' until he reached the top and 'became / Another *Thing* and *Name*'), to the royalists (the 'losing party' that is blamed for 'those false *Moves* that break the *Game*'), and most pointedly to the final defeat of the cause of Charles I (due to 'th' *ill Conduct* of the *Mated King*'); and he saw it as 'a bold stroke' to single out Brutus, 'a regicide as well as a republican', for praise 'at this juncture'.[108] Ruth Nevo accepted these readings and regarded the Brutus ode in particular as 'fervent in its admiration of the archetypal republican "usurper"', comparing it with Marvell's verse tribute to Cromwell on the first anniversary of the Protectorate.[109] Doubt was cast on this straightforward approach to the Brutus ode when critics began to emphasize the implications of its ending, in which Cowley sets Christian patience and fortitude against the pagan hero's worship of '*Virtue*' as 'the most solid *Good*, and greatest *Deitie*', to which he sacrificed his life by committing suicide after his defeat at Philippi, not long before the beginning of the Christian era:

> A few years more, so soon hadst thou not dy'ed,
> Would have confounded *Humane Virtues* pride,
> And shew'd thee a *God crucifi'ed*.   (p. 197)

James Keough sees parallels between Cromwell and Caesar – 'for each had put an end to Civil Wars and each was aspiring to kingship' – and between Brutus and Cowley, who is writing 'from a deep despair similar to that which engendered Brutus's suicidal decision' but who clings to his Christian belief that 'what appears unjust to man will prove just in God's overall plan'.[110] In the context of the Engagement and the Protectorate, 'the ode functions as a poetic statement of a defeated royalist's acceptance of Cromwellian rule'.[111] For T. R. Langley, Cowley's Brutus is also the despairing idealist rather than the king-killer, but the poem itself supports Sprat's interpretation of Cowley's political motives, warning royalists against 'acts of suicidal desperation' in the Christian hope that those 'prepared to be patient may yet live to witness a change for the better'. The 'Republican smokescreen' with which the poet sought to conceal 'his Royalist intentions' was so thick, however, that he was misunderstood by his friends as well as by his enemies.[112] Anselment and Corns also deny a pro-Cromwellian stance in the Pindarics: the former highlights the quest of a 'troubled spirit' for consolation first in the bleak determinism of 'Destinie' – which ascribes the moves of all the chess-pieces to the operation of an *'unseen Hand'* – and then in the 'decidedly more Christian patience' of 'Brutus'; and the latter suggests that Cowley discovered in the fate of the Roman idealist the sombre lesson that 'the best of political causes perishes through a mixture of chance (or fate) and the malice of corrupt adversaries'.[113]

Commentators have paused uneasily over the charge in 'Destinie' that 'the conquer'd *Pieces'* are swept from the board by 'th' *ill Conduct* of the *Mated King'*, seeing it as a criticism of the royal martyr or his son, each of whom 'has made errors (palpably), but of a practical, not ethical, kind'.[114] The phrase fits more aptly into the postwar world of competing royalist factions if it is read as a comment not on the poor leadership (*'Conduct'*) of the King (whether Charles I or Charles II) but on the way he was or is led by those responsible for royal policy – and Cowley had good reason for resentment against both Hyde and Jermyn. Another more deeply personal pain may inform the troubled question provoked by his contemplation of the suicide of Brutus:

> What joy can *humane things* to us afford,
> When we see perish thus by odde events,
>   *Ill men*, and wretched *Accidents*,
> The best *Cause* and best *Man* that ever drew a *Sword?* (p. 196)

From his youthful anxiety about the danger that Lord Falkland was exposed to in the expedition to Scotland in 1639 to the grief-stricken lament over the death in battle that Falkland seems to have deliberately courted in 1643, Cowley had always regarded the patron of the Great Tew circle as the embodiment of those civilized values which, for men like him, the Civil War had been fought to preserve. Now, as a prisoner of the Protectorate, he considers the temptation that Falkland had apparently succumbed to at Newbury – which has its parallel in Vaughan's yearning to join his dead brother in the late 1640s – but finds, in the image of 'a *God crucifi'ed'*, the faith that will enable him to live on through the dark days of political despair.

The most detailed analysis of the complete collection of Pindarics, has demonstrated that it is 'not a mere miscellany' but 'a sequence with a very definite political sub-text'; and that the poet who had spent some years handling the ciphers in which Charles and Henrietta Maria carried on their correspondence was sending his own 'coded message to the people of England'.[115] Even the two opening odes, which are

translations from Pindaric originals, can be accommodated to the overarching political scheme as secret tributes to Charles I and his son; and
the twelve 'imitations' that follow, with 'Destinie' and 'Brutus' at their
centre, all reflect in different ways the dilemma of a royalist 'who was
employing the license of an ancient poetic mode to speak what he could
not otherwise'.[116] The sequence ends as it began with two translations,
this time of carefully selected passages from the Old Testament.[117] In the
first, Isaiah evokes the 'dreadful *Host* of *Judgments*' that God is preparing
for the disobedient inhabitants of a 'cursed *Land*'; and in the second,
derived from the Book of Exodus, the poet indicts the Israelites for lying
in 'black *Egyptian Slavery*' and submitting to 'vile Drudgerie' instead of
heeding the '*Prophets* and *Apostles*' who come 'To call us home, / Home
to the promis'd *Canaan* above', and then describes the plagues visited by
a wrathful God upon 'th' *Egyptian Prince*' who is, like England's Protector, 'Hard of *Belief* and *Will*'. The ode ends with Pharoah's army
engulfed by the waters of the Red Sea and the Israelites freed from their
long captivity, so that the entire sequence pursues the course charted in
the two parts of *Silex Scintillans*, from despair to deliverance. And, as
Revard presents it, the literary method used in these final odes is very
similar to that used by the Breconshire royalist in such poems as 'The
Mutinie' and 'L'Envoy': 'Cowley takes these Puritan readings of Scripture and turns them on their head, identifying the Royalists with the
prophets and the chosen people whom the kingly Moses will lead to the
promised land.'[118]

The scheme of *Poems* (1656) was completed with four books of a
projected epic, the last of which gives an account of the origins of the
Jewish monarchy and the characters of King Saul and his son Jonathan
and appears to have been written or revised shortly before publication.
Trotter is convinced that *Davideis* 'expresses anti-monarchist sentiments'
and reads Book IV as 'a statement about the nature of power and
authority, and particularly about the consequences of the abuse of
authority'.[119] One passage gives an impression of Jewish history under
the Judges that is not unlike the summary in *Cooper's Hill* of the en-
croachments of tyrannical kings upon the liberties established at Runnymede in Magna Carta: from time to time, 'well-form'd *Spirits*' are
raised by God 'To free the groaning *Nation*, and to give / *Peace* first, and
then the *Rules* in *Peace* to live', but their '*Rules* and *Pattern*' do not outlive
them and 'The *hungry Rich* all near them did devour, / Their *Judge* was
Appetite, and their *Law* was *Power*'.[120] In this reading, Jonathan represents
an unrealizable ideal to set against the reality of kingly tyranny and
Cowley's biblical epic, like *The Civil War* before it, could not be

continued because its literary model broke down under the mounting
pressure of political despair.[121] In his insistence that Cowley had lost his
faith in monarchy itself, however, Trotter overlooks the significance of
the titular hero, David, who returned in triumph to Jerusalem and
whose story represented the abiding truth that 'heroic virtue begins with
conformity to the divine will and grows with adversity'.[122] But even
among critics who recognize the poet's steadfast royalism, the import of
Davideis for readers in 1656 is no more easily decipherable than the rest
of Cowley's enigmatic volume. Anselment, for example, finds in the
poetic treatment of the story told in the First Book of Samuel a 'redemp-
tive pattern seen in the patience of heroes and the rhythms of time',
which was designed to reassure 'royalists confronting the bleak prospects of the Interregnum' that 'the destruction of one monarchy is not
the destruction of all monarchy'.[123] For Corns, however, Cowley's
'would-be prophetic account of the triumph of the royalist underground' came up against 'the hard reality of Cromwellian domination'
in 1655 and was one more 'royalist fantasy' frustrated by history.[124]

Oliver Cromwell's death on 3 September 1658 did not result in a
resurgence of support for the Stuart cause. There was widespread
backing for his son Richard, whose succession to the Protectorship
raised 'hopes for normalcy under one who had had so little hand in the
arbitrary measures of the 1650s, and was so little identified with the
warriors' cause of the 1640s'.[125] Such was the unlikelihood of an imminent return of Charles II that laudatory elegies on the dead Protector
were produced not only by the veteran puritan, George Wither, and
Milton's assistant as Latin Secretary, Andrew Marvell, but also by
Edmund Waller, who had returned from exile in 1653 and made his
peace with the republic, by Cowley's friend Thomas Sprat, and by John
Dryden, who was destined to become the major poetic voice in the
political and cultural world that was 'restored' in 1660.[126] The negative
view of Cromwell's character and career was expressed by Thomas
Shipman and Abraham Cowley, though neither committed his work to
print until it was safe to do so. Shipman's 'The Arch-Traitor. 1659.
Upon the Death of Oliver Cromwell' emphasized the equal contribution made by the '*Muses*' and the '*Cavaleers*' to the royalist cause:

> the time affords
> *Poets* to use their *Pens*, and those their *Swords*:
> The *Tyrant* knew by both he might be harm'd;
> So *Playes* he voted down, and them disarm'd.

It also castigated those who had abused their art in eulogizing the dead usurper: 'Base! that in verse *Rebellion* should appear; / As though *Apollo* were turn'd *Presbyter*.'[127]

In a much longer retrospective in prose and verse, entitled 'A Discourse By way of a Vision, Concerning the Government of Oliver Cromwell', Cowley tells of his visionary encounter on the night of the Protector's funeral with 'the figure of a man taller than a Gyant', which is both Cromwell and the Devil and which seems to owe something to the frontispiece of Hobbes's *Leviathan*:

His body was naked, but that nakedness adorn'd, or rather deform'd all over, with several figures, after the manner of the antient *Britons*, painted upon it: and I perceived that most of them were the representation of the late battels in our civil Wars, and (if I be not much mistaken) it was the battle of *Naseby* that was drawn upon his Breast. His Eyes were like burning Brass, and there were three Crowns of the same metal (as I guest) and that lookt as red-hot too, upon his head. He held in his right hand a Sword that was yet bloody ... and in his left hand a thick Book, upon the back of which was written in Letters of Gold, Acts, Ordinances, Protestations, Covenants, Engagements, Declarations, Remonstrances, &c.[128]

The evil angel, who claims to be 'His Highness, the Protector of the Common-wealth of *England, Scotland* and *Ireland*', defends his lately deceased human counterpart against the poet's charges of dissimulation, usurpation and oppression. The virulence of the analysis of Cromwell's personality and abuse of power leaves no doubt about Cowley's attitude towards the regime he had sought to placate in the preface of 1656 and, indeed, it reads more like an act of private psychological exorcism than the attempt at public rehabilitation that it must have appeared to be when it was published in 1661.

Richard Cromwell failed to provide the stability that the country needed. His dissolution of Parliament on 22 April and resignation on 24 May 1659 inaugurated a period of turmoil in which various expedients were tried and discarded: the Rump was recalled on 6 May and dismissed by the Army, in which Lambert was now the dominant general, on 13 October; an attempt at military rule collapsed and the soldiers restored the Rump again on 24 December. Growing fears of anarchy and the threat from Lambert brought Fairfax out of retirement on 30 December to secure York for a Parliament and on 2 January 1660, General George Monck crossed the Scottish border and began to march towards London, which he reached on 3 February. Monck forced the Rump to re-admit members excluded by Pride in 1648 and on 16 March the Long Parliament dissolved itself.[129] While arrangements were being made for a new Parliament to be freely elected, Charles II issued the Declaration of Breda on 4 April, promising a general pardon and religious toleration in the event of his being recalled.

During this period of uncertainty, royalist polemicists became active again, putting the case for a restoration of the monarchy as the only way of settling the government on a firm basis. John Evelyn, for example, couched *An Apology for the Royal Party* (London, [4 November] 1659) in the form of a letter to 'a Person of the Late Councel of State'. Besides looking back over the deceptions, miseries and injustices of the past decade – in which 'that proud *Leviathan*', Cromwell, was hailed as 'the *Moses*, the *Man of God*, the *Joshua*, the *Saviour* of *Israel*' (p. 3) – he glances with contempt at the 'wretched *Interludes*, *Farces* and *Fantasms*' (p. 3) of recent months and the '*pseudo-politicks* and irreligious Principles' (p. 5) of the soldiers, before pronouncing the royalists 'the only honest men which have appeared upon the stage' (p. 8) and answering various objections to the return of Charles II.

The Convention Parliament, composed of both Lords and Commons, assembled on 25 April and the King landed at Dover on 25 May 1660. He was greeted by cheering crowds when he entered London on 29 May and by an outpouring of prose welcomes and loyal verses by, among others, Edmund Waller, Sir William Davenant, Martin Lluellyn, Alexander Brome, Charles Cotton, Katherine Philips, Abraham Cowley and John Dryden.[130] But that is the start of another story of another world, in which the heir of the Royal Martyr 'scattered his Maker's image through the land', the 'antient way' of Edward Symmons and Henry Vaughan was never quite restored in the re-established Church of England, and the old-fashioned piety of 'loyal converts' like Francis Quarles was superseded by the sceptical rationalism of survivors like Davenant and a new generation of courtier-poets, like the son of General Wilmot, the Earl of Rochester.

Notes

INTRODUCTION

1 Ronald Hutton, 'The Structure of the Royalist Party, 1642–1646', *Historical Journal*, 24 (1981), 553–69; 553.

2 G. E. Aylmer, 'Collective Mentalities in Mid Seventeenth-Century England: II. Royalist Attitudes', *Transactions of the Royal Historical Society*, 5th series, 37 (1987), 1–30; 1.

3 Kevin Sharpe and Steven N. Zwicker, *Politics of Discourse: The Literature and History of Seventeenth-Century England* (Berkeley and Los Angeles, 1987), note 23, p. 298.

4 Russell, *FBM*, p. 526.

5 See Paul H. Hardacre, *The Royalists During the Puritan Revolution* (The Hague, 1956); James W. Daly, 'The Idea of Absolute Monarchy in Seventeenth-Century England', *Historical Journal*, 21 (1978), 227–50; Daly, 'The Implications of Royalist Politics, 1642–1646', *Historical Journal*, 27 (1984), 745–55; Daly, *Sir Robert Filmer and English Political Thought* (Toronto, 1979); Joyce Lee Malcolm, *Caesar's Due: Loyalty and King Charles 1642–1646* (London, 1983).

6 See L. J. Reeve, *Charles I and the Road to Personal Rule* (Cambridge, 1989); Peter Donald, *An Uncounselled King: Charles I and the Scottish Troubles, 1637–1641* (Cambridge, 1990); Glenn Burgess, 'The Divine Right of Kings Reconsidered', *English Historical Review*, 107 (1992), 837–61; Kevin Sharpe, *The Personal Rule of Charles I* (New Haven and London, 1992); David L. Smith, *Constitutional Royalism and the Search for Settlement, c. 1640–1649* (Cambridge, 1994).

7 Lois Potter, *Secret Rites and Secret Writing: Royalist Literature, 1641–1660* (Cambridge, 1989), p. 3.

8 See Thomas, *JB*; Annabel Patterson, *Censorship and Interpretation: The Conditions of Writing and Reading in Early Modern England* (Madison, 1984); Kevin Sharpe, *Criticism and Compliment: The Politics of Literature in the England of Charles I* (Cambridge, 1987); Anselment, *LR*.

9 Thomas N. Corns, *Uncloistered Virtue: English Political Literature, 1640–1660* (Oxford, 1992); Gerald M. MacLean, *Time's Witness: Historical Representation in English Poetry, 1603–1660* (Madison, 1990); Dale B. J. Randall, *Winter Fruit: English Drama 1642–1660* (Lexington, 1995); Susan Wiseman, *Drama and*

349

Politics in the English Civil War (Cambridge, 1998); James Loxley, *RP*; Steven N. Zwicker, *Lines of Authority: Politics and English Literary Culture, 1649–1689* (Ithaca and London, 1993). This growing interest in the royalist perspective is also evident in *The English Civil Wars in the Literary Imagination*, ed. Claude J. Summers and Ted-Larry Pebworth (Columbia and London, 1999), which contains essays by various hands on Mildmay Fane, Herrick, Cleveland, Lovelace, Vaughan, *Cooper's Hill*, and Katherine Philips.

10 Patterson, *Censorship and Interpretation*, p. 47; David Norbrook, *Poetry and Politics in the English Renaissance* (London, 1984), p. 8.

11 See Tessa Watt, *Cheap Print and Popular Piety, 1550–1640* (Cambridge, 1993); Dagmar Freist, *Governed by Opinion: Politics, Religion and the Dynamics of Communication in Stuart London 1637–1645* (London and New York, 1997).

12 Arthur F. Marotti, *Manuscript, Print, and the English Renaissance Lyric* (Ithaca and London, 1995), p. 34.

13 Freist, *Governed by Opinion*, p. 19.

14 J. P. Kenyon, *The Stuart Constitution 1603–1688: Documents and Commentary* (Cambridge, 1966), p. 18.

15 From *Commons Debates, 1628*, II, pp. 391, 452, quoted in Christopher Hill, 'Political Discourse in Early Seventeenth-Century England', *Politics and People in Revolutionary England: Essays in Honour of Ivan Roots*, ed. Colin Jones, Malyn Newitt and Stephen Roberts (Oxford, 1986), pp. 41–64; p. 57.

16 Kenyon, *Stuart Constitution*, p. 17. Pym was speaking on 4 June 1628.

17 William M. Lamont, *Godly Rule: Politics and Religion, 1603–60* (London, 1969), pp. 94–5.

18 Conal Condren, *The Language of Politics in Seventeenth-Century England* (Basingstoke, 1994), p. 36.

19 *Ibid.*, pp. 37–8.

20 Kevin Sharpe, *Politics and Ideas in Early Stuart England: Essays and Studies* (London and New York, 1989), p. 65.

21 Austin Woolrych, 'Court, Country and City Revisited', *History*, 65 (1980), 236–45; 236.

22 Sharpe, *Criticism and Compliment*, p. 27.

23 J. S. A. Adamson, 'Chivalry and Political Culture in Caroline England', *Culture and Politics in Early Stuart England*, ed. Kevin Sharpe and Peter Lake (London and Basingstoke, 1994), pp. 161–97; p. 182.

24 Martin Butler, *Theatre and Crisis 1632–1642* (Cambridge, [1984] 1987), p. 11.

25 R. Malcolm Smuts, *Court Culture and the Origins of a Royalist Tradition in Early Stuart England* (Philadelphia, 1987), p. 218.

1: THE HALCYON DAYS: 1628–1637

1 'A Discourse by Way of Vision, Concerning the Government of *Oliver Cromwell*', *CowleyE*, pp. 343–4.

2 *Memoires of the Reigne of King Charles I* (London, 1701), p. 46.

3 Clarendon, I, 162.

4 'Thomas Carew, Sir John Suckling, and Richard Lovelace', *Cambridge Companion to English Poetry: Donne to Marvell*, ed. Thomas N. Corns (Cambridge, 1993), pp. 200–20; p. 201.

5 'To his Noble Friend Mr. *Richard Lovelace*, upon his Poems', in *Poems and Letters of Andrew Marvell*, ed. H. M. Margoliouth, 2 vols. (1927), 3rd. edn. revised by Pierre Legouis with the collaboration of E. E. Duncan-Jones (Oxford, 1971), I, p. 3.

6 Wormald, *Clarendon*, p. 181.

7 See Raymond A. Anselment, 'Clarendon and the Caroline Myth of Peace', *Journal of British Studies*, 23 (1984), 37–54.

8 See Graham Parry, *The Golden Age Restor'd: The Culture of the Stuart Court, 1603–1642* (Manchester, 1981), pp. 184–229; R. Malcolm Smuts, *Court Culture and the Origins of a Royalist Tradition in Early Stuart England* (Philadelphia, 1987); Kevin Sharpe, *Criticism and Compliment: The Politics of Literature in the England of Charles I* (Cambridge, 1987).

9 See Charles Carlton, *Charles I: The Personal Monarch* (London, 1984), pp. 111–17; L. J. Reeve, *Charles I and the Road to Personal Rule* (Cambridge, 1989), pp. 35–9.

10 Reeve, *Road to Personal Rule*, pp. 30, 37.

11 Letter written by Secretary Coke, quoted in Kevin Sharpe, *The Personal Rule of Charles I* (New Haven and London, 1992), p. 65.

12 'LXVI An Epigram to the Queen, then Lying in. 1630', *Ben Jonson: Complete Poems*, ed. George Parfitt (Harmondsworth, 1975), p. 208.

13 See Ann Baynes Coiro, '"A ball of strife": Caroline Poetry and Royal Marriage', *The Royal Image: Representations of Charles I*, ed. Thomas N. Corns (Cambridge, 1999), pp. 26–46.

14 'Upon the King's happy Returne from Scotland', *Poems of Henry King*, ed. Margaret Crum (Oxford, 1965), pp. 81–2.

15 See Dolores Palomo, 'The Halcyon Moment of Stillness in Royalist Poetry', *Huntington Library Quarterly*, 44 (1981), 205–21.

16 Smuts, *Court Culture*, p. 249.

17 Michael P. Parker, '"All are not born (Sir) to the Bay": "Jack" Suckling, "Tom" Carew, and the Making of a Poet', *English Literary Renaissance*, 12 (1982), 341–68; 342. See also Kevin Sharpe, *Politics and Ideas in Early Stuart England : Essays and Studies* (London and New York, 1989), pp. 230–58.

18 *Poems of Thomas Carew with his Masque Coelum Britannicum*, ed. Rhodes Dunlap (Oxford, 1949), pp. 89–90.

19 See John Peacock, 'The Politics of Portraiture', in *Culture and Politics in Early Stuart England*, ed. Kevin Sharpe and Peter Lake (Basingstoke, 1994), pp. 199–228; p. 226; David Howarth, *Images of Rule: Art and Politics in the English Renaissance, 1485–1649* (Basingstoke, 1997), pp. 136–43.

20 For the musical culture of the court of Charles I, see Jonathan P. Wainwright, 'The King's Music', *Royal Image*, ed. Corns, pp. 162–75; and for the Caroline masque, see Sharpe, *Criticism and Compliment*, pp. 179–264; Martin Butler, 'Reform or Reverence? The Politics of the Caroline Masque,'

Theatre and Government Under the Early Stuarts, ed. J. R. Mulryne and Margaret Shewring (Cambridge, 1993), pp. 118–56.

21 *Ben Jonson*, ed. C. H. Herford and Percy and Evelyn Simpson, 11 vols. (Oxford, 1925–1952), VII, pp. 735–43.

22 Smuts, *Court Culture*, p. 237.

23 *Sir Richard Fanshawe: Shorter Poems and Translations*, ed. N. W. Bawcutt (Liverpool, 1964), p. 7.

24 Eclogue I, 'The Shepheards Oracles', in *QCW*, III, p. 203.

25 Ruth Nevo, *The Dial of Virtue: A Study of Poems on Affairs of State in the Seventeenth Century* (Princeton, 1963), p. 20.

26 See Jonathan Goldberg, *James I and the Politics of Literature: Jonson, Shakespeare, Donne and Their Contemporaries* (Stanford, 1989), pp. 29–32; Kevin Sharpe, 'The Image of Virtue: the Court and Household of Charles I, 1625–1642', *The English Court from the Wars of the Roses to the Civil War*, ed. David Starkey (London, 1987), pp. 226–60.

27 M. L. Donnelly, 'Caroline Royalist Panegyric and the Disintegration of a Symbolic Mode', *"The Muses Commonweale": Poetry and Politics in the Seventeenth Century*, ed. Claude J. Summers and Ted-Larry Pebworth (Columbia, 1988), pp. 163–76; pp. 163–4.

28 *Ibid.*, p. 164.

29 'On His Majesty's Return Out of Scotland, 1633', quoted from Cowley's *Juvenilia* in Nevo, *Dial of Virtue*, p. 26.

30 *King*, ed. Crum, pp. 81–2; *CPP*, pp. 449–50.

31 There were poems on the death of Gustavus Adolphus by, among others, Dudley North, Robert Gomersall, Henry King, Richard Fanshawe, Francis Quarles, and Thomas Randolph; and the third part of *The Swedish Intelligencer* (London, 1633), appended nine verse elegies to a prose character of the dead hero.

32 Smuts, *Court Culture*, p. 252.

33 *Poems and Masques of Aurelian Townshend*, ed. Cedric C. Brown (Reading, 1983), p. 48.

34 Sharpe, *Politics and Ideas*, p. 255.

35 See Michael P. Parker, 'Carew's Politics of Pastoral: Virgilian Pretexts in the 'Answer to Aurelian Townshend'', *John Donne Journal*, 1 (1982), 101–16; Joanne Altieri, 'Responses to a Waning Mythology in Carew's Political Poetry', *Studies in English Literature*, 26 (1986), 107–24.

36 'In answer of an Elegiacall Letter upon the death of the King of *Sweden* from *Aurelian Townshend*, inviting me to write on that subject', *Carew*, ed. Dunlap, pp. 74–7.

37 For details of the Ship Money controversy, see Sharpe, *Personal Rule*, pp. 545–95.

38 David Underdown, *Revel, Riot, and Rebellion: Popular Politics and Culture in England: 1603–1660* (Oxford, 1987), p. 63.

39 David Loewenstein, 'Politics and Religion', in *Cambridge Companion: Donne to Marvell*, ed. Corns, p. 16.

40 Sharpe, *Personal Rule*, pp. 328–45.
41 *Ibid.*, pp. 317–21.
42 *Ibid.*, pp. 322–8.
43 *Poems of Edmund Waller*, ed. G. Thorn Drury, 2 vols. (London, 1893), I, pp. 16–18.
44 Stephen Orgel, *The Illusion of Power: Political Theater in the English Renaissance* (Berkeley and Los Angeles, 1975), p. 83; Parry, *Golden Age Restor'd*, p. 196.
45 Sharpe, *Criticism and Compliment*, p. 232.
46 For other recent assessments of Carew, see Diana Benet, 'Carew's Monarchy of Wit','*The Muses Common-weale*', ed. Summers and Pebworth, pp. 80–91; John Kerrigan, 'Thomas Carew', *Proceedings of the British Academy*, 74 (1988), 311–50; Anthony Low, *The Reinventing of Love: Poetry, Politics and Culture from Sidney to Milton* (Cambridge, 1993), pp. 132–57.
47 The text of *Coelum Britannicum* is in *Carew*, ed. Dunlap, pp. 151–85.
48 '"To that secure fix'd state": The Function of the Caroline Masque Form', *The Court Masque*, ed. David Lindley (Manchester, 1984), pp. 78–93; p. 86.
49 Altieri, 'Waning Mythology', 112.
50 C. V. Wedgwood, *Poetry and Politics Under the Stuarts* (Cambridge, 1960), pp. 47–8.
51 See R. M. Smuts, 'The Puritan Followers of Henrietta Maria in the 1630s', *English Historical Review*, 93 (1978), 26–45.
52 See Martin Butler, 'Entertaining the Palatine Prince: Plays on Foreign Affairs 1635–1637', *English Literary Renaissance*, 13 (1983), 319–44.
53 Sharpe, *Personal Rule*, p. 536.

2: THE BISHOPS' WARS AND THE SHORT PARLIAMENT: JULY
1637–OCTOBER 1640

1 *The Life of Edward Earl of Clarendon... Written by Himself*, 3 vols. (Oxford, 1759), I, p. 71.
2 For a summary of the relations between Scotland and the first two Stuart kings of England, see Peter Donald, *An Uncounselled King: Charles I and the Scottish Troubles, 1637–1641* (Cambridge, 1990), pp. 1–42.
3 See Kevin Sharpe, *The Personal Rule of Charles I* (New Haven and London, 1992), pp. 783–7.
4 See Donald, *Uncounselled King*, pp. 78–118.
5 The poem was first printed in *The Poems of George Daniel, Esq., of Beswick, Yorkshire (1616–1657)*, ed. Revd. Alexander B. Grosart, 4 vols. (Blackburn, 1878), I, pp. 161–90.
6 Details of Daniel's extensive knowledge of classical and contemporary poetry are given in *The Selected Poems of George Daniel of Beswick 1616–1657*, ed. Thomas B. Stroup (Lexington, 1959), pp. xix–xxii.
7 'To the Queen Mother of France, Upon her Landing', *Poems of Edmund Waller*, ed. G. Thorn Drury, 2 vols. (London, 1893), I, pp. 35–6.

8 See Mark Charles Fissel, *The Bishops' Wars: Charles I's Campaigns against Scotland, 1638–1640* (Cambridge, 1994), pp. 3–39.
9 Quoted in Donald, *Uncounselled King*, pp. 132–3.
10 Sharpe, *Personal Rule*, pp. 813, 821.
11 Clarendon, VII, 220.
12 *Waller*, ed. Thorn Drury, I, pp. 75–6.
13 *CowleyP*, pp. 19–20.
14 Letters 36 and 37, *SNW*, pp. 140–2.
15 *Aubrey's Brief Lives*, ed. Oliver Lawson Dick (Harmondsworth, 1972), p. 450.
16 See Appendix A, *SNW*, pp. 204–5.
17 Letter 38, *SNW*, pp. 142–4.
18 Letter 42, *SNW*, pp. 147–8.
19 'To Lucasta, Going to the Warres', *Poems of Richard Lovelace*, ed. C. H. Wilkinson (Oxford, 1930), p. 18.
20 'To Generall *Goring*, after the pacification at *Berwicke*', *ibid.*, pp. 81–2.
21 Gerald Hammond, *Fleeting Things: English Poets and Poems, 1616–1660* (Cambridge, Mass., 1990), p. 29.
22 See Michael Parker, '"To my friend G. N. from Wrest": Carew's Secular Masque', in *Classic and Cavalier: Essays on Jonson and the Sons of Ben*, ed. Claude J. Summers and Ted-Larry Pebworth (Pittsburgh, 1982), pp. 171–91.
23 *Poems of Thomas Carew with his Masque Coelum Britannicum*, ed. Rhodes Dunlap (Oxford, 1949), pp. 86–9.
24 Joanne Altieri, 'Responses to a Waning Mythology in Carew's Political Poetry', *Studies in English Literature*, 26 (1986), 107–24; 122.
25 Parker, 'Carew's Secular Masque', p. 189.
26 Quoted by T. J. B. Spencer in the introduction to his edition of *Salmacida Spolia* in *A Book of Masques: In Honour of Allardyce Nicoll* (Cambridge, 1967), p. 340.
27 For the text of *Salmacida Spolia*, see Spencer, *A Book of Masques*, pp. 347–62.
28 For different readings, see Kevin Sharpe, *Criticism and Compliment: The Politics of Literature in the England of Charles I* (Cambridge, 1987), pp. 254–6; Graham Parry, *The Golden Age Restor'd: The Culture of the Stuart Court, 1603–1642* (Manchester, 1981), pp. 202–3; Martin Butler, 'Politics and the Masque: *Salmacida Spolia*', *Literature and the English Civil War*, ed. Thomas Healey and Jonathan Sawday (Cambridge, 1990), pp. 59–74; pp. 65–9.
29 C. V. Wedgwood, *Truth and Opinion: Historical Essays* (London, 1960), pp. 139–56; p. 155.
30 Derek Hirst, *Authority and Conflict: England 1603–1658* (London, 1986), p. 188.
31 Martin Parker, 'An Exact Description of the Manner how His Majestie and his Nobles went to the Parliament', licensed 9 April 1640, quoted from *Cavalier and Puritan: Ballads and Broadsides Illustrating the Period of the Great Rebellion 1640–1660*, ed. Hyder E. Rollins (New York, 1923), p. 78.
32 John K. Gruenfelder, 'The Election of the Short Parliament, 1640', *Early Stuart Studies: Essays in Honor of David Harris Willson*, ed. Howard S. Reinmouth, Jr (Minneapolis, 1970), pp. 180–230; pp. 183, 219, 230.

33 *Ibid.*, p. 185. For the pro-Scots contingent in the Short Parliament, see Russell, *FBM*, pp. 99–100.

34 See Donald, *Uncounselled King*, pp. 223–6.

35 *Proceedings of the Short Parliament of 1640*, ed. Esther S. Cope in collaboration with Willson H. Coates, Camden 4th Series, vol. 19 (London, 1977), pp. 118–20. The last phrase is a reference to a letter from the Covenanters to Louis XIII requesting French intercession on their behalf, which had fallen into the hands of the English King.

36 *Ibid.*, pp. 135–6.

37 *Ibid.*, pp. 249–50.

38 *Ibid.*, pp. 146, 149.

39 *Ibid.*, pp. 187–8.

40 See Russell, *FBM*, pp. 122–3.

41 See Esther S. Cope, 'The Short Parliament of 1640 and Convocation', *Journal of Ecclesiastical History*, 25 (1974), 167–84.

42 See Robin Clifton, 'The Popular Fear of Catholics During the English Revolution', *Past and Present*, No. 52 (1971), 23–55; 25–6.

43 *CP*, p. 4.

44 Fissel, *Bishops' Wars*, p. 47.

45 See Russell, *FBM*, pp. 147–57.

46 For the text of *Brennoralt*, see *Works of Sir John Suckling: The Plays*, ed. L.A. Beaurline (Oxford, 1971), pp. 183–236.

47 See Russell, *FBM*, p. 164.

48 Fissel, *Bishops' Wars*, p. 1.

3: THE LONG PARLIAMENT AND THE TRIAL OF STRAFFORD: NOVEMBER 1640–MAY 1641

1 Clayton Roberts, 'The Earl of Bedford and the Coming of the English Revolution', *Journal of Modern History*, 49 (1977), 600–16; 601. For a full account of the political make-up of the Long Parliament, see D. Brunton and D. H. Pennington, *Members of the Long Parliament* (London, 1954), Chapter 1.

2 Clarendon, III, 1.

3 Russell, *FBM*, pp. 206–7.

4 See Peter Donald, *An Uncounselled King: Charles I and the Scottish Troubles, 1637–1641* (Cambridge, 1990), pp. 275 ff.

5 Wedgwood, *KP*, p. 330.

6 Conrad Russell, *The Crisis of Parliaments: English History 1509–1660* (Oxford, 1971), p. 333.

7 Clarendon, III, 1.

8 J. P. Kenyon, *The Stuart Constitution 1603–1688: Documents and Commentary* (Cambridge, 1966), pp. 204–5.

9 See C. V. Wedgwood, *Thomas Wentworth: First Earl of Strafford 1593–1641: A Revaluation* (London, 1961), pp. 314–21.

10 The text of this letter is in *SNW*, pp. 163–7.

11 This untitled letter was printed in Part III of Dudley North's *A Forest Promiscuous* (London, 1659), pp. 231–3.

12 See Fletcher, *Outbreak*, p. 91.

13 Letter 45, in *The Knyvett Letters (1620–1644)*, ed. Bertram Schofield (London, 1949), pp. 96–7.

14 See introduction to Quarles's *Hosanna and Threnodes*, ed. John Horden (Liverpool, 1960), pp. xxii–xxviii.

15 Quoted by Gordon S. Haight, 'Francis Quarles in the Civil War', *Review of English Studies*, 12 (1936), 147–64; 148.

16 The text is in *QCW*, III, pp. 288–312.

17 Karl Josef Höltgen, *Francis Quarles 1592–1644* (Tubingen, 1978), pp. 278–80.

18 Haight, 'Quarles in the Civil War', 148–50.

19 For Ussher's patronage of Quarles, see Masoodul Hasan, *Francis Quarles: A Study of his Life and Poetry* (Aligarh, India, 1966), pp. 5–7.

20 The text is in *Mildmay Fane's Raguaillo D'Oceano and Candy Restored 1641*, ed. Clifford Leech (Louvain, 1938), pp. 103–34.

21 *Ibid.*, pp. 40–1; Martin Butler, *Theatre and Crisis 1632–1642* (Cambridge, [1984] 1987), p. 123.

22 Russell, *FBM*, p. 207.

23 *CPP*, pp. 533–5. I assume the poem was written for New Year's Day 1641.

24 Letter 46, *Knyvett Letters*, ed. Schofield, pp. 98–100.

25 Quoted in Roberts, 'Earl of Bedford', 602.

26 Quoted in Russell, *FBM*, p. 238. For different accounts of the political manoeuvrings, see Paul Christianson, 'The Peers, the People, and Parliamentary Management in the First Six Months of the Long Parliament', *Journal of Modern History*, 49 (1977), 575–99; Derek Hirst, 'Unanimity in the Commons, Aristocratic Intrigues and the Origins of the English Civil War', *Journal of Modern History*, 50 (1978), 51–71; and Sheila Lambert, 'The Opening of the Long Parliament', *Historical Journal*, 27 (1984), 265–87.

27 Russell, *FBM*, p. 243.

28 *Ibid.*, p. 247.

29 *Ibid.*, p. 239.

30 *Sir William Davenant: The Shorter Poems, and Songs from the Plays and Masques*, ed. A. M. Gibbs (Oxford, 1972), pp. 139–40.

31 Gerald Hammond, *Fleeting Things: English Poets and Poems 1626–1660* (Cambridge, Mass., 1990), pp. 38–9.

32 See Caroline M. Hibbard, *Charles I and the Popish Plot* (Chapel Hill, 1983), pp. 182–3, 189.

33 Lambert plays down the constitutional issue and places the passing of the Triennial Act in the context of a deal over the granting of subsidies ('Opening of Long Parliament', 276–7).

34 Quoted by Christianson, 'Peers', 588.

35 Quoted by Christianson, *ibid.*, 589.

36 Wedgwood, *KP*, p. 362.

37 Fletcher, *Outbreak*, p. 4.

38 Russell, *FBM*, p. 270.

39 See Wedgwood, *Wentworth*, p. 333; and for more information about the use of the press to incite public opinion against Strafford, see Terence Kilburn and Anthony Milton, 'The Public Context of the Trial and Execution of Strafford', in *The Political World of Thomas Wentworth, Earl of Strafford, 1621–1641*, ed. J. F. Merritt (Cambridge, 1996), pp. 230–51; pp. 232–5.

40 Quoted in Fletcher, *Outbreak* , p. 7.

41 Quoted in Charles Carlton, *Charles I: The Personal Monarch* (London, 1983), p. 224.

42 North, *A Forest Promiscuous*, Part III, pp. 233–5.

43 Kenyon, *Stuart Constitution*, p. 210.

44 *Ibid.*, pp. 211–2.

45 See Fletcher, *Outbreak*, p. 12; O Hehir, *HD*, p. 31.

46 See Clarendon, III, 164, 165.

47 See Conrad Russell, 'First Army Plot of 1641', *Transactions of the Royal Historical Society*, 38 (1988), 85–106.

48 Quoted in Carlton, *Charles I*, p. 225.

49 See Elizabeth Hamilton, *Henrietta Maria* (London, 1976), p. 173.

50 '*On the Marriage of the Lady* Mary *to the Prince of* Aurange *his Son. 1641*'', *CPP*, pp. 539–41.

51 Kenyon, *Stuart Constitution*, p. 223.

52 These are Vane's figures, given by Russell, *FBM*, p. 297.

53 Quoted in Wedgwood, *KP*, p. 385.

54 Clarendon, III, 192.

55 *Plays and Poems of Henry Glapthorne*, 2 vols. (London, 1874), II, pp. 251–3.

56 This early manuscript version is printed as a footnote to the first published text of 1668 in *Poetical Works of Sir John Denham*, ed. Theodore Howard Banks, Jr (New Haven, 1928), p. 153.

57 Kilburn and Milton note that there were seven editions in 1641 of Strafford's final summing-up at his trial ('Public Context', p. 239).

58 *Sir Richard Fanshawe: Shorter Poems and Translations*, ed. N.W. Bawcutt (Liverpool, 1964), pp. 67–8.

59 Clarendon, III, 203.

60 Hammond, *Fleeting Things*, p. 48.

61 See *CP*, pp. xxxiii–xxxiv. The text of the poem is on p. 66.

62 See C. V. Wedgwood, *Poetry and Politics Under the Stuarts* (Cambridge, 1960), pp. 66–7.

4: THE BEGINNINGS OF CONSTITUTIONAL ROYALISM: MAY–OCTOBER 1641

1 Russell, *FBM*, pp. 330, 301.

2 *Ibid.*, p. 358.

3 See Alan Everitt, *The Community of Kent and the Great Rebellion 1640–1660*

(Leicester, [1966] 1973), pp. 84–94; William M. Lamont, *Politics and Religion, 1603–1660* (London, 1969), pp. 83–93; Derek Hirst, 'The Defection of Sir Edward Dering, 1640–1641', *Historical Journal*, 15 (1972), 193–208.

4   *A Collection of Speeches Made by Sir Edward Dering* (1642), pp. 33, 35.

5   *QCW*, III, pp. 233–6. For the date of composition, see Masoodul Hasan, *Francis Quarles: A Study of his Life and Poetry* (Aligarh, India, 1966), pp. 307–11.

6   Hasan, *Quarles*, p. 308.

7   For accounts of popular violence at this time, see John Morrill, *The Revolt of the Provinces: Conservatives and Radicals in the English Civil War 1630–1650* (London and New York, 1980), pp. 34–5; David Underdown, *Revel, Riot and Rebellion: Popular Politics and Culture in England 1603–1660* (Oxford, 1987), pp. 136–41.

8   See *SNW*, pp. lviii–lxi.

9   Quoted in Alfred Harbage, *Sir William Davenant: Poet Adventurer 1606–1668* (New York, [1935] 1971), pp. 81–7.

10 See Russell, *FBM*, pp. 331–2.

11 Fletcher, *Outbreak*, p. 48.

12 Quoted in John M. Wallace, '*Cooper's Hill*: The Manifesto of Parliamentary Royalism, 1641', *ELH*, 41 (1974), 505.

13 See Caroline M. Hibbard, *Charles I and the Popish Plot* (Chapel Hill, 1983), pp. 207–8.

14 Russell, *FBM*, p. 371.

15 Fletcher, *Outbreak*, p. 47.

16 Russell, *FBM*, p. 361.

17 Bennett, *CW*, pp. 87–8.

18 Fletcher, *Outbreak*, p. 100.

19 Smith, *CR*, p. 80.

20 See O Hehir, *EH*, pp. 41–73.

21 *Ibid.*, pp. 25, 32.

22 Earl R. Wasserman, *The Subtler Language: Critical Readings of Neoclassic and Romantic Poems* (Baltimore, 1959), p. 48. A political reading of Denham's poem was first mooted by Rufus Putney, 'The View from Cooper's Hill', *University of Colorado Studies*, 6 (1957), 13–22.

23 Wasserman, *Subtler Language*, pp. 47–8, 50, 79.

24 O Hehir, *EH*, pp. 27, 209.

25 Wallace, '*Cooper's Hill*', 496–7, 532.

26 *Ibid.*, 495, 502, 500, 534.

27 James Turner, *The Politics of Landscape: Rural Scenery and Society in English Poetry 1630– 1660* (Oxford, 1979), p. 57.

28 *Ibid.*, pp. 51, 61.

29 O Hehir, *EH*, pp. 13, 19–20.

30 Ruth Nevo, *The Dial of Virtue: A Study of Poems on Affairs of State in the Seventeenth Century* (Princeton, 1963), pp. 36–7.

31 All quotations from Draft I are from O Hehir, *EH*, pp. 79–90.

32 Wallace, '*Cooper's Hill*', 497.

33 Loxley, *RP*, p. 86.
34 William Rockett, '"Courts make not Kings, but Kings the Court": *Cooper's Hill* and the Constitutional Crisis of 1642', *Restoration: Studies in English Literary Culture*, 17 (1993), 1–14; 1.
35 Wasserman, *Subtler Language*, p. 49; O Hehir, *EH*, p. 30; Wallace, '*Cooper's Hill*', 525–6.
36 Rockett, '"Courts make not Kings"', 2.
37 O Hehir, *EH*, p. 179.
38 Wallace, '*Cooper's Hill*', 498.
39 See Wasserman, *Subtler Language*, pp. 53–61 and O Hehir, *EH*, pp. 165–76.
40 See O Hehir's notes and commentary, *EH*, pp. 119, 187–9.
41 Wallace, '*Cooper's Hill*', 499.
42 See O Hehir's notes on Henry VIII, *EH*, pp. 120–1.
43 Quoted in Russell, *FBM*, p. 245.
44 See Wallace, '*Cooper's Hill*', 506–9; O Hehir, *EH*, pp. 194–5.
45 *Mildmay Fane's Raguaillo D'Oceano 1640 and Candy Restored 1641*, ed. Clifford Leech (Louvain, 1938), p. 132; *QCW*, III, p. 309.
46 J. P. Kenyon, *The Stuart Constitution 1603–1688: Documents and Commentary* (Cambridge, 1966), p. 212.
47 See Wallace, '*Cooper's Hill*', 510–11.
48 O Hehir, *EH*, p. 201; Wallace, '*Cooper's Hill*', 516.
49 O Hehir, *EH*, pp. 203–5.
50 Wasserman, *Subtler Language*, p. 73.
51 Nevo, *Dial of Virtue*, p. 35.
52 O Hehir, *EH*, p. 31.
53 Wallace, '*Cooper's Hill*', 517–20.
54 O Hehir, *EH*, p. 206.
55 Quoted, along with other instances of this imagery, in Wallace, '*Cooper's Hill*', 523.
56 Wasserman, *Subtler Language*, p. 79.
57 Wallace, '*Cooper's Hill*', 535.
58 O Hehir, *EH*, p. 209.
59 Smith, *CR*, p. 80.

5: THE EMERGENCE OF THE CONSTITUTIONAL ROYALISTS: OCTOBER 1641–MARCH 1642

1 Quoted in Donald Nicholas, *Mr Secretary Nicholas (1593–1669): His Life and Letters* (London, 1955), p. 143.
2 Fletcher, *Outbreak*, pp. 159, 124.
3 See Russell, *FBM*, pp. 409–10.
4 See Fletcher, *Outbreak*, pp. 133–4.
5 See Russell, *FBM*, pp. 411–12.
6 Fletcher, *Outbreak*, pp. 134–5.
7 Smith, *CR*, pp. 78, 79.

8 *The Life of Edward Earl of Clarendon … Written by Himselfe*, 3 vols. (Oxford, 1759), I, pp. 82–3.

9 Wormald, *Clarendon*, p. 18.

10 *Ibid.*, p. 14.

11 See Fletcher, *Outbreak*, pp. 130–2.

12 *The Journal of Sir Simmonds D'Ewes: From the First Recess of the Long Parliament to the Withdrawal of King Charles from London*, ed. Willson Havelock Coates (New Haven, 1942), pp. 14–15.

13 Ashton, *ECW*, p. 138.

14 *Journal*, ed. Coates, p. 45.

15 Quoted in *Secretary Nicholas*, p. 144.

16 Caroline M. Hibbard, *Charles I and the Popish Plot* (Chapel Hill, 1983), p. 214.

17 See Keith J. Lindley, 'The Impact of the 1641 Rebellion upon England and Wales, 1641–1645', *Irish Historical Studies*, 18 (1972), 143–76; 144–5.

18 All the phrases in this paragraph are quoted from title pages.

19 Bennett, *CW*, p. 93. For other views, see Hibbard, *Charles I and the Popish Plot*, p. 214; Conrad Russell, 'The British Background to the Irish Rebellion of 1641', *Historical Research: The Bulletin of the Institute of Historical Research*, 61 (1988), 166–82; 177–9.

20 *Journal*, ed. Coates, p. 94.

21 Quoted in J. P. Kenyon, *The Stuart Constitution 1603–1688: Documents and Commentary* (Cambridge, 1966), p. 228.

22 See Vernon F. Snow, 'Essex and the Aristocratic Opposition to the Early Stuarts', *Journal of Modern History*, 32 (1960), 224–33; 231–2.

23 Fletcher, *Outbreak*, p. 145.

24 *Ibid.*, pp. 81–90.

25 Kenyon, *Stuart Constitution*, p. 231.

26 Fletcher, *Outbreak*, p. 146.

27 Clarendon, IV, 49.

28 Wormald, *Clarendon*, p. 22.

29 *Journal*, ed. Coates, pp. 151, 183.

30 *A Collection of Speeches Made by Sir Edward Dering* (London, 1642), pp. 71, 66.

31 Quoted in Wormald, *Clarendon*, p. 25.

32 *Ibid.*, pp. 28, 29.

33 Fletcher, *Outbreak*, pp. 156, 157.

34 See Valerie Pearl, *London and the Outbreak of the Puritan Revolution: City Government and National Politics, 1625–1643* (Oxford, 1961), pp. 122–8.

35 Fletcher, *Outbreak*, pp. 161–2.

36 Bernard Capp, *The World of John Taylor the Water-Poet 1578–1653* (Oxford, 1994), p. 144.

37 *King Charles His Entertainment, and Londons Loyaltie. Being a true Relation, and description, of the manner, of the Cities welcome, and, expression of the Subjects love to His Royall Majestie, at his Return from SCOTLAND* (London, 1641). The poem is on pp. 5–6.

38 John Bond, *King Charles his welcome home, Or A Congratulation of all his loving*

Subjects in thankfulnesse to God for his Majesties safe and happie returne from Scotland (London, 1641).

39 John Cragge, *Great Britains Prayers in This dangerous time of Contagion Together with a Congratulatory for the Entertainment of his Majesty out of Scotland* (London?, 1641).

40 Loxley, *RP*, pp. 68–9.

41 The poem is printed among the dubious attributions in Appendix I of *VW*. A note on p. 762 gives details of a Fellow named Henry Vaughan and a Gentleman-Commoner named Herbert Vaughan, both of whom were at Jesus College at the time, but points out that only Henry Vaughan, the Silurist, is known to have composed verse in English.

42 Loxley, *RP*, pp. 69–70.

43 'An Ode upon the return of his Majestie' by Cowley and the titleless poem by Cleveland are on sigg. K1^{r-v} and L1^{v}–L2^{r}, respectively. They are quoted from modern editions: *CowleyP*, pp. 22–4; *CP*, pp. 2–3.

44 Ruth Nevo, *The Dial of Virtue: A Study of Poems on Affairs of State in the Seventeenth Century* (Princeton, 1963), p. 42; Lee A. Jacobus, *John Cleveland* (Boston, Mass., 1975), p. 105.

45 A. D. Cousins, 'The Cavalier World and John Cleveland,' *Studies in Philology*, 78 (1981), 61–86; 75.

46 'Upon the Kings Returne to the City of London', *Parnassus Biceps or Several Choice Pieces of Poetry 1656*, ed. G. Thorn-Drury (London, 1927), pp. 50–3.

47 See Pearl, *London and the Puritan Revolution*, pp. 127–8.

48 *Ibid.*, pp. 129–30. (See also Fletcher, *Outbreak*, pp. 162–3.)

49 Smith, *CR*, p. 84.

50 *Life of Clarendon*, I, pp. 85–6.

51 Ashton, *ECW*, p. 145.

52 Wormald, *Clarendon*, pp. 36–42.

53 See Fletcher, *Outbreak*, pp. 171–2; Russell, *FBM*, pp. 439–44.

54 *Journal*, ed. Coates, p. 366.

55 See Wedgwood, *KW*, p. 49.

56 Russell, *FBM*, p. 446.

57 Clarendon, IV, 126.

58 See Smith, *CR*, pp. 86–7.

59 Wormald, *Clarendon*, pp. 45–6.

60 Wedgwood, *KW*, p. 24.

61 For the rise of 'The London Pamphlet Market' in the early 1640s, see Dagmar Freist, *Governed by Opinion: Politics, Religion and the Dynamics of Communication in Stuart London 1637–1645* (London and New York, 1997), pp. 87–124.

62 Nigel Smith, *Literature and Revolution in England 1640–1660* (New Haven and London, 1994), p. 24.

63 See David Stevenson, 'A Revolutionary Regime and the Press: The Scottish Covenanters and their Printers, 1638–1651', *The Library*, 6th series, 7 (1985), 321–5.

362

64 Sheila Lambert, 'The Beginning of Printing for the House of Commons, 1640–1642', *The Library*, 6th series, 3 (1981), 43–61; 49–50.

65 See Richard Cust, 'News and Politics in Early Seventeenth-Century England', *Past and Present*, No. 112 (1986), 60–90.

66 See Joseph Frank, *The Beginnings of the English Newspaper 1620–1660* (Cambridge, Mass., 1961), pp. 20–4.

67 See Fredrick Seaton Siebert, *Freedom of the Press in England 1476–1776: The Rise and Decline of Government Controls* (Urbana, 1952), pp. 203–7.

68 Smith, *Literature and Revolution*, p. 306.

69 *CP*, pp. 23–6.

70 *Ibid.*, p. 103.

71 Cousins, 'Cavalier World', 82.

72 See Raman Selden, *English Verse Satire 1590–1765* (London, 1978), pp. 55–6.

73 Margaret Anne Doody, *The Daring Muse: Augustan Poetry Reconsidered* (Cambridge, 1985), p. 40.

74 Cousins, 'Cavalier World', 62, 79.

75 See Ann Baynes Coiro, 'Milton and Class Identity: The Publication of *Areopagitica* and the 1645 *Poems*', *Journal of Mediaeval and Renaissance Studies*, 22 (1992), 261–89; 265.

76 See *CP*, pp. xxii–xli.

77 Wedgwood, *KW*, p. 51.

78 Pearl, *London and the Puritan Revolution*, p. 139.

79 Clarendon, IV, 158–9.

80 *Ibid.*, IV, 195.

81 See Fletcher, *Outbreak*, pp. 184–5.

82 Russell, *FBM*, pp. 452–3.

83 Smith, *CR*, p. 88.

84 See Elizabeth Hamilton, *Henrietta Maria* (London, 1976), pp. 184–5.

85 See Russell, *FBM*, pp. 464–5.

86 Dering, *Collection of Speeches*, title page. For details of Dering's career, see William M. Lamont, *Politics and Religion, 1603–1660* (London, 1969), pp. 83–93; Derek Hirst, 'The Defection of Sir Edward Dering, 1640–1641', *Historical Journal*, 15 (1972), 193–208.

87 O Hehir, *EH*, p. 217. The text of Draft II is on pp. 93–105.

88 *Ibid.*, p. 215.

89 *Ibid.*, pp. 216–7.

90 *Ibid.*, p. 217.

91 Clarendon, IV, 167.

92 Wedgwood, *KW*, p. 68.

93 Smith, *CR*, p. 95.

94 See Lois G. Schwoerer, '"The Fittest Subject for a King's Quarrel": An Essay on the Militia Controversy 1641–1642', *Journal of British Studies*, 11 (1971), 45–76; 60–1.

95 See Joan E. Hartman, 'Restyling the King: Clarendon Writes Charles I', *Pamphlet Wars: Prose in the English Revolution*, ed. James Holstun, special

issue of *Prose Studies: History, Theory, Criticism*, 14 (1991), 45–59.

96 Russell, *FBM*, pp. 478, 487.
97 *CowleyE*, pp. 178, 220.
98 *Ibid.*, p. 161.
99 See O Hehir, *HD*, p. 38.
100 *The Poetical Works of Sir John Denham*, ed. Theodore Howard Banks, Jr (New Haven, 1928), p. 45, cites Thomas Herbert's *Some Yeares Travels into Divers Parts of Asia and Afrique* (1634) as the source of *The Sophy*. Quotations are from the text of Denham's play given in this edition, pp. 232–309.
101 O Hehir, *HD*, pp. 42–3; John M. Wallace, '"Examples Are Best Precepts": Readers and Meanings in Seventeenth-Century Poetry', *Critical Inquiry*, 1 (1974–5), 273–90; 274.
102 Fletcher, *Outbreak*, p. 191.
103 Quotations are from *Poetical Works*, ed. Banks, pp. 128–9. For the circulation of Denham's poem in manuscript, see Peter Beal, *Index of English Literary Manuscripts*, Vol. II, Part 1 (London and New York, 1987), pp. 331, 342–3.

6: THE BEGINNING OF HOSTILITIES: MARCH 1642–APRIL 1643

1 See Russell, *FBM*, pp. 495–6, 502.
2 See Wedgwood, *KW*, pp. 80–1, 89–92.
3 See Alan Everitt, *The Community of Kent and the Great Rebellion 1640–1660* (Leicester, [1966] 1973), pp. 95–104; T. P. S. Woods, *Prelude to Civil War 1642: Mr Justice Malet and the Kentish Petitions* (Salisbury, 1980), pp. 30–46. Woods reprints the text of the March petition in Appendix II, pp. 141–4.
4 Everitt, *Community of Kent*, p. 96.
5 Russell, *FBM*, p. 499.
6 See Woods, *Prelude*, pp. 47–75.
7 *Ibid.*, pp. 82–5.
8 See *Poems of Richard Lovelace*, ed. C. H. Wilkinson (Oxford, 1930), p. 277; the text of the poem is on pp. 78–9. For manuscripts, see Peter Beal, *Index of English Literary Manuscripts*, Vol. II, Part 1 (London and New York, 1993), pp. 9–10.
9 Anselment, *LR*, p. 104.
10 This text is in *Lovelace*, ed. Wilkinson, pp. 48–51. For date, see H. M. Margoliouth, review of Wilkinson's edition, *Review of English Studies*, 3 (1927), 89–95; 94.
11 Margoliouth, review of *Poems of Lovelace*, 94.
12 Gerald Hammond, 'Richard Lovelace and the Uses of Obscurity', *Proceedings of the British Academy*, 71 (1985), 203–34; 216.
13 Wedgwood, *KW*, p. 82; Russell, *FBM*, p. 504.
14 See Russell, *FBM*, pp. 504–11 for arguments on both sides.
15 See Russell, *ibid.*, p. 512; Fletcher, *Outbreak*, pp. 322–3; Joyce Lee Malcolm, *Caesar's Due: Loyalty and King Charles 1642–1646* (London, 1983), pp. 19–21.

16 Loxley, *RP*, p. 76.
17 *The Knyvett Letters (1620–1644)*, ed. Bertram Schofield (London, 1949), Letter 48, pp. 101–5.
18 See *Collected Works of Abraham Cowley*, Vol. I, ed. Thomas Calhoun, Laurence Hyworth and Allan Pritchard (Newark, 1989), pp. 320–6 for title, attribution and date. The text is on pp. 94–101. See Notes *passim* for connections with Donne's satires.
19 See Paul S. Seaver, *The Puritan Lectureships: The Politics of Religious Dissent 1560–1662* (Stanford, 1970), pp. 267–72.
20 Michael Mendle, *Henry Parker and the English Civil War: The Political Thought of the Public's "privado"* (Cambridge, 1995), pp. 81–5.
21 Fletcher, *Outbreak*, p. 261.
22 Quoted in Russell, *FBM*, p. 515.
23 Quoted in Michael Mendle, *Dangerous Positions: Mixed Government, the Estates of the Realm and the Making of the Answer to the xix Propositions* (Alabama, 1985), p. 15.
24 Smith, *CR*, pp. 90, 91.
25 Ronald Hutton, 'The Structure of the Royalist Party, 1642–1646', *Historical Journal*, 24 (1981), 553–69; 554–6.
26 For Charles's activities in July, see Malcolm, *Caesar's Due*, pp. 34–9.
27 Hutton, 'Structure of Royalist Party', 556.
28 Fletcher, *Outbreak*, pp. 367, 373.
29 *Ibid.*, p. 264.
30 *Rules to Know a Royall King, from a Disloyall Subject* (London, [28 July] 1642).
31 O Hehir, *EH*, pp. 56, 218. The text of Draft III is on pp. 109–34.
32 *Ibid.*, p. 223.
33 *Ibid.*, p. 226.
34 See O Hehir, *HD*, pp. 55–61.
35 The text of 'Eclogue IV' is in *Selected Poems of George Daniel of Beswick 1616–1657*, ed. Thomas B. Stroup (Kentucky, 1959), pp. 172–9. All five eclogues were first printed in *Poems of George Daniel, Esq., of Beswick, Yorkshire (1616–1657)*, ed. Alexander B. Grosart, 2 vols. (Boston, Lincolnshire, 1878), II, pp. 135–205.
36 See Thomas B. Stroup, 'George Daniel: Cavalier Poet', *Renaissance Papers*, 4 (1959), 39–51; 39–40.
37 John Taylor, *A Reply* (London, 1641), p. 6.
38 *A Plea for Prerogative: Or, Give Caesar his Due* (London, 1642).
39 Harold F. Brooks lists several examples in 'English Verse Satire, 1640–1660: Prolegomenon', *The Seventeenth Century*, 3 (1989), 17–46; 24.
40 The poem was printed in *A Royal Arbor of Loyal Poesie, Consisting of Poems and Songs . . . Composed by Thomas Jordan* (London, 1663), pp. 78–80.
41 *Ibid.*, pp. 7–9. There is another version, entitled 'Pym's *Anarchy*', in *Rump: Or an Exact Collection of the Choycest Poems and Songs Relating to the Late Times* (London, 1662), pp. 68–9.
42 Printed in *Rump*, pp. 17–19.

43 *Ibid.*, pp. 47–9.
44 *A Puritane Set Forth In his Lively Colours* (London, 1642).
45 Malcolm, *Caesar's Due*, pp. 149, 164.
46 Clarendon, V, 449.
47 Quoted in Donald Nicholas, *Mr Secretary Nicholas (1593–1669): His Life and Letters* (London, 1955), p. 171.
48 See Peter Young, *Edgehill 1642: The Campaign and the Battle* (Moreton-in-the Marsh, [1967] 1998), p. 70. For Charles's successful method of recruitment by commissioning individual supporters to raise a regiment of regular soldiers, see Ronald Hutton, 'The Royalist War Effort', in *Reactions to the English Civil War: 1642–1649*, ed. John Morrill (Basingstoke, 1982), pp. 51–66; pp. 52–4.
49 Patrick Morrah, *Prince Rupert of the Rhine* (London, 1976), p. 78.
50 Young, *Edgehill*, pp. 130, 132, 136.
51 See Wedgwood, *KW*, pp. 140–2; Bennett, *CV*, pp. 155–8.
52 Bennett, *ibid.*, p. 161.
53 See O Hehir, *HD*, pp. 60–2.
54 Wedgwood, *KW*, p. 148.
55 See Gardiner, *History*, I, pp. 89–93.
56 See Roy Sherwood, *The Civil War in the Midlands 1642–1651* (Stroud, 1992), pp. 32–3.
57 Mendle, *Henry Parker*, p. 90.
58 *Ibid.*, p. 90.
59 *Ibid.*, pp. 5–69.
60 Mendle disputes the attribution of this tract to Sir John Spelman (*Henry Parker*, pp. 105–7).
61 For the attribution of this tract to Spelman rather than Digges, see Mendle, *Henry Parker*, pp. 105–7.
62 J. W. Daly, 'John Bramhall and The Theoretical Problems of Royalist Moderation', *Journal of British Studies*, 11 (1971), 26–44; 26. See also John Sanderson, '*Serpent-Salve*, 1643: the Royalism of John Bramhall', *Journal of Ecclesiastical History*, 25 (1974), 1–14.
63 J. W. Allen, *English Political Thought 1603–1644* (New York [1938], 1967), p. 482; Daly, 'John Bramhall', 26.
64 Mendle, *Henry Parker*, p. 104.
65 Quoted from a letter to the Earl of Ormond in Malcolm, *Caesar's Due*, p. 149.
66 *The Wishing Common-wealths Men: Or, A Queint Dialogue* (London, [25 August] 1642).
67 *A Treatise of Monarchy* (1643), reprinted in *Divine Right and Democracy: An Anthology of Political Writing in Stuart England*, ed. David Wootton (Harmondsworth, 1986), p. 210.
68 *The Soveraignty of Kings* (London, [21 November] 1642).
69 *A Whisper in the Eare: Or a Discourse between the Kings Majesty and the High Court of Parliament.*(Oxford, [9 January] 1643), sigg. A2ᵛ–A3ʳ.

70 *A Letter Sent by An Oxford Scholler To his Quondam Schoolemaster* (1643), p. 1.

71 *A Deep Sigh Breathd Through the Lodgings at White-Hall, Deploring the Absence of the COURT, And the Miseries of the Pallace* (London, [4 October] 1642), sig. A2ʳ.

72 'White-Hall. A Poem. Written 1642' [Thomason 4 March 1643], *Plays and Poems of Henry Glapthorne*, 2 vols. (London, 1874), II, pp. 239–50.

73 *An Humble Desired Union Betweene Prerogative and Priviledge* (London, [8 November] 1642).

74 Bernard Capp, *The World of John Taylor the Water-Poet 1578–1653* (Oxford, 1994), p. 170.

75 *CP*, pp. 33–8. For its date, see headnote, p. 123.

76 Loxley, *RP*, p. 90.

77 'The Saint's Encouragement', *BP*, I, 207–8.

78 For other examples, see Brooks, 'English Verse Satire', 23–4.

79 The text is in *The Poetical Works of Sir John Denham*, ed. Theodore Howard Banks, Jr (New Haven, 1928), pp. 122–7.

80 Thomason's copy of a broadside version, *Mr Hampdens speech occasioned upon the Londoners Petition for Peace*, is dated 23 March 1643.

81 *Collected Works of Cowley*, I, p. 339.

82 *Ibid.*, I, pp. 337, 341–3, and 104–11 for Cowley's authorship, his movements in 1643 and the text of the poem.

83 Anselment, *LR*, p. 160.

84 See Fredrick Seaton Siebert, *Freedom of the Press in England 1476–1776: The Rise and Decline of Government Controls* (Urbana, 1952), pp. 205–6.

85 See Laurence Hanson, 'The King's Printer at York and Shrewsbury, 1642–1643', *The Library*, 4th series, 23 (1943), 129–31.

86 Thomas, *JB*, p. 29.

87 *Ibid.*, pp. 27, 31–5.

88 *Mercurius Aulicus* (Week 1, 1 January 1643), p. 1.

89 Thomas, *JB*, pp. 29, 65.

90 See Wedgwood, *KW*, pp. 167, 175.

91 Gardiner, *History*, I, 105.

92 Wedgwood, *KW*, p. 169.

93 Nicholas, *Mr Secretary Nicholas*, p. 179.

94 *Political Ideas of the English Civil Wars 1641–1649: A Collection of Representative Texts with a Commentary*, ed. Andrew Sharp (Harlow, 1983), p. 117.

7: LEARNING TO WRITE THE WAR: APRIL–SEPTEMBER 1643

1 *Making the News: An Anthology of the Newsbooks of Revolutionary England 1641–1660*, ed. Joad Raymond (Moreton-in-the Marsh, 1993), p. 20.

2 Thomas, *JB*, p. 67.

3 *Ibid.*, pp. 67, 69.

4 *Ibid.*, pp. 89–90.

5 See J. S. Morrill, *The Revolt of the Provinces: Conservatives and Radicals in the English Civil War 1630–1650* (London, [1976] 1980), pp. 95–7.

6 *The Knyvett Letters (1620–1644)*, ed. Bertram Schofield (London, 1949), Letters 52 and 51, pp. 109–10.

7 *Certaine Informations from Severall parts of the Kingdom*, No. 17, p. 131.

8 See Gardiner, *History*, I, pp. 135–9.

9 *Poetical Works of Sir John Denham*, ed. Theodore Howard Banks, Jr (New Haven, 1928), pp. 13–14.

10 See Gardiner, *History*, I, pp. 145–8.

11 Ashton, *ECW*, p. 210.

12 *Ibid.*, p. 210. See also Wormald, *Clarendon*, pp. 127–8.

13 See Ashton, *ECW*, p. 211.

14 *Mr Waller's Speech in the House of Commons, On Tuesday the fourth of July, 1643* (London, 1643), p. 3.

15 See Bennett, *CW*, pp. 160–2.

16 See Laurence Kaplan, 'Presbyterians and Independents in 1643', *English Historical Review*, 84 (1969), 244–56; 246–7.

17 Gardiner, *History*, I, p. 155; see also Wormald, *Clarendon*, pp. 130–1.

18 Nigel Smith, *Literature and Revolution in England 1640–1660* (New Haven and London, 1994), pp. 340–1.

19 *Ibid.*, p. 341.

20 See Daniel Woolf, 'Conscience, Constancy and Ambition in the Career and Writings of James Howell', *Public Duty and Private Conscience in Seventeenth-Century England, Essays Presented to G. E. Aylmer*, ed. John Morrill, Paul Slack and Daniel Woolf (Oxford, 1993), 243–78; pp. 262–3 for the complex printing history of these two pamphlets, which were revised in the late 1650s and reissued under the title *Casuall Discourses, and Interlocutions betwixt Patricius and Peregrin* along with other works by Howell in 1661. Quotations are from the 1643 edition in the Thomason collection.

21 The fruits of many years spent in Europe are gathered in Howell's *Instructions for Forreine Travell* (London, 1642).

22 Smith, *Literature and Revolution*, p. 341.

23 *Ibid.*, p. 341.

24 For the invocation of a chivalric 'trial by battle' by Essex and other military leaders during the early years of the civil war, see J. S. A. Adamson, 'The Baronial Context of the English Civil War', *Transactions of the Royal Historical Society*, 5th series, 40 (1990), 93–120; 102–5.

25 See Wedgwood, *KW*, pp. 223–4.

26 *Memoirs of the Verney Family during the Seventeenth Century*, compiled by Frances Parthenope Verney and Margaret M. Verney, 3rd edn., 2 vols (London, 1925), I, pp. 295–6.

27 E. M. Symonds, 'The Diary of John Greene (1635–1657)', *English Historical Review*, 43 (1928), 385–94; 392.

28 Donald Nicholas, *Mr Secretary Nicholas (1593–1669): His Life and Letters* (London, 1955), pp. 181, 183–4.

29 *Knyvett Letters*, Letter 57, p. 119.

30 See Alan Everitt, *The Community of Kent and the Great Rebellion 1640–1660*

(Leicester, [1966] 1973), pp. 187–200.

31   *Knyvett Letters*, Letter 61, p. 124–5.

32   *Ibid.*, Letter 62, p. 126.

33   See Gardiner, *History*, I, pp. 199–202.

34   Thomas, *JB*, p. 76.

35   *Ibid.*, p. 105.

36   See Rosalind K. Marshall, *Henrietta Maria: The Intrepid Queen* (London, 1990), pp. 105–6.

37   *CPP*, pp. 554–5. In the Oxford volume, the poem is on sigg. D1^v–D2^r.

38   Quoted in John Stucley, *Sir Bevill Grenvile and His Times: 1596–1643* (Chichester, 1983), pp. 127, 148.

39   G. E. Aylmer, 'Collective Mentalities in Mid Seventeenth-Century England: II. Royalist Attitudes', *Transactions of the Royal Historical Society*, 5th series, 37 (1987), 1–30; 30.

40   P. R. Newman, 'The King's Servants: Conscience, Principle and Sacrifice in Armed Royalism', *Public Duty and Private Conscience*, pp. 225–41; p. 240. See also Newman's *The Old Service: Royalist Regimental Colonels and the Civil War, 1642–1646* (Manchester, 1993), pp. 20–65.

41   See Derek Hirst, 'The Place of Principle', *Past and Present*, No. 92 (1981), 79–99.

42   Loxley, *RP*, pp. 79–80.

43   *Ibid.*, p. 80.

44   Quoted from the text in *CPP*, pp. 555–8. In the Oxford volume, the poem is on pp. 8–11.

45   For conditions during a seventeenth-century battle, see Charles Carlton, 'The Impact of the Fighting', in *The Impact of the English Civil War*, ed. John Morrill (London, 1991), pp. 22–7.

46   *The Cambridge Royalist Imprisoned* [31 July 1643].

47   Thomas, *JB*, p. 98.

48   Anselment, *LR*, p. 130.

49   'An Ode. 1643,' in *BP*, I, pp. 14–15.

50   *Ibid.*, pp. 205–6.

51   See Thomas, *JB*, p. 255.

52   *BP*, I, pp. 185–91.

53   *Denham*, ed. Banks, pp. 133–4.

54   John Taylor, *The Noble Cavalier Caracterised and a Rebellious Caviller Cauterised* (Oxford, 1643).

55   See Thomas, *JB*, pp. 106–10.

56   *Making the News*, ed. Raymond, p. 21.

57   Wedgwood, *KW*, p. 223.

58   See Gardiner, *History*, I, pp. 182–3, 202–4.

59   Quoted in Roy Sherwood, *The Civil War in the Midlands: 1642–1651* (Stroud, [1974] 1992), p. 59.

60   *A Letter sent to LONDON from a Spie at OXFORD, Written by Owle-light, Intercepted by Moon-light, Printed in the Twi-light, Dispersed by Day-light, and may be Read by Candle-light* (Oxford, 1643).

61 For information about their movements in 1643, see *Collected Works of Abraham Cowley*, Vol. I, ed. Thomas O. Calhoun, Laurence Heyworth and Allan Pritchard (Newark, 1989), p. 342 and *CP*, p. xvi.

62 Lee A. Jacobus, *John Cleveland* (Boston, 1975), p. 90.

63 *CP*, pp. 26–8.

64 A. D. Cousins, 'The Cavalier World of John Cleveland,' *Studies in Philology*, 78 (1981), 61–86; 83.

65 *CowleyP*, p. 9.

66 This text was included in *CowleyE*, pp. 465–81.

67 See Allan Pritchard, 'Six Letters by Cowley', *Review of English Studies*, new series 18 (1967), 253–63; 256 note 3; *Abraham Cowley: The Civil War*, ed. Allan Pritchard (Toronto, 1973). Pritchard's edition was later incorporated into the first volume of *Collected Works*, ed. Calhoun where the poem appears on pp. 114–62. Quotations are from this text and the accompanying commentary and notes.

68 *Collected Works*, I, p. 359.

69 These sentiments were omitted in later editions of *Poems* and are not included in Waller's edition.

70 *Collected Works*, I, pp. 270, 266; David Trotter, *The Poetry of Abraham Cowley* (Basingstoke, 1979), pp. 7, 16; Anselment, *LR*, p. 161.

71 Gerald M. MacLean, *Time's Witness: Historical Representation in English Poetry, 1603–1660* (Madison, 1990), pp. 208, 202.

72 David Norbrook, *Writing the English Republic: Poetry, Rhetoric and Politics, 1627–1660* (Cambridge, 1999), pp. 85, 86.

73 *Collected Works*, I, p. 365.

74 *Ibid.*, pp. 263–4.

75 *Ibid.*, pp. 274, 390 note 69.

76 These last lines are not in any of the versions of 'Book 1' alone. Pritchard thinks it likely that 'the last leaf was torn away and lost as the manuscript passed around' (*Collected Works*, I, p. 279).

77 Loxley, *RP*, p. 87; MacLean, *Time's Witness*, p. 209.

78 Thomas Sprat, 'An Account of the Life and Writings of Mr Abraham Cowley,' in *The Works of Abraham Cowley* (London, 1668), sig. A2^v.

79 Loxley, *RP*, p. 87.

80 See *Collected Works*, I, p. 440, note on lines 621–2.

81 See Arthur H. Nethercot, *Abraham Cowley: The Muses' Hannibal* (New York, 1967), pp. 90–2.

8: DECLINING FORTUNES: FROM NEWBURY TO MARSTON MOOR: SEPTEMBER 1643–JUNE 1644

1 Ashton, *ECW*, p. 207.

2 *CPP*, p. 21.

3 *Ibid.*, pp. 560–3.

4 See Gardiner, *History*, I, pp. 229–30.

5　Bennett, *CW*, p. 165; Ashton, *ECW*, p. 203.

6　Wedgwood, *KW*, p. 260.

7　*A Short View of the Life and Actions of the Late Deceased John Pim Esquire* (London, [12 December] 1643), sig. A4ᵛ.

8　*A Narrative of the Disease and Death of that Noble Gentleman, John Pym Esquire* (London, [30 December] 1643), p. 1.

9　*Mercurius Aquaticus, Or, The Water-Poets Answer to All that hath or shall be Writ by Mercurius Britanicus* (Oxford, [Madan December] 1643), sig. C3ᵛ.

10　Bennett, *CW*, p. 165.

11　Wedgwood, *KW*, p. 238.

12　Quoted in Donald Nicholas, *Mr Secretary Nicholas (1593–1669): His Life and Letters* (London, 1955), pp. 186–7.

13　'To W.[illiam] M.[arquess] of N.[ewcastle]', *Poems of James Shirley*, ed. Ray Livingstone Armstrong (New York, 1941), p. 11.

14　E. M. Symonds, 'The Diary of John Greene (1635–1657)', *English Historical Review*, 43 (1928), 385–94; 393.

15　A. D. Cousins, 'The Cavalier World and John Cleveland', *Studies in Philology*, 78 (1981), pp. 61–86; 84. The poem is quoted from *CP*, pp. 29–32.

16　Lee A. Jacobus, *John Cleveland* (Boston, 1974), p. 105.

17　See Ashton, *ECW* pp. 211–13.

18　Gardiner, *History*, I, pp. 307–8.

19　*The Knyvett Letters (1620–1644)*, transcribed and ed. Bertram Schofield (London, 1949), Letter 64, p. 128.

20　*Nicholas: Life and Letters*, pp. 189–90.

21　See Frederick John Varley, *The Siege of Oxford: An Account of Oxford during the Civil War, 1642–1646* (Oxford, 1932), p. 49.

22　Thomas, *JB*, p. 78.

23　*A Declaration of the Lords and Commons of Parliament Assembled at Oxford, Of their Proceedings Touching a Treatie for Peace, and the Refusall Thereof* (Oxford, 19 March 1644), p. 1.

24　Ashton, *ECW*, p. 214.

25　J. W. Allen, *English Political Thought: 1603–1644* (New York, [1938], 1967), p. 494.

26　Smith, *CR*, p. 226.

27　Michael Mendle, *Henry Parker and the English Civil War* (Cambridge, 1995), p. 104.

28　See Thomas, *JB*, p. 107.

29　James Daly, 'The Idea of Absolute Monarchy in Seventeenth-Century England', *Historical Journal*, 21 (1978), 227–50; 239.

30　Smith, *CR*, p. 230.

31　*Ibid.*, p. 244.

32　Johann P. Sommerville, 'From Suarez to Filmer: A Reappraisal', *Historical Journal*, 25 (1982), 525–40; 537–8.

33　Daly, 'Idea of Absolute Monarchy', 244.

34　For the debate about the date of the composition of *Patriarcha* and Filmer's other works, see *Patriarcha and Other Writings*, ed. Johann P. Sommerville (Cambridge, 1991), pp. xxxii–xxxiv.

35 For details of Filmer's life, see *Patriarcha and Other Political Works of Sir Robert Filmer*, ed. Peter Laslett (Oxford, 1949), pp. 2–7.

36 *The Grand Question Concerning Taking up Armes against the King Answered* (Oxford, [11 October] 1643), p. 12 [misnumbered p. 6].

37 *The Soveraignes Power, and the Subjects Duty* (Oxford, [Madan 5 March] 1644), pp. 1, 29.

38 *The Kings Cause Rationally, Briefly, and Plainly Debated* (Oxford, [25 March] 1644), p. 45.

39 Nigel Smith, *Literature and Revolution in England 1640–1660* (New Haven and London, 1994), p. 105.

40 *Mercurius, &c. not – Veridicus, nor yet – Mutus; But – Cambro – (or if you please) – honest – Britannus* (No. 2, 31 January to 6 February, 1644), p. 10.

41 *A Declaration by Sir Edward Dering* (London, 1 April 1644), pp. 1, 2, 10–11, 3.

42 Ashton, *ECW*, p. 211. For details of Dering's last months, see Alan Everitt, *The Community of Kent and the Great Rebellion 1640–1660* (Leicester, [1966] 1973), pp. 205–8.

43 *QCW*, I, p. 139.

44 *Ibid.*, I, p. 140.

45 *Ibid.*, I, p. 146.

46 The full text is given in Peter Young, *Marston Moor 1644: The Campaign and the Battle* (Moreton-in-the-Marsh, [1970] 1998), pp. 78–9.

47 See Gardiner, *History*, I, pp. 353–4.

48 *Knyvett Letters*, ed. Schofield, Letter 81, p. 160.

49 *Mercurius Aulicus* (Week 26, 29 June 1644), p. 1060.

50 See Gardiner, *History*, I, p. 371.

51 *QCW*, I, p. 144.

52 Richard Ollard, *Clarendon and His Friends* (Oxford, 1988), p. 30.

53 Madan dates it November 1642; Gardiner gives its 'supposed' date as 13 October 1643 (*History*, I, p. 281).

54 *A Sermon Preached before His Majesty at Reading* (Oxford, [Madan 18 June] 1644), pp. 11, 13, 14.

55 See Gardiner, *History*, I, pp. 281–3.

56 *A Sermon Preached at the Publique Fast the Ninth of Feb. in St Maries Oxford*, (Oxford, [8 March] 1644), p. 36; *A Sermon Preached at the Publique Fast the Twelfth Day of April. At St Maries Oxford* (Oxford, [8 May] 1644), pp. 1, 11.

57 *A Military Sermon ... Preached at Shrewsbury March 3. 1643* [i.e. 1644] (Oxford, [Madan 27 June] 1644), sig. A2ᵛ.

58 G. E. Aylmer, 'Collective Mentalities in Mid Seventeenth-Century England: II. Royalist Attitudes', *Transactions of the Royal Historical Society*, 5th series, 37 (1987), 1–30; 23.

59 See Wedgwood, *KW*, p. 316.

60 *Mercurius Davidicus, Or a Patterne of Loyall Devotion*.(Oxford, [9 October] 1643); *A Manuall of Prayers: Collected for the Use of Gentlemen Soldiers* (Oxford, 1643); *The*

Cavaliers New Common-Prayer Booke (York, [Madan 8 September] 1644).

61 *Richard Symonds's Diary of the Marches of the Royal Army*, ed. C. E. Long (Camden Society, 1859; reprinted Cambridge, 1997), p. 30.

62 Madan identifies this as a counterfeit imprint used by a London printer.

63 Quoted from Thomason's copy, dated 8 July and 'saide to be printed at Bristoll', pp. 4, 23.

64 Lois Potter, *Secret Rites and Secret Writing: Royalist Literature 1641–1660* (Cambridge, 1989), p. 27.

65 *Davids Three Mighties: Or Sovereignties Three Champions: Being the Three Prime Reformers of the Protestant Religion, Luther, Calvin, Tindal, Faithfully Cited, and Affectionately Presented to all the misled People of England* (Oxford, [10 April] 1644), sig. A3^r.

66 *Ibid.*, sig. A3^r.

67 'The Riddle', *BP*, I, p. 172.

68 *Mad Verse, Sad Verse, Glad Verse and Bad Verse* (Oxford, [10 May] 1644), pp. 1, 3, 7.

69 *England's Tears, for the Present Wars* (London, May 1644), in *The Harleian Miscellany*, VIII (London, 1746).

70 *Ibid.*, pp. 244–5.

71 *Britannicae Virtutis Imago. Or, The Effigies of True Fortitude* (Oxford, [3 July] 1644).

72 Thomas, *JB*, p. 37.

9: DEFEAT, CAPTIVITY AND EXILE: JULY 1644–SEPTEMBER 1647

1 See Elizabeth Hamilton, *Henrietta Maria* (London, 1976), pp. 208–10.

2 See J. S. A. Adamson, 'The Baronial Context of the English Civil War', *Transactions of the Royal Historical Society*, 5th series, 40 (1990), 93–120; 111–12.

3 The text of Essex's letter is given in *Richard Symonds's Diary of the Marches of the Royal Army*, ed. C. E. Long (Camden Society, 1859; reprinted Cambridge, 1997), p. 53. Symonds charts the progress of the King's campaign throughout 1644 in detail.

4 See Ian Roy, 'George Digby, Royalist Intrigue and the Collapse of the Cause', *Soldiers, Writers and Statesmen of the English Revolution*, ed. Ian Gentles, John Morrill and Blair Worden (Cambridge, 1998), pp. 68–90; p. 84.

5 See C. V. Wedgwood, *Montrose* (Stroud, [1952] 1998), pp. 61–78.

6 Bennett, *CV*, pp. 237, 240.

7 Derek Hirst, *England in Conflict, 1603–1660: Kingdom, Community, Commonwealth* (London, 1999), p. 220.

8 J. W. Allen, *English Political Thought: 1603–1644* ([1938] New York, 1967), pp. 520–1.

9 M. Pricket, *An Appeale to the Reverend and Learned Synod of Divines: for Resolution of the grand Controversie of these times; Concerning Kings* (Oxford, [8 August] 1644).

10 John Maxwell, *An Answer By Letter to a Worthy Gentleman Who desired of a Divine some reasons by which it might appeare how Inconsistent PRESBYTERIAL Govern-*

ment is with MONARCHY (Oxford, [Madan 5 October] 1644).

11 Quoted from *QCW*, I, pp. 147–57.
12 *Ibid.*, I, pp. 159–77.
13 Gordon S. Haight, 'Francis Quarles in the Civil War', *Review of English Studies*, 12 (1936), 147–64; 158–9.
14 See Thomas, *JB*, pp. 114–16.
15 *CP*, p. 74.
16 *BP*, I, pp. 211–13.
17 Madan provides this information about the early editions.
18 The text is quoted from the Scolar Press fascimile reprint of Cleveland's *Poems* (1653) (Menston, 1971), pp. 88–94.
19 Sharon Achinstein, 'The Politics of Babel in the English Revolution', in *Pamphlet Wars: Prose in the English Revolution*, special issue of *Prose Studies: History, Theory, Criticism*, 14: 3 (1991), 14–44; 33.
20 *Ibid.*, 32–3.
21 See the discussion of *The Character of a London Diurnall-Maker* by Achinstein, *Pamphlet Wars*, 29.
22 *Ibid.*, 32.
23 Wedgwood, *KW*, p. 368.
24 Adamson, 'Baronial Context', 115–18.
25 Quoted by Adamson, *ibid.*, 112.
26 See Gardiner, *History*, II, pp. 82–4, 86–90.
27 Hirst, *England in Conflict*, p. 224.
28 Lawrence Kaplan, *Politics and Religion during the English Revolution: The Scots and the Long Parliament 1643–1645* (New York, 1976), p. 98.
29 E. M. Symonds, 'The Diary of John Greene (1635–1657) II', *English Historical Review*, 43 (1928), 598–604; 602.
30 John Morrill, 'The Church in England, 1642–1649', *Reactions to the English Civil War 1642–1649*, ed. John Morrill (London and Basingstoke, 1982), pp. 89–114; p. 96.
31 *Episcopacy and Presbytery Considered, According to the severall Respects, which may command a Church-Government, and oblige good Christians to it* (Oxford, [Madan January] 1645), pp. 1–2.
32 *Considerations of present use concerning The Danger Resulting from the Change of our Church-Government* (Oxford, [February] 1645), p. 1.
33 *Certaine Scruples and Doubts of Conscience about taking the Solemn League and Covenant* ([20 January] 1645), pp. 9, 6.
34 *A Review of the Covenant* (London, 1661), p. 1. Thomason collected the first (anonymous) London edition on 22 July 1644; Madan dates the Oxford edition, January 1645.
35 *Scripture Vindicated from the Mis-apprehensions, Mis-interpretations, and Mis-applications of Mr Stephen Marshall, In his Sermon Preached before the Commons House of Parliament, Feb. 23. 1641* (Oxford, [February] 1645).
36 *A Full and Satisfactorie Answere to the Archbishop of Canterburies Speech* (London, 1645); *The Life and Death of William Lawd, Late Archbishop of Canterburie* (London, [31 January] 1645).

37 *A Briefe Relation of the Death and Sufferings of The Most Reverend and Renowned Prelate the L. Archbishop of Canterbury* (Oxford, [Madan 6 February] 1645).

38 For the use of theatrical metaphors in response to the death of Charles I, see Nancy Klein Maguire, 'The Theatrical Mask/Masque of Politics: The Case of Charles I', *Journal of British Studies*, 28 (1989), 1–22.

39 *CP*, pp. 38–9.

40 *Crop-Eare Curried* (Oxford, [17 February] 1645).

41 David Underdown, *Revel, Riot and Rebellion: Popular Politics and Culture in England 1603–1660* (Oxford, [1985] 1987), p. 156. For other accounts of the Clubmen, see John Morrill, *The Revolt of the Provinces: Conservatives and Radicals in the English Civil War 1630–1650* (London, [1976] 1980), pp. 98–111 and Roy Sherwood, *The Civil War in the Midlands 1642–1651* (Stroud, 1992), pp. 125–8.

42 Wedgwood, *KW*, p. 394.

43 See Ian Roy, 'The Royalist Council of War, 1642–1646', *Bulletin of the Institute of Historical Research*, 35 (1962), 150–68; 166–8.

44 For the two letters to the Queen in May, see Gardiner, *History*, II, p. 181 and Kaplan, *Politics and Religion*, p. 113.

45 See Wedgwood, *Montrose*, pp. 86–94.

46 *A Letter to A Friend, Shewing, The illegull proceedings of the two Houses of Parliament: And observing GOD's averseness to their Actions.*(London, [15 May] 1645).

47 *The Judgement of an Old Grand-Jury-Man of Oxfordshire, Concerning the Breaking Up of the Late Treaty Begun at Uxbridge* (Oxford, [23 May] 1645).

48 *Rebels Anathematized, And Anatomized* (Oxford, [Madan 18 May] 1645), p. 3.

49 *Oxford Besiedged, Surprised, Taken, and Pittifully Entred on Monday the Second of June last, 1645 by the valiant Forces of the London and Westminster Parliament* (Oxford, [Madan 10 June] 1645).

50 Donald Nicholas, *Mr Secretary Nicholas (1593–1660): His Life and Letters* (London, 1955), p. 208.

51 See Roy, 'Council of War', pp. 166–7; Ronald Hutton, 'The Structure of the Royalist Party, 1642–1646', *Historical Journal*, 24 (1981), 553–69; 566.

52 Hirst, *England in Conflict*, p. 230.

53 See Roy, 'George Digby', pp. 87–8.

54 Wedgwood, *KW*, p. 473.

55 *The Loyall Subject's Retiring-Roome, Opened in A Sermon at St Maries, on the 13th day of July ... 1645* (Oxford, [13 July] 1645), p. 2.

56 *England's Iliads in a Nut-Shell* (Oxford, [Madan 17 July] 1645), sigg. A2^{r-v}.

57 *Alter Britanniae Heros* (Oxford, 1645).

58 See Michael Mendle, *Henry Parker and the English Civil War* (Cambridge, 1995), pp. 25–6.

59 For accounts of the controversy over the publication of the letters, see Lois Potter, *Secret Rites and Secret Writing: Royalist Literature, 1641–1660* (Cambridge, 1989), pp. 57–67; Joad Raymond, 'Popular Representations of Charles I', *The Royal Image: Representations of Charles I*, ed. Thomas N. Corns (Cambridge, 1999), pp. 47–73; pp. 57–60.

60 Numbers 90–91 are reprinted in *Making the News: An Anthology of the Newsbooks*

of Revolutionary England: 1641–1660, ed. Joad Raymond (Moreton-in-the-Marsh, 1993), pp. 339–48.

61 Raymond, 'Popular Representations', p. 58.

62 'A Satyr, Occasioned by the Author's Survey of a Scandalous Pamphlet, intituled *The King's Cabinet opened*', reprinted in *Rump. Or an Exact Collection of the Choycest Poems and Songs Relating to the Late Times* (London, 1662), pp. 169–78.

63 *Some Observations upon Occasion of the Publishing their Majesties Letters* (Oxford, [8 August] 1645), pp. 1–2.

64 *A Letter in which The Arguments of the Annotator And three other Speeches Upon their Majesties Letters Published in London, are Examined and Answered* (Oxford, [12 August] 1645).

65 *A Key to the Kings Cabinet* (Oxford, [21 August] 1645).

66 Reprinted in *Making the News*, p. 348.

67 See Thomas, *JB*, pp. 117–19.

68 *Ibid.*, p. 117.

69 *A Discourse Discovering some Mysteries of our New State* (Oxford, [26 September] 1645), pp. 29, 37.

70 See Thomas, *JB*, p. 124.

71 *Parliaments Power, In Lawes for Religion* (Oxford, [25 August] 1645).

72 *No Peace 'till the King Prosper* (Oxford, [Madan 18 August] 1645), p. 3.

73 *A Letter Sent from a Gentleman in Oxford, To His Friend in London; Concerning the Justice of the King's Cause* (Oxford, [Madan April] 1646), p. 4.

74 See F. E. Hutchinson, *Henry Vaughan: A Life and Interpretation* (Oxford, 1947), pp. 48–50.

75 See 'To my Ingenuous Friend, R. W.' and 'A Rhapsodie', *VW*, pp. 3–4, 10–12.

76 For a discussion of this and other translations printed in *Olor Iscanus* (London, 1651), see my article '"Feathering some slower hours": Henry Vaughan's Verse Translations', *Scintilla* 4 (2000), 142–61.

77 *VW*, pp. 71, 67–8.

78 *Henry Vaughan: The Complete Poems*, ed. Alan Rudrum (Harmondsworth, 1976), p. 516. The poem is quoted from *VW*, pp. 77–8.

79 See Sir Frederick Rees, 'Breconshire During the Civil War', *Brycheiniog*, 8 (1962), 2–3; Edward Parry, 'Charles I in South Wales, July to September 1645', *Brycheiniog*, 29 (1996–1997), 39–45.

80 See Hutchinson, *Life*, pp. 64–5.

81 'An elegie on the death of Mr. R. W. slain in the late unfortunate differences at *Routon* Heath, neer *Chester*, 1645', *VW*, pp. 49–51.

82 'Upon a Cloke lent him by Mr. *J. Ridsley*', *ibid.*, pp. 52–4.

83 Quoted by Rees, 'Breconshire During the Civil War', 4.

84 Symonds, *Diary*, p. 263.

85 See Hutchinson, *Life*, pp. 65–6; Rees, 'Breconshire', 4–5.

86 'To his retired friend, an Invitation to *Brecknock*', in *VW*, pp. 46–8.

87 '*To his Learned Friend and Loyal Fellow-Prisoner*, Thomas Powel *of* Cant. *Doctor*

of Divinity', in *VW*, pp. 623–4.

88 See James D. Simmonds, 'Henry Vaughan's "Fellow-Prisoner"', *English Studies*, 45 (1964), 454–7.

89 *CP*, pp. 6–9.

90 Lee A. Jacobus, *John Cleveland* (Boston, 1975), p. 75.

91 *VW*, pp. 625–6.

92 'An Ecloge: Spoken by Hilas and Strephon', *Poems of George Daniel, Esq., of Beswick Yorkshire (1616–1657)*, ed. Revd. Alexander B. Grosart, 4 vols (Blackburn, 1878), II, 192–205.

93 Loxley, *RP*, p. 139.

94 *Mercurius Rusticus: Or, The Countries Complaint of the Murthers, Robberies, Plunderings, and other Outrages, Committed by the Sectaries of this late flourishing Kingdome* (Oxford, [April] 1646).

95 See Thomas, *JB*, pp. 129–32.

96 See Bernard Capp, *The World of John Taylor the Water-Poet: 1578–1653* (Oxford, 1994), pp. 153–5.

97 See Arthur H. Nethercot, *Sir William Davenant: Poet Laureate and Playwright-Manager* (New York, [1938] 1967), pp. 216–24, 227–33.

98 Gardiner, *History*, III, p. 213.

99 David Underdown, *Pride's Purge: Politics in the Puritan Revolution* (Oxford, 1971), p. 76.

100 *Ibid.*, p. 81.

101 Robert Ashton, *Counter-Revolution: The Second Civil War and its Origins, 1646–1648* (New Haven and London, 1994), p. 27.

102 *Judge Jenkins Remonstrance* ([21 February] 1647), p. 8; *Lex Terrae* (No title-page [April 1647]), pp. 1, 7, 9.

103 *The Royall, and the Royallist's Plea* ([3 June] 1647), pp. 1, 5.

104 David Jenkins, *A Discourse Touching the Inconveniences of a Long continued Parliament* ([17 June] 1647).

105 *Royalty and Loyalty or A Short Survey of the Power of Kings over their Subjects: and the Duty of Subjects to their Kings* ([7 July] 1647), p. 62.

106 *Prima Pars. De Comparatis Comparandis ... or the justification of King Charles comparatively against the Parliament* (Oxford [3 July] 1647), p. 1. Parts II and III appeared in November 1647 and May 1648. See Valerie Pearl, 'The "Royal Independents" in the English Civil War', *Transactions of the Royal Historical Society*, 5th series, 18 (1968), 69–96.

107 *The Divine Right of Government: ... More Particularly of Monarchie; the onely Legitimate and Natural spece of Politique Government* ([9 September] 1647), sigg. (a)1^v, A2^r.

108 Οχλο-μεχια, *Or The Peoples War* ([7 June] 1647), p. 1.

109 Potter, *Secret Rites*, p. 135.

110 *Lex Terrae*, p. 2; *Divine Right*, sig. (a)3^r.

111 *Epistolae Ho-Elianae: The Familiar Letters of James Howell*, ed. Joseph Jacobs (London, 1890), p. 355. This is Number XLVII in Jacobs' edition, which reflects the revised, expanded and reordered editions of *Familiar Letters*

published in 1647, 1650 and 1655, which added dates and places of composition, some of them erroneous. All page references are to Jacobs.

112 'A Royalist Rewriting of George Herbert: *His Majesties Complaint to his Subjects* (1647)', *Modern Philology*, 89 (1991), pp. 211–24; p. 218. Gottlieb prints the full text of the parody on pp. 219–24.

113 Annabel Patterson, *Censorship and Interpretation: The Conditions of Writing and Reading in Early Modern England* (Madison, 1984), p. 211.

114 *Parnassus Biceps or Several Choice Pieces of Poetry* (1656), ed. G. Thorn -Drury (London, 1927), pp. 107, 109. For the ascription of this poem to L'Estrange and the manuscripts of 'To Althea', see *The Poems of Richard Lovelace*, ed. C. H. Wilkinson (Oxford, [1930] 1968), pp. 277–85.

115 *A Loyall Song of the Royall Feast, kept by the Prisoners in the Towre in August, with the names, titles and characters of every Prisoner* (n.d.).

116 J. W. Saunders, 'The Stigma of Print: A Note on the Social Bases of Tudor Poetry', *Essays in Criticism*, 1 (1951), 139–64; 141.

117 Ann Baynes Coiro, 'Milton and Class Identity: the Publication of *Areopagitica* and the 1645 *Poems*', *Journal of Medieval and Renaissance Studies*, 22 (1992), 261–89; 265.

118 Arthur F. Marotti, *Manuscript, Print and the English Renaissance Lyric* (Ithaca and London, 1995), pp. 247, 259.

119 *Ibid.*, p. 261.

120 Warren Chernaik, 'Books as Memorials: The Politics of Consolation', *Yearbook of English Studies*, 21 (1991), 207–17; 209, 212; Thomas Corns, 'Thomas Carew, Sir John Suckling and Richard Lovelace', *The Cambridge Companion to English Poetry: Donne to Marvell*, ed. Thomas N. Corns (Cambridge, 1993), pp. 200–50; p. 201.

121 Loxley, *RP*, p. 223.

122 For dates and other details of publication, see the prefatory note to the Scolar Press reprint of Waller, *Poems 1645* (Menston, 1971).

123 Along with his other addresses to the reader, this is reprinted by John Curtis Reed, 'Humphrey Moseley, Publisher', *Oxford Bibliographical Society Proceedings and Papers*, 2 (1927–1930), 61–131; 76.

124 *Ibid.*, p. 76.

125 QCW, III, p. 236. Some time in 1645, after the death of the author, one of the Oxford printers issued a volume containing *The Loyall Convert, The New Distemper* and *The Whipper Whipt* under the general title *The Profest Royalist*.

126 *Works of George Herbert*, ed. F. E. Hutchinson (Oxford, 1941), p. lx.

127 *Poems &c. By James Shirley* (London, 1646), p. 79.

128 *VW*, p. 2.

129 See James D. Simmonds, *Masques of God: Form and Theme in the Poetry of Henry Vaughan* (Pittsburgh, 1972), p. 87.

130 *VW*, pp. 20–1.

131 Knevet's collection of devotional verse is printed in *The Shorter Poems of Ralph Knevet*, ed. Amy M. Charles (Ohio, 1966), pp. 275–396.

132 See Nathan Comfort Starr, '*The Concealed Fansyes*: A Play by Lady Jane

Cavendish and Lady Elizabeth Brackley', *Publications of the Modern Language Association*, 46 (1931), 802–38 (containing the text of the play); Margaret J. M. Ezell, '"To be your Daughter in your Pen": The Social Functions of Literature in the Writings of Lady Elizabeth Brackley and Lady Jane Cavendish', *Huntington Library Quarterly*, 51 (1988), 281–96; Dale B. J. Randall, *Winter Fruit: English Drama 1642–1660* (Lexington, 1995), pp. 321–6.

133 See *Minor Poems of Joseph Beaumont, D. D. 1616–1699*, ed. Eloise Robinson (London, 1914); P. G. Stanwood, 'A Portrait of Stuart Orthodoxy', *Church Quarterly Review*, 165 (1964), 27–39.

134 *Selected Poems of George Daniel of Beswick 1616–1657*, ed. Thomas B. Stroup (Lexington, 1959), p. 168.

10: TRIAL AND MARTYRDOM: SEPTEMBER 1647–JANUARY 1649

1 Derek Hirst, *England in Conflict, 1603–1660: Kingdom, Community, Commonwealth* (London, 1999), p. 246.

2 David Underdown, *Pride's Purge: Politics in the Puritan Revolution* (Oxford, 1971), p. 87.

3 Hirst, *England in Conflict*, p. 246; Underdown, *ibid.*, p. 88.

4 Robert Ashton, *Counter-Revolution: The Second Civil War and its Origins, 1646–1648* (New Haven and London, 1994), p. 424.

5 See Charles Carlton, *Charles I: The Personal Monarch* (London, [1983] 1984), p. 318.

6 *The Kings Most Excellent Majesties Wellcome to his owne House, Truly called the Honour of Hampton Court* (London, 1647), reprinted in *Works of John Taylor, the Water-Poet*, ed. Charles Hindley (London, 1876), pp. 1, 2, 3, 5.

7 See Joseph Frank, *Cromwell's Press Agent: A Critical Biography of Marchamont Nedham, 1620–1678* (Lanham, 1980), pp. 44–5.

8 See Thomas, *JB*, pp. 152–60.

9 *Ibid.*, pp. 151–2.

10 *The Assembly-man; Written in the Year 1647* (London, 1663), p. 5. For an analysis of this 'Character', which circulated widely in manuscript before it was printed, see Thomas, *JB*, pp. 146–9.

11 Reprinted in *Cavalier and Puritan: Ballads and Broadsides Illustrating the Period of the Great Rebellion 1640–1660*, ed. Hyder E Rollins (New York, 1923), pp. 185–7.

12 'Cromwell's *Panegyrick, upon his riding in triumph over the baffled City of* London', in *BP*, I, pp. 348–50.

13 Thomas Swadlin, *Loyall Subjects. Or the Blessed Mans Encouragement, Upon the Kings retyrement from Hampton Court . . . Delivered in a Sermon, November the 14th. 1647* ([London], 1647), pp. 6, 17.

14 C[harles] G[erbier], *The Modest Cavallieres Advice* ([29 November] 1647), pp. 3, 5, 4.

15 See Royce MacGillivray, *Restoration Historians and the English Civil War* (The

Hague, 1974), pp. 16–19.

16 *Relations and Observations, Historicall and Politick, upon the PARLIAMENT, begun Anno Dom. 1640* (1648).

17 See C. H. Firth, 'Clarendon's *History of the Rebellion*. Part I. The Original "History"', *English Historical Review*, 19 (1904), 26–54; 27, 52.

18 Clarendon, IX, 3.

19 Quoted by George Watson, 'The Reader in Clarendon's *History of the Rebellion*', *Review of English Studies*, new series 25 (1974), 396–409; 396.

20 Letter dated 14 August 1646, quoted in Firth, 'Clarendon's *History*', p. 27.

21 Clarendon, I, 1–2.

22 Watson, 'Reader in Clarendon's *History*', p. 407; Nigel Smith, *Literature and Revolution in England 1640–1660* (New Haven and London, 1994), p. 345.

23 Claude J. Summers, 'Herrick's Political Counterplots', *Studies in English Literature*, 25 (1985), 165–82; 165.

24 Thomas N. Corns, *Uncloistered Virtue: English Political Literature, 1640–1660* (Oxford, 1992), p. 308.

25 See Leah S. Marcus, 'Herrick's *Hesperides* and the "Proclamation made for May"', *Studies in Philology*, 76 (1979), 49–74 and *idem, The Politics of Mirth: Jonson, Herrick, Milton, Marvell, and the Defense of Old Holiday Pastimes* (Chicago and London, 1986).

26 Corns, *Uncloistered Virtue*, p. 307.

27 Summers, 'Counterplots', 174.

28 *Robert Herrick's Hesperides and the Epigram Book Tradition* (Baltimore, 1988), pp. 4–6, 9.

29 See Leah S. Marcus, 'Herrick's *Noble Numbers* and the Politics of Playfulness', *English Literary Renaissance*, 7 (1977), 108–26; David W. Landrum, '"To Seek of God": Enthusiasm and the Anglican Response in Robert Herrick's *Noble Numbers*', *Studies in Philology*, 89 (1992), 244–55.

30 Summers, 'Counterplots', 174.

31 *Poetical Works of Robert Herrick*, ed. L. C. Martin (Oxford, 1956), pp. 398–9.

32 Sir John Berkeley's memoirs, quoted in Ashton, *Counter-Revolution*, p. 208.

33 *Otia Sacra* (London, 1648), p. 157.

34 '*To my Worthy Friend Mr* Peter Lilly: *on that excellent Picture of his Majesty, and the Duke of Yorke, drawne by him at* Hampton-Court', in *The Poems of Richard Lovelace*, ed. C. H. Wilkinson (Oxford, [1930] 1968), p. 57.

35 Raymond A. Anselment, '"Clouded Majesty": Richard Lovelace, Sir Peter Lely, and the Royalist Spirit', *Studies in Philology*, 86 (1989), 367–87; 379; Corns, *Uncloistered Virtue*, p. 245.

36 *BP*, I, pp. 293–4.

37 'An Elegy on Sir Charls Lucas, and Sir George Lisle', *Poems of Henry King*, ed. Margaret Crum (Oxford, 1965), pp. 101–10.

38 Gilbert Burnet, *The Memoires of the Lives and Actions of James and William Dukes of Hamilton and Castleherald* (London, 1677), p. 203.

39 *A Vindication of King Charles: Or, A Loyal Subjects Duty* (London, [November] 1648), p. a3^v.

40 *The Image of the King: Charles I and Charles II* (London, [1979] 1993), p. 46.
41 Underdown, *Pride's Purge*, p. 106.
42 William Goffe, quoted by Godfrey Davies, *The Early Stuarts 1603–1660*, 2nd edn. (Oxford, 1959), p. 154.
43 Quoted by C. V. Wedgwood, *The Trial of Charles I* (London, [1964] 1967), p. 33.
44 See Underdown, *Pride's Purge*, Chapter 6, pp. 143–63.
45 See Davies, *Early Stuarts*, p. 160.
46 See Wedgwood, *Trial*, p. 227.
47 Joad Raymond, 'Popular Representations of Charles I', *The Royal Image: Representations of Charles I*, ed. Thomas N. Corns (Cambridge, 1999), pp. 47–73; p. 62.
48 See John W. Packer, *The Transformation of Anglicanism: 1643–1660 with special reference to Henry Hammond* (Manchester, 1969), pp. 176–7.
49 Underdown, *Pride's Purge*, p. 177.
50 Joseph Frank, *The Beginnings of the English Newspaper 1620–1660* (Cambridge, Mass., 1961), p. 170.
51 *Ibid.*, pp. 163–4.
52 See Fredrick S. Siebert, *Freedom of the Press in England 1476–1776: The Rise and Decline of Government Controls* (Urbana, 1952), pp. 216–17.
53 Wedgwood, *Trial*, p. 222.
54 *King Charles His Tryal* (London, 1649).
55 *The Kings Speech on the Scaffold* (London, 1649).
56 Quoted from *Politics, Religion and Literature in the Seventeenth Century*, ed. William Lamont and Sybil Oldfield (London, 1975), p. 143.
57 *Eikon Basilike: The Portraiture of His Sacred Majesty in His Solitudes and Sufferings*, ed. Philip A. Knachel (Ithaca, New York, 1966), p. xi. Quotations are from this edition.
58 Two books by the Revd Christopher Wordsworth, *'Who Wrote Eikon Basilike?': Considered and Answered in Two Letters* (London, 1824) and *Documentary Supplement to 'Who Wrote Eikon Basilike?'* (London, 1825), discuss and reprint the evidence then available. Francis F. Madan has assembled all that is currently known about its authorship and printing in the appendices to *A New Bibliography of the Eikon Basilike of King Charles the First*, Oxford Bibliographical Society Publications, new series 3 (1949). The iconographical aspects of the work are discussed by Richard Helgerson, 'Milton Reads the King's Book: Print, Performance, and the Making of a Bourgeois Idol', *Criticism*, 29 (1987), 1–25.
59 *Lines of Authority: Politics and English Literary Culture, 1649–1689* (Ithaca and London, [1993] 1996), pp. 43, 50. For other recent discussions of literary aspects of the text itself, see Corns, *Uncloistered Virtue*, pp. 80–91; Elizabeth Skerpan Wheeler, '*Eikon Basilike* and the rhetoric of self-representation,' in *Royal Image*, ed. Corns, pp. 122–40.
60 This evidence is from *The Princely Pellican* (London, [June] 1649), pp. 4–7,

21–22. Madan attributes it to John Ashburnham.

61 Both Major Huntington and Dr Dillingham, Master of Emmanuel College, Cambridge, claimed to have seen part of the manuscript at Holdenby (Madan, *New Bibliography*, p. 128, note 12).

62 *Ibid.*, p. 128.

63 *Ibid.*, p. 128.

64 See Charles E. Doble, 'Notes and Queries on the *Eikon Basilike* II,' *The Academy*, No. 577 (26 May 1883), 367–68; 368.

65 For sources of the evidence drawn upon in this paragraph and derived from Madan, see Robert Wilcher, 'What was the King's Book for?: The Evolution of *Eikon Basilike*', *The Yearbook of English Studies*, 21 (1991), 218–28; 221–3.

66 Helgerson, 'Milton Reads the King's Book', 1. See also Kevin Sharpe, 'Private Conscience and Public Duty in the Writings of Charles I', *Historical Journal*, 40 (1997), 643–65.

67 Since Chapter 28, 'Meditations Upon Death', was added by Gauden.

11: LAMENTING THE KING: 1649

1 'An Horatian Ode upon Cromwell's return from Ireland', *Poems and Letters of Andrew Marvell*, ed. H. M. Margoliouth, 2 vols. (Oxford, 1927), 3rd edn., revised by Pierre Legouis with the collaboration of E. E. Duncan-Jones (Oxford, 1971), I, pp. 88–9.

2 *A Plea for the King, and Kingdome; By way of Answer to the late Remonstrance of the Army, Presented to the House of Commons on Monday Novemb. 20* (London, 1648), p. 27.

3 'The Whitehall Debates' (13 January 1649), *Puritanism and Liberty: Being the Army Debates (1647–1649) from the Clarke Manuscripts*, ed. A. S. P. Woodhouse, 2nd edn. (London, 1974), p. 176.

4 Alvise Contarini, Venetian Ambassador at Munster, writing to the Doge and Senate, 26 February 1649, quoted in *The Puritan Revolution: A Documentary History*, ed. Stuart E. Prall (London, 1968), p. 193.

5 Clarendon, XI, 238; Sir Philip Warwick, *Memoires of the Reigne of King Charles I* (London, 1701), p. 309.

6 See Nancy Klein Maguire, 'The Theatrical Mask/Masque of Politics: The Case of Charles I', *Journal of British Studies*, 28 (1989), 1–22.

7 Warwick, *Memoires*, pp. 339, 344.

8 David Underdown, *Royalist Conspiracy in England 1649–1660* (New Haven, 1960), p. 5.

9 See Roger Hainsworth, *The Swordsmen in Power: War and Politics under the English Republic 1649–1660* (Stroud, 1997), pp. 22–4.

10 *Ibid.*, pp. 28–38.

11 See Bennett, *CW*, pp. 328–32.

12 See Fredrick Seaton Siebert, *Freedom of the Press in England 1476–1776: The Rise and Decline of Government Controls* (Urbana, 1952), pp. 216–17, 221–3.

13 Lois Potter, *Secret Rites and Secret Writing: Royalist Literature, 1641–1660* (Cambridge, 1989), p. 18.

14 *God and the King: Or, The Divine Constitution of the Supreme Magistrate* (London, [5 April] 1649), p. 2.

15 *King Charles the First, No Man of Blood: But A Martyr for his People* (London, [25 June] 1649), p. 66.

16 For discussions of the play, see Dale B. J. Randall, *Winter Fruit: English Drama 1642–1660* (Lexington, 1993), pp. 103–9; Susan Wiseman, *Drama and Politics in the English Civil War* (Cambridge, 1998), pp. 62–9.

17 *The Princely Pellican. Royall Resolves Presented In Sundry Choice Observations, Extracted from his Majesties Divine Meditations: With Satisfactory Reasons to the whole Kingdome, that His Sacred Person was the onely Author of them* (London, [2 June] 1649), pp. 1, 3. For an account of the ensuing controversy, see Potter, *Secret Rites*, pp. 176–84.

18 *Complete Prose Works of John Milton*, ed. Don M. Wolfe et al., 8 vols (New Haven, 1953–1982), III, p. 342–3.

19 Hugh Trevor-Roper, *Historical Essays* (London, 1957), p. 210.

20 Helen W. Randall, 'The Rise and Fall of a Martyrology: Sermons on Charles I' *Huntington Library Quarterly*, 10 (1946–7), 135–67; 137, 140–2.

21 Thomas Warmstrey, *A Handkerchiefe for Loyal Mourners. Or, A Cordial for Drooping Spirits* ([1649], quotations from 1659 edition).

22 Loxley, *RP*, pp. 192–3.

23 Potter, *Secret Rites*, pp. 186–7.

24 Quoted from *Poems by J. C. With Additions never before Printed* (1653) (reprinted Menston, 1971), p. 81.

25 *Poems of Henry King*, ed. Margaret Crum (Oxford, 1965), pp. 110–17, 117–32.

26 *Regale Lectum Miseriae; Or, A Kingly Bed of Misery* (London, [18 April] 1649), p. 34.

27 *Jeremias Redivivus: Or, An Elegiacall Lamentation on the Death of our English Josias, Charles the First, King of Great Britaine, &c. Publiquely Murdered by His Calvino-Judaicall Subjects* (London, [30 May] 1649), pp. 1–2.

28 Printed in *Poems by J. C.* (1653), p. 86–7.

29 *King*, ed. Crum, p. 124.

30 *Ibid.*, pp. 130–1.

31 'An Elegie,' *Vaticinium Votivum* (London, [11 March] 1649), p. 69.

32 'On the Death of King Charles', in *BP*, I, p. 296.

33 Dennis Kay, *Melodious Tears: The English Funeral Elegy from Spenser to Milton* (Oxford, 1990), p. 5.

34 *Ibid.*, pp. 29, 90, 94–5, 4.

35 Ruth Wallerstein, *Studies in Seventeenth-Century Poetic* (Madison and Milwaukee, 1965), p. 65.

36 Ronald Berman, *Henry King and the Seventeenth Century* (London, 1964), p. 18.

37 *A Flattering Elegie, Upon the death of King Charles: The cleane contrary way* (1649), p. 4.

38 *King*, ed. Crum, pp. 131–2.

39 'On the Kings death,' *BP*, I, p. 298.
40 'Upon the Death of King CHARLES the First', printed in *Poems by J.C.*, p. 88.
41 Gerald MacLean, *Time's Witness: Historical Representation in English Poetry, 1603–1660* (Madison, 1990), p. 215.
42 I have argued elsewhere the case for identifying Vaughan's Daphnis as Charles I. (See Robert Wilcher, '"Daphnis: An Elegiac Eclogue" by Henry Vaughan', *Durham University Journal*, new series 36 (1974), 25–40.) The elegy was published in Vaughan's late gathering of poetry, *Thalia Rediviva* (1678), and was thought by F. E. Hutchinson to have been 'originally written on the death of William Vaughan or some other young friend who died before 1649' and then adapted, by the addition of lines 113–18, 'to commemorate his twin brother' who died in 1666 (*Henry Vaughan: A Life and Interpretation* (Oxford, 1947), p. 221). Graeme J. Watson has since argued that the poem belongs entirely to 1666 and reflects the disillusionment felt by royalists in the years following the restoration of the monarchy ('Political Change and Continuity of Vision in Henry Vaughan's "Daphnis. An Elegiac Eclogue"', *Studies in Philology*, 83 (1986), 158–81). His argument ignores the allusions to the *Eikon Basilike* in Vaughan's text and foists onto the Welsh poet a London perspective rather than the specifically local context that I find in the poem. To take one example, he links the 'publick plagues and woes' of line 124 with the Great Plague and the Great Fire of 1665 and 1666; it is just as likely that Vaughan, who manifestly read a good deal of contemporary verse, was echoing the invocation of the Egyptian plagues in printed elegies on the King.
43 Peter Sacks, *The English Elegy: Studies in the Genre from Spenser to Yeats* (Baltimore and London, 1985), p. 20.
44 The poem is quoted from *VW*, pp. 676–80.
45 See Hutchinson, *Life*, pp. 95–7.
46 *VW*, p. 58.
47 See Hutchinson, *Life*, pp. 109–11.
48 *Ibid.*, pp. 96–7, 146–7.
49 For a comparison of the two elegies, see Cedric C. Brown, 'The Death of Righteous Men: Prophetic Gesture in Vaughan's "Daphnis" and Milton's *Lycidas*', *George Herbert Journal*, 7 (1984), 1–24.
50 Quoted in Martin's notes, *VW*, p. 747.
51 Hutchinson, *Life*, pp. 20, 29.
52 The epitaph first appeared in the supplementary matter added in Dugard's edition of 15 March 1649. It is quoted from *Eikon Basilike*, ed. Philip A. Knachel (Ithaca, New York, 1966), p. 195.
53 See Randall, 'Martyrology,' 135–6.
54 It is mentioned by Horace, *Carmina*, I, xii, 47.
55 *Eikon Basilike*, ed. Knachel, Chapter 15, p. 92.
56 Margarita Stocker, *Apocalyptic Marvell* (Brighton, 1986), p. 271.
57 The poem is quoted from *Poems and Letters of Marvell*, I, pp. 27–9.

58 Stocker, *Apocalyptic Marvell*, p. 273.
59 *Ibid.*, pp. 275, 285.
60 *Ibid.*, p. 286.
61 *Ibid.*, p. 289.
62 *Ibid.*, p. 298–9.
63 *Ibid.*, p. 305.
64 Thomas N. Corns, *Uncloistered Virtue: English Political Literature, 1640–1660* (Oxford, 1992), p. 79.

12: COPING WITH DEFEAT AND WAITING FOR THE KING: 1649–1660

1 For the insurrection in Kent, see Alan Everitt, *The Community of Kent and the Great Rebellion 1640–1660* (Leicester, [1966] 1973), pp. 240–70.
2 See *Poems of Richard Lovelace*, ed. C. H. Wilkinson (Oxford, [1930] 1968), pp. li–lii.
3 *Ibid.*, p. xlvii.
4 'Amyntor's Grove', *ibid.*, pp. 71–4.
5 'The Grasse-hopper', *ibid.*, pp. 38–40.
6 Anselment, *LR*, p. 99.
7 'Calling Lucasta from her Retirement', *Lovelace*, ed. Wilkinson, pp. 105–6.
8 Gerald Hammond reads these lines as 'a resolve to live obscurely', in 'Richard Lovelace and the Uses of Obscurity', *Proceedings of the British Academy*, 71 (1985), 203–34; 225.
9 'To his Noble Friend Mr. Richard Lovelace, upon his Poems', *Lovelace*, ed. Wilkinson, p. 8.
10 'Aramantha. A Pastorall', *ibid.*, pp. 107–18.
11 Paul H. Hardacre, *The Royalists During the Puritan Revolution* (The Hague, 1956), p. 64.
12 *Otia Sacra* (London, 1648), pp. 135, 174.
13 *Ibid.*, p. 8.
14 *The Cavalier Mode: From Jonson to Cotton* (Princeton, 1971), pp. 179–80.
15 James D. Simmonds, *Masques of God: Form and Theme in the Poetry of Henry Vaughan* (Pittsburgh, 1972), pp. 85–137; Eluned Brown, 'Henry Vaughan's Biblical Landscape', *Essays and Studies*, new series 30 (1977), 50–60; 51; Jonathan F. S. Post, *Henry Vaughan: The Unfolding Vision* (Princeton, 1982), pp. 118, 189. See also Claude J. Summers and Ted-Larry Pebworth, 'Herbert, Vaughan, and Public Concerns in Private Modes', *George Herbert Journal*, 3 (1979–80), 1–21; Robert Wilcher, '"Then keep the ancient way!" A Study of Henry Vaughan's *Silex Scintillans*', *Durham University Journal*, new series 45 (1983), 11–24; Janet E. Halley, 'Versions of the Self and the Politics of Privacy in *Silex Scintillans*', *George Herbert Journal*, 7 (1983–4), 51–71; Graeme J. Watson, 'The Temple in "The Night": Henry Vaughan and the Collapse of the Established Church', *Modern Philology*, 84 (1986), 144–61; Chris Fitter, 'Henry Vaughan's Landscapes of Military Occupa-

tion', *Essays in Criticism*, 42 (1992), 123–47; Robert Wilcher, '"The Present Times Are Not / To Snudge In": Henry Vaughan, *The Temple*, and the Pressure of History', *George Herbert: Sacred and Profane*, ed. Helen Wilcox and Richard Todd (Amsterdam, 1995), pp. 185–94; Peter W. Thomas, 'The Language of Light: Henry Vaughan and the Puritans', *Scintilla*, 3 (1999), 9–29.

16 'The Date of Henry Vaughan's *Silex Scintillans*', *Notes and Queries*, new series 7 (1960), 64–5.

17 M. M. Mahood, *Poetry and Humanism* (London, 1950), p. 290.

18 *VW*, p. 410. All quotations from Vaughan's work are from this edition.

19 'Henry Vaughan's Ceremony of Innocence', *Essays and Studies*, new series 26 (1973), 35–52.

20 For a fuller discussion of the complex relationship between this poem and the work of George Herbert, see Robert Wilcher, 'Henry Vaughan and the Church', *Scintilla*, 2 (1998), 90–104; 94–8.

21 See David Underdown, *Royalist Conspiracy in England 1649–1660* (New Haven, 1960), pp. 10–11.

22 See Alfred Harbage, *Sir William Davenant: Poet Venturer 1606–1668* (New York, [1935] 1971), pp. 110–12; Mary Edmond, *Rare Sir William Davenant* (Manchester 1987), p. 103.

23 Both texts are printed in *Sir William Davenant's Gondibert*, ed. David F. Gladish (Oxford, 1971), pp. 3–55.

24 Harbage, *Davenant*, p. 197; Edmond, *Rare Sir William*, p. 105.

25 *Lines of Authority: Politics and English Literary Culture, 1649–1689* (Ithaca and London, 1993), pp. 26, 17.

26 *Ibid.*, p. 21.

27 The postscript is in *Gondibert*, ed. Gladish, pp. 250–2.

28 *Ibid.*, pp. 269–70.

29 *VW*, pp. 64–5.

30 See O Hehir, *HD*, pp. 91–6.

31 Harbage, *Davenant*, p. 187; *Gondibert*, ed. Gladish, p. x.

32 *Gondibert*, ed. Gladish, p. 73.

33 Along with his other addresses to the reader, this is reprinted by John Curtis Reed, 'Humphrey Moseley, Publisher', *Oxford Bibliographical Society Proceedings and Papers*, 2 (1927–30), 61–131; 82.

34 *Minor Poets of the Caroline Period*, ed. George Saintsbury, 3 vols. (Oxford, 1905), I, pp. 447–8.

35 See *Poems and Translations of Thomas Stanley*, ed. Galbraith Miller Crump (Oxford, 1962), p. xxv.

36 *Ibid.*, pp. xxvi–xxvii; see also *The Poems of James Shirley*, ed. Ray Livingstone Armstrong (New York, 1941), pp. 65–6.

37 See William R. Parker, 'Henry Vaughan and his Publishers', *The Library*, 4th series, 20 (1940), 401–11; Harold R. Walley, 'The Strange Case of *Olor Iscanus*', *Review of English Studies*, 18 (1942), 27–37; E. L. Marilla, '"The Publisher to the Reader" of *Olor Iscanus*', *Review of English Studies*, 24 (1948),

36–41; James D. Simmonds, 'The Publication of *Olor Iscanus*', *Modern Language Notes*, 76 (1961), 404–8.

38 *VW*, p. 38.

39 Austin Woolrych, *Commonwealth to Protectorate* (Oxford, 1982), pp. 9, 15.

40 See Bennett, *CW*, pp. 339–45. For an account of Charles II's adventures, see Richard Ollard, *The Escape of Charles II After the Battle of Worcester* (London, 1966).

41 Underdown, *Royalist Conspiracy*, p. 57.

42 See Joseph Frank, *The Beginnings of the English Newspaper 1620–1660* (Cambridge, Mass., 1961), pp. 208–9.

43 Quoted by C. H. Firth, 'The Royalists Under the Protectorate', *English Historical Review*, 52 (1937), 634–48; 634.

44 *Ibid*, p. 641.

45 See Hardacre, *Royalists*, pp. 76–9.

46 See Quentin Skinner, 'Conquest and Consent: Thomas Hobbes and the Engagement Controversy', *The Interregnum: The Quest for Settlement 1646–1660*, ed. G. E. Aylmer (London and Basingstoke, 1972), pp. 79–98.

47 *Philosophicall Rudiments Concerning Government and Society* (1651), quoted from *Divine Right and Democracy: An Anthology of Political Writing in Stuart England*, ed. David Wootton (Harmondsworth, 1986), p. 467.

48 *Leviathan* (London, 1914), Part II, Chapter 21, p. 116.

49 Underdown, *Royalist Conspiracy*, p. 58.

50 Derek Hirst, *England in Conflict, 1603–1660: Kingdom, Community, Commonwealth* (London, 1999), p. 275.

51 See Blair Worden, *The Rump Parliament 1648–1653* (Cambridge, 1974), Chapters 13–17; Woolrych, *Commonwealth*, pp. 68–102.

52 Derek Massarella, 'The Politics of the Army and the Quest for Settlement', in *'Into Another Mould': Aspects of the Interregnum*, ed. Ivan Roots, 2nd edn. (London, 1998), pp. 101–37; p. 114.

53 See Woolrych, *Commonwealth*, pp. 352–62.

54 Bennett, *CW*, pp. 345–6.

55 'The Church in England, 1642–1649', *Reactions to the English Civil War 1642–1649*, ed. John Morrill (London and Basingstoke, 1982), pp. 89–114; p. 101.

56 A. M. Johnson, 'Wales during the Commonwealth and Protectorate', in *Puritans and Revolutionaries: Essays in Seventeenth-Century History presented to Christopher Hill*, ed. Donald Pennington and Keith Thomas (Oxford, 1978), pp. 233–56; p. 237. See also Stephen Roberts, 'Religion, Politics and Welshness, 1649–1660', *"Into Another Mould"*, ed. Roots, pp. 30–46.

57 See W. S. K. Thomas, *Stuart Wales: 1603–1714* (Landysul, 1988), pp. 67–9.

58 See F. E. Hutchinson, *Henry Vaughan: A Life and Interpretation* (Oxford, 1947), p. 111.

59 John N. Wall, *Transformations of the Word: Spenser, Herbert, Vaughan* (Athens, Georgia, 1988), p. 275.

60 *Childhood and Cultural Despair: A Theme and Variations in Seventeenth-Century*

Literature (Pittsburgh, 1978), pp. 171–2.

61 Post, *Unfolding Vision*, p. 117.

62 Simmonds, *Masques of God*, p. 13.

63 See Frank, *English Newspaper*, pp. 195–6, 203–5.

64 See Thomas, *JB*, pp. 180–3.

65 Zwicker, *Lines of Authority*, p. 60.

66 H. J. Oliver, 'The Composition and Revisions of *The Compleat Angler*', *Modern Language Review*, 42 (1947), 295–313; 309.

67 David Hill Radcliffe, '"Study to Be Quiet": Genre and Politics in Izaak Walton's *Compleat Angler*', *English Literary Renaissance*, 22 (1992), 95–111; 100, 97.

68 *The Compleat Angler: 1653–1676*, ed. Jonquil Bevan (Oxford, 1983), p. 59. Further quotations are from this comparative edition.

69 Zwicker, *Lines of Authority*, pp. 63, 71, 67.

70 *Ibid.*, p. 73.

71 Introduction, *Compleat Angler*, ed. Bevan, p. 4.

72 This play on words is suggested by Nigel Smith, *Literature and Revolution in England, 1640–1660* (New Haven and London, 1994), p. 328. The connection between angling and loyal membership of the Church of England had been suggested earlier by B. D. Greenslade, '*The Compleat Angler* and the Sequestered Clergy', *Review of English Studies*, new series, 5 (1954), 361–6.

73 Cotton's poems were published in 1689, two years after his death. They are quoted from *Poems of Charles Cotton*, ed. John Buxton (London, 1958).

74 See Hardacre, *Royalists*, pp. 74–5.

75 John Buxton, *A Tradition of Poetry* (London, 1967), p. 144.

76 Quoted from Appendix in *Compleat Angler*, ed. Bevan, pp. 434–5.

77 *BP*, I, pp. 145–6. Further quotations are from this edition.

78 *Collected Works of Katherine Philips: The Matchless Orinda*, ed. Patrick Thomas, 2 vols. (Stump Cross, 1990), I, pp. 157, 162. Further quotations are from this edition.

79 Ellen Moody, 'Orinda, Rosania, Lucasia *et aliae*: Towards a New Edition of the Works of Katherine Philips', *Philological Quarterly*, 66 (1987), 325–53; 329.

80 Carol Barash, *English Women's Poetry, 1649–1714: Politics, Community, and Linguistic Authority* (Oxford, 1996), p. 62.

81 See *Works of Philips*, ed. Thomas, pp. 3–5.

82 *Ibid.*, p. 6.

83 Barash, *Women's Poetry*, p. 63.

84 *Ibid.*, pp. 71–5.

85 *Ibid.*, p. 67.

86 *Ibid.*, p. 56.

87 See Roland Mathias, 'The Making of a Royalist,' *Scintilla*, 3 (1999), 107–20; 113–16.

88 Hirst, *England in Conflict*, p. 285.

89 See Underdown, *Royalist Conspiracy*, pp. 149–53, 273–84.

90 See *Ibid.*, pp. 73–88.

91 See O Hehir, *HD*, pp. 98–100, 113–17.

92 Thomas, *JB*, pp. 192–3.

93 See O Hehir, *EH*, p. 137. The 1655/1668 version of the poem is on pp. 139–62.

94 *Ibid.*, p. 238.

95 *Ibid.*, pp. 246, 248.

96 See Arthur H. Nethercot, *Abraham Cowley: The Muse's Hannibal* (London, 1931), pp. 142–8, 155–6.

97 'Preface to *Poems*', reprinted in *Critical Essays of the Seventeenth Century*, ed. J. E. Spingarn, 2 vols. (Oxford [1908], 1957), II, pp. 77–90.

98 Nethercot, *Cowley*, p. 160; Sprat's 'Account of the Life and Writings', *The Works of Mr Abraham Cowley* (London, 1668).

99 Zwicker, *Lines of Authority*, p. 27.

100 Nethercot, *Cowley*, p. 150.

101 *Ibid.*, p. 150.

102 Sprat, 'Account', sig. a3^v.

103 Quoted in Hardacre, *Royalists*, p. 125.

104 Thomas N. Corns, *Uncloistered Virtue: English Political Literature 1640–1660* (Oxford, 1992), pp. 253, 256.

105 Zwicker, *Lines of Authority*, p. 29.

106 The preface to 'Pindarique Odes' is in *CowleyP*, pp. 155–6.

107 Nethercot, *Cowley*, p. 152.

108 *Ibid.*, pp. 152–3. The two odes are in *CowleyP*, pp. 192–4, 195–7.

109 *The Dial of Virtue: A Study of Poems on Affairs of State in the Seventeenth Century* (Princeton, 1963), p. 119.

110 'Cowley's Brutus Ode: Historical Precepts and the Politics of Defeat,' *Texas Studies in Literature and Language*, 19 (1977), 382–91; 383, 387, 388.

111 *Ibid.*, 384.

112 'Abraham Cowley's "Brutus": Royalist or Republican?' *Yearbook of English Studies*, 6 (1976), 41–52; 49, 52.

113 Anselment, *LR*, pp. 173–4; Corns, *Uncloistered Virtue*, p. 265.

114 Corns, *ibid.*, p. 264.

115 Stella Revard, 'Cowley's *Pindarique Odes* and the Politics of the Interregnum', *Criticism*, 35 (1993), 391–418; 404, 395.

116 *Ibid.*, 403.

117 'The 34. Chapter of the Prophet *Isaiah*' and '*The Plagues of* Egypt' are in *CowleyP*, pp. 211–38.

118 Revard, '*Pindarique Odes*', 409.

119 David Trotter, *The Poetry of Abraham Cowley* (London and Basingstoke, 1979), pp. 83, 85.

120 *CowleyP*, pp. 366–7.

121 See Trotter, *Poetry of Cowley*, p. 100.

122 Anselment, *LR*, p. 167.

123 *Ibid.*, p. 172.

124 Corns, *Uncloistered Virtue*, pp. 267–8.

125 Hirst, *England in Conflict*, p. 316.
126 See Charles S. Hensley, 'Wither, Waller and Marvell: Panegyrists for the Protector', *Ariel*, 3 (1972), 5–16; 11–16.
127 *Carolina: Or, Loyal Poems* (London, 1683), pp. 36–7.
128 *CowleyE*, pp. 345–6.
129 See Hirst, *England in Conflict*, pp. 318–27.
130 See Nevo, *Dial of Virtue*, pp. 138–50.

Index